SCRIBBLING WOMEN

SHORT STORIES BY 19TH-CENTURY AMERICAN WOMEN

SCRIBBLING WOMEN

SHORT STORIES BY 19TH-CENTURY AMERICAN WOMEN

Selected and introduced by
ELAINE SHOWALTER
Princeton University

Consultant Editor for this volume
CHRISTOPHER BIGSBY
University of East Anglia

Rutgers University Press
New Brunswick, New Jersey

First published in Great Britain 1996
J. M. Dent
Orion Publishing Group
Orion House
5 Upper St Martin's Lane
London WC2H 9EA

First published in the United States 1997
Rutgers University Press
New Brunswick, New Jersey

Library of Congress Cataloging-in-Publication
Data and British Library Cataloging-in-Publication
Data is available upon request.

ISBN 0-8135-2392-3 (cloth)
ISBN 0-8135-2393-1 (pbk.)

Printed in Great Britain

CONTENTS

NOTE ON THE AUTHORS

LOUISA MAY ALCOTT was born in 1832 in Germantown, Pennsylvania, the second of four daughters of the famous transcendental philosopher Amos Bronson and his wife Abba May Alcott. Raised in Concord, Massachusetts, she was taught by her father and also introduced to men of great influence, including Ralph Waldo Emerson, Nathaniel Hawthorne and Henry David Thoreau. After serving as an army nurse in the Civil War in 1862, Alcott published her first acclaimed work, *Hospital Sketches* (1863). The same year 'My Contraband; or, The Brothers' – first called 'The Brothers' – was published in *Atlantic Monthly* in its November issue and later reprinted in *Camp and Fireside Stories*. The story centered around issues of slavery and dispossession. Alcott rewrote her favorite novel *Moods* (1864) at least three times. Between 1863 and 1869 she wrote gothic thrillers published under a pseudonym. Her landmark novel *Little Women* (1868) gained her the most fame for its original portrayals of young American women. Its success led to financial security, as well as many sequels including *An Old-Fashioned Girl* (1870), *Little Men* (1871), *Eight Cousins* (1875), *Rose in Bloom* (1876) and *Jo's Boys* (1891). Alcott participated in the women's suffrage and temperance movements during the last decade of her life. Although she is best known for the domestic fiction of *Little Women*, she also wrote adult fiction later in life. She died in Boston in 1888.

WILLA CATHER was born in 1873 in Black Creek, Virginia, the daughter of Charles and Virginia Cather. In 1883, the family moved to Nebraska where Cather identified with the immigrant population she would later write about in *My Ántonia* (1918), her most canonized novel. In Red Cloud, Willa sometimes called herself William and was known for her eccentricity and cross-dressing. At the University of Nebraska she studied English literature and became a scathing drama critic for several

Nebraska newspapers. After graduation Cather settled in Pittsburgh and became the editor of *Home Monthly*. In 1899 she met, and soon after lived with, Isabelle McClung. Cather's stories, poems and articles appeared in the *Library*, while she taught high school to support herself. In 1902, she traveled to Europe with McClung, but it was not until the next year that her career as a writer began in earnest. She published several stories in *McClure's Magazine* and then *The Troll Garden* collection including 'Paul's Case' in 1905. After accepting a *McClure's* editorship in 1906, Cather lived with lifelong companion Edith Lewis in New York City. The same year she met Sarah Orne Jewett, who became her literary mentor, urging Cather to devote herself entirely to fiction. She left journalism in 1911 and published her first novel *Alexander's Bridge* (1912), followed by *O Pioneers!* (1913), *The Song of the Lark* (1915) and *My Ántonia*. In 1923, *One of Ours* was awarded the Pulitzer Prize. Cather moved on to consider fictions of romance with *A Lost Lady* (1923) and *My Mortal Enemy* (1926), and time and history in *The Professor's House* (1925), *Death Comes for the Archbishop* (1927) and *Shadows on the Rock* (1931). After her father's death in 1928, Cather travelled across country periodically to visit her mother, who was now living in a sanitarium. In the 1930s, Cather's writing slowed. She published only two novels, *Obscure Destinies* (1932), set in Nebraska, and *Lucy Gayheart* (1935). The *Not Under Forty* collection appeared in 1936 and her last novel, *Sapphira and the Slave Girl*, came out in 1940. She died in 1947.

KATE CHOPIN was born in 1850 in St Louis, Missouri, the daughter of Thomas and Eliza Faris O'Flaherty. Her father was an Irish immigrant; her mother a member of the St Louis aristocracy. After her father died in 1855 in a railroad accident, Kate was raised in a house run by three generations of widowed women. She received an unconventional education from her great-grandmother, who spoke to her only in French and told her tales of Old St Louis. In 1860, she started school with the Madames of Sacred Heart. In 1863, Kate's brother George died fighting for the Confederacy in the Civil War, and her great-grandmother died a month later. Kate rejoined society in 1870 to marry Oscar Chopin, raising six children in New Orleans. After her husband's death in 1882, she returned to St Louis to begin her life as a writer. Chopin's first novel, *At Fault* (1890), was considered a failure, but she wrote over sixty short stories, and enjoyed commercial success. The collections *Bayou Folk* (1894) and *A Night in Arcadie* (1897) established her reputation as a local colorist for her descriptions of Creoles and Arcadians in Louisiana. 'Desirée's Baby', one of her best known stories, appeared in *Vogue* in 1894. But it was her novel *The Awakening* (1899) that transformed Chopin's reputation. Both she and the novel were scornfully condemned by a deluge of criticism. Chopin wrote 'The Storm' shortly after her famous novel, but it was never published, and she produced only seven more stories until her death from a stroke in 1904.

REBECCA HARDING DAVIS was born in 1831 in Washington, Pennsylvania, the first of five children of Rachel Leet and Richard Harding. At the time of her birth, her parents lived in Huntsville, Alabama. When Davis was five years old, her family moved north, settling in Wheeling, Virginia. Rebecca was taught at home by her mother and then by tutors. At fourteen she entered the Washington Female Seminary, graduating with highest honors in 1848 and giving the valedictory address. After returning home to help with the younger children, she continued to study through her brother, Wilson, a student at the exclusively male Washington College. In 1861, *Atlantic Monthly* published 'Life in the Iron Mills', which was hailed for its realism and for introducing the industrial revolution into literature. After its success, she sent a manuscript to be published serially in the *Atlantic* as *A Story of To-day*, later published in book form as *Margaret Howth* (1862). Originally, when she sent editor James T. Fields the manuscript, he complained it was too gloomy, so Davis altered her text. It was the first of many instances in her literary career when she would be guided by other hands, including those of Clark Davis, a poor apprentice lawyer whom she married in 1863. He convinced her to write 'potboilers' for *Peterson's Magazine*. Davis embarked upon a dual career, writing lucrative thrillers for popular magazines while submitting more serious articles to the *Atlantic* and *Scribners*. In 1864, she published 'The Wife's Story' in the *Atlantic*, an account of the mental breakdown she suffered as a result of the conflict between wifely and artistic duties. *Waiting for the Verdict* (1868) explored the experience of slaves, freed

slaves, and mulattos after the Civil War; *John Andross* followed
in 1874. Later works included *Silhouettes of American Life*
(1892) and *Bits of Gossip* (1904). Although Davis wrote
throughout her lifetime, many critics feel that she did not fulfill
the potential of 'Life in the Iron Mills' because of the compromises forced upon her. She died in 1910.

MARY E. WILKINS FREEMAN was born in 1852 in Randolph,
Massachusetts, the second child of Warren Wilkins, a carpenter,
and Eleanor Winthrop Wilkins. At fifteen she moved to Brattle-
boro, Vermont. By the time she was thirty-one, Mary was the
sole survivor of her family, outliving her sister and her parents.
Her first significant publication, 'The Two Lovers', appeared
in *Harper's Bazaar* on 31 March 1883. The same year, she
moved back to Randolph and lived with her childhood friend,
Mary John Wales, and her family. During the 1880s, she
continued to write short stories for *Harper's* under the editorship of Mary Louise Booth, who became her trusted friend. Her
first two collections were composed primarily of previously
published stories: *A Humble Romance and Other Stories* (1887)
included the story 'Old Woman Magoun', and *A New England
Nun and Other Stories* (1891) included 'Sister Liddy' and
'A Poetess'. These two works established Freeman's reputation
as a New England regionalist and short story writer. She went
on to experiment with the novel in her later years because the
genre offered more critical status and financial reward. *Pem-
broke* (1894) was her greatest critical success. At forty-nine she
married Charles Manning Freeman, a New Jersey physician.
After her marriage, Freeman's writing took a conventional
turn with the novels *Madelon* (1896), *Jerome, A Poor Man*
(1897) and *The Portion of Labor* (1901). She also wrote her
spiritual autobiography, *By the Light of the Soul*. She died in
1930.

CHARLOTTE PERKINS GILMAN was born in 1860 in Hartford,
Connecticut, the daughter of Frederick Beecher and Mary A.
Fritch Perkins. Her father left the family soon after her birth,
and Charlotte received only suggested reading lists from him
during her childhood. Her formal education was a brief attendance at Rhode Island School of Design. In 1884 she married
Charles Walter Stetson. Ten months later, their only child

Katherine was born, an event which led to an extended period of depression for Gilman. On her husband's recommendation, she sought the medical attention of S. Weir Mitchell, a prominent doctor in the study of women's nervous disorders. Gilman later wrote 'The Yellow Wallpaper' based on this experience. In 1888 she took the dramatic step of leaving her husband and moving to Pasadena, California, with her daughter in order to regain her sanity. She was formally divorced in 1892. In 1898 Gilman published *Women and Economics*, a 'feminist manifesto' that gained her fame and established her voice as a women's rights reformer. *Concerning Children* (1900) and *The Home* (1904) expanded on her arguments in *Women and Economics*, suggesting that economic dependence on men can stunt women's mental growth. In 1900 Gilman married her first cousin George Houghton Gilman, a lawyer from New York, and settled in a relationship which proved happy and sustaining. In 1909 Gilman began a seven-year editorship of *Forerunner*, her own monthly periodical. *Forerunner* published two of her novels, *What Diantha Did* (1910) and *The Crux* (1911), as well as a non-fiction work, *Man-Made World* (1911). Gilman's other fiction included the utopian novels *Moving the Mountain* (1911), *Herland* (1915) and *With Her in Ourland* (1916). When her husband died in 1934, she moved from their home in Norwich, Connecticut, to Pasadena to live with her daughter's family. The next year, having been diagnosed with breast cancer, she committed suicide with chloroform. Her autobiography, *The Living of Charlotte Perkins Gilman*, was published in 1935, the year of her death.

SUSAN GLASPELL was born in 1876 and raised in Davenport, Iowa, the daughter of Elmer S. and Alice K. Glaspell. She was educated in public schools and matriculated at Drake University. After graduation in 1899, Susan became a correspondent for the *Des Moines Daily News* and in 1900 did graduate work at the University of Chicago. She wrote such popular fiction as her first novel, *The Glory and the Conquered* (1909), and short stories for *Harper's* and *Ladies Home Journal*. In 1913 she married George Cram Cook, an aspiring director, and a year later moved to Provincetown, Massachusetts, to found the Provincetown Players. Later the Cooks became founders of the Playwrights' Theater in Greenwich Village, where Eugene

O'Neill, Edna St Vincent Millay, John Reed and Michael Gold joined Glaspell as the leading playwrights. Her novels *The Visioning* (1911) and *Fidelity* (1915) questioned and challenged social norms. Glaspell wrote ten plays during this period, including *Suppressed Desires* (1914), *Tickless Time* (1918) and *Close the Book* (1917). *Trifles* (1916), considered her masterpiece, deals with the themes of guilt and female solidarity, and she later rewrote it as 'A Jury of Her Peers'. In *The Outside* (1917) and *The Verge* (1921), Glaspell portrayed women's rebellion. In 1922, she left for Greece with her husband, who died there in 1924. While still traveling in Europe she met and married Norman Matson with whom she produced *The Comic Artist* in 1928. In 1931, she divorced Matson and won the Pulitzer Prize for *Alison's House*, a play based on the life of Emily Dickinson. Glaspell returned to the theater in 1936 as the head of the Midwest Play Bureau for two years. She wrote three other plays which tried to maintain optimism in the face of the Great Depression before dying in 1948.

FRANCES HARPER was born in 1825 in Baltimore, Maryland, the daughter of free black parents. She was orphaned at three and lived with her uncle, William Watkins, who ran an academy for free colored youth. Harper received an uncommonly diverse education. In 1850 she taught sewing as the first female teacher at Union Seminary in Columbus, Ohio. The next year, she took a teaching position in Little York, Pennsylvania. After pledging herself to the anti-slavery cause, Harper moved to Philadelphia to educate herself about its networks. She began speaking publicly in 1854 and became a lecturer for the Anti-Slavery Society of Maine. During this time, she also wrote *Poems on Miscellaneous Subjects*, all copies of which are lost. From 1856 to 1859, Harper traveled, lecturing in the Northeast and Canada. She published 'The Two Offers' in *Anglo-African* in 1859. A year later, she married Fenton Harper from Cincinnati, settling in Columbus where their daughter Mary was born. After her husband's death in 1864, she resumed lecturing and writing: *Moses: A Story of the Nile* (1865) is considered her best work. She also published *Sketches on a Southern Life* (1872), based on her tours of the South between 1865 and 1872. *Iola Leroy* (1892) was the first black novel set in the Reconstruction. Harper followed it with a series of poetry collections: *The*

Sparrow's Fall and Other Poems (*c.* 1895), *Poems* (1895) and *Light Beyond Darkness* (n.d.). She died in 1911.

SARAH ORNE JEWETT was born in 1849 in South Berwick, Maine, the second daughter of Caroline Frances Perry and Theodore Herman Jewett, a wealthy country doctor. She was educated at Miss Raynes's School and Berwick Academy, but often was absent due to ill health. Financially independent throughout her life, Jewett published her first short story 'Jenny Garrow's Lovers' in 1868 in the *Flag of Our Union*. 'Mr Bruce' appeared the following year in the *Atlantic Monthly*. While she continued to publish other short stories such as 'The Shore House' in 1873 in the *Atlantic*, Jewett also wrote moral stories for young girls. *Deephaven* (1877), her first collection, was set in a fictitious seaport town. After its arrival publishers consistently collected her stories into book form, including *Play Days* (1878), *Old Friends and New* (1879) and *Country By-ways* (1881). In 1878, Dr Jewett died. However, Jewett gained a close friend, Annie Fields, widow of the editor of the *Atlantic Monthly*. Jewett spent winters with Mrs Fields in the literary circles of Boston. The novel *A Country Doctor* (1884) attracted attention abroad and was followed by *A March Island* (1885). In 1886, she published '*A White Heron' and Other Stories*, with the allegorical title story that made her famous. Jewett's masterpiece, *The Country of the Pointed Firs* (1896), solidified her reputation as a prominent American woman regionalist. In 1901 *The Tory Lover* ran serially in the *Atlantic* while two books for girls appeared: *Betty Leicester* (1890) and *Betty Leicester's Christmas* (1899). In 1901 Jewett was the first woman ever to receive an honorary Litt.D. from Bowdoin College. The next year she had an accident that ended her career. In March 1909 Jewett suffered a stroke and returned to Berwick where she died in June of that year.

ELIZABETH STUART PHELPS was born in 1815 in Andover, Massachusetts, to Abigail Clark, a long-term invalid, and Moses Stuart, professor of sacred literature at Andover Theological Seminary. Educated at Andover's Abbot Academy, she left home at sixteen and studied at Boston's Mount Vernon School while living with the family of Jacob Abbot. She returned to Andover in 1834 due to a chronic cerebral disease which eventually caused her death. In 1842 she married Austin Phelps, and moved to Boston where he had accepted a pastorate. In 1844 her daughter was born and christened Mary Gray, but she would take her mother's name upon her death. In 1848 the family once more returned to Andover, and she had two sons, Moses Stuart and Amos Lawrence. Phelps's literary success came late in her life; she died a year after the publication of *The Sunny Side or The Country Minister's Wife*, a book internationally recognized for portraying the hardships and triumphs of domestic life. Phelps's 'The Angel Over The Right Shoulder', a separately published short story, appeared in 1852, the year of her death. The story has been much anthologized because of its documentation of one woman's struggle to mediate between her literary work and domestic duties. Also in 1852 *A Peep at 'Number Five' or A Chapter in the Life of a City Pastor* was published. Her husband also published two of her collections after her death: *The Last Leaf from Sunny Side* (1853) and *The Tell-Tale or Home Secrets told by Old Travellers* (1853). Phelps's literary legacy lived on through her daughter who wrote *The Story of Avis* (1877) and her own autobiography, *Chapters from a Life* (1896).

CATHARINE SEDGWICK was born in 1789 in Stockbridge, Massachusetts, the third daughter of Pamela Dwight and Theodore Sedgwick. Her father was a self-made man who won political influence, becoming both a senator and a state representative. Throughout Catharine's youth her mother suffered from illness and depression, so the seven children were raised by a black servant, Elizabeth Freeman. Catharine attended school briefly but was primarily educated at home. Both her parents died early in her life, her mother in 1807 and her father in 1813, so it was her brothers' encouragement that led to the publication of her first novel, *A New England Tale* (1822), originally a Unitarian tract. Its immediate success was followed by *Redwood* (1824). With her third novel, *Hope Leslie* (1827), considered by many critics to be her best, she became the most famous American woman writer of her day. The work deals with the conflict between English settlers and the native Americans already inhabiting the land. *Clarence*, a more urban and contemporary novel, followed in 1830. With *The Linwoods* (1835), Sedgwick returned to historical romance, the genre for which she is best known. During 1835, she moved from adult fiction to moral tales, juvenile stories and etiquette books, and wrote her most famous didactic novels, *Home* (1835), *The Poor Rich Man and the Rich Poor Man* (1836) and *Live and Let Live* (1837). In 1857, she published *Married or Single?*, a novel that urged women not to marry for financial gain or prestige, but rather to cultivate their independence and marry only for admiration and respect. Sedgwick herself never married, but often acted as a surrogate mother to her brothers' children. During her lifetime, she was widely praised, alongside James Fenimore Cooper, Washington Irving and William Cullen Bryant, as part of the founding generation of American literature. However, Sedgwick distinguished herself from her male contemporaries by focusing on a female-centered world and changing the literary stereotyping of women through her more complex portrayals. She died in 1867.

HARRIET PRESCOTT SPOFFORD was born in 1835 in Calais, Maine, the oldest of five children of Sarah Bridges and Joseph Prescott. Throughout her childhood, her family suffered financially so she only attended school when they could afford it. In 1849 the mother and children moved to Newburyport Massachusetts, to live with a married sister while Harriet's father tried to renew his fortunes out West. Harriet attended the Putnam Free School, gaining a community of friends who shared her literary interests. She wrote for the school paper and composed hymns and dramatic dialogues. At sixteen, she won a prize for an essay on *Hamlet*. In 1853, the family moved to Derry, New Hampshire, where Harriet completed her formal education at Pinkerton Academy. Her first work, 'Life', dates back to this period. In 1856 her father returned, having fallen ill, and her mother soon became an invalid as well. Harriet began writing to support her family. In 1858 she submitted the detective story, 'In a Cellar', to the *Atlantic Monthly*. Although the publisher at first doubted her authorship of such a sophisticated tale, it proved to be well received. In 1860 she published her first novel, *Sir Rohan's Ghost*, a supernatural tale. *The Amber Gods and Other Stories* followed in 1863, and her second novel, *Azarian*, in 1864. An extremely productive writer, Spofford also wrote poems, novellas, children's books, literary essays, books on domestic issues, travel books and personal reminiscences. She married Richard Spofford in 1865. Their only child died in infancy. Though popular by the turn of the century for works such as *A Scarlet Poppy and Other Stories* (1894), *Old Madame and Other Tragedies* (1900) and *Old Washington* (1906), Spofford's critical reputation steadily declined until it was revived with the appearance of *The Elder People* (1920). She died in 1921.

EDITH WHARTON was born in 1862 in New York City, the daughter of George and Lucretia Rhinelander Jones. The family was part of the wealthy, traditional society of Old New York, and Edith was educated by governesses in modern languages and manners. She read extensively of her own accord in her father's library and traveled with her parents in Europe. At twenty-three Edith married Edward Robbins Wharton. She published 'Mrs Manstey's View' in 1891, and her first volume of fiction, *The Greater Inclination*, in 1899. The year before, Wharton suffered a nervous breakdown and, like Charlotte Perkins Gilman before her, was treated by Siles Weir Mitchell. Despite her illness, her novel *The Valley of Decisions* appeared in 1902. *The House of Mirth* (1905) established her critical reputation. It was followed by *The Reef* (1912) and *The Custom of the Country* (1913). That same year she divorced her husband and moved to Paris. *The Age of Innocence*, which many critics consider her best work, was published in 1920 and awarded the Pulitzer Prize in 1921, the first given to a woman. Wharton was also granted an honorary degree from Yale and a Gold Medal from the Academy of Arts and Letters in 1924. In 1934 she published her autobiography *A Backward Glance*. Wharton died in her house near Paris of a stroke in 1937.

CONSTANCE FENIMORE WOOLSON was born in 1840 in Clare-mont, New Hampshire, the daughter of Charles Jarvis and Hannah Cooper Pomeroy Woolson, and the great-niece of James Fenimore Cooper. After the death of three sisters from scarlet fever, the family moved to Cleveland. Constance attended school there and then enrolled in Madame Chegary's School in New York. After her father's death in 1859, Woolson and her mother traveled extensively. When her mother died in 1879, she went to Europe with her sister, Clare Benedict, and did not return to America. Woolson's first children's book, *The Old Stone House*

(1872), was published under a pseudonym. *Anne* (1880), the collection *Castle Nowhere: Lake Country Sketches* (1878), based on observations of Mackinac Island, and *Rodman the Keeper: Southern Sketches* (1880) were published before she left for Europe. 'Miss Grief' was first published in *Lippincott's Magazine* in 1880 shortly after her departure. While abroad, Woolson wrote a number of works set in Europe such as *Dorothy and Other Italian Stories* (1895), including 'At the Château of Corinne', and *The Front Yard and Other Stories* (1896). She also continued to publish works set in America, such as the novella *For the Major* (1883) and three novels: *East Angels* (1886), *Jupiter Lights* (1889) and *Horace Chase* (1874). Although she never married, two male literary confidants influenced her career: Clarence Steadman, whom she met vacationing in St Augustine, and Henry James, whom she met in 1880. The latter became her lifelong and intimate friend. Known primarily for her contribution to the local color movement, Woolson also explored descriptions of small town life and the international theme. She suffered bouts of depression throughout her life, and some critics speculate that the two-story fall which caused her death in Venice in 1894 was a suicide.

NOTE ON THE EDITORS

ELAINE SHOWALTER is Avalon Professor of the Humanities at Princeton University. Her books on women writers include *A Literature of Their Own* and *Sister's Choice: Tradition and Change in American Women's Writing*.

CATHERINE SAINT LOUIS was born in Longmeadow, Massachusetts. She graduated in June 1996 from Princeton University with a BA in English and American studies. While at Princeton, she was a Mellon Minority Undergraduate fellow. She plans to read for her M.Phil. in English at Oxford University this fall.

STUART BURROWS was born in Bromley, England. He received a BA in English and History from the University of Southampton in 1989 and an MA in English from Northeastern University, Boston, in 1994. He is currently a PhD candidate in the English Department at Princeton University.

CHRONOLOGY OF THE AUTHORS' LIVES

Year   Age   Life

1789   Birth of Catharine Sedgwick

CHRONOLOGY OF THEIR TIMES

Year	Artistic Context	Historical Events
1784	Hannah Adams (1755–1831), probably the first professional woman writer in the US, publishes *Alphabetical Compendium of the Various Sects*	
1789		French Revolution George Washington becomes president of the US
1790	Ann Eliza Bleecker (1752–83) writes on the American frontier at war	
1794	Ann Radcliffe, *The Mysteries of Udolpho*	
1796	Sarah W. A. Morton co-authors (with William Brown) first novel published in the US, *The Power of Sympathy*	
1797	Ann Radcliffe, *The Italian*	Birth of Sojourner Truth, abolitionist orator
1798	Hannah Webster Foster (1759–1879), *The Boarding School*, a manual for young ladies	
1801	Tabitha Gilman Tenney (1762–1837), *Female Quixoticism*	Thomas Jefferson becomes president of the US
1808		Import of slaves into US banned
1810	Birth of Margaret Harper (d. 1850)	
1811	Jane Austen, *Sense and Sensibility*	
1812		US and Britain at war (to 1814)

Year   *Age*   *Life*

1815   Birth of Elizabeth Stuart Phelps

1822   33   Catharine Sedgwick, *A New England Tale*

1825   Birth of Frances Harper

1827   38   Catharine Sedgwick, *Hope Leslie*

1831   Birth of Rebecca Harding Davis
1832   Birth of Louisa May Alcott

1835   Birth of Harriet Prescott Spofford

1840   Birth of Constance Fenimore Woolson

Year	Artistic Context	Historical Events
1813	Jane Austen, *Pride and Prejudice, Mansfield Park*	
1815		Napoleon defeated at Battle of Waterloo
1816	Mary Shelley, *Frankenstein* Jane Austen, *Emma*	
1819	Irving, *The Sketch Book of Geoffrey Crayon*	
1824		The first strike by women takes place in Pawtucket, Rhode Island
1826	Fenimore Cooper, *The Last of the Mohicans*	
1827	Susan Bogert Warner (1819–55), *The Wide, Wide World* – first American book to sell 1 million copies	
1829	Frances Wright begins publication of *The Free Enquirer*	
1830	Birth of Emily Dickinson (d. 1886)	
1833	Lydia Maria Child, *Appeal in Favor of . . . Africans*	
1834		American Female Moral Reform Society (AFMR) formed
1835	Lydia Maria Child, *A History of the Condition of Women*	Publication of *The Advocate*, AFMR Society's journal, begins
1836	*Letters on the Difficulties of Religion*, by Catharine Esther Beecher (1800–78)	Wesleyan College in Macon, Georgia, the first chartered women's college in America, opens
1839	The mill girls of Lowell, Massachusetts, begin publishing *The Lowell Offering*, a monthly magazine of poetry, fiction and essays	

Year   Age   Life

Year	Age	Life
1849		Birth of Sarah Orne Jewett
1850		Birth of Kate Chopin
1851	36	Elizabeth Stuart Phelps, *The Sunny Side* or *The Country Minister's Wife*
1852		Birth of Mary E. Wilkins Freeman
	37	Death of Elizabeth Stuart Phelps
1857	68	Catharine Sedgwick, *Married or Single?*
1860		Birth of Charlotte Perkins Gilman
	25	Harriet Prescott Spofford publishes her first novel, *Sir Rohan's Ghost*, anonymously
1861	30	Rebecca Harding Davis, 'Life in the Iron Mills'
1862		Birth of Edith Wharton
	31	Rebecca Harding Davis, *Margaret Howth*
1863	28	Harriet Prescott Spofford, *The Amber Gods and Other Stories*
	31	Louisa May Alcott, *Hospital Sketches*

Year	Artistic Context	Historical Events
1841	Emerson, *Essays*	Brook Farm established
1845	Margaret Fuller, *Women in the Nineteenth Century*	
1847	Charlotte Brontë, *Jane Eyre* Emily Brontë, *Wuthering Heights*	
1848	Poe, *Tales of the Grotesque and Arabesque*	*Seneca Falls Declaration of Rights and Sentiments* delivered; Elizabeth Cady Stanton and Lucretia Mott organize Seneca Falls Convention 1848 revolutions in Europe
1850	Hawthorne, *The Scarlet Letter*	
1851	Melville, *Moby Dick*	
1852	Harriet Beecher Stowe, *Uncle Tom's Cabin*	
1853		Paulina Davis publishes *Una*, the first women's rights magazine in the US
1854	Thoreau, *Walden*	Formation of the Republican Party
1855	Walt Whitman, *Leaves of Grass*	Crimean War
1857	Flaubert, *Madame Bovary* Elizabeth Gaskell, *Life of Charlotte Brontë*	Matrimonial Causes Act makes divorce possible in England without an Act of Parliament
1859	Darwin, *The Origin of Species* George Eliot, *Adam Bede* *Our Nig* by Harriet Wilson, first novel by an African-American woman, published	
1860	George Eliot, *The Mill on the Floss*	Abraham Lincoln elected US president
1861	Harriet Davies, *Incidents in the Life of a Slave Girl*	American Civil War declared

Year	Age	Life
1865	40	Frances Harper, *Moses: A Story of the Nile*
1867	78	Death of Catharine Sedgwick
1868	36	Louisa May Alcott, *Little Women*
	53	Elizabeth Stuart Phelps, *The Gates Ajar*
1873		Birth of Willa Cather
1876		Birth of Susan Glaspell
1877	28	Sarah Orne Jewett publishes first collection of stories, *Deephaven*
		Phelps's daughter, *The Story of Avis*
1880	40	Constance Fenimore Woolson, *Rodman the Keeper: Southern Sketches*

Year	Artistic Context	Historical Events
1865	Carroll, *Alice's Adventures in Wonderland*	President Lincoln assassinated; Andrew Johnson becomes US president; Civil War ends Belle Boyd, after being captured by the union, writes *Belle Boyd, in Camp and Prison* Thirteenth Amendment to the Constitution, abolishing slavery, goes to the states for ratification
1866	Augusta Jane Evans Wilson (1835–1909), *St Elmo*	
1869	J. S. Mill, *The Subjection of Women*	Elizabeth Cady Stanton, Martha Coffin, Pelham Wright and Susan B. Anthony found the National Woman Suffrage Association (NWSA); American Woman Suffrage Association founded by Lucy Stone and Julia Ward Howe; Wyoming Territory grants women the vote
1871	George Eliot, *Middlemarch*	
1872	Birth of Eleanor Hallowell Abbott (d. 1958)	
1876	Twain, *Tom Sawyer*	
1878	*The Leavemouth Case*, reputedly the first detective novel by an American woman, published by Anna Katharine Green	

Year	Artistic Context	Historical Events
1881	James, *The Portrait of a Lady* Elizabeth Cady Stanton, Susan B. Anthony and Matilda Joslyn Gage compile and publish *History of Woman Suffrage* (to 1886)	Clara Barton founds the National Society for the Red Cross
1883	Lillie Devereux Blake, *Woman's Place To-day*	
1884	Twain, *The Adventures of Huckleberry Finn* Helen Hunt Jackson, *Ramona*	
1887	Birth of Edna Ferber (d. 1968)	
1889		Jane Adams and Ellen Gates Starr found Hull House in Chicago, dedicated to community service
1890	Emily Dickinson, *Poems*	National Woman Suffrage Association and the American Woman Suffrage Association merge to form the National American Woman Suffrage Association
1893	Birth of Dorothy Parker (d. 1967)	
1895	Elizabeth Cady Stanton, *Woman's Bible*	
1896		National Association of Colored Women formed
1900	Freud, *The Interpretation of Dreams* Dreiser, *Sister Carrie*	

Year   Age   Life

Year	Age	Life
1904	54	Death of Kate Chopin
1905	43	Edith Wharton, *The House of Mirth*
1909	60	Death of Sarah Orne Jewett
1910	79	Death of Rebecca Harding Davis
1911	49	Edith Wharton, *Ethan Frome*
	86	Death of Frances Harper
1912	39	Willa Cather publishes first novel, *Alexander's Bridge*
1916	40	Susan Glaspell, *Trifles*
1918	45	Willa Cather, *My Ántonia*
1920	85	Harriet Prescott Spofford, *The Elder People*
1921	59	Edith Wharton's, *The Age of Innocence* wins Pulitzer Prize
	86	Death of Harriet Prescott Spofford
1923	50	Willa Cather's *One of Ours* wins Pulitzer Prize
1930	78	Death of Mary E. Wilkins Freeman
1931	55	Susan Glaspell's *Alison's House* wins the Pulitzer Prize
1934	72	Edith Wharton, *A Backward Glance,* her autobiography

Year	Artistic Context	Historical Events
1903	DuBois, *The Souls of Black Folk*	
1914		First World War begins
1918	Joyce, *Ulysses*	First World War ends
1920		The Nineteenth Amendment, giving women the vote in America, is ratified
1922	T. S. Eliot, *The Wasteland*	Rebecca Latimer Felton is the first woman appointed to US Senate
1923	Edna St Vincent Millay wins Pulitzer Prize for *The Ballad of The Harp-Weaver*, *A Few Figs From Thistles* and eight sonnets in *American Poetry, 1922, a Miscellany*	
1925	Scott Fitzgerald, *The Great Gatsby*	Nellie Tayloe Ross becomes first American Woman governor
1926	Amy Lowell wins Pulitzer Prize for *What's O'Clock*	
1927	Virginia Woolf, *To The Lighthouse*	
1929	Faulkner, *The Sound and the Fury* Hemingway, *A Farewell to Arms*	
1931		Jane Addams shares the Nobel Prize for peace with Nicholas Murray Butler

Year	Age	Life
1935	75	Death of Charlotte Perkins Gilman *The Living of Charlotte Perkins Gilman* published
1937	75	Death of Edith Wharton
1938		Edith Wharton, *The Buccaneers*
1940	67	Willa Cather publishes her last novel, *Sapphira and the Slave Girl*
1947	74	Death of Willa Cather
1948	72	Death of Susan Glaspell

Year	Artistic Context	Historical Events
1938	Pearl S. Buck becomes first American woman to win the Nobel Prize for Literature	
1939	Steinbeck, *The Grapes of Wrath*	Second World War begins
1940	Richard Wright, *Native Son*	
1942	Ellen Glasgow's *In This Our Life* wins Pulitzer Prize	
1945		Second World War ends
1947		Dr Gerty T. Cori first woman to be awarded the Nobel Prize in medicine or physiology

INTRODUCTION

'America is now wholly given over to a d——d mob of scribbling women', wrote Nathaniel Hawthorne in 1855 to his publisher, William Ticknor, 'and I should have no chance of success while the public taste is occupied with their trash.' Generations of critics took Hawthorne's disdainful words about the popular women story writers of his day as definitive. In his influential study *American Renaissance* (1960), F. O. Matthiessen placed the male writers of the 1850s, including Hawthorne, Melville and Emerson, at the center of the American literary tradition, and relegated women writers to the margins. In his book on *The Feminine Fifties* (1940), Fred Lewis Pattee described the scribbling women as fervid, fatuous and florid. Unlike nineteenth-century English women writers, like Jane Austen, the Brontës and George Eliot, whose work was included in the very highest ranks of the national literature, nineteenth-century 'American women writers have systematically been dismissed, scattered, ignored'.[1]

As Nina Baym, an eminent scholar of Hawthorne, has noted, his disparaging words about his female contemporaries 'constitute the threshold which all of us who work on women's writing of the nineteenth century have been forced to cross in order to get to work'.[2] But in recent years, a new generation of feminist historians and literary critics have rediscovered this fiction and redefined its significance. Scribbling women are now regarded as 'those who refuse to be silenced by critical standards that trivialize the subjects of women's lives, and who write with energy, intelligence, and commitment'.[3]

This anthology aims to introduce readers to a sampling of the best short stories by nineteenth-century American women writers, from Catharine Sedgwick, one of the first American best-sellers, to Edith Wharton. It includes stories that have become classics of social protest, such as Rebecca Harding Davis's 'Life in the Iron Mills' and Charlotte Perkins Gilman's 'The Yellow

Wallpaper'; stories that will acquaint readers with unfamiliar writers, like Harriet Prescott Spofford and Elizabeth Stuart Phelps, and unfamiliar stories by well-known writers, like Louisa May Alcott and Kate Chopin. Here, too, is Frances Harper's 'The Two Offers', one of the earliest stories published by an African-American woman. Competition with men in the literary market and the woman's struggle to combine a literary career with a domestic life were important themes of these stories. Mary E. Wilkins Freeman in 'A Poetess' and Constance Fenimore Woolson in 'Miss Grief' used the tensions between male and female literary culture as the subject of haunting tales of disappointment and loss. Susan Glaspell, in 'A Jury of Her Peers', used a murder case to challenge literary judgments as well as legal ones.

Besides energy, intelligence and commitment, these stories share a wide-ranging imaginative vision and raise questions we are still debating today. Americans have long claimed the short story as their national literary genre, and nineteenth-century women writers did their best work in this genre. The novel carried the aesthetic freight of the male literary tradition, and the high standards of the Victorian Golden Age. It demanded a commitment of time many American women could not afford, and a set of conventions not always appropriate to the American experience. But the short story was a flexible and innovative form, responsive to the scenes, dialects and conflicts of various regions and classes.

American book-publishing began around 1800, despite the absence of copyright which made pirated English novels comparatively inexpensive. By mid-century, literary centers had developed in Boston, New York and Philadelphia. Women writers played an important part in American literary culture. Literary annuals, gift books and women's magazines, like *Godey's Lady's Book*, became important outlets for women's stories and poems. By the late 1840s, in *Female Poets of America*, the editor Rufus Griswold declared his pride in 'the increased degree to which women among us are taking a leading part in literature ... The proportion of female writers at this moment in America far exceeds that which the present or any other age in England exhibits.'

At the same time, writes the literary historian Michael Davitt Bell, 'a pronounced differentiation of "masculine" and "feminine" American fiction began to emerge as the major fault line in the American literary landscape'.[4] Women were praised as long as they adhered to the precepts of the domestic codes of the time. They were discouraged from discussing politics or seeking literary fame. As Sarah Hale, editor of *Godey's*, wrote to the abolitionist Lydia Maria Child, 'The precepts and examples of the Saviour should be the guide of woman's benevolent efforts. In no case did He lend aid or encouragement to the agitation of political questions.'[5]

As Hawthorne's remarks about literary success and public taste imply, women and men were competing for readers in the new marketplaces of American publishing. But if 'there was anxiety or antagonism between these male and female "traditions", it flowed almost exclusively in one direction. Writers like Hawthorne and Melville aroused little professional anxiety in popular women writers.'[6] As Baym explained in *Woman's Fiction: A Guide to Novels by and about Women in America 1820–1870*, American 'women authors tended not to think of themselves as artists or justify themselves in the language of art until the 1870s and after ... [Their work] did not make the sorts of claims on its readers that "art" does – the dimensions of formal self-consciousness, attachment to or quarrel with a grand tradition, aesthetic seriousness, all are missing.'[7] This modesty certainly reflected cultural attitudes toward art and femininity. As Jane Tompkins points out, before the Civil War women 'were seen as instruments of spiritual and moral refinement, existing to ennoble and spiritualize men. Thus, they share with works of art the status of a vehicle of inspiration, existing not as ends in themselves, but as elevating influences.'[8]

Nonetheless, antebellum women writers used parable, parody, sensationalism and satire to undermine the feminine stereotypes to which they were consigned. 'We shall take care to deal with the subject after a desultory, unsystematic, and feminine manner', writes Caroline Kirkland in 'Literary Women'. 'We repudiate learning; we disdain accuracy, we abjure logic. We shall aim only at the pretty prattle which is conceded to our sex as a right, and admired as a charm.'[9] In 'Behind a Mask', published under her pseudonym, A. M. Barnard, Louisa May Alcott's heroine, Jean Muir, pretends to be the demure feminine creature men expect, and plots brilliantly to get her revenge. Constance Fenimore Woolson's character 'Miss Grief' dies unpublished because she cannot alter her imaginative vision to fit the polite conventions of her editors. Indeed, even if 'these writers in different ways advertised their conformity to contemporary ideas of women's proper sphere', they were turning to short fiction to express their deepest private feelings.[10] Moreover, as Douglas notes, their sentimentalist sensibility was also a disguise. 'Their outwardly decorous lives and fairly conservative political stands have served, as they were intended to do, to obscure the fact that women authors . . . in America at this time were part of a wider movement which defied ancient conventions and claimed wider experience as woman's due.'[11]

American women swept into the field of publishing in part because 'literature was a profession but could be made to look unprofessional. It enabled its practitioners to do a man's job, for a man's pay, in a woman's clothes . . . In short, American women were drawn to writing just when it became a possible business, and they were among the first to sense and develop its business potential.'[12] Moreover, while American women writers have expressed discomfort with fame and often stressed spiritual or maternal motives for their work, conditions of the marketplace may actually have favored them. Nineteenth-century author-publisher relationships were relatively congenial to women. As women writers were 'ladies', so, too, did their publishers regard themselves as 'gentlemen'. Publishers valued 'personal relationships, noncommercial aims, and moral guardianship', and, thus, the entrepreneurial side of women's writing was facilitated by business styles that did not require new or 'unfeminine' skills.[13]

American women's writing was influenced by the English tradition, but it also transformed and expanded that tradition in terms of its own historical, cultural and racial contexts. Catharine Sedgwick dedicated her first novel, *A New England Tale* (1822), to Maria Edgeworth; other American women writers expressed admiration for Elizabeth Barrett Browning and George Eliot. Sarah Hale recalled that as a child 'of all the books I saw, few were written by Americans and none by *women*'. She read Mrs Radcliffe's gothic novel *The Mysteries of Udolpho* as a girl, and was thrilled: 'It was the most fascinating I ever read . . . written by a woman! How happy it made me! The wish to promote the reputation of my own sex, and to do something for my own country, were among the earliest mental emotions I can recollect.'[14] Constance Fenimore Woolson's 'At the Château of Corinne' pays tribute to the intellectual heroine of an influential novel by Madame de Staël. By far the most popular of the English women novelists, however, was Charlotte Brontë, and *Jane Eyre* was the most beloved book.

The Civil War was a pivotal episode in the history of American women's fiction; it launched the careers of such writers as Harriet Beecher Stowe and Louisa May Alcott. The literary historian David Reynolds finds the Civil War period so rich in important work by women that he calls the ten years between 1855 and 1865 'the American Women's Renaissance'.[15] After the Civil War, the gentlemanly publishers were driven out by businessmen, who were indifferent to 'feminine' values and more interested in impersonal profits. Moreover, the postwar generation of women writers saw themselves as artists rather than moralists; Constance Fenimore Woolson noted that earlier women writers had 'favored the beautiful at the expense of strength'. However, she argued that 'literature must not refuse to deal with the ugly and the commonplace and even the shockingly unpleasant'.[16]

Many of these writers, including Mary E. Wilkins Freeman and Sarah Orne Jewett, set their fiction in the rural areas of New England that had been devastated by the Civil War, where only old men, single women, clergymen and a few little boys had been left behind. Their lonely spinster heroines protest against the confining circumstances of their lives in rebellions that range from passive resistance to outright violence. They, too, were living in an age that favored the development of the short story as a major art form and a uniquely American genre. In 1887, *Harper's* editorialized that 'Americans have ... brought the short story nearer perfection in the all-round sense ... and for reasons very simple and near at hand. It might be argued from the national hurry and impatience that it was a literary form peculiarly adapted to the American temperament.'[17] The prestigious *Atlantic Monthly* echoed the idea in 1892: 'American writers ... have taken the short story as their province ... [T]here is no sign that the art is anywhere so rich, so varied, or so fresh as it is with us ... It appears to have become in truth, the national mode of utterance in the things of the imagination, and, taking its own wherever it finds it, the short story has become more and more variously expressive.'[18]

The 1890s were transitional years in the formation of an American feminine aesthetic. Local Colorists, who specialised in fiction about particular regions of the country, were experimenting with an ethnographic realism that may have helped them deal with hitherto forbidden subject matter. Kate Chopin's stories about the Creoles of Louisiana bayou, with their themes of interracial love and intense female sexuality, are among the most important examples of the genre. New Women writers like Charlotte Perkins Gilman were also experimenting with new narrative forms and with feminist themes. While the previous generation solved the conflict between art and the domestic ideal by rejecting the role of 'artist', the New Woman chose art over maternity and domesticity. In Gilman's much-anthologized 'The Yellow Wallpaper', a young mother suffering from post-partum depression goes mad when she is deprived of social contact and literary activity.

With the appearance of Edith Wharton and Willa Cather, who made their debuts as short story writers in the 1890s, American women's fiction achieved critical acclaim as well as popular success. At the turn of the century, their stories were widely read as examples of the best the country had to offer. By the end of World War I, however, American critical hostility toward female authorship once again stigmatized women's writing. A nation taking new pride in its cultural heritage after the war saw only weakness and sentimentality in the contributions women had made to the national literature. In the years following the armistice, women writers were gradually but systematically eliminated from the canon of American literature as it was anthologized, studied and taught. In 1918, the editors of the first major literary history of the United States announced that 'a truly American art ... should embody the values of a manly culture'.[19]

The final story in this collection, Susan Glaspell's 'A Jury of Her Peers', raises both legal and aesthetic questions about women's place in American culture. In 1917, when it was published, American women could not vote or serve on juries, and they had scant representation on the editorial boards of critical journals and literary histories. Glaspell asks whether this double standard gives women the right to take the law into their own hands, and whether a peer is someone who shares a common language. Are women the only accurate judges of women's work? Glaspell anticipates both contemporary discussions of the differences between male and female forms of communication and expression and theories of a female aesthetic in art.

Glaspell's own career, however, suggests that these differences are cultural and political rather than natural or psychological. A celebrated writer and dramatist at the beginning of the century, often compared to Eugene O'Neill, Glaspell's reputation declined throughout the century. In the forty years following her death in 1948, only one book and a single article about her work appeared. Glaspell was revived only when research specifically devoted to women writers began, and when 'A Jury of Her Peers' was rediscovered. But its skill and depth will be apparent to all thoughtful readers today. As nineteenth-century scribbling women find new juries of readers at the end of the twentieth century, they will successfully plead their own critical case.

ELAINE SHOWALTER

References

1. Elizabeth Ammons, *Conflicting Stories: American Women Writers at the Turn into the Twentieth Century* (New York: Oxford University Press, 1991), p. ix.
2. Nina Baym, 'Rewriting the Scribbling Women', in *Legacy* 2 (1985), p. 4.
3. Mary Wyer, 'Scribbling Women', in *Oxford Guide to American Women's Writing*, ed., Cathy M. Davidson and Linda Wagner-Martin (New York: Oxford University Press, 1995), p. 782.
4. Michael Davitt Bell, 'Conditions of Literary Vocation', in *The Cambridge History of American Literature* II, ed., Sacvan Bercovitch (Cambridge: Cambridge University Press, 1995), p. 43.
5. See Ann Douglas, 'The "Scribbling Women" and Fanny Fern: Why Women Wrote', *American Quarterly* 23 (1971): pp. 4–24.
6. Bell, p. 121.
7. Baym, *Woman's Fiction* (Ithaca: Cornell University Press, 1977), p. 32.
8. Jane Tompkins, 'Introduction', to Susan Warner, *The Wide, Wide World* (New York: Paxman, 1851), p. 607.
9. Caroline Kirkland, 'Literary Women'.
10. Bell, p. 82.

11. Ann Douglas, 'The Literature of Impoverishment', *Women's Studies* I (1972), p. 5.
12. Douglas, p. 6.
13. See Susan Coultrap-McQuin, *Doing Literary Business: American Women Writers in the Nineteenth Century* (Chapel Hill: University of North Carolina Press, 1990), p. 28.
14. Sarah J. Hale, *Woman's Record* (New York: Harper & Brothers, 1852), p. 869.
15. See David Reynolds, *Beneath the American Renaissance* (New York: Alfred A. Knopf, 1988), p. 387.
16. Fred Lewis Pattee, 'Constance Fenimore Woolson and the South', in *South Atlantic Quarterly* 38 (1939), p. 132.
17. 'Editor's Study', *Harper's* (1887), p. 484.
18. 'The Short Story', *Atlantic Monthly* (February 1892), p. 261.
19. William B. Cairns, ed., *History of American Literature* (New York: Johnson Reprint Corp., 1969), p. 15.

SCRIBBLING WOMEN
SHORT STORIES BY
19TH-CENTURY AMERICAN WOMEN

CATHARINE SEDGWICK

Cacoethes Scribendi

1830

BY THE AUTHOR OF *HOPE LESLIE*

> *Glory and gain the industrious tribe provoke.**
>
> POPE

The little secluded and quiet village of H. lies at no great
distance from our 'literary emporium.' It was never remarked or
remarkable for anything, save one mournful preeminence, to
those who sojourned within its borders – it was duller even than
common villages. The young men of the better class all emi-
grated. The most daring spirits adventured on the sea. Some
went to Boston; some to the south; and some to the west; and
left a community of women who lived like nuns, with the
advantage of more liberty and fresh air, but without the
consolation and excitement of a religious vow. Literally, there
was not a single young gentleman in the village – nothing in
manly shape to which these desperate circumstances could give
the form and quality and use of a beau. Some dashing city
blades, who once strayed from the turnpike to this sequestered
spot, averred that the girls stared at them as if, like Miranda,
they would have exclaimed –

> 'What is't? a spirit?
> Lord, how it looks about! Believe me, sir,
> It carries a brave form: – But 'tis a spirit.'*

A peculiar fatality hung over this devoted place. If death seized
on either head of a family, he was sure to take the husband;
every woman in H was a widow or maiden; and it is a sad fact,
that when the holiest office of the church was celebrated, they
were compelled to borrow deacons from an adjacent village.
But, incredible as it may be, there was no great diminution of

happiness in consequence of the absence of the nobler sex.
Mothers were occupied with their children and housewifery,
and the young ladies read their books with as much interest as
if they had lovers to discuss them with, and worked their frills
and capes as diligently, and wore them as complacently, as if
they were to be seen by manly eyes. Never were there pleasanter
gatherings or parties (for that was the word even in their
nomenclature) than those of the young girls of H. There was no
mincing – no affectation – no hope of passing for what they
were not – no envy of the pretty and fortunate – no insolent
triumph over the plain and demure and neglected, – but all was
good will and good humour. They were a pretty circle of girls –
a garland of bright fresh flowers. Never were there more
sparkling glances, – never sweeter smiles – nor more of them.
Their present was all health and cheerfulness; and their future,
not the gloomy perspective of dreary singleness, for somewhere
in the passage of life they were sure to be mated. Most of the
young men who had abandoned their native soil, as soon as they
found themselves *getting along*, loyally returned to lay their
fortunes at the feet of the companions of their childhood.

The girls made occasional visits to Boston, and occasional
journeys to various parts of the country, for they were all enter-
prising and independent, and had the characteristic New England avidity for seizing a 'privilege;' and in these various ways,
to borrow a phrase of their good grandames, 'a door was opened
for them,' and in due time they fulfilled the destiny of women.

We spoke strictly, and à la lettre, when we said that in the
village of H. there was not a single *beau*. But on the outskirts of
the town, at a pleasant farm, embracing hill and valley, upland
and meadow land; in a neat house, looking to the south, with
true economy of sunshine and comfort, and overlooking the
prettiest winding stream that ever sent up its sparkling beauty
to the eye, and flanked on the north by a rich maple grove,
beautiful in spring and summer, and glorious in autumn, and
the kindest defense in winter; – on this farm and in this house
dwelt a youth, to fame unknown, but known and loved by every
inhabitant of H., old and young, grave and gay, lively and
severe. Ralph Hepburn was one of nature's favourites. He had a
figure that would have adorned courts and cities; and a face that
adorned human nature, for it was full of good humour, kind-
heartedness, spirit, and intelligence; and driving the plough or

wielding the scythe, his cheek flushed with manly and profitable exercise, he looked as if he had been moulded in a poet's fancy – as farmers look in Georgics and Pastorals.* His gifts were by no means all external. He wrote verses in every album in the village, and very pretty album verses they were, and numerous too – for the number of albums was equivalent to the whole female population. He was admirable at pencil sketches; and once with a little paint, the refuse of a house painting, he achieved an admirable portrait of his grandmother and her cat. There was, to be sure, a striking likeness between the two figures, but he was limited to the same colours for both; and besides, it was not out of nature, for the old lady and her cat had purred together in the chimney corner, till their physiognomies bore an obvious resemblance to each other. Ralph had a talent for music too. His voice was the sweetest of all the Sunday choir, and one would have fancied, from the bright eyes that were turned on him from the long line and double lines of treble and counter singers, that Ralph Hepburn was a note book, or that the girls listened with their eyes as well as their ears. Ralph did not restrict himself to psalmody. He had an ear so exquisitely susceptible to the 'touches of sweet harmony,' that he discovered, by the stroke of his axe, the musical capacities of certain species of wood, and he made himself a violin of chestnut, and drew strains from it, that if they could not create a soul under the ribs of death, could make the prettiest feet and the lightest hearts dance, an achievement far more to Ralph's taste than the aforesaid miracle. In short, it seemed as if nature, in her love of compensation, had showered on Ralph all the gifts that are usually diffused through a community of beaux. Yet Ralph was no prodigy; none of his talents were in excess, but all in moderate degree. No genius was ever so good humoured, so useful, so practical; and though, in his small and modest way, a Crichton,* he was not, like most universal geniuses, good for nothing for any particular office in life. His farm was not a pattern farm – a prize farm for an agricultural society, but in wonderful order considering – his miscellaneous pursuits. He was the delight of his grandfather for his sagacity in hunting bees – the old man's favourite, in truth his only pursuit. He was so skilled in woodcraft that the report of his gun was as certain a signal of death as the tolling of a church bell. The fish always caught at his bait. He manufactured half his farming utensils, improved upon old inventions, and struck out some new ones; tamed partridges – the most untameable of all the feathered tribe; domesticated squirrels; rivalled Scheherazade herself in telling stories, strange and long – the latter quality being essential at a country fireside; and, in short, Ralph made a perpetual holiday of a life of labour.

Every girl in the village street knew when Ralph's wagon or sleigh traversed it; indeed, there was scarcely a house to which the horses did not, as if by instinct, turn up while their master greeted its fair tenants. This state of affairs had continued for two winters and two summers since Ralph came to his majority and, by the death of his father, to the sole proprietorship of the 'Hepburn farm,' – the name his patrimonial acres had obtained from the singular circumstance (in our *moving* country) of their having remained in the same family for four generations. Never was the matrimonial destiny of a young lord, or heir just come to his estate, more thoroughly canvassed than young Hepburn's by mothers, aunts, daughters, and nieces. But Ralph, perhaps from sheer good heartedness, seemed reluctant to give to one the heart that diffused rays of sunshine through the whole village.

With all decent people he eschewed the doctrines of a certain erratic female lecturer on the odious monopoly of marriage, yet Ralph, like a tender hearted judge, hesitated to place on a single brow the crown matrimonial which so many deserved, and which, though Ralph was far enough from a coxcomb, he could not but see so many coveted.

Whether our hero perceived that his mind was becoming elated or distracted with this general favour, or that he observed a dawning of rivalry among the fair competitors, or whatever was the cause, the fact was, that he by degrees circumscribed his visits, and finally concentrated them in the family of his aunt Courland.

Mrs Courland was a widow, and Ralph was the kindest of nephews to her, and the kindest of cousins to her children. To their mother he seemed their guardian angel. That the five lawless, daring little urchins did not drown themselves when they were swimming, nor shoot themselves when they were shooting, was, in her eyes, Ralph's merit; and then 'he was so attentive to Alice, her only daughter – a brother could not be kinder.' But who would not be kind to Alice? she was a sweet girl of seventeen, not beautiful, not handsome perhaps, – but pretty enough – with soft hazel eyes, a profusion of light brown hair, always in the neatest trim, and a mouth that could not but be lovely and loveable, for all kind and tender affections were playing about it. Though Alice was the only daughter of a doting mother, the only sister of five loving boys, the only niece of three single, fond aunts, and, last and greatest, the only cousin of our only beau, Ralph Hepburn, no girl of seventeen was ever more disinterested, unassuming, unostentatious, and unspoiled. Ralph and Alice had always lived on terms of cousinly affection – an affection of a neutral tint that they never thought of being shaded into the deep dye of a more tender passion. Ralph rendered her all cousinly offices. If he had twenty damsels to escort, not an uncommon case, he never forgot Alice. When he returned from any little excursion, he always brought some graceful offering to Alice.

He had lately paid a visit to Boston. It was at the season of the periodical inundation of annuals. He brought two of the prettiest to Alice. Ah! little did she think they were to prove Pandora's box to her. Poor simple girl! she sat down to read them, as if an annual were meant to be read, and she was honestly interested and charmed. Her mother observed her delight. 'What have you there, Alice?' she asked. 'Oh the prettiest story, mamma! – two such tried faithful lovers, and married at last! It ends beautifully: I hate love stories that don't end in marriage.'

'And so do I, Alice,' exclaimed Ralph, who entered at the moment, and for the first time Alice felt her cheeks tingle at his approach. He had brought a basket, containing a choice plant he had obtained for her, and she laid down the annual and went with him to the garden to see it set by his own hand.

Mrs Courland seized upon the annual with avidity. She had imbibed a literary taste in Boston, where the best and happiest years of her life were passed. She had some literary ambition too. She read the *North American Review** from beginning to end, and she fancied no conversation could be sensible or improving that was not about books. But she had been effectually prevented, by the necessities of a narrow income, and by the unceasing wants of five teasing boys, from indulging her literary inclinations; for Mrs Courland, like all New England women, had been taught to consider domestic duties as the first temporal duties of her sex. She had recently seen some of the native productions with which the press is daily teeming, and which certainly have a tendency to dispel our early illusions about the craft of authorship. She had even felt some obscure intimations, within her secret soul, that she might herself become an author. The annual was destined to fix her fate. She opened it – the publisher had written the names of the authors of the anonymous pieces against their productions. Among them she found some of the familiar friends of her childhood and youth.

If, by a sudden gift of second sight, she had seen them enthroned as kings and queens, she would not have been more astonished. She turned to their pieces, and read them, as perchance no one else ever did, from beginning to end – faithfully. Not a sentence – a sentence! not a word was skipped. She paused to consider commas, colons, and dashes. All the art and magic of authorship were made level to her comprehension, and when she closed the book, she *felt a call* to become an author, and before she retired to bed she obeyed the call, as if it had been, in truth, a divinity stirring within her. In the morning she presented an article to *her* public, consisting of her own family and a few select friends. All applauded, and every voice, save one, was unanimous for publication – that one was Alice. She was a modest, prudent girl; she feared failure, and feared notoriety still more. Her mother laughed at her childish scruples. The piece was sent off, and in due time graced the pages of an annual. Mrs Courland's fate was now decided. She had, to use her own phrase, started in the career of letters, and she was no Atalanta* to be seduced from her straight onward way. She was a social, sympathetic, good hearted creature too, and she could not bear to go forth in the golden field to reap alone.

She was, besides, a prudent woman, as most of her country-women are, and the little pecuniary equivalent for this delightful exercise of talents was not overlooked. Mrs Courland, as we have somewhere said, had three single sisters – worthy women they were – but nobody ever dreamed of their taking to authorship. She, however, held them all in sisterly estimation. Their talents were magnified as the talents of persons who live in a circumscribed sphere are apt to be, particularly if seen through the dilating medium of affection.

Miss Anne, the oldest, was fond of flowers, a successful cultivator, and a diligent student of the science of botany. All this taste and knowledge, Mrs Courland thought, might be turned to excellent account; and she persuaded Miss Anne to write a little book entitled 'Familiar Dialogues on Botany.' The second sister, Miss Ruth, had a turn for education ('bachelor's wives and maid's children are always well taught'), and Miss Ruth undertook a popular treatise on that subject. Miss Sally, the youngest, was the saint of the family, and she doubted about the propriety of a literary occupation, till her scruples were overcome by the fortunate suggestion that her coup d'essai should be a Saturday night book entitled 'Solemn Hours,' – and solemn hours they were to their unhappy readers. Mrs Courland next besieged her old mother. 'You know, mamma,' she said, 'you have such a precious fund of anecdotes of the revolution and the French war, and you talk just like the 'Annals of the Parish,' and I am certain you can write a book fully as good.'

'My child, you are distracted! I write a dreadful poor hand, and I never learned to spell – no girls did in my time.'

'Spell! that is not of the least consequence – the printers correct the spelling.'

But the honest old lady would not be tempted on the crusade, and her daughter consoled herself with the reflection that if she would not write, she was an admirable subject to be written about, and her diligent fingers worked off three distinct stories in which the old lady figured.

Mrs Courland's ambition, of course, embraced within its widening circle her favourite nephew Ralph. She had always thought him a genius, and genius in her estimation was the philosopher's stone. In his youth she had laboured to persuade his father to send him to Cambridge, but the old man uniformly replied that Ralph 'was a smart lad on the farm, and steady, and by that he knew he was no genius.' As Ralph's character was developed, and talent after talent broke forth, his aunt renewed her lamentations over his ignoble destiny. That Ralph was useful, good, and happy – the most difficult and rare results achieved in life – was nothing, so long as he was but a farmer in H. Once she did half persuade him to turn painter, but his good sense and filial duty triumphed over her eloquence, and suppressed the hankerings after distinction that are innate in every human breast, from the little ragged chimneysweep that hopes to be a *boss*, to the political aspirant whose bright goal is the presidential chair.

Now Mrs Courland fancied Ralph might climb the steep of fame without quitting his farm; occasional authorship was compatible with his vocation. But alas! she could not persuade Ralph to pluck the laurels that she saw ready grown to his hand. She was not offended, for she was the best natured woman in the world, but she heartily pitied him, and seldom mentioned his name without repeating that stanza of Gray's, inspired for the consolation of hopeless obscurity:

'Full many a gem of purest ray serene,' etc.*

Poor Alice's sorrows we have reserved to the last, for they were heaviest. 'Alice,' her mother said, 'was gifted; she was well educated, well informed; she was every thing necessary to be an author.' But Alice resisted; and, though the gentlest, most complying of all good daughters, she would have resisted to the death – she would as soon have stood in a pillory as appeared in print. Her mother, Mrs Courland, was not an obstinate woman, and gave up in despair. But still our poor heroine was destined to be the victim of this *cacoethes scribendi*;* for Mrs Courland divided the world into two classes, or rather parts – authors and subjects for authors; the one active, the other passive. At first blush one would have thought the village of H. rather a barren field for such a reaper as Mrs Courland, but her zeal and indefatigableness worked wonders. She converted the stern scholastic divine of H. into as much of a La Roche* as she could describe; a tall wrinkled bony old woman, who reminded her of Meg Merrilies,* sat for a witch; the school master for an Ichabod Crane;* a poor half witted boy was made to utter as much pathos and sentiment and wit as she could put into his lips; and a crazy vagrant was a God-send to her. Then every 'wide spreading elm,' 'blasted pine,' or 'gnarled oak,' flourished on her pages. The village church and school house stood there according to their actual dimensions. One old *pilgrim* house was as prolific as haunted tower or ruined abbey. It was surveyed outside, ransacked inside, and again made habitable for the reimbodied spirits of its founders.

The most kind hearted of women, Mrs Courland's interests came to be so at variance with the prosperity of the little community of H., that a sudden calamity, a death, a funeral, were fortunate events to her. To do her justice she felt them in a twofold capacity. She wept as a woman, and exulted as an author. The days of the calamities of authors have passed by. We have all wept over Otway* and shivered at the thought of Tasso.* But times are changed. The lean sheaf is devouring the full one. A new class of sufferers has arisen, and there is nothing more touching in all the memoirs Mr D'Israeli* has collected, than the trials of poor Alice, tragi-comic though they were. Mrs Courland's new passion ran most naturally in the worn channel of maternal affection. Her boys were too purely boys for her art – but Alice, her sweet Alice, was preeminently lovely in the new light in which she now placed every object. Not an incident of her life but was inscribed on her mother's memory, and thence transferred to her pages, by way of precept, or example, or pathetic or ludicrous circumstance. She regretted now, for the first time, that Alice had no lover whom she might introduce among her dramatis personæ. Once her thoughts did glance on Ralph, but she had not quite merged the woman in the author; she knew instinctively that Alice would be particularly offended at being thus paired with Ralph. But Alice's *public life* was not limited to her mother's productions. She was the darling niece of her three aunts. She had studied botany with the eldest, and Miss Anne had recorded in her private diary all her favourite's clever remarks during their progress in the science. This diary was now a mine of gold to her, and faithfully worked up for a circulating medium. But, most trying of all to poor Alice, was the attitude in which she appeared in her aunt Sally's 'solemn hours.' Every aspiration of piety to which her young lips had given utterance was there *printed*. She felt as if she were condemned to say her prayers in the market place. Every act of kindness, every deed of charity, she had ever performed, were produced to the public. Alice would have been consoled if she had known how small that public was; but, as it was, she felt like a modest country girl when she first enters an apartment, hung on every side with mirrors, when, shrinking from observation, she sees in every direction her image multiplied and often distorted; for, notwithstanding Alice's dutiful respect for her good aunts, and her consciousness of their affectionate intentions, she could not but perceive that they were unskilled painters. She grew afraid to speak or to act, and from being the most artless, frank, and, at home, social little creature in the world, she became as silent and as stiff as a statue. And, in the circle of her young associates, her natural

gaiety was constantly checked by their winks and smiles, and
broader allusions to her multiplied portraits; for they had
instantly recognized them through the thin veil of feigned names
of persons and places. They called her a blue stocking* too; for
they had the vulgar notion that every body must be tinged that
lived under the same roof with an author. Our poor victim was
afraid to speak of a book – worse than that, she was afraid to
touch one, and the last Waverley novel actually lay in the house
a month before she opened it. She avoided wearing even a blue
ribbon, as fearfully as a forsaken damsel shuns the colour of
green.

It was during the height of this literary fever in the Courland
family, that Ralph Hepburn, as has been mentioned, concentrated all his visiting there. He was of a compassionate disposition, and he knew Alice was, unless relieved by him, in solitary
possession of their once social parlour, while her mother and
aunts were driving their quills in their several apartments.

Oh! what a changed place was that parlour! Not the tower of
Babel, after the builders had forsaken it, exhibited a sadder
reverse; not a Lancaster school, when the boys have left it, a
more striking contrast. Mrs Courland and her sisters were all
'talking women,' and too generous to encroach on one another's
rights and happiness. They had acquired the power to hear and
speak simultaneously. Their parlour was the general gathering
place, a sort of village exchange, where all the innocent gossips,
old and young, met together. 'There are tongues in trees,' and
surely there seemed to be tongues in the very walls of that vocal
parlour. Every thing there had a social aspect. There was
something agreeable and conversable in the litter of netting and
knitting work, of sewing implements, and all the signs and
shows of happy female occupation.

Now, all was as orderly as a town drawing room in company
hours. Not a sound was heard there save Ralph's and Alice's
voices, mingling in soft and suppressed murmurs, as if afraid of
breaking the chain of their aunt's ideas, or, perchance, of too
rudely jarring a tenderer chain. One evening, after tea, Mrs
Courland remained with her daughter, instead of retiring, as
usual, to her writing desk. – 'Alice, my dear,' said the good
mother, 'I have noticed for a few days past that you look out of
spirits. You will listen to nothing I say on that subject; but if
you would try it, my dear, if you would only try it, you would

find there is nothing so tranquillizing as the occupation of writing.'

'I shall never try it, mamma.'

'You are afraid of being called a blue stocking. Ah! Ralph, how are you?' – Ralph entered at this moment – 'Ralph, tell me honestly, do you not think it a weakness in Alice to be so afraid of blue stockings?'

'It would be a pity, aunt, to put blue stockings on such pretty feet as Alice's.'

Alice blushed and smiled, and her mother said – 'Nonsense, Ralph; you should bear in mind the celebrated saying of the Edinburgh wit – "no matter how blue the stockings are, if the petticoats are long enough to hide them."'

'Hide Alice's feet! Oh aunt, worse and worse!'

'Better hide her feet, Ralph, than her talents – that is a sin for which both she and you will have to answer. Oh! you and Alice need not exchange such significant glances! You are doing yourselves and the public injustice, and you have no idea how easy writing is.'

'Easy writing, but hard reading, aunt.'

'That's false modesty, Ralph. If I had but your opportunities to collect materials' – Mrs Courland did not know that in literature, as in some species of manufacture, the most exquisite productions are wrought from the smallest quantity of raw material – 'There's your journey to New York, Ralph,' she continued, 'you might have made three capital articles out of that. The revolutionary officer would have worked up for the "Legendary;" the mysterious lady for the "Token;" and the man in black for the "Remember Me;" – all founded on fact, all romantic and pathetic.'

'But mamma,' said Alice, expressing in words what Ralph's arch smile expressed almost as plainly, 'you know the officer drank too much; and the mysterious lady turned out to be a runaway milliner; and the man in black – oh! what a theme for a pathetic story! – the man in black was a widower, on his way to Newhaven, where he was to select his third wife from three *recommended* candidates.'

'Pshaw! Alice: do you suppose it is necessary to tell things precisely as they are?'

'Alice is wrong, aunt, and you are right; and if she will open her writing desk for me, I will sit down this moment, and write a story – a true story – true from beginning to end; and if it moves you, my dear aunt, if it meets your approbation, my destiny is decided.'

Mrs Courland was delighted; she had slain the giant, and she saw fame and fortune smiling on her favourite. She arranged the desk for him herself; she prepared a folio sheet of paper, folded the ominous margins; and was so absorbed in her bright visions, that she did not hear a little by-talk between Ralph and Alice, nor see the tell-tale flush on their cheeks, nor notice the perturbation with which Alice walked first to one window and then to another, and finally settled herself to that best of all sedatives – hemming a ruffle. Ralph chewed off the end of his quill, mended his pen twice, though his aunt assured him 'printers did not mind the penmanship,' and had achieved a single line when Mrs Courland's vigilant eye was averted by the entrance of her servant girl, who put a packet into her hands. She looked at the direction, cut the string, broke the seals, and took out a periodical fresh from the publisher. She opened at the first article – a strangely mingled current of maternal pride and literary triumph rushed through her heart and brightened her face. She whispered to the servant a summons to all her sisters to the parlour, and an intimation, sufficiently intelligible to them, of her joyful reason for interrupting them.

Our readers will sympathize with her, and with Alice too, when we disclose to them the secret of her joy. The article in question was a clever composition written by our devoted Alice when she was at school. One of her fond aunts had preserved it; and aunts and mother had combined in the pious fraud of giving it to the public, unknown to Alice. They were perfectly aware of her determination never to be an author. But they fancied it was the mere timidity of an unfledged bird; and that when, by their innocent artifice, she found that her pinions could soar in a literary atmosphere, she would realize the sweet fluttering sensations they had experienced at their first flight. The good souls all hurried to the parlour, eager to witness the coup de théatre. Miss Sally's pen stood emblematically erect in her turban; Miss Ruth, in her haste, had overset her inkstand, and the drops were trickling down her white dressing, or, as she now called it, writing gown; and Miss Anne had a wild flower in her hand, as she hoped, of an undescribed species, which, in her joyful agitation, she most unluckily picked to pieces. All bit their lips to keep impatient congratulation from bursting forth. Ralph was so intent on his writing, and Alice on her hemming, that neither noticed the irruption; and Mrs Courland was obliged twice to speak to her daughter before she could draw her attention.

'Alice, look here – Alice, my dear.'

'What is it, mamma? something new of yours?'

'No; guess again, Alice.'

'Of one of my aunts, of course?'

'Neither, dear, neither. Come and look for yourself, and see if you can then tell whose it is.'

Alice dutifully laid aside her work, approached and took the book. The moment her eye glanced on the fatal page, all her apathy vanished – deep crimson overspread her cheeks, brow, and neck. She burst into tears of irrepressible vexation, and threw the book into the blazing fire.

The gentle Alice! Never had she been guilty of such an ebullition of temper. Her poor dismayed aunts retreated; her mother looked at her in mute astonishment; and Ralph, struck with her emotion, started from the desk, and would have asked an explanation, but Alice exclaimed – 'Don't say any thing about it, mamma – I cannot bear it now.'

Mrs Courland knew instinctively that Ralph would sympathize entirely with Alice, and quite willing to avoid an éclaircissement, she said – 'Some other time, Ralph, I'll tell you the whole. Show me now what you have written. How have you begun?'

Ralph handed her the paper with a novice's trembling hand.

'Oh! how very little! and so scratched and interlined! but never mind – "c'est le premier pas qui coute."'

While making these general observations, the good mother was getting out and fixing her spectacles, and Alice and Ralph had retreated behind her. Alice rested her head on his shoulder, and Ralph's lips were not far from her ear. Whether he was soothing her ruffled spirit, or what he was doing, is not recorded. Mrs Courland read and re-read the sentence. She dropped a tear on it. She forgot her literary aspirations for Ralph and Alice – forgot she was herself an author – forgot every thing but the mother; and rising, embraced them both as her dear children, and expressed, in her raised and moistened eye, consent to their union, which Ralph had dutifully and prettily asked in that short and true story of his love for his sweet cousin Alice.

*

In due time the village of H. was animated with the celebration of Alice's nuptials: and when her mother and aunts saw her the happy mistress of the Hepburn farm, and the happiest of wives, they relinquished, without a sigh, the hope of ever seeing her an author.

ELIZABETH STUART PHELPS

The Angel Over The Right Shoulder

1852

'There! a woman's work is never done,' said Mrs James. 'I thought, for once, I was through; but just look at that lamp, now! it will not burn, and I must go and spend half an hour over it.'

'Don't you wish you had never been married?' said Mr James, with a good-natured laugh.

'Yes' – rose to her lips, but was checked by a glance at the group upon the floor where her husband was stretched out, and two little urchins with sparkling eyes and glowing cheeks were climbing and tumbling over him, as if they found in this play the very essence of fun.

She did say, 'I should like the good, without the evil, if I could have it.'

'You have no evils to endure,' replied her husband.

'That is just all you gentlemen know about it. What would you think, if you could not get an uninterrupted half hour to yourself, from morning till night? I believe you would give up trying to do anything.'

'There is no need of that; all you want, is *system*. If you arranged your work systematically, you would find that you could command your time.'

'Well,' was the reply, 'all I wish is, that you could just follow me around for one day, and see what I have to do. If you could reduce it all to system, I think you would show yourself a genius.'

When the lamp was trimmed, the conversation was resumed. Mr James had employed the 'half hour,' in meditating on this subject.

'Wife,' said he, as she came in, 'I have a plan to propose to you, and I wish you to promise me beforehand, that you will

accede to it. It is to be an experiment, I acknowledge, but I wish it to have a fair trial. Now to please me, will you promise?'

Mrs James hesitated. She felt almost sure that his plan would be quite impracticable, for what does a man know of a woman's work? Yet she promised.

'Now I wish you,' said he, 'to set apart two hours of every day for your own private use. Make a point of going to your room, and locking yourself in; and also make up your mind to let the work which is not done, go undone, if it must. Spend this time on just those things which will be most profitable to yourself. I shall bind you to your promise for one month – then, if it has proved a total failure, we will devise something else.'

'When shall I begin?'

'Tomorrow.'

The morrow came. Mrs James had chosen the two hours before dinner as being, on the whole, the most convenient and the least liable to interruption. They dined at one o'clock. She wished to finish her morning work, get dressed for the day, and enter her room at eleven.

Hearty as were her efforts to accomplish this, the hour of eleven found her with her work but half done; yet, true to her promise, she left all, retired to her room and locked the door.

With some interest and hope, she immediately marked out a course of reading and study, for these two precious hours: then arranging her table, her books, pen and paper, she commenced a schedule of her work with much enthusiasm. Scarcely had she dipped her pen in ink, when she heard the tramping of little feet along the hall, and then a pounding at her door.

'Mamma! mamma! I cannot find my mittens, and Hannah is going to slide without me.'

'Go to Amy, my dear; mamma is busy.'

'So Amy busy too; she say she can't leave baby.'

The child began to cry, still standing close to the fastened door. Mrs James knew the easiest, and indeed the only way of settling the trouble, was to go herself and hunt up the missing mittens. Then a parley must be held with Frank, to induce him to wait for his sister, and the child's tears must be dried, and little hearts must be all set right before the children went out to play; and so favorable an opportunity must not be suffered to slip, without impressing on young minds the importance of having a 'place for everything, and everything in its place.' This took time; and when Mrs James returned to her study, her watch told her that *half* her portion had gone. Quietly resuming her work, she was endeavoring to mend her broken train of thought, when heavier steps were heard in the hall, and the fastened door was once more besieged. Now, Mr James must be admitted.

'Mary,' said he, 'cannot you come and sew a string on for me? I do believe there is not a bosom in my drawer in order, and I am in a great hurry. I ought to have been down town an hour ago.'

The schedule was thrown aside, the work-basket taken, and Mrs James followed him. She soon sewed on the tape, but then a button needed fastening; and, at last, a rip in his glove was to be mended. As Mrs James stitched away on the glove, a smile lurked in the corners of her mouth, which her husband observed.

'What are you laughing at?' asked he.

'To think how famously your plan works.'

'I declare!' said he, 'is this your study hour? I am sorry, but what can a man do? He cannot go down town without a shirt-bosom!'

'Certainly not,' said his wife, quietly.

When her liege lord was fairly equipped and off, Mrs James returned to her room. A half an hour yet remained to her, and of this she determined to make the most. But scarcely had she resumed her pen, when there was another disturbance in the entry. Amy had returned from walking out with the baby, and she entered the nursery with him, that she might get him to sleep. Now it happened that the only room in the house which Mrs James could have to herself with a fire, was the one adjoining the nursery. She had become so accustomed to the ordinary noise of the children, that it did not disturb her; but the very extraordinary noise which master Charley sometimes felt called upon to make, when he was fairly on his back in the cradle, did disturb the unity of her thoughts. The words which she was reading rose and fell with the screams and lulls of the child, and she felt obliged to close her book, until the storm was over. When quiet was restored in the cradle, the children came in from sliding, crying with cold fingers; and just as she was going to them, the dinner-bell rang.

'How did your new plan work this morning?' inquired Mr James.

'Famously,' was the reply; 'I read about seventy pages of German, and as many more in French.'

'I am sure *I* did not hinder you long.'

'No – yours was only one of a dozen interruptions.'

'O, well! you must not get discouraged. Nothing succeeds well the first time. Persist in your arrangement, and by and by the family will learn that if they want anything of you, they must wait until after dinner.'

'But what can a man do?' replied his wife; 'he cannot go down town without a shirt-bosom.'

'I was in a bad case,' replied Mr James, 'it may not happen again. I am anxious to have you try the month out faithfully, and then we will see what has come of it.'

The second day of trial was a stormy one. As the morning was dark, Bridget overslept, and consequently breakfast was too late by an hour. This lost hour Mrs James could not recover. When the clock struck eleven, she seemed but to have commenced her morning's work, so much remained to be done. With mind disturbed and spirits depressed, she left her household matters 'in the suds,' as they were, and punctually retired to her study. She soon found, however, that she could not fix her attention upon any intellectual pursuit. Neglected duties haunted her, like ghosts around the guilty conscience. Perceiving that she was doing nothing with her books, and not wishing to lose the morning wholly, she commenced writing a letter. Bridget interrupted her before she had proceeded far on the first page.

'What, ma'am, shall we have for dinner? No marketing ha'n't come.'

'Have some steaks, then.'

'We ha'n't got none, ma'am.'

'I will send out for some, directly.'

Now there was no one to send but Amy, and Mrs James knew it. With a sigh, she put down her letter and went into the nursery.

'Amy, Mr James has forgotten our marketing. I should like to have you run over to the provision store, and order some beef-steaks; I will stay with the baby.'

Amy was not much pleased to be sent out on this errand. She remarked, that she 'must change her dress first.'

'Be as quick as possible,' said Mrs James, 'for I am particularly engaged at this hour.'

Amy neither obeyed, nor disobeyed, but managed to take her own time, without any very deliberate intention to do so. Mrs James, hoping to get along with a sentence or two, took her German book into the nursery. But this arrangement was not to master Charley's mind. A fig did he care for German, but 'the kitties' he must have, whether or no – and kitties he would find in that particular book – so he turned its leaves over in great haste. Half of the time on the second day of trial had gone when Amy returned, and Mrs James, with a sigh, left the nursery. Before one o'clock, she was twice called into the kitchen to superintend some important dinner arrangement, and thus it turned out that she did not finish one page of her letter.

On the third morning the sun shone, and Mrs James rose early, made every provision which she deemed necessary for dinner, and for the comfort of her family; and then, elated by her success, in good spirits, and with good courage, she entered her study precisely at eleven o'clock, and locked her door. Her books were opened, and the challenge given to a hard German lesson. Scarcely had she made the first onset, when the door-bell was heard to ring, and soon Bridget, coming nearer and nearer, – then, tapping at the door.

'Somebodies wants to see you in the parlor, ma'am.'

'Tell them I am engaged, Bridget.'

'I told 'em you were to home, ma'am, and they sent up their names, but I ha'n't got 'em, jist.'

There was no help for it – Mrs James must go down to receive her callers. She had to smile when she felt little like it – to be sociable when her thoughts were busy with her task. Her friends made a long call – they had nothing else to do with their time, and when they went, others came. In very unsatisfactory chit-chat, her morning slipped away.

On the next day, Mr James invited company to tea, and her morning was devoted to preparing for it; she did not enter her study. On the day following, a sick-head-ache confined her to bed; and on Saturday, the care of the baby devolved upon her, as Amy had extra work to do. Thus passed the first week.

True to her promise, Mrs James patiently persevered for a month, in her efforts to secure for herself this little fragment of her broken time, but with what success, the first week's history can tell. With its close, closed the month of December.

On the last day of the old year, she was so much occupied in her preparations for the morrow's festival, that the last hour of the day was approaching, before she made her good night's call in the nursery. She first went to the crib and looked at the baby. There he lay in his innocence and beauty, fast asleep. She softly stroked his golden hair – she kissed gently his rosy cheek – she pressed the little dimpled hand in hers; and then carefully drawing the coverlet over it, tucked it in, – and stealing yet another kiss, she left him to his peaceful dreams, – and sat down on her daughter's bed. She also slept sweetly, with her dolly hugged to her bosom. At this her mother smiled, but soon grave thoughts entered her mind, and these deepened into sad ones. She thought of her disappointment and the failure of her plans. To her, not only the past month but the whole past year, seemed to have been one of fruitless effort – all broken and disjointed – even her hours of religious duty had been encroached upon, and disturbed. She had accomplished nothing, that she could see, but to keep her house and family in order, and even this, to her saddened mind, seemed to have been but indifferently done. She was conscious of yearnings for a more earnest life than this. Unsatisfied longings for something which she had not attained, often clouded what, otherwise, would have been a bright day to her; and yet the causes of these feelings seemed to lie in a dim and misty region, which her eye could not penetrate.

What then did she need? To see some *results* from her life's work? To know that a golden cord bound her life-threads together into *unity* of purpose – notwithstanding they seemed, so often, single and broken?

She was quite sure that she felt no desire to shrink from duty, however humble, but she sighed for some comforting assurance of what *was duty*. Her employments, conflicting as they did with her tastes, seemed to her frivolous and useless. It seemed to her that there was some better way of living, which she, from deficiency in energy of character, or of principle, had failed to discover. As she leaned over her child, her tears fell fast upon its young brow.

Most earnestly did she wish, that she could shield that child from the disappointments and mistakes and self-reproach from which the mother was then suffering; that the little one might take up life where she could give it to her – all mended by her own experience. It would have been a comfort to have felt that, in fighting the battle, she had fought for both; yet she knew that so it could not be – that for ourselves must we all learn what are those things which 'make for our peace.'

The tears were in her eyes, as she gave the goodnight to her sleeping daughter; then, with soft steps, she entered an adjoining room, and there fairly kissed out the old year on another chubby cheek, which nestled among the pillows. At length she sought her own rest.

Soon she found herself in a singular place. She was traversing a vast plain. No trees were visible, save those which skirted the distant horizon, and on their broad tops rested wreaths of golden clouds. Before her was a female, who was journeying towards that region of light. Little children were about her, now in her arms, now running by her side, and as they travelled, she occupied herself in caring for them. She taught them how to place their little feet; she gave them timely warnings of the pit-falls; she gently lifted them over the stumbling-blocks. When they were weary, she soothed them by singing of that brighter land, which she kept ever in view, and towards which she seemed hastening with her little flock. But what was most remarkable was, that, all unknown to her, she was constantly watched by two angels, who reposed on two golden clouds which floated above her. Before each was a golden book, and a pen of gold. One angel, with mild and loving eyes, peered constantly over her right shoulder; another, kept as strict watch over her left. Not a deed, not a word, not a look, escaped their notice. When a good deed, word, look, went from her, the angel over the right shoulder, with a glad smile, wrote it down in his book; when an evil, however trivial, the angel over the left shoulder recorded it in his book, – then, with sorrowful eyes, followed the pilgrim until he observed penitence for the wrong, upon which he dropped a tear on the record, and blotted it out, and both angels rejoiced.

To the looker-on, it seemed that the traveller did nothing which was worthy of such careful record.

Sometimes, she did but bathe the weary feet of her little children, but the angel over the *right shoulder* – wrote it down. Sometimes, she did but patiently wait to lure back a little truant who had turned his face away from the distant light, but the angel over the *right shoulder* – wrote it down. Sometimes, she did but soothe an angry feeling or raise a drooping eyelid, or kiss away a little grief; but the angel over the right shoulder – *wrote it down.*

Sometimes, her eye was fixed so intently on that golden horizon, and she became so eager to make progress thither, that the little ones, missing her care, did languish or stray. Then it was that the angel over the *left shoulder*, lifted his golden pen, and made the entry, and followed her with sorrowful eyes, until he could blot it out. Sometimes, she seemed to advance rapidly, but in her haste the little ones had fallen back, and it was the sorrowing angel who recorded her progress. Sometimes, so intent was she to gird up her loins, and have her lamp trimmed and burning, that the little children wandered away quite into forbidden paths, and it was the angel over the *left shoulder* who recorded her diligence.

Now the observer as she looked, felt that this was a faithful and true record, and was to be kept to that journey's end. The strong clasps of gold on those golden books, also impressed her with the conviction that, when they were closed, it would only be for a future opening.

Her sympathies were warmly enlisted for the gentle traveller, and with a beating heart she quickened her steps that she might overtake her. She wished to tell her of the angels keeping watch above her – to entreat her to be faithful and patient to the end – for her life's work was all written down – every item of it – and the *results* would be known when those golden books should be unclasped. She wished to beg of her to think no duty trivial which must be done, for over her right shoulder and over her left were recording angels, who would surely take note of all!

Eager to warn the traveller of what she had seen, she touched her. The traveller turned, and she recognized or seemed to recognize *herself*. Startled and alarmed, she awoke in tears. The gray light of morning struggled through the half-open shutter, the door was ajar, and merry faces were peeping in.

'Wish you a happy new year, mamma!' – 'Wish you a *Happy new Year*!' – 'A happy noo ear!'

She returned the merry greeting most heartily. It seemed to her as if she had entered upon a new existence. She had found her way through the thicket in which she had been entangled, and a light was now about her path. The *Angel over the Right Shoulder* whom she had seen in her dream, would bind up in his golden book her life's work, if it were but well done. He required of her no great deeds, but faithfulness and patience to the end of the race which was set before her. Now she could see, plainly enough, that, though it was right and important for her to cultivate her own mind and heart, it was equally right and equally important, to meet and perform faithfully all those little household cares and duties on which the comfort and virtue of her family depended; for into these things the angels carefully looked – and these duties and cares acquired a dignity from the strokes of that golden pen – they could not be neglected without danger.

Sad thoughts and sadder misgivings – undefined yearnings and ungratified longings seemed to have taken their flight with the Old Year, and it was with fresh resolution and cheerful hope, and a happy heart, she welcomed the *Glad* New Year. The *Angel over the Right Shoulder* would go with her, and if she were found faithful, would strengthen and comfort her to its close.

FRANCES HARPER

The Two Offers

1852

'What is the matter with you, Laura, this morning? I have been watching you this hour, and in that time you have commenced a half-dozen letters and torn them all up. What matter of such grave moment is puzzling your dear little head, that you do not know how to decide?'

'Well, it is an important matter: I have two offers for marriage, and I do not know which to choose.'

'I should accept neither, or to say the least, not at present.'

'Why not?'

'Because I think a woman who is undecided between two offers has not love enough for either to make a choice; and in that very hesitation, indecision, she has a reason to pause and seriously reflect, lest her marriage, instead of being an affinity of souls or a union of hearts, should only be a mere matter of bargain and sale, or an affair of convenience and selfish interest.'

'But I consider them both very good offers, just such as many a girl would gladly receive. But to tell you the truth, I do not think that I regard either as a woman should the man she chooses for her husband. But then if I refuse, there is the risk of being an old maid, and that is not to be thought of.'

'Well, suppose there is? Is that the most dreadful fate that can befall a woman? Is there not more intense wretchedness in an ill-assorted marriage, more utter loneliness in a loveless home, than in the lot of the old maid who accepts her earthly mission as a gift from God and strives to walk the path of life with earnest and unfaltering steps?'

'Oh! what a little preacher you are. I really believe that you were cut out for an old maid – that when nature formed you she put in a double portion of intellect to make up for a deficiency of love; and yet you are kind and affectionate. But I do not think that you know anything of the grand, overmastering passion, or the deep necessity of woman's heart for loving.'

'Do you think so?' resumed the first speaker, and bending over her work she quietly applied herself to the knitting that had lain neglected by her side during this brief conversation. But as she did so, a shadow flitted over her pale and intellectual brow, a mist gathered in her eyes, and a slight quivering of the lips revealed a depth of feeling to which her companion was a stranger.

But before I proceed with my story, let me give you a slight history of the speakers. They were cousins who had met life under different auspices. Laura Lagrange was the only daughter of rich and indulgent parents who had spared no pains to make her an accomplished lady. Her cousin, Janette Alston, was the child of parents rich only in goodness and affection. Her father had been unfortunate in business and, dying before he could retrieve his fortunes, left his business in an embarrassed state. His widow was unacquainted with his business affairs, and when the estate was settled, hungry creditors had brought their claims and the lawyers had received their fees, she found herself homeless and almost penniless, and she, who had been sheltered in the warm clasp of loving arms, found them too powerless to shield her from the pitiless pelting storms of adversity. Year after year she struggled with poverty and wrestled with want, till her toilworn hands became too feeble to hold the shattered chords of existence, and her tear-dimmed eyes grew heavy with the slumber of death.

Her daughter had watched over her with untiring devotion, had closed her eyes in death and gone out into the busy, restless world, missing a precious tone from the voices of earth, a beloved step from the paths of life. Too self-reliant to depend on the charity of relations, she endeavored to support herself by her own exertions, and she had succeeded. Her path for a while was marked with struggle and trial, but instead of uselessly repining she met them bravely, and her life became not a thing of ease and indulgence, but of conquest, victory and accomplishments.

At the time when this conversation took place, the deep trials of her life had passed away. The achievements of her genius had won her a position in the literary world, where she shone as one of its bright particular stars. And with her fame came a competence of worldly means, which gave her leisure for improvement and the riper development of her rare talents. And she, that pale, intellectual woman, whose genius gave life and vivacity to the social circle and whose presence threw a halo of beauty and grace around the charmed atmosphere in which she moved, had at one period of her life known the mystic and solemn strength of an all-absorbing love. Years faded into the misty past had seen the kindling of her eye, the quick flushing of her cheek and the wild throbbing of her heart at tones of a voice long since hushed to the stillness of death. Deeply, wildly, passionately, she had loved. . . . This love quickened her talents, inspired her genius and threw over her life a tender and spiritual earnestness.

And then came a fearful shock, a mournful waking from that 'dream of beauty and delight.' A shadow fell around her path; it came between her and the object of her heart's worship. First a few cold words, estrangement, and then a painful separation: the old story of woman's pride. . . . And thus faded out from that young heart her bright, brief and saddened dream of life. Faint and spirit-broken, she turned from the scenes associated with the memory of the loved and lost. She tried to break the chain of sad associations that bound her to the mournful past; and so . . . her genius gathered strength from suffering, and wondrous power and brilliancy from the agony she hid within the desolate chambers of her soul . . . and turning, with an earnest and shattered spirit to life's duties and trials, she found a calmness and strength that she had only imagined in her dreams of poetry and song.

We will now pass over a period of ten years, and the cousins have met again. In that calm and lovely woman, in whose eyes is a depth of tenderness tempering the flashes of her genius, whose looks and tones are full of sympathy and love, we recognize the once smitten and stricken Janette Alston. The bloom of her girlhood had given way to a higher type of spiritual beauty, as if some unseen hand had been polishing and refining the temple in which her lovely spirit found its habitation. . . .

Never in the early flush of womanhood, when an absorbing love had lit up her eyes and glowed in her life, had she appeared so interesting as when, with a countenance which seemed overshadowed with a spiritual light, she bent over the deathbed of a young woman just lingering at the shadowy gates of the unseen land.

'Has he come?' faintly but eagerly exclaimed the dying woman. 'Oh! how I have longed for his coming, and even in death he forgets me.'

'Oh, do not say so, dear Laura. Some accident may have detained him,' said Janette to her cousin; for on that bed, from whence she will never rise, lies the once beautiful and light-hearted Laura Lagrange, the brightness of whose eyes had long since been dimmed with tears, and whose voice had become like a harp whose every chord is tuned to sadness – whose faintest thrill and loudest vibrations are but the variations of agony. A heavy hand was laid upon her once warm and bounding heart, and a voice came whispering through her soul that she must die. But to her the tidings was a message of deliverance – a voice hushing her wild sorrows to the calmness of resignation and hope.

Life had grown so weary upon her head – the future looked so hopeless – she had no wish to tread again the track where thorns had pierced her feet and clouds overcast her sky, and she hailed the coming of death's angel as the footsteps of a welcome friend. And yet, earth had one object so very dear to her weary heart. It was her absent and recreant husband; for, since that conversation [ten years earlier], she had accepted one of her offers and become a wife. But before she married she learned that great lesson of human experience and woman's life – to love the man who bowed at her shrine, a willing worshipper.

He had a pleasing address, raven hair, flashing eyes, a voice of thrilling sweetness and lips of persuasive eloquence; and being well versed in the ways of the world, he won his way to her heart and she became his bride, and he was proud of his prize. Vain and superficial in his character, he looked upon marriage not as a divine sacrament for the soul's development and human progression, but as the title deed that gave him possession of the woman he thought he loved. But alas for her, the laxity of his principles had rendered him unworthy of the deep and undying devotion of a pure-hearted woman. But, for a while, he hid from her his true character, and she blindly loved him, and for a short period was happy in the consciousness of being beloved. Though sometimes a vague unrest would fill her soul, when, overflowing with a sense of the good, the beautiful and the true, she would turn to him but find no response to the deep yearnings of her soul – no appreciation of life's highest realities, its solemn grandeur and significant importance. Their souls never met, and soon she found a void in her bosom that his earthborn love could not fill. He did not satisfy the wants of her mental and moral nature: between him and her there was no affinity of minds, no intercommunion of souls.

Talk as you will of woman's deep capacity for loving – of the strength of her affectional nature. I do not deny it. But will the mere possession of any human love fully satisfy all the demands of her whole being? You may paint her in poetry or fiction as a frail vine, clinging to her brother man for support and dying when deprived of it, and all this may sound well enough to please the imaginations of schoolgirls, or lovelorn maidens. But woman – the true woman – if you would render her happy, it needs more than the mere development of her affectional nature. Her conscience should be enlightened, her faith in the true and right established, and scope given to her heaven-endowed and God-given faculties. The true aim of female education should be, not a development of one or two, but all the faculties of the human soul, because no perfect womanhood is developed by imperfect culture. Intense love is often akin to intense suffering, and to trust the whole wealth of woman's nature on the frail bark of human love may often be like trusting a cargo of gold and precious gems to a bark that has never battled with the storm or buffeted the waves. Is it any wonder, then, that so many life-barks ... are stranded on the shoals of existence, mournful beacons and solemn warnings for the thoughtless, to whom marriage is a careless and hasty rushing together of the affections? Alas, that an institution so fraught with good for humanity should be so perverted, and that state of life which should be filled with happiness become so replete with misery. And this was the fate of Laura Lagrange.

For a brief period after her marriage her life seemed like a bright and beautiful dream, full of hope and radiant with joy. And then there came a change: he found other attractions that lay beyond the pale of home influences. The gambling saloon had power to win him from her side; he had lived in an element of unhealthy and unhallowed excitements, and the society of a loving wife, the pleasures of a well-regulated home, were enjoyments too tame for one who had vitiated his tastes by the pleasures of sin. There were charmed houses of vice, built upon dead men's loves, where, amid a flow of song, laughter, wine and careless mirth, he would spend hour after hour, forgetting the cheek that was paling through his neglect, heedless of the tear-dimmed eyes peering anxiously into the darkness, waiting or watching his return.

The influence of old associations was upon him. In early life, home had been to him a place of ceilings and walls, not a true home built upon goodness, love and truth. It was a place where velvet carpets hushed his tread, where images of loveliness and beauty, invoked into being by painter's art and sculptor's skill, pleased the eye and gratified the taste, where magnificence surrounded his way and costly clothing adorned his person; but it was not the place for the true culture and right development of his soul. His father had been too much engrossed in making money and his mother in spending it, in striving to maintain a fashionable position in society and shining in the eyes of the world, to give the proper direction to the character of their wayward and impulsive son. His mother put beautiful robes upon his body but left ugly scars upon his soul; she pampered his appetite but starved his spirit. . . .

That parental authority which should have been preserved as a string of precious pearls, unbroken and unscattered, was simply the administration of chance. At one time obedience was enforced by authority, at another time by flattery and promises, and just as often it was not enforced. . . . His early associations were formed as chance directed, and from his want of home training, his character received a bias, his life a shade, which ran through every avenue of his existence and darkened all his future hours. . . .

Before a year of his married life had waned, his young wife had learned to wait and mourn his frequent and uncalled-for absence. More than once had she seen him come home from his midnight haunts, the bright intelligence of his eye displaced by the drunkard's stare, and his manly gait changed to the inebriate's stagger; and she was beginning to know the bitter agony that is compressed in the mournful words

'drunkard's wife.'

And then there came a bright but brief episode in her experience. The angel of life gave to her existence a deeper meaning and loftier significance: she sheltered in the warm clasp of her loving arms a dear babe, a precious child whose love filled every chamber of her heart. . . . How many lonely hours were beguiled by its winsome ways, its answering smiles and fond caresses! How exquisite and solemn was the feeling that thrilled her heart when she clasped the tiny hands together and taught her dear child to call God 'Our Father'!

What a blessing was that child! The father paused in his headlong career, awed by the strange beauty and precocious intellect of his child; and the mother's life had a better expression through her ministrations of love. And then there came hours of bitter anguish, shading the sunlight of her home and hushing the music of her heart. The angel of death bent over the couch of her child and beckoned it away. Closer and closer the mother strained her child to her wildly heaving breast and struggled with the heavy hand that lay upon its heart. Love and agony contended with death. . . .

But death was stronger than love and mightier than agony, and won the child for the land of crystal founts and deathless flowers, and the poor stricken mother sat down beneath the shadow of her mighty grief, feeling as if a great light had gone out from her soul and that the sunshine had suddenly faded around her path. She turned in her deep anguish to the father of her child, the loved and cherished dead. For a while his words were kind and tender, his heart seemed subdued and his tenderness fell upon her worn and weary heart like rain on perishing flowers, or cooling waters to lips all parched with thirst and scorched with fever. But the change was evanescent; the influence of unhallowed associations and evil habits had vitiated and poisoned the springs of his existence. They had bound him in their meshes, and he lacked the moral strength to break his fetters and stand erect in all the strength and dignity of a true manhood, making life's highest excellence his ideal and striving to gain it.

And yet moments of deep contrition would sweep over him, when he would resolve to abandon the wine cup forever, when he was ready to forswear the handling of another card, and he would try to break away from the associations that he felt were working his ruin. But when the hour of temptation came his strength was weakness, his earnest purposes were cobwebs, his well-meant resolutions ropes of sand – and thus passed year after year of the married life of Laura Lagrange. She tried to hide her agony from the public gaze, to smile when her heart was almost breaking. But year after year her voice grew fainter and sadder, her once light and bounding step grew slower and faltering.

Year after year she wrestled with agony and strove with despair, till the quick eyes of her brother read, in the paling of her cheek and the dimming eye, the secret anguish of her worn and weary spirit. On that wan, sad face he saw the death tokens, and he knew the dark wing of the mystic angel swept coldly around her path.

'Laura,' said her brother to her one day, 'you are not well, and I think you need our mother's tender care and nursing. You are daily losing strength, and if you will go I will accompany you.'

At first she hesitated; she shrank almost instinctively from presenting that pale, sad face to the loved ones at home. . . . But then a deep yearning for home sympathy woke within her a passionate longing for love's kind words, for tenderness and heart support, and she resolved to seek the home of her childhood and lay her weary head upon her mother's bosom, to be folded again in her loving arms, to lay that poor, bruised and aching heart where it might beat and throb closely to the loved ones at home.

A kind welcome awaited her. All that love and tenderness could devise was done to bring the bloom to her cheek and the light to her eye. But it was all in vain; hers was a disease that no medicine could cure, no earthly balm would heal. It was a slow wasting of the vital forces, the sickness of the soul. The unkindness and neglect of her husband lay like a leaden weight upon her heart. . . .

And where was he that had won her love and then cast it aside as a useless thing, who rifled her heart of its wealth and spread bitter ashes upon its broken altars? He was lingering away from her when the death damps were gathering on her brow, when his name was trembling on her lips! Lingering away! when she was watching his coming, though the death films were gathering before her eyes and earthly things were fading from her vision.

'I think I hear him now,' said the dying woman, 'surely that is his step,' but the sound died away in the distance.

Again she started from an uneasy slumber: 'That is his voice! I am so glad he has come.'

Tears gathered in the eyes of the sad watchers by that dying bed, for they knew that she was deceived. He had not returned. For her sake they wished his coming. Slowly the hours waned away, and then came the sad, soul-sickening thought that she was forgotten, forgotten in the last hour of human need, forgotten when the spirit, about to be dissolved, paused for the last time on the threshold of existence, a weary watcher at the gates of death.

'He has forgotten me,' again she faintly murmured, and the last tears she would ever shed on earth sprung to her mournful eyes, and ... a few broken sentences issued from her pale and quivering lips. They were prayers for strength, and earnest pleading for him who had desolated her young life by turning its sunshine to shadows, its smiles to tears.

'He has forgotten me,' she murmured again, 'but I can bear it; the bitterness of death is passed, and soon I hope to exchange the shadows of death for the brightness of eternity, the rugged paths of life for the golden streets of glory, and the care and turmoils of earth for the peace and rest of heaven.'

Her voice grew fainter and fainter; they saw the shadows that never deceive flit over her pale and faded face and knew that the death angel waited to soothe their weary one to rest, to calm the throbbing of her bosom and cool the fever of her brain. And amid the silent hush of their grief the freed spirit, refined through suffering and brought into divine harmony through the spirit of the living Christ, passed over the dark waters of death as on a bridge of light, over whose radiant arches hovering angels bent. They parted the dark locks from her marble brow, closed the waxen lids over the once bright and laughing eye and left her to the dreamless slumber of the grave.

Her cousin turned from that deathbed a sadder and wiser woman. She resolved more earnestly than ever to make the world better by her example, gladder by her presence, and to kindle the fires of her genius on the altars of universal love and truth. She had a higher and better object in all her writings than the mere acquisition of gold or acquirement of fame. She felt that she had a high and holy mission on the battlefield of existence – that life was not given her to be frittered away in nonsense or wasted away in trifling pursuits. She would willingly espouse an unpopular cause, but not an unrighteous one.

In her the downtrodden slave found an earnest advocate; the

flying fugitive remembered her kindness as he stepped cautiously through our Republic to gain his freedom in a monarchial land, having broken the chains on which the rust of centuries had gathered. Little children learned to name her with affection; the poor called her blessed as she broke her bread to the pale lips of hunger.

Her life was like a beautiful story, only it was clothed with the dignity of reality and invested with the sublimity of truth. True, she was an old maid; no husband brightened her life with his love or shaded it with his neglect. No children nestling lovingly in her arms called her mother. No one appended Mrs to her name.

She was indeed an old maid, not vainly striving to keep up an appearance of girlishness when 'departed' was written on her youth, not vainly pining at her loneliness and isolation. The world was full of warm, loving hearts, and her own beat in unison with them. Neither was she always sentimentally sighing for something to love; objects of affection were all around her, and the world was not so wealthy in love that it had no use for hers. In blessing others she made a life and benediction, and as old age descended peacefully and gently upon her, she had learned one of life's most precious lessons: that true happiness consists not so much in the fruition of our wishes as in the regulation of desires and the full development and right culture of our whole natures.

HARRIET PRESCOTT SPOFFORD

Circumstance

1860

She had remained, during all that day, with a sick neighbor, –
those eastern wilds of Maine in that epoch frequently making
neighbors and miles synonymous, – and so busy had she been
with care and sympathy that she did not at first observe the
approaching night. But finally the level rays, reddening the
snow, threw their gleam upon the wall, and, hastily donning
cloak and hood, she bade her friends farewell and sallied forth
on her return. Home lay some three miles distant, across a
copse, a meadow, and a piece of woods, – the woods being a
fringe on the skirts of the great forests that stretch far away into
the North. That home was one of a dozen log-houses lying a
few furlongs apart from each other, with their half-cleared
demesnes* separating them at the rear from a wilderness untrod-
den save by stealthy native or deadly panther tribes.

She was in a nowise exalted frame of spirit, – on the contrary,
rather depressed by the pain she had witnessed and the fatigue
she had endured; but in certain temperaments such a condition
throws open the mental pores, so to speak, and renders one
receptive of every influence. Through the little copse she walked
slowly, with her cloak folded about her, lingering to imbibe the
sense of shelter, the sunset filtered in purple through the mist of
woven spray and twig, the companionship of growth not
sufficiently dense to band against her, the sweet homefeeling of
a young and tender wintry wood. It was therefore just on the
edge of the evening that she emerged from the place and began
to cross the meadowland. At one hand lay the forest to which
her path wound; at the other the evening star hung over a tide
of failing orange that slowly slipped down the earth's broad side
to sadden other hemispheres with sweet regret. Walking rapidly
now, and with her eyes wide-open, she distinctly saw in the air

before her what was not there a moment ago, a winding-sheet, – cold, white, and ghastly, waved by the likeness of four wan hands, – that rose with a long inflation, and fell in rigid folds, while a voice, shaping itself from the hollowness above, spectral and melancholy, sighed, – 'The Lord have mercy on the people! The Lord have mercy on the people!' Three times the sheet with its corpse-covering outline waved beneath the pale hands, and the voice, awful in its solemn and mysterious depth, sighed, 'The Lord have mercy on the people!' Then all was gone, the place was clear again, the gray sky was obstructed by no deathly blot; she looked about her, shook her shoulders decidedly, and, pulling on her hood, went forward once more.

She might have been a little frightened by such an apparition, if she had led a life of less reality than frontier settlers are apt to lead; but dealing with hard fact does not engender a flimsy habit of mind, and this woman was too sincere and earnest in her character, and too happy in her situation, to be thrown by antagonism, merely, upon superstitious fancies and chimeras of the second-sight. She did not even believe herself subject to an hallucination, but smiled simply, a little vexed that her thought could have framed such a glamour from the day's occurrences, and not sorry to lift the bough of the warder of the woods and enter and disappear in their sombre path. If she had been imaginative, she would have hesitated at her first step into a region whose dangers were not visionary; but I suppose that the thought of a little child at home would conquer that propensity in the most habituated. So, biting a bit of spicy birch, she went along. Now and then she came to a gap where the trees had been partially felled, and here she found that the lingering twilight was explained by that peculiar and perhaps electric film which sometimes sheathes the sky in diffused light for many hours before a brilliant aurora. Suddenly, a swift shadow, like the fabulous flying-dragon, writhed through the air before her, and she felt herself instantly seized and borne aloft. It was that wild beast – the most savage and serpentine and subtle and fearless of our latitudes – known by hunters as the Indian Devil,* and he held her in his clutches on the broad floor of a swinging fir-bough. His long sharp claws were caught in her clothing, he worried them sagaciously a little, then, finding that ineffectual to free them, he commenced licking her bare arm with his rasping tongue and pouring over her the wide streams of his hot, foetid breath. So quick had this flashing action been that the woman had had no time for alarm; moreover, she was not of the screaming kind: but now, as she felt him endeavoring to disentangle his claws, and the horrid sense of her fate smote her, and she saw instinctively the fierce plunge of those weapons, the long strips of living flesh torn from her bones, the agony, the quivering disgust, itself a worse agony, – while by her side, and holding her in his great lithe embrace, the monster crouched, his white tusks whetting and gnashing, his eyes glaring through all the darkness like balls of red fire, – a shriek, that rang in every forest hollow, that startled every winter-housed thing, that stirred and woke the least needle of the tasselled pines, tore through her lips. A moment afterward, the beast left the arm, once white, now crimson, and looked up alertly.

She did not think at this instant to call upon God. She called upon her husband. It seemed to her that she had but one friend in the world; that was he; and again the cry, loud, clear, prolonged, echoed through the woods. It was not the shriek that disturbed the creature at his relish; he was not born in the woods to be scared of an owl, you know; what then? It must have been the echo, most musical, most resonant, repeated and yet repeated, dying with long sighs of sweet sound, vibrated from rock to river and back again from depth to depth of cave and cliff. Her thought flew after it; she knew, that, even if her husband heard it, he yet could not reach her in time; she saw that while the beast listened he would not gnaw, – and this she *felt* directly, when the rough, sharp, and multiplied stings of his tongue retouched her arm. Again her lips opened by instinct, but the sound that issued thence came by reason. She had heard that music charmed wild beasts, – just this point between life and death intensified every faculty, – and when she opened her lips the third time, it was not for shrieking, but for singing.

A little thread of melody stole out, a rill of tremulous motion; it was the cradle-song with which she rocked her baby; – how could she sing that? And then she remembered the baby sleeping rosily one the long settee before the fire, – the father cleaning his gun, with one foot on the green wooden rundle, – the merry light from the chimney dancing out and through the room, on the rafters of the ceiling with their tassels of onions and herbs, on the log walls painted with lichens and festooned with apples, on the king's-arm slung across the shelf with the old pirate'scutlass, on the snow-pile of the bed, and on the great brass clock, – dancing, too, and lingering on the baby, with his fringed-gentian eyes, his chubby fists clenched on the pillow, and his fine breezy hair fanning with the motion of his father's foot. All this struck her in one, and made a sob of her breath, and she ceased.

Immediately the long red tongue thrust forth again. Before it touched, a song sprang to her lips, a wild sea-song, such as some sailor might be singing far out on trackless blue water that night, the shrouds whistling with frost and the sheets glued in ice, – a song with the wind in its burden and the spray in its chorus. The monster raised his head and flared the fiery eyeballs upon her, then fretted the imprisoned claws a moment and was quiet; only the breath like the vapor from some hell-pit still swathed her. Her voice, at first faint and fearful, gradually lost its quaver, grew under her control and subject to her modulation; it rose on long swells, it fell in subtile cadences, now and then its tones pealed out like bells from distant belfries on fresh sonorous mornings. She sung the song through, and, wondering lest his name of Indian Devil were not his true name, and if he would not detect her, she repeated it. Once or twice now, indeed, the beast stirred uneasily, turned, and made the bough sway at his movement. As she ended, he snapped his jaws together, and tore away the fettered member, curling it under him with a snarl, – when she burst into the gayest reel that ever answered a fiddle-bow. How many a time she had heard her husband play it on the homely fiddle made by himself from birch and cherrywood! how many a time she had seen it danced on the floor of their one room, to the patter of wooden clogs and the rustle of homespun petticoat! how many a time she had danced it herself! – and did she not remember once, as they joined clasps for eight-hands-round, how it had lent its gay, bright measure to her life? And here she was singing it alone, in the forest, at midnight, to a wild beast! As she sent her voice trilling up and down its quick oscillations between joy and pain, the creature who grasped her uncurled his paw and scratched the bark from the bough; she must vary the spell; and her voice spun leaping along the projecting points of tune of a hornpipe. Still singing, she felt herself twisted about with a low growl and a lifting of the red lip from the glittering teeth; she broke the hornpipe's thread, and commenced unravelling a lighter, livelier thing, an Irish jig.

Up and down and round about her voice flew, the beast threw back his head so that the diabolical face fronted hers, and the torrent of his breath prepared her for his feast as the anaconda slimes his prey. Franticly she darted from tune to tune; his restless movements followed her. She tired herself with dancing and vivid national airs, growing feverish and singing spasmodically as she felt her horrid tomb yawning wider. Touching in this manner all the slogan and keen clan cries, the beast moved again, but only to lay the disengaged paw across her with heavy satisfaction. She did not dare to pause; through the clear cold air, the frosty starlight, she sang. If there were yet any tremor in the tone, it was not fear, – she had learned the secret of sound at last; nor could it be chill, – far too high a fever throbbed her pulses; it was nothing but the thought of the log-house and of what might be passing within it. She fancied the baby stirring in his sleep and moving his pretty lips, – her husband rising and opening the door, looking out after her, and wondering at her absence. She fancied the light pouring through the chink and then shut in again with all the safety and comfort and joy, her husband taking down the fiddle and playing lightly with his head inclined, playing while she sang, while she sang for her life to an Indian Devil. Then she knew he was fumbling for and finding some shining fragment and scoring it down the yellowing-hair, and unconsciously her voice forsook the wild wartunes and drifted into the half-gay, half-melancholy 'Rosin the Bow.'

Suddenly she woke pierced with a pang, and the daggered tooth penetrating her flesh; – dreaming of safety, she had ceased singing and lost it. The beast had regained the use of all his limbs, and now, standing and raising his back, bristling and foaming, with sounds that would have been like hisses but for their deep and fearful sonority, he withdrew step by step toward the trunk of the tree, still with his flaming balls upon her. She was all at once free, on one end of the bough, twenty feet from the ground. She did not measure the distance, but rose to drop herself down, careless of any death, so that it were not this. Instantly, as if he scanned her thoughts, the creature bounded forward with a yell and caught her again in his dreadful hold. It might be that he was not greatly famished; for, as she suddenly flung up her voice again, he settled himself composedly on the bough, still clasping her with invincible pressure to his rough, ravenous breast, and listening in a fascination to the sad, strange

U-la-lu that now moaned forth in loud, hollow tones above him. He half closed his eyes, and sleepily reopened and shut them again.

What rending pains were close at hand! Death! and what a death! worse than any other that is to be named! Water, be it cold or warm, that which buoys up blue icefields, or which bathes tropical coasts with currents of balmy bliss, is yet a gentle conqueror, kisses as it kills, and draws you down gently through darkening fathoms to its heart. Death at the sword is the festival of trumpet and bugle and banner, with glory ringing out around you and distant hearts thrilling through yours. No gnawing disease can bring such hideous end as this; for that is a fiend bred of your own flesh, and this – is it a fiend, this living lump of appetites? What dread comes with the thought of perishing in flames! but fire, let it leap and hiss never so hotly, is something too remote, too alien, to inspire us with such loathly horror as a wild beast; if it have a life, that life is too utterly beyond our comprehension. Fire is not half ourselves; as it devours, arouses neither hatred nor disgust; is not to be known by the strength of our lower natures let loose; does not drip our blood into our faces with foaming chaps, nor mouth nor slaver above us with vitality. Let us be ended by fire, and we are ashes, for the winds to bear, the leaves to cover; let us be ended by wild beasts, and the base, cursed thing howls with us forever through the forest. All this she felt as she charmed him, and what force it lent to her song God knows. If her voice should fail! If the damp and cold should give her any fatal hoarseness! If all the silent powers of the forest did not conspire to help her! The dark, hollow night rose indifferently over her; the wide, cold air breathed rudely past her, lifted her wet hair and blew it down again; the great boughs swung with a ponderous strength, now and then clashed their iron lengths together and shook off a sparkle of icy spears or some long-lain weight of snow from their heavy shadows. The green depths were utterly cold and silent and stern. These beautiful haunts that all the summer were hers and rejoiced to share with her their bounty, these heavens that had yielded their largess, these stems that had thrust their blossoms into her hands, all these friends of three moons ago forgot her now and knew her no longer.

Feeling her desolation, wild, melancholy, forsaken songs rose thereon from that frightful aerie, – weeping, wailing tunes, that sob among the people from age to age, and overflow with otherwise unexpressed sadness, – all rude, mournful ballads, – old tearful strains, that Shakespeare heard the vagrants sing, and that rise and fall like the wind and tide, – sailor-songs, to be heard only in lone mid-watches beneath the moon and stars, – ghastly rhyming romances, such as that famous one of the Lady Margaret,* when

> 'She slipped on her gown of green
>   A piece below the knee, –
> And 't was all a long cold winter's night
>   A dead corse followed she.'

Still the beast lay with closed eyes, yet never relaxing his grasp. Once a half-whine of enjoyment escaped him, – he fawned his fearful head upon her; once he scored her cheek with his tongue – savage caresses that hurt like wounds. How weary she was! and yet how terribly awake! How fuller and fuller of dismay grew the knowledge that she was only prolonging her anguish and playing with death! How appalling the thought that with her voice ceased her existence! Yet she could not sing forever; her throat was dry and hard; her very breath was a pain; her mouth was hotter than any desert-worn pilgrim's; – if she could but drop upon her burning tongue one atom of the ice that glittered about her! – but both of her arms were pinioned in the giant's vice. She remembered the winding-sheet, and for the first time in her life shivered with spiritual fear. Was it hers? She asked herself, as she sang, what sins she had committed, what life she had led, to find her punishment so soon and in these pangs, – and then she sought eagerly for some reason why her husband was not up and abroad to find her. He failed her, – her one sole hope in life; and without being aware of it, her voice forsook the songs of suffering and sorrow for old Covenanting hymns, – hymns with which her mother had lulled her, which the class-leader pitched in the chimney-corners, – grand and sweet Methodist hymns, brimming with melody and with all fantastic involutions of tune to suit that ecstatic worship, – hymns full of the beauty of holiness, steadfast, relying, sanctified by the salvation they had lent to those in worse extremity than hers, – for they had found themselves in the grasp of hell, while she was but in the jaws of death. Out of this strange music, peculiar to one character of faith, and than which there is none more beautiful in its degree nor owning a more potent sway of sound, her voice soared into the glorified chants of churches. What to her was death by cold or famine or wild beasts? 'Though He slay me, yet will I trust in him,' she sang. High and clear through the frore fair night, the level moonbeams splintering in the wood, the scarce glints of stars in the shadowy roof of branches, these sacred anthems rose, – rose as a hope from despair, as some snowy spray of flower-bells from blackest mould. Was she not in God's hands? Did not the world swing at his will? If this were in his great plan of providence, was it not best, and should she not accept it?

'He is the Lord our God; his judgments are in all the earth.'

Oh, sublime faith of our fathers, where utter self-sacrifice alone was true love, the fragrance of whose unrequired subjection was pleasanter than that of golden censers swung in purple-vapored chancels!

Never ceasing in the rhythm of her thoughts, articulated in music as they thronged, the memory of her first communion flashed over her. Again she was in that distant place on that sweet spring morning. Again the congregation rustled out, and the few remained, and she trembled to find herself among them. How well she remembered the devout, quiet faces, too accustomed to the sacred feast to glow with their inner joy! how well the snowy linen at the altar, the silver vessels slowly and silently shifting! and as the cup approached and passed, how the sense of delicious perfume stole in and heightened the transport of her prayer, and she had seemed, looking up through the windows where the sky soared blue in constant freshness, to feel all heaven's balms dripping from the portals, and to scent the lilies of eternal peace! Perhaps another would not have felt so much ecstasy as satisfaction on that occasion; but it is a true, if a later disciple, who has said, 'The Lord bestoweth his blessings there, where he findeth the vessels empty.'

'And does it need the walls of a church to renew my communion?' she asked. 'Does not every moment stand a temple four-square to God? And in that morning, with its buoyant sunlight, was I any dearer to the Heart of the World than now? – "My beloved is mine, and I am his,"' she sang over and over again, with all varied inflection and profuse tune. How gently all the winter-wrapt things bent toward her then! into what relation with her had they grown! how this common dependence was the spell of their intimacy! how at one with Nature had she become! how all the night and the silence and the forest seemed to hold its breath, and to send its soul up to God in her singing! It was no longer despondency, that singing. It was neither prayer nor petition. She had left imploring, 'How long wilt thou forget me, O Lord? Lighten mine eyes, lest I sleep the sleep of death! For in death there is no remembrance of thee,' – with countless other such fragments of supplication. She cried rather, 'Yea, though I walk through the valley of the shadow of death, I will fear no evil: for thou art with me; thy rod and thy staff, they comfort me,' – and lingered, and repeated, and sang again, 'I shall be satisfied, when I awake, with thy likeness.'

Then she thought of the Great Deliverance, when he drew her up out of many waters, and the flashing old psalm pealed forth triumphantly:

'The Lord descended from above,
    and bow'd the heavens hie:
And underneath his feet he cast
    the darknesse of the skie.
On cherubs and on cherubins
    full royally he road:
And on the wings of all the winds
    came flying all abroad.'

She forgot how recently, and with what a strange pity for her own shapeless form that was to be, she had quaintly sung, –

'O lovely appearance of death!
    What sight upon earth is so fair?
Not all the gay pageants that breathe,
    Can with a dead body compare!'

She remembered instead, – 'In thy presence is fulness of joy; at thy right hand there are pleasures forevermore. God will redeem my soul from the power of the grave: for he shall receive me. He will swallow up death in victory.' Not once now did she say, 'Lord, how long wilt thou look on; rescue my soul from their destructions, my darling from the lions,' – for she knew that the young lions roar after their prey and seek their meat from God. 'O Lord, thou preservest man and beast!' she said.

She had no comfort or consolation in this season, such as sustained the Christian martyrs in the amphitheatre. She was not dying for her faith; there were no palms in heaven for her to wave; but how many a time had she declared, – 'I had rather be a doorkeeper in the house of my God, than to dwell in the tents of wickedness!' And as the broad rays here and there broke through the dense covert of shade and lay in rivers of lustre on crystal sheathing and frozen fretting of trunk and limb and on the great spaces of refraction, they builded up visibly that house, the shining city on the hill, and singing, 'Beautiful for situation, the joy of the whole earth, is Mount Zion, on the sides of the North, the city of the Great King,' her vision climbed to that higher picture where the angel shows the dazzling thing, the holy Jerusalem descending out of heaven from God, with its splendid battlements and gates of pearls, and its foundations, the eleventh a jacinth, the twelfth an amethyst, – with its great white throne, and the rainbow round about it, in sight like unto an emerald: 'And there shall be no night there, – for the Lord God giveth them light,' she sang.

What whisper of dawn now rustled through the wilderness? How the night was passing? And still the beast crouched upon the bough, changing only the posture of his head, that again he might command her with those charmed eyes; – half their fire was gone; she could almost have released herself from his custody; yet, had she stirred, no one knows what malevolent instinct might have dominated anew. But of that she did not dream; long ago stripped of any expectation, she was experiencing in her divine rapture how mystically true it is that 'he that dwelleth in the secret place of the Most High shall abide under the shadow of the Almighty.'

Slow clarion cries now wound from the distance as the cocks caught the intelligence of day and re-echoed it faintly from farm to farm, – sleepy sentinels of night, sounding the foe's invasion, and translating that dim intuition to ringing notes of warning. Still she chanted on. A remote crash of brushwood told of some other beast on his depredations, or some night-belated traveller groping his way through the narrow path. Still she chanted on. The far, faint echoes of the chanticleers died into distance, the crashing of the branches grew nearer. No wild beast that, but a man's step, – a man's form in the moonlight, stalwart and strong, – on one arm slept a little child, in the other hand he held his gun. Still she chanted on.

Perhaps, when her husband last looked forth, he was half

ashamed to find what a fear he felt for her. He knew she would never leave the child so long but for some direst need, – and yet he may have laughed at himself, as he lifted and wrapped it with awkward care, and, loading his gun and strapping on his horn, opened the door again and closed it behind him, going out and plunging into the darkness and dangers of the forest. He was more singularly alarmed than he would have been willing to acknowledge; as he had sat with his bow hovering over the strings, he had half believed to hear her voice mingling gayly with the instrument, till he paused and listened if she were not about to lift the latch and enter. As he drew nearer the heart of the forest, that intimation of melody seemed to grow more actual, to take body and breath, to come and go on long swells and ebbs of the night-breeze, to increase with tune and words, till a strange shrill singing grew ever clearer, and, as he stepped into an open space of moonbeams, far up in the branches, rocked by the wind, and singing, 'How beautiful upon the mountains are the feet of him that bringeth good tidings, that publisheth peace,' he saw his wife, – his wife, – but, great God in heaven! how? Some mad exclamation escaped him, but without diverting her. The child knew the singing voice, though never heard before in that unearthly key, and turned toward it through the veiling dreams. With a celerity almost instantaneous, it lay, in the twinkling of an eye, on the ground at the father's feet, while his gun was raised to his shoulder and levelled at the monster covering his wife with shaggy form and flaming gaze, – his wife so ghastly white, so rigid, so stained with blood, her eyes so fixedly bent above, and her lips, that had indurated into the chiselled pallor of marble, parted only with that flood of solemn song.

I do not know if it were the mother-instinct that for a moment lowered her eyes, – those eyes, so lately riveted on heaven, now suddenly seeing all life-long bliss possible. A thrill of joy pierced and shivered through her like a weapon, her voice trembled in its course, her glance lost its steady strength, fever-flushes chased each other over her face, yet she never once ceased chanting. She was quite aware, that, if her husband shot now, the ball must pierce her body before reaching any vital part of the beast, – and yet better that death, by his hand, than the other. But this her husband also knew, and he remained motionless, just covering the creature with the sight. He dared not fire, lest some wound not mortal should break the spell exercised by her voice, and the beast, enraged with pain, should rend her in atoms; moreover, the light was too uncertain for his aim. So he waited. Now and then he examined his gun to see if the damp were injuring its charge, now and then he wiped the great drops from his forehead. Again the cocks crowed with the passing hour, – the last time they were heard on that night. Cheerful home sound then, how full of safety and all comfort and rest it seemed! what sweet morning incidents of sparkling fire and sunshine, of gay household bustle, shining dresser, and cooing baby, of steaming cattle in the yard, and brimming milk-pails at the door! what pleasant voices! what laughter! what security! and here –

Now, as she sang on in the slow, endless, infinite moments, the fervent vision of God's peace was gone. Just as the grave had lost its sting, she was snatched back again to the arms of earthly hope. In vain she tried to sing, 'There remaineth a rest for the people of God,' – her eyes trembled on her husband's, and she could only think of him, and of the child, and of happiness that yet might be, but with what a dreadful gulf of doubt between! She shuddered now in the suspense; all calm forsook her; she was tortured with dissolving heats or frozen with icy blasts; her face contracted, growing small and pinched; her voice was hoarse and sharp, – every tone cut like a knife, – the notes became heavy to lift, – withheld by some hostile pressure, – impossible. One gasp, a convulsive effort, and there was silence, – she had lost her voice.

The beast made a sluggish movement, – stretched and fawned like one awaking, – then, as if he would have yet more of the enchantment, stirred her slightly with his muzzle. As he did so, a sidelong hint of the man standing below with the raised gun smote him; he sprung round furiously, and, seizing his prey, was about to leap into some unknown airy den of the topmost branches now waving to the slow dawn. The late moon had rounded through the sky so that her gleam at last fell full upon the bough with fairy frosting; the wintry morning light did not yet penetrate the gloom. The woman, suspended in mid-air an instant, cast only one agonized glance beneath, – but across and through it, ere the lids could fall, shot a withering sheet of flame, – a rifle-crack, half-heard, was lost in the terrible yell of desperation that bounded after it and filled her ears with savage echoes, and in the wide arc of some eternal descent she was falling; – but the beast fell under her.

I think that the moment following must have been too sacred for us, and perhaps the three have no special interest again till they issue from the shadows of the wilderness upon the white hills that skirt their home. The father carries the child hushed again into slumber, the mother follows with no such feeble step as might be anticipated. It is not time for reaction, – the tension not yet relaxed, the nerves still vibrant, she seems to herself like some one newly made; the night was a dream; the present stamped upon her in deep satisfaction, neither weighed nor compared with the past; if she has the careful tricks of former habit, it is as an automaton; and as they slowly climb the steep under the clear gray vault and the paling morning star, and as she stops to gather a spray of the red-rose berries or a feathery tuft of dead grasses for the chimney-piece of the log-house, or a handful of brown cones for the child's play, – of these quiet, happy folk you would scarcely dream how lately they had stolen from under the banner and encampment of the great King Death. The husband proceeds a step or two in advance; the wife lingers over a singular foot-print in the snow, stoops and examines it, then looks up with a hurried word. Her husband stands alone on the hill, his arms folded across the babe, his gun fallen, – stands defined as a silhouette against the pallid sky. What is there in their home, lying below and yellowing in the light, to fix him with such a stare? She springs to his side. There is no home there. The log-house, the barns, the neighboring farms, the fences, are all blotted out and mingled in one smoking ruin. Desolation and death were indeed there, and beneficence and life in the forest. Tomahawk and scalping-knife, descending during that night, had left behind them only this work of their accomplished hatred and one subtle foot-print in the snow.

For the rest, – the world was all before them, where to choose.*

REBECCA HARDING DAVIS

Life in the Iron Mills

1861

Is this the end?
O Life, as futile, then, as frail!
What hope of answer of redress?*

A cloudy day: do you know what that is in a town of iron-works? The sky sank down before dawn, muddy, flat, immovable. The air is thick, clammy with the breath of crowded human beings. It stifles me. I open the window, and, looking out, can scarcely see through the rain the grocer's shop opposite, where a crowd of drunken Irishmen are puffing Lynchburg tobacco in their pipes. I can detect the scent through all the foul smells ranging loose in the air.

The idiosyncrasy of this town is smoke. It rolls sullenly in slow folds from the great chimneys of the iron-foundries, and settles down in black, slimy pools on the muddy streets. Smoke on the wharves, smoke on the dingy boats, on the yellow river, – clinging in a coating of greasy soot to the house-front, the two faded poplars, the faces of the passers-by. The long train of mules, dragging masses of pig-iron through the narrow street, have a foul vapor hanging to their reeking sides. Here, inside, is a little broken figure of an angel pointing upward from the mantel-shelf; but even its wings are covered with smoke, clotted and black. Smoke everywhere! A dirty canary chirps desolately in a cage beside me. Its dream of green fields and sunshine is a very old dream, – almost worn out, I think.

From the back-window I can see a narrow brick-yard sloping down to the river-side, strewed with rain-butts* and tubs. The river, dull and tawny-colored, (*la belle rivière!*)* drags itself sluggishly along, tired of the heavy weight of boats and coal-barges. What wonder? When I was a child, I used to fancy a

look of weary, dumb appeal upon the face of the negro-like
river slavishly bearing its burden day after day. Something of
the same idle notion comes to me today, when from the street-
window I look on the slow stream of human life creeping past,
night and morning, to the great mills. Masses of men, with dull,
besotted faces bent to the ground, sharpened here and there by
pain or cunning; skin and muscle and flesh begrimed with smoke
and ashes; stooping all night over boiling caldrons of metal,
laired by day in dens of drunkenness and infamy; breathing
from infancy to death an air saturated with fog and grease and
soot, vileness for soul and body. What do you make of a case
like that, amateur psychologist? You call it an altogether serious
thing to be alive: to these men it is a drunken jest, a joke, –
horrible to angels perhaps, to them commonplace enough. My
fancy about the river was an idle one: it is no type of such a life.
What if it be stagnant and slimy here? It knows that beyond
there waits for it odorous sunlight, – quaint old gardens, dusky
with soft, green foliage of apple-trees, and flushing crimson with
roses, – air, and fields, and mountains. The future of the Welsh
puddler* passing just now is not so pleasant. To be stowed
away, after his grimy work is done, in a hole in the muddy
graveyard, and after that, – *not* air, nor green fields, nor curious
roses.

Can you see how foggy the day is? As I stand here, idly
tapping the window-pane, and looking out through the rain at
the dirty back-yard and the coal-boats below, fragments of an
old story float up before me, – a story of this old house into
which I happened to come today. You may think it a tiresome
story enough, as foggy as the day, sharpened by no sudden
flashes of pain or pleasure. – I know: only the outline of a dull
life, that long since, with thousands of dull lives like its own,
was vainly lived and lost: thousands of them, – massed, vile,
slimy lives, like those of the torpid lizards in yonder stagnant
water-butt. – Lost? There is a curious point for you to settle, my
friend, who study psychology in a lazy, *dilettante* way. Stop a
moment. I am going to be honest. This is what I want you to
do. I want you to hide your disgust, take no heed to your clean
clothes, and come right down with me, – here, into the thickest
of the fog and mud and foul effluvia. I want you to hear this
story. There is a secret down here, in this nightmare fog, that
has lain dumb for centuries: I want to make it a real thing to

you. You, Egoist, or Pantheist, or Arminian,* busy in making straight paths for your feet on the hills, do not see it clearly, – this terrible question which men here have gone mad and died trying to answer. I dare not put this secret into words. I told you it was dumb. These men, going by with drunken faces and brains full of unawakened power, do not ask it of Society or of God. Their lives ask it; their deaths ask it. There is no reply. I will tell you plainly that I have a great hope; and I bring it to you to be tested. It is this: that this terrible dumb question is its own reply; that it is not the sentence of death we think it, but, from the very extremity of its darkness, the most solemn prophecy which the world has known of the Hope to come. I dare make my meaning no clearer, but will only tell my story. It will, perhaps, seem to you as foul and dark as this thick vapor about us, and as pregnant with death; but if your eyes are free as mine are to look deeper, no perfume-tinted dawn will be so fair with promise of the day that shall surely come.

My story is very simple, – only what I remember of the life of one of these men, – a furnace-tender in one of Kirby & John's rolling-mills, – Hugh Wolfe. You know the mills? They took the great order for the Lower Virginia railroads there last winter; run usually with about a thousand men. I cannot tell why I choose the half-forgotten story of this Wolfe more than that of myriads of these furnace-hands. Perhaps because there is a secret underlying sympathy between that story and this day with its impure fog and thwarted sunshine, – or perhaps simply for the reason that this house is the one where the Wolfes lived. There were the father and son, – both hands, as I said, in one of Kirby & John's mills for making railroad-iron, – and Deborah, their cousin, a picker* in some of the cotton-mills. The house was rented then to half a dozen families. The Wolfes had two of the cellar-rooms. The old man, like many of the puddlers and feeders* of the mills, was Welsh, – had spent half of his life in the Cornish tin-mines. You may pick the Welsh emigrants, Cornish miners, out of the throng passing the windows, any day. They are a trifle more filthy; their muscles are not so brawny; they stoop more. When they are drunk, they neither yell, nor shout, nor stagger, but skulk along like beaten hounds. A pure, unmixed blood, I fancy: shows itself in the slight angular bodies and sharply-cut facial lines. It is nearly thirty years since the Wolfes lived here. Their lives were like those of their class:

incessant labor, sleeping in kennel-like rooms, eating rank pork and molasses, drinking – God and the distillers only know what; with an occasional night in jail, to atone for some drunken excess. Is that all of their lives? – of the portion given to them and these their duplicates swarming the streets today? – nothing beneath? – all? So many a political reformer will tell you, – and many a private reformer, too, who has gone among them with a heart tender with Christ's charity, and come out outraged, hardened.

One rainy night, about eleven o'clock, a crowd of half-clothed women stopped outside of the cellar-door. They were going home from the cotton-mill.

'Goodnight, Deb,' said one, a mulatto, steadying herself against the gas-post. She needed the post to steady her. So did more than one of them.

'Dah's a ball to Miss Potts' tonight. Ye'd best come.'

'Inteet, Deb, if hur'll come, hur'll hef fun,' said a shrill Welsh voice in the crowd.

Two or three dirty hands were thrust out to catch the gown of the woman, who was groping for the latch of the door.

'No.'

'No? Where's Kit Small, then?'

'Begorra! on the spools.* Alleys behint, though we helped her, we dud. An wid ye! Let Deb alone! It's ondacent frettin' a quite body. Be the powers, an' we'll have a night of it! there'll be lashin's o' drink, – the Vargent be blessed and praised for 't!'

They went on, the mulatto inclining for a moment to show fight, and drag the woman Wolfe off with them; but, being pacified, she staggered away.

Deborah groped her way into the cellar, and, after considerable stumbling, kindled a match, and lighted a tallow dip, that sent a yellow glimmer over the room. It was low, damp, – the earthen floor covered with a green, slimy moss, – a fetid air smothering the breath. Old Wolfe lay asleep on a heap of straw, wrapped in a torn horse-blanket. He was a pale, meek little man, with a white face and red rabbit-eyes. The woman Deborah was like him; only her face was even more ghastly, her lips bluer, her eyes more watery. She wore a faded cotton gown and a slouching bonnet. When she walked, one could see that she was deformed, almost a hunchback. She trod softly, so as not to waken him, and went through into the room beyond.

There she found by the half-extinguished fire an iron saucepan filled with cold boiled potatoes, which she put upon a broken chair with a pint-cup of ale. Placing the old candlestick beside this dainty repast, she untied her bonnet, which hung limp and wet over her face, and prepared to eat her supper. It was the first food that had touched her lips since morning. There was enough of it, however: there is not always. She was hungry, – one could see that easily enough, – and not drunk, as most of her companions would have been found at this hour. She did not drink, this woman, – her face told that, too, – nothing stronger than ale. Perhaps the weak, flaccid wretch had some stimulant in her pale life to keep her up, – some love or hope, it might be, or urgent need. When that stimulant was gone, she would take to whiskey. Man cannot live by work alone. While she was skinning the potatoes, and munching them, a noise behind her made her stop.

'Janey!' she called, lifting the candle and peering into the darkness. 'Janey, are you there?'

A heap of ragged coats was heaved up, and the face of a young girl emerged, staring sleepily at the woman.

'Deborah,' she said, at last, 'I'm here the night.'

'Yes, child, Hur's welcome,' she said, quietly eating on.

The girl's face was haggard and sickly; her eyes were heavy with sleep and hunger: real Milesian* eyes they were, dark, delicate blue, glooming out from black shadows with a pitiful fright.

'I was alone,' she said, timidly.

'Where's the father?' asked Deborah, holding out a potato, which the girl greedily seized.

'He's beyant, – wid Haley, – in the stone house.' (Did you ever hear the word *jail* from an Irish mouth?) 'I came here. Hugh told me never to stay me-lone.'

'Hugh?'

'Yes.'

A vexed frown crossed her face. The girl saw it, and added quickly, –

'I have not seen Hugh the day, Deb. The old man says his watch lasts till the mornin'.'

The woman sprang up, and hastily began to arrange some bread and flitch* in a tin pail, and to pour her own measure of ale into a bottle. Tying on her bonnet, she blew out the candle.

'Lay ye down, Janey dear,' she said, gently, covering her with the old rags. 'Hur can eat the potatoes, if hur's hungry.'

'Where are ye goin', Deb? The rain's sharp.'

'To the mill, with Hugh's supper.'

'Let him bide till th' morn. Sit ye down.'

'No, no,' – sharply pushing her off. 'The boy'll starve.'

She hurried from the cellar, while the child wearily coiled herself up for sleep. The rain was falling heavily, as the woman, pail in hand, emerged from the mouth of the alley, and turned down the narrow street, that stretched out, long and black, miles before her. Here and there a flicker of gas lighted an uncertain space of muddy footwalk and gutter; the long rows of houses, except an occasional lager-bier shop, were closed; now and then she met a band of mill-hands skulking to or from their work.

Not many even of the inhabitants of a manufacturing town know the vast machinery of system by which the bodies of workmen are governed, that goes on unceasingly from year to year. The hands of each mill are divided into watches that relieve each other as regularly as the sentinels of an army. By night and day the work goes on, the unsleeping engines groan and shriek, the fiery pools of metal boil and surge. Only for a day in the week, in half-courtesy to public censure, the fires are partially veiled; but as soon as the clock strikes midnight, the great furnaces break forth with renewed fury, the clamor begins with fresh, breathless vigor, the engines sob and shriek like 'gods in pain.'

As Deborah hurried down through the heavy rain, the noise of these thousand engines sounded through the sleep and shadow of the city like far-off thunder. The mill to which she was going lay on the river, a mile below the city-limits. It was far, and she was weak, aching from standing twelve hours at the spools. Yet it was her almost nightly walk to take this man his supper, though at every square she sat down to rest, and she knew she should receive small word of thanks.

Perhaps, if she had possessed an artist's eye, the picturesque oddity of the scene might have made her step stagger less, and the path seem shorter; but to her the mills were only 'summat deilish to look at by night.'

The road leading to the mills had been quarried from the solid rock, which rose abrupt and bare on one side of the cinder-covered road, while the river, sluggish and black, crept past on the other. The mills for rolling iron are simply immense tent-like roofs, covering acres of ground, open on every side. Beneath these roofs Deborah looked in on a city of fires, that burned hot and fiercely in the night. Fire in every horrible form: pits of flame waving in the wind; liquid metal-flames writhing in tortuous streams through the sand; wide caldrons filled with boiling fire, over which bent ghastly wretches stirring the strange brewing; and through all, crowds of half-clad men, looking like revengeful ghosts in the red light, hurried, throwing masses of glittering fire. It was like a street in Hell. Even Deborah muttered, as she crept through, "T looks like t' Devil's place!' It did, – in more ways than one.

She found the man she was looking for, at last, heaping coal on a furnace. He had not time to eat his supper; so she went behind the furnace, and waited. Only a few men were with him, and they noticed her only by a 'Hyur comes t' hunchback, Wolfe.'

Deborah was stupid with sleep; her back pained her sharply; and her teeth chattered with cold, with the rain that soaked her clothes and dripped from her at every step. She stood, however, patiently holding the pail, and waiting.

'Hout, woman! ye look like a drowned cat. Come near to the fire,' – said one of the men, approaching to scrape away the ashes.

She shook her head. Wolfe had forgotten her. He turned, hearing the man, and came closer.

'I did no' think; gi' me my supper, woman.'

She watched him eat with a painful eagerness. With a woman's quick instinct, she saw that he was not hungry, – was eating to please her. Her pale, watery eyes began to gather a strange light.

'Is't good, Hugh? T'ale was a bit sour, I feared.'

'No, good enough.' He hesitated a moment. 'Ye're tired, poor lass! Bide here till I go. Lay down there on that heap of ash, and go to sleep.'

He threw her an old coat for a pillow, and turned to his work. The heap was the refuse of the burnt iron, and was not a hard bed; the half-smothered warmth, too, penetrated her limbs, dulling their pain and cold shiver.

Miserable enough she looked, lying there on the ashes like a limp, dirty rag, – yet not an unfitting figure to crown the scene of hopeless discomfort and veiled crime: more fitting, if one looked deeper into the heart of things, – at her thwarted woman's form, her colorless life, her waking stupor that smothered pain and hunger, – even more fit to be a type of her class. Deeper yet if one could look, was there nothing worth reading in this wet, faded thing, half-covered with ashes? no story of a soul filled with groping passionate love, heroic unselfishness, fierce jealousy? of years of weary trying to please the one human being whom she loved, to gain one look of real heart-kindness from him? If anything like this were hidden beneath the pale, bleared eyes, and dull, washed-out-looking face, no one had ever taken the trouble to read its faint signs: not the half-clothed furnace-tender, Wolfe, certainly. Yet he was kind to her: it was his nature to be kind, even to the very rats that swarmed in the cellar; kind to her in just the same way. She knew that. And it might be that very knowledge had given to her face its apathy and vacancy more than her low, torpid life. One sees that dead, vacant look steal sometimes over the rarest, finest of women's faces, – in the very midst, it may be, of their warmest summer's day; and then one can guess at the secret of intolerable solitude that lies hid beneath the delicate laces and brilliant smile. There was no warmth, no brilliancy, no summer for this woman; so the stupor and vacancy had time to gnaw into her face perpetually. She was young, too, though no one guessed it; so the gnawing was the fiercer.

She lay quiet in the dark corner, listening, through the monotonous din and uncertain glare of the works, to the dull plash of the rain in the far distance, – shrinking back whenever the man Wolfe happened to look towards her. She knew, in spite of all his kindness, that there was that in her face and form which made him loathe the sight of her. She felt by instinct, although she could not comprehend it, the finer nature of the man, which made him among his fellow-workmen something unique, set apart. She knew, that, down under all the vileness and coarseness of his life, there was a groping passion for whatever was beautiful and pure, – that his soul sickened with disgust at her deformity, even when his words were kindest. Through this dull consciousness, which never left her, came, like a sting, the recollection of the dark blue eyes and lithe figure of the little Irish girl she had left in the cellar. The recollection struck through even her stupid intellect with a vivid glow of beauty and of grace. Little Janey, timid, helpless, clinging to Hugh as her only friend: that was the sharp thought, the bitter thought, that drove into the glazed eyes a fierce light of pain. You laugh at it? Are pain and jealousy less savage realities down here in this place I am taking you to than in your own house or your own heart, – your heart, which they clutch at sometimes? The note is the same, I fancy, be the octave high or low.

If you could go into this mill where Deborah lay, and drag out from the hearts of these men the terrible tragedy of their lives, taking it as a symptom of the disease of their class, no ghost Horror would terrify you more. A reality of soul-starvation, of living death, that meets you every day under the besotted faces on the street, – I can paint nothing of this, only give you the outside outlines of a night, a crisis in the life of one man: whatever muddy depth of soul-history lies beneath you can read according to the eyes God has given you.

Wolfe, while Deborah watched him as a spaniel its master, bent over the furnace with his iron pole, unconscious of her scrutiny, only stopping to receive orders. Physically, Nature had promised the man but little. He had already lost the strength and instinct vigor of a man, his muscles were thin, his nerves weak, his face (a meek, woman's face) haggard, yellow with consumption. In the mill he was known as one of the girl-men: 'Molly Wolfe' was his *sobriquet*. He was never seen in the cockpit, did not own a terrier, drank but seldom; when he did, desperately. He fought sometimes, but was always thrashed, pommelled to a jelly. The man was game enough, when his blood was up: but he was no favorite in the mill; he had the taint of school-learning on him, – not to a dangerous extent, only a quarter or so in the free-school in fact, but enough to ruin him as a good hand in a fight.

For other reasons, too, he was not popular. Not one of themselves, they felt that, though outwardly as filthy and ash-covered; silent, with foreign thoughts and longings breaking out through his quietness in innumerable curious ways: this one, for instance. In the neighboring furnace-buildings lay great heaps of the refuse from the ore after the pig-metal is run. *Korl** we call it here: a light, porous substance, of a delicate, waxen, flesh-colored tinge. Out of the blocks of this korl, Wolfe, in his off-hours from the furnace, had a habit of chipping and moulding figures, – hideous, fantastic enough, but sometimes strangely beautiful: even the mill-men saw that, while they jeered at him. It was a curious fancy in the man, almost a passion. The few hours for rest he spent hewing and hacking with his blunt knife, never speaking, until his watch came again, – working at one figure for months, and, when it was finished, breaking it to pieces perhaps, in a fit of disappointment. A morbid, gloomy man, untaught, unled, left to feed his soul in grossness and crime, and hard, grinding labor.

I want you to come down and look at this Wolfe, standing there among the lowest of his kind, and see him just as he is, that you may judge him justly when you hear the story of this night. I want you to look back, as he does every day, at his birth in vice, his starved infancy; to remember the heavy years he has groped through as boy and man, – the slow, heavy years of constant, hot work. So long ago he began, that he thinks sometimes he has worked there for ages. There is no hope that it will ever end. Think that God put into this man's soul a fierce thirst for beauty, – to know it, to create it; to *be* – something, he knows not what, – other than he is. There are moments when a passing cloud, the sun glinting on the purple thistles, a kindly smile, a child's face, will rouse him to a passion of pain, – when his nature starts up with a mad cry of rage against God, man, whoever it is that has forced this vile, slimy life upon him. With all this groping, this mad desire, a great blind intellect stumbling through wrong, a loving poet's heart, the man was by habit only a coarse, vulgar laborer, familiar with sights and words you would blush to name. Be just: when I tell you about this night, see him as he is. Be just, – not like man's law, which seizes on one isolated fact, but like God's judging angel, whose clear, sad eye saw all the countless cankering days of this man's life, all the countless nights, when, sick with starving, his soul fainted in him, before it judged him for this night, the saddest of all.

I called this night the crisis of his life. If it was, it stole on him unawares. These great turning-days of life cast no shadow before, slip by unconsciously. Only a trifle, a little turn of the rudder, and the ship goes to heaven or hell.

Wolfe, while Deborah watched him, dug into the furnace of melting iron with his pole, dully thinking only how many rails the lump would yield. It was late, – nearly Sunday morning; another hour, and the heavy work would be done, – only the furnaces to replenish and cover for the next day. The workmen were growing more noisy, shouting, as they had to do, to be heard over the deep clamor of the mills. Suddenly they grew less boisterous, – at the far end, entirely silent. Something unusual had happened. After a moment, the silence came nearer; the men stopped their jeers and drunken choruses. Deborah, stupidly lifting up her head, saw the cause of the quiet. A group of five or six men were slowly approaching, stopping to examine each furnace as they came. Visitors often came to see the mills after night: except by growing less noisy, the men took no notice of them. The furnace where Wolfe worked was near the bounds of the works; they halted there hot and tired: a walk over one of these great foundries is no trifling task. The woman, drawing out of sight, turned over to sleep. Wolfe, seeing them stop, suddenly roused from his indifferent stupor, and watched them keenly. He knew some of them: the overseer, Clarke, – a son of Kirby, one of the millowners, – and a Doctor May, one of the town-physicians. The other two were strangers. Wolfe came closer. He seized eagerly every chance that brought him into contact with this mysterious class that shone down on him perpetually with the glamour of another order of being. What made the difference between them? That was the mystery of his life. He had a vague notion that perhaps tonight he could find it out. One of the strangers sat down on a pile of bricks, and beckoned young Kirby to his side.

'This *is* hot, with a vengeance. A match, please?' – lighting his cigar. 'But the walk is worth the trouble. If it were not that you must have heard it so often, Kirby, I would tell you that your works look like Dante's Inferno.'

Kirby laughed.

'Yes. Yonder is Farinata* himself in the burning tomb,' – pointing to some figure in the shimmering shadows.

'Judging from some of the faces of your men,' said the other, 'they bid fair to try the reality of Dante's vision, some day.'

Young Kirby looked curiously around, as if seeing the faces of his hands for the first time.

'They're bad enough, that's true. A desperate set, I fancy. Eh, Clarke?'

The overseer did not hear him. He was talking of net profits just then, – giving, in fact, a schedule of the annual business of the firm to a sharp peering little Yankee, who jotted down notes on a paper laid on the crown of his hat: a reporter for one of the city-papers getting up a series of reviews of the leading manufactories. The other gentlemen had accompanied them merely for amusement. They were silent until the notes were finished, drying their feet at the furnaces, and sheltering their faces from the intolerable heat. At last the overseer concluded with –

'I believe that is a pretty fair estimate, Captain.'

'Here, some of you men!' said Kirby, 'bring up those boards. We may as well sit down, gentlemen, until the rain is over. It cannot last much longer at this rate.'

'Pig-metal,' mumbled the reporter, 'um! – coal facilities – um! – hands employed, twelve hundred – bitumen – um! – all right, I believe, Mr Clarke – sinking-fund – what did you say was your sinking-fund?'*

'Twelve hundred hands?' said the stranger, the young man who had first spoken. 'Do you control their votes, Kirby?'

'Control? No.' The young man smiled complacently. 'But my father brought seven hundred votes to the polls for his candidate last November. No force-work, you understand, – only a speech or two, a hint to form themselves into a society, and a bit of red and blue bunting to make them a flag. The Invincible Roughs, – I believe that is their name. I forget the motto: "Our country's hope," I think.'

There was a laugh. The young man talking to Kirby sat with an amused light in his cool gray eye, surveying critically the half-clothed figures of the puddlers, and the slow swing of their brawny muscles. He was a stranger in the city, – spending a couple of months in the borders of a Slave State, to study the institutions of the South, – a brother-in-law of Kirby's, – Mitchell. He was an amateur gymnast, – hence his anatomical eye; a patron, in a *blasé* way, of the prize-ring; a man who sucked the essence out of a science or philosophy in an indifferent, gentlemanly way; who took Kant, Novalis, Humboldt,* for what they were worth in his own scales; accepting all, despising nothing, in heaven, earth, or hell, but one-idead men; with a temper yielding and brilliant as summer water, until his Self was touched, when it was ice, though brilliant still. Such men are not rare in the States.

As he knocked the ashes from his cigar, Wolfe caught with a quick pleasure the contour of the white hand, the blood-glow of a red ring he wore. His voice, too, and that of Kirby's, touched him like music, – low, even, with chording cadences. About this man Mitchell hung the impalpable atmosphere belonging to the thoroughbred gentleman. Wolfe, scraping away the ashes beside him, was conscious of it, did obeisance to it with his artist sense, unconscious that he did so.

The rain did not cease. Clarke and the reporter left the mills; the others, comfortably seated near the furnace, lingered, smoking and talking in a desultory way. Greek would not have been more unintelligible to the furnace-tenders, whose presence they soon forgot entirely. Kirby drew out a newspaper from his pocket and read aloud some article, which they discussed eagerly. At every sentence, Wolfe listened more and more like a dumb, hopeless animal, with a duller, more stolid look creeping over his face, glancing now and then at Mitchell, marking acutely every smallest sign of refinement, then back to himself, seeing as in a mirror his filthy body, his more stained soul.

Never! He had no words for such a thought, but he knew now, in all the sharpness of the bitter certainty, that between them there was a great gulf never to be passed. Never!

The bells of the mills rang for midnight. Sunday morning had dawned. Whatever hidden message lay in the tolling bells floated past these men unknown. Yet it was there. Veiled in the solemn music ushering the risen saviour was a key-note to solve the darkest secrets of a world gone wrong, – even this social riddle which the brain of the grimy puddler grappled with madly tonight.

The men began to withdraw the metal from the caldrons. The mills were deserted on Sundays, except by the hands who fed the fires, and those who had no lodgings and slept usually on the ash-heaps. The three strangers sat still during the next hour, watching the men cover the furnaces, laughing now and then at some jest of Kirby's.

'Do you know,' said Mitchell, 'I like this view of the works better than when the glare was fiercest? These heavy shadows and the amphitheatre of smothered fires are ghostly, unreal. One could fancy these red smouldering lights to be the half-shut eyes of wild beasts, and the spectral figures their victims in the den.'

Kirby laughed. 'You are fanciful. Come, let us get out of the den. The spectral figures, as you call them, are a little too real for me to fancy a close proximity in the darkness, – unarmed, too.'

The others rose, buttoning their over-coats, and lighting cigars.

'Raining, still,' said Doctor May, 'and hard. Where did we leave the coach, Mitchell?'

'At the other side of the works. – Kirby, what's that?'

Mitchell started back, half-frightened, as, suddenly turning a corner, the white figure of a woman faced him in the darkness, – a woman, white, of giant proportions, crouching on the ground, her arms flung out in some wild gesture of warning.

'Stop! Make that fire burn there!' cried Kirby, stopping short.

The flame burst out, flashing the gaunt figure into bold relief.

Mitchell drew a long breath.

'I thought it was alive,' he said, going up curiously.

The others followed.

'Not marble, eh?' asked Kirby, touching it.

One of the lower overseers stopped.

'Korl, Sir.'

'Who did it?'

'Can't say. Some of the hands; chipped it out in off-hours.'

'Chipped to some purpose, I should say. What a flesh-tint the stuff has! Do you see, Mitchell?'

'I see.'

He had stepped aside where the light fell boldest on the figure, looking at it in silence. There was not one line of beauty or grace in it: a nude woman's form, muscular, grown coarse with labor, the powerful limbs instinct with some one poignant longing. One idea: there it was in the tense, rigid muscles, the clutching hands, the wild, eager face, like that of a starving wolf's. Kirby and Doctor May walked around it, critical, curious. Mitchell stood aloof, silent. The figure touched him strangely.

'Not badly done,' said Doctor May. 'Where did the fellow learn that sweep of the muscles in the arm and hand? Look at them! They are groping, – do you see? – clutching: the peculiar action of a man dying of thirst.'

'They have ample facilities for studying anatomy,' sneered Kirby, glancing at the half-naked figures.

'Look,' continued the Doctor, 'at this bony wrist, and the

strained sinews of the instep! A working woman, – the very type of her class.'

'God forbid!' muttered Mitchell.

'Why?' demanded May. 'What does the fellow intend by the figure? I cannot catch the meaning.'

'Ask him,' said the other, dryly. 'There he stands,' – pointing to Wolfe, who stood with a group of men, leaning on his ash-rake.

The Doctor beckoned him with the affable smile which kind-hearted men put on, when talking with these people.

'Mr Mitchell has picked you out as the man who did this, – I'm sure I don't know why. But what did you mean by it?'

'She be hungry.'

Wolfe's eyes answered Mitchell, not the Doctor.

'Oh-h! But what a mistake you have made, my fine fellow! You have given no sign of starvation to the body. It is strong, – terribly strong. It has the mad, half-despairing gesture of drowning.'

Wolfe stammered, glanced appealingly at Mitchell, who saw the soul of the thing, he knew. But the cool, probing eyes were turned on himself now, – mocking, cruel, relentless.

'Not hungry for meat,' the furnace-tender said at last.

'What then? Whiskey?' jeered Kirby, with a coarse laugh.

Wolfe was silent a moment, thinking.

'I dunno,' he said, with a bewildered look. 'It mebbe. Summat to make her live, I think, – like you. Whiskey ull do it, in a way.'

The young man laughed again. Mitchell flashed a look of disgust somewhere, – not at Wolfe.

'May,' he broke out impatiently, 'are you blind? Look at that woman's face! It asks questions of God, and says, "I have a right to know." Good God, how hungry it is!'

They looked a moment; then May turned to the mill-owner: –

'Have you many such hands as this? What are you going to do with them? Keep them at puddling iron?'

Kirby shrugged his shoulders. Mitchell's look had irritated him.

'Ce n'est pas mon affaire.* I have no fancy for nursing infant geniuses. I suppose there are some stray gleams of mind and soul among these wretches. The Lord will take care of his own;

or else they can work out their own salvation. I have heard you call our American system a ladder which any man can scale. Do you doubt it? Or perhaps you want to banish all social ladders, and put us all on a flat table-land, – eh, May?'

The Doctor looked vexed, puzzled. Some terrible problem lay hid in this woman's face, and troubled these men. Kirby waited for an answer, and, receiving none, went on, warming with his subject.

'I tell you, there's something wrong that no talk of "*Liberté*" or "*Égalité*" will do away. If I had the making of men, these men who do the lowest part of the world's work should be machines, – nothing more, – hands. It would be kindness. God help them! What are taste, reason, to creatures who must live such lives as that?' He pointed to Deborah, sleeping on the ash-heap. 'So many nerves to sting them to pain. What if God had put your brain, with all its agony of touch, into your fingers, and bid you work and strike with that?'

'You think you could govern the world better?' laughed the Doctor.

'I do not think at all.'

'That is true philosophy. Drift with the stream, because you cannot dive deep enough to find bottom, eh?'

'Exactly,' rejoined Kirby. 'I do not think. I wash my hands of all social problems, – slavery, caste, white or black. My duty to my operatives has a narrow limit, – the pay-hour on Saturday night. Outside of that, if they cut korl, or cut each other's throats, (the more popular amusement of the two,) I am not responsible.'

The Doctor sighed, – a good honest sigh, from the depths of his stomach.

'God help us! Who is responsible?'

'Not I, I tell you,' said Kirby, testily. 'What has the man who pays them money to do with their souls' concerns, more than the grocer or butcher who takes it?'

'And yet,' said Mitchell's cynical voice, 'look at her! How hungry she is!'

Kirby tapped his boot with his cane. No one spoke. Only the dumb face of the rough image looking into their faces with the awful question, 'What shall we do to be saved?'* Only Wolfe's face, with its heavy weight of brain, its weak, uncertain mouth, its desperate eyes, out of which looked the soul of his class, –

only Wolfe's face turned towards Kirby's. Mitchell laughed, – a cool, musical laugh.

'Money has spoken!' he said, seating himself lightly on a stone with the air of an amused spectator at a play. 'Are you answered?' – turning to Wolfe his clear, magnetic face.

Bright and deep and cold as Arctic air, the soul of the man lay tranquil beneath. He looked at the furnace-tender as he had looked at a rare mosaic in the morning; only the man was the more amusing study of the two.

'Are you answered? Why, May, look at him! "*De profundis clamavi.*"* Or, to quote in English, "Hungry and thirsty, his soul faints in him." And so Money sends back its answer into the depths through you, Kirby! Very clear the answer, too! – I think I remember reading the same words somewhere: – washing your hands in Eau de Cologne, and saying, "I am innocent of the blood of this man. See ye to it!"'*

Kirby flushed angrily.

'You quote Scripture freely.'

'Do I not quote correctly? I think I remember another line, which may amend my meaning: "Inasmuch as ye did it unto one of the least of these, ye did it unto me."* Deist? Bless you, man, I was raised on the milk of the Word. Now, Doctor, the pocket of the world having uttered its voice, what has the heart to say? You are a philanthropist, in a small way, – *n'est ce pas?** Here, boy, this gentleman can show you how to cut korl better, – or your destiny. Go on, May!'

'I think a mocking devil possesses you tonight,' rejoined the Doctor, seriously.

He went to Wolfe and put his hand kindly on his arm. Something of a vague idea possessed the Doctor's brain that much good was to be done here by a friendly word or two: a latent genius to be warmed into life by a waited-for sun-beam. Here it was: he had brought it. So he went on complacently: –

'Do you know, boy, you have it in you to be a great sculptor, a great man? – do you understand?' (talking down to the capacity of his hearer: it is a way people have with children, and men like Wolfe,) – 'to live a better, stronger life than I, or Mr Kirby here? A man may make himself anything he chooses. God has given you stronger powers than many men, – me, for instance.'

May stopped, heated, glowing with his own magnanimity.

And it was magnanimous. The puddler had drunk in every word, looking through the Doctor's flurry, and generous heat, and self-approval, into his will, with those slow, absorbing eyes of his.

'Make yourself what you will. It is your right.'

'I know,' quietly. 'Will you help me?'

Mitchell laughed again. The Doctor turned now, in a passion, –

'You know, Mitchell, I have not the means. You know, if I had, it is in my heart to take this boy and educate him for' –

'The glory of God, and the glory of John May.'

May did not speak for a moment; then, controlled, he said, –

'Why should one be raised, when myriads are left? – I have not the money, boy,' to Wolfe, shortly.

'Money?' He said it over slowly, as one repeats the guessed answer to a riddle, doubtfully. 'That is it? Money?'

'Yes, money, – that is it,' said Mitchell, rising, and drawing his furred coat about him. 'You've found the cure for all the world's diseases. – Come, May, find your good-humor, and come home. This damp wind chills my very bones. Come and preach your Saint-Simonian* doctrines tomorrow to Kirby's hands. Let them have a clear idea of the rights of the soul, and I'll venture next week they'll strike for higher wages. That will be the end of it.'

'Will you send the coach-driver to this side of the mills?' asked Kirby, turning to Wolfe.

He spoke kindly: it was his habit to do so. Deborah, seeing the puddler go, crept after him. The three men waited outside. Doctor May walked up and down, chafed. Suddenly he stopped.

'Go back, Mitchell! You say the pocket and the heart of the world speak without meaning to these people. What has its head to say? Taste, culture, refinement? Go!'

Mitchell was leaning against a brick wall. He turned his head indolently, and looked into the mills. There hung about the place a thick, unclean odor. The slightest motion of his hand marked that he perceived it, and his insufferable disgust. That was all. May said nothing, only quickened his angry tramp.

'Besides,' added Mitchell, giving a corollary to his answer, 'it would be of no use. I am not one of them.'

'You do not mean' – said May, facing him.

'Yes, I mean just that. Reform is born of need, not pity. No vital movement of the people's has worked down, for good or evil; fermented, instead, carried up the heaving, cloggy mass. Think back through history, and you will know it. What will this lowest deep – thieves, Magdalens,* negroes – do with the light filtered through ponderous Church creeds, Baconian theories, Goethe schemes?* Some day, out of their bitter need will be thrown up their light-bringer, – their Jean Paul, their Cromwell, their Messiah.'*

'Bah!' was the Doctor's inward criticism. However, in practice, he adopted the theory; for, when, night and morning, afterwards, he prayed that power might be given these degraded souls to rise, he glowed at heart, recognizing an accomplished duty.

Wolfe and the woman had stood in the shadow of the works as the coach drove off. The Doctor had held out his hand in a frank, generous way, telling him to 'take care of himself, and to remember it was his right to rise.' Mitchell had simply touched his hat, as to an equal, with a quiet look of thorough recognition. Kirby had thrown Deborah some money, which she found, and clutched eagerly enough. They were gone now, all of them. The man sat down on the cinder-road, looking up into the murky sky.

''T be late, Hugh. Wunnot hur come?'

He shook his head doggedly, and the woman crouched out of his sight against the wall. Do you remember rare moments when a sudden light flashed over yourself, your world, God? when you stood on a mountain-peak, seeing your life as it might have been, as it is? one quick instant, when custom lost its force and everyday usage? when your friend, wife, brother, stood in a new light? your soul was bared, and the grave, – a foretaste of the nakedness of the Judgment-Day? So it came before him, his life, that night. The slow tides of pain he had borne gathered themselves up and surged against his soul. His squalid daily life, the brutal coarseness eating into his brain, as the ashes into his skin: before, these things had been a dull aching into his consciousness; tonight, they were reality. He gripped the filthy red shirt that clung, stiff with soot, about him, and tore it savagely from his arm. The flesh beneath was muddy with grease and ashes, – and the heart beneath that! And the soul? God knows.

Then flashed before his vivid poetic sense the man who had left him, – the pure face, the delicate, sinewy limbs, in harmony with all he knew of beauty or truth. In his cloudy fancy he had pictured a Something like this. He had found it in this Mitchell, even when he idly scoffed at his pain: a Man all-knowing, all-seeing, crowned by Nature, reigning, – the keen glance of his eye falling like a sceptre on other men. And yet his instinct taught him that he too – He! He looked at himself with sudden loathing, sick, wrung his hands with a cry, and then was silent. With all the phantoms of his heated, ignorant fancy, Wolfe had not been vague in his ambitions. They were practical, slowly built up before him out of his knowledge of what he could do. Through years he had day by day made this hope a real thing to himself, – a clear, projected figure of himself, as he might become.

Able to speak, to know what was best, to raise these men and women working at his side up with him: sometimes he forgot this defined hope in the frantic anguish to escape, – only to escape, – out of the wet, the pain, the ashes, somewhere, anywhere, – only for one moment of free air on a hill-side, to lie down and let his sick soul throb itself out in the sunshine. But tonight he panted for life. The savage strength of his nature was roused; his cry was fierce to God for justice.

'Look at me!' he said to Deborah, with a low, bitter laugh, striking his puny chest savagely. 'What am I worth, Deb? Is it my fault that I am no better? My fault? My fault?'

He stopped, stung with a sudden remorse, seeing her hunchback shape writhing with sobs. For Deborah was crying thankless tears, according to the fashion of women.

'God forgi' me, woman! Things go harder wi' you nor me. It's a worse share.'

He got up and helped her to rise; and they went doggedly down the muddy street, side by side.

'It's all wrong,' he muttered, slowly, – 'all wrong! I dunnot understan'. But it'll end some day.'

'Come home, Hugh!' she said, coaxingly; for he had stopped, looking around bewildered.

'Home, – and back to the mill!' He went on saying this over to himself, as if he would mutter down every pain in this dull despair.

She followed him through the fog, her blue lips chattering with cold. They reached the cellar at last. Old Wolfe had been drinking since she went out, and had crept nearer the door. The girl Janey slept heavily in the corner. He went up to her, touching softly the worn white arm with his fingers. Some bitterer thought stung him, as he stood there. He wiped the drops from his forehead, and went into the room beyond, livid, trembling. A hope, trifling, perhaps, but very dear, had died just then out of the poor puddler's life, as he looked at the sleeping, innocent girl, – some plan for the future, in which she had borne a part. He gave it up that moment, then and forever. Only a trifle, perhaps, to us: his face grew a shade paler, – that was all. But, somehow, the man's soul, as God and the angels looked down on it, never was the same afterwards.

Deborah followed him into the inner room. She carried a candle, which she placed on the floor, closing the door after her. She had seen the look on his face, as he turned away: her own grew deadly. Yet, as she came up to him her eyes glowed. He was seated on an old chest, quiet, holding his face in his hands.

'Hugh!' she said, softly.

He did not speak.

'Hugh, did hur hear what the man said, – him with the clear voice? Did hur hear? Money, money, – that it wud do all?'

He pushed her away, – gently, but he was worn out; her rasping tone fretted him.

'Hugh!'

The candle flared a pale yellow light over the cobwebbed brick walls, and the woman standing there. He looked at her. She was young, in deadly earnest; her faded eyes, and wet, ragged figure caught from their frantic eagerness a power akin to beauty.

'Hugh, it is true! Money ull do it! Oh, Hugh, boy, listen till me! He said it true! It is money!'

'I know. Go back! I do not want you here.'

'Hugh, it is t' last time. I'll never worrit hur again.'

There were tears in her voice now, but she choked them back.

'Hear till me only tonight! If one of t' witch people wud come, them we heard of t' home, and gif hur all hur wants, what then? Say, Hugh!'

'What do you mean?'

'I mean money.'

Her whisper shrilled through his brain.

'If one of t' witch dwarfs wud come from t' lane moors tonight, and gif hur money, to go out, – *out*, I say, – out, lad, where t' sun shines, and t' heath grows, and t' ladies walk in silken gownds, and God stays all t' time, – where t' man lives that talked to us tonight, – Hugh knows, – Hugh could walk there like a king!'

He thought the woman mad, tried to check her, but she went on, fierce in her eager haste.

'If I were t' witch dwarf, if I had t' money, wud hur thank me? Wud hur take me out o' this place wid hur and Janey? I wud not come into the gran' house hur wud build, to vex hur wid t' hunch, – only at night, when t' shadows were dark, stand far off to see hur.'

Mad? Yes! Are many of us mad in this way?

'Poor Deb! poor Deb!' he said, soothingly.

'It is here,' she said, suddenly jerking into his hand a small roll. 'I took it! I did it! Me, me! – not hur! I shall be hanged, I shall be burnt in hell, if anybody knows I took it! Out of his pocket, as he leaned against t' bricks. Hur knows?'

She thrust it into his hand, and then, her errand done, began to gather chips together to make a fire, choking down hysteric sobs.

'Has it come to this?'

That was all he said. The Welsh Wolfe blood was honest. The roll was a small green pocket-book containing one or two gold pieces, and a check for an incredible amount, as it seemed to the poor puddler. He laid it down, hiding his face again in his hands.

'Hugh, don't be angry wud me! It's only poor Deb, – hur knows?'

He took the long skinny fingers kindly in his.

'Angry? God help me, no! Let me sleep. I am tired.'

He threw himself heavily down on the wooden bench, stunned with pain and weariness. She brought some old rags to cover him.

It was late on Sunday evening before he awoke. I tell God's truth, when I say he had then no thought of keeping this money. Deborah had hid it in his pocket. He found it there. She watched him eagerly, as he took it out.

'I must gif it to him,' he said, reading her face.

'Hur knows,' she said with a bitter sigh of disappointment. 'But it is hur right to keep it.'

His right! The word struck him. Doctor May had used the

same. He washed himself, and went out to find this man Mitchell. His right! Why did this chance word cling to him so obstinately? Do you hear the fierce devils whisper in his ear, as he went slowly down the darkening street?

The evening came on, slow and calm. He seated himself at the end of an alley leading into one of the larger streets. His brain was clear tonight, keen, intent, mastering. It would not start back, cowardly, from any hellish temptation, but meet it face to face. Therefore the great temptation of his life came to him veiled by no sophistry, but bold, defiant, owning its own vile name, trusting to one bold blow for victory.

He did not deceive himself. Theft! That was it. At first the word sickened him; then he grappled with it. Sitting there on a broken cart-wheel, the fading day, the noisy groups, the church-bells' tolling passed before him like a panorama, while the sharp struggle went on within. This money! He took it out, and looked at it. If he gave it back, what then? He was going to be cool about it.

People going by to church saw only a sickly mill-boy watching them quietly at the alley's mouth. They did not know that he was mad, or they would not have gone by so quietly: mad with hunger; stretching out his hands to the world, that had given so much to them, for leave to live the life God meant him to live. His soul within him was smothering to death; he wanted so much, thought so much, and *knew* – nothing. There was nothing of which he was certain, except the mill and things there. Of God and heaven he had heard so little, that they were to him what fairy-land is to a child: something real, but not here; very far off. His brain, greedy, dwarfed, full of thwarted energy and unused powers, questioned these men and women going by, coldly, bitterly, that night. Was it not his right to live as they, – a pure life, a good, true-hearted life, full of beauty and kind words? He only wanted to know how to use the strength within him. His heart warmed, as he thought of it. He suffered himself to think of it longer. If he took the money?

Then he saw himself as he might be, strong, helpful, kindly. The night crept on, as this one image slowly evolved itself from the crowd of other thoughts and stood triumphant. He looked at it. As he might be! What wonder, if it blinded him to delirium, – the madness that underlies all revolution, all progress, and all fall?

You laugh at the shallow temptation? You see the error underlying its argument so clearly, – that to him a true life was one of full development rather than self-restraint? that he was deaf to the higher tone in a cry of voluntary suffering for truth's sake than in the fullest flow of spontaneous harmony? I do not plead his cause. I only want to show you the mote in my brother's eye: then you can see clearly to take it out.

The money, – there it lay on his knee, a little blotted slip of paper, nothing in itself; used to raise him out of the pit; something straight from God's hand. A thief! Well, what was it to be a thief? He met the question at last, face to face, wiping the clammy drops of sweat from his forehead. God made this money – the fresh air, too – for his children's use. He never made the difference between poor and rich. The Something who looked down on him that moment through the cool gray sky had a kindly face, he knew, – loved his children alike. Oh, he knew that!

There were times when the soft floods of color in the crimson and purple flames, or the clear depth of amber in the water below the bridge, had somehow given him a glimpse of another world than this, – of an infinite depth of beauty and of quiet somewhere, – somewhere, – a depth of quiet and rest and love. Looking up now, it became strangely real. The sun had sunk quite below the hills, but his last rays struck upward, touching the zenith. The fog had risen, and the town and river were steeped in its thick, gray damp; but overhead, the sun-touched smoke-clouds opened like a cleft ocean, – shifting, rolling seas of crimson mist, waves of billowy silver veined with blood-scarlet, inner depths unfathomable of glancing light. Wolfe's artist-eye grew drunk with color. The gates of that other world! Fading, flashing before him now! What, in that world of Beauty, Content, and Right, were the petty laws, the mine and thine, of mill-owners and mill-hands?

A consciousness of power stirred within him. He stood up. A man, – he thought, stretching out his hands, – free to work, to live, to love! Free! His right! He folded the scrap of paper in his hand. As his nervous fingers took it in, limp and blotted, so his soul took in the mean temptation, lapped it in fancied rights, in dreams of improved existences, drifting and endless as the cloud-seas of color. Clutching it, as if the tightness of his hold would strengthen his sense of possession, he went aimlessly down the street. It was his watch at the mill. He need not go, need never go again, thank God! – shaking off the thought with unspeakable loathing.

Shall I go over the history of the hours of that night? how the man wandered from one to another of his old haunts, with a half-consciousness of bidding them farewell, – lanes and alleys and back-yards where the mill-hands lodged, – noting, with a new eagerness, the filth and drunkenness, the pig-pens, the ash-heaps covered with potato-skins, the bloated, pimpled women at the doors, – with a new disgust, a new sense of sudden triumph, and, under all, a new, vague dread, unknown before, smothered down, kept under, but still there? It left him but once during the night, when, for the second time in his life, he entered a church. It was a sombre Gothic pile, where the stained light lost itself in far-retreating arches; built to meet the requirements and sympathies of a far other class than Wolfe's. Yet it touched, moved him uncontrollably. The distances, the shadows, the still, marble figures, the mass of silent kneeling worshippers, the mysterious music, thrilled, lifted his soul with a wonderful pain. Wolfe forgot himself, forgot the new life he was going to live, the mean terror gnawing underneath. The voice of the speaker strengthened the charm; it was clear, feeling, full, strong. An old man, who had lived much, suffered much; whose brain was keenly alive, dominant; whose heart was summer-warm with charity. He taught it tonight. He held up Humanity in its grand total; showed the great world-cancer to his people. Who could show it better? He was a Christian reformer; he had studied the age thoroughly; his outlook at man had been free, worldwide, over all time. His faith stood sublime upon the Rock of Ages; his fiery zeal guided vast schemes by which the gospel was to be preached to all nations. How did he preach it tonight? In burning, light-laden words he painted the incarnate Life, Love, the universal Man: words that became reality in the lives of these people, – that lived again in beautiful words and actions, trifling, but heroic. Sin, as he defined it, was a real foe to them; their trials, temptations, were his. His words passed far over the furnace-tender's grasp, toned to suit another class of culture; they sounded in his ears a very pleasant song in an unknown tongue. He meant to cure this world-cancer with a steady eye that had never glared with hunger, and a hand that neither poverty nor strychnine-whiskey had taught to shake.

In this morbid, distorted heart of the Welsh puddler he had failed.

Wolfe rose at last, and turned from the church down the street. He looked up; the night had come on foggy, damp; the golden mists had vanished, and the sky lay dull and ash-colored. He wandered again aimlessly down the street, idly wondering what had become of the cloud-sea of crimson and scarlet. The trial-day of this man's life was over, and he had lost the victory. What followed was mere drifting circumstance, – a quicker walking over the path, – that was all. Do you want to hear the end of it? You wish me to make a tragic story out of it? Why, in the police-reports of the morning paper you can find a dozen such tragedies: hints of shipwrecks unlike any that ever befell on the high seas; hints that here a power was lost to heaven, – that there a soul went down where no tide can ebb or flow. Commonplace enough the hints are, – jocose sometimes, done up in rhyme.

Doctor May, a month after the night I have told you of, was reading to his wife at breakfast from this fourth column of the morning-paper: an unusual thing, – these police-reports not being, in general, choice reading for ladies; but it was only one item he read.

'Oh, my dear! You remember that man I told you of, that we saw at Kirby's mill? – that was arrested for robbing Mitchell? Here he is; just listen: – 'Circuit Court. Judge Day. Hugh Wolfe, operative in Kirby & John's Loudon Mills. Charge, grand larceny. Sentence, nineteen years' hard labor in penitentiary.' – Scoundrel! Serves him right! After all our kindness that night! Picking Mitchell's pocket at the very time!'

His wife said something about the ingratitude of that kind of people, and then they began to talk of something else.

Nineteen years! How easy that was to read! What a simple word for Judge Day to utter! Nineteen years! Half a lifetime!

Hugh Wolfe sat on the window-ledge of his cell, looking out. His ankles were ironed. Not usual in such cases; but he had made two desperate efforts to escape. 'Well,' as Haley, the jailer, said, 'small blame to him! Nineteen years' imprisonment was not a pleasant thing to look forward to.' Haley was very good-natured about it, though Wolfe had fought him savagely.

'When he was first caught,' the jailer said afterwards, in telling the story, 'before the trial, the fellow was cut down at once, –

laid there on that pallet like a dead man, with his hands over his eyes. Never saw a man so cut down in my life. Time of the trial, too, came the queerest dodge of any customer I ever had. Would choose no lawyer. Judge gave him one, of course. Gibson it was. He tried to prove the fellow crazy; but it wouldn't go. Thing was plain as day-light: money found on him. 'Twas a hard sentence, – all the law allows; but it was for 'xample's sake. These mill-hands are gettin' onbearable. When the sentence was read, he just looked up, and said the money was his by rights, and that all the world had gone wrong. That night, after the trial, a gentleman came to see him here, name of Mitchell, – him as he stole from. Talked to him for an hour. Thought he came for curiosity, like. After he was gone, thought Wolfe was remarkable quiet, and went into his cell. Found him very low; bed all bloody. Doctor said he had been bleeding at the lungs. He was as weak as a cat; yet, if ye'll b'lieve me, he tried to get a-past me and get out. I just carried him like a baby, and threw him on the pallet. Three days after, he tried it again: that time reached the wall. Lord help you! he fought like a tiger, – giv' some terrible blows. Fightin' for life, you see; for he can't live long, shut up in the stone crib down yonder. Got a death-cough now. 'T took two of us to bring him down that day; so I just put the irons on his feet. There he sits, in there. Goin' tomorrow, with a batch more of 'em. That woman, hunchback, tried with him, – you remember? – she's only got three years. 'Complice. But *she's* a woman, you know. He's been quiet ever since I put on irons: giv' up, I suppose. Looks white, sick-lookin'. It acts different on 'em, bein' sentenced. Most of 'em gets reckless, devilish-like. Some prays awful, and sings them vile songs of the mills, all in a breath. That woman, now, she's desper't'. Been beggin' to see Hugh, as she calls him, for three days. I'm a-goin' to let her in. She don't go with him. Here she is in this next cell. I'm a-goin' now to let her in.'

He let her in. Wolfe did not see her. She crept into a corner of the cell, and stood watching him. He was scratching the iron bars of the window with a piece of tin which he had picked up, with an idle, uncertain, vacant stare, just as a child or idiot would do.

'Tryin' to get out, old boy?' laughed Haley. 'Them irons will need a crow-bar beside your tin, before you can open 'em.'

Wolfe laughed, too, in a senseless way.

'I think I'll get out,' he said.

'I believe his brain's touched,' said Haley, when he came out.

The puddler scraped away with the tin for half an hour. Still Deborah did not speak. At last she ventured nearer, and touched his arm.

'Blood?' she said, looking at some spots on his coat with a shudder.

He looked up at her. 'Why, Deb!' he said, smiling, – such a bright, boyish smile, that it went to poor Deborah's heart directly, and she sobbed and cried out loud.

'Oh, Hugh, lad! Hugh! dunnot look at me, when it wur my fault! To think I brought hur to it! And I loved hur so! Oh, lad, I dud!'

'The confession, even in this wretch, came with the woman's blush through the sharp cry.

He did not seem to hear her, – scraping away diligently at the bars with the bit of tin.

Was he going mad? She peered closely into his face. Something she saw there made her draw suddenly back, – something which Haley had not seen, that lay beneath the pinched, vacant look it had caught since the trial, or the curious gray shadow that rested on it. That gray shadow, – yes, she knew what that meant. She had often seen it creeping over women's faces for months, who died at last of slow hunger or consumption. That meant death, distant, lingering: but this – Whatever it was the woman saw, or thought she saw, used as she was to crime and misery, seemed to make her sick with a new horror. Forgetting her fear of him, she caught his shoulders, and looked keenly, steadily, into his eyes.

'Hugh!' she cried, in a desperate whisper, – 'oh, boy, not that! for God's sake, not *that*!'

The vacant laugh went off his face, and he answered her in a muttered word or two that drove her away. Yet the words were kindly enough. Sitting there on his pallet, she cried silently a hopeless sort of tears, but did not speak again. The man looked up furtively at her now and then. Whatever his own trouble was, her distress vexed him with a momentary sting.

It was market-day. The narrow window of the jail looked down directly on the carts and wagons drawn up in a long line, where they had unloaded. He could see, too, and hear distinctly the clink of money as it changed hands, the busy crowd of

whites and blacks shoving, pushing one another, and the chaffering* and swearing at the stalls. Somehow, the sound, more
than anything else had done, wakened him up, – made the whole
real to him. He was done with the world and the business of it.
He let the tin fall, and looked out, pressing his face close to the
rusty bars. How they crowded and pushed! And he, – he should
never walk that pavement again! There came Neff Sanders, one
of the feeders at the mill, with a basket on his arm. Sure enough,
Neff was married the other week. He whistled, hoping he would
look up; but he did not. He wondered if Neff remembered he
was there, – if any of the boys thought of him up there, and
thought that he never was to go down that old cinder-road
again. Never again! He had not quite understood it before; but
now he did. Not for days or years, but never! – that was it.

How clear the light fell on that stall in front of the market!
and how like a picture it was, the dark-green heaps of corn, and
the crimson beets, and golden melons! There was another with
game: how the light flickered on that pheasant's breast, with the
purplish blood dripping over the brown feathers! He could see
the red shining of the drops, it was so near. In one minute he
could be down there. It was just a step. So easy, as it seemed, so
natural to go! Yet it could never be – not in all the thousands of
years to come – that he should put his foot on the street again!
He thought of himself with a sorrowful pity, as of some one
else. There was a dog down in the market, walking after his
master with such a stately, grave look! – only a dog, yet he
could go backwards and forwards just as he pleased: he had
good luck! Why, the very vilest cur, yelping there in the gutter,
had not lived his life, had been free to act out whatever thought
God had put into his brain; while he – No, he would not think
of that! He tried to put the thought away, and to listen to a
dispute between a countryman and a woman about some meat;
but it would come back. He, what had he done to bear this?

Then came the sudden picture of what might have been, and
now. He knew what it was to be in the penitentiary, – how it
went with men there. He knew how in these long years he
should slowly die, but not until soul and body had become
corrupt and rotten, – how, when he came out, if he lived to
come, even the lowest of the mill-hands would jeer him, – how
his hands would be weak, and his brain senseless and stupid. He
believed he was almost that now. He put his hand to his head,

with a puzzled, weary look. It ached, his head, with thinking. He tried to quiet himself. It was only right, perhaps; he had done wrong. But was there right or wrong for such as he? What was right? And who had ever taught him? He thrust the whole matter away. A dark, cold quiet crept through his brain. It was all wrong; but let it be! It was nothing to him more than the others. Let it be!

The door grated, as Haley opened it.

'Come, my woman! Must lock up for t' night. Come, stir yerself!'

She went up and took Hugh's hand.

'Goodnight, Deb,' he said, carelessly.

She had not hoped he would say more; but the tired pain on her mouth just then was bitterer than death. She took his passive hand and kissed it.

'Hur'll never see Deb again!' she ventured, her lips growing colder and more bloodless.

What did she say that for? Did he not know it? Yet he would not be impatient with poor old Deb. She had trouble of her own, as well as he.

'No, never again,' he said, trying to be cheerful.

She stood just a moment, looking at him. Do you laugh at her, standing there, with her hunchback, her rags, her bleared, withered face, and the great despised love tugging at her heart?

'Come, you!' called Haley, impatiently.

She did not move.

'Hugh!' she whispered.

It was to be her last word. What was it?

'Hugh, boy, not THAT!'

He did not answer. She wrung her hands, trying to be silent, looking in his face in an agony of entreaty. He smiled again, kindly.

'It is best, Deb. I cannot bear to be hurted any more.'

'Hur knows,' she said, humbly.

'Tell my father goodbye; and – and kiss little Janey.'

She nodded, saying nothing, looked in his face again, and went out of the door. As she went, she staggered.

'Drinkin' today?' broke out Haley, pushing her before him. 'Where the Devil did you get it? Here, in with ye!' and he shoved her into her cell, next to Wolfe's, and shut the door.

Along the wall of her cell there was a crack low down by the floor, through which she could see the light from Wolfe's. She had discovered it days before. She hurried in now, and, kneeling down by it, listened, hoping to hear some sound. Nothing but the rasping of the tin on the bars. He was at his old amusement again. Something in the noise jarred on her ear, for she shivered as she heard it. Hugh rasped away at the bars. A dull old bit of tin, not fit to cut korl with.

He looked out of the window again. People were leaving the market now. A tall mulatto girl, following her mistress, her basket on her head, crossed the street just below, and looked up. She was laughing; but, when she caught sight of the haggard face peering out through the bars, suddenly grew grave, and hurried by. A free, firm step, a clear-cut olive face, with a scarlet turban tied on one side, dark, shining eyes, and on the head the basket poised, filled with fruit and flowers, under which the scarlet turban and bright eyes looked out half-shadowed. The picture caught his eye. It was good to see a face like that. He would try tomorrow, and cut one like it. *Tomorrow!* He threw down the tin, trembling, and covered his face with his hands. When he looked up again, the daylight was gone.

Deborah, crouching near by on the other side of the wall, heard no noise. He sat on the side of the low pallet, thinking. Whatever was the mystery which the woman had seen on his face, it came out now slowly, in the dark there, and became fixed, – a something never seen on his face before. The evening was darkening fast. The market had been over for an hour; the rumbling of the carts over the pavement grew more infrequent: he listened to each, as it passed, because he thought it was to be for the last time. For the same reason, it was, I suppose, that he strained his eyes to catch a glimpse of each passer-by, wondering who they were, what kind of homes they were going to, if they had children, – listening eagerly to every chance word in the street, as if – (God be merciful to the man! what strange fancy was this?) – as if he never should hear human voices again.

It was quite dark at last. The street was a lonely one. The last passenger, he thought, was gone. No, – there was a quick step: Joe Hill, lighting the lamps. Joe was a good old chap; never passed a fellow without some joke or other. He remembered once seeing the place where he lived with his wife. 'Granny Hill' the boys called her. Bedridden she was; but so kind as Joe was to her! kept the room so clean! – and the old woman, when he was there, was laughing at 'some of t' lad's foolishness.' The step was far down the street; but he could see him place the ladder, run up, and light the gas. A longing seized him to be spoken to once more.

'Joe!' he called, out of the grating. 'Goodbye, Joe!'

The old man stopped a moment, listening uncertainly; then hurried on. The prisoner thrust his hand out of the window, and called again, louder; but Joe was too far down the street. It was a little thing; but it hurt him, – this disappointment.

'Goodbye, Joe!' he called, sorrowfully enough.

'Be quiet!' said one of the jailers, passing the door, striking on it with his club.

Oh, that was the last, was it?

There was an inexpressible bitterness on his face, as he lay down on the bed, taking the bit of tin, which he had rasped to a tolerable degree of sharpness, in his hand, – to play with, it may be. He bared his arms, looking intently at their corded veins and sinews. Deborah, listening in the next cell, heard a slight clicking sound, often repeated. She shut her lips tightly, that she might not scream, the cold drops of sweat broke over her, in her dumb agony.

'Hur knows best,' she muttered at last, fiercely clutching the boards where she lay.

If she could have seen Wolfe, there was nothing about him to frighten her. He lay quite still, his arms outstretched, looking at the pearly stream of moonlight coming into the window. I think in that one hour that came then he lived back over all the years that had gone before. I think that all the low, vile life, all his wrongs, all his starved hopes, came then, and stung him with a farewell poison that made him sick unto death. He made neither moan nor cry, only turned his worn face now and then to the pure light, that seemed so far off, as one that said, 'How long, O Lord? how long?'*

The hour was over at last. The moon, passing over her nightly path, slowly came nearer, and threw the light across his bed on his feet. He watched it steadily, as it crept up, inch by inch, slowly. It seemed to him to carry with it a great silence. He had been so hot and tired there always in the mills! The years had been so fierce and cruel! There was coming now quiet and coolness and sleep. His tense limbs relaxed, and settled in a calm languor. The blood ran fainter and slow from his heart. He did not think now with a savage anger of what might be and was not; he was conscious only of deep stillness creeping over him. At first he saw a sea of faces: the mill-men, – women he had known, drunken and bloated, – Janeys timid and pitiful, – poor old Debs: then they floated together like a mist, and faded away, leaving only the clear, pearly moonlight.

Whether, as the pure light crept up the stretched-out figure, it brought with it calm and peace, who shall say? His dumb soul was alone with God in judgment. A Voice may have spoken for it from far-off Calvary, 'Father, forgive them, for they know not what they do!'* Who dare say? Fainter and fainter the heart rose and fell, slower and slower the moon floated from behind a cloud, until, when at last its full tide of white splendor swept over the cell, it seemed to wrap and fold into a deeper stillness the dead figure that never should move again. Silence deeper than the Night! Nothing that moved, save the black nauseous stream of blood dripping slowly from the pallet to the floor!

There was outcry and crowd enough in the cell the next day. The coroner and his jury, the local editors, Kirby himself, and boys with their hands thrust knowingly into their pockets and heads on one side, jammed into the corners. Coming and going all day. Only one woman. She came late, and outstayed them all. A Quaker, or Friend, as they call themselves. I think this woman was known by that name in heaven. A homely body, coarsely dressed in gray and white. Deborah (for Haley had let her in) took notice of her. She watched them all – sitting on the end of the pallet, holding his head in her arms – with the ferocity of a watch-dog, if any of them touched the body. There was no meekness, or sorrow, in her face; the stuff out of which murderers are made, instead. All the time Haley and the woman were laying straight the limbs and cleaning the cell, Deborah sat still, keenly watching the Quaker's face. Of all the crowd there that day, this woman alone had not spoken to her, – only once or twice had put some cordial to her lips. After they all were gone, the woman, in the same still, gentle way, brought a vase of wood-leaves and berries, and placed it by the pallet, then opened the narrow window. The fresh air blew in, and swept the woody fragrance over the dead face. Deborah looked up with a quick wonder.

'Did hur know my boy wud like it? Did hur know Hugh?'

'I know Hugh now.'

The white fingers passed in a slow, pitiful way over the dead, worn face. There was a heavy shadow in the quiet eyes.

'Did hur know where they'll bury Hugh?' said Deborah in a shrill tone, catching her arm.

This had been the question hanging on her lips all day.

'In t' town-yard? Under t' mud and ash? T' lad'll smother, woman! He wur born on t' lane moor, where t' air is frick* and strong. Take hur out, for God's sake, take hur out where t' air blows!'

The Quaker hesitated, but only for a moment. She put her strong arm around Deborah and led her to the window.

'Thee sees the hills, friend, over the river? Thee sees how the light lies warm there, and the winds of God blow all the day? I live there, – where the blue smoke is, by the trees. Look at me.' She turned Deborah's face to her own, clear and earnest. 'Thee will believe me? I will take Hugh and bury him there tomorrow.'

Deborah did not doubt her. As the evening wore on, she leaned against the iron bars, looking at the hills that rose far off, through the thick sodden clouds, like a bright, unattainable calm. As she looked, a shadow of their solemn repose fell on her face: its fierce discontent faded into a pitiful, humble quiet. Slow, solemn tears gathered in her eyes: the poor weak eyes turned so hopelessly to the place where Hugh was to rest, the grave heights looking higher and brighter and more solemn than ever before. The Quaker watched her keenly. She came to her at last, and touched her arm.

'When thee comes back,' she said, in a low, sorrowful tone, like one who speaks from a strong heart deeply moved with remorse or pity, 'thee shall begin thy life again, – there on the hills. I came too late; but not for thee, – by God's help, it may be.'

Not too late. Three years after, the Quaker began her work. I end my story here. At evening-time it was light. There is no need to tire you with the long years of sunshine, and fresh air, and slow, patient Christ-love, needed to make healthy and hopeful this impure body and soul. There is a homely pine house, on one of these hills, whose windows overlook broad, wooded slopes and clover-crimsoned meadows, – niched into the very place where the light is warmest, the air freest. It is the Friends' meeting-house. Once a week they sit there, in their grave, earnest way, waiting for the Spirit of Love to speak, opening their simple hearts to receive His words. There is a woman, old, deformed, who takes a humble place among them: waiting like them: in her gray dress, her worn face, pure and meek, turned now and then to the sky. A woman much loved by these silent, restful people; more silent than they, more humble, more loving. Waiting: with her eyes turned to hills higher and purer than these on which she lives, – dim and far off now, but to be reached some day. There may be in her heart some latent hope to meet there the love denied her here, – that she shall find him whom she lost, and that then she will not be all-unworthy. Who blames her? Something is lost in the passage of every soul from one eternity to the other, – something pure and beautiful, which might have been and was not: a hope, a talent, a love, over which the soul mourns, like Esau* deprived of his birthright. What blame to the meek Quaker, if she took her lost hope to make the hills of heaven more fair?

Nothing remains to tell that the poor Welsh puddler once lived, but this figure of the mill-woman cut in korl. I have it here in a corner of my library. I keep it hid behind a curtain, – it is such a rough, ungainly thing. Yet there are about it touches, grand sweeps of outline, that show a master's hand. Sometimes, – tonight, for instance, – the curtain is accidentally drawn back, and I see a bare arm stretched out imploringly in the darkness, and an eager, wolfish face watching mine: a wan, woful face, through which the spirit of the dead korl-cutter looks out, with its thwarted life, its mighty hunger, its unfinished work. Its pale, vague lips seem to tremble with a terrible question. 'Is this the End?' they say, – 'nothing beyond? – no more?' Why, you tell me you have seen that look in the eyes of dumb brutes, – horses dying under the lash. I know.

The deep of the night is passing while I write. The gas-light wakens from the shadows here and there the objects which lie scattered through the room: only faintly, though; for they belong to the open sunlight. As I glance at them, they each recall some task or pleasure of the coming day. A half-moulded child's head; Aphrodite;* a bough of forest-leaves; music; work; homely fragments, in which lie the secrets of all eternal truth and beauty. Prophetic all! Only this dumb, woful face seems to belong to and end with the night. I turn to look at it. Has the power of its desperate need commanded the darkness away? While the room

is yet steeped in heavy shadow, a cool, gray light suddenly
touches its head like a blessing hand, and its groping arm points
through the broken cloud to the far East, where, in the flickering,
nebulous crimson, God has set the promise of the Dawn.

Marcia

1876

One winter morning a few years ago the mail brought me a roll of MS. (with one stamp too many, as if to bribe the post to care for so precious a thing) and a letter. Every publisher, editor, or even the obscurest of writers receives such packages so often as to know them at a glance. Half a dozen poems and a story – a blur of sunsets, duchesses, violets, bad French, and worse English; not a solid grain of common-sense, not a hint of reality or even of possibility, in the whole of it. The letter – truth in every word: formal, hard, practical, and the meaning of it a woman's cry for bread for her hungry children. Each woman who writes such a letter fancies she is the first, that its pathos will move hard-hearted editors, and that the extent of her need will supply the lack of wit, wisdom, or even grammar in her verses or story. Such appeals pour in literally by the thousand every year to every publishing office. The sickly daughter of a poor family; the wife of a drunken husband; a widow; children that must be fed and clothed. What was the critic's honest opinion of her work? how much would it bring in dollars and cents? etc., etc.

I did not open the letter that day. When we reach middle age we have learned, through rough experiences, how many trage-dies there are in our street or under our own roof which will be none the better for our handling, and are apt, selfishly, to try to escape the hearing of them.

This letter, however, when I opened it next morning, proved to be not of a tragical sort. The writer was 'not dependent on her pen for support;' she 'had vowed herself to literature;' she 'was resolved to assist in the Progress of humanity.' Scarcely had I laid down the letter when I was told that she waited below to see me. The card she sent up was a bit of the fly-leaf of a book. cut oblong with scissors, and the name – Miss Barr – written in imitation of engraving. Her back was toward me when I came down, and I had time to read the same sham stylishness written all over her thin little person. The sleazy black silk was looped in the prevailing fashion, a sweeping white plume drooped from the cheap hat, and on her hands were washed cotton gloves.

Instead of the wizened features of the 'dead beat' which I expected, she turned on me a child's face: an ugly face, I believe other women called it, but one of the most innocent and honest in the world. Her brown eyes met yours eagerly, full of a joyous good-fellowship for every thing and every body alive. She poured out her story, too, in a light-hearted way, and in the lowest, friendliest of voices. To see the girl was to be her ally. 'People will do any thing for me – but publish my manuscripts,' she said.

She came from Mississippi; had been the only white child on a poor plantation on the banks of the Yazoo. 'I have only had such teaching as my mother could give: she had but two years with a governess. We had no books nor newspapers, except an occasional copy of a magazine sent to us by friends in the North.' Her mother was the one central figure in the world to her then. In our after-intercourse she talked of her continually. 'She is a little woman – less than I; but she has one of the finest minds in the world,' she would cry. 'The sight of any thing beautiful or the sound of music sways her as the wind does a reed. But she never was twenty miles from the plantation; she has read nothing, knows nothing. My father thinks women are like mares – only useful to bring forth children. My mother's children all died in babyhood but me. There she has lived all her life, with the swamp on one side and the forest of live-oak on the other: nothing to do, nothing to think of. Oh, it was frightful! With a mind like hers, any woman would go mad, with that eternal forest and swamp, and the graves of her dead babies just in sight! She rubbed snuff a good deal to quiet herself, but of late years she has taken opium.'

'And you?'

'I left her. I hoped to do something for us both. My mind is not of as high order as hers, but it is very different from that of most women. I shall succeed some day,' in the most matter-of-fact tones. 'As soon as I knew that I was a poet I determined to come to Philadelphia and go straight to real publishers and real editors. In my country nobody had ever seen a man who had written a book. Ever since I came here I find how hard it is to

find out any thing about the business of authorship. Medicine,
or law, or blacksmithing – every body knows the workings of
those trades, but people with pens in their hands keep the secret
of their craft like Freemasons,' laughing.

'You came alone?'

'Quite alone. I hired a little room over a baker's shop in Pine
Street. They are a very decent couple, the baker and his wife. I
board myself, and send out my manuscripts. They always come
back to me.'

'Where do you send them?'

'Oh, every where. I can show you printed forms of rejection
from every magazine and literary newspaper in the country,'
opening and shutting again a black sachel on her lap. 'I have
written three novels, and sent them to the ——s' and ——s'. They
sent them back as unavailable. But they never read them. I trick
them this a-way: I put a loose blue thread between the third and
fourth pages of the manuscript, and it is always there when it
comes back.' Her voice broke a little, but she winked her brown
eyes and laughed bravely.

'How long have you been here?'

'Three years.'

'Impossible! You are but a child.'

'I am twenty. I had an article published once in a Sunday
paper,' producing a slip about two inches long.

Three years, and only that little grain of success! She had
supported herself meanwhile, as I learned afterward, by sewing
men's socks for a firm in Germantown.

'You are ready to give up now?'

'No; not if it were ten years instead of three.'

Yet I can swear there was not a drop of New England blood
in her little body. One was certain, against all reason, that
she would succeed. When even such puny creatures as this take
the world by the throat in that fashion, they are sure to conquer
it.

Her books and poems must, I think, have seemed unique to
any editor. The spelling was atrocious; the errors of grammar
in every line beyond remedy. The lowest pupil in our public
schools would have detected her ignorance on the first page.
There was, too, in all she said or wrote an occasional gross
indecency, such as a child might show: her life on the plantation explained it. Like Juliet, she spoke the language of her

nurse. But even Shakespeare's nurse and Juliet would not be allowed nowadays to chatter at will in the pages of a family magazine.

But in all her ignorance, mistakes, and weaknesses there was no trace of imitation. She plagiarized nobody. There was none of the usual talk of countesses, heather, larks, or emotions of which she knew nothing. She painted over and over again her own home on the Yazoo: the hot still sunshine, the silence of noon, the swamp, the slimy living things in the stagnant ponds, the semi-tropical forest, the house and negro quarters, with all their dirt and dreary monotony. It was a picture which remained in the mind strong and vivid as a desert by Gérôme* or a moor by Boughton.*

There could be but one kind of advice to give her – to put away pen and ink, and for three years at least devote herself to hard study. She would, of course, have none of such counsel. The popular belief in the wings of genius, which can carry it over hard work and all such obstacles as ignorance of grammar or even the spelling-book, found in her a marked example. Work was for commonplace talent, not for those whose veins were full of the divine ichor.

Meanwhile she went on sewing socks, and sending off her great yellow envelopes, with stamps to bring them back.

'Stamps and paper count up so fast!' she said, with a laugh, into which had grown a pitiful quaver. She would take not a penny of aid. 'I shall not starve. When the time has come for me to know that I have failed, I can go back to my own country and live like the other women there.'

Meanwhile her case very nearly reached starvation. I remember few things more pathetic than the damp, forlorn little figure in a shabby water-proof, black sachel in hand, which used to come to my door through the snows and drenching rains that winter. Her shoes were broken, and her hands shriveled blue with cold. But a plated gilt chain or a scarlet ribbon used to flaunt somewhere over the meagre, scant poverty. Sometimes she brought news with her. She had work given her – to collect a column of jokes for a Sunday paper, by which she made three dollars a week. But she lost it from trying to insert her own matter, which could not well be reckoned as funny sayings. One day she came flushed with excitement. Somebody had taken her through the Academy of Design and a private gallery of engravings then on exhibition. She had a keen, just eye for form and color, and the feeling of a true artist for both.

'That is what I could have done,' she said, after keeping silence a long while. 'But what chance had I? I never even saw a picture at home, except those which were cut out of illustrated papers. There seemed to be no way for me but to write.'

It was suggested to her that she might find the other way even now. Painting, designing, wood-engraving, were expressions for a woman's mind, even though, like her own, it was 'one of the finest in the world.'

She did not smile. 'It is too late,' she said. 'I will go on as I have begun. But it is a pity my mother and I had not known of such things.'

After that her light-hearted courage seemed to give way. She persevered, but it was with dogged, indomitable resolution, and little hope.

One day in the spring I was summoned to see a visitor on business. I found a tall, lank young man stalking up and down the room, the most noticeable point about him the shock of red hair and whisker falling over his neck and greasy coat collar. The face was that of an ignorant, small-minded man. But it was candid and not sensual.

He came straight toward me. 'Is Marcia Barr here?'

'No; she has been gone for an hour.'

He damned his luck in a white heat of rage, which must, I thought, have required some time to kindle. Indeed, I found he had been pacing up and down the street half the morning, having seen her come in. She had gone out by a side door.

'I caught a glimpse of her half a mile off. I have come to Philadelphia three times this year to find her. Good God! how rank poor she is! Where does she live?'

I could not tell him, as Marcia had long ago left the baker's, and changed her quarters every month.

'And I reckon I'll have to wait until she comes hyah again. Tell her it's Zack Biron, the overseer's son, on – on business.'

He was not long in unveiling his business, which any woman would soon have guessed. He had come to bring Marcia home and marry her. He had always 'wanted her,' and the old colonel, her father, had promised he should marry her provided he could bring her back from her mad flight. The colonel was dead, and he was now 'runnin' the plantation for ole madam. She's no better than a walkin' corpse, with that damned drug she chews. She can't keep still now: walks, walks incessant about the place, with her eyes set an' the skin clingin' to her bones. I couldn't 'a borne it, I ashuah you, but for the sake of findin' Marcia.'

Two months passed, in which he haunted the house. But Marcia did not come. She had begun to frequent newspaper offices, and occasionally was given a trifling bit of work by the managers of the reporting corps – a description of the dresses at a Männerchor ball to write, or a puff of some coming play, etc. She came at last to tell me of what she had done.

'It is miserable work. I would rather sew the heels of stockings; but the stocking looms have stopped, and I must live a little longer, at any rate. I think I have something to say, if people only would hear it.'

I told her of Biron and his chase for her.

'I saw him outside the window the last time I was here. That was the reason I went out by the side street. I knew he was looking for me. You will not tell him I have been here?'

'But, Marcia, the man seems honest and kindly – '

'If he found me,' in the same quiet tone, 'he would marry me and take me back to the plantation.'

'And you are not ready to give up?'

'No, I will not give up. I shall get into the right groove at last,' with the infectious little laugh which nobody could resist.

The water-proof cloak was worn down quite into the cotton by this time, and the straw hat had been darned around the ragged edge. But there was a cheap red rose in it. Her cheekbones showed high, and her eyes shone out of black hollows.

'No, I have no cough, and I don't need medicine,' she said, irritably, when questioned. 'I have had plenty of offers of help. But I'd rather steal than take alms.' She rose hastily and buttoned her cloak.

'This man Biron waits only a word to come to you. He is faithful as a dog.'

She nodded carelessly. Biron, or a return to her old home, held no part in her world, it was plain to see.

I was out of the city for several months. A few weeks after my return I saw in the evening paper one day, in the usual list of crimes and casualties, an item headed '*Pitiable Case*. – A young woman named Burr was arrested yesterday on charge of theft, and taken to the Central Station. About eleven o'clock the other women in the cell where she was confined perceiving that she lay on a bench breathing in a stertorous manner, summoned Lieutenant Pardy, who found life to be almost extinct. A physician was called, who discovered that the woman had swallowed some poisonous drug. With her first breath of returning consciousness she protested her innocence of the charge. She appears to have been in an extreme state of want. But little hope is entertained of her recovery. Miss Burr is favorably known, we believe, as a writer of some ability for the daily press.'

In spite of the difference of name, it must be Marcia.

When we reached the Central Station we were told that her discharge was already procured. She had friends who knew what wires to work. In the outer room were half a dozen young men, reporters, a foreman of a printing-room, and one or two women, dramatic or musical critics. There is as eager an *esprit de corps* among that class of journalists as among actors. They were all talking loudly, and zealous in defense of 'little Marty,' as they called her, whom they declared to be 'a dunce so far as head went, but pure and guileless as a child.'

'I knew she was devilishly hard up,' said one, 'but never suspected she was starving. She would not borrow a dollar, she had that pride in her.'

Marcia was still in the cell, lying on an iron stretcher. The Mississippian, Biron, was with her, kneeling on the floor in his shirt sleeves, chafing her hand. He had taken off his coat to wrap about her.

'I've a good Quaker nurse and a room ready for her at the Continental the minute she can be moved,' he whispered. 'Look a-here!' turning down the poor bit of lace and red ribbon at her throat, his big hairy hand shaking. 'Them bones is a'most through the skin! The doctor says it's hunger – hunger! And *I* was eatin' three solid meals a day – like a beast!'

Hunger had almost done its work. There was but a feeble flicker of life left in the emaciated little body; not enough to know or speak to us when at last she opened her dull eyes.

'None o' them folks need consarn themselves any furder about her,' said Biron, savagely. 'She'll come home to her own now, thank God, and be done with rubbishy book-makers. Mrs Biron will live like a lady.'

Two or three weeks later, the most splendid of hired phaetons stopped at my door, and Mr and Mrs Biron sent up their cards. Mr Biron was glowing with happiness. It asserted itself offensively somehow in the very jingling of his watch chain and tie of his cravat.

'We return immediately to the plantation,' he said, grandiloquently. 'I reckon largely on the effect of her native air in restorin' Mrs Biron to health.'

Marcia was magnificent in silk and plumes, the costliest that her owner's money could buy. Her little face was pale, however, and she looked nobody in the eye.

'We leave for the South to-morrow,' she said, calmly, 'and I shall not return to Philadelphia. I have no wish to return.'

'Shall I send you books or papers, Marcia?'

'No, I thank you; nothing.'

When they rose to go, her husband said, 'Mrs Biron has some – rubbish she wishes to leave with you. Hyah!' calling out of the window. 'You nigger, bring that thah bag!'

It was the old black sachel. Marcia took it in her white-gloved hands, half opened it, shut it quickly, came up closer.

'These are my manuscripts,' she said. 'Will you burn them for me? All: do not leave a line, a word. I could not do it.'

I took the sachel, and they departed. Mr Biron was vehement in his protestations of friendship and invitations to visit the plantation. But Marcia did not say a word, even of farewell.

LOUISA MAY ALCOTT

My Contraband*

1863

Doctor Franck came in as I sat sewing up the rents in an old shirt, that Tom might go tidily to his grave. New shirts were needed for living, and there was no wife or mother to 'dress him handsome when he went to meet the Lord,' as one woman said, describing the fine funeral she had pinched herself to give her son.

'Miss Dane, I'm in a quandary,' began the Doctor, with that expression of countenance which says as plainly as words, 'I want to ask a favor, but I wish you'd save me the trouble.'

'Can I help you out of it?'

'Faith! I don't like to propose it, but you certainly can, if you please.'

'Then name it, I beg.'

'You see a Reb has just been brought in crazy with typhoid; a bad case every way; a drunken, rascally little captain somebody took the trouble to capture, but whom nobody wants to take the trouble to cure. The wards are full, the ladies worked to death, and willing to be for our own boys, but rather slow to risk their lives for a Reb. Now, you've had the fever, you like queer patients, your mate will see to your ward for a while, and I will find you a good attendant. The fellow won't last long, I fancy; but he can't die without some sort of care, you know. I've put him in the fourth story of the west wing, away from the rest. It is airy, quiet, and comfortable there. I'm on that ward, and will do my best for you in every way. Now, then, will you go?'

'Of course I will, out of perversity, if not common charity; for some of these people think that because I'm an abolitionist I am also a heathen, and I should rather like to show them that, though I cannot quite love my enemies, I am willing to take care of them.'

'Very good; I thought you'd go; and speaking of abolition reminds me that you can have a contraband for servant, if you like. It is that fine mulatto fellow who was found burying his rebel master after the fight, and, being badly cut over the head, our boys brought him along. Will you have him?'

'By all means, – for I'll stand to my guns on that point, as on the other; these black boys are far more faithful and handy than some of the white scamps given me to serve, instead of being served by. But is this man well enough?'

'Yes, for that sort of work, and I think you'll like him. He must have been a handsome fellow before he got his face slashed; not much darker than myself; his master's son, I dare say, and the white blood makes him rather high and haughty about some things. He was in a bad way when he came in, but vowed he'd die in the street rather than turn in with the black fellows below; so I put him up in the west wing, to be out of the way, and he's seen to the captain all the morning. When can you go up?'

'As soon as Tom is laid out, Skinner moved, Haywood washed, Marble dressed, Charley rubbed, Downs taken up, Upham laid down, and the whole forty fed.'

We both laughed, though the Doctor was on his way to the dead-house and I held a shroud on my lap. But in a hospital one learns that cheerfulness is one's salvation; for, in an atmosphere of suffering and death, heaviness of heart would soon paralyze usefulness of hand, if the blessed gift of smiles had been denied us.

In an hour I took possession of my new charge, finding a dissipated-looking boy of nineteen or twenty raving in the solitary little room, with no one near him but the contraband in the room adjoining. Feeling decidedly more interest in the black man than in the white, yet remembering the Doctor's hint of his being 'high and haughty,' I glanced furtively at him as I scattered chloride of lime about the room to purify the air, and settled matters to suit myself. I had seen many contrabands, but never one so attractive as this. All colored men are called 'boys,' even if their heads are white; this boy was five-and-twenty at least, strong-limbed and manly, and had the look of one who never had been cowed by abuse or worn with oppressive labor. He sat on his bed doing nothing; no book, no pipe, no pen or paper anywhere appeared, yet anything less indolent or listless than his attitude and expression I never saw. Erect he sat, with a hand on either knee, and eyes fixed on the bare wall opposite, so rapt in some absorbing thought as to be unconscious of my presence, though the door stood wide open and my movements were by no means noiseless. His face was half averted, but I instantly approved the Doctor's taste, for the profile which I saw possessed all the attributes of comeliness belonging to his mixed race. He was more quadroon than mulatto, with Saxon features, Spanish complexion darkened by exposure, color in lips and cheek, waving hair, and an eye full of the passionate melancholy which in such men always seems to utter a mute protest against the broken law that doomed them at their birth. What could he be thinking of? The sick boy cursed and raved, I rustled to and fro, steps passed the door, bells rang, and the steady rumble of army-wagons came up from the street, still he never stirred. I had seen colored people in what they call 'the black sulks,' when, for days, they neither smiled nor spoke, and scarcely ate. But this was something more than that; for the man was not dully brooding over some small grievance; he seemed to see an all-absorbing fact or fancy recorded on the wall, which was a blank to me. I wondered if it were some deep wrong or sorrow, kept alive by memory and impotent regret; if he mourned for the dead master to whom he had been faithful to the end; or if the liberty now his were robbed of half its sweetness by the knowledge that some one near and dear to him still languished in the hell from which he had escaped. My heart quite warmed to him at that idea; I wanted to know and comfort him; and, following the impulse of the moment, I went in and touched him on the shoulder.

In an instant the man vanished and the slave appeared. Freedom was too new a boon to have wrought its blessed changes yet; and as he started up, with his hand at his temple, and an obsequious 'Yes, Missis,' any romance that had gathered round him fled away, leaving the saddest of all sad facts in living guise before me. Not only did the manhood seem to die out of him, but the comeliness that first attracted me; for, as he turned, I saw the ghastly wound that had laid open cheek and forehead. Being partly healed, it was no longer bandaged, but held together with strips of that transparent plaster which I never see without a shiver, and swift recollections of the scenes with which it is associated in my mind. Part of his black hair had been shorn away, and one eye was nearly closed; pain so distorted, and the cruel sabre-cut so marred that portion of his face, that, when I saw it, I felt as if a fine medal had been suddenly reversed, showing me a far more striking type of human suffering and wrong than Michael Angelo's bronze prisoner.* By one of those inexplicable processes that often teach us how little we understand ourselves, my purpose was suddenly changed; and, though I went in to offer comfort as a friend, I merely gave an order as a mistress.

'Will you open these windows? this man needs more air.'

He obeyed at once, and, as he slowly urged up the unruly sash, the handsome profile was again turned toward me, and again I was possessed by my first impression so strongly that I involuntarily said, –

'Thank you.'

Perhaps it was fancy, but I thought that in the look of mingled surprise and something like reproach which he gave me, there was also a trace of grateful pleasure. But he said, in that tone of spiritless humility these poor souls learn so soon, –

'I isn't a white man, Missis, I'se a contraband.'

'Yes, I know it; but a contraband is a free man, and I heartily congratulate you.'

He liked that; his face shone, he squared his shoulders, lifted his head, and looked me full in the eye with a brisk, –

'Thank ye, Missis; anything more to do fer yer?'

'Doctor Franck thought you would help me with this man, as there are many patients and few nurses or attendants. Have you had the fever?'

'No, Missis.'

'They should have thought of that when they put him here; wounds and fevers should not be together. I'll try to get you moved.'

He laughed a sudden laugh: if he had been a white man, I should have called it scornful; as he was a few shades darker than myself, I suppose it must be considered an insolent, or at least an unmannerly one.

'It don't matter, Missis. I'd rather be up here with the fever than down with those niggers; and there isn't no other place fer me.'

Poor fellow! that was true. No ward in all the hospital would take him in to lie side by side with the most miserable white

wreck there. Like the bat in Æsop's fable,* he belonged to
neither race; and the pride of one and the helplessness of the
other, kept him hovering alone in the twilight a great sin has
brought to overshadow the whole land.

'You shall stay, then; for I would far rather have you than my
lazy Jack. But are you well and strong enough?'

'I guess I'll do, Missis.'

He spoke with a passive sort of acquiescence, – as if it did not
much matter if he were not able, and no one would particularly
rejoice if he were.

'Yes, I think you will. By what name shall I call you?'

'Bob, Missis.'

Every woman has her pet whim; one of mine was to teach the
men self-respect by treating them respectfully. Tom, Dick, and
Harry would pass, when lads rejoiced in those familiar abbrevi-
ations; but to address men often old enough to be my father in
that style did not suit my old-fashioned ideas of propriety. This
'Bob' would never do; I should have found it as easy to call the
chaplain 'Gus' as my tragical-looking contraband by a title so
strongly associated with the tail of a kite.

'What is your other name?' I asked. 'I like to call my
attendants by their last names rather than by their first.'

'I'se got no other, Missis; we has our masters' names, or do
without. Mine's dead, and I won't have anything of his 'bout
me.'

'Well, I'll call you Robert, then, and you may fill this pitcher
for me, if you will be so kind.'

He went; but, through all the tame obedience years of
servitude had taught him, I could see that the proud spirit his
father gave him was not yet subdued, for the look and gesture
with which he repudiated his master's name were a more
effective declaration of independence than any Fourth-of-July
orator could have prepared.

We spent a curious week together. Robert seldom left his
room, except upon my errands; and I was a prisoner all day,
often all night, by the bedside of the rebel. The fever burned
itself rapidly away, for there seemed little vitality to feed it in
the feeble frame of this old young man, whose life had been
none of the most righteous, judging from the revelations made
by his unconscious lips; since more than once Robert authoritatively silenced him, when my gentler hushings were of no avail,

and blasphemous wanderings or ribald camp-songs made my cheeks burn and Robert's face assume an aspect of disgust. The captain was the gentleman in the world's eye, but the contraband was the gentleman in mine; – I was a fanatic, and that accounts for such depravity of taste, I hope. I never asked Robert of himself, feeling that somewhere there was a spot still too sore to bear the lightest touch; but, from his language, manner, and intelligence, I inferred that his color had procured for him the few advantages within the reach of a quick-witted, kindly-treated slave. Silent, grave, and thoughtful, but most serviceable, was my contraband; glad of the books I brought him, faithful in the performance of the duties I assigned to him, grateful for the friendliness I could not but feel and show toward him. Often I longed to ask what purpose was so visibly altering his aspect with such daily deepening gloom. But I never dared, and no one else had either time or desire to pry into the past of this specimen of one branch of the chivalrous 'F.F.Vs.'*

On the seventh night, Dr Franck suggested that it would be well for some one, besides the general watchman of the ward, to be with the captain, as it might be his last. Although the greater part of the two preceding nights had been spent there, of course I offered to remain, – for there is a strange fascination in these scenes, which renders one careless of fatigue and unconscious of fear until the crisis is past.

'Give him water as long as he can drink, and if he drops into a natural sleep, it may save him. I'll look in at midnight, when some change will probably take place. Nothing but sleep or a miracle will keep him now. Goodnight.'

Away went the Doctor; and, devouring a whole mouthful of grapes, I lowered the lamp, wet the captain's head, and sat down on a hard stool to begin my watch. The captain lay with his hot, haggard face turned toward me, filling the air with his poisonous breath, and feebly muttering, with lips and tongue so parched that the sanest speech would have been difficult to understand. Robert was stretched on his bed in the inner room, the door of which stood ajar, that a fresh draught from his open window might carry the fever-fumes away through mine. I could just see a long, dark figure, with the lighter outline of a face, and, having little else to do just then, I fell to thinking of this curious contraband, who evidently prized his freedom highly, yet seemed in no haste to enjoy it. Dr Franck had offered to send him on to safer quarters, but he had said, 'No, thank yer, sir, not yet,' and then had gone away to fall into one of those black moods of his, which began to disturb me, because I had no power to lighten them. As I sat listening to the clocks from the steeples all about us, I amused myself with planning Robert's future, as I often did my own, and had dealt out to him a generous hand of trumps wherewith to play this game of life which hitherto had gone so cruelly against him, when a harsh choked voice called, –

'Lucy!'

It was the captain, and some new terror seemed to have gifted him with momentary strength.

'Yes, here's Lucy,' I answered, hoping that by following the fancy I might quiet him, – for his face was damp with the clammy moisture, and his frame shaken with the nervous tremor that so often precedes death. His dull eye fixed upon me, dilating with a bewildered look of incredulity and wrath, till he broke out fiercely, –

'That's a lie! she's dead, – and so's Bob, damn him!'

Finding speech a failure, I began to sing the quiet tune that had often soothed delirium like this; but hardly had the line, –

> 'See gentle patience smile on pain,'

passed my lips, when he clutched me by the wrist, whispering like one in mortal fear, –

'Hush! she used to sing that way to Bob, but she never would to me. I swore I'd whip the devil out of her, and I did; but you know before she cut her throat she said she'd haunt me, and there she is!'

He pointed behind me with an aspect of such pale dismay, that I involuntarily glanced over my shoulder and started as if I had seen a veritable ghost; for, peering from the gloom of that inner room, I saw a shadowy face, with dark hair all about it, and a glimpse of scarlet at the throat. An instant showed me that it was only Robert leaning from his bed's foot, wrapped in a gray army-blanket, with his red shirt just visible above it, and his long hair disordered by sleep. But what a strange expression was on his face! The unmarred side was toward me, fixed and motionless as when I first observed it, – less absorbed now, but more intent. His eye glittered, his lips were apart like one who listened with every sense, and his whole aspect reminded me of a hound to which some wind had brought the scent of unsuspected prey.

'Do you know him, Robert? Does he mean you?'

'Laws, no, Missis; they all own half-a-dozen Bobs: but hearin' my name woke me; that's all.'

He spoke quite naturally, and lay down again, while I returned to my charge, thinking that this paroxysm was probably his last. But by another hour I perceived a hopeful change; for the tremor had subsided, the cold dew was gone, his breathing was more regular, and Sleep, the healer, had descended to save or take him gently away. Doctor Franck looked in at midnight, bade me keep all cool and quiet, and not fail to administer a certain draught as soon as the captain woke. Very much relieved, I laid my head on my arms, uncomfortably folded on the little table, and fancied I was about to perform one of the feats which practice renders possible, – 'sleeping with one eye open,' as we say: a half-and-half doze, for all senses sleep but that of hearing; the faintest murmur, sigh, or motion will break it, and give one back one's wits much brightened by the brief permission to 'stand at ease.' On this night the experiment was a failure, for previous vigils, confinement, and much care had rendered naps a dangerous indulgence. Having roused half-a-dozen times in an hour to find all quiet, I dropped my heavy head on my arms, and, drowsily resolving to look up again in fifteen minutes, fell fast asleep.

The striking of a deep-voiced clock awoke me with a start. 'That is one,' thought I; but, to my dismay, two more strokes followed, and in remorseful haste I sprang up to see what harm my long oblivion had done. A strong hand put me back into my seat, and held me there. It was Robert. The instant my eye met his my heart began to beat, and all along my nerves tingled that electric flash which foretells a danger that we cannot see. He was very pale, his mouth grim, and both eyes full of sombre fire; for even the wounded one was open now, all the more sinister for the deep scar above and below. But his touch was steady, his voice quiet, as he said, –

'Sit still, Missis; I won't hurt yer, nor scare yer, ef I can help it, but yer waked too soon.'

'Let me go, Robert, – the captain is stirring, – I must give him something.'

'No, Missis, yer can't stir an inch. Look here!'

Holding me with one hand, with the other he took up the glass in which I had left the draught, and showed me it was empty.

'Has he taken it?' I asked, more and more bewildered.

'I flung it out o' winder, Missis; he'll have to do without.'

'But why, Robert? why did you do it?'

''Kase I hate him!'

Impossible to doubt the truth of that; his whole face showed it, as he spoke through his set teeth, and launched a fiery glance at the unconscious captain. I could only hold my breath and stare blankly at him, wondering what mad act was coming next. I suppose I shook and turned white, as women have a foolish habit of doing when sudden danger daunts them; for Robert released my arm, sat down upon the bedside just in front of me, and said, with the ominous quietude that made me cold to see and hear, –

'Don't yer be frightened, Missis; don't try to run away, fer the door's locked and the key in my pocket; don't yer cry out, fer yer'd have to scream a long while, with my hand on yer mouth, 'efore yer was heard. Be still, an' I'll tell yer what I'm gwine to do.'

'Lord help us! he has taken the fever in some sudden, violent way, and is out of his head. I must humor him till some one comes'; in pursuance of which swift determination, I tried to say, quite composedly, –

'I will be still and hear you; but open the window. Why did you shut it?'

'I'm sorry I can't do it, Missis; but yer'd jump out, or call, if I did, an' I'm not ready yet. I shut it to make yer sleep, an' heat would do it quicker'n anything else I could do.'

The captain moved, and feebly muttered 'Water!' Instinctively I rose to give it to him, but the heavy hand came down upon my shoulder, and in the same decided tone Robert said, –

'The water went with the physic; let him call.'

'Do let me go to him! he'll die without care!'

'I mean he shall; – don't yer meddle, if yer please, Missis.'

In spite of his quiet tone and respectful manner, I saw murder in his eyes, and turned faint with fear; yet the fear excited me, and, hardly knowing what I did, I seized the hands that had seized me, crying, –

'No, no; you shall not kill him! It is base to hurt a helpless man. Why do you hate him? He is not your master.'

'He's my brother.'

I felt that answer from head to foot, and seemed to fathom what was coming, with a prescience vague, but unmistakable. One appeal was left to me, and I made it.

'Robert, tell me what it means? Do not commit a crime and make me accessory to it. There is a better way of righting wrong than by violence; – let me help you find it.'

My voice trembled as I spoke, and I heard the frightened flutter of my heart; so did he, and if any little act of mine had ever won affection or respect from him, the memory of it served me then. He looked down, and seemed to put some question to himself; whatever it was, the answer was in my favor, for when his eyes rose again, they were gloomy, but not desperate.

'I *will* tell yer, Missis; but mind, this makes no difference; the boy is mine. I'll give the Lord a chance to take him fust: if He don't, I shall.'

'Oh, no! remember he is your brother.'

An unwise speech; I felt it as it passed my lips, for a black frown gathered on Robert's face, and his strong hands closed with an ugly sort of grip. But he did not touch the poor soul gasping there behind him, and seemed content to let the slow suffocation of that stifling room end his frail life.

'I'm not like to forgit dat, Missis, when I've been thinkin' of it all this week. I knew him when they fetched him in, an' would 'a' done it long 'fore this, but I wanted to ask where Lucy was; he knows, – he told tonight, – an' now he's done for.'

'Who is Lucy?' I asked hurriedly, intent on keeping his mind busy with any thought but murder.

With one of the swift transitions of a mixed temperament like this, at my question Robert's deep eyes filled, the clenched hands were spread before his face, and all I heard were the broken words, –

'My wife, – he took her – '

In that instant every thought of fear was swallowed up in burning indignation for the wrong, and a perfect passion of pity for the desperate man so tempted to avenge an injury for which there seemed no redress but this. He was no longer slave or contraband, no drop of black blood marred him in my sight, but an infinite compassion yearned to save, to help, to comfort him. Words seemed so powerless I offered none, only put my hand on his poor head, wounded, homeless, bowed down with grief for which I had no cure, and softly smoothed the long, neglected hair, pitifully wondering the while where was the wife who must have loved this tender-hearted man so well.

The captain moaned again, and faintly whispered, 'Air!' but I never stirred. God forgive me! just then I hated him as only a woman thinking of a sister woman's wrong could hate. Robert looked up; his eyes were dry again, his mouth grim. I saw that, said, 'Tell me more,' and he did; for sympathy is a gift the poorest may give, the proudest stoop to receive.

'Yer see, Missis, his father, – I might say ours, ef I warn't ashamed of both of 'em, – his father died two years ago, an' left us all to Marster Ned, – that's him here, eighteen then. He always hated me, I looked so like old Marster: he don't, – only the light skin an' hair. Old Marster was kind to all of us, me 'specially, an' bought Lucy off the next plantation down there in South Carolina, when he found I liked her. I married her, all I could; it warn't much, but we was true to one another till Marster Ned come home a year after an' made hell fer both of us. He sent my old mother to be used up in his rice-swamp in Georgy; he found me with my pretty Lucy, an' though young Miss cried, an' I prayed to him on my knees, an' Lucy run away, he wouldn't have no mercy; he brought her back, an' – took her.'

'Oh, what did you do?' I cried, hot with helpless pain and passion.

How the man's outraged heart sent the blood flaming up into his face and deepened the tones of his impetuous voice, as he stretched his arm across the bed, saying, with a terribly expressive gesture, –

'I half murdered him, an' tonight I'll finish.'

'Yes, yes – but go on now; what came next?'

He gave me a look that showed no white man could have felt a deeper degradation in remembering and confessing these last acts of brotherly oppression.

'They whipped me till I couldn't stand, an' then they sold me further South. Yer thought I was a white man once, – look here!'

With a sudden wrench he tore the shirt from neck to waist, and on his strong, brown shoulders showed me furrows deeply ploughed, wounds which, though healed, were ghastlier to me than any in that house. I could not speak to him, and, with the

pathetic dignity a great grief lends the humblest sufferer, he
ended his brief tragedy by simply saying, –

'That's all, Missis. I'se never seen her since, an' now I never
shall in this world, – maybe not in t'other.'

'But, Robert, why think her dead? The captain was wandering
when he said those sad things; perhaps he will retract them
when he is sane. Don't despair; don't give up yet.'

'No, Missis, I 'spect he's right; she was too proud to bear that
long. It's like her to kill herself. I told her to, if there was no
other way; an' she always minded me, Lucy did. My poor girl!
Oh, it warn't right! No, by God, it warn't!'

As the memory of this bitter wrong, this double bereavement,
burned in his sore heart, the devil that lurks in every strong
man's blood leaped up; he put his hand upon his brother's
throat, and, watching the white face before him, muttered low
between his teeth, –

'I'm lettin' him go too easy; there's no pain in this; we a'n't
even yet. I wish he knew me. Marster Ned! it's Bob; where's
Lucy?'

From the captain's lips there came a long faint sigh, and
nothing but a flutter of the eyelids showed that he still lived. A
strange stillness filled the room as the elder brother held the
younger's life suspended in his hand, while wavering between a
dim hope and a deadly hate. In the whirl of thoughts that went
on in my brain, only one was clear enough to act upon. I must
prevent murder, if I could, – but how? What could I do up there
alone, locked in with a dying man and a lunatic? – for any mind
yielded utterly to any unrighteous impulse is mad while the
impulse rules it. Strength I had not, nor much courage, neither
time nor will for stratagem, and chance only could bring me
help before it was too late. But one weapon I possessed, – a
tongue, – often a woman's best defence; and sympathy, stronger
than fear, gave me power to use it. What I said Heaven only
knows, but surely Heaven helped me; words burned on my lips,
tears streamed from my eyes, and some good angel prompted
me to use the one name that had power to arrest my hearer's
hand and touch his heart. For at that moment I heartily believed
that Lucy lived, and this earnest faith roused in him a like belief.

He listened with the lowering look of one in whom brute
instinct was sovereign for the time, – a look that makes the
noblest countenance base. He was but a man, – a poor,

untaught, outcast, outraged man. Life had few joys for him; the
world offered him no honors, no success, no home, no love.
What future would this crime mar? and why should he deny
himself that sweet, yet bitter morsel called revenge? How many
white men, with all New England's freedom, culture, Christian-
ity, would not have felt as he felt then? Should I have reproached
him for a human anguish, a human longing for redress, all now
left him from the ruin of his few poor hopes? Who had taught
him that self-control, self-sacrifice, are attributes that make men
masters of the earth, and lift them nearer heaven? Should I have
urged the beauty of forgiveness, the duty of devout submission?
He had no religion, for he was no saintly 'Uncle Tom,' and
Slavery's black shadow seemed to darken all the world to him,
and shut out God. Should I have warned him of penalties, of
judgments, and the potency of law? What did he know of
justice, or the mercy that should temper that stern virtue, when
every law, human and divine, had been broken on his hearth-
stone? Should I have tried to touch him by appeals to filial duty,
to brotherly love? How had his appeals been answered? What
memories had father and brother stored up in his heart to plead
for either now? No, – all these influences, these associations,
would have proved worse than useless, had I been calm enough
to try them. I was not; but instinct, subtler than reason, showed
me the one safe clue by which to lead this troubled soul from
the labyrinth in which it groped and nearly fell. When I paused,
breathless, Robert turned to me, asking, as if human assurances
could strengthen his faith in Divine Omnipotence, –

'Do you believe, if I let Marster Ned live, the lord will give
me back my Lucy?'

'As surely as there is a Lord, you will find her here or in the
beautiful hereafter, where there is no black or white, no master
and no slave.'

He took his hand from his brother's throat, lifted his eyes
from my face to the wintry sky beyond, as if searching for that
blessed country, happier even than the happy North. Alas, it
was the darkest hour before the dawn! – there was no star
above, no light below but the pale glimmer of the lamp that
showed the brother who had made him desolate. Like a blind
man who believes there is a sun, yet cannot see it, he shook his
head, let his arms drop nervelessly upon his knees, and sat there
dumbly asking that question which many a soul whose faith is

firmer fixed than his has asked in hours less dark than this, –
'Where is God?' I saw the tide had turned, and strenuously tried
to keep this rudderless life-boat from slipping back into the
whirlpool wherein it had been so nearly lost.

'I have listened to you, Robert; now hear me, and heed what
I say, because my heart is full of pity for you, full of hope for
your future, and a desire to help you now. I want you to go
away from here, from the temptation of this place, and the sad
thoughts that haunt it. You have conquered yourself once, and I
honor you for it, because, the harder the battle, the more
glorious the victory; but it is safer to put a greater distance
between you and this man. I will write you letters, give you
money, and send you to good old Massachusetts to begin your
new life a freeman, – yes, and a happy man; for when the
captain is himself again, I will learn where Lucy is, and move
heaven and earth to find and give her back to you. Will you do
this, Robert?'

Slowly, very slowly, the answer came; for the purpose of a
week, perhaps a year, was hard to relinquish in an hour.

'Yes, Missis, I will.'

'Good! Now you are the man I thought you, and I'll work for
you with all my heart. You need sleep, my poor fellow; go, and
try to forget. The captain is alive, and as yet you are spared that
sin. No, don't look there; I'll care for him. Come, Robert, for
Lucy's sake.'

Thank Heaven for the immortality of love! for when all other
means of salvation failed, a spark of this vital fire softened the
man's iron will, until a woman's hand could bend it. He let me
take from him the key, let me draw him gently away, and lead
him to the solitude which now was the most healing balm I
could bestow. Once in his little room, he fell down on his bed
and lay there, as if spent with the sharpest conflict of his life. I
slipped the bolt across his door, and unlocked my own, flung up
the window, steadied myself with a breath of air, then rushed to
Doctor Franck. He came; and till dawn we worked together,
saving one brother's life, and taking earnest thought how best
to secure the other's liberty. When the sun came up as blithely
as if it shone only upon happy homes, the Doctor went to
Robert. For an hour I heard the murmur of their voices; once I
caught the sound of heavy sobs, and for a time a reverent hush,
as if in the silence that good man were ministering to soul as

well as body. When he departed he took Robert with him, pausing to tell me he should get him off as soon as possible, but not before we met again.

Nothing more was seen of them all day; another surgeon came to see the captain, and another attendant came to fill the empty place. I tried to rest, but could not, with the thought of poor Lucy tugging at my heart, and was soon back at my post again, anxiously hoping that my contraband had not been too hastily spirited away. Just as night fell there came a tap, and, opening, I saw Robert literally 'clothed, and in his right mind.' The Doctor had replaced the ragged suit with tidy garments, and no trace of the tempestuous night remained but deeper lines upon the forehead, and the docile look of a repentant child. He did not cross the threshold, did not offer me his hand, – only took off his cap, saying, with a traitorous falter in his voice, –

'God bless yer, Missis! I'm gwine.'

I put out both my hands, and held his fast.

'Goodby, Robert! Keep up good heart, and when I come home to Massachusetts we'll meet in a happier place than this. Are you quite ready, quite comfortable for your journey?'

'Yes, Missis, yes; the Doctor's fixed everything! I'se gwine with a friend of his; my papers are all right, an' I'm as happy as I can be till I find' –

He stopped there; then went on, with a glance into the room, –

'I'm glad I didn't do it, an' I thank yer, Missis, fer hinderin' me – thank yer hearty; but I'm afraid I hate him jest the same.'

Of course he did; and so did I; for these faulty hearts of ours cannot turn perfect in a night, but need frost and fire, wind and rain, to ripen and make them ready for the great harvest-home. Wishing to divert his mind, I put my poor mite into his hand, and, remembering the magic of a certain little book, I gave him mine, on whose dark cover whitely shone the Virgin Mother and the Child, the grand history of whose life the book contained. The money went into Robert's pocket with a grateful murmur, the book into his bosom, with a long look and a tremulous –

'I never saw *my* baby, Missis.'

I broke down then; and though my eyes were too dim to see, I felt the touch of lips upon my hands, heard the sound of departing feet, and knew my contraband was gone.

When one feels an intense dislike, the less one says about the subject of it the better; therefore I shall merely record that the captain lived, – in time was exchanged; and that, whoever the other party was, I am convinced the Government got the best of the bargain. But long before this occurred, I had fulfilled my promise to Robert; for as soon as my patient recovered strength of memory enough to make his answer trustworthy, I asked, without any circumlocution, –

'Captain Fairfax, where is Lucy?'

And too feeble to be angry, surprised, or insincere, he straightway answered, –

'Dead, Miss Dane.'

'And she killed herself when you sold Bob?'

'How the devil did you know that?' he muttered, with an expression half-remorseful, half-amazed; but I was satisfied, and said no more.

Of course this went to Robert, waiting far away there in a lonely home, – waiting, working, hoping for his Lucy. It almost broke my heart to do it; but delay was weak, deceit was wicked; so I sent the heavy tidings, and very soon the answer came, – only three lines; but I felt that the sustaining power of the man's life was gone.

'I tort I'd never see her any more; I'm glad to know she's out of trouble. I thank yer, Missis; an' if they let us, I'll fight fer yer till I'm killed, which I hope will be 'fore long.'

Six months later he had his wish, and kept his word.

Every one knows the story of the attack on Fort Wagner;* but we should not tire yet of recalling how our Fifty-Fourth, spent with three sleepless nights, a day's fast, and a march under the July sun, stormed the fort as night fell, facing death in many shapes, following their brave leaders through a fiery rain of shot and shell, fighting valiantly for 'God and Governor Andrew,' – how the regiment that went into action seven hundred strong, came out having had nearly half its number captured, killed, or wounded, leaving their young commander to be buried, like a chief of earlier times, with his body-guard around him, faithful to the death. Surely, the insult turns to honor, and the wide grave needs no monument but the heroism that consecrates it in our sight; surely, the hearts that held him nearest, see through their tears a noble victory in the seeming sad defeat; and surely, God's benediction was bestowed, when this loyal soul answered, as Death called the roll, 'Lord, here am I, with the brothers Thou hast given me!'

The future must show how well that fight was fought; for though Fort Wagner once defied us, public prejudice is down; and through the cannon-smoke of that black night, the manhood of the colored race shines before many eyes that would not see, rings in many ears that would not hear, wins many hearts that would not hitherto believe.

When the news came that we were needed, there was none so glad as I to leave teaching contrabands, the new work I had taken up, and go to nurse 'our boys,' as my dusky flock so proudly called the wounded of the Fifty-Fourth. Feeling more satisfaction, as I assumed my big apron and turned up my cuffs, than if dressing for the President's levee, I fell to work in Hospital No. 10 at Beaufort. The scene was most familiar, and yet strange; for only dark faces looked up at me from the pallets so thickly laid along the floor, and I missed the sharp accent of my Yankee boys in the slower, softer voices calling cheerily to one another, or answering my questions with a stout, 'We'll never give it up, Missis, till the last Reb's dead,' or, 'If our people's free, we can afford to die.'

Passing from bed to bed, intent on making one pair of hands do the work of three, at least, I gradually washed, fed, and bandaged my way down the long line of sable heroes, and coming to the very last, found that he was my contraband. So old, so worn, so deathly weak and wan, I never should have known him but for the deep scar on his cheek. That side lay uppermost, and caught my eye at once; but even then I doubted, such an awful change had come upon him, when, turning to the ticket just above his head, I saw the name, 'Robert Dane.' That both assured and touched me, for, remembering that he had no name, I knew that he had taken mine. I longed for him to speak to me, to tell how he had fared since I lost sight of him, and let me perform some little service for him in return for many he had done for me; but he seemed asleep; and as I stood re-living that strange night again, a bright lad, who lay next him softly waving an old fan across both beds, looked up and said, –

'I guess you know him, Missis?'

'You are right. Do you?'

'As much as any one was able to, Missis.'

'Why do you say "was," as if the man were dead and gone?'

'I s'pose because I know he'll have to go. He's got a bad jab in the breast, an' is bleedin' inside, the Doctor says. He don't suffer any, only gets weaker 'n' weaker every minute. I've been fannin' him this long while, an' he's talked a little; but he don't know me now, so he's most gone, I guess.'

There was so much sorrow and affection in the boy's face, that I remembered something, and asked, with redoubled interest, –

'Are you the one that brought him off? I was told about a boy who nearly lost his life in saving that of his mate.'

I dare say the young fellow blushed, as any modest lad might have done; I could not see it, but I heard the chuckle of satisfaction that escaped him, as he glanced from his shattered arm and bandaged side to the pale figure opposite.

'Lord, Missis, that's nothin'; we boys always stan' by one another, an' I warn't goin' to leave him to be tormented any more by them cussed Rebs. He's been a slave once, though he don't look half so much like it as me, an' I was born in Boston.'

He did not; for the speaker was as black as the ace of spades, – being a sturdy specimen, the knave of clubs would perhaps be a fitter representative, – but the dark freeman looked at the white slave with the pitiful, yet puzzled expression I have so often seen on the faces of our wisest men, when this tangled question of Slavery presented itself, asking to be cut or patiently undone.

'Tell me what you know of this man; for, even if he were awake, he is too weak to talk.'

'I never saw him till I joined the regiment, an' no one 'peared to have got much out of him. He was a shut-up sort of feller, an' didn't seem to care for anything but gettin' at the Rebs. Some say he was the fust man of us that enlisted; I know he fretted till we were off, an' when we pitched into Old Wagner, he fought like the devil.'

'Were you with him when he was wounded? How was it?'

'Yes, Missis. There was somethin' queer about it; for he 'peared to know the chap that killed him, an' the chap knew him. I don't dare to ask, but I rather guess one owned the other some time; for, when they clinched, the chap sung out, 'Bob!' an' Dane, 'Marster Ned!' – then they went at it.'

I sat down suddenly, for the old anger and compassion struggled in my heart, and I both longed and feared to hear what was to follow.

'You see, when the Colonel, – Lord keep an' send him back to us! – it a'n't certain yet, you know, Missis, though it's two days ago we lost him, – well, when the Colonel shouted, "Rush on, boys, rush on!" Dane tore away as if he was goin' to take the fort alone; I was next him, an' kept close as we went through the ditch an' up the wall. Hi! warn't that a rusher!' and the boy flung up his well arm with a whoop, as if the mere memory of that stirring moment came over him in a gust of irrepressible excitement.

'Were you afraid?' I said, asking the question women often put, and receiving the answer they seldom fail to get.

'No, Missis!' – emphasis on the 'Missis' – 'I never thought of anything but the damn' Rebs, that scalp, slash, an' cut our ears off, when they git us. I was bound to let daylight into one of 'em at least, an' I did. Hope he liked it!'

'It is evident that you did. Now go on about Robert, for I should be at work.'

'He was one of the fust up; I was just behind, an' though the whole thing happened in a minute, I remember how it was, for all I was yellin' an' knockin' round like mad. Just where we were, some sort of an officer was wavin' his sword an' cheerin' on his men; Dane saw him by a big flash that come by; he flung away his gun, give a leap, an' went at that feller as if he was Jeff, Beauregard, an' Lee,* all in one. I scrabbled after as quick as I could, but was only up in time to see him git the sword straight through him an' drop into the ditch. You needn't ask what I did next, Missis, for I don't quite know myself; all I'm clear about is, that I managed somehow to pitch that Reb into the fort as dead as Moses, git hold of Dane, an' bring him off. Poor old feller! we said we went in to live or die; he said he went in to die, an' he's done it.'

I had been intently watching the excited speaker; but as he regretfully added those last words I turned again, and Robert's eyes met mine, – those melancholy eyes, so full of an intelligence that proved he had heard, remembered, and reflected with that preternatural power which often outlives all other faculties. He knew me, yet gave no greeting; was glad to see a woman's face, yet had no smile wherewith to welcome it; felt that he was dying, yet uttered no farewell. He was too far across the river to return or linger now; departing thought, strength, breath, were spent in one grateful look, one murmur of submission to the last pang he could ever feel. His lips moved, and, bending to them, a whisper chilled my cheek, as it shaped the broken words, –

'I'd 'a' done it, – but it's better so, – I'm satisfied.'

Ah! well he might be, – for, as he turned his face from the shadow of the life that was, the sunshine of the life to be touched it with a beautiful content, and in the drawing of a breath my contraband found wife and home, eternal liberty and God.

Behind a Mask; or, A Woman's Power

1866

1 Jean Muir

'Has she come?'

'No, Mamma, not yet.'

'I wish it were well over. The thought of it worries and excites me. A cushion for my back, Bella.'

And poor, peevish Mrs Coventry sank into an easy chair with a nervous sigh and the air of a martyr, while her pretty daughter hovered about her with affectionate solicitude.

'Who are they talking of, Lucia?' asked the languid young man lounging on a couch near his cousin, who bent over her tapestry work with a happy smile on her usually haughty face.

'The new governess, Miss Muir. Shall I tell you about her?'

'No, thank you. I have an inveterate aversion to the whole tribe. I've often thanked heaven that I had but one sister, and she a spoiled child, so that I have escaped the infliction of a governess so long.'

'How will you bear it now?' asked Lucia.

'Leave the house while she is in it.'

'No, you won't. You're too lazy, Gerald,' called out a younger and more energetic man, from the recess where he stood teasing his dogs.

'I'll give her a three days' trial; if she proves endurable I shall not disturb myself; if, as I am sure, she is a bore, I'm off anywhere, anywhere out of her way.'

'I beg you won't talk in that depressing manner, boys. I dread the coming of a stranger more than you possibly can, but Bella *must* not be neglected; so I have nerved myself to endure this woman, and Lucia is good enough to say she will attend to her after tonight.'

'Don't be troubled, Mamma. She is a nice person, I dare say, and when once we are used to her, I've no doubt we shall be glad to have her, it's so dull here just now. Lady Sydney said she was a quiet, accomplished, amiable girl, who needed a home, and would be a help to poor stupid me, so try to like her for my sake.'

'I will, dear, but isn't it getting late? I do hope nothing has happened. Did you tell them to send a carriage to the station for her, Gerald?'

'I forgot it. But it's not far, it won't hurt her to walk' was the languid reply.

'It was indolence, not forgetfulness, I know. I'm very sorry; she will think it so rude to leave her to find her way so late. Do go and see to it, Ned.'

'Too late, Bella, the train was in some time ago. Give your orders to me next time, Mother, and I'll see that they are obeyed,' said Edward.

'Ned is just at an age to make a fool of himself for any girl who comes in his way. Have a care of the governess, Lucia, or she will bewitch him.'

Gerald spoke in a satirical whisper, but his brother heard him and answered with a good-humored laugh.

'I wish there was any hope of your making a fool of yourself in that way, old fellow. Set me a good example, and I promise to follow it. As for the governess, she is a woman, and should be treated with common civility. I should say a little extra kindness wouldn't be amiss, either, because she is poor, and a stranger.'

'That is my dear, good-hearted Ned! We'll stand by poor little Muir, won't we?' And running to her brother, Bella stood on tiptoe to offer him a kiss which he could not refuse, for the rosy lips were pursed up invitingly, and the bright eyes full of sisterly affection.

'I do hope she has come, for, when I make an effort to see anyone, I hate to make it in vain. Punctuality is *such* a virtue, and I know this woman hasn't got it, for she promised to be here at seven, and now it is long after,' began Mrs Coventry, in an injured tone.

Before she could get breath for another complaint, the clock struck seven and the doorbell rang.

'There she is!' cried Bella, and turned toward the door as if to go and meet the newcomer.

But Lucia arrested her, saying authoritatively, 'Stay here, child. It is her place to come to you, not yours to go to her.'

'Miss Muir,' announced a servant, and a little black-robed figure stood in the doorway. For an instant no one stirred, and the governess had time to see and be seen before a word was uttered. All looked at her, and she cast on the household group a keen glance that impressed them curiously; then her eyes fell, and bowing slightly she walked in. Edward came forward and received her with the frank cordiality which nothing could daunt or chill.

'Mother, this is the lady whom you expected. Miss Muir, allow me to apologize for our apparent neglect in not sending for you. There was a mistake about the carriage, or, rather, the lazy fellow to whom the order was given forgot it. Bella, come here.'

'Thank you, no apology is needed. I did not expect to be sent for.' And the governess meekly sat down without lifting her eyes.

'I am glad to see you. Let me take your things,' said Bella, rather shyly, for Gerald, still lounging, watched the fireside group with languid interest, and Lucia never stirred. Mrs Coventry took a second survey and began:

'You were punctual, Miss Muir, which pleases me. I'm a sad invalid, as Lady Sydney told you, I hope; so that Miss Coventry's lessons will be directed by my niece, and you will go to her for directions, as she knows what I wish. You will excuse me if I ask you a few questions, for Lady Sydney's note was very brief, and I left everything to her judgment.'

'Ask anything you like, madam,' answered the soft, sad voice.

'You are Scotch, I believe.'

'Yes, madam.'

'Are your parents living?'

'I have not a relation in the world.'

'Dear me, how sad! Do you mind telling me your age?'

'Nineteen.' And a smile passed over Miss Muir's lips, as she folded her hands with an air of resignation, for the catechism was evidently to be a long one.

'So young! Lady Sydney mentioned five-and-twenty, I think, didn't she, Bella?'

'No, Mamma, she only said she thought so. Don't ask such questions. It's not pleasant before us all,' whispered Bella.

A quick, grateful glance shone on her from the suddenly lifted eyes of Miss Muir, as she said quietly, 'I wish I was thirty, but, as I am not, I do my best to look and seem old.'

Of course, every one looked at her then, and all felt a touch of pity at the sight of the pale-faced girl in her plain black dress, with no ornament but a little silver cross at her throat. Small, thin, and colorless she was, with yellow hair, gray eyes, and sharply cut, irregular, but very expressive features. Poverty seemed to have set its bond stamp upon her, and life to have had for her more frost than sunshine. But something in the lines of the mouth betrayed strength, and the clear, low voice had a curious mixture of command and entreaty in its varying tones. Not an attractive woman, yet not an ordinary one; and, as she sat there with her delicate hands lying in her lap, her head bent, and a bitter look on her thin face, she was more interesting than many a blithe and blooming girl. Bella's heart warmed to her at once, and she drew her seat nearer, while Edward went back to his dogs that his presence might not embarrass her.

'You have been ill, I think,' continued Mrs Coventry, who considered this fact the most interesting of all she had heard concerning the governess.

'Yes, madam, I left the hospital only a week ago.'

'Are you quite sure it is safe to begin teaching so soon?'

'I have no time to lose, and shall soon gain strength here in the country, if you care to keep me.'

'And you are fitted to teach music, French, and drawing?'

'I shall endeavor to prove that I am.'

'Be kind enough to go and play an air or two. I can judge by your touch; I used to play finely when a girl.'

Miss Muir rose, looked about her for the instrument, and seeing it at the other end of the room went toward it, passing Gerald and Lucia as if she did not see them. Bella followed, and in a moment forgot everything in admiration. Miss Muir played like one who loved music and was perfect mistress of her art. She charmed them all by the magic of this spell; even indolent Gerald sat up to listen, and Lucia put down her needle, while Ned watched the slender white fingers as they flew, and wondered at the strength and skill which they possessed.

'Please sing,' pleaded Bella, as a brilliant overture ended.

With the same meek obedience Miss Muir complied, and began a little Scotch melody, so sweet, so sad, that the girl's eyes filled, and Mrs Coventry looked for one of her many pocket-handkerchiefs. But suddenly the music ceased, for, with a vain attempt to support herself, the singer slid from her seat and lay before the startled listeners, as white and rigid as if struck with death. Edward caught her up, and, ordering his brother off the couch, laid her there, while Bella chafed her hands, and her mother rang for her maid. Lucia bathed the poor girl's temples, and Gerald, with unwonted energy, brought a glass of wine. Soon Miss Muir's lips trembled, she sighed, then murmured, tenderly, with a pretty Scotch accent, as if wandering in the past, 'Bide wi' me, Mither, I'm sae sick an sad here all alone.'

'Take a sip of this, and it will do you good, my dear,' said Mrs Coventry, quite touched by the plaintive words.

The strange voice seemed to recall her. She sat up, looked about her, a little wildly, for a moment, then collected herself and said, with a pathetic look and tone, 'Pardon me. I have been on my feet all day, and, in my eagerness to keep my appointment, I forgot to eat since morning. I'm better now; shall I finish the song?'

'By no means. Come and have some tea,' said Bella, full of pity and remorse.

'Scene first, very well done,' whispered Gerald to his cousin.

Miss Muir was just before them, apparently listening to Mrs Coventry's remarks upon fainting fits; but she heard, and looked over her shoulders with a gesture like Rachel.* Her eyes were gray, but at that instant they seemed black with some strong emotion of anger, pride, or defiance. A curious smile passed over her face as she bowed, and said in her penetrating voice, 'Thanks. The last scene shall be still better.'

Young Coventry was a cool, indolent man, seldom conscious of any emotion, any passion, pleasurable or otherwise; but at the look, the tone of the governess, he experienced a new sensation, indefinable, yet strong. He colored and, for the first time in his life, looked abashed. Lucia saw it, and hated Miss Muir with a sudden hatred; for, in all the years she had passed with her cousin, no look or word of hers had possessed such power. Coventry was himself again in an instant, with no trace of that passing change, but a look of interest in his usually dreamy eyes, and a touch of anger in his sarcastic voice.

'What a melodramatic young lady! I shall go tomorrow.'

Lucia laughed, and was well pleased when he sauntered away

to bring her a cup of tea from the table where a little scene was just taking place. Mrs Coventry had sunk into her chair again, exhausted by the flurry of the fainting fit. Bella was busied about her; and Edward, eager to feed the pale governess, was awkwardly trying to make the tea, after a beseeching glance at his cousin which she did not choose to answer. As he upset the caddy and uttered a despairing exclamation, Miss Muir quietly took her place behind the urn, saying with a smile, and a shy glance at the young man, 'Allow me to assume my duty at once, and serve you all. I understand the art of making people comfortable in this way. The scoop, please. I can gather this up quite well alone, if you will tell me how your mother likes her tea.'

Edward pulled a chair to the table and made merry over his mishaps, while Miss Muir performed her little task with a skill and grace that made it pleasant to watch her. Coventry lingered a moment after she had given him a steaming cup, to observe her more nearly, while he asked a question or two of his brother. She took no more notice of him than if he had been a statue, and in the middle of the one remark he addressed to her, she rose to take the sugar basin to Mrs Coventry, who was quite won by the modest, domestic graces of the new governess.

'Really, my dear, you are a treasure; I haven't tasted such tea since my poor maid Ellis died. Bella never makes it good, and Miss Lucia always forgets the cream. Whatever you do you seem to do well, and that is *such* a comfort.'

'Let me always do this for you, then. It will be a pleasure, madam.' And Miss Muir came back to her seat with a faint color in her cheek which improved her much.

'My brother asked if young Sydney was at home when you left,' said Edward, for Gerald would not take the trouble to repeat the question.

Miss Muir fixed her eyes on Coventry, and answered with a slight tremor of the lips, 'No, he left home some weeks ago.'

The young man went back to his cousin, saying, as he threw himself down beside her, 'I shall not go tomorrow, but wait till the three days are out.'

'Why?' demanded Lucia.

Lowering his voice he said, with a significant nod toward the governess, 'Because I have a fancy that she is at the bottom of

Sydney's mystery. He's not been himself lately, and now he is gone without a word. I rather like romances in real life, if they are not too long, or difficult to read.'

'Do you think her pretty?'

'Far from it, a most uncanny little specimen.'

'Then why fancy Sydney loves her?'

'He is an oddity, and likes sensations and things of that sort.'

'What do you mean, Gerald?'

'Get the Muir to look at you, as she did at me, and you will understand. Will you have another cup, Juno?'*

'Yes, please.' She liked to have him wait upon her, for he did it to no other woman except his mother.

Before he could slowly rise, Miss Muir glided to them with another cup on the salver; and, as Lucia took it with a cold nod, the girl said under her breath, 'I think it honest to tell you that I possess a quick ear, and cannot help hearing what is said anywhere in the room. What you say of me is of no consequence, but you may speak of things which you prefer I should not hear; therefore, allow me to warn you.' And she was gone again as noiselessly as she came.

'How do you like that?' whispered Coventry, as his cousin sat looking after the girl, with a disturbed expression.

'What an uncomfortable creature to have in the house! I am very sorry I urged her coming, for your mother has taken a fancy to her, and it will be hard to get rid of her,' said Lucia, half angry, half amused.

'Hush, she hears every word you say. I know it by the expression of her face, for Ned is talking about horses, and she looks as haughty as ever you did, and that is saying much. Faith, this is getting interesting.'

'Hark, she is speaking; I want to hear,' and Lucia laid her hand on her cousin's lips. He kissed it, and then idly amused himself with turning the rings to and fro on the slender fingers.

'I have been in France several years, madam, but my friend died and I came back to be with Lady Sydney, till – ' Muir paused an instant, then added, slowly, 'till I fell ill. It was a contagious fever, so I went of my own accord to the hospital, not wishing to endanger her.'

'Very right, but are you sure there is no danger of infection now?' asked Mrs Coventry anxiously.

'None, I assure you. I have been well for some time, but did not leave because I preferred to stay there, than to return to Lady Sydney.'

'No quarrel, I hope? No trouble of any kind?'

'No quarrel, but – well, why not? You have a right to know, and I will not make a foolish mystery out of a very simple thing. As your family, only, is present, I may tell the truth. I did not go back on the young gentleman's account. Please ask no more.'

'Ah, I see. Quite prudent and proper, Miss Muir. I shall never allude to it again. Thank you for your frankness. Bella, you will be careful not to mention this to your young friends; girls gossip sadly, and it would annoy Lady Sydney beyond everything to have this talked of.'

'Very neighborly of Lady S. to send the dangerous young lady here, where there are *two* young gentlemen to be captivated. I wonder why she didn't keep Sydney after she had caught him,' murmured Coventry to his cousin.

'Because she had the utmost contempt for a titled fool.' Miss Muir dropped the words almost into his ear, as she bent to take her shawl from the sofa corner.

'How the deuce did she get there?' ejaculated Coventry, looking as if he had received another sensation. 'She has spirit, though, and upon my word I pity Sydney, if he did try to dazzle her, for he must have got a splendid dismissal.'

'Come and play billiards. You promised, and I hold you to your word,' said Lucia, rising with decision, for Gerald was showing too much interest in another to suit Miss Beaufort.

'I am, as ever, your most devoted. My mother is a charming woman, but I find our evening parties slightly dull, when only my own family are present. Good night, Mamma.' He shook hands with his mother, whose pride and idol he was, and, with a comprehensive nod to the others, strolled after his cousin.

'Now they are gone we can be quite cozy, and talk over things, for I don't mind Ned any more than I do his dogs,' said Bella, settling herself on her mother's footstool.

'I merely wish to say, Miss Muir, that my daughter has never had a governess and is sadly backward for a girl of sixteen. I want you to pass the mornings with her, and get her on as rapidly as possible. In the afternoon you will walk or drive with her, and in the evening sit with us here, if you like, or amuse yourself as you please. While in the country we are very quiet, for I cannot bear much company, and when my sons want gaiety, they go away for it. Miss Beaufort oversees the servants, and takes my place as far as possible. I am very delicate and keep my room till evening, except for an airing at noon. We will try each other for a month, and I hope we shall get on quite comfortably together.'

'I shall do my best, madam.'

One would not have believed that the meek spiritless voice which uttered these words was the same that had startled Coventry a few minutes before, nor that the pale, patient face could ever have kindled with such sudden fire as that which looked over Miss Muir's shoulder when she answered her young host's speech.

Edward thought within himself, Poor little woman! She has had a hard life. We will try and make it easier while she is here; and began his charitable work by suggesting that she might be tired. She acknowledged she was, and Bella led her away to a bright, cozy room, where with a pretty little speech and a goodnight kiss she left her.

When alone Miss Muir's conduct was decidedly peculiar. Her first act was to clench her hands and mutter between her teeth, with passionate force, 'I'll not fail again if there is power in a woman's wit and will!' She stood a moment motionless, with an expression of almost fierce disdain on her face, then shook her clenched hand as if menacing some unseen enemy. Next she laughed, and shrugged her shoulders with a true French shrug, saying low to herself, 'Yes, the last scene *shall* be better than the first. *Mon dieu*, how tired and hungry I am!'

Kneeling before the one small trunk which held her worldly possessions, she opened it, drew out a flask, and mixed a glass of some ardent cordial, which she seemed to enjoy extremely as she sat on the carpet, musing, while her quick eyes examined every corner of the room.

'Not bad! It will be a good field for me to work in, and the harder the task the better I shall like it. *Merci*, old friend. You put heart and courage into me when nothing else will. Come, the curtain is down, so I may be myself for a few hours, if actresses ever are themselves.'

Still sitting on the floor she unbound and removed the long abundant braids from her head, wiped the pink from her face, took out several pearly teeth, and slipping off her dress appeared herself indeed, a haggard, worn, and moody woman of thirty at least. The metamorphosis was wonderful, but the disguise was more in the expression she assumed than in any art of costume or false adornment. Now she was alone, and her mobile features settled into their natural expression, weary, hard, bitter. She had been lovely once, happy, innocent, and tender; but nothing of all this remained to the gloomy woman who leaned there brooding over some wrong, or loss, or disappointment which had darkened all her life. For an hour she sat so, sometimes playing absently with the scanty locks that hung about her face, sometimes lifting the glass to her lips as if the fiery draught warmed her cold blood; and once she half uncovered her breast to eye with a terrible glance the scar of a newly healed wound. At last she rose and crept to bed, like one worn out with weariness and mental pain.

2 A Good Beginning

Only the housemaids were astir when Miss Muir left her room next morning and quietly found her way into the garden. As she walked, apparently intent upon the flowers, her quick eye scrutinized the fine old house and its picturesque surroundings.

'Not bad,' she said to herself, adding, as she passed into the adjoining park, 'but the other may be better, and I will have the best.'

Walking rapidly, she came out at length upon the wide green lawn which lay before the ancient hall where Sir John Coventry lived in solitary splendor. A stately old place, rich in oaks, well-kept shrubberies, gay gardens, sunny terraces, carved gables, spacious rooms, liveried servants, and every luxury befitting the ancestral home of a rich and honorable race. Miss Muir's eyes brightened as she looked, her step grew firmer, her carriage prouder, and a smile broke over her face; the smile of one well pleased at the prospect of the success of some cherished hope. Suddenly her whole air changed, she pushed back her hat, clasped her hands loosely before her, and seemed absorbed in girlish admiration of the fair scene that could not fail to charm any beauty-loving eye. The cause of this rapid change soon appeared. A hale, handsome man, between fifty and sixty, came through the little gate leading to the park, and, seeing the young stranger, paused to examine her. He had only time for a glance, however; she seemed conscious of his presence in a moment, turned with a startled look, uttered an exclamation of surprise, and looked as if hesitating whether to speak or run away. Gallant Sir John took off his hat and said, with an old-fashioned courtesy which became him well, 'I beg your pardon for disturbing you, young lady. Allow me to atone for it by inviting you to walk where you will, and gather what flowers you like. I see you love them, so pray make free with those about you.'

With a charming air of maidenly timidity and artlessness, Miss Muir replied, 'Oh, thank you, sir! But it is I who should ask pardon for trespassing. I never should have dared if I had not known that Sir John was absent. I always wanted to see this fine old place, and ran over the first thing, to satisfy myself.'

'And *are* you satisfied?' he asked, with a smile.

'More than satisfied – I'm charmed; for it is the most beautiful spot I ever saw, and I've seen many famous seats, both at home and abroad,' she answered enthusiastically.

'The Hall is much flattered, and so would its master be if he heard you,' began the gentleman, with an odd expression.

'I should not praise it to him – at least, not as freely as I have to you, sir,' said the girl, with eyes still turned away.

'Why not?' asked her companion, looking much amused.

'I should be afraid. Not that I dread Sir John; but I've heard so many beautiful and noble things about him, and respect him so highly, that I should not dare to say much, lest he should see how I admire and – '

'And what, young lady? Finish, if you please.'

'I was going to say, love him. I will say it, for he is an old man, and one cannot help loving virtue and bravery.'

Miss Muir looked very earnest and pretty as she spoke, standing there with the sunshine glinting on her yellow hair, delicate face, and downcast eyes. Sir John was not a vain man, but he found it pleasant to hear himself commended by this unknown girl, and felt redoubled curiosity to learn who she was. Too well bred to ask, or to abash her by avowing what she seemed unconscious of, he left both discoveries to chance; and when she turned, as if to retrace her steps, he offered her the handful of hothouse flowers which he held, saying, with a gallant bow, 'In Sir John's name let me give you my little nosegay, with thanks for your good opinion, which, I assure you, is not entirely deserved, for I know him well.'

Miss Muir looked up quickly, eyed him an instant, then dropped her eyes, and, coloring deeply, stammered out, 'I did not know – I beg your pardon – you are too kind, Sir John.'

He laughed like a boy, asking, mischievously, 'Why call me Sir John? How do you know that I am not the gardener or the butler?'

'I did not see your face before, and no one but yourself would say that any praise was undeserved,' murmured Miss Muir, still overcome with girlish confusion.

'Well, well, we will let that pass, and the next time you come we will be properly introduced. Bella always brings her friends to the Hall, for I am fond of young people.'

'I am not a friend. I am only Miss Coventry's governess.' And Miss Muir dropped a meek curtsy. A slight change passed over Sir John's manner. Few would have perceived it, but Miss Muir felt it at once, and bit her lips with an angry feeling at her heart. With a curious air of pride, mingled with respect, she accepted the still offered bouquet, returned Sir John's parting bow, and tripped away, leaving the old gentleman to wonder where Mrs Coventry found such a piquant little governess.

'That is done, and very well for a beginning,' she said to herself as she approached the house.

In a green paddock close by fed a fine horse, who lifted up his head and eyed her inquiringly, like one who expected a greeting. Following a sudden impulse, she entered the paddock and, pulling a handful of clover, invited the creature to come and eat. This was evidently a new proceeding on the part of a lady, and the horse careered about as if bent on frightening the newcomer away.

'I see,' she said aloud, laughing to herself. 'I am not your master, and you rebel. Nevertheless, I'll conquer you, my fine brute.'

Seating herself in the grass, she began to pull daisies, singing idly the while, as if unconscious of the spirited prancings of the horse. Presently he drew nearer, sniffing curiously and eyeing her with surprise. She took no notice, but plaited the daisies and sang on as if he was not there. This seemed to pique the petted creature, for, slowly approaching, he came at length so close that he could smell her little foot and nibble at her dress. Then she offered the clover, uttering caressing words and making soothing sounds, till by degrees and with much coquetting, the horse permitted her to stroke his glossy neck and smooth his mane.

It was a pretty sight – the slender figure in the grass, the high-spirited horse bending his proud head to her hand. Edward Coventry, who had watched the scene, found it impossible to restrain himself any longer and, leaping the wall, came to join the group, saying, with mingled admiration and wonder in countenance and voice, 'Good morning, Miss Muir. If I had not seen your skill and courage proved before my eyes, I should be alarmed for your safety. Hector is a wild, wayward beast, and has damaged more than one groom who tried to conquer him.'

'Good morning, Mr Coventry. Don't tell tales of this noble creature, who has not deceived my faith in him. Your grooms did not know how to win his heart, and so subdue his spirit without breaking it.'

Miss Muir rose as she spoke, and stood with her hand on Hector's neck while he ate the grass which she had gathered in the skirt of her dress.

'You have the secret, and Hector* is your subject now, though heretofore he has rejected all friends but his master. Will you give him his morning feast? I always bring him bread and play with him before breakfast.'

'Then you are not jealous?' And she looked up at him with eyes so bright and beautiful in expression that the young man wondered he had not observed them before.

'Not I. Pet him as much as you will; it will do him good. He is a solitary fellow, for he scorns his own kind and lives alone, like his master,' he added, half to himself.

'Alone, with such a happy home, Mr Coventry?' And a softly compassionate glance stole from the bright eyes.

'That was an ungrateful speech, and I retract it for Bella's sake. Younger sons have no position but such as they can make for themselves, you know, and I've had no chance yet.'

'Younger sons! I thought – I beg pardon.' And Miss Muir paused, as if remembering that she had no right to question.

Edward smiled and answered frankly, 'Nay, don't mind me. You thought I was the heir, perhaps. Whom did you take my brother for last night?'

'For some guest who admired Miss Beaufort. I did not hear his name, nor observe him enough to discover who he was. I saw only your kind mother, your charming little sister, and – '

She stopped there, with a half-shy, half-grateful look at the young man which finished the sentence better than any words. He was still a boy, in spite of his one-and-twenty years, and a little color came into his brown cheek as the eloquent eyes met his and fell before them.

'Yes, Bella is a capital girl, and one can't help loving her. I know you'll get her on, for, really, she is the most delightful little dunce. My mother's ill health and Bella's devotion to her have prevented our attending to her education before. Next winter, when we go to town, she is to come out, and must be prepared for that great event, you know,' he said, choosing a safe subject.

'I shall do my best. And that reminds me that I should report myself to her, instead of enjoying myself here. When one has been ill and shut up a long time, the country is so lovely one is apt to forget duty for pleasure. Please remind me if I am negligent, Mr Coventry.'

'That name belongs to Gerald. I'm only Mr Ned here,' he said as they walked toward the house, while Hector followed to the wall and sent a sonorous farewell after them.

Bella came running to meet them, and greeted Miss Muir as if she had made up her mind to like her heartily. 'What a lovely bouquet you have got! I never can arrange flowers prettily, which vexes me, for Mamma is so fond of them and cannot go out herself. You have charming taste,' she said, examining the graceful posy which Miss Muir had much improved by adding feathery grasses, delicate ferns, and fragrant wild flowers to Sir John's exotics.

Putting them into Bella's hand, she said, in a winning way, 'Take them to your mother, then, and ask her if I may have the pleasure of making her a daily nosegay; for I should find real delight in doing it, if it would please her.'

'How kind you are! Of course it would please her. I'll take them to her while the dew is still on them.' And away flew Bella, eager to give both the flowers and the pretty message to the poor invalid.

Edward stopped to speak to the gardener, and Miss Muir went up the steps alone. The long hall was lined with portraits, and pacing slowly down it she examined them with interest. One caught her eye, and, pausing before it, she scrutinized it carefully. A young, beautiful, but very haughty female face. Miss Muir suspected at once who it was, and gave a decided nod, as if she saw and caught at some unexpected chance. A soft rustle behind her made her look around, and, seeing Lucia, she bowed, half turned, as if for another glance at the picture, and said, as if involuntarily, 'How beautiful it is! May I ask if it is an ancestor, Miss Beaufort?'

'It is the likeness of my mother' was the reply, given with a softened voice and eyes that looked up tenderly.

'Ah, I might have known, from the resemblance, but I scarcely saw you last night. Excuse my freedom, but Lady Sydney treated me as a friend, and I forget my position. Allow me.'

As she spoke, Miss Muir stooped to return the handkerchief which had fallen from Lucia's hand, and did so with a humble mien which touched the other's heart; for, though a proud, it was also a very generous one.

'Thank you. Are you better, this morning?' she said, graciously. And having received an affirmative reply, she added, as she walked on, 'I will show you to the breakfast room, as Bella is not here. It is a very informal meal with us, for my aunt is never down and my cousins are very irregular in their hours. You can always have yours when you like, without waiting for us, if you are an early riser.'

Bella and Edward appeared before the others were seated, and Miss Muir quietly ate her breakfast, feeling well satisfied with her hour's work. Ned recounted her exploit with Hector, Bella delivered her mother's thanks for the flowers, and Lucia more than once recalled, with pardonable vanity, that the governess had compared her to her lovely mother, expressing by a look as much admiration for the living likeness as for the painted one. All kindly did their best to make the pale girl feel at home, and their cordial manner seemed to warm and draw her out; for soon she put off her sad, meek air and entertained them with gay anecdotes of her life in Paris, her travels in Russia when governess in Prince Jermadoff's family, and all manner of witty stories that kept them interested and merry long after the meal was over. In the middle of an absorbing adventure, Coventry came in, nodded lazily, lifted his brows, as if surprised at seeing the governess there, and began his breakfast as if the ennui of another day had already taken possession of him. Miss Muir stopped short, and no entreaties could induce her to go on.

'Another time I will finish it, if you like. Now Miss Bella and I should be at our books.' And she left the room, followed by her pupil, taking no notice of the young master of the house, beyond a graceful bow in answer to his careless nod.

'Merciful creature! she goes when I come, and does not make life unendurable by moping about before my eyes. Does she belong to the moral, the melancholy, the romantic, or the dashing class, Ned?' said Gerald, lounging over his coffee as he did over everything he attempted.

'To none of them; she is a capital little woman. I wish you had seen her tame Hector this morning.' And Edward repeated his story.

'Not a bad move on her part,' said Coventry in reply. 'She must be an observing as well as an energetic young person, to discover your chief weakness and attack it so soon. First tame the horse, and then the master. It will be amusing to watch the game, only I shall be under the painful necessity of checkmating you both, if it gets serious.'

'You needn't exert yourself, old fellow, on my account. If I was not above thinking ill of an inoffensive girl, I should say you were the prize best worth winning, and advise you to take care of your own heart, if you've got one, which I rather doubt.'

'I often doubt it, myself; but I fancy the little Scotchwoman will not be able to satisfy either of us upon that point. How does your highness like her?' asked Coventry of his cousin, who sat near him.

'Better than I thought I should. She is well bred, unassuming, and very entertaining when she likes. She has told us some of the wittiest stories I've heard for a long time. Didn't our laughter wake you?' replied Lucia.

'Yes. Now atone for it by amusing me with a repetition of these witty tales.'

'That is impossible; her accent and manner are half the charm,' said Ned. 'I wish you had kept away ten minutes longer, for your appearance spoilt the best story of all.'

'Why didn't she go on?' asked Coventry, with a ray of curiosity.

'You forgot that she overheard us last night, and must feel

that you consider her a bore. She has pride, and no woman forgets speeches like those you made,' answered Lucia.

'Or forgives them, either, I believe. Well, I must be resigned to languish under her displeasure then. On Sydney's account I take a slight interest in her; not that I expect to learn anything from her, for a woman with a mouth like that never confides or confesses anything. But I have a fancy to see what captivated him; for captivated he was, beyond a doubt, and by no lady whom he met in society. Did you ever hear anything of it, Ned?' asked Gerald.

'I'm not fond of scandal or gossip, and never listen to either.' With which remark Edward left the room.

Lucia was called out by the housekeeper a moment after, and Coventry left to the society most wearisome to him, namely his own. As he entered, he had caught a part of the story which Miss Muir had been telling, and it had excited his curiosity so much that he found himself wondering what the end could be and wishing that he might hear it.

What the deuce did she run away for, when I came in? he thought. If she *is* amusing, she must make herself useful; for it's intensely dull, I own, here, in spite of Lucia. Hey, what's that?

It was a rich, sweet voice, singing a brilliant Italian air, and singing it with an expression that made the music doubly delicious. Stepping out of the French window, Coventry strolled along the sunny terrace, enjoying the song with the relish of a connoisseur. Others followed, and still he walked and listened, forgetful of weariness or time. As one exquisite air ended, he involuntarily applauded. Miss Muir's face appeared for an instant, then vanished, and no more music followed, though Coventry lingered, hoping to hear the voice again. For music was the one thing of which he never wearied, and neither Lucia nor Bella possessed skill enough to charm him. For an hour he loitered on the terrace or the lawn, basking in the sunshine, too indolent to seek occupation or society. At length Bella came out, hat in hand, and nearly stumbled over her brother, who lay on the grass.

'You lazy man, have you been dawdling here all this time?' she said, looking down at him.

'No, I've been very busy. Come and tell me how you've got on with the little dragon.'

'Can't stop. She bade me take a run after my French, so that I might be ready for my drawing, and so I must.'

'It's too warm to run. Sit down and amuse your deserted brother, who has had no society but bees and lizards for an hour.'

He drew her down as he spoke, and Bella obeyed; for, in spite of his indolence, he was one to whom all submitted without dreaming of refusal.

'What have you been doing? Muddling your poor little brains with all manner of elegant rubbish?'

'No, I've been enjoying myself immensely. Jean is *so* interesting, so kind and clever. She didn't bore me with stupid grammar, but just talked to me in such pretty French that I got on capitally, and like it as I never expected to, after Lucia's dull way of teaching it.'

'What did you talk about?'

'Oh, all manner of things. She asked questions, and I answered, and she corrected me.'

'Questions about our affairs, I suppose?'

'Not one. She don't care two sous for us or our affairs. I thought she might like to know what sort of people we were, so I told her about Papa's sudden death, Uncle John, and you, and Ned; but in the midst of it she said, in her quiet way, "You are getting too confidential, my dear. It is not best to talk too freely of one's affairs to strangers. Let us speak of something else."'

'What were you talking of when she said that, Bell?'

'You.'

'Ah, then no wonder she was bored.'

'She was tired of my chatter, and didn't hear half I said; for she was busy sketching something for me to copy, and thinking of something more interesting than the Coventrys.'

'How do you know?'

'By the expression of her face. Did you like her music, Gerald?'

'Yes. Was she angry when I clapped?'

'She looked surprised, then rather proud, and shut the piano at once, though I begged her to go on. Isn't Jean a pretty name?'

'Not bad; but why don't you call her Miss Muir?'

'She begged me not. She hates it, and loves to be called Jean, alone. I've imagined such a nice little romance about her, and someday I shall tell her, for I'm sure she has had a love trouble.'

'Don't get such nonsense into your head, but follow Miss Muir's well-bred example and don't be curious about other people's affairs. Ask her to sing tonight; it amuses me.'

'She won't come down, I think. We've planned to read and work in my boudoir, which is to be our study now. Mamma will stay in her room, so you and Lucia can have the drawing room all to yourselves.'

'Thank you. What will Ned do?'

'He will amuse Mamma, he says. Dear old Ned! I wish you'd stir about and get him his commission. He is so impatient to be doing something and yet so proud he won't ask again, after you have neglected it so many times and refused Uncle's help.'

'I'll attend to it very soon; don't worry me, child. He will do very well for a time, quietly here with us.'

'You always say that, yet you know he chafes and is unhappy at being dependent on you. Mamma and I don't mind; but he is a man, and it frets him. He said he'd take matters into his own hands soon, and then you may be sorry you were so slow in helping him.'

'Miss Muir is looking out of the window. You'd better go and take your run, else she will scold.'

'Not she. I'm not a bit afraid of her, she's so gentle and sweet. I'm fond of her already. You'll get as brown as Ned, lying here in the sun. By the way, Miss Muir agrees with me in thinking him handsomer than you.'

'I admire her taste and quite agree with her.'

'She said he was manly, and that was more attractive than beauty in a man. She does express things so nicely. Now I'm off.' And away danced Bella, humming the burden of Miss Muir's sweetest song.

'"Energy is more attractive than beauty in a man." She is right, but how the deuce *can* a man be energetic, with nothing to expend his energies upon?' mused Coventry, with his hat over his eyes.

A few moments later, the sweep of a dress caught his ear. Without stirring, a sidelong glance showed him Miss Muir coming across the terrace, as if to join Bella. Two stone steps led down to the lawn. He lay near them, and Miss Muir did not see him till close upon him. She started and slipped on the last step, recovered herself, and glided on, with a glance of unmistakable contempt as she passed the recumbent figure of the apparent sleeper. Several things in Bella's report had nettled him, but this look made him angry, though he would not own it, even to himself.

'Gerald, come here, quick!' presently called Bella, from the rustic seat where she stood beside her governess, who sat with her hand over her face as if in pain.

Gathering himself up, Coventry slowly obeyed, but involuntarily quickened his pace as he heard Miss Muir say, 'Don't call him; *he* can do nothing' for the emphasis on the word 'he' was very significant.

'What is it, Bella?' he asked, looking rather wider awake than usual.

'You startled Miss Muir and made her turn her ankle. Now help her to the house, for she is in great pain; and don't lie there anymore to frighten people like a snake in the grass,' said his sister petulantly.

'I beg your pardon. Will you allow me?' And Coventry offered his arm.

Miss Muir looked up with the expression which annoyed him and answered coldly, 'Thank you, Miss Bella will do as well.'

'Permit me to doubt that.' And with a gesture too decided to be resisted, Coventry drew her arm through his and led her into the house. She submitted quietly, said the pain would soon be over, and when settled on the couch in Bella's room dismissed him with the briefest thanks. Considering the unwonted exertion he had made, he thought she might have been a little more grateful, and went away to Lucia, who always brightened when he came.

No more was seen of Miss Muir till teatime; for now, while the family were in retirement, they dined early and saw no company. The governess had excused herself at dinner, but came down in the evening a little paler than usual and with a slight limp in her gait. Sir John was there, talking with his nephew, and they merely acknowledged her presence by the sort of bow which gentlemen bestow on governesses. As she slowly made her way to her place behind the urn, Coventry said to his brother, 'Take her a footstool, and ask her how she is, Ned.' Then, as if necessary to account for his politeness to his uncle, he explained how he was the cause of the accident.

'Yes, yes. I understand. Rather a nice little person, I fancy.

Not exactly a beauty, but accomplished and well bred, which is better for one of her class.'

'Some tea, Sir John?' said a soft voice at his elbow, and there was Miss Muir, offering cups to the gentlemen.

'Thank you, thank you,' said Sir John, sincerely hoping she had overheard him.

As Coventry took his, he said graciously, 'You are very forgiving, Miss Muir, to wait upon me, after I have caused you so much pain.'

'It is my duty, sir' was her reply, in a tone which plainly said, 'but not my pleasure.' And she returned to her place, to smile, and chat, and be charming, with Bella and her brother.

Lucia, hovering near her uncle and Gerald, kept them to herself, but was disturbed to find that their eyes often wandered to the cheerful group about the table, and that their attention seemed distracted by the frequent bursts of laughter and fragments of animated conversation which reached them. In the midst of an account of a tragic affair which she endeavored to make as interesting and pathetic as possible, Sir John burst into a hearty laugh, which betrayed that he had been listening to a livelier story than her own. Much annoyed, she said hastily, 'I knew it would be so! Bella has no idea of the proper manner in which to treat a governess. She and Ned will forget the difference of rank and spoil that person for her work. She is inclined to be presumptuous already, and if my aunt won't trouble herself to give Miss Muir a hint in time, I shall.'

'Wait till she has finished that story, I beg of you,' said Coventry, for Sir John was already off.

'If you find that nonsense so entertaining, why don't you follow Uncle's example? I don't need you.'

'Thank you. I will.' And Lucia was deserted.

But Miss Muir had ended and, beckoning to Bella, left the room, as if quite unconscious of the honor conferred upon her or the dullness she left behind her. Ned went up to his mother, Gerald returned to make his peace with Lucia, and, bidding them goodnight, Sir John turned homeward. Strolling along the terrace, he came to the lighted window of Bella's study, and wishing to say a word to her, he half pushed aside the curtain and looked in. A pleasant little scene. Bella working busily, and near her in a low chair, with the light falling on her fair hair and delicate profile, sat Miss Muir, reading aloud. 'Novels!' thought

Sir John, and smiled at them for a pair of romantic girls. But
pausing to listen a moment before he spoke, he found it was no
novel, but history, read with a fluency which made every fact
interesting, every sketch of character memorable, by the dramatic effect given to it. Sir John was fond of history, and failing
eyesight often curtailed his favorite amusement. He had tried
readers, but none suited him, and he had given up the plan.
Now as he listened, he thought how pleasantly the smoothly
flowing voice would wile away his evenings, and he envied Bella
her new acquisition.

A bell rang, and Bella sprang up, saying, 'Wait for me a
minute. I must run to Mamma, and then we will go on with this
charming prince.'

Away she went, and Sir John was about to retire as quietly as
he came, when Miss Muir's peculiar behavior arrested him for
an instant. Dropping the book, she threw her arms across the
table, laid her head down upon them, and broke into a passion
of tears, like one who could bear restraint no longer. Shocked
and amazed, Sir John stole away; but all that night the kind-
hearted gentleman puzzled his brains with conjectures about his
niece's interesting young governess, quite unconscious that she
intended he should do so.

3 Passion and Pique

For several weeks the most monotonous tranquillity seemed to
reign at Coventry House, and yet, unseen, unsuspected, a storm
was gathering. The arrival of Miss Muir seemed to produce a
change in everyone, though no one could have explained how
or why. Nothing could be more unobtrusive and retiring than
her manners. She was devoted to Bella, who soon adored her,
and was only happy when in her society. She ministered in many
ways to Mrs Coventry's comfort, and that lady declared there
never was such a nurse. She amused, interested and won Edward
with her wit and womanly sympathy. She made Lucia respect
and envy her for her accomplishments, and piqued indolent
Gerald by her persistent avoidance of him, while Sir John was

charmed with her respectful deference and the graceful little attentions she paid him in a frank and artless way, very winning to the lonely old man. The very servants liked her; and instead of being, what most governesses are, a forlorn creature hovering between superiors and inferiors, Jean Muir was the life of the house, and the friend of all but two.

Lucia disliked her, and Coventry distrusted her; neither could exactly say why, and neither owned the feeling, even to themselves. Both watched her covertly yet found no shortcoming anywhere. Meek, modest, faithful, and invariably sweet-tempered – they could complain of nothing and wondered at their own doubts, though they could not banish them.

It soon came to pass that the family was divided, or rather that two members were left very much to themselves. Pleading timidity, Jean Muir kept much in Bella's study and soon made it such a pleasant little nook that Ned and his mother, and often Sir John, came in to enjoy the music, reading, or cheerful chat which made the evenings so gay. Lucia at first was only too glad to have her cousin to herself, and he too lazy to care what went on about him. But presently he wearied of her society, for she was not a brilliant girl, and possessed few of those winning arts which charm a man and steal into his heart. Rumors of the merrymakings that went on reached him and made him curious to share them; echoes of fine music went sounding through the house, as he lounged about the empty drawing room; and peals of laughter reached him while listening to Lucia's grave discourse.

She soon discovered that her society had lost its charm, and the more eagerly she tried to please him, the more signally she failed. Before long Coventry fell into a habit of strolling out upon the terrace of an evening, and amusing himself by passing and repassing the window of Bella's room, catching glimpses of what was going on and reporting the result of his observations to Lucia, who was too proud to ask admission to the happy circle or to seem to desire it.

'I shall go to London tomorrow, Lucia,' Gerald said one evening, as he came back from what he called 'a survey,' looking very much annoyed.

'To London?' exclaimed his cousin, surprised.

'Yes, I must bestir myself and get Ned his commission, or it will be all over with him.'

'How do you mean?'

'He is falling in love as fast as it is possible for a boy to do it. That girl has bewitched him, and he will make a fool of himself very soon, unless I put a stop to it.'

'I was afraid she would attempt a flirtation. These persons always do, they are such a mischief-making race.'

'Ah, but there you are wrong, as far as little Muir is concerned. She does not flirt, and Ned has too much sense and spirit to be caught by a silly coquette. She treats him like an elder sister, and mingles the most attractive friendliness with a quiet dignity that captivates the boy. I've been watching them, and there he is, devouring her with his eyes, while she reads a fascinating novel in the most fascinating style. Bella and Mamma are absorbed in the tale, and see nothing; but Ned makes himself the hero, Miss Muir the heroine, and lives the love scene with all the ardor of a man whose heart has just waked up. Poor lad! Poor lad!'

Lucia looked at her cousin, amazed by the energy with which he spoke, the anxiety in his usually listless face. The change became him, for it showed what he might be, making one regret still more what he was. Before she could speak, he was gone again, to return presently, laughing, yet looking a little angry.

'What now?' she asked.

' "Listeners never hear any good of themselves" is the truest of proverbs. I stopped a moment to look at Ned, and heard the following flattering remarks. Mamma is gone, and Ned was asking little Muir to sing that delicious barcarole* she gave us the other evening.

' "Not now, not here," she said.

' "Why not? You sang it in the drawing room readily enough," said Ned, imploringly.

' "That is a very different thing," and she looked at him with a little shake of the head, for he was folding his hands and doing the passionate pathetic.

' "Come and sing it there then," said innocent Bella. "Gerald likes your voice so much, and complains that you will never sing to him."

' "He never asks me," said Muir, with an odd smile.

' "He is too lazy, but he wants to hear you."

' "When he asks me, I will sing – if I feel like it." And she shrugged her shoulders with a provoking gesture of indifference.

' "But it amuses him, and he gets so bored down here," began stupid little Bella. "Don't be shy or proud, Jean, but come and entertain the poor old fellow."

' "No, thank you. I engaged to teach Miss Coventry, not to amuse Mr Coventry" was all the answer she got.

' "You amuse Ned, why not Gerald? Are you afraid of him?" asked Bella.

'Miss Muir laughed, such a scornful laugh, and said, in that peculiar tone of hers, "I cannot fancy anyone being *afraid* of your elder brother."

' "I am, very often, and so would you be, if you ever saw him angry." And Bella looked as if I'd beaten her.

' "Does he ever wake up enough to be angry?" asked that girl, with an air of surprise. Here Ned broke into a fit of laughter, and they are at it now, I fancy, by the sound.'

'Their foolish gossip is not worth getting excited about, but I certainly would send Ned away. It's no use trying to get rid of "that girl," as you say, for my aunt is as deluded about her as Ned and Bella, and she really does get the child along splendidly. Dispatch Ned, and then she can do no harm,' said Lucia, watching Coventry's altered face as he stood in the moonlight, just outside the window where she sat.

'Have you no fears for me?' he asked smiling, as if ashamed of his momentary petulance.

'No, have you for yourself?' And a shade of anxiety passed over her face.

'I defy the Scotch witch to enchant me, except with her music,' he added, moving down the terrace again, for Jean was singing like a nightingale.

As the song ended, he put aside the curtain, and said, abruptly, 'Has anyone any commands for London? I am going there tomorrow.'

'A pleasant trip to you,' said Ned carelessly, though usually his brother's movements interested him extremely.

'I want quantities of things, but I must ask Mamma first.' And Bella began to make a list.

'May I trouble you with a letter, Mr Coventry?'

Jean Muir turned around on the music stool and looked at him with the cold keen glance which always puzzled him.

He bowed, saying, as if to them all, 'I shall be off by the early train, so you must give me your orders tonight.'

'Then come away, Ned, and leave Jean to write her letter.'

And Bella took her reluctant brother from the room.

'I will give you the letter in the morning,' said Miss Muir, with a curious quiver in her voice, and the look of one who forcibly suppressed some strong emotion.

'As you please.' And Coventry went back to Lucia, wondering who Miss Muir was going to write to. He said nothing to his brother of the purpose which took him to town, lest a word should produce the catastrophe which he hoped to prevent; and Ned, who now lived in a sort of dream, seemed to forget Gerald's existence altogether.

With unwonted energy Coventry was astir seven next morning. Lucia gave him his breakfast, and as he left the room to order the carriage, Miss Muir came gliding downstairs, very pale and heavy-eyed (with a sleepless, tearful night, he thought) and, putting a delicate little letter into his hand, said hurriedly, 'Please leave this at Lady Sydney's, and if you see her, say "I have remembered."'

Her peculiar manner and peculiar message struck him. His eye involuntarily glanced at the address of the letter and read young Sydney's name. Then, conscious of his mistake, he thrust it into his pocket with a hasty 'Good morning,' and left Miss Muir standing with one hand pressed on her heart, the other half extended as if to recall the letter.

All the way to London, Coventry found it impossible to forget the almost tragical expression of the girl's face, and it haunted him through the bustle of two busy days. Ned's affair was put in the way of being speedily accomplished, Bella's commissions were executed, his mother's pet delicacies provided for her, and a gift for Lucia, whom the family had given him for his future mate, as he was too lazy to choose for himself.

Jean Muir's letter he had not delivered, for Lady Sydney was in the country and her townhouse closed. Curious to see how she would receive his tidings, he went quietly in on his arrival at home. Everyone had dispersed to dress for dinner except Miss Muir, who was in the garden, the servant said.

'Very well; I have a message for her'; and, turning, the 'young master,' as they called him, went to seek her. In a remote corner he saw her sitting alone, buried in thought. As his step roused her, a look of surprise, followed by one of satisfaction, passed over her face, and, rising, she beckoned to him with an almost eager gesture. Much amazed, he went to her and offered the letter, saying kindly, 'I regret that I could not deliver it. Lady Sydney is in the country, and I did not like to post it without your leave. Did I do right?'

'Quite right, thank you very much – it is better so.' And with an air of relief, she tore the letter to atoms, and scattered them to the wind.

More amazed than ever, the young man was about to leave her when she said, with a mixture of entreaty and command, 'Please stay a moment. I want to speak to you.'

He paused, eyeing her with visible surprise, for a sudden color dyed her cheeks, and her lips trembled. Only for a moment, then she was quite self-possessed again. Motioning him to the seat she had left, she remained standing while she said, in a low, rapid tone full of pain and of decision:

'Mr Coventry, as the head of the house I want to speak to you, rather than to your mother, of a most unhappy affair which has occurred during your absence. My month of probation ends today; your mother wishes me to remain; I, too, wish it sincerely, for I am happy here, but I ought not. Read this, and you will see why.'

She put a hastily written note into his hand and watched him intently while he read it. She saw him flush with anger, bite his lips, and knit his brows, then assume his haughtiest look, as he lifted his eyes and said in his most sarcastic tone, 'Very well for a beginning. The boy has eloquence. Pity that it should be wasted. May I ask if you have replied to this rhapsody?'

'I have.'

'And what follows? He begs you "to fly with him, to share his fortunes, and be the good angel of his life." Of course you consent?'

There was no answer, for, standing erect before him, Miss Muir regarded him with an expression of proud patience, like one who expected reproaches, yet was too generous to resent them. Her manner had its effect. Dropping his bitter tone, Coventry asked briefly, 'Why do you show me this? What can I do?'

'I show it that you may see how much in earnest "the boy" is, and how open I desire to be. You can control, advise, and comfort your brother, and help me to see what is my duty.'

'You love him?' demanded Coventry bluntly.

'No!' was the quick, decided answer.

'Then why make him love you?'

'I never tried to do it. Your sister will testify that I have endeavored to avoid him as I – ' And he finished the sentence with an unconscious tone of pique, 'As you have avoided me.'

She bowed silently, and he went on:

'I will do you the justice to say that nothing can be more blameless than your conduct toward myself; but why allow Ned to haunt you evening after evening? What could you expect of a romantic boy who had nothing to do but lose his heart to the first attractive woman he met?'

A momentary glisten shone in Jean Muir's steel-blue eyes as the last words left the young man's lips; but it was gone instantly, and her voice was full of reproach, as she said, steadily, impulsively, 'If the "romantic boy" had been allowed to lead the life of a man, as he longed to do, he would have had no time to lose his heart to the first sorrowful girl whom he pitied. Mr Coventry, the fault is yours. Do not blame your brother, but generously own your mistake and retrieve it in the speediest, kindest manner.'

For an instant Gerald sat dumb. Never since his father died had anyone reproved him; seldom in his life had he been blamed. It was a new experience, and the very novelty added to the effect. He saw his fault, regretted it, and admired the brave sincerity of the girl in telling him of it. But he did not know how to deal with the case, and was forced to confess not only past negligence but present incapacity. He was as honorable as he was proud, and with an effort he said frankly, 'You are right, Miss Muir. I *am* to blame, yet as soon as I saw the danger, I tried to avert it. My visit to town was on Ned's account; he will have his commission very soon, and then he will be sent out of harm's way. Can I do more?'

'No, it is too late to send him away with a free and happy heart. He must bear his pain as he can, and it may help to make a man of him,' she said sadly.

'He'll soon forget,' began Coventry, who found the thought of gay Ned suffering an uncomfortable one.

'Yes, thank heaven, that is possible, for men.'

Miss Muir pressed her hands together, with a dark expression on her half-averted face. Something in her tone, her manner, touched Coventry; he fancied that some old wound bled, some bitter memory awoke at the approach of a new lover. He was young, heart-whole, and romantic, under all his cool nonchalance of manner. This girl, who he fancied loved his friend and who was beloved by his brother, became an object of interest to him. He pitied her, desired to help her, and regretted his past distrust, as a chivalrous man always regrets injustice to a woman. She was happy here, poor, homeless soul, and she should stay. Bella loved her, his mother took comfort in her, and when Ned was gone, no one's peace would be endangered by her winning ways, her rich accomplishments. These thoughts swept through his mind during a brief pause, and when he spoke, it was to say gently:

'Miss Muir, I thank you for the frankness which must have been painful to you, and I will do my best to be worthy of the confidence which you repose in me. You were both discreet and kind to speak only to me. This thing would have troubled my mother extremely, and have done no good. I shall see Ned, and try and repair my long neglect as promptly as possible. I know you will help me, and in return let me beg of you to remain, for he will soon be gone.'

She looked at him with eyes full of tears, and there was no coolness in the voice that answered softly, 'You are too kind, but I had better go; it is not wise to stay.'

'Why not?'

She colored beautifully, hesitated, then spoke out in the clear, steady voice which was her greatest charm, 'If I had known there were sons in this family, I never should have come. Lady Sydney spoke only of your sister, and when I found two gentlemen, I was troubled, because – I am so unfortunate – or rather, people are so kind as to like me more than I deserve. I thought I could stay a month, at least, as your brother spoke of going away, and you were already affianced, but – '

'I am not affianced.'

Why he said that, Coventry could not tell, but the words passed his lips hastily and could not be recalled. Jean Muir took the announcement oddly enough. She shrugged her shoulders with an air of extreme annoyance, and said almost rudely, 'Then you should be; you will be soon. But that is nothing to me. Miss Beaufort wishes me gone, and I am too proud to remain and become the cause of disunion in a happy family. No, I will go, and go at once.'

She turned away impetuously, but Edward's arm detained her, and Edward's voice demanded, tenderly, 'Where will you go, my Jean?'

The tender touch and name seemed to rob her of her courage and calmness, for, leaning on her lover, she hid her face and sobbed audibly.

'Now don't make a scene, for heaven's sake,' began Coventry impatiently, as his brother eyed him fiercely, divining at once what had passed, for his letter was still in Gerald's hand and Jean's last words had reached her lover's ear.

'Who gave you the right to read that, and to interfere in my affairs?' demanded Edward hotly.

'Miss Muir' was the reply, as Coventry threw away the paper.

'And you add to the insult by ordering her out of the house,' cried Ned with increasing wrath.

'On the contrary, I beg her to remain.'

'The deuce you do! And why?'

'Because she is useful and happy here, and I am unwilling that your folly should rob her of a home which she likes.'

'You are very thoughtful and devoted all at once, but I beg you will not trouble yourself. Jean's happiness and home will be my care now.'

'My dear boy, do be reasonable. The thing is impossible. Miss Muir sees it herself; she came to tell me, to ask how best to arrange matters without troubling my mother. I've been to town to attend to your affairs, and you may be off now very soon.'

'I have no desire to go. Last month it was the wish of my heart. Now I'll accept nothing from you.' And Edward turned moodily away from his brother.

'What folly! Ned, you *must* leave home. It is all arranged and cannot be given up now. A change is what you need, and it will make a man of you. We shall miss you, of course, but you will be where you'll see something of life, and that is better for you than getting into mischief here.'

'Are you going away, Jean?' asked Edward, ignoring his brother entirely and bending over the girl, who still hid her face and wept. She did not speak, and Gerald answered for her.

'No, why should she if you are gone?'

'Do you mean to stay?' asked the lover eagerly of Jean.

'I wish to remain, but – ' She paused and looked up. Her eyes went from one face to the other, and she added decidedly, 'Yes, I must go, it is not wise to stay even when you are gone.'

Neither of the young men could have explained why that hurried glance affected them as it did, but each felt conscious of a willful desire to oppose the other. Edward suddenly felt that his brother loved Miss Muir, and was bent on removing her from his way. Gerald had a vague idea that Miss Muir feared to remain on his account, and he longed to show her that he was quite safe. Each felt angry, and each showed it in a different way, one being violent, the other satirical.

'You are right, Jean, this is not the place for you; and you must let me see you in a safer home before I go,' said Ned, significantly.

'It strikes me that this will be a particularly safe home when your dangerous self is removed,' began Coventry, with an aggravating smile of calm superiority.

'And *I* think that I leave a more dangerous person than myself behind me, as poor Lucia can testify.'

'Be careful what you say, Ned, or I shall be forced to remind you that I am master here. Leave Lucia's name out of this disagreeable affair, if you please.'

'You *are* master here, but not of me, or my actions, and you have no right to expect obedience or respect, for you inspire neither. Jean, I asked you to go with me secretly; now I ask you openly to share my fortune. In my brother's presence I ask, and *will* have an answer.'

He caught her hand impetuously, with a defiant look at Coventry, who still smiled, as if at boy's play, though his eyes were kindling and his face changing with the still, white wrath which is more terrible than any sudden outburst. Miss Muir looked frightened; she shrank away from her passionate young lover, cast an appealing glance at Gerald, and seemed as if she longed to claim his protection yet dared not.

'Speak!' cried Edward, desperately. 'Don't look to him, tell me truly, with your own lips, do you, can you love me, Jean?'

'I have told you once. Why pain me by forcing another hard reply,' she said pitifully, still shrinking from his grasp and seeming to appeal to his brother.

'You wrote a few lines, but I'll not be satisfied with that. You shall answer; I've seen love in your eyes, heard it in your voice, and I know it is hidden in your heart. You fear to own it; do not hesitate, no one can part us – speak, Jean, and satisfy me.'

Drawing her hand decidedly away, she went a step nearer Coventry, and answered, slowly, distinctly, though her lips trembled, and she evidently dreaded the effect of her words, 'I will speak, and speak truly. You have seen love in my face; it is in my heart, and I do not hesitate to own it, cruel as it is to force the truth from me, but this love is not for you. Are you satisfied?'

He looked at her with a despairing glance and stretched his hand toward her beseechingly. She seemed to fear a blow, for suddenly she clung to Gerald with a faint cry. The act, the look of fear, the protecting gesture Coventry involuntarily made were too much for Edward, already excited by conflicting passions. In a paroxysm of blind wrath, he caught up a large pruning knife left there by the gardener, and would have dealt his brother a fatal blow had he not warded it off with his arm. The stroke fell, and another might have followed had not Miss Muir with unexpected courage and strength wrested the knife from Edward and flung it into the little pond near by. Coventry dropped down upon the seat, for the blood poured from a deep wound in his arm, showing by its rapid flow that an artery had been severed. Edward stood aghast, for with the blow his fury passed, leaving him overwhelmed with remorse and shame.

Gerald looked up at him, smiled faintly, and said, with no sign of reproach or anger, 'Never mind, Ned. Forgive and forget. Lend me a hand to the house, and don't disturb anyone. It's not much, I dare say.' But his lips whitened as he spoke, and his strength failed him. Edward sprang to support him, and Miss Muir, forgetting her terrors, proved herself a girl of uncommon skill and courage.

'Quick! Lay him down. Give me your handkerchief, and bring some water,' she said, in a tone of quiet command. Poor Ned obeyed and watched her with breathless suspense while she tied the handkerchief tightly around the arm, thrust the handle of his riding whip underneath, and pressed it firmly above the severed artery to stop the dangerous flow of blood.

'Dr Scott is with your mother, I think. Go and bring him here' was the next order; and Edward darted away, thankful to do anything to ease the terror which possessed him. He was gone some minutes, and while they waited Coventry watched the girl as she knelt beside him, bathing his face with one hand while with the other she held the bandage firmly in its place. She was pale, but quite steady and self-possessed, and her eyes shone with a strange brilliancy as she looked down at him. Once, meeting his look of grateful wonder, she smiled a reassuring smile that made her lovely, and said, in a soft, sweet tone never used to him before, 'Be quiet. There is no danger. I will stay by you till help comes.'

Help did come speedily, and the doctor's first words were 'Who improvised that tourniquet?'

'She did,' murmured Coventry.

'Then you may thank her for saving your life. By Jove! It was capitally done'; and the old doctor looked at the girl with as much admiration as curiosity in his face.

'Never mind that. See to the wound, please, while I run for bandages, and salts, and wine.'

Miss Muir was gone as she spoke, so fleetly that it was in vain to call her back or catch her. During her brief absence, the story was told by repentant Ned and the wound examined.

'Fortunately I have my case of instruments with me,' said the doctor, spreading on the bench a long array of tiny, glittering implements of torture. 'Now, Mr Ned, come here, and hold the arm in that way, while I tie the artery. Hey! That will never do. Don't tremble so, man, look away and hold it steadily.'

'I can't!' And poor Ned turned faint and white, not at the sight but with the bitter thought that he had longed to kill his brother.

'I will hold it,' and a slender white hand lifted the bare and bloody arm so firmly, steadily, that Coventry sighed a sigh of relief, and Dr Scott fell to work with an emphatic nod of approval.

It was soon over, and while Edward ran in to bid the servants beware of alarming their mistress, Dr Scott put up his instruments and Miss Muir used salts, water, and wine so skillfully that Gerald was able to walk to his room, leaning on the old man, while the girl supported the wounded arm, as no sling could be made on the spot. As he entered the chamber, Coventry turned, put out his left hand, and with much feeling in his fine eyes said simply, 'Miss Muir, I thank you.'

The color came up beautifully in her pale cheeks as she pressed the hand and without a word vanished from the room.

Lucia and the housekeeper came bustling in, and there was no
lack of attendance on the invalid. He soon wearied of it, and
sent them all away but Ned, who remorsefully haunted the
chamber, looking like a comely young Cain and feeling like an
outcast.

'Come here, lad, and tell me all about it. I was wrong to be
domineering. Forgive me, and believe that I care for your
happiness more sincerely than for my own.'

These frank and friendly words healed the breach between
the two brothers and completely conquered Ned. Gladly did he
relate his love passages, for no young lover ever tires of that
amusement if he has a sympathizing auditor, and Gerald *was*
sympathetic now. For an hour did he lie listening patiently
to the history of the growth of his brother's passion. Emotion
gave the narrator eloquence, and Jean Muir's character was
painted in glowing colors. All her unsuspected kindness to those
about her was dwelt upon; all her faithful care, her sisterly
interest in Bella, her gentle attentions to their mother, her sweet
forbearance with Lucia, who plainly showed her dislike, and
most of all, her friendly counsel, sympathy, and regard for Ned
himself.

'She would make a man of me. She puts strength and courage
into me as no one else can. She is unlike any girl I ever saw;
there's no sentimentality about her; she is wise, and kind, and
sweet. She says what she means, looks you straight in the eye,
and is as true as steel. I've tried her, I know her, and – ah,
Gerald, I love her so!'

Here the poor lad leaned his face into his hands and sighed a
sigh that made his brother's heart ache.

'Upon my soul, Ned, I feel for you; and if there was no
obstacle on her part, I'd do my best for you. She loves Sydney,
and so there is nothing for it but to bear your fate like a man.'

'Are you sure about Sydney? May it not be some one else?'
and Ned eyed his brother with a suspicious look.

Coventry told him all he knew and surmised concerning his
friend, not forgetting the letter. Edward mused a moment, then
seemed relieved, and said frankly, 'I'm glad it's Sydney and not
you. I can bear it better.'

'Me!' ejaculated Gerald, with a laugh.

'Yes, you; I've been tormented lately with a fear that you
cared for her, or rather, she for you.'

'You jealous young fool! We never see or speak to one another scarcely, so how could we get up a tender interest?'

'What do you lounge about on that terrace for every evening? And why does she get fluttered when your shadow begins to come and go?' demanded Edward.

'I like the music and don't care for the society of the singer, that's why I walk there. The fluttering is all your imagination; Miss Muir isn't a woman to be fluttered by a man's shadow.' And Coventry glanced at his useless arm.

'Thank you for that, and for not saying "little Muir," as you generally do. Perhaps it was my imagination. But she never makes fun of you now, and so I fancied she might have lost her heart to the "young master." Women often do, you know.'

'She used to ridicule me, did she?' asked Coventry, taking no notice of the latter part of his brother's speech, which was quite true nevertheless.

'Not exactly, she was too well bred for that. But sometimes when Bella and I joked about you, she'd say something so odd or witty that it was irresistible. You're used to being laughed at, so you don't mind, I know, just among ourselves.'

'Not I. Laugh away as much as you like,' said Gerald. But he did mind, and wanted exceedingly to know what Miss Muir had said, yet was too proud to ask. He turned restlessly and uttered a sigh of pain.

'I'm talking too much; it's bad for you. Dr Scott said you must be quiet. Now go to sleep, if you can.'

Edward left the bedside but not the room, for he would let no one take his place. Coventry tried to sleep, found it impossible, and after a restless hour called his brother back.

'If the bandage was loosened a bit, it would ease my arm and then I could sleep. Can you do it, Ned?'

'I dare not touch it. The doctor gave orders to leave it till he came in the morning, and I shall only do harm if I try.'

'But I tell you it's too tight. My arm is swelling and the pain is intense. It can't be right to leave it so. Dr Scott dressed it in a hurry and did it too tight. Common sense will tell you that,' said Coventry impatiently.

'I'll call Mrs Morris; she will understand what's best to be done.' And Edward moved toward the door, looking anxious.

'Not she, she'll only make a stir and torment me with her chatter. I'll bear it as long as I can, and perhaps Dr Scott will come tonight. He said he would if possible. Go to your dinner, Ned. I can ring for Neal if I need anything. I shall sleep if I'm alone, perhaps.'

Edward reluctantly obeyed, and his brother was left to himself. Little rest did he find, however, for the pain of the wounded arm grew unbearable, and, taking a sudden resolution, he rang for his servant.

'Neal, go to Miss Coventry's study, and if Miss Muir is there, ask her to be kind enough to come to me. I'm in great pain, and she understands wounds better than anyone else in the house.'

With much surprise in his face, the man departed and a few moments after the door noiselessly opened and Miss Muir came in. It had been a very warm day, and for the first time she had left off her plain black dress. All in white, with no ornament but her fair hair, and a fragrant posy of violets in her belt, she looked a different woman from the meek, nunlike creature one usually saw about the house. Her face was as altered as her dress, for now a soft color glowed in her cheeks, her eyes smiled shyly, and her lips no longer wore the firm look of one who forcibly repressed every emotion. A fresh, gentle, and charming woman she seemed, and Coventry found the dull room suddenly brightened by her presence. Going straight to him, she said simply, and with a happy, helpful look very comforting to see, 'I'm glad you sent for me. What can I do for you?'

He told her, and before the complaint was ended, she began loosening the bandages with the decision of one who understood what was to be done and had faith in herself.

'Ah, that's relief, that's comfort!' ejaculated Coventry, as the last tight fold fell away. 'Ned was afraid I should bleed to death if he touched me. What will the doctor say to us?'

'I neither know nor care. I shall say to him that he is a bad surgeon to bind it so closely, and not leave orders to have it untied if necessary. Now I shall make it easy and put you to sleep, for that is what you need. Shall I? May I?'

'I wish you would, if you can.'

And while she deftly rearranged the bandages, the young man watched her curiously. Presently he asked, 'How came you to know so much about these things?'

'In the hospital where I was ill, I saw much that interested me, and when I got better, I used to sing to the patients sometimes.'

'Do you mean to sing to me?' he asked, in the submissive tone men unconsciously adopt when ill and in a woman's care.

'If you like it better than reading aloud in a dreamy tone,' she answered, as she tied the last knot.

'I do, much better,' he said decidedly.

'You are feverish. I shall wet your forehead, and then you will be quite comfortable.' She moved about the room in the quiet way which made it a pleasure to watch her, and, having mingled a little cologne with water, bathed his face as unconcernedly as if he had been a child. Her proceedings not only comforted but amused Coventry, who mentally contrasted her with the stout, beer-drinking matron who had ruled over him in his last illness.

'A clever, kindly little woman,' he thought, and felt quite at his ease, she was so perfectly easy herself.

'There, now you look more like yourself,' she said with an approving nod as she finished, and smoothed the dark locks off his forehead with a cool, soft hand. Then seating herself in a large chair near by, she began to sing, while tidily rolling up the fresh bandages which had been left for the morning. Coventry lay watching her by the dim light that burned in the room, and she sang on as easily as a bird, a dreamy, low-toned lullaby, which soothed the listener like a spell. Presently, looking up to see the effect of her song, she found the young man wide awake, and regarding her with a curious mixture of pleasure, interest, and admiration.

'Shut your eyes, Mr Coventry,' she said, with a reproving shake of the head, and an odd little smile.

He laughed and obeyed, but could not resist an occasional covert glance from under his lashes at the slender white figure in the great velvet chair. She saw him and frowned.

'You are very disobedient; why won't you sleep?'

'I can't, I want to listen. I'm fond of nightingales.'

'Then I shall sing no more, but try something that has never failed yet. Give me your hand, please.'

Much amazed, he gave it, and, taking it in both her small ones, she sat down behind the curtain and remained as mute and motionless as a statue. Coventry smiled to himself at first, and wondered which would tire first. But soon a subtle warmth seemed to steal from the soft palms that enclosed his own, his heart beat quicker, his breath grew unequal, and a thousand fancies danced through his brain. He sighed, and said dreamily, as he turned his face toward her, 'I like this.' And in the act of speaking, seemed to sink into a soft cloud which encompassed him about with an atmosphere of perfect repose. More than this he could not remember, for sleep, deep and dreamless, fell upon him, and when he woke, daylight was shining in between the curtains, his hand lay alone on the coverlet, and his fair-haired enchantress was gone.

4 A Discovery

For several days Coventry was confined to his room, much against his will, though everyone did their best to lighten his irksome captivity. His mother petted him, Bella sang, Lucia read, Edward was devoted, and all the household, with one exception, were eager to serve the young master. Jean Muir never came near him, and Jean Muir alone seemed to possess the power of amusing him. He soon tired of the others, wanted something new; recalled the piquant character of the girl and took a fancy into his head that she would lighten his ennui. After some hesitation, he carelessly spoke of her to Bella, but nothing came of it, for Bella only said Jean was well, and very busy doing something lovely to surprise Mamma with. Edward complained that he never saw her, and Lucia ignored her existence altogether. The only intelligence the invalid received was from the gossip of two housemaids over their work in the next room. From them he learned that the governess had been 'scolded' by Miss Beaufort for going to Mr Coventry's room; that she had taken it very sweetly and kept herself carefully out of the way of both young gentlemen, though it was plain to see that Mr Ned was dying for her.

Mr Gerald amused himself by thinking over this gossip, and quite annoyed his sister by his absence of mind.

'Gerald, do you know Ned's commission has come?'

'Very interesting. Read on, Bella.'

'You stupid boy! You don't know a word I say,' and she put down the book to repeat her news.

'I'm glad of it; now we must get him off as soon as possible –

that is, I suppose he will want to be off as soon as possible.'
And Coventry woke up from his reverie.

'You needn't check yourself, I know all about it. I think Ned
was very foolish, and that Miss Muir has behaved beautifully.
It's quite impossible, of course, but I wish it wasn't, I do so like
to watch lovers. You and Lucia are so cold you are not a bit
interesting.'

'You'll do me a favor if you'll stop all that nonsense about
Lucia and me. We are not lovers, and never shall be, I fancy. At
all events, I'm tired of the thing, and wish you and Mamma
would let it drop, for the present at least.'

'Oh Gerald, you know Mamma has set her heart upon it, that
Papa desired it, and poor Lucia loves you so much. How can
you speak of dropping what will make us all so happy?'

'It won't make me happy, and I take the liberty of thinking
that this is of some importance. I'm not bound in any way, and
don't intend to be till I am ready. Now we'll talk about Ned.'

Much grieved and surprised, Bella obeyed, and devoted herself
to Edward, who very wisely submitted to his fate and prepared
to leave home for some months. For a week the house was in a
state of excitement about his departure, and everyone but Jean
was busied for him. She was scarcely seen; every morning she
gave Bella her lessons, every afternoon drove out with Mrs
Coventry, and nearly every evening went up to the Hall to read
to Sir John, who found his wish granted without exactly
knowing how it had been done.

The day Edward left, he came down from bidding his mother
goodbye, looking very pale, for he had lingered in his sister's
little room with Miss Muir as long as he dared.

'Goodbye, dear. Be kind to Jean,' he whispered as he kissed
his sister.

'I will, I will,' returned Bella, with tearful eyes.

'Take care of Mamma, and remember Lucia,' he said again,
as he touched his cousin's beautiful cheek.

'Fear nothing. I will keep them apart,' she whispered back,
and Coventry heard it.

Edward offered his hand to his brother, saying, significantly,
as he looked him in the eye, 'I trust you, Gerald.'

'You may, Ned.'

Then he went, and Coventry tired himself with wondering
what Lucia meant. A few days later he understood.

Now Ned is gone, little Muir will appear, I fancy, he said to himself; but 'little Muir' did not appear, and seemed to shun him more carefully than she had done her lover. If he went to the drawing room in the evening hoping for music, Lucia alone was there. If he tapped at Bella's door, there was always a pause before she opened it, and no sign of Jean appeared though her voice had been audible when he knocked. If he went to the library, a hasty rustle and the sound of flying feet betrayed that the room was deserted at his approach. In the garden Miss Muir never failed to avoid him, and if by chance they met in hall or breakfast room, she passed him with downcast eyes and the briefest, coldest greeting. All this annoyed him intensely, and the more she eluded him, the more he desired to see her – from a spirit of opposition, he said, nothing more. It fretted and yet it entertained him, and he found a lazy sort of pleasure in thwarting the girl's little maneuvers. His patience gave out at last, and he resolved to know what was the meaning of this peculiar conduct. Having locked and taken away the key of one door in the library, he waited till Miss Muir went in to get a book for his uncle. He had heard her speak to Bella of it, knew that she believed him with his mother, and smiled to himself as he stole after her. She was standing in a chair, reaching up, and he had time to see a slender waist, a pretty foot, before he spoke.

'Can I help you, Miss Muir?'

She started, dropped several books, and turned scarlet, as she said hurriedly, 'Thank you, no; I can get the steps.'

'My long arm will be less trouble. I've got but one, and that is tired of being idle, so it is very much at your service. What will you have?'

'I – I – you startled me so I've forgotten.' And Jean laughed, nervously, as she looked about her as if planning to escape.

'I beg your pardon, wait till you remember, and let me thank you for the enchanted sleep you gave me ten days ago. I've had no chance yet, you've shunned me so pertinaciously.'

'Indeed I try not to be rude, but – ' She checked herself, and turned her face away, adding, with an accent of pain in her voice, 'It is not my fault, Mr Coventry. I only obey orders.'

'Whose orders?' he demanded, still standing so that she could not escape.

'Don't ask; it is one who has a right to command where you are concerned. Be sure that it is kindly meant, though it may seem folly to us. Nay, don't be angry, laugh at it, as I do, and let me run away, please.'

She turned, and looked down at him with tears in her eyes, a smile on her lips, and an expression half sad, half arch, which was altogether charming. The frown passed from his face, but he still looked grave and said decidedly, 'No one has a right to command in this house but my mother or myself. Was it she who bade you avoid me as if I was a madman or a pest?'

'Ah, don't ask. I promised not to tell, and you would not have me break my word, I know.' And still smiling, she regarded him with a look of merry malice which made any other reply unnecessary. It was Lucia, he thought, and disliked his cousin intensely just then. Miss Muir moved as if to step down; he detained her, saying earnestly, yet with a smile, 'Do you consider me the master here?'

'Yes,' and to the word she gave a sweet, submissive intonation which made it expressive of the respect, regard, and confidence which men find pleasantest when women feel and show it. Unconsciously his face softened, and he looked up at her with a different glance from any he had ever given her before.

'Well, then, will you consent to obey me if I am not tyrannical or unreasonable in my demands?'

'I'll try.'

'Good! Now frankly, I want to say that all this sort of thing is very disagreeable to me. It annoys me to be a restraint upon anyone's liberty or comfort, and I beg you will go and come as freely as you like, and not mind Lucia's absurdities. She means well, but hasn't a particle of penetration or tact. Will you promise this?'

'No.'

'Why not?'

'It is better as it is, perhaps.'

'But you called it folly just now.'

'Yes, it seems so, and yet – ' She paused, looking both confused and distressed.

Coventry lost patience, and said hastily, 'You women are such enigmas I never expect to understand you! Well, I've done my best to make you comfortable, but if you prefer to lead this sort of life, I beg you will do so.'

'I *don't* prefer it; it is hateful to me. I like to be myself, to have my liberty, and the confidence of those about me. But I

cannot think it kind to disturb the peace of anyone, and so I try
to obey. I've promised Bella to remain, but I will go rather than
have another scene with Miss Beaufort or with you.'

Miss Muir had burst out impetuously, and stood there with a
sudden fire in her eyes, sudden warmth and spirit in her face
and voice that amazed Coventry. She was angry, hurt, and
haughty, and the change only made her more attractive, for not
a trace of her former meek self remained. Coventry was electri-
fied, and still more surprised when she added, imperiously, with
a gesture as if to put him aside, 'Hand me that book and move
away. I wish to go.'

He obeyed, even offered his hand, but she refused it, stepped
lightly down, and went to the door. There she turned, and with
the same indignant voice, the same kindling eyes and glowing
cheeks, she said rapidly, 'I know I have no right to speak in this
way. I restrain myself as long as I can, but when I can bear no
more, my true self breaks loose, and I defy everything. I am tired
of being a cold, calm machine; it is impossible with an ardent
nature like mine, and I shall try no longer. I cannot help it if
people love me. I don't want their love. I only ask to be left in
peace, and why I am tormented so I cannot see. I've neither
beauty, money, nor rank, yet every foolish boy mistakes my
frank interest for something warmer, and makes me miserable.
It is my misfortune. Think of me what you will, but beware of
me in time, for against my will I may do you harm.'

Almost fiercely she had spoken, and with a warning gesture
she hurried from the room, leaving the young man feeling as if
a sudden thunder-gust had swept through the house. For several
minutes he sat in the chair she left, thinking deeply. Suddenly he
rose, went to his sister, and said, in his usual tone of indolent
good nature, 'Bella, didn't I hear Ned ask you to be kind to
Miss Muir?'

'Yes, and I try to be, but she is so odd lately.'

'Odd! How do you mean?'

'Why, she is either as calm and cold as a statue, or restless
and queer; she cries at night, I know, and sighs sadly when she
thinks I don't hear. Something is the matter.'

'She frets for Ned perhaps,' began Coventry.

'Oh dear, no; it's a great relief to her that he is gone. I'm
afraid that she likes someone very much, and someone don't
like her. Can it be Mr Sydney?'

'She called him a "titled fool" once, but perhaps that didn't mean anything. Did you ever ask her about him?' said Coventry, feeling rather ashamed of his curiosity, yet unable to resist the temptation of questioning unsuspecting Bella.

'Yes, but she only looked at me in her tragical way, and said, so pitifully, "My little friend, I hope you will never have to pass through the scenes I've passed through, but keep your peace unbroken all your life." After that I dared say no more. I'm very fond of her, I want to make her happy, but I don't know how. Can you propose anything?'

'I was going to propose that you make her come among us more, now Ned is gone. It must be dull for her, moping about alone. I'm sure it is for me. She is an entertaining little person, and I enjoy her music very much. It's good for Mamma to have gay evenings; so you bestir yourself, and see what you can do for the general good of the family.'

'That's all very charming, and I've proposed it more than once, but Lucia spoils all my plans. She is afraid you'll follow Ned's example, and that is so silly.'

'Lucia is a – no, I won't say fool, because she has sense enough when she chooses; but I wish you'd just settle things with Mamma, and then Lucia can do nothing but submit,' said Gerald angrily.

'I'll try, but she goes up to read to Uncle, you know, and since he has had the gout, she stays later, so I see little of her in the evening. There she goes now. I think she will captivate the old one as well as the young one, she is so devoted.'

Coventry looked after her slender black figure, just vanishing through the great gate, and an uncomfortable fancy took possession of him, born of Bella's careless words. He sauntered away, and after eluding his cousin, who seemed looking for him, he turned toward the Hall, saying to himself, I will see what is going on up here. Such things have happened. Uncle is the simplest soul alive, and if the girl is ambitious, she can do what she will with him.

Here a servant came running after him and gave him a letter, which he thrust into his pocket without examining it. When he reached the Hall, he went quietly to his uncle's study. The door was ajar, and looking in, he saw a scene of tranquil comfort, very pleasant to watch. Sir John leaned in his easy chair with one foot on a cushion. He was dressed with his usual care and, in spite of the gout, looked like a handsome, well-preserved old gentleman. He was smiling as he listened, and his eyes rested complacently on Jean Muir, who sat near him reading in her musical voice, while the sunshine glittered on her hair and the soft rose of her cheek. She read well, yet Coventry thought her heart was not in her task, for once when she paused, while Sir John spoke, her eyes had an absent expression, and she leaned her head upon her hand, with an air of patient weariness.

Poor girl! I did her great injustice; she has no thought of captivating the old man, but amuses him from simple kindness. She is tired. I'll put an end to her task; and Coventry entered without knocking.

Sir John received him with an air of polite resignation, Miss Muir with a perfectly expressionless face.

'Mother's love, and how are you today, sir?'

'Comfortable, but dull, so I want you to bring the girls over this evening, to amuse the old gentleman. Mrs King has got out the antique costumes and trumpery, as I promised Bella she should have them, and tonight we are to have a merrymaking, as we used to do when Ned was here.'

'Very well, sir, I'll bring them. We've all been out of sorts since the lad left, and a little jollity will do us good. Are you going back, Miss Muir?' asked Coventry.

'No, I shall keep her to give me my tea and get things ready. Don't read anymore, my dear, but go and amuse yourself with the pictures, or whatever you like,' said Sir John; and like a dutiful daughter she obeyed, as if glad to get away.

'That's a very charming girl, Gerald,' began Sir John as she left the room. 'I'm much interested in her, both on her own account and on her mother's.'

'Her mother's! What do you know of her mother?' asked Coventry, much surprised.

'Her mother was Lady Grace Howard, who ran away with a poor Scotch minister twenty years ago. The family cast her off, and she lived and died so obscurely that very little is known of her except that she left an orphan girl at some small French pension. This is the girl, and a fine girl, too. I'm surprised that you did not know this.'

'So am I, but it is like her not to tell. She is a strange, proud creature. Lady Howard's daughter! Upon my word, that is a discovery,' and Coventry felt his interest in his sister's governess much increased by this fact; for, like all wellborn Englishmen, he valued rank and gentle blood even more than he cared to own.

'She has had a hard life of it, this poor little girl, but she has a brave spirit, and will make her way anywhere,' said Sir John admiringly.

'Did Ned know this?' asked Gerald suddenly.

'No, she only told me yesterday. I was looking in the *Peerage** and chanced to speak of the Howards. She forgot herself and called Lady Grace her mother. Then I got the whole story, for the lonely little thing was glad to make a confidant of someone.'

'That accounts for her rejection of Sydney and Ned: she knows she is their equal and will not snatch at the rank which is hers by right. No, she's not mercenary or ambitious.'

'What do you say?' asked Sir John, for Coventry had spoken more to himself than to his uncle.

'I wonder if Lady Sydney was aware of this?' was all Gerald's answer.

'No, Jean said she did not wish to be pitied, and so told nothing to the mother. I think the son knew, but that was a delicate point, and I asked no questions.'

'I shall write to him as soon as I discover his address. We have been so intimate I can venture to make a few inquiries about Miss Muir, and prove the truth of her story.'

'Do you mean to say that you doubt it?' demanded Sir John angrily.

'I beg your pardon, Uncle, but I must confess I have an instinctive distrust of that young person. It is unjust, I dare say, yet I cannot banish it.'

'Don't annoy me by expressing it, if you please. I have some penetration and experience, and I respect and pity Miss Muir heartily. This dislike of yours may be the cause of her late melancholy, hey, Gerald?' And Sir John looked suspiciously at his nephew.

Anxious to avert the rising storm, Coventry said hastily as he turned away, 'I've neither time nor inclination to discuss the matter now, sir, but will be careful not to offend again. I'll take your message to Bella, so goodbye for an hour, Uncle.'

And Coventry went his way through the park, thinking within himself, The dear old gentleman is getting fascinated, like poor Ned. How the deuce does the girl do it? Lady Howard's daughter, yet never told us; I don't understand that.

5 How The Girl Did It

At home he found a party of young friends, who hailed with delight the prospect of a revel at the Hall. An hour later, the blithe company trooped into the great saloon, where preparations had already been made for a dramatic evening.

Good Sir John was in his element, for he was never so happy as when his house was full of young people. Several persons were chosen, and in a few moments the curtains were withdrawn from the first of these impromptu tableaux. A swarthy, darkly bearded man lay asleep on a tiger skin, in the shadow of a tent. Oriental arms and drapery surrounded him; an antique silver lamp burned dimly on a table where fruit lay heaped in costly dishes, and wine shone redly in half-emptied goblets. Bending over the sleeper was a woman robed with barbaric splendor. One hand turned back the embroidered sleeve from the arm which held a scimitar; one slender foot in a scarlet sandal was visible under the white tunic; her purple mantle swept down from snowy shoulders; fillets of gold bound her hair, and jewels shone on neck and arms. She was looking over her shoulder toward the entrance of the tent, with a steady yet stealthy look, so effective that for a moment the spectators held their breath, as if they also heard a passing footstep.

'Who is it?' whispered Lucia, for the face was new to her.

'Jean Muir,' answered Coventry, with an absorbed look.

'Impossible! She is small and fair,' began Lucia, but a hasty 'Hush, let me look!' from her cousin silenced her.

Impossible as it seemed, he was right nevertheless; for Jean Muir it was. She had darkened her skin, painted her eyebrows, disposed some wild black locks over her fair hair, and thrown such an intensity of expression into her eyes that they darkened and dilated till they were as fierce as any southern eyes that ever flashed. Hatred, the deepest and bitterest, was written on her sternly beautiful face, courage glowed in her glance, power spoke in the nervous grip of the slender hand that held the weapon, and the indomitable will of the woman was expressed – even the firm pressure of the little foot half hidden in the tiger skin.

'Oh, isn't she splendid?' cried Bella under her breath.

'She looks as if she'd use her sword well when the time comes,' said someone admiringly.

'Good night to Holofernes; his fate is certain,' added another.

'He is the image of Sydney, with that beard on.'

'Doesn't she look as if she really hated him?'

'Perhaps she does.'

Coventry uttered the last exclamation, for the two which preceded it suggested an explanation of the marvelous change in Jean. It was not all art: the intense detestation mingled with a savage joy that the object of her hatred was in her power was too perfect to be feigned; and having the key to a part of her story, Coventry felt as if he caught a glimpse of the truth. It was but a glimpse, however, for the curtain dropped before he had half analyzed the significance of that strange face.

'Horrible! I'm glad it's over,' said Lucia coldly.

'Magnificent! Encore! Encore!' cried Gerald enthusiastically.

But the scene was over, and no applause could recall the actress. Two or three graceful or gay pictures followed, but Jean was in none, and each lacked the charm which real talent lends to the simplest part.

'Coventry, you are wanted,' called a voice. And to everyone's surprise, Coventry went, though heretofore he had always refused to exert himself when handsome actors were in demand.

'What part am I to spoil?' he asked, as he entered the green room, where several excited young gentlemen were costuming and attitudinizing.

'A fugitive cavalier. Put yourself into this suit, and lose no time asking questions. Miss Muir will tell you what to do. She is in the tableau, so no one will mind you,' said the manager pro tem, throwing a rich old suit toward Coventry and resuming the painting of a moustache on his own boyish face.

A gallant cavalier was the result of Gerald's hasty toilet, and when he appeared before the ladies a general glance of admiration was bestowed upon him.

'Come along and be placed; Jean is ready on the stage.' And Bella ran before him, exclaiming to her governess, 'Here he is, quite splendid. Wasn't he good to do it?'

Miss Muir, in the charming prim and puritanical dress of a Roundhead damsel,* was arranging some shrubs, but turned suddenly and dropped the green branch she held, as her eye met the glittering figure advancing toward her.

'You!' she said with a troubled look, adding low to Bella, 'Why did you ask *him*? I begged you not.'

'He is the only handsome man here, and the best actor if he likes. He won't play usually, so make the most of him.' And Bella was off to finish powdering her hair for 'The Marriage à la Mode.'

'I was sent for and I came. Do you prefer some other person?' asked Coventry, at a loss to understand the half-anxious, half-eager expression of the face under the little cap.

It changed to one of mingled annoyance and resignation as she said, 'It is too late. Please kneel here, half behind the shrubs; put down your hat, and – allow me – you are too elegant for a fugitive.'

As he knelt before her, she disheveled his hair, pulled his lace collar awry, threw away his gloves and sword, and half untied the cloak that hung about his shoulders.

'That is better; your paleness is excellent – nay, don't spoil it. We are to represent the picture which hangs in the Hall. I need tell you no more. Now, Roundheads, place yourselves, and then ring up the curtain.'

With a smile, Coventry obeyed her; for the picture was of two lovers, the young cavalier kneeling, with his arm around the waist of the girl, who tries to hide him with her little mantle, and presses his head to her bosom in an ecstasy of fear, as she glances back at the approaching pursuers. Jean hesitated an instant and shrank a little as his hand touched her; she blushed deeply, and her eyes fell before his. Then, as the bell rang, she threw herself into her part with sudden spirit. One arm half covered him with her cloak, the other pillowed his head on the muslin kerchief folded over her bosom, and she looked backward with such terror in her eyes that more than one chivalrous young spectator longed to hurry to the rescue. It lasted but a moment; yet in that moment Coventry experienced another new sensation. Many women had smiled on him, but he had remained heart-whole, cool, and careless, quite unconscious of the power which a woman possesses and knows how to use, for the weal or woe of man. Now, as he knelt there with a soft arm about him, a slender waist yielding to his touch, and a maiden heart throbbing against his cheek, for the first time in his life he felt the indescribable spell of womanhood, and looked the ardent lover to perfection. Just as his face assumed this new and most becoming aspect, the curtain dropped, and clamorous encores recalled him to the fact that Miss Muir was trying to escape from his hold, which had grown painful in its unconscious pressure. He sprang up, half bewildered, and looking as he had never looked before.

'Again! Again!' called Sir John. And the young men who played the Roundheads, eager to share in the applause begged for a repetition in new attitudes.

'A rustle has betrayed you, we have fired and shot the brave girl, and she lies dying, you know. That will be effective; try it, Miss Muir,' said one. And with a long breath, Jean complied.

The curtain went up, showing the lover still on his knees, unmindful of the captors who clutched him by the shoulder, for at his feet the girl lay dying. Her head was on his breast, now, her eyes looked full into his, no longer wild with fear, but eloquent with the love which even death could not conquer. The power of those tender eyes thrilled Coventry with a strange delight, and set his heart beating as rapidly as hers had done. She felt his hands tremble, saw the color flash into his cheek, knew that she had touched him at last, and when she rose it was with a sense of triumph which she found it hard to conceal. Others thought it fine acting; Coventry tried to believe so; but Lucia set her teeth, and, as the curtain fell on that second picture, she left her place to hurry behind the scenes, bent on putting an end to such dangerous play. Several actors were complimenting the mimic lovers. Jean took it merrily, but Coventry, in spite of himself, betrayed that he was excited by something deeper than mere gratified vanity.

As Lucia appeared, his manner changed to its usual indifference; but he could not quench the unwonted fire of his eyes, or keep all trace of emotion out of his face, and she saw this with a sharp pang.

'I have come to offer my help. You must be tired, Miss Muir. Can I relieve you?' said Lucia hastily.

'Yes, thank you. I shall be very glad to leave the rest to you, and enjoy them from the front.'

So with a sweet smile Jean tripped away, and to Lucia's dismay Coventry followed.

'I want you, Gerald; please stay,' she cried.

'I've done my part – no more tragedy for me tonight.' And he was gone before she could entreat or command.

There was no help for it; she must stay and do her duty, or expose her jealousy to the quick eyes about her. For a time she bore it; but the sight of her cousin leaning over the chair she had left and chatting with the governess, who now filled it, grew unbearable, and she dispatched a little girl with a message to Miss Muir.

'Please, Miss Beaufort wants you for Queen Bess,* as you are the only lady with red hair. Will you come?' whispered the child, quite unconscious of any hidden sting in her words.

'Yes, dear, willingly though I'm not stately enough for Her Majesty, nor handsome enough,' said Jean, rising with an untroubled face, though she resented the feminine insult.

'Do you want an Essex?* I'm all dressed for it,' said Coventry, following to the door with a wistful look.

'No, Miss Beaufort said *you* were not to come. She doesn't want you both together,' said the child decidedly.

Jean gave him a significant look, shrugged her shoulders, and went away smiling her odd smile, while Coventry paced up and down the hall in a curious state of unrest, which made him forgetful of everything till the young people came gaily out to supper.

'Come, bonny Prince Charlie,* take me down, and play the lover as charmingly as you did an hour ago. I never thought you had so much warmth in you,' said Bella, taking his arm and drawing him on against his will.

'Don't be foolish, child. Where is – Lucia?'

Why he checked Jean's name on his lips and substituted another's, he could not tell; but a sudden shyness in speaking of her possessed him, and though he saw her nowhere, he would not ask for her. His cousin came down looking lovely in a classical costume; but Gerald scarcely saw her, and, when the merriment was at its height, he slipped away to discover what had become of Miss Muir.

Alone in the deserted drawing room he found her, and paused to watch her a moment before he spoke; for something in her attitude and face struck him. She was leaning wearily back in the great chair which had served for a throne. Her royal robes were still unchanged, though the crown was off and all her fair hair hung about her shoulders. Excitement and exertion made her brilliant, the rich dress became her wonderfully, and an air of luxurious indolence changed the meek governess into a charming woman. She leaned on the velvet cushions as if she were used to such support; she played with the jewels which had crowned her as carelessly as if she were born to wear them; her attitude was full of negligent grace, and the expression of her face half proud, half pensive, as if her thoughts were bitter-sweet.

One would know she was wellborn to see her now. Poor girl, what a burden a life of dependence must be to a spirit like hers! I wonder what she is thinking of so intently. And Coventry indulged in another look before he spoke.

'Shall I bring you some supper, Miss Muir?'

'Supper!' she ejaculated, with a start. 'Who thinks of one's body when one's soul is – ' She stopped there, knit her brows, and laughed faintly as she added, 'No, thank you. I want nothing but advice, and that I dare not ask of anyone.'

'Why not?'

'Because I have no right.'

'Everyone has a right to ask help, especially the weak of the strong. Can I help you? Believe me, I most heartily offer my poor services.'

'Ah, you forget! This dress, the borrowed splendor of these jewels, the freedom of this gay evening, the romance of the part you played, all blind you to the reality. For a moment I cease to be a servant, and for a moment you treat me as an equal.'

It was true; he *had* forgotten. That soft, reproachful glance touched him, his distrust melted under the new charm, and he answered with real feeling in voice and face, 'I treat you as an equal because you *are* one; and when I offer help, it is not to my sister's governess alone, but to Lady Howard's daughter.'

'Who told you that?' she demanded, sitting erect.

'My uncle. Do not reproach him. It shall go no further, if you forbid it. Are you sorry that I know it?'

'Yes.'

'Why?'

'Because I will not be pitied!' And her eyes flashed as she made a half-defiant gesture.

'Then, if I may not pity the hard fate which has befallen an innocent life, may I admire the courage which meets adverse fortune so bravely, and conquers the world by winning the respect and regard of all who see and honor it?'

Miss Muir averted her face, put up her hand, and answered hastily, 'No, no, not that! Do not be kind; it destroys the only barrier now left between us. Be cold to me as before, forget what I am, and let me go on my way, unknown, unpitied, and unloved!'

Her voice faltered and failed as the last word was uttered, and she bent her face upon her hand. Something jarred upon Coventry in this speech, and moved him to say, almost rudely, 'You need have no fears for me. Lucia will tell you what an iceberg I am.'

'Then Lucia would tell me wrong. I have the fatal power of reading character; I know you better than she does, and I see – ' There she stopped abruptly.

'What? Tell me and prove your skill,' he said eagerly.

Turning, she fixed her eyes on him with a penetrating power that made him shrink as she said slowly, 'Under the ice I see fire, and warn you to beware lest it prove a volcano.'

For a moment he sat dumb, wondering at the insight of the girl; for she was the first to discover the hidden warmth of a nature too proud to confess its tender impulses, or the ambitions that slept till some potent voice awoke them. The blunt, almost stern manner in which she warned him away from her only made her more attractive; for there was no conceit or arrogance in it, only a foreboding fear emboldened by past suffering to be frank. Suddenly he spoke impetuously:

'You are right! I am not what I seem, and my indolent indifference is but the mask under which I conceal my real self. I could be as passionate, as energetic and aspiring as Ned, if I had any aim in life. I have none, and so I am what you once called me, a thing to pity and despise.'

'I never said that!' cried Jean indignantly.

'Not in those words, perhaps; but you looked it and thought it, though you phrased it more mildly. I deserved it, but I shall deserve it no longer. I am beginning to wake from my disgraceful idleness, and long for some work that shall make a man of me. Why do you go? I annoy you with my confessions. Pardon me. They are the first I ever made; they shall be the last.'

'No, oh no! I am too much honored by your confidence; but

is it wise, is it loyal to tell *me* your hopes and aims? Has not Miss Beaufort the first right to be your confidante?'

Coventry drew back, looking intensely annoyed, for the name recalled much that he would gladly have forgotten in the novel excitement of the hour. Lucia's love, Edward's parting words, his own reserve so strangely thrown aside, so difficult to resume. What he would have said was checked by the sight of a half-open letter which fell from Jean's dress as she moved away. Mechanically he took it up to return it, and, as he did so, he recognized Sydney's handwriting. Jean snatched it from him, turning pale to the lips as she cried, 'Did you read it? What did you see? Tell me, tell me, on your honor!'

'On my honor, I saw nothing but this single sentence, "By the love I bear you, believe what I say." No more, as I am a gentleman. I know the hand, I guess the purport of the letter, and as a friend of Sydney, I earnestly desire to help you, if I can. Is this the matter upon which you want advice?'

'Yes.'

'Then let me give it?'

'You cannot, without knowing all, and it is so hard to tell!'

'Let me guess it, and spare you the pain of telling. May I?' And Coventry waited eagerly for her reply, for the spell was still upon him.

Holding the letter fast, she beckoned him to follow, and glided before him to a secluded little nook, half boudoir, half conservatory. There she paused, stood an instant as if in doubt, then looked up at him with confiding eyes and said decidedly, 'I will do it; for, strange as it may seem, you are the only person to whom I *can* speak. You know Sydney, you have discovered that I am an equal, you have offered your help. I accept it; but oh, do not think me unwomanly! Remember how alone I am, how young, and how much I rely upon your sincerity, your sympathy!'

'Speak freely. I am indeed your friend.' And Coventry sat down beside her, forgetful of everything but the soft-eyed girl who confided in him so entirely.

Speaking rapidly, Jean went on, 'You know that Sydney loved me, that I refused him and went away. But you do not know that his importunities nearly drove me wild, that he threatened to rob me of my only treasure, my good name, and that, in desperation, I tried to kill myself. Yes, mad, wicked as it was, I did long to end the life which was, at best, a burden, and under his persecution had become a torment. You are shocked, yet what I say is the living truth. Lady Sydney will confirm it, the nurses at the hospital will confess that it was not a fever which brought me there; and here, though the external wound is healed, my heart still aches and burns with the shame and indignation which only a proud woman can feel.'

She paused and sat with kindling eyes, glowing cheeks, and both hands pressed to her heaving bosom, as if the old insult roused her spirit anew. Coventry said not a word, for surprise, anger, incredulity, and admiration mingled so confusedly in his mind that he forgot to speak, and Jean went on, 'That wild act of mine convinced him of my indomitable dislike. He went away, and I believed that this stormy love of his would be cured by absence. It is not, and I live in daily fear of fresh entreaties, renewed persecution. His mother promised not to betray where I had gone, but he found me out and wrote to me. The letter I asked you to take to Lady Sydney was a reply to his, imploring him to leave me in peace. You failed to deliver it, and I was glad, for I thought silence might quench hope. All in vain; this is a more passionate appeal than ever, and he vows he will never desist from his endeavors till I give another man the right to protect me. I *can* do this – I am sorely tempted to do it, but I rebel against the cruelty. I love my freedom, I have no wish to marry at this man's bidding. What can I do? How can I free myself? Be my friend, and help me!'

Tears streamed down her cheeks, sobs choked her words, and she clasped her hands imploringly as she turned toward the young man in all the abandonment of sorrow, fear, and supplication. Coventry found it hard to meet those eloquent eyes and answer calmly, for he had no experience in such scenes and knew not how to play his part. It is this absurd dress and that romantic nonsense which makes me feel so unlike myself, he thought, quite unconscious of the dangerous power which the dusky room, the midsummer warmth and fragrance, the memory of the 'romantic nonsense,' and, most of all, the presence of a beautiful, afflicted woman had over him. His usual self-possession deserted him, and he could only echo the words which had made the strongest impression upon him:

'You *can* do this, you are tempted to do it. Is Ned the man who can protect you?'

'No' was the soft reply.

'Who then?'

'Do not ask me. A good and honorable man; one who loves me well, and would devote his life to me; one whom once it would have been happiness to marry, but now – '

There her voice ended in a sigh, and all her fair hair fell down about her face, hiding it in a shining veil.

'Why not now? This is a sure and speedy way of ending your distress. Is it impossible?'

In spite of himself, Gerald leaned nearer, took one of the little hands in his, and pressed it as he spoke, urgently, compassionately, nay, almost tenderly. From behind the veil came a heavy sigh, and the brief answer, 'It is impossible.'

'Why, Jean?'

She flung her hair back with a sudden gesture, drew away her hand, and answered, almost fiercely, 'Because I do not love him! Why do you torment me with such questions? I tell you I am in a sore strait and cannot see my way. Shall I deceive the good man, and secure peace at the price of liberty and truth? Or shall I defy Sydney and lead a life of dread? If he menaced my life, I should not fear; but he menaces that which is dearer than life – my good name. A look, a word can tarnish it; a scornful smile, a significant shrug can do me more harm than any blow; for I am a woman – friendless, poor, and at the mercy of his tongue. Ah, better to have died, and so have been saved the bitter pain that has come now!'

She sprang up, clasped her hands over her head, and paced despairingly through the little room, not weeping, but wearing an expression more tragical than tears. Still feeling as if he had suddenly stepped into a romance, yet finding a keen pleasure in the part assigned him, Coventry threw himself into it with spirit, and heartily did his best to console the poor girl who needed help so much. Going to her, he said as impetuously as Ned ever did, 'Miss Muir – nay, I will say Jean, if that will comfort you – listen, and rest assured that no harm shall touch you if I can ward it off. You are needlessly alarmed. Indignant you may well be, but, upon my life, I think you wrong Sydney. He is violent, I know, but he is too honorable a man to injure you by a light word, an unjust act. He did but threaten, hoping to soften you. Let me see him, or write to him. He is my friend; he will listen to me. Of that I am sure.'

'Be sure of nothing. When a man like Sydney loves and is thwarted in his love, nothing can control his headstrong will. Promise me you will not see or write to him. Much as I fear and despise him, I will submit, rather than any harm should befall you – or your brother. You promise me, Mr Coventry?'

He hesitated. She clung to his arm with unfeigned solicitude in her eager, pleading face, and he could not resist it.

'I promise; but in return you must promise to let me give what help I can; and, Jean, never say again that you are friendless.'

'You are so kind! God bless you for it. But I dare not accept your friendship; *she* will not permit it, and I have no right to mar her peace.'

'Who will not permit it?' he demanded hotly.

'Miss Beaufort.'

'Hang Miss Beaufort!' exclaimed Coventry, with such energy that Jean broke into a musical laugh, despite her trouble. He joined in it, and, for an instant they stood looking at one another as if the last barrier were down, and they were friends indeed. Jean paused suddenly, with the smile on her lips, the tears still on her cheek, and made a warning gesture. He listened: the sound of feet mingled with calls and laughter proved that they were missed and sought.

'That laugh betrayed us. Stay and meet them. I cannot.' And Jean darted out upon the lawn. Coventry followed; for the thought of confronting so many eyes, so many questions, daunted him, and he fled like a coward. The sound of Jean's flying footsteps guided him, and he overtook her just as she paused behind a rose thicket to take breath.

'Fainthearted knight! You should have stayed and covered my retreat. Hark! they are coming! Hide! Hide!' she panted, half in fear, half in merriment, as the gay pursuers rapidly drew nearer.

'Kneel down; the moon is coming out and the glitter of your embroidery will betray you,' whispered Jean, as they cowered behind the roses.

'Your arms and hair will betray you. "Come under my plaiddie," as the song says.' And Coventry tried to make his velvet cloak cover the white shoulders and fair locks.

'We are acting our parts in reality now. How Bella will enjoy the thing when I tell her!' said Jean as the noises died away.

'Do not tell her,' whispered Coventry.

'And why not?' she asked, looking up into the face so near her own, with an artless glance.

'Can you not guess why?'

'Ah, you are so proud you cannot bear to be laughed at.'

'It is not that. It is because I do not want you to be annoyed by silly tongues; you have enough to pain you without that. I am your friend, now, and I do my best to prove it.'

'So kind, so kind! How can I thank you?' murmured Jean. And she involuntarily nestled closer under the cloak that sheltered both.

Neither spoke for a moment, and in the silence the rapid beating of two hearts was heard. To drown the sound, Coventry said softly, 'Are you frightened?'

'No, I like it,' she answered, as softly, then added abruptly, 'But why do we hide? There is nothing to fear. It is late. I must go. You are kneeling on my train. Please rise.'

'Why in such haste? This flight and search only adds to the charm of the evening. I'll not get up yet. Will you have a rose, Jean?'

'No, I will not. Let me go, Mr Coventry, I insist. There has been enough of this folly. You forget yourself.'

She spoke imperiously, flung off the cloak, and put him from her. He rose at once, saying, like one waking suddenly from a pleasant dream, 'I do indeed forget myself.'

Here the sound of voices broke on them, nearer than before. Pointing to a covered walk that led to the house, he said, in his usually cool, calm tone, 'Go in that way; I will cover your retreat.' And turning, he went to meet the merry hunters.

Half an hour later, when the party broke up, Miss Muir joined them in her usual quiet dress, looking paler, meeker, and sadder than usual. Coventry saw this, though he neither looked at her nor addressed her. Lucia saw it also, and was glad that the dangerous girl had fallen back into her proper place again, for she had suffered much that night. She appropriated her cousin's arm as they went through the park, but he was in one of his taciturn moods, and all her attempts at conversation were in vain. Miss Muir walked alone, singing softly to herself as she followed in the dusk. Was Gerald so silent because he listened to that fitful song? Lucia thought so, and felt her dislike rapidly deepening to hatred.

When the young friends were gone, and the family were

exchanging goodnights among themselves, Jean was surprised by Coventry's offering his hand, for he had never done it before, and whispering, as he held it, though Lucia watched him all the while, 'I have not given my advice, yet.'

'Thanks, I no longer need it. I have decided for myself.'

'May I ask how?'

'To brave my enemy.'

'Good! But what decided you so suddenly?'

'The finding of a friend.' And with a grateful glance she was gone.

6 On The Watch

'If you please, Mr Coventry, did you get the letter last night?' were the first words that greeted the 'young master' as he left his room next morning.

'What letter, Dean? I don't remember any,' he answered, pausing, for something in the maid's manner struck him as peculiar.

'It came just as you left for the Hall, sir. Benson ran after you with it, as it was marked "Haste." Didn't you get it, sir?' asked the woman, anxiously.

'Yes, but upon my life, I forgot all about it till this minute. It's in my other coat, I suppose, if I've not lost it. That absurd masquerading put everything else out of my head.' And speaking more to himself than to the maid, Coventry turned back to look for the missing letter.

Dean remained where she was, apparently busy about the arrangement of the curtains at the hall window, but furtively watching meanwhile with a most unwonted air of curiosity.

'Not there, I thought so!' she muttered, as Coventry impatiently thrust his hand into one pocket after another. But as she spoke, an expression of amazement appeared in her face, for suddenly the letter was discovered.

'I'd have sworn it wasn't there! I don't understand it, but she's a deep one, or I'm much deceived.' And Dean shook her head like one perplexed, but not convinced.

Coventry uttered an exclamation of satisfaction on glancing at the address and, standing where he was, tore open the letter.

Dear C:

I'm off to Baden. Come and join me, then you'll be out of harm's way; for if you fall in love with J. M. (and you can't escape if you stay where she is), you will incur the trifling inconvenience of having your brains blown out by

Yours truly, F. R. Sydney

'The man is mad!' ejaculated Coventry, staring at the letter while an angry flush rose to his face. 'What the deuce does he mean by writing to me in that style? Join him – not I! And as for the threat, I laugh at it. Poor Jean! This headstrong fool seems bent on tormenting her. Well, Dean, what are you waiting for?' he demanded, as if suddenly conscious of her presence.

'Nothing, sir; I only stopped to see if you found the letter. Beg pardon, sir.'

And she was moving on when Coventry asked, with a suspicious look, 'What made you think it was lost? You seem to take an uncommon interest in my affairs today.'

'Oh dear, no, sir. I felt a bit anxious, Benson is so forgetful, and it was me who sent him after you, for I happened to see you go out, so I felt responsible. Being marked that way, I thought it might be important so I asked about it.'

'Very well, you can go, Dean. It's all right, you see.'

'I'm not so sure of that,' muttered the woman, as she curtsied respectfully and went away, looking as if the letter had *not* been found.

Dean was Miss Beaufort's maid, a grave, middle-aged woman with keen eyes and a somewhat grim air. Having been long in the family, she enjoyed all the privileges of a faithful and favorite servant. She loved her young mistress with an almost jealous affection. She watched over her with the vigilant care of a mother and resented any attempt at interference on the part of others. At first she had pitied and liked Jean Muir, then distrusted her, and now heartily hated her, as the cause of the increased indifference of Coventry toward his cousin. Dean knew the depth of Lucia's love, and though no man, in her eyes, was worthy of her mistress, still, having honored him with her regard, Dean felt bound to like him, and the late change in his manner disturbed the maid almost as much as it did the mistress.

She watched Jean narrowly, causing that amiable creature much amusement but little annoyance, as yet, for Dean's slow English wit was no match for the subtle mind of the governess. On the preceding night, Dean had been sent up to the Hall with costumes and had there seen something which much disturbed her. She began to speak of it while undressing her mistress, but Lucia, being in an unhappy mood, had so sternly ordered her not to gossip that the tale remained untold, and she was forced to bide her time.

Now I'll see how *she* looks after it; though there's not much to be got out of *her* face, the deceitful hussy, thought Dean, marching down the corridor and knitting her black brows as she went.

'Good morning, Mrs Dean. I hope you are none the worse for last night's frolic. You had the work and we the play,' said a blithe voice behind her; and turning sharply, she confronted Miss Muir. Fresh and smiling, the governess nodded with an air of cordiality which would have been irresistible with anyone but Dean.

'I'm quite well, thank you, miss,' she returned coldly, as her keen eye fastened on the girl as if to watch the effect of her words. 'I had a good rest when the young ladies and gentlemen were at supper, for while the maids cleaned up, I sat in the "little anteroom."'

'Yes, I saw you, and feared you'd take cold. Very glad you didn't. How is Miss Beaufort? She seemed rather poorly last night' was the tranquil reply, as Jean settled the little frills about her delicate wrists. The cool question was a return shot for Dean's hint that she had been where she could oversee the interview between Coventry and Miss Muir.

'She is a bit tired, as any *lady* would be after such an evening. People who are *used* to *play-acting* wouldn't mind it, perhaps, but Miss Beaufort don't enjoy *romps* as much as *some* do.'

The emphasis upon certain words made Dean's speech as impertinent as she desired. But Jean only laughed, and as Coventry's step was heard behind them, she ran downstairs, saying blandly, but with a wicked look, 'I won't stop to thank you now, lest Mr Coventry should bid me goodmorning, and so increase Miss Beaufort's indisposition.'

Dean's eyes flashed as she looked after the girl with a wrathful face, and went her way, saying grimly, 'I'll bide my time, but I'll get the better of her yet.'

Fancying himself quite removed from 'last night's absurdity,' yet curious to see how Jean would meet him, Coventry lounged into the breakfast room with his usual air of listless indifference. A languid nod and murmur was all the reply he vouchsafed to the greetings of cousin, sister, and governess as he sat down and took up his paper.

'Have you had a letter from Ned?' asked Bella, looking at the note which her brother still held.

'No' was the brief answer.

'Who then? You look as if you had received bad news.'

There was no reply, and, peeping over his arm, Bella caught sight of the seal and exclaimed, in a disappointed tone, 'It is the Sydney crest. I don't care about the note now. Men's letters to each other are not interesting.'

Miss Muir had been quietly feeding one of Edward's dogs, but at the name she looked up and met Coventry's eyes, coloring so distressfully that he pitied her. Why he should take the trouble to cover her confusion, he did not stop to ask himself, but seeing the curl of Lucia's lip, he suddenly addressed her with an air of displeasure, 'Do you know that Dean is getting impertinent? She presumes too much on her age and your indulgence, and forgets her place.'

'What has she done?' asked Lucia coldly.

'She troubles herself about my affairs and takes it upon herself to keep Benson in order.'

Here Coventry told about the letter and the woman's evident curiosity.

'Poor Dean, she gets no thanks for reminding you of what you had forgotten. Next time she will leave your letters to their fate, and perhaps it will be as well, if they have such a bad effect upon your temper, Gerald.'

Lucia spoke calmly, but there was an angry color in her cheek as she rose and left the room. Coventry looked much annoyed, for on Jean's face he detected a faint smile, half pitiful, half satirical, which disturbed him more than his cousin's insinuation. Bella broke the awkward silence by saying, with a sigh, 'Poor Ned! I do so long to hear again from him. I thought a letter had come for some of us. Dean said she saw one bearing his writing on the hall table yesterday.'

'She seems to have a mania for inspecting letters. I won't allow it. Who was the letter for, Bella?' said Coventry, putting down his paper.

'She wouldn't or couldn't tell, but looked very cross and told me to ask you.'

'Very odd! I've had none,' began Coventry.

'But I had one several days ago. Will you please read it, and my reply?' And as she spoke, Jean laid two letters before him.

'Certainly not. It would be dishonorable to read what Ned intended for no eyes but your own. You are too scrupulous in one way, and not enough so in another, Miss Muir.' And Coventry offered both the letters with an air of grave decision, which could not conceal the interest and surprise he felt.

'You are right. Mr Edward's note *should* be kept sacred, for in it the poor boy has laid bare his heart to me. But mine I beg you will read, that you may see how well I try to keep my word to you. Oblige me in this, Mr Coventry; I have a right to ask it of you.'

So urgently she spoke, so wistfully she looked, that he could not refuse and, going to the window, read the letter. It was evidently an answer to a passionate appeal from the young lover, and was written with consummate skill. As he read, Gerald could not help thinking, If this girl writes in this way to a man whom she does *not* love, with what a world of power and passion would she write to one whom she *did* love. And this thought kept returning to him as his eye went over line after line of wise argument, gentle reproof, good counsel, and friendly regard. Here and there a word, a phrase, betrayed what she had already confessed, and Coventry forgot to return the letter, as he stood wondering who was the man whom Jean loved.

The sound of Bella's voice recalled him, for she was saying, half kindly, half petulantly, 'Don't look so sad, Jean. Ned will outlive it, I dare say. You remember you said once men never died of love, though women might. In his one note to me, he spoke so beautifully of you, and begged me to be kind to you for his sake, that I try to be with all my heart, though if it was anyone but you, I really think I should hate them for making my dear boy so unhappy.'

'You are too kind, Bella, and I often think I'll go away to relieve you of my presence; but unwise and dangerous as it is to stay, I haven't the courage to go. I've been so happy here.' And as she spoke, Jean's head dropped lower over the dog as it nestled to her affectionately.

Before Bella could utter half the loving words that sprang to her lips, Coventry came to them with all languor gone from face and mien, and laying Jean's letter before her, he said, with an undertone of deep feeling in his usually emotionless voice, 'A right womanly and eloquent letter, but I fear it will only increase the fire it was meant to quench. I pity my brother more than ever now.'

'Shall I send it?' asked Jean, looking straight up at him, like one who had entire reliance on his judgment.

'Yes, I have not the heart to rob him of such a sweet sermon upon self-sacrifice. Shall I post it for you?'

'Thank you; in a moment.' And with a grateful look, Jean dropped her eyes. Producing her little purse, she selected a penny, folded it in a bit of paper, and then offered both letter and coin to Coventry, with such a pretty air of business, that he could not control a laugh.

'So you won't be indebted to me for a penny? What a proud woman you are, Miss Muir.'

'I am; it's a family failing.' And she gave him a significant glance, which recalled to him the memory of who she was. He understood her feeling, and liked her the better for it, knowing that he would have done the same had he been in her place. It was a little thing, but if done for effect, it answered admirably, for it showed a quick insight into his character on her part, and betrayed to him the existence of a pride in which he sympathized heartily. He stood by Jean a moment, watching her as she burnt Edward's letter in the blaze of the spirit lamp under the urn.

'Why do you do that?' he asked involuntarily.

'Because it is my duty to forget' was all her answer.

'Can you always forget when it becomes a duty?'

'I wish I could! I wish I could!'

She spoke passionately, as if the words broke from her against her will, and, rising hastily, she went into the garden, as if afraid to stay.

'Poor, dear Jean is very unhappy about something, but I can't discover what it is. Last night I found her crying over a rose, and now she runs away, looking as if her heart was broken. I'm glad I've got no lessons.'

'What kind of a rose?' asked Coventry from behind his paper as Bella paused.

'A lovely white one. It must have come from the Hall; we have none like it. I wonder if Jean was ever going to be married, and lost her lover, and felt sad because the flower reminded her of bridal roses.'

Coventry made no reply, but felt himself change countenance as he recalled the little scene behind the rose hedge, where he gave Jean the flower which she had refused yet taken. Presently, to Bella's surprise, he flung down the paper, tore Sydney's note to atoms, and rang for his horse with an energy which amazed her.

'Why, Gerald, what has come over you? One would think Ned's restless spirit had suddenly taken possession of you. What are you going to do?'

'I'm going to work' was the unexpected answer, as Coventry turned toward her with an expression so rarely seen on his fine face.

'What has waked you up all at once?' asked Bella, looking more and more amazed.

'You did,' he said, drawing her toward him.

'I! When? How?'

'Do you remember saying once that energy was better than beauty in a man, and that no one could respect an idler?'

'I never said anything half so sensible as that. Jean said something like it once, I believe, but I forgot. Are you tired of doing nothing, at last, Gerald?'

'Yes, I neglected my duty to Ned, till he got into trouble, and now I reproach myself for it. It's not too late to do other neglected tasks, so I'm going at them with a will. Don't say anything about it to anyone, and don't laugh at me, for I'm in earnest, Bell.'

'I know you are, and I admire and love you for it, my dear old boy,' cried Bella enthusiastically, as she threw her arms about his neck and kissed him heartily. 'What will you do first?' she asked, as he stood thoughtfully smoothing the bright head that leaned upon his shoulder, with that new expression still clear and steady in his face.

'I'm going to ride over the whole estate, and attend to things as a master should; not leave it all to Bent, of whom I've heard many complaints, but have been too idle to inquire about them.

I shall consult Uncle, and endeavor to be all that my father was in his time. Is that a worthy ambition, dear?'

'Oh, Gerald, let me tell Mamma. It will make her so happy. You are her idol, and to hear you say these things, to see you look so like dear Papa, would do more for her spirits than all the doctors in England.'

'Wait till I prove what my resolution is worth. When I have really done something, then I'll surprise Mamma with a sample of my work.'

'Of course you'll tell Lucia?'

'Not on any account. It is a little secret between us, so keep it till I give you leave to tell it.'

'But Jean will see it at once; she knows everything that happens, she is so quick and wise. Do you mind her knowing?'

'I don't see that I can help it if she is so wonderfully gifted. Let her see what she can, I don't mind her. Now I'm off.' And with a kiss to his sister, a sudden smile on his face, Coventry sprang upon his horse and rode away at a pace which caused the groom to stare after him in blank amazement.

Nothing more was seen of him till dinnertime, when he came in so exhilarated by his brisk ride and busy morning that he found some difficulty in assuming his customary manner, and more than once astonished the family by talking animatedly on various subjects which till now had always seemed utterly uninteresting to him. Lucia was amazed, his mother delighted, and Bella could hardly control her desire to explain the mystery; but Jean took it very calmly and regarded him with the air of one who said, 'I understand, but you will soon tire of it.' This nettled him more than he would confess, and he exerted himself to silently contradict that prophecy.

'Have you answered Mr Sydney's letter?' asked Bella, when they were all scattered about the drawing room after dinner.

'No,' answered her brother, who was pacing up and down with restless steps, instead of lounging near his beautiful cousin.

'I ask because I remembered that Ned sent a message for him in my last note, as he thought you would know Sydney's address. Here it is, something about a horse. Please put it in when you write,' and Bella laid the note on the writing table nearby.

'I'll send it at once and have done with it,' muttered Coventry and, seating himself, he dashed off a few lines, sealed and sent the letter, and then resumed his march, eyeing the three young ladies with three different expressions, as he passed and repassed. Lucia sat apart, feigning to be intent upon a book, and her handsome face looked almost stern in its haughty composure, for though her heart ached, she was too proud to own it. Bella now lay on the sofa, half asleep, a rosy little creature, as unconsciously pretty as a child. Miss Muir sat in the recess of a deep window, in a low lounging chair, working at an embroidery frame with a graceful industry pleasant to see. Of late she had worn colors, for Bella had been generous in gifts, and the pale blue muslin which flowed in soft waves about her was very becoming to her fair skin and golden hair. The close braids were gone, and loose curls dropped here and there from the heavy coil wound around her well-shaped head. The tip of one dainty foot was visible, and a petulant little gesture which now and then shook back the falling sleeve gave glimpses of a round white arm. Ned's great hound lay nearby, the sunshine flickered on her through the leaves, and as she sat smiling to herself, while the dexterous hands shaped leaf and flower, she made a charming picture of all that is most womanly and winning; a picture which few men's eyes would not have liked to rest upon.

Another chair stood near her, and as Coventry went up and down, a strong desire to take it possessed him. He was tired of his thoughts and wished to be amused by watching the changes of the girl's expressive face, listening to the varying tones of her voice, and trying to discover the spell which so strongly attracted him in spite of himself. More than once he swerved from his course to gratify his whim, but Lucia's presence always restrained him, and with a word to the dog, or a glance from the window, as pretext for a pause, he resumed his walk again. Something in his cousin's face reproached him, but her manner of late was so repellent that he felt no desire to resume their former familiarity, and, wishing to show that he did not consider himself bound, he kept aloof. It was a quiet test of the power of each woman over this man; they instinctively felt it, and both tried to conquer. Lucia spoke several times, and tried to speak frankly and affably; hut her manner was constrained, and Coventry, having answered politely, relapsed into silence. Jean said nothing, but silently appealed to eye and ear by the pretty picture she made of herself, the snatches of song she softly sang, as if forgetting that she was not alone, and a shy glance now and then, half wistful, half merry, which was more alluring than graceful figure or sweet voice. When she had tormented Lucia and tempted Coventry long enough, she quietly asserted her supremacy in a way which astonished her rival, who knew nothing of the secret of her birth, which knowledge did much to attract and charm the young man. Letting a ball of silk escape from her lap, she watched it roll toward the promenader, who caught and returned it with an alacrity which added grace to the trifling service. As she took it, she said, in the frank way that never failed to win him, 'I think you must be tired; but if exercise is necessary, employ your energies to some purpose and put your mother's basket of silks in order. They are in a tangle, and it will please her to know that you did it, as your brother used to do.'

'Hercules* at the distaff,' said Coventry gaily, and down he sat in the long-desired seat. Jean put the basket on his knee, and as he surveyed it, as if daunted at his task, she leaned back, and indulged in a musical little peal of laughter charming to hear. Lucia sat dumb with surprise, to see her proud, indolent cousin obeying the commands of a governess, and looking as if he heartily enjoyed it. In ten minutes she was as entirely forgotten as if she had been miles away; for Jean seemed in her wittiest, gayest mood, and as she now treated the 'young master' like an equal, there was none of the former meek timidity. Yet often her eyes fell, her color changed, and the piquant sallies faltered on her tongue, as Coventry involuntarily looked deep into the fine eyes which had once shone on him so tenderly in that mimic tragedy. He could not forget it, and though neither alluded to it, the memory of the previous evening seemed to haunt both and lend a secret charm to the present moment. Lucia bore this as long as she could, and then left the room with an air of an insulted princess; but Coventry did not, and Jean feigned not to see her go. Bella was fast asleep, and before he knew how it came to pass, the young man was listening to the story of his companion's life. A sad tale, told with wonderful skill, for soon he was absorbed in it. The basket slid unobserved from his knee, the dog was pushed away, and, leaning forward, he listened eagerly as the girl's low voice recounted all the hardships, loneliness, and grief of her short life. In the midst of a touching episode she started, stopped, and looked straight before her, with an intent expression which changed to one of intense

contempt, and her eye turned to Coventry's, as she said, pointing
to the window behind him, 'We are watched.'

'By whom?' he demanded, starting up angrily.

'Hush, say nothing, let it pass. I am used to it.'

'But *I* am not, and I'll not submit to it. Who was it, Jean?' he
answered hotly.

She smiled significantly at a knot of rose-colored ribbon,
which a little gust was blowing toward them along the terrace.
A black frown darkened the young man's face as he sprang out
of the long window and went rapidly out of sight, scrutinizing
each green nook as he passed. Jean laughed quietly as she
watched him, and said softly to herself, with her eyes on the
fluttering ribbon, 'That was a fortunate accident, and a happy
inspiration. Yes, my dear Mrs Dean, you will find that playing
the spy will only get your mistress as well as yourself into
trouble. You would not be warned, and you must take the
consequences, reluctant as I am to injure a worthy creature like
yourself.'

Soon Coventry was heard returning. Jean listened with suspended breath to catch his first words, for he was not alone.

'Since you insist that it was you and not your mistress, I let it
pass, although I still have my suspicions. Tell Miss Beaufort I
desire to see her for a few moments in the library. Now go,
Dean, and be careful for the future, if you wish to stay in my
house.'

The maid retired, and the young man came in looking both
ireful and stern.

'I wish I had said nothing, but I was startled, and spoke
involuntarily. Now you are angry, and I have made fresh trouble
for poor Miss Lucia. Forgive me as I forgive her, and let it pass.
I have learned to bear this surveillance, and pity her causeless
jealousy,' said Jean, with a self-reproachful air.

'I will forgive the dishonorable act, but I cannot forget it, and
I intend to put a stop to it. I am not betrothed to my cousin, as
I told you once, but you, like all the rest, seem bent on believing
that I am. Hitherto I have cared too little about the matter to
settle it, but now I shall prove beyond all doubt that I am free.'

As he uttered the last word, Coventry cast on Jean a look that
affected her strangely. She grew pale, her work dropped on her
lap, and her eyes rose to his, with an eager, questioning
expression, which slowly changed to one of mingled pain and

pity, as she turned her face away, murmuring in a tone of tender sorrow, 'Poor Lucia, who will comfort her?'

For a moment Coventry stood silent, as if weighing some fateful purpose in his mind. As Jean's rapt sigh of compassion reached his ear, he had echoed it within himself, and half repented of his resolution; then his eye rested on the girl before him looking so lonely in her sweet sympathy for another that his heart yearned toward her. Sudden fire shot into his eye, sudden warmth replaced the cold sternness of his face, and his steady voice faltered suddenly, as he said, very low, yet very earnestly, 'Jean, I have tried to love her, but I cannot. Ought I to deceive her, and make myself miserable to please my family?'

'She is beautiful and good, and loves you tenderly; is there no hope for her?' asked Jean, still pale, but very quiet, though she held one hand against her heart, as if to still or hide its rapid beating.

'None,' answered Coventry.

'But can you not learn to love her? Your will is strong, and most men would not find it a hard task.'

'I cannot, for something stronger than my own will controls me.'

'What is that?' And Jean's dark eyes were fixed upon him, full of innocent wonder.

His fell, and he said hastily, 'I dare not tell you yet.'

'Pardon! I should not have asked. Do not consult me in this matter; I am not the person to advise you. I can only say that it seems to me as if any man with an empty heart would be glad to have so beautiful a woman as your cousin.'

'My heart is not empty,' began Coventry, drawing a step nearer, and speaking in a passionate voice. 'Jean, I *must* speak; hear me. I cannot love my cousin, because I love you.'

'Stop!' And Jean sprang up with a commanding gesture. 'I will not hear you while any promise binds you to another. Remember your mother's wishes, Lucia's hopes, Edward's last words, your own pride, my humble lot. You forget yourself, Mr Coventry. Think well before you speak, weigh the cost of this act, and recollect who I am before you insult me by any transient passion, any false vows.'

'I have thought, I do weigh the cost, and I swear that I desire to woo you as humbly, honestly as I would any lady in the land. You speak of my pride. Do I stoop in loving my equal in rank?

You speak of your lowly lot, but poverty is no disgrace, and the courage with which you bear it makes it beautiful. I should have broken with Lucia before I spoke, but I could not control myself. My mother loves you, and will be happy in my happiness. Edward must forgive me, for I have tried to do my best, but love is irresistible. Tell me, Jean, is there any hope for me?'

He had seized her hand and was speaking impetuously, with ardent face and tender tone, but no answer came, for as Jean turned her eloquent countenance toward him, full of maiden shame and timid love, Dean's prim figure appeared at the door, and her harsh voice broke the momentary silence, saying, sternly, 'Miss Beaufort is waiting for you, sir.'

'Go, go at once, and be kind, for my sake, Gerald,' whispered Jean, for he stood as if deaf and blind to everything but her voice, her face.

As she drew his head down to whisper, her cheek touched his, and regardless of Dean, he kissed it, passionately, whispering back, 'My little Jean! For your sake I can be anything.'

'Miss Beaufort is waiting. Shall I say you will come, sir?' demanded Dean, pale and grim with indignation.

'Yes, yes, I'll come. Wait for me in the garden, Jean.' And Coventry hurried away, in no mood for the interview but anxious to have it over.

As the door closed behind him, Dean walked up to Miss Muir, trembling with anger, and laying a heavy hand on her arm, she said below her breath, 'I've been expecting this, you artful creature. I saw your game and did my best to spoil it, but you are too quick for me. You think you've got him. There you are mistaken; for as sure as my name is Hester Dean, I'll prevent it, or Sir John shall.'

'Take your hand away and treat me with proper respect, or you will be dismissed from this house. Do you know who I am?' And Jean drew herself up with a haughty air, which impressed the woman more deeply than her words. 'I am the daughter of Lady Howard and, if I choose it, can be the wife of Mr Coventry.'

Dean drew back amazed, yet not convinced. Being a well-trained servant, as well as a prudent woman, she feared to overstep the bounds of respect, to go too far, and get her mistress as well as herself into trouble.

So, though she still doubted Jean, and hated her more than

ever, she controlled herself. Dropping a curtsy, she assumed her usual air of deference, and said, meekly, 'I beg pardon, miss. If I'd known, I should have conducted myself differently, of course, but ordinary governesses make so much mischief in a house, one can't help mistrusting them. I don't wish to meddle or be overbold, but being fond of my dear young lady, I naturally take her part, and must say that Mr Coventry has not acted like a gentleman.'

'Think what you please, Dean, but I advise you to say as little as possible if you wish to remain. I have not accepted Mr Coventry yet, and if he chooses to set aside the engagement his family made for him, I think he has a right to do so. Miss Beaufort would hardly care to marry him against his will, because he pities her for her unhappy love,' and with a tranquil smile, Miss Muir walked away.

7 The Last Chance

'She will tell Sir John, will she? Then I must be before her, and hasten events. It will be as well to have all sure before there can be any danger. My poor Dean, you are no match for me, but you may prove annoying, nevertheless.'

These thoughts passed through Miss Muir's mind as she went down the hall, pausing an instant at the library door, for the murmur of voices was heard. She caught no word, and had only time for an instant's pause as Dean's heavy step followed her. Turning, Jean drew a chair before the door, and, beckoning to the woman, she said, smiling still, 'Sit here and play watchdog. I am going to Miss Bella, so you can nod if you will.'

'Thank you, miss. I will wait for my young lady. She may need me when this hard time is over.' And Dean seated herself with a resolute face.

Jean laughed and went on; but her eyes gleamed with sudden malice, and she glanced over her shoulder with an expression which boded ill for the faithful old servant.

'I've got a letter from Ned, and here is a tiny note for you,' cried Bella as Jean entered the boudoir. 'Mine is a very odd, hasty letter, with no news in it, but his meeting with Sydney. I hope yours is better, or it won't be very satisfactory.'

As Sydney's name passed Bella's lips, all the color died out of Miss Muir's face, and the note shook with the tremor of her hand. Her very lips were white, but she said calmly, 'Thank you. As you are busy, I'll go and read my letter on the lawn.' And before Bella could speak, she was gone.

Hurrying to a quiet nook, Jean tore open the note and read the few blotted lines it contained.

> I have seen Sydney; he has told me all; and, hard as I found it to believe, it was impossible to doubt, for he has discovered proofs which cannot be denied. I make no reproaches, shall demand no confession or atonement, for I cannot forget that I once loved you. I give you three days to find another home, before I return to tell the family who you are. Go at once, I beseech you, and spare me the pain of seeing your disgrace.

Slowly, steadily she read it twice over, then sat motionless, knitting her brows in deep thought. Presently she drew a long breath, tore up the note, and rising, went slowly toward the Hall, saying to herself, 'Three days, only three days! Can it be accomplished in so short a time? It shall be, if wit and will can do it, for it is my last chance. If this fails, I'll not go back to my old life, but end all at once.'

Setting her teeth and clenching her hands, as if some memory stung her, she went on through the twilight, to find Sir John waiting to give her a hearty welcome.

'You look tired, my dear. Never mind the reading tonight; rest yourself, and let the book go,' he said kindly, observing her worn look.

'Thank you, sir. I am tired, but I'd rather read, else the book will not be finished before I go.'

'Go, child! Where are you going?' demanded Sir John, looking anxiously at her as she sat down.

'I will tell you by-and-by, sir.' And opening the book, Jean read for a little while.

But the usual charm was gone; there was no spirit in the voice of the reader, no interest in the face of the listener, and soon he said, abruptly, 'My dear, pray stop! I cannot listen with a divided mind. What troubles you? Tell your friend, and let him comfort you.'

As if the kind words overcame her, Jean dropped the book, covered up her face, and wept so bitterly that Sir John was much alarmed; for such a demonstration was doubly touching in one who usually was all gaiety and smiles. As he tried to soothe her, his words grew tender, his solicitude full of a more than paternal anxiety, and his kind heart overflowed with pity and affection for the weeping girl. As she grew calmer, he urged her to be frank, promising to help and counsel her, whatever the affliction or fault might be.

'Ah, you are too kind, too generous! How can I go away and leave my one friend?' sighed Jean, wiping the tears away and looking up at him with grateful eyes.

'Then you do care a little for the old man?' said Sir John with an eager look, an involuntary pressure of the hand he held.

Jean turned her face away, and answered, very low, 'No one ever was so kind to me as you have been. Can I help caring for you more than I can express?'

Sir John was a little deaf at times, but he heard that, and looked well pleased. He had been rather thoughtful of late, had dressed with unusual care, been particularly gallant and gay when the young ladies visited him, and more than once, when Jean paused in the reading to ask a question, he had been forced to confess that he had not been listening; though, as she well knew, his eyes had been fixed upon her. Since the discovery of her birth, his manner had been peculiarly benignant, and many little acts had proved his interest and goodwill. Now, when Jean spoke of going, a panic seized him, and desolation seemed about to fall upon the old Hall. Something in her unusual agitation struck him as peculiar and excited his curiosity. Never had she seemed so interesting as now, when she sat beside him with tearful eyes, and some soft trouble in her heart which she dared not confess.

'Tell me everything, child, and let your friend help you if he can.' Formerly he said 'father' or 'the old man,' but lately he always spoke of himself as her 'friend.'

'I will tell you, for I have no one else to turn to. I must go away because Mr Coventry has been weak enough to love me.'

'What, Gerald?' cried Sir John, amazed.

'Yes; today he told me this, and left me to break with Lucia;

so I ran to you to help me prevent him from disappointing his mother's hopes and plans.'

Sir John had started up and paced down the room, but as Jean paused he turned toward her, saying, with an altered face, 'Then you do not love him? Is it possible?'

'No, I do not love him,' she answered promptly.

'Yet he is all that women usually find attractive. How is it that you have escaped, Jean?'

'I love someone else' was the scarcely audible reply.

Sir John resumed his seat with the air of a man bent on getting at a mystery, if possible.

'It will be unjust to let you suffer for the folly of these boys, my little girl. Ned is gone, and I was sure that Gerald was safe; but now that his turn has come, I am perplexed, for he cannot be sent away.'

'No, it is I who must go; but it seems so hard to leave this safe and happy home, and wander away into the wide, cold world again. You have all been too kind to me, and now separation breaks my heart.'

A sob ended the speech, and Jean's head went down upon her hands again. Sir John looked at her a moment, and his fine old face was full of genuine emotion, as he said slowly, 'Jean, will you stay and be a daughter to the solitary old man?'

'No, sir' was the unexpected answer.

'And why not?' asked Sir John, looking surprised, but rather pleased than angry.

'Because I could not be a daughter to you; and even if I could, it would not be wise, for the gossips would say you were not old enough to be the adopted father of a girl like me. Sir John, young as I am, I know much of the world, and am sure that this kind plan is impractical; but I thank you from the bottom of my heart.'

'Where will you go, Jean?' asked Sir John, after a pause.

'To London, and try to find another situation where I can do no harm.'

'Will it be difficult to find another home?'

'Yes. I cannot ask Mrs Coventry to recommend me, when I have innocently brought so much trouble into her family; and Lady Sydney is gone, so I have no friend.'

'Except John Coventry. I will arrange all that. When will you go, Jean?'

'Tomorrow.'

'So soon!' And the old man's voice betrayed the trouble he was trying to conceal.

Jean had grown very calm, but it was the calmness of desperation. She had hoped that the first tears would produce the avowal for which she waited. It had not, and she began to fear that her last chance was slipping from her. Did the old man love her? If so, why did he not speak? Eager to profit by each moment, she was on the alert for any hopeful hint, any propitious word, look, or act, and every nerve was strung to the utmost.

'Jean, may I ask one question?' said Sir John.

'Anything of me, sir.'

'This man whom you love – can he not help you?'

'He could if he knew, but he must not.'

'If he knew what? Your present trouble?'

'No. My love.'

'He does know this, then?'

'No, thank heaven! And he never will.'

'Why not?'

'Because I am too proud to own it.'

'He loves you, my child?'

'I do not know – I dare not hope it,' murmured Jean.

'Can I not help you here? Believe me, I desire to see you safe and happy. Is there nothing I can do?'

'Nothing, nothing.'

'May I know the name?'

'No! No! Let me go; I cannot bear this questioning!' And Jean's distressful face warned him to ask no more.

'Forgive me, and let me do what I may. Rest here quietly. I'll write a letter to a good friend of mine, who will find you a home, if you leave us.'

As Sir John passed into his inner study, Jean watched him with despairing eyes and wrung her hands, saying to herself, Has all my skill deserted me when I need it most? How can I make him understand, yet not overstep the bounds of maiden modesty? He is so blind, so timid, or so dull he will not see, and time is going fast. What shall I do to open his eyes?

Her own eyes roved about the room, seeking for some aid from inanimate things, and soon she found it. Close behind the couch where she sat hung a fine miniature of Sir John. At first her eye rested on it as she contrasted its placid comeliness with the unusual pallor and disquiet of the living face seen through the open door, as the old man sat at his desk trying to write and casting covert glances at the girlish figure he had left behind him. Affecting unconsciousness of this, Jean gazed on as if forgetful of everything but the picture, and suddenly, as if obeying an irresistible impulse, she took it down, looked long and fondly at it, then, shaking her curls about her face, as if to hide the act, pressed it to her lips and seemed to weep over it in an uncontrollable paroxysm of tender grief. A sound startled her, and like a guilty thing, she turned to replace the picture; but it dropped from her hand as she uttered a faint cry and hid her face, for Sir John stood before her, with an expression which she could not mistake.

'Jean, why did you do that?' he asked, in an eager, agitated voice.

No answer, as the girl sank lower, like one overwhelmed with shame. Laying his hand on the bent head, and bending his own, he whispered, 'Tell me, is the name John Coventry?'

Still no answer, but a stifled sound betrayed that his words had gone home.

'Jean, shall I go back and write the letter, or may I stay and tell you that the old man loves you better than a daughter?'

She did not speak, but a little hand stole out from under the falling hair, as if to keep him. With a broken exclamation he seized it, drew her up into his arms, and laid his gray head on her fair one, too happy for words. For a moment Jean Muir enjoyed her success; then, fearing lest some sudden mishap should destroy it, she hastened to make all secure. Looking up with well-feigned timidity and half-confessed affection, she said softly, 'Forgive me that I could not hide this better. I meant to go away and never tell it, but you were so kind it made the parting doubly hard. Why did you ask such dangerous questions? Why did you look, when you should have been writing my dismissal?'

'How could I dream that you loved me, Jean, when you refused the only offer I dared make? Could I be presumptuous enough to fancy you would reject young lovers for an old man like me?' asked Sir John caressing her.

'You are not old, to me, but everything I love and honor!' interrupted Jean, with a touch of genuine remorse, as this generous, honorable gentleman gave her both heart and home, unconscious of deceit. 'It is I who am presumptuous, to dare to love one so far above me. But I did not know how dear you were to me till I felt that I must go. I ought not to accept this happiness. I am not worthy of it; and you will regret your kindness when the world blames you for giving a home to one so poor, and plain, and humble as I.'

'Hush, my darling. I care nothing for the idle gossip of the world. If you are happy here, let tongues wag as they will. I shall be too busy enjoying the sunshine of your presence to heed anything that goes on about me. But, Jean, you are sure you love me? It seems incredible that I should win the heart that has been so cold to younger, better men than I.'

'Dear Sir John, be sure of this, I love you truly. I will do my best to be a good wife to you, and prove that, in spite of my many faults, I possess the virtue of gratitude.'

If he had known the strait she was in, he would have understood the cause of the sudden fervor of her words, the intense thankfulness that shone in her face, the real humility that made her stoop and kiss the generous hand that gave so much. For a few moments she enjoyed and let him enjoy the happy present, undisturbed. But the anxiety which devoured her, the danger which menaced her, soon recalled her, and forced her to wring yet more from the unsuspicious heart she had conquered.

'No need of letters now,' said Sir John, as they sat side by side, with the summer moonlight glorifying all the room. 'You have found a home for life; may it prove a happy one.'

'It is not mine yet, and I have a strange foreboding that it never will be,' she answered sadly.

'Why, my child?'

'Because I have an enemy who will try to destroy my peace, to poison your mind against me, and to drive me out from my paradise, to suffer again all I have suffered this last year.'

'You mean that mad Sydney of whom you told me?'

'Yes. As soon as he hears of this good fortune to poor little Jean, he will hasten to mar it. He is my fate; I cannot escape him, and wherever he goes my friends desert me; for he has the power and uses it for my destruction. Let me go away and hide before he comes, for, having shared your confidence, it will break my heart to see you distrust and turn from me, instead of loving and protecting.'

'My poor child, you are superstitious. Be easy. No one can harm you now, no one would dare attempt it. And as for my deserting you, that will soon be out of my power, if I have my way.'

'How, dear Sir John?' asked Jean, with a flutter of intense relief at her heart, for the way seemed smoothing before her.

'I will make you my wife at once, if I may. This will free you from Gerald's love, protect you from Sydney's persecution, give you a safe home, and me the right to cherish and defend with heart and hand. Shall it be so, my child?'

'Yes; but oh, remember that I have no friend but you! Promise me to be faithful to the last – to believe in me, to trust me, protect and love me, in spite of all misfortunes, faults, and follies. I will be true as steel to you, and make your life as happy as it deserves to be. Let us promise these things now, and keep the promises unbroken to the end.'

Her solemn air touched Sir John. Too honorable and upright himself to suspect falsehood in others, he saw only the natural impulse of a lovely girl in Jean's words, and, taking the hand she gave him in both of his, he promised all she asked, and kept that promise to the end. She paused an instant, with a pale, absent expression, as if she searched herself, then looked up clearly in the confiding face above her, and promised what she faithfully performed in afteryears.

'When shall it be, little sweetheart? I leave all to you, only let it be soon, else some gay young lover will appear, and take you from me,' said Sir John, playfully, anxious to chase away the dark expression which had stolen over Jean's face.

'Can you keep a secret?' asked the girl, smiling up at him, all her charming self again.

'Try me.'

'I will. Edward is coming home in three days. I must be gone before he comes. Tell no one of this; he wishes to surprise them. And if you love me, tell nobody of your approaching marriage. Do not betray that you care for me until I am really yours. There will be such a stir, such remonstrances, explanations, and reproaches that I shall be worn out, and run away from you all to escape the trial. If I could have my wish, I would go to some quiet place tomorrow and wait till you come for me. I know so little of such things, I cannot tell how soon we may be married; not for some weeks, I think.'

'Tomorrow, if we like. A special license permits people to marry when and where they please. My plan is better than yours. Listen, and tell me if it can be carried out. I will go to town tomorrow, get the license, invite my friend, the Reverend Paul Fairfax, to return with me, and tomorrow evening you come at your usual time, and, in the presence of my discreet old servants, make me the happiest man in England. How does this suit you, my little Lady Coventry?'

The plan which seemed made to meet her ends, the name which was the height of her ambition, and the blessed sense of safety which came to her filled Jean Muir with such intense satisfaction that tears of real feeling stood in her eyes, and the glad assent she gave was the truest word that had passed her lips for months.

'We will go abroad or to Scotland for our honeymoon, till the storm blows over,' said Sir John, well knowing that this hasty marriage would surprise or offend all his relations, and feeling as glad as Jean to escape the first excitement.

'To Scotland, please. I long to see my father's home,' said Jean, who dreaded to meet Sydney on the continent.

They talked a little longer, arranging all things, Sir John so intent on hurrying the event that Jean had nothing to do but give a ready assent to all his suggestions. One fear alone disturbed her. If Sir John went to town, he might meet Edward, might hear and believe his statements. Then all would be lost. Yet this risk must be incurred, if the marriage was to be speedily and safely accomplished; and to guard against the meeting was Jean's sole care. As they went through the park – for Sir John insisted upon taking her home – she said, clinging to his arm:

'Dear friend, bear one thing in mind, else we shall be much annoyed, and all our plans disarranged. Avoid your nephews; you are so frank your face will betray you. They both love me, are both hot-tempered, and in the first excitement of the discovery might be violent. You must incur no danger, no disrespect for my sake; so shun them both till we are safe – particularly Edward. He will feel that his brother has wronged him, and that you have succeeded where he failed. This will irritate him, and I fear a stormy scene. Promise to avoid both for a day or two; do not listen to them, do not see them, do not write to or receive letters from them. It is foolish, I know; but you are all I have, and I am haunted by a strange foreboding that I am to lose you.'

Touched and flattered by her tender solicitude, Sir John promised everything, even while he laughed at her fears. Love blinded the good gentleman to the peculiarity of the request; the novelty, romance, and secrecy of the affair rather bewildered though it charmed him; and the knowledge that he had out-rivaled three young and ardent lovers gratified his vanity more than he would confess. Parting from the girl at the garden gate, he turned homeward, feeling like a boy again, and loitered back, humming a love lay, quite forgetful of evening damps, gout, and the five-and-fifty years which lay so lightly on his shoulders since Jean's arms had rested there. She hurried toward the house, anxious to escape Coventry; but he was waiting for her, and she was forced to meet him.

'How could you linger so long, and keep me in suspense?' he said reproachfully, as he took her hand and tried to catch a glimpse of her face in the shadow of her hat brim. 'Come and rest in the grotto. I have so much to say, to hear and enjoy.'

'Not now; I am too tired. Let me go in and sleep. Tomorrow we will talk. It is damp and chilly, and my head aches with all this worry.' Jean spoke wearily, yet with a touch of petulance, and Coventry, fancying that she was piqued at his not coming for her, hastened to explain with eager tenderness.

'My poor little Jean, you do need rest. We wear you out, among us, and you never complain. I should have come to bring you home, but Lucia detained me, and when I got away I saw my uncle had forestalled me. I shall be jealous of the old gentleman, if he is so devoted. Jean, tell me one thing before we part; I am free as air, now, and have a right to speak. Do you love me? Am I the happy man who has won your heart? I dare to think so, to believe that this telltale face of yours has betrayed you, and to hope that I have gained what poor Ned and wild Sydney have lost.'

'Before I answer, tell me of your interview with Lucia. I have a right to know,' said Jean.

Coventry hesitated, for pity and remorse were busy at his heart when he recalled poor Lucia's grief. Jean was bent on hearing the humiliation of her rival. As the young man paused, she frowned, then lifted up her face wreathed in softest smiles, and laying her hand on his arm, she said, with most effective emphasis, half shy, half fond, upon his name, 'Please tell me, Gerald!'

He could not resist the look, the touch, the tone, and taking the little hand in his, he said rapidly, as if the task was distasteful to him, 'I told her that I did not, could not love her; that I had submitted to my mother's wish, and, for a time, had felt tacitly bound to her, though no words had passed between us. But now I demanded my liberty, regretting that the separation was not mutually desired.'

'And she – what did she say? How did she bear it?' asked Jean, feeling in her own woman's heart how deeply Lucia's must have been wounded by that avowal.

'Poor girl! It was hard to bear, but her pride sustained her to the end. She owned that no pledge tied me, fully relinquished any claim my past behavior had seemed to have given her, and prayed that I might find another woman to love me as truly, tenderly as she had done. Jean, I felt like a villain; and yet I never plighted my word to her, never really loved her, and had a perfect right to leave her, if I would.'

'Did she speak of me?'

'Yes.'

'What did she say?'

'Must I tell you?'

'Yes, tell me everything. I know she hates me and I forgive her, knowing that I should hate any woman whom *you* loved.'

'Are you jealous, dear?'

'Of you, Gerald?' And the fine eyes glanced up at him, full of a brilliancy that looked like the light of love.

'You make a slave of me already. How do you do it? I never obeyed a woman before. Jean, I think you are a witch. Scotland is the home of weird, uncanny creatures, who take lovely shapes for the bedevilment of poor weak souls. Are you one of those fair deceivers?'

'You are complimentary,' laughed the girl. 'I *am* a witch, and one day my disguise will drop away and you will see me as I am, old, ugly, bad and lost. Beware of me in time. I've warned you. Now love me at your peril.'

Coventry had paused as he spoke, and eyed her with an unquiet look, conscious of some fascination which conquered yet brought no happiness. A feverish yet pleasurable excitement possessed him; a reckless mood, making him eager to obliterate the past by any rash act, any new experience which his passion brought. Jean regarded him with a wistful, almost woeful face, for one short moment; then a strange smile broke over it, as she spoke in a tone of malicious mockery, under which lurked the bitterness of a sad truth. Coventry looked half bewildered, and his eye went from the girl's mysterious face to a dimly lighted window, behind whose curtains poor Lucia hid her aching heart, praying for him the tender prayers that loving women give to those whose sins are all forgiven for love's sake. His heart smote him, and a momentary feeling of repulsion came over him, as he looked at Jean. She saw it, felt angry, yet conscious of a sense of relief; for now that her own safety was so nearly secured, she felt no wish to do mischief, but rather a desire to undo what was already done, and be at peace with all the world. To recall him to his allegiance, she sighed and walked on, saying gently yet coldly, 'Will you tell me what I ask before I answer your question, Mr Coventry?'

'What Lucia said of you? Well, it was this, "Beware of Miss Muir. We instinctively distrusted her when we had no cause. I believe in instincts, and mine have never changed, for she has not tried to delude me. Her art is wonderful; I feel yet cannot explain or detect it, except in the working of events which her hand seems to guide. She has brought sorrow and dissension into this hitherto happy family. We are all changed, and this girl has done it. Me she can harm no further; you she will ruin, if she can. Beware of her in time, or you will bitterly repent your blind infatuation!"'

'And what answer did you make?' asked Jean, as the last words came reluctantly from Coventry's lips.

'I told her that I loved you in spite of myself, and would make you my wife in the face of all opposition. Now, Jean, your answer.'

'Give me three days to think of it. Goodnight.' And gliding from him, she vanished into the house, leaving him to roam about half the night, tormented with remorse, suspense, and the old distrust which would return when Jean was not there to banish it by her art.

8 Suspense

All the next day, Jean was in a state of the most intense anxiety, as every hour brought the crisis nearer, and every hour might bring defeat, for the subtlest human skill is often thwarted by some unforeseen accident. She longed to assure herself that Sir John was gone, but no servants came or went that day, and she could devise no pretext for sending to glean intelligence. She dared not go herself, lest the unusual act should excite suspicion, for she never went till evening. Even had she determined to venture, there was no time, for Mrs Coventry was in one of her nervous states, and no one but Miss Muir could amuse her; Lucia was ill, and Miss Muir must give orders; Bella had a studious fit, and Jean must help her. Coventry lingered about the house for several hours, but Jean dared not send him, lest some hint of the truth might reach him. He had ridden away to his new duties when Jean did not appear, and the day dragged on wearisomely. Night came at last, and as Jean dressed for the late dinner, she hardly knew herself when she stood before her mirror, excitement lent such color and brilliancy to her countenance. Remembering the wedding which was to take place that evening, she put on a simple white dress and added a cluster of white roses in bosom and hair. She often wore flowers, but in spite of her desire to look and seem as usual, Bella's first words as she entered the drawing room were 'Why, Jean, how like a bride you look; a veil and gloves would make you quite complete!'

'You forget one other trifle, Bell,' said Gerald, with eyes that brightened as they rested on Miss Muir.

'What is that?' asked his sister.

'A bridegroom.'

Bella looked to see how Jean received this, but she seemed quite composed as she smiled one of her sudden smiles, and merely said, 'That trifle will doubtless be found when the time comes. Is Miss Beaufort too ill for dinner?'

'She begs to be excused, and said you would be willing to take her place, she thought.'

As innocent Bella delivered this message, Jean glanced at Coventry, who evaded her eye and looked ill at ease.

A little remorse will do him good, and prepare him for repentance after the grand *coup*, she said to herself, and was particularly gay at dinnertime, though Coventry looked often at Lucia's empty seat, as if he missed her. As soon as they left the table, Miss Muir sent Bella to her mother; and, knowing that Coventry would not linger long at his wine, she hurried away to the Hall. A servant was lounging at the door, and of him she asked, in a tone which was eager in spite of all efforts to be calm, 'Is Sir John at home?'

'No, miss, he's just gone to town.'

'Just gone! When do you mean?' cried Jean, forgetting the relief she felt in hearing of his absence in surprise at his late departure.

'He went half an hour ago, in the last train, miss.'

'I thought he was going early this morning; he told me he should be back this evening.'

'I believe he did mean to go, but was delayed by company. The steward came up on business, and a load of gentlemen called, so Sir John could not get off till night, when he wasn't fit to go, being worn out, and far from well.'

'Do you think he will be ill? Did he look so?' And as Jean spoke, a thrill of fear passed over her, lest death should rob her of her prize.

'Well, you know, miss, hurry of any kind is bad for elderly gentlemen inclined to apoplexy. Sir John was in a worry all day, and not like himself. I wanted him to take his man, but he wouldn't; and drove off looking flushed and excited like. I'm anxious about him, for I know something is amiss to hurry him off in this way.'

'When will he be back, Ralph?'

'Tomorrow noon, if possible; at night, certainly, he bid me tell anyone that called.'

'Did he leave no note or message for Miss Coventry, or someone of the family?'

'No, miss, nothing.'

'Thank you.' And Jean walked back to spend a restless night and rise to meet renewed suspense.

The morning seemed endless, but noon came at last, and under the pretense of seeking coolness in the grotto, Jean stole away to a slope whence the gate to the Hall park was visible. For two long hours she watched, and no one came. She was just turning away when a horseman dashed through the gate and came galloping toward the Hall. Heedless of everything but the uncontrollable longing to gain some tidings, she ran to meet him, feeling assured that he brought ill news. It was a young man from the station, and as he caught sight of her, he drew bridle, looking agitated and undecided.

'Has anything happened?' she cried breathlessly.

'A dreadful accident on the railroad, just the other side of Croydon. News telegraphed half an hour ago,' answered the man, wiping his hot face.

'The noon train? Was Sir John in it? Quick, tell me all!'

'It was that train, miss, but whether Sir John was in it or not, we don't know; for the guard is killed, and everything is in such confusion that nothing can be certain. They are at work getting out the dead and wounded. We heard that Sir John was expected, and I came up to tell Mr Coventry, thinking he would wish to go down. A train leaves in fifteen minutes; where shall I find him? I was told he was at the Hall.'

'Ride on, ride on! And find him if he is there. I'll run home and look for him. Lose no time. Ride! Ride!' And turning, Jean sped back like a deer, while the man tore up the avenue to rouse the Hall.

Coventry was there, and went off at once, leaving both Hall and house in dismay. Fearing to betray the horrible anxiety that possessed her, Jean shut herself up in her room and suffered untold agonies as the day wore on and no news came. At dark a sudden cry rang through the house, and Jean rushed down to learn the cause. Bella was standing in the hall, holding a letter, while a group of excited servants hovered near her.

'What is it?' demanded Miss Muir, pale and steady, though her heart died within her as she recognised Gerald's handwriting. Bella gave her the note, and hushed her sobbing to hear again the heavy tidings that had come.

Dear Bella:

Uncle is safe; he did not go in the noon train. But several persons are sure that Ned was there. No trace of him as yet, but many bodies are in the river, under the ruins of the bridge, and I am doing my best to find the poor lad, if he is there. I have sent to all his haunts in town, and as he has not been seen, I hope it is a false report and he is safe with his regiment. Keep this from my mother till we are sure. I write you, because Lucia is ill. Miss Muir will comfort and sustain you. Hope for the best, dear.

Yours, G. C.

Those who watched Miss Muir as she read these words wondered at the strange expressions which passed over her face, for the joy which appeared there as Sir John's safety was made known did not change to grief or horror at poor Edward's possible fate. The smile died on her lips, but her voice did not falter, and in her downcast eyes shone an inexplicable look of something like triumph. No wonder, for if this was true, the danger which menaced her was averted for a time, and the marriage might be consummated without such desperate haste. This sad and sudden event seemed to her the mysterious fulfilment of a secret wish; and though startled she was not daunted but inspirited, for fate seemed to favor her designs. She did comfort Bella, control the excited household, and keep the rumors from Mrs Coventry all that dreadful night.

At dawn Gerald came home exhausted, and bringing no tiding of the missing man. He had telegraphed to the headquarters of the regiment and received a reply, stating that Edward had left for London the previous day, meaning to go home before returning. The fact of his having been at the London station was also established, but whether he left by the train or not was still uncertain. The ruins were still being searched, and the body might yet appear.

'Is Sir John coming at noon?' asked Jean, as the three sat together in the rosy hush of dawn, trying to hope against hope.

'No, he had been ill, I learned from young Gower, who is just from town, and so had not completed his business. I sent him word to wait till night, for the bridge won't be passable till then. Now I must try and rest an hour; I've worked all night and have no strength left. Call me the instant any messenger arrives.'

With that Coventry went to his room, Bella followed to wait on him, and Jean roamed through house and grounds, unable to rest. The morning was far spent when the messenger arrived. Jean went to receive his tidings, with the wicked hope still lurking at her heart.

'Is he found?' she asked calmly, as the man hesitated to speak.

'Yes, ma'am.'

'You are sure?'

'I am certain, ma'am, though some won't say till Mr Coventry comes to look.'

'Is he alive?' And Jean's white lips trembled as she put the question.

'Oh no, ma'am, that warn't possible, under all them stones and water. The poor young gentleman is so wet, and crushed, and torn, no one would know him, except for the uniform, and the white hand with the ring on it.'

Jean sat down, very pale, and the man described the finding of the poor shattered body. As he finished, Coventry appeared, and with one look of mingled remorse, shame, and sorrow, the elder brother went away, to find and bring the younger home. Jean crept into the garden like a guilty thing, trying to hide the satisfaction which struggled with a woman's natural pity, for so sad an end for this brave young life.

'Why waste tears or feign sorrow when I must be glad?' she muttered, as she paced to and fro along the terrace. 'The poor boy is out of pain, and I am out of danger.'

She got no further, for, turning as she spoke, she stood face to face with Edward! Bearing no mark of peril on dress or person, but stalwart and strong as ever, he stood there looking at her, with contempt and compassion struggling in his face. As if turned to stone, she remained motionless, with dilated eyes, arrested breath, and paling cheek. He did not speak but watched her silently till she put out a trembling hand, as if to assure herself by touch that it was really he. Then he drew back, and as if the act convinced as fully as words, she said slowly, 'They told me you were dead.'

'And you were glad to believe it. No, it was my comrade, young Courtney, who unconsciously deceived you all, and lost his life, as I should have done, if I had not gone to Ascot after seeing him off yesterday.'

'To Ascot?' echoed Jean, shrinking back, for Edward's eye was on her, and his voice was stern and cold.

'Yes; you know the place. I went there to make inquiries concerning you and was well satisfied. Why are you still here?'

'The three days are not over yet. I hold you to your promise. Before night I shall be gone; till then you will be silent, if you have honor enough to keep your word.'

'I have.' Edward took out his watch and, as he put it back, said with cool precision, 'It is now two, the train leaves for

London at half-past six; a carriage will wait for you at the side door. Allow me to advise you to go then, for the instant dinner is over I shall speak.' And with a bow he went into the house, leaving Jean nearly suffocated with a throng of contending emotions.

For a few minutes she seemed paralyzed; but the native energy of the woman forbade utter despair, till the last hope was gone. Frail as that now was, she still clung to it tenaciously, resolving to win the game in defiance of everything. Springing up, she went to her room, packed her few valuables, dressed herself with care, and then sat down to wait. She heard a joyful stir below, saw Coventry come hurrying back, and from a garrulous maid learned that the body was that of young Courtney. The uniform being the same as Edward's and the ring, a gift from him, had caused the men to believe the disfigured corpse to be that of the younger Coventry. No one but the maid came near her; once Bella's voice called her, but some one checked the girl, and the call was not repeated. At five an envelope was brought her, directed in Edward's hand, and containing a check which more than paid a year's salary. No word accompanied the gift, yet the generosity of it touched her, for Jean Muir had the relics of a once honest nature, and despite her falsehood could still admire nobleness and respect virtue. A tear of genuine shame dropped on the paper, and real gratitude filled her heart, as she thought that even if all else failed, she was not thrust out penniless into the world, which had no pity for poverty.

As the clock struck six, she heard a carriage drive around and went down to meet it. A servant put on her trunk, gave the order, 'To the station, James,' and she drove away without meeting anyone, speaking to anyone, or apparently being seen by anyone. A sense of utter weariness came over her, and she longed to lie down and forget. But the last chance still remained, and till that failed, she would not give up. Dismissing the carriage, she seated herself to watch for the quarter-past-six train from London, for in that Sir John would come if he came at all that night. She was haunted by the fear that Edward had met and told him. The first glimpse of Sir John's frank face would betray the truth. If he knew all, there was no hope, and she would go her way alone. If he knew nothing, there was yet time for the marriage; and once his wife, she knew she was safe, because for the honor of his name he would screen and protect her.

Up rushed the train, out stepped Sir John, and Jean's heart died within her. Grave, and pale, and worn he looked, and leaned heavily on the arm of a portly gentleman in black. The Reverend Mr Fairfax, why has he come, if the secret is out? thought Jean, slowly advancing to meet them and fearing to read her fate in Sir John's face. He saw her, dropped his friend's arm, and hurried forward with the ardor of a young man, exclaiming, as he seized her hand with a beaming face, a glad voice, 'My little girl! Did you think I would never come?'

She could not answer, the reaction was too strong, but she clung to him, regardless of time or place, and felt that her last hope had not failed. Mr Fairfax proved himself equal to the occasion. Asking no questions, he hurried Sir John and Jean into a carriage and stepped in after them with a bland apology. Jean was soon herself again, and, having told her fears at his delay, listened eagerly while he related the various mishaps which had detained him.

'Have you seen Edward?' was her first question.

'Not yet, but I know he has come, and have heard of his narrow escape. I should have been in that train, if I had not been delayed by the indisposition which I then cursed, but now bless. Are you ready, Jean? Do you repent your choice, my child?'

'No, no! I am ready, I am only too happy to become your wife, dear, generous Sir John,' cried Jean, with a glad alacrity, which touched the old man to the heart, and charmed the Reverend Mr Fairfax, who concealed the romance of a boy under his clerical suit.

They reached the Hall. Sir John gave orders to admit no one and after a hasty dinner sent for his old housekeeper and his steward, told them of his purpose, and desired them to witness his marriage. Obedience had been the law of their lives, and Master could do nothing wrong in their eyes, so they played their parts willingly, for Jean was a favorite at the Hall. Pale as her gown, but calm and steady; she stood beside Sir John, uttering her vows in a clear tone and taking upon herself the vows of a wife with more than a bride's usual docility. When the ring was fairly on, a smile broke over her face. When Sir John kissed and called her his 'little wife,' she shed a tear or two of sincere happiness; and when Mr Fairfax addressed her as 'my lady,' she laughed her musical laugh, and glanced up at a picture of Gerald with eyes full of exultation. As the servants left the room, a message was brought from Mrs Coventry, begging Sir John to come to her at once.

'You will not go and leave me so soon?' pleaded Jean, well knowing why he was sent for.

'My darling, I must.' And in spite of its tenderness, Sir John's manner was too decided to be withstood.

'Then I shall go with you,' cried Jean, resolving that no earthly power should part them.

9 Lady Coventry

When the first excitement of Edward's return had subsided, and before they could question him as to the cause of this unexpected visit, he told them that after dinner their curiosity should be gratified, and meantime he begged them to leave Miss Muir alone, for she had received bad news and must not be disturbed. The family with difficulty restrained their tongues and waited impatiently. Gerald confessed his love for Jean and asked his brother's pardon for betraying his trust. He had expected an outbreak, but Edward only looked at him with pitying eyes, and said sadly, 'You too! I have no reproaches to make, for I know what you will suffer when the truth is known.'

'What do you mean?' demanded Coventry.

'You will soon know, my poor Gerald, and we will comfort one another.'

Nothing more could be drawn from Edward till dinner was over, the servants gone, and all the family alone together. Then pale and grave, but very self-possessed, for trouble had made a man of him, he produced a packet of letters, and said, addressing himself to his brother, 'Jean Muir has deceived us all. I know her story; let me tell it before I read her letters.'

'Stop! I'll not listen to any false tales against her. The poor girl has enemies who belie her!' cried Gerald, starting up.

'For the honor of the family, you must listen, and learn what fools she has made of us. I can prove what I say, and convince you that she has the art of a devil. Sit still ten minutes, then go, if you will.'

Edward spoke with authority, and his brother obeyed him with a foreboding heart.

'I met Sydney, and he begged me to beware of her. Nay, listen, Gerald! I know she has told her story, and that you believe it; but her own letters convict her. She tried to charm Sydney as she did us, and nearly succeeded in inducing him to marry her. Rash and wild as he is, he is still a gentleman, and when an incautious word of hers roused his suspicions, he refused to make her his wife. A stormy scene ensued, and, hoping to intimidate him, she feigned to stab herself as if in despair. She did wound herself, but failed to gain her point and insisted upon going to a hospital to die. Lady Sydney, good, simple soul, believed the girl's version of the story, thought her son was in the wrong, and when he was gone, tried to atone for his fault by finding Jean Muir another home. She thought Gerald was soon to marry Lucia, and that I was away, so sent her here as a safe and comfortable retreat.'

'But, Ned, are you sure of all this? Is Sydney to be believed?' began Coventry, still incredulous.

'To convince you, I'll read Jean's letter before I say more. They were written to an accomplice and were purchased by Sydney. There was a compact between the two women, that each should keep the other informed of all adventures, plots and plans, and share whatever good fortune fell to the lot of either. Thus Jean wrote freely, as you shall judge. The letters concern us alone. The first was written a few days after she came.

'Dear Hortense:

'Another failure. Sydney was more wily than I thought. All was going well, when one day my old fault beset me, I took too much wine, and I carelessly owned that I had been an actress. He was shocked, and retreated. I got up a scene, and gave myself a safe little wound, to frighten him. The brute was not frightened, but coolly left me to my fate. I'd have died to spite him, if I dared, but as I didn't, I lived to torment him. As yet, I have had no chance, but I will not forget him. His mother is a poor, weak creature, whom I could use as I would, and through her I found an excellent place. A sick mother, silly daughter, and two eligible sons. One is engaged to a handsome iceberg, but that only renders him more interesting in my eyes, rivalry adds so much to the charm of one's conquests. Well, my dear, I went, got up in the meek style, intending to do the pathetic; but before I saw the family, I was so angry I could hardly control myself. Through the indolence of Monsieur the young master, no carriage was sent for me, and I intend he shall atone for that rudeness by-and-by. The younger son, the mother, and the girl received me patronizingly, and I understood the simple souls at once. Monsieur (as I shall call him, as names are unsafe) was unapproachable, and took no pains to conceal his dislike of governesses. The cousin was lovely, but detestable with her pride, her coldness, and her very visible adoration of Monsieur, who let her worship him, like an inanimate idol as he is. I hated them both, of course, and in return for their insolence shall torment her with jealousy, and teach him how to woo a woman by making his heart ache. They are an intensely proud family, but I can humble them all, I think, by captivating the sons, and when they have committed themselves, cast them off, and marry the old uncle, whose title takes my fancy.'

'She never wrote that! It is impossible. A woman could not do it,' cried Lucia indignantly, while Bella sat bewildered and Mrs Coventry supported herself with salts and fan. Coventry went to his brother, examined the writing, and returned to his seat, saying, in a tone of suppressed wrath, 'She did write it. I posted some of those letters myself. Go on, Ned.'

'I made myself useful and agreeable to the amiable ones, and overheard the chat of the lovers. It did not suit me, so I fainted away to stop it, and excite interest in the provoking pair. I thought I had succeeded, but Monsieur suspected me and showed me that he did. I forgot my meek role and gave him a stage look. It had a good effect, and I shall try it again. The man is well worth winning, but I prefer the title, and as the uncle is a hale, handsome gentleman, I can't wait for him to die, though Monsieur is very charming, with his elegant languor, and his heart so fast asleep no woman has had power to wake it yet. I told my story, and they believed it, though I had the audacity to say I was but nineteen, to talk Scotch, and bashfully confess that Sydney wished to marry me. Monsieur knows S. and evidently suspects something. I must watch him and keep the truth from him, if possible.

'I was very miserable that night when I got alone. Something in the atmosphere of this happy home made me wish I was anything but what I am. As I sat there trying to pluck up my spirits, I thought of the days when I was lovely and young, good and gay. My glass showed me an old woman of thirty, for my false locks were off, my paint gone, and my face was without its mask. Bah! how I hate sentiment! I drank your health from your own little flask, and went to bed to dream that I was playing Lady Tartuffe* – as I am. Adieu, more soon.'

No one spoke as Edward paused, and taking up another letter, he read on:

'My Dear Creature:

'All goes well. Next day I began my task, and having caught a hint of the character of each, tried my power over them. Early in the morning I ran over to see the Hall. Approved of it highly, and took the first step toward becoming its mistress, by piquing the curiosity and flattering the pride of its master. His estate is his idol; I praised it with a few artless compliments to himself, and he was charmed. The cadet of the family adores horses. I risked my neck to pet his beast, and he was charmed. The little girl is romantic about flowers; I made a posy and was sentimental, and she was charmed. The fair icicle loves her departed mamma, I had raptures over an old picture, and she thawed. Monsieur is used to being worshipped. I took no notice of him, and by the natural perversity of human nature, he began to take notice of me. He likes music; I sang, and stopped when he'd listened long enough to want more. He is lazily fond of being amused; I showed him my skill, but refused to exert it in his behalf. In short, I gave him no peace till he began to wake up. In order to get rid of the boy, I fascinated him, and he was sent away. Poor lad, I rather liked him, and if the title had been nearer would have married him.

'Many thanks for the honor.' And Edward's lip curled with intense scorn. But Gerald sat like a statue, his teeth set, his eyes fiery, his brows bent, waiting for the end.

'The passionate boy nearly killed his brother, but I turned the affair to good account, and bewitched Monsieur by playing nurse, till Vashti* (the icicle) interfered. Then I enacted injured virtue, and kept out of his way, knowing that he would miss me. I mystified him about S. by sending a letter where S. would not get it, and got up all manner of soft scenes to win this proud creature. I get on well and meanwhile privately fascinate Sir J. by being daughterly and devoted. He is a worthy old man, simple as a child, honest as the day, and generous as a prince. I shall be a happy woman if I win him, and you shall share my good fortune; so wish me success.

'This is the third, and contains something which will surprise you,' Edward said, as he lifted another paper.

'Hortense:

'I've done what I once planned to do on another occasion. You know my handsome, dissipated father married a lady of rank for his second wife. I never saw Lady H——d but once, for I was kept out of the way. Finding that this good Sir J. knew something of her when a girl, and being sure that he did not know of the death of her little daughter, I boldly said I was the child, and told a pitiful tale of my early life. It worked like a charm; he told Monsieur, and both felt the most chivalrous compassion for Lady Howard's daughter, though before they had secretly looked down on me, and my real poverty and my lowliness. That boy pitied me with an honest warmth and never waited to learn my birth. I don't forget that and shall repay it if I can. Wishing to bring Monsieur's affair to a successful crisis, I got up a theatrical evening and was in my element. One little event I must tell you, because I committed an actionable offense and was nearly discovered. I did not go down to supper, knowing that the moth would return to flutter about the candle, and preferring that the fluttering should be done in private, as Vashti's jealousy is getting uncontrollable. Passing through the gentlemen's dressing room, my quick eye caught sight of a letter lying among the costumes. It was no stage affair, and an odd sensation of fear ran through me as I recognized the hand of S. I had feared this, but I believe in chance; and having found the letter, I examined it. You know I can imitate almost any hand. When I read in this paper the whole story of my affair with S., truly told, and also that he had made inquiries into my past life and discovered the truth, I was in a fury. To be so near success and fail was terrible, and I resolved to risk everything. I opened the letter by means of a heated knife blade under the seal, therefore the envelope was perfect; imitating S.'s hand, I penned a few lines in his hasty style, saying he was at Baden, so that if Monsieur answered, the reply would not reach him, for he is in London, it seems. This letter I put into the pocket whence the other must have fallen, and was just congratulating myself on this narrow escape, when Dean, the maid of Vashti, appeared as if watching me. She had evidently seen the letter in my hand, and suspected something. I took no notice of her, but must be careful, for she is on the watch. After this the evening closed with strictly private theatricals, in which Monsieur and myself were the only actors. To make sure that he received my version of the story first, I told him a romantic story of S.'s persecution, and he believed it. This I followed up by a moonlight episode behind a rose hedge, and sent the young gentleman home in a half-dazed condition. What fools men are!'

'She is right!' muttered Coventry, who had flushed scarlet with shame and anger, as his folly became known and Lucia listened in astonished silence.

'Only one more, and my distasteful task will be nearly over,' said Edward, unfolding the last of the papers. 'This is not a letter, but a copy of one written three nights ago. Dean boldly ransacked Jean Muir's desk while she was at the Hall, and, fearing to betray the deed by keeping the letter, she made a hasty copy which she gave me today, begging me to save the family from disgrace. This makes the chain complete. Go now, if you will, Gerald. I would gladly spare you the pain of hearing this.'

'I will not spare myself; I deserve it. Read on,' replied Coventry, guessing what was to follow and nerving himself to hear it. Reluctantly his brother read these lines:

'The enemy has surrendered! Give me joy, Hortense; I can be the wife of this proud monsieur, if I will. Think what an honor for the divorced wife of a disreputable actor. I laugh at the farce and enjoy it, for I only wait till the prize I desire is fairly mine, to turn and reject this lover who has proved himself false to brother, mistress, and his own conscience. I resolved to be revenged on both, and I have kept my word. For my sake he cast off the beautiful woman who truly loved him; he forgot his promise to his brother, and put by his pride to beg of me the worn-out heart that is not worth a good man's love. Ah well, I am satisfied, for Vashti has suffered the sharpest pain a proud woman can endure, and will feel another pang when I tell her that I scorn her recreant lover, and give him back to her, to deal with as she will.'

Coventry started from his seat with a fierce exclamation, but Lucia bowed her face upon her hands, weeping, as if the pang had been sharper than even Jean foresaw.

'Send for Sir John! I am mortally afraid of this creature. Take her away; do something to her. My poor Bella, what a companion for you! Send for Sir John at once!' cried Mrs Coventry incoherently, and clasped her daughter in her arms, as if Jean Muir would burst in to annihilate the whole family. Edward alone was calm.

'I have already sent, and while we wait, let me finish this story. It is true that Jean is the daughter of Lady Howard's husband, the pretended clergyman, but really a worthless man who married her for her money. Her own child died, but this girl, having beauty, wit and a bold spirit, took her fate into her own hands, and became an actress. She married an actor, led a reckless life for some years; quarreled with her husband, was divorced, and went to Paris; left the stage, and tried to support herself as governess and companion. You know how she fared with the Sydneys, how she has duped us, and but for this discovery would have duped Sir John. I was in time to prevent this, thank heaven. She is gone; no one knows the truth but Sydney and ourselves; he will be silent, for his own sake; we will be for ours, and leave this dangerous woman to the fate which will surely overtake her.'

'Thank you, it has overtaken her, and a very happy one she finds it.'

A soft voice uttered the words, and an apparition appeared at the door, which made all start and recoil with amazement – Jean Muir leaning on the arm of Sir John.

'How dare you return?' began Edward, losing the self-control so long preserved. 'How dare you insult us by coming back to enjoy the mischief you have done? Uncle, you do not know that woman!'

'Hush, boy, I will not listen to a word, unless you remember where you are,' said Sir John, with a commanding gesture.

'Remember your promise: love me, forgive me, protect me, and do not listen to their accusations,' whispered Jean, whose quick eye had discovered the letters.

'I will; have no fears, my child,' he answered, drawing her nearer as he took his accustomed place before the fire, always lighted when Mrs Coventry was down.

Gerald, who had been pacing the room excitedly, paused behind Lucia's chair as if to shield her from insult; Bella clung to her mother; and Edward, calming himself by a strong effort, handed his uncle the letters, saying briefly, 'Look at those, sir, and let them speak.'

'I will look at nothing, hear nothing, believe nothing which can in any way lessen my respect and affection for this young lady. She has prepared me for this. I know the enemy who is unmanly enough to belie and threaten her. I know that you both are unsuccessful lovers, and this explains your unjust, uncourteous treatment now. We all have committed faults and follies. I freely forgive Jean hers, and desire to know nothing of them from your lips. If she has innocently offended, pardon it for my sake, and forget the past.'

'But, Uncle, we have proofs that this woman is not what she seems. Her own letters convict her. Read them, and do not blindly deceive yourself,' cried Edward, indignant at his uncle's words.

A low laugh startled them all, and in an instant they saw the cause of it. While Sir John spoke, Jean had taken the letters from the hand which he had put behind him, a favorite gesture of his, and, unobserved, had dropped them on the fire. The mocking laugh, the sudden blaze, showed what had been done. Both young men sprang forward, but it was too late; the proofs were ashes, and Jean Muir's bold, bright eyes defied them, as she said, with a disdainful little gesture, 'Hands off, gentlemen! You may degrade yourselves to the work of detectives, but I am not a prisoner yet. Poor Jean Muir you might harm, but Lady Coventry is beyond your reach.'

'Lady Coventry!' echoed the dismayed family, in varying tones of incredulity, indignation, and amazement.

'Aye, my dear and honored wife,' said Sir John, with a protecting arm about the slender figure at his side; and in the act, the words, there was a tender dignity that touched the listeners with pity and respect for the deceived man. 'Receive her as such, and for my sake, forbear all further accusation,' he continued steadily. 'I know what I have done. I have no fear that I shall repent it. If I am blind, let me remain so till time opens my eyes. We are going away for a little while, and when we return, let the old life return again, unchanged, except that Jean makes sunshine for me as well as for you.'

No one spoke, for no one knew what to say. Jean broke the silence, saying coolly, 'May I ask how those letters came into your possession?'

'In tracing out your past life, Sydney found your friend Hortense. She was poor, money bribed her, and your letters were given up to him as soon as received. Traitors are always betrayed in the end,' replied Edward sternly.

Jean shrugged her shoulders, and shot a glance at Gerald, saying with her significant smile, 'Remember that, monsieur, and allow me to hope that in wedding you will be happier than in wooing. Receive my congratulations, Miss Beaufort, and let me beg of you to follow my example, if you would keep your lovers.'

Here all the sarcasm passed from her voice, the defiance from her eye, and the one unspoiled attribute which still lingered in this woman's artful nature shone in her face, as she turned toward Edward and Bella at their mother's side.

'You have been kind to me,' she said, with grateful warmth. 'I thank you for it, and will repay it if I can. To you I will acknowledge that I am not worthy to be this good man's wife, and to you I will solemnly promise to devote my life to his happiness. For his sake forgive me, and let there be peace between us.'

There was no reply, but Edward's indignant eyes fell before hers. Bella half put out her hand, and Mrs Coventry sobbed as if some regret mingled with her resentment. Jean seemed to expect no friendly demonstration, and to understand that they forbore for Sir John's sake, not for hers, and to accept their contempt as her just punishment.

'Come home, love, and forget all this,' said her husband, ringing the bell, and eager to be gone. 'Lady Coventry's carriage.'

And as he gave the order, a smile broke over her face, for the sound assured her that the game was won. Pausing an instant on the threshold before she vanished from their sight, she looked backward, and fixing on Gerald the strange glance he remembered well, she said in her penetrating voice, 'Is not the last scene better than the first?'

MARY E. WILKINS FREEMAN

A New England Nun

1891

It was late in the afternoon, and the light was waning. There was a difference in the look of the tree shadows out in the yard. Somewhere in the distance cows were lowing and a little bell was tinkling; now and then a farm-wagon tilted by, and the dust flew; some blue-shirted laborers with shovels over their shoulders plodded past; little swarms of flies were dancing up and down before the people's faces in the soft air. There seemed to be a gentle stir arising over everything for the mere sake of subsidence – a very premonition of rest and hush and night.

This soft diurnal commotion was over Louisa Ellis also. She had been peacefully sewing at her sitting-room window all the afternoon. Now she quilted her needle carefully into her work, which she folded precisely, and laid in a basket with her thimble and thread and scissors. Louisa Ellis could not remember that ever in her life she had mislaid one of these little feminine appurtenances, which had become, from long use and constant association, a very part of her personality.

Louisa tied a green apron round her waist, and got out a flat straw hat with a green ribbon. Then she went into the garden with a little blue crockery bowl, to pick some currants for her tea. After the currants were picked she sat on the back doorstep and stemmed them, collecting the stems carefully in her apron, and afterwards throwing them into the hen-coop. She looked sharply at the grass beside the step to see if any had fallen there.

Louisa was slow and still in her movements; it took her a long time to prepare her tea; but when ready it was set forth with as much grace as if she had been a veritable guest to her own self. The little square table stood exactly in the centre of the kitchen, and was covered with a starched linen cloth whose border pattern of flowers glistened. Louisa had a damask napkin on her tea-tray, where were arranged a cut-glass tumbler full of tea-spoons, a silver cream-pitcher, a china sugar-bowl, and one pink china cup and saucer. Louisa used china every day – something which none of her neighbors did. They whispered about it among themselves. Their daily tables were laid with common crockery, their sets of best china stayed in the parlor closet, and Louisa Ellis was no richer nor better bred than they. Still she would use the china. She had for her supper a glass dish full of sugared currants, a plate of little cakes, and one of light white biscuits. Also a leaf or two of lettuce, which she cut up daintily. Louisa was very fond of lettuce, which she raised to perfection in her little garden. She ate quite heartily, though in a delicate, pecking way; it seemed almost surprising that any considerable bulk of the food should vanish.

After tea she filled a plate with nicely baked thin corn-cakes, and carried them out into the back-yard.

'Cæsar!' she called. 'Cæsar! Cæsar!'

There was a little rush, and the clank of a chain, and a large yellow-and-white dog appeared at the door of his tiny hut, which was half hidden among the tall grasses and flowers. Louisa patted him and gave him the corn-cakes. Then she returned to the house and washed the tea-things, polishing the china carefully. The twilight had deepened; the chorus of the frogs floated in at the open window wonderfully loud and shrill, and once in a while a long sharp drone from a tree-toad pierced it. Louisa took off her green gingham apron, disclosing a shorter one of pink and white print. She lighted her lamp, and sat down again with her sewing.

In about half an hour Joe Dagget came. She heard his heavy step on the walk, and rose and took off her pink-and-white apron. Under that was still another – white linen with a little cambric edging on the bottom; that was Louisa's company apron. She never wore it without her calico sewing apron over it unless she had a guest. She had barely folded the pink and white one with methodical haste and laid it in a table-drawer when the door opened and Joe Dagget entered.

He seemed to fill up the whole room. A little yellow canary that had been asleep in his green cage at the south window woke up and fluttered wildly, beating his little yellow wings against the wires. He always did so when Joe Dagget came into the room.

'Goodevening,' said Louisa. She extended her hand with a kind of solemn cordiality.

'Goodevening, Louisa,' returned the man, in a loud voice.

She placed a chair for him, and they sat facing each other, with the table between them. He sat bolt-upright, toeing out his heavy feet squarely, glancing with a good-humored uneasiness around the room. She sat gently erect, folding her slender hands in her white-linen lap.

'Been a pleasant day,' remarked Dagget.

'Real pleasant,' Louisa assented, softly. 'Have you been haying?' she asked, after a little while.

'Yes, I've been haying all day, down in the ten-acre lot. Pretty hot work.'

'It must be.'

'Yes, it's pretty hot work in the sun.'

'Is your mother well today?'

'Yes, mother's pretty well.'

'I suppose Lily Dyer's with her now?'

Dagget colored. 'Yes, she's with her,' he answered, slowly.

He was not very young, but there was a boyish look about his large face. Louisa was not quite as old as he, her face was fairer and smoother, but she gave people the impression of being older.

'I suppose she's a good deal of help to your mother,' she said, further.

'I guess she is; I don't know how mother'd get along without her,' said Dagget, with a sort of embarrassed warmth.

'She looks like a real capable girl. She's pretty-looking too,' remarked Louisa.

'Yes, she is pretty fair looking.'

Presently Dagget began fingering the books on the table. There was a square red autograph album, and a Young Lady's Gift-Book which had belonged to Louisa's mother. He took them up one after the other and opened them; then laid them down again, the album on the Gift-Book.

Louisa kept eyeing them with mild uneasiness. Finally she rose and changed the position of the books, putting the album underneath. That was the way they had been arranged in the first place.

Dagget gave an awkward little laugh. 'Now what difference did it make which book was on top?' said he.

Louisa looked at him with a deprecating smile. 'I always keep them that way,' murmured she.

'You do beat everything,' said Dagget, trying to laugh again. His large face was flushed.

He remained about an hour longer, then rose to take leave. Going out, he stumbled over a rug, and trying to recover himself, hit Louisa's work-basket on the table, and knocked it on the floor.

He looked at Louisa, then at the rolling spools; he ducked himself awkwardly toward them, but she stopped him. 'Never mind,' said she; 'I'll pick them up after you're gone.'

She spoke with a mild stiffness. Either she was a little disturbed, or his nervousness affected her, and made her seem constrained in her effort to reassure him.

When Joe Dagget was outside he drew in the sweet evening air with a sigh, and felt much as an innocent and perfectly well-intentioned bear might after his exit from a china shop.

Louisa, on her part, felt much as the kind-hearted, long-suffering owner of the china shop might have done after the exit of the bear.

She tied on the pink, then the green apron, picked up all the scattered treasures and replaced them in her work-basket, and straightened the rug. Then she set the lamp on the floor, and began sharply examining the carpet. She even rubbed her fingers over it, and looked at them.

'He's tracked in a good deal of dust,' she murmured. 'I thought he must have.'

Louisa got a dust-pan and brush, and swept Joe Dagget's track carefully.

If he could have known it, it would have increased his perplexity and uneasiness, although it would not have disturbed his loyalty in the least. He came twice a week to see Louisa Ellis, and every time, sitting there in her delicately sweet room, he felt as if surrounded by a hedge of lace. He was afraid to stir lest he should put a clumsy foot or hand through the fairy web, and he had always the consciousness that Louisa was watching fearfully lest he should.

Still the lace and Louisa commanded perforce his perfect respect and patience and loyalty. They were to be married in a month, after a singular courtship which had lasted for a matter of fifteen years. For fourteen out of the fifteen years the two had not once seen each other, and they had seldom exchanged letters. Joe had been all those years in Australia, where he had gone to make his fortune, and where he had stayed until he made it. He would have stayed fifty years if it had taken so long, and come home feeble and tottering, or never come home at all, to marry Louisa.

But the fortune had been made in the fourteen years, and he had come home now to marry the woman who had been patiently and unquestioningly waiting for him all that time.

Shortly after they were engaged he had announced to Louisa his determination to strike out into new fields, and secure a competency before they should be married. She had listened and assented with the sweet serenity which never failed her, not even when her lover set forth on that long and uncertain journey. Joe, buoyed up as he was by his sturdy determination, broke down a little at the last, but Louisa kissed him with a mild blush, and said goodby.

'It won't be for long,' poor Joe had said, huskily; but it was for fourteen years.

In that length of time much had happened. Louisa's mother and brother had died, and she was all alone in the world. But greatest happening of all – a subtle happening which both were too simple to understand – Louisa's feet had turned into a path, smooth maybe under a calm, serene sky, but so straight and unswerving that it could only meet a check at her grave, and so narrow that there was no room for any one at her side.

Louisa's first emotion when Joe Dagget came home (he had not apprised her of his coming) was consternation, although she would not admit it to herself, and he never dreamed of it. Fifteen years ago she had been in love with him – at least she considered herself to be. Just at that time, gently acquiescing with and falling into the natural drift of girlhood, she had seen marriage ahead as a reasonable feature and a probable desirability of life. She had listened with calm docility to her mother's views upon the subject. Her mother was remarkable for her cool sense and sweet, even temperament. She talked wisely to her daughter when Joe Dagget presented himself, and Louisa accepted him with no hesitation. He was the first lover she had ever had.

She had been faithful to him all these years. She had never dreamed of the possibility of marrying any one else. Her life, especially for the last seven years, had been full of a pleasant peace, she had never felt discontented nor impatient over her lover's absence; still she had always looked forward to his return and their marriage as the inevitable conclusion of things. However, she had fallen into a way of placing it so far in the future that it was almost equal to placing it over the boundaries of another life.

When Joe came she had been expecting him, and expecting to be married for fourteen years, but she was as much surprised and taken aback as if she had never thought of it.

Joe's consternation came later. He eyed Louisa with an instant confirmation of his old admiration. She had changed but little. She still kept her pretty manner and soft grace, and was, he considered, every whit as attractive as ever. As for himself, his stent was done; he had turned his face away from fortune-seeking, and the old winds of romance whistled as loud and sweet as ever through his ears. All the song which he had been wont to hear in them was Louisa; he had for a long time a loyal belief that he heard it still, but finally it seemed to him that although the winds sang always that one song, it had another name. But for Louisa the wind had never more than murmured; now it had gone down, and everything was still. She listened for a little while with half-wistful attention; then she turned quietly away and went to work on her wedding clothes.

Joe had made some extensive and quite magnificent alterations in his house. It was the old homestead; the newly-married couple would live there, for Joe could not desert his mother, who refused to leave her old home. So Louisa must leave hers. Every morning, rising and going about among her neat maidenly possessions, she felt as one looking her last upon the faces of dear friends. It was true that in a measure she could take them with her, but, robbed of their old environments, they would appear in such new guises that they would almost cease to be themselves. Then there were some peculiar features of her happy solitary life which she would probably be obliged to relinquish altogether. Sterner tasks than these graceful but half-needless ones would probably devolve upon her. There would be a large house to care for; there would be company to entertain; there would be Joe's rigorous and feeble old mother to wait upon; and it would be contrary to all thrifty village traditions for her to keep more than one servant. Louisa had a little still, and she used to occupy herself pleasantly in summer weather with distilling the sweet and aromatic essences from roses and peppermint and spearmint. By-and-by her still must be laid away. Her store of essences was already considerable, and there would be no time for her to distil for the mere pleasure of it. Then Joe's mother would think it foolishness; she had already hinted her opinion in the matter. Louisa dearly loved to sew a linen seam, not always for use, but for the simple, mild pleasure which she took in it. She would have been loath to confess how more than once she had ripped a seam for the mere delight of sewing it together again. Sitting at her window during long sweet afternoons, drawing her needle gently through the dainty fabric, she was peace itself. But there was small chance of such foolish comfort in the future. Joe's mother, domineering, shrewd old matron that she was even in her old age, and very likely even Joe himself, with his honest masculine rudeness, would laugh and frown down all these pretty but senseless old maiden ways.

Louisa had almost the enthusiasm of an artist over the mere order and cleanliness of her solitary home. She had throbs of genuine triumph at the sight of the window-panes which she had polished until they shone like jewels. She gloated gently over her orderly bureau-drawers, with their exquisitely folded contents redolent with lavender and sweet clover and very purity. Could she be sure of the endurance of even this? She had visions, so startling that she half repudiated them as indelicate, of coarse masculine belongings strewn about in endless litter; of dust and disorder arising necessarily from a coarse masculine presence in the midst of all this delicate harmony.

Among her forebodings of disturbance, not the least was with regard to Cæsar. Cæsar was a veritable hermit of a dog. For the greater part of his life he had dwelt in his secluded hut, shut out from the society of his kind and all innocent canine joys. Never had Cæsar since his early youth watched at a woodchuck's hole; never had he known the delights of a stray bone at a neighbor's kitchen door. And it was all on account of a sin committed when hardly out of his puppyhood. No one knew the possible depth of remorse of which this mild-visaged, altogether inno-cent-looking old dog might be capable; but whether or not he had encountered remorse, he had encountered a full measure of righteous retribution. Old Cæsar seldom lifted up his voice in a growl or a bark; he was fat and sleepy; there were yellow rings which looked like spectacles around his dim old eyes; but there was a neighbor who bore on his hand the imprint of several of Cæsar's sharp white youthful teeth, and for that he had lived at the end of a chain, all alone in a little hut, for fourteen years. The neighbor, who was choleric and smarting with the pain of his wound, had demanded either Cæsar's death or complete ostracism. So Louisa's brother, to whom the dog had belonged, had built him his little kennel and tied him up. It was now fourteen years since, in a flood of youthful spirits, he had inflicted that memorable bite, and with the exception of short excursions, always at the end of the chain, under the strict guardianship of his master or Louisa, the old dog had remained a close prisoner. It is doubtful if, with his limited ambition, he took much pride in the fact, but it is certain that he was possessed of considerable cheap fame. He was regarded by all the children in the village and by many adults as a very monster of ferocity. St George's dragon could hardly have surpassed in evil repute Louisa Ellis's old yellow dog. Mothers charged their children with solemn emphasis not to go too near to him, and the children listened and believed greedily, with a fascinated appetite for terror, and ran by Louisa's house stealthily, with many sidelong and backward glances at the terrible dog. If perchance he sounded a hoarse bark, there was a panic. Wayfarers chancing into Louisa's yard eyed him with respect, and inquired if the chain were stout. Cæsar at large might have seemed a very ordinary dog, and excited no comment whatever; chained, his reputation overshadowed him, so that he lost his own proper outlines and looked darkly vague and enormous. Joe Dagget, however, with his good-humored sense and shrewdness, saw him as he was. He strode valiantly up to him and patted him on the head, in spite of Louisa's soft clamor of warning, and even attempted to set him loose. Louisa grew so alarmed that he desisted, but kept announcing his opinion in the matter quite forcibly at intervals. 'There ain't a better-natured dog in town,' he would say, 'and it's downright cruel to keep him tied up there. Some day I'm going to take him out.'

Louisa had very little hope that he would not, one of these days, when their interests and possessions should be more completely fused in one. She pictured to herself Cæsar on the rampage through the quiet and unguarded village. She saw innocent children bleeding in his path. She was herself very fond of the old dog, because he had belonged to her dead brother, and he was always very gentle with her; still she had great faith in his ferocity. She always warned people not to go too near him. She fed him on ascetic fare of corn-mush and cakes, and never fired his dangerous temper with heating and sanguinary diet of flesh and bones. Louisa looked at the old dog munching his simple fare, and thought of her approaching marriage and trembled. Still no anticipation of disorder and confusion in lieu of sweet peace and harmony, no forebodings of Cæsar on the rampage, no wild fluttering of her little yellow canary, were sufficient to turn her a hair's-breadth. Joe Dagget had been fond of her and working for her all these years. It was not for her, whatever came to pass, to prove untrue and break his heart. She put the exquisite little stitches into her wedding-garments, and the time went on until it was only a week before her wedding-day. It was a Tuesday evening, and the wedding was to be a week from Wednesday.

There was a full moon that night. About nine o'clock Louisa strolled down the road a little way. There were harvest-fields on either hand, bordered by low stone walls. Luxuriant clumps of bushes grew beside the wall, and trees – wild cherry and old apple-trees – at intervals. Presently Louisa sat down on the wall and looked about her with mildly sorrowful reflectiveness. Tall shrubs of blueberry and meadow-sweet, all woven together and tangled with blackberry vines and horsebriers, shut her in on either side. She had a little clear space between them. Opposite her, on the other side of the road, was a spreading tree; the moon shone between its boughs, and the leaves twinkled like silver. The road was bespread with a beautiful shifting dapple of silver and shadow; the air was full of a mysterious sweetness. 'I wonder if it's wild grapes?' murmured Louisa. She sat there some time. She was just thinking of rising, when she heard footsteps and low voices, and remained quiet. It was a lonely place, and she felt a little timid. She thought she would keep still in the shadow and let the persons, whoever they might be, pass her.

But just before they reached her the voices ceased, and the footsteps. She understood that their owners had also found seats upon the stone wall. She was wondering if she could not steal away unobserved, when the voice broke the stillness. It was Joe Dagget's. She sat still and listened.

The voice was announced by a loud sigh, which was as

familiar as itself. 'Well,' said Dagget, 'you've made up your mind, then, I suppose?'

'Yes,' returned another voice; 'I'm going day after tomorrow.'

'That's Lily Dyer,' thought Louisa to herself. The voice embodied itself in her mind. She saw a girl tall and full-figured, with a firm, fair face, looking fairer and firmer in the moonlight, her strong yellow hair braided in a close knot. A girl full of a calm rustic strength and bloom, with a masterful way which might have beseemed a princess. Lily Dyer was a favorite with the village folk; she had just the qualities to arouse the admiration. She was good and handsome and smart. Louisa had often heard her praises sounded.

'Well,' said Joe Dagget, 'I ain't got a word to say.'

'I don't know what you could say,' returned Lily Dyer.

'Not a word to say,' repeated Joe, drawing out the words heavily. Then there was a silence. 'I ain't sorry,' he began at last, 'that that happened yesterday – that we kind of let on how we felt to each other. I guess it's just as well we knew. Of course I can't do anything any different. I'm going right on an' get married next week. I ain't going back on a woman that's waited for me fourteen years, an' break her heart.'

'If you should jilt her tomorrow, I wouldn't have you,' spoke up the girl, with sudden vehemence.

'Well, I ain't going to give you the chance,' said he; 'but I don't believe you would, either.'

'You'd see I wouldn't. Honor's honor, an' right's right. An' I'd never think anything of any man that went against 'em for me or any other girl; you'd find that out, Joe Dagget.'

'Well, you'll find out fast enough that I ain't going against 'em for you or any other girl,' returned he. Their voices sounded almost as if they were angry with each other. Louisa was listening eagerly.

'I'm sorry you feel as if you must go away,' said Joe, 'but I don't know but it's best.'

'Of course it's best. I hope you and I have got common-sense.'

'Well, I suppose you're right.' Suddenly Joe's voice got an undertone of tenderness. 'Say, Lily,' said he, 'I'll get along well enough myself, but I can't bear to think – You don't suppose you're going to fret much over it?'

'I guess you'll find out I sha'n't fret much over a married man.'

'Well, I hope you won't – I hope you won't, Lily. God knows I do. And – I hope – one of these days – you'll – come across somebody else – '

'I don't see any reason why I shouldn't.' Suddenly her tone changed. She spoke in a sweet, clear voice, so loud that she could have been heard across the street. 'No, Joe Dagget,' said she, 'I'll never marry any other man as long as I live. I've got good sense, an' I ain't going to break my heart nor make a fool of myself; but I'm never going to be married, you can be sure of that. I ain't that sort of a girl to feel this way twice.'

Louisa heard an exclamation and a soft commotion behind the bushes; then Lily spoke again – the voice sounded as if she had risen. 'This must be put a stop to,' said she. 'We've stayed here long enough. I'm going home.'

Louisa sat there in a daze, listening to their retreating steps. After a while she got up and slunk softly home herself. The next day she did her housework methodically; that was as much a matter of course as breathing; but she did not sew on her wedding-clothes. She sat at her window and meditated. In the evening Joe came. Louisa Ellis had never known that she had any diplomacy in her, but when she came to look for it that night she found it, although meek of its kind, among her little feminine weapons. Even now she could hardly believe that she had heard aright, and that she would not do Joe a terrible injury should she break her troth-plight. She wanted to sound him without betraying too soon her own inclinations in the matter. She did it successfully, and they finally came to an understanding; but it was a difficult thing, for he was as afraid of betraying himself as she.

She never mentioned Lily Dyer. She simply said that while she had no cause of complaint against him, she had lived so long in one way that she shrank from making a change.

'Well, I never shrank, Louisa,' said Dagget. 'I'm going to be honest enough to say that I think maybe it's better this way; but if you'd wanted to keep on, I'd have stuck to you till my dying day. I hope you know that.'

'Yes, I do,' said she.

That night she and Joe parted more tenderly than they had done for a long time. Standing in the door, holding each other's hands, a last great wave of regretful memory swept over them.

'Well, this ain't the way we've thought it was all going to end, is it, Louisa?' said Joe.

She shook her head. There was a little quiver on her placid face.

'You let me know if there's ever anything I can do for you,' said he. 'I ain't ever going to forget you, Louisa.' Then he kissed her, and went down the path.

Louisa, all alone by herself that night, wept a little, she hardly knew why; but the next morning, on waking, she felt like a queen who, after fearing lest her domain be wrested away from her, sees it firmly insured in her possession.

Now the tall weeds and grasses might cluster around Cæsar's little hermit hut, the snow might fall on its roof year in and year out, but he never would go on a rampage through the unguarded village. Now the little canary might turn itself into a peaceful yellow ball night after night, and have no need to wake and flutter with wild terror against its bars. Louisa could sew linen seams, and distil roses, and dust and polish and fold away in lavender, as long as she listed. That afternoon she sat with her needle-work at the window, and felt fairly steeped in peace. Lily Dyer, tall and erect and blooming, went past; but she felt no qualm. If Louisa Ellis had sold her birthright she did not know it, the taste of the pottage was so delicious, and had been her sole satisfaction for so long. Serenity and placid narrowness had become to her as the birthright itself. She gazed ahead through a long reach of future days strung together like pearls in a rosary, every one like the others, and all smooth and flawless and innocent, and her heart went up in thankfulness. Outside was the fervid summer afternoon; the air was filled with the sounds of the busy harvest of men and birds and bees; there were halloos, metallic clatterings, sweet calls, and long hummings. Louisa sat, prayerfully numbering her days, like an uncloistered nun.

A Poetess

1891

The garden-patch at the right of the house was all a gay spangle with sweet-peas and red-flowering beans, and flanked with feathery asparagus. A woman in blue was moving about there. Another woman, in a black bonnet, stood at the front door of the house. She knocked and waited. She could not see from where she stood the blue-clad woman in the garden. The house was very close to the road, from which a tall evergreen hedge separated it, and the view to the side was in a measure cut off.

The front door was open; the woman had to reach to knock on it, as it swung into the entry. She was a small woman and quite young, with a bright alertness about her which had almost the effect of prettiness. It was to her what greenness and crispness are to a plant. She poked her little face forward, and her sharp pretty eyes took in the entry and a room at the left, of which the door stood open. The entry was small and square and unfurnished, except for a well-rubbed old card-table against the back wall. The room was full of green light from the tall hedge, and bristling with grasses and flowers and asparagus stalks.

'Betsey, you there?' called the woman. When she spoke, a yellow canary, whose cage hung beside the front door, began to chirp and twitter.

'Betsey, you there?' the woman called again. The bird's chirps came in a quick volley; then he began to trill and sing.

'She ain't there,' said the woman. She turned and went out of the yard through the gap in the hedge; then she looked around. She caught sight of the blue figure in the garden. 'There she is,' said she.

She went around the house to the garden. She wore a gay cashmere-patterned calico dress with her mourning bonnet, and she held it carefully away from the dewy grass and vines.

The other woman did not notice her until she was close to her and said, 'Good-mornin', Betsey.' Then she started and turned around.

'Why, Mis' Caxton! That you?' said she.

'Yes. I've been standin' at your door for the last half-hour. I was jest goin' away when I caught sight of you out here.'

In spite of her brisk speech her manner was subdued. She drew down the corners of her mouth sadly.

'I declare I'm dreadful sorry you had to stan' there so long!' said the other woman.

She set a pan partly filled with beans on the ground, wiped her hands, which were damp and green from the wet vines, on her apron, then extended her right one with a solemn and sympathetic air.

'It don't make much odds, Betsey,' replied Mrs Caxton. 'I ain't got much to take up my time nowadays.' She sighed heavily as she shook hands, and the other echoed her.

'We'll go right in now. I'm dreadful sorry you stood there so long,' said Betsey.

'You'd better finish pickin' your beans.'

'No; I wa'n't goin' to pick any more. I was jest goin' in.'

'I declare, Betsey Dole, I shouldn't think you'd got enough for a cat!' said Mrs Caxton, eying the pan.

'I've got pretty near all there is. I guess I've got more flowerin' beans than eatin' ones, anyway.'

'I should think you had,' said Mrs Caxton, surveying the row of bean-poles topped with swarms of delicate red flowers. 'I should think they were pretty near all flowerin' ones. Had any peas?'

'I didn't have more'n three or four messes. I guess I planted sweet-peas mostly. I don't know hardly how I happened to.'

'Had any summer squash?'

'Two or three. There's some more set, if they ever get ripe. I planted some gourds. I think they look real pretty on the kitchen shelf in the winter.'

'I should think you'd got a sage bed big enough for the whole town.'

'Well, I have got a pretty good-sized one. I always liked them blue sage-blows. You'd better hold up your dress real careful goin' through here, Mis' Caxton, or you'll get it wet.'

The two women picked their way through the dewy grass, around a corner of the hedge, and Betsey ushered her visitor into the house.

'Set right down in the rockin-chair,' said she. 'I'll jest carry these beans out into the kitchen.'

'I should think you'd better get another pan and string 'em, or you won't get 'em done for dinner.'

'Well, mebbe I will, if you'll excuse it, Mis' Caxton. The beans had ought to boil quite a while; they're pretty old.'

Betsey went into the kitchen and returned with a pan and an old knife. She seated herself opposite Mrs Caxton, and began to string and cut the beans.

'If I was in your place I shouldn't feel as if I'd got enough to boil a kettle for,' said Mrs Caxton, eying the beans. 'I should 'most have thought when you didn't have any more room for a garden than you've got that you'd planted more real beans and peas instead of so many flowerin' ones. I'd rather have a good mess of green peas boiled with a piece of salt pork than all the sweet-peas you could give me. I like flowers well enough, but I never set up for a butterfly, an' I want something else to live on.' She looked at Betsey with pensive superiority.

Betsey was near-sighted; she had to bend low over the beans in order to string them. She was fifty years old, but she wore her streaky light hair in curls like a young girl. The curls hung over her faded cheeks and almost concealed them. Once in a while she flung them back with a childish gesture which sat strangely upon her.

'I dare say you're in the right of it,' she said, meekly.

'I know I am. You folks that write poetry wouldn't have a single thing to eat growin' if they were left alone. And that brings to mind what I come for. I've been thinkin' about it ever since – our – little Willie – left us.' Mrs Caxton's manner was suddenly full of shamefaced dramatic fervor, her eyes reddened with tears.

Betsey looked up inquiringly, throwing back her curls. Her face took on unconsciously lines of grief so like the other woman's that she looked like her for the minute.

'I thought maybe,' Mrs Caxton went on, tremulously, 'you'd be willin' to – write a few lines.'

'Of course I will, Mis' Caxton. I'll be glad to, if I can do 'em to suit you,' Betsey said, tearfully.

'I thought jest a few – lines. You could mention how – handsome he was, and good, and I never had to punish him but once in his life, and how pleased he was with his little new suit, and what a sufferer he was, and – how we hope he is at rest – in a better land.'

'I'll try, Mis' Caxton, I'll try,' sobbed Betsey. The two women wept together for a few minutes.

'It seems as if – I couldn't have it so sometimes,' Mrs Caxton said, brokenly. 'I keep thinkin' he's in the other – room. Every time I go back home when I've been away it's like – losin' him again. Oh, it don't seem as if I could go home and not find him there – it don't, it don't! Oh, you don't know anything about it, Betsey. You never had any children!'

'I don't s'pose I do, Mis' Caxton; I don't s'pose I do.'

Presently Mrs Caxton wiped her eyes. 'I've been thinkin',' said she, keeping her mouth steady with an effort, 'that it would be real pretty to have – some lines printed on some sheets of white paper with a neat black border. I'd like to send some to my folks, and one to the Perkinses in Brigham, and there's a good many others I thought would value 'em.'

'I'll do jest the best I can, Mis' Caxton, an' be glad to. It's little enough anybody can do at such times.'

Mrs Caxton broke out weeping again. 'Oh, it's true, it's true, Betsey!' she sobbed. 'Nobody can do anything, and nothin' amounts to anything – poetry or anything else – when he's *gone*. Nothin' can bring him back. Oh, what shall I do, what shall I do?'

Mrs Caxton dried her tears again, and arose to take leave. 'Well, I must be goin', or Wilson won't have any dinner,' she said, with an effort at self-control.

'Well, I'll do jest the best I can with the poetry,' said Betsey. 'I'll write it this afternoon.' She had set down her pan of beans and was standing beside Mrs Caxton. She reached up and straightened her black bonnet, which had slipped backward.

'I've got to get a pin,' said Mrs Caxton, tearfully. 'I can't keep it anywheres. It drags right off my head, the veil is so heavy.'

Betsey went to the door with her visitor. 'It's dreadful dusty, ain't it?' she remarked, in that sad, contemptuous tone with which one speaks of discomforts in the presence of affliction.

'Terrible,' replied Mrs Caxton. 'I wouldn't wear my black dress in it nohow; a black bonnet is bad enough. This dress is 'most too good. It's enough to spoil everything. Well, I'm much obliged to you, Betsey, for bein' willin' to do that.'

'I'll do jest the best I can, Mis' Caxton.'

After Betsey had watched her visitor out of the yard she returned to the sitting-room and took up the pan of beans. She looked doubtfully at the handful of beans all nicely strung and cut up. 'I declare I don't know what to do,' said she. 'Seems as if I should kind of relish these, but it's goin' to take some time to cook 'em, tendin' the fire an' everything, an' I'd ought to go to work on that poetry. Then, there's another thing, if I have 'em today, I can't tomorrow. Mebbe I shall take more comfort thinkin' about 'em. I guess I'll leave 'em over till tomorrow.'

Betsey carried the pan of beans out into the kitchen and set them away in the pantry. She stood scrutinizing the shelves like a veritable Mother Hubbard. There was a plate containing three or four potatoes and a slice of cold boiled pork, and a spoonful of red jelly in a tumbler; that was all the food in sight. Betsey stooped and lifted the lid from an earthen jar on the floor. She took out two slices of bread. 'There!' said she. 'I'll have this bread and that jelly this noon, an' tonight I'll have a kind of dinner-supper with them potatoes warmed up with the pork. An' then I can sit right down an' go to work on that poetry.'

It was scarcely eleven o'clock, and not time for dinner. Betsey returned to the sitting-room, got an old black portfolio and pen and ink out of the chimney cupboard, and seated herself to work. She meditated, and wrote one line, then another. Now and then she read aloud what she had written with a solemn intonation. She sat there thinking and writing, and the time went on. The twelve-o'clock bell rang, but she never noticed it; she had quite forgotten the bread and jelly. The long curls drooped over her cheeks; her thin yellow hand, cramped around the pen, moved slowly and fitfully over the paper. The light in the room was dim and green, like the light in an arbor, from the tall hedge before the windows. Great plumy bunches of asparagus waved over the tops of the looking-glass; a framed sampler, a steel engraving of a female head taken from some old magazine, and sheaves of dried grasses hung on or were fastened to the walls; vases and tumblers of flowers stood on the shelf and table. The air was heavy and sweet.

Betsey in this room, bending over her portfolio, looked like the very genius of gentle, old-fashioned, sentimental poetry. It seemed as if one, given the premises of herself and the room,

could easily deduce what she would write, and read without
seeing those lines wherein flowers rhymed sweetly with vernal
bowers, home with beyond the tomb, and heaven with even.

The summer afternoon wore on. It grew warmer and closer;
the air was full of the rasping babble of insects, with the cicadas
shrilling over them; now and then a team passed, and a dust
cloud floated over the top of the hedge; the canary at the door
chirped and trilled, and Betsey wrote poor little Willie Caxton's
obituary poetry.

Tears stood in her pale blue eyes; occasionally they rolled
down her cheeks, and she wiped them away. She kept her
handkerchief in her lap with her portfolio. When she looked
away from the paper she seemed to see two childish forms in
the room – one purely human, a boy clad in his little girl
petticoats, with a fair chubby face; the other in a little straight
white night-gown, with long, shining wings, and the same face.
Betsey had not enough imagination to change the face. Little
Willie Caxton's angel was still himself to her, although decked
in the paraphernalia of the resurrection.

'I s'pose I can't feel about it nor write about it anything the
way I could if I'd had any children of my own an' lost 'em. I
s'pose it *would* have come home to me different,' Betsey
murmured once, sniffing. A soft color flamed up under her curls
at the thought. For a second the room seemed all aslant with
white wings, and smiling with the faces of children that had
never been. Betsey straightened herself as if she were trying to
be dignified to her inner consciousness. 'That's one trouble I've
been clear of, anyhow,' said she; 'an' I guess I can enter into her
feelin's considerable.'

She glanced at a great pink shell on the shelf, and remembered
how she had often given it to the dead child to play with when
he had been in with his mother, and how he had put it to his ear
to hear the sea.

'Dear little fellow!' she sobbed, and sat awhile with her
handkerchief at her face.

Betsey wrote her poem upon backs of old letters and odd
scraps of paper. She found it difficult to procure enough paper
for fair copies of her poems when composed; she was forced to
be very economical with the first draft. Her portfolio was piled
with a loose litter of written papers when she at length arose
and stretched her stiff limbs. It was near sunset; men with

dinner-pails were tramping past the gate, going home from their work.

Betsey laid the portfolio on the table. 'There! I've wrote sixteen verses,' said she, 'an' I guess I've got everything in. I guess she'll think that's enough. I can copy it off nice tomorrow. I can't see tonight to do it, anyhow.'

There were red spots on Betsey's cheeks; her knees were unsteady when she walked. She went into the kitchen and made a fire, and set on the tea-kettle. 'I guess I won't warm up them potatoes tonight,' said she; 'I'll have the bread an' jelly, an' save 'em for breakfast. Somehow I don't seem to feel so much like 'em as I did, an' fried potatoes is apt to lay heavy at night.'

When the kettle boiled, Betsey drank her cup of tea and soaked her slice of bread in it; then she put away her cup and saucer and plate, and went out to water her garden. The weather was so dry and hot it had to be watered every night. Betsey had to carry the water from a neighbor's well; her own was dry. Back and forth she went in the deepening twilight, her slender body strained to one side with the heavy water-pail, until the garden-mould looked dark and wet. Then she took in the canary-bird, locked up her house, and soon her light went out. Often on these summer nights Betsey went to bed without lighting a lamp at all. There was no moon, but it was a beautiful starlight night. She lay awake nearly all night, thinking of her poem. She altered several lines in her mind.

She arose early, made herself a cup of tea, and warmed over the potatoes, then sat down to copy the poem. She wrote it out on both sides of note-paper, in a neat, cramped hand. It was the middle of the afternoon before it was finished. She had been obliged to stop work and cook the beans for dinner, although she begrudged the time. When the poem was fairly copied, she rolled it neatly and tied it with a bit of black ribbon; then she made herself ready to carry it to Mrs Caxton's.

It was a hot afternoon. Betsey went down the street in her thinnest dress – an old delaine,* with delicate bunches of faded flowers on a faded green ground. There was a narrow green belt ribbon around her long waist. She wore a green barège bonnet, stiffened with rattans, scooping over her face, with her curls pushed forward over her thin cheeks in two bunches, and she carried a small green parasol with a jointed handle. Her costume was obsolete, even in the little country village where she lived.

She had worn it every summer for the last twenty years. She made no more change in her attire than the old perennials in her garden. She had no money with which to buy new clothes, and the old satisfied her. She had come to regard them as being as unalterably a part of herself as her body.

Betsey went on, setting her slim, cloth-gaitered feet daintily in the hot sand of the road. She carried her roll of poetry in a black-mitted hand. She walked rather slowly. She was not very strong; there was a limp feeling in her knees; her face, under the green shade of her bonnet, was pale and moist with the heat.

She was glad to reach Mrs Caxton's and sit down in her parlor, damp and cool and dark as twilight, for the blinds and curtains had been drawn all day. Not a breath of the fervid out-door air had penetrated it.

'Come right in this way; it's cooler than the sittin'-room,' Mrs Caxton said; and Betsey sank into the haircloth rocker and waved a palm-leaf fan.

Mrs Caxton sat close to the window in the dim light, and read the poem. She took out her handkerchief and wiped her eyes as she read. 'It's beautiful, beautiful,' she said, tearfully, when she had finished. 'It's jest as comfortin' as it can be, and you worked that in about his new suit so nice. I feel real obliged to you, Betsey, and you shall have one of the printed ones when they're done. I'm goin' to see to it right off.'

Betsey flushed and smiled. It was to her as if her poem had been approved and accepted by one of the great magazines. She had the pride and self-wonderment of recognized genius. She went home buoyantly, under the wilting sun, after her call was done. When she reached home there was no one to whom she could tell her triumph, but the hot spicy breath of the evergreen hedge and the fervent sweetness of the sweet-peas seemed to greet her like the voices of friends.

She could scarcely wait for the printed poem. Mrs Caxton brought it, and she inspected it, neatly printed in its black border. She was quite overcome with innocent pride.

'Well, I don't know but it does read pretty well,' said she.

'It's beautiful,' said Mrs Caxton, fervently. 'Mr White said he never read anything any more touchin', when I carried it to him to print. I think folks are goin' to think a good deal of havin' it. I've had two dozen printed.'

It was to Betsey like a large edition of a book. She had written obituary poems before, but never one had been printed in this sumptuous fashion. 'I declare I think it would look pretty framed!' said she.

'Well, I don't know but it would,' said Mrs Caxton. 'Anybody might have a neat little black frame, and it would look real appropriate.'

'I wonder how much it would cost?' said Betsey.

After Mrs Caxton had gone, she sat long, staring admiringly at the poem, and speculating as to the cost of a frame. 'There ain't no use; I can't have it nohow, not if it don't cost more'n a quarter of a dollar,' said she.

Then she put the poem away and got her supper. Nobody knew how frugal Betsey Dole's suppers and breakfasts and dinners were. Nearly all her food in the summer came from the scanty vegetables which flourished between the flowers in her garden. She ate scarcely more than her canary-bird, and sang as assiduously. Her income was almost infinitesimal: the interest at a low per cent of a tiny sum in the village savings-bank, the remnant of her father's little hoard after his funeral expenses had been paid. Betsey had lived upon it for twenty years, and considered herself well-to-do. She had never received a cent for her poems; she had not thought of such a thing as possible. The appearance of this last in such shape was worth more to her than its words represented in as many dollars.

Betsey kept the poem pinned on the wall under the looking-glass; if any one came in, she tried with delicate hints to call attention to it. It was two weeks after she received it that the downfall of her innocent pride came.

One afternoon Mrs Caxton called. It was raining hard. Betsey could scarcely believe it was she when she went to the door and found her standing there.

'Why, Mis' Caxton!' said she. 'Ain't you wet to your skin?'

'Yes, I guess I be, pretty near. I s'pose I hadn't ought to come 'way down here in such a soak; but I went into Sarah Rogers's a minute after dinner, and something she said made me so mad, I made up my mind I'd come down here and tell you about it if I got drowned.' Mrs Caxton was out of breath; rain-drops trickled from her hair over her face; she stood in the door and shut her umbrella with a vicious shake to scatter the water from it. 'I don't know what you're goin' to do with this,' said she; 'it's drippin'.'

'I'll take it out an' put it in the kitchen sink.'

'Well, I'll take off my shawl here too, and you can hang it out in the kitchen. I spread this shawl out. I thought it would keep the rain off me some. I know one thing, I'm goin' to have a waterproof if I live.'

When the two women were seated in the sitting-room, Mrs Caxton was quiet for a moment. There was a hesitating look on her face, fresh with the moist wind, with strands of wet hair clinging to the temples.

'I don't know as I had ought to tell you,' she said, doubtfully.

'Why hadn't you ought to?'

'Well, I don't care; I'm goin' to, anyhow. I think you'd ought to know, an' it ain't so bad for you as it is for me. It don't begin to be. I put considerable money into 'em. I think Mr White was pretty high, myself.'

Betsey looked scared. 'What is it?' she asked, in a weak voice.

Sarah Rogers says that the minister told her Ida that that poetry you wrote was jest as poor as it could be, an' it was in dreadful bad taste to have it printed an' sent round that way. What do you think of that?'

Betsey did not reply. She sat looking at Mrs Caxton as a victim whom the first blow had not killed might look at her executioner. Her face was like a pale wedge of ice between her curls.

Mrs Caxton went on. 'Yes, she said that right to my face, word for word. An' there was something else. She said the minister said that you had never wrote anything that could be called poetry, an' it was a dreadful waste of time. I don't s'pose he thought 'twas comin' back to you. You know he goes with Ida Rogers, an' I s'pose he said it to her kind of confidential when she showed him the poetry. There! I gave Sarah Rogers one of them nice printed ones, an' she acted glad enough to have it. Bad taste! H'm! If anybody wants to say anything against that beautiful poetry, printed with that nice black border, they can. I don't care if it's the minister, or who it is. I don't care if he does write poetry himself, an' has had some printed in a magazine. Maybe his ain't quite so fine as he thinks 'tis. Maybe them magazine folks jest took his for lack of something better. I'd like to have you send that poetry there. Bad taste! I jest got right up. "Sarah Rogers," says I, "I hope you won't never do anything yourself in any worse taste." I trembled so I could hardly speak, and I made up my mind I'd come right straight over here.'

Mrs Caxton went on and on. Betsey sat listening, and saying nothing. She looked ghastly. Just before Mrs Caxton went home she noticed it. 'Why, Betsey Dole,' she cried, 'you look as white as a sheet. You ain't takin' it to heart as much as all that comes to, I hope. Goodness, I wish I hadn't told you!'

'I'd a good deal ruther you told me,' replied Betsey, with a certain dignity. She looked at Mrs Caxton. Her back was as stiff as if she were bound to a stake.

'Well, I thought you would,' said Mrs Caxton, uneasily; 'and you're dreadful silly if you take it to heart, Betsey, that's all I've got to say. Goodness, I guess I don't, and it's full as hard on me as 'tis on you!'

Mrs Caxton arose to go. Betsey brought her shawl and umbrella from the kitchen, and helped her off. Mrs Caxton turned on the door-step and looked back at Betsey's white face. 'Now don't go to thinkin' about it any more,' said she. 'I ain't goin' to. It ain't worth mindin'. Everybody knows what Sarah Rogers is. Goodby.'

'Goodby, Mis' Caxton,' said Betsey. She went back into the sitting-room. It was a cold rain, and the room was gloomy and chilly. She stood looking out of the window, watching the rain pelt on the hedge. The bird-cage hung at the other window. The bird watched her with his head on one side; then he begun to chirp.

Suddenly Betsey faced about and began talking. It was not as if she were talking to herself; it seemed as if she recognized some other presence in the room. 'I'd like to know if it's fair,' said she. 'I'd like to know if you think it's fair. Had I ought to have been born with the wantin' to write poetry if I couldn't write it – had I? Had I ought to have been let to write all my life, an' not know before there wa'n't any use in it? Would it be fair if that canary-bird there, that ain't never done anything but sing, should turn out not to be singin'? Would it, I'd like to know? S'pose them sweet-peas shouldn't be smellin' the right way? I ain't been dealt with as fair as they have, I'd like to know if I have.'

The bird trilled and trilled. It was as if the golden down on his throat bubbled. Betsey went across the room to a cupboard beside the chimney. On the shelves were neatly stacked newspapers and little white rolls of writing-paper. Betsey began clearing the shelves. She took out the newspapers first, got the scissors, and cut a poem neatly out of the corner of each. Then she took up the clipped poems and the white rolls in her apron, and carried them into the kitchen. She cleaned out the stove carefully, removing every trace of ashes; then she put in the papers, and set them on fire. She stood watching them as their edges curled and blackened, then leaped into flame. Her face twisted as if the fire were curling over it also. Other women might have burned their lovers' letters in agony of heart. Betsey had never had any lover, but she was burning all the love-letters that had passed between her and life. When the flames died out she got a blue china sugar-bowl from the pantry and dipped the ashes into it with one of her thin silver teaspoons; then she put on the cover and set it away in the sitting-room cupboard.

The bird, who had been silent while she was out, began chirping again. Betsey went back to the pantry and got a lump of sugar, which she stuck between the cage wires. She looked at the clock on the kitchen shelf as she went by. It was after six. 'I guess I don't want any supper tonight,' she muttered.

She sat down by the window again. The bird pecked at his sugar. Betsey shivered and coughed. She had coughed more or less for years. People said she had the old-fashioned consumption. She sat at the window until it was quite dark; then she went to bed in her little bedroom out of the sitting-room. She shivered so she could not hold herself upright crossing the room. She coughed a great deal in the night.

Betsey was always an early riser. She was up at five the next morning. The sun shone, but it was very cold for the season. The leaves showed white in a north wind, and the flowers looked brighter than usual, though they were bent with the rain of the day before. Betsey went out in the garden to straighten her sweet-peas.

Coming back, a neighbor passing in the street eyed her curiously. 'Why, Betsey, you sick?' said she.

'No; I'm kinder chilly, that's all,' replied Betsey.

But the woman went home and reported that Betsey Dole looked dreadfully, and she didn't believe she'd ever see another summer.

It was now late August. Before October it was quite generally recognized that Betsey Dole's life was nearly over. She had no relatives, and hired nurses were rare in this little village. Mrs Caxton came voluntarily and took care of her, only going home to prepare her husband's meals. Betsey's bed was moved into the sitting-room, and the neighbors came every day to see her, and brought little delicacies. Betsey had talked very little all her life; she talked less now, and there was a reticence about her which somewhat intimidated the other women. They would look pityingly and solemnly at her, and whisper in the entry when they went out.

Betsey never complained; but she kept asking if the minister had got home. He had been called away by his mother's illness, and returned only a week before Betsey died.

He came over at once to see her. Mrs Caxton ushered him in one afternoon.

'Here's Mr Lang come to see you, Betsey,' said she, in the tone she would have used towards a little child. She placed the rocking-chair for the minister, and was about to seat herself, when Betsey spoke:

'Would you mind goin' out in the kitchen jest a few minutes, Mis' Caxton?' said she.

Mrs Caxton arose, and went out with an embarrassed trot. Then there was silence. The minister was a young man – a country boy who had worked his way through a country college. He was gaunt and awkward, but sturdy in his loose clothes. He had a homely, impetuous face, with a good forehead.

He looked at Betsey's gentle, wasted face, sunken in the pillow, framed by its clusters of curls; finally he began to speak in the stilted fashion, yet with a certain force by reason of his unpolished honesty, about her spiritual welfare. Betsey listened quietly; now and then she assented. She had been a church member for years. It seemed now to the young man that this elderly maiden, drawing near the end of her simple, innocent life, had indeed her lamp, which no strong winds of temptation had ever met, well trimmed and burning.

When he paused, Betsey spoke. 'Will you go to the cupboard side of the chimney and bring me the blue sugar-bowl on the top shelf?' said she, feebly.

The young man stared at her a minute; then he went to the cupboard, and brought the sugar-bowl to her. He held it, and Betsey took off the lid with her weak hand. 'Do you see what's in there?' said she.

'It looks like ashes.'

'It's – the ashes of all – the poetry I – ever wrote.'

'Why, what made you burn it, Miss Dole?'

'I found out it wa'n't worth nothin'.'

The minister looked at her in a bewildered way. He began to question if she were not wandering in her mind. He did not once suspect his own connection with the matter.

Betsey fastened her eager, sunken eyes upon his face. 'What I want to know is – if you'll 'tend to – havin' this – buried with me.'

The minister recoiled. He thought to himself that she certainly was wandering.

'No, I ain't out of my head,' said Betsey. 'I know what I'm sayin'. Maybe it's queer soundin', but it's a notion I've took. If you'll – 'tend to it, I shall be – much obliged. I don't know anybody else I can ask.'

'Well, I'll attend to it, if you wish me to, Miss Dole,' said the minister, in a serious, perplexed manner. She replaced the lid on the sugar-bowl, and left it in his hands.

'Well, I shall be much obliged if you will 'tend to it; an' now there's something else,' said she.

'What is it, Miss Dole?'

She hesitated a moment. 'You write poetry, don't you?'

The minister colored. 'Why, yes; a little sometimes.'

'It's good poetry, ain't it? They printed some in a magazine.'

The minister laughed confusedly. 'Well, Miss Dole. I don't know how good poetry it may be, but they did print some in a magazine.'

Betsey lay looking at him. 'I never wrote none that was – good,' she whispered, presently; 'but I've been thinkin' – if you would jest write a few – lines about me – afterward – I've been thinkin' that – mebbe my – dyin' was goin' to make me – a good subject for – poetry, if I never wrote none. If you would jest write a few lines.'

The minister stood holding the sugar-bowl; he was quite pale with bewilderment and sympathy. 'I'll – do the best I can, Miss Dole,' he stammered.

'I'll be much obliged,' said Betsey, as if the sense of grateful obligation was immortal like herself. She smiled, and the sweetness of the smile was as evident through the drawn lines of her mouth as the old red in the leaves of a withered rose. The sun was setting; a red beam flashed softly over the top of the hedge and lay along the opposite wall; then the bird in his cage began to chirp. He chirped faster and faster until he trilled into a triumphant song.

Old Woman Magoun

1909

The hamlet of Barry's Ford is situated in a sort of high valley among the mountains. Below it the hills lie in moveless curves like a petrified ocean; above it they rise in green-cresting waves which never break. It is *Barry's* Ford because at one time the Barry family was the most important in the place; and *Ford* because just at the beginning of the hamlet the little turbulent Barry River is fordable. There is, however, now a rude bridge across the river.

Old Woman Magoun was largely instrumental in bringing the bridge to pass. She haunted the miserable little grocery, wherein whiskey and hands of tobacco* were the most salient features of the stock in trade, and she talked much. She would elbow herself into the midst of a knot of idlers and talk.

'That bridge ought to be built this very summer,' said Old Woman Magoun. She spread her strong arms like wings, and sent the loafers, half laughing, half angry, flying in every direction. 'If I were a *man*,' said she, 'I'd go out this very minute and lay the fust log. If I were a passel* of lazy men layin' round, I'd start up for once in my life, I would.' The men cowered visibly – all except Nelson Barry; he swore under his breath and strode over to the counter.

Old Woman Magoun looked after him majestically. 'You can cuss all you want to, Nelson Barry,' said she; 'I ain't afraid of you. I don't expect you to lay ary log of the bridge, but I'm goin' to have it built this very summer.' She did. The weakness of the masculine element in Barry's Ford was laid low before such strenuous feminine assertion.

Old Woman Magoun and some other women planned a treat – two sucking pigs, and pies, and sweet cake – for a reward after the bridge should be finished. They even viewed leniently the increased consumption of ardent spirits.

'It seems queer to me,' Old Woman Magoun said to Sally Jinks, 'that men can't do nothin' without havin' to drink and chew to keep their sperits up. Lord! I've worked all my life and never done nuther.'

'Men is different,' said Sally Jinks.

'Yes, they be,' assented Old Woman Magoun, with open contempt.

The two women sat on a bench in front of Old Woman Magoun's house, and little Lily Barry, her granddaughter, sat holding her doll on a small mossy stone near by. From where they sat they could see the men at work on the new bridge. It was the last day of the work.

Lily clasped her doll – a poor old rag thing – close to her childish bosom, like a little mother, and her face, round which curled her long yellow hair, was fixed upon the men at work. Little Lily had never been allowed to run with the other children of Barry's Ford. Her grandmother had taught her everything she knew – which was not much, but tending at least to a certain measure of spiritual growth – for she, as it were, poured the goodness of her own soul into this little receptive vase of another. Lily was firmly grounded in her knowledge that it was wrong to lie or steal or disobey her grandmother. She had also learned that one should be very industrious. It was seldom that Lily sat idly holding her doll-baby, but this was a holiday because of the bridge. She looked only a child, although she was nearly fourteen; her mother had been married at sixteen. That is, Old Woman Magoun said that her daughter, Lily's mother, had married at sixteen; there had been rumors, but no one had dared openly gainsay the old woman. She said that her daughter had married Nelson Barry, and he had deserted her. She had lived in her mother's house, and Lily had been born there, and she had died when the baby was only a week old. Lily's father, Nelson Barry, was the fairly dangerous degenerate of a good old family. Nelson's father before him had been bad. He was now the last of the family, with the exception of a sister of feeble intellect, with whom he lived in the old Barry house. He was a middle-aged man, still handsome. The shiftless population of Barry's Ford looked up to him as to an evil deity. They wondered how Old Woman Magoun dared brave him as she did. But Old Woman Magoun had within her a mighty sense of reliance upon herself as being on the right track in the midst of a maze of evil, which gave her courage. Nelson Barry had manifested no interest whatever in his daughter. Lily seldom saw her father.

She did not often go to the store which was his favorite haunt. Her grandmother took care that she should not do so.

However, that afternoon she departed from her usual custom and sent Lily to the store.

She came in from the kitchen, whither she had been to baste the roasting pig. 'There's no use talkin',' said she, 'I've got to have some more salt. I've jest used the very last I had to dredge* over that pig. I've got to go to the store.'

Sally Jinks looked at Lily. 'Why don't you send her?' she asked.

Old Woman Magoun gazed irresolutely at the girl. She was herself very tired. It did not seem to her that she could drag herself up the dusty hill to the store. She glanced with covert resentment at Sally Jinks. She thought that she might offer to go. But Sally Jinks said again, 'Why don't you let her go?' and looked with a languid eye at Lily holding her doll on the stone.

Lily was watching the men at work on the bridge, with her childish delight in a spectacle of any kind, when her grandmother addressed her.

'Guess I'll let you go down to the store an' git some salt, Lily,' said she.

The girl turned uncomprehending eyes upon her grandmother at the sound of her voice. She had been filled with one of the innocent reveries of childhood. Lily had in her the making of an artist or a poet. Her prolonged childhood went to prove it, and also her retrospective eyes, as clear and blue as blue light itself, which seemed to see past all that she looked upon. She had not come of the old Barry family for nothing. The best of the strain was in her, along with the splendid stanchness in humble lines which she had acquired from her grandmother.

'Put on your hat,' said Old Woman Magoun; 'the sun is hot, and you might git a headache.' She called the girl to her, and put back the shower of fair curls under the rubber band which confined the hat. She gave Lily some money, and watched her knot it into a corner of her little cotton handkerchief. 'Be careful you don't lose it,' said she, 'and don't stop to talk to anybody, for I am in a hurry for that salt. Of course, if anybody speaks to you answer them polite, and then come right along.'

Lily started, her pocket-handkerchief weighted with the small silver dangling from one hand, and her rag doll carried over her shoulder like a baby. The absurd travesty of a face peeped forth from Lily's yellow curls. Sally Jinks looked after her with a sniff.

'She ain't goin' to carry that rag doll to the store?' said she.

'She likes to,' replied Old Woman Magoun, in a half-shamed yet defiantly extenuating voice.

'Some girls at her age is thinkin' about beaux instead of rag dolls,' said Sally Jinks.

The grandmother bristled, 'Lily ain't big nor old for her age,' said she. 'I ain't in any hurry to have her git married. She ain't none too strong.'

'She's got a good color,' said Sally Jinks. She was crocheting white cotton lace, making her thick fingers fly. She really knew how to do scarcely anything except to crochet that coarse lace; somehow her heavy brain or her fingers had mastered that.

'I know she's got a beautiful color,' replied Old Woman Magoun, with an odd mixture of pride and anxiety, 'but it comes an' goes.'

'I've heard that was a bad sign,' remarked Sally Jinks, loosening some thread from her spool.

'Yes, it is,' said the grandmother. 'She's nothin' but a baby, though she's quicker than most to learn.'

Lily Barry went on her way to the store. She was clad in a scanty short frock of blue cotton; her hat was tipped back, forming an oval frame for her innocent face. She was very small, and walked like a child, with the clap-clap of little feet of babyhood. She might have been considered, from her looks, under ten.

Presently she heard footsteps behind her; she turned around a little timidly to see who was coming. When she saw a handsome, well-dressed man, she felt reassured. The man came alongside and glanced down carelessly at first, then his look deepened. He smiled, and Lily saw he was very handsome indeed, and that his smile was not only reassuring but wonderfully sweet and compelling.

'Well, little one,' said the man, 'where are you bound, you and your dolly?'

'I am going to the store to buy some salt for grandma,' replied Lily, in her sweet treble. She looked up in the man's face, and he fairly started at the revelation of its innocent beauty. He regulated his pace by hers, and the two went on together. The man did not speak again at once. Lily kept glancing timidly up at him, and every time that she did so the man smiled and her confidence increased. Presently when the man's hand grasped her little childish one hanging by her side, she felt a complete trust in him. Then she smiled up at him. She felt glad that this nice man had come along, for just here the road was lonely.

After a while the man spoke. 'What is your name, little one?' he asked, caressingly.

'Lily Barry.'

The man started. 'What is your father's name?'

'Nelson Barry,' replied Lily.

The man whistled. 'Is your mother dead?'

'Yes, sir.'

'How old are you, my dear?'

'Fourteen,' replied Lily.

The man looked at her with surprise. 'As old as that?'

Lily suddenly shrank from the man. She could not have told why. She pulled her little hand from his, and he let it go with no remonstrance. She clasped both her arms around her rag doll, in order that her hand should not be free for him to grasp again.

She walked a little farther away from the man, and he looked amused.

'You still play with your doll?' he said, in a soft voice.

'Yes, sir,' replied Lily. She quickened her pace and reached the store.

When Lily entered the store, Hiram Gates, the owner, was behind the counter. The only man besides in the store was Nelson Barry. He sat tipping his chair back against the wall; he was half asleep, and his handsome face was bristling with a beard of several days' growth and darkly flushed. He opened his eyes when Lily entered, the strange man following. He brought his chair down on all fours, and he looked at the man – not noticing Lily at all – with a look compounded of defiance and uneasiness.

'Hullo, Jim!' he said.

'Hullo, old man!' returned the stranger.

Lily went over to the counter and asked for the salt, in her pretty little voice. When she had paid for it and was crossing the store, Nelson Barry was on his feet.

'Well, how are you, Lily? It is Lily, isn't it?' he said.

'Yes, sir,' replied Lily, faintly.

Her father bent down and, for the first time in her life, kissed her, and the whiskey odor of his breath came into her face.

Lily involuntarily started, and shrank away from him. Then she rubbed her mouth violently with her little cotton handkerchief, which she held gathered up with the rag doll.

'Damn it all! I believe she is afraid of me,' said Nelson Barry, in a thick voice.

'Looks a little like it,' said the other man, laughing.

'It's that damned old woman,' said Nelson Barry. Then he smiled again at Lily. 'I didn't know what a pretty little daughter I was blessed with,' said he, and he softly stroked Lily's pink cheek under her hat.

Now Lily did not shrink from him. Hereditary instincts and nature itself were asserting themselves in the child's innocent, receptive breast.

Nelson Barry looked curiously at Lily. 'How old are you, anyway, child?' he asked.

'I'll be fourteen in September,' replied Lily.

'But you still play with your doll?' said Barry, laughing kindly down at her.

Lily hugged her doll more tightly, in spite of her father's kind voice. 'Yes, sir,' she replied.

Nelson glanced across at some glass jars filled with sticks of candy. 'See here, little Lily, do you like candy?' said he.

'Yes, sir.'

'Wait a minute.'

Lily waited while her father went over to the counter. Soon he returned with a package of the candy.

'I don't see how you are going to carry so much,' he said, smiling. 'Suppose you throw away your doll?'

Lily gazed at her father and hugged the doll tightly, and there was all at once in the child's expression something mature. It became the reproach of a woman. Nelson's face sobered.

'Oh, it's all right, Lily,' he said; 'keep your doll. Here, I guess you can carry this candy under your arm.'

Lily could not resist the candy. She obeyed Nelson's instructions for carrying it, and left the store laden. The two men also left, and walked in the opposite direction, talking busily.

When Lily reached home, her grandmother, who was watching for her, spied at once the package of candy.

'What's that?' she asked, sharply.

'My father gave it to me,' answered Lily, in a faltering voice. Sally regarded her with something like alertness.

'Your father?'

'Yes, ma'am.'

'Where did you see him?'

'In the store.'

'He gave you this candy?'

'Yes, ma'am.'

'What did he say?'

'He asked me how old I was, and – '

'And what?'

'I don't know,' replied Lily; and it really seemed to her that she did not know, she was so frightened and bewildered by it all, and, more than anything else, by her grandmother's face as she questioned her.

Old Woman Magoun's face was that of one upon whom a long-anticipated blow had fallen. Sally Jinks gazed at her with a sort of stupid alarm.

Old Woman Magoun continued to gaze at her grandchild with that look of terrible solicitude, as if she saw the girl in the clutch of a tiger. 'You can't remember what else he said?' she asked, fiercely, and the child began to whimper softly.

'No, ma'am,' she sobbed. 'I – don't know, and – '

'And what? Answer me.'

'There was another man there. A real handsome man.'

'Did he speak to you?' asked Old Woman Magoun.

'Yes ma'am; he walked along with me a piece,' confessed Lily, with a sob of terror and bewilderment.

'What did *he* say to you?' asked Old Woman Magoun, with a sort of despair.

Lily told, in her little, faltering, frightened voice, all of the conversation which she could recall. It sounded harmless enough, but the look of the realization of a long-expected blow never left her grandmother's face.

The sun was getting low, and the bridge was nearing completion. Soon the workmen would be crowding into the cabin for their promised supper. There became visible in the distance, far up the road, the heavily plodding figure of another woman who had agreed to come and help. Old Woman Magoun turned again to Lily.

'You go right upstairs to your own chamber now,' said she.

'Good land! ain't you goin' to let that poor child stay up and see the fun?' said Sally Jinks.

'You jest mind your own business,' said Old Woman Magoun, forcibly, and Sally Jinks shrank. 'You go right up there now, Lily,' said the grandmother, in a softer tone, 'and grandma will bring you up a nice plate of supper.'

'When be you goin' to let that girl grow up?' asked Sally Jinks, when Lily had disappeared.

'She'll grow up in the Lord's good time,' replied Old Woman Magoun, and there was in her voice something both sad and threatening. Sally Jinks again shrank a little.

Soon the workmen came flocking noisily into the house. Old Woman Magoun and her two helpers served the bountiful supper. Most of the men had drunk as much as, and more than, was good for them, and Old Woman Magoun had stipulated that there was to be no drinking of anything except coffee during supper.

'I'll git you as good a meal as I know how,' she said, 'but if I see ary one of you drinkin' a drop, I'll run you all out. If you want anything to drink, you can go up to the store afterward. That's the place for you to go to, if you've got to make hogs of yourselves. I ain't goin' to have no hogs in my house.'

Old Woman Magoun was implicitly obeyed. She had a curious authority over most people when she chose to exercise it. When the supper was in full swing, she quietly stole upstairs and carried some food to Lily. She found the girl, with the rag doll in her arms, crouching by the window in her little rocking-chair – a relic of her infancy, which she still used.

'What a noise they are makin', grandma!' she said, in a terrified whisper, as her grandmother placed the plate before her on a chair.

'They've 'most all of 'em been drinkin'. They air a passel of hogs,' replied the old woman.

'Is the man that was with – with my father down there?' asked Lily, in a timid fashion. Then she fairly cowered before the look in her grandmother's eyes.

'No, he ain't; and what's more, he never will be down there if I can help it,' said Old Woman Magoun, in a fierce whisper. 'I know who he is. They can't cheat me. He's one of them Willises – that family the Barrys married into. They're worse than the

Barrys, ef they *have* got money. Eat your supper, and put him out of your mind, child.'

It was after Lily was asleep, when Old Woman Magoun was alone, clearing away her supper dishes, that Lily's father came. The door was closed, and he knocked, and the old woman knew at once who was there. The sound of that knock meant as much to her as the whir of a bomb to the defender of a fortress. She opened the door, and Nelson Barry stood there.

'Good evening, Mrs Magoun,' he said.

Old Woman Magoun stood before him, filling up the doorway with her firm bulk.

'Good evening, Mrs Magoun,' said Nelson Barry again.

'I ain't got no time to waste,' replied the old woman, harshly. 'I've got my supper dishes to clean up after them men.'

She stood there and looked at him as she might have looked at a rebellious animal which she was trying to tame. The man laughed.

'It's no use,' said he. 'You know me of old. No human being can turn me from my way when I am once started in it. You may as well let me come in.'

Old Woman Magoun entered the house, and Barry followed her.

Barry began without any preface. 'Where is the child?' asked he.

'Upstairs. She has gone to bed.'

'She goes to bed early.'

'Children ought to,' returned the old woman, polishing a plate.

Barry laughed. 'You are keeping her a child a long while,' he remarked, in a soft voice which had a sting in it.

'She *is* a child,' returned the old woman, defiantly.

'Her mother was only three years older when Lily was born.'

The old woman made a sudden motion toward the man which seemed fairly menacing. Then she turned again to her dish-washing.

'I want her,' said Barry.

'You can't have her,' replied the old woman, in a still stern voice.

'I don't see how you can help yourself. You have always acknowledged that she was my child.'

The old woman continued her task, but her strong back heaved. Barry regarded her with an entirely pitiless expression.

'I am going to have the girl, that is the long and short of it,' he said, 'and it is for her best good, too. You are a fool, or you would see it.'

'Her best good?' muttered the old woman.

'Yes, her best good. What are you going to do with her, anyway? The girl is a beauty, and almost a woman grown, although you try to make out that she is a baby. You can't live forever.'

'The Lord will take care of her,' replied the old woman, and again she turned and faced him, and her expression was that of a prophetess.

'Very well, let Him,' said Barry, easily. 'All the same I'm going to have her, and I tell you it is for her best good. Jim Willis saw her this afternoon, and – '

Old Woman Magoun looked at him. 'Jim Willis!' she fairly shrieked.

'Well, what of it?'

'One of them Willises!' repeated the old woman, and this time her voice was thick. It seemed almost as if she were stricken with paralysis. She did not enunciate clearly.

The man shrank a little. 'Now what is the need of your making such a fuss?' he said. 'I will take her, and Isabel will look out for her.'

'Your half-witted sister?' said Old Woman Magoun.

'Yes, my half-witted sister. She knows more than you think.'

'More wickedness.'

'Perhaps. Well, a knowledge of evil is a useful thing. How are you going to avoid evil if you don't know what it is like? My sister and I will take care of my daughter.'

The old woman continued to look at the man, but his eyes never fell. Suddenly her gaze grew inconceivably keen. It was as if she saw through all externals.

'I know what it is!' she cried. 'You have been playing cards and you lost, and this is the way you will pay him.'

Then the man's face reddened, and he swore under his breath.

'Oh, my God!' said the old woman; and she really spoke with her eyes aloft as if addressing something outside of them both. Then she turned again to her dish-washing.

The man cast a dogged look at her back. 'Well, there is no use talking. I have made up my mind,' said he, 'and you know me and what that means. I am going to have the girl.'

'When?' said the old woman, without turning around.

'Well, I am willing to give you a week. Put her clothes in good order before she comes.'

The old woman made no reply. She continued washing dishes. She even handled them so carefully that they did not rattle.

'You understand,' said Barry. 'Have her ready a week from today.'

'Yes,' said Old Woman Magoun, 'I understand.'

Nelson Barry, going up the mountain road, reflected that Old Woman Magoun had a strong character, that she understood much better than her sex in general the futility of withstanding the inevitable.

'Well,' he said to Jim Willis when he reached home, 'the old woman did not make such a fuss as I expected.'

'Are you going to have the girl?'

'Yes; a week from today. Look here, Jim; you've got to stick to your promise.'

'All right,' said Willis. 'Go you one better.'

The two were playing at cards in the old parlor, once magnificent, now squalid, of the Barry house. Isabel, the half-witted sister, entered, bringing some glasses on a tray. She had learned with her feeble intellect some tricks, like a dog. One of them was the mixing of sundry drinks. She set the tray on a little stand near the two men, and watched them with her silly simper.

'Clear out now and go to bed,' her brother said to her, and she obeyed.

Early the next morning Old Woman Magoun went up to Lily's little sleeping-chamber, and watched her a second as she lay asleep, with her yellow locks spread over the pillow. Then she spoke. 'Lily,' said she – 'Lily, wake up. I am going to Greenham across the new bridge, and you can go with me.'

Lily immediately sat up in bed and smiled at her grandmother. Her eyes were still misty, but the light of awakening was in them.

'Get right up,' said the old woman. 'You can wear your new dress if you want to.'

Lily gurgled with pleasure like a baby. 'And my new hat?' asked she.

'I don't care.'

Old Woman Magoun and Lily started for Greenham before Barry Ford, which kept late hours, was fairly awake. It was three miles to Greenham. The old woman said that, since the horse was a little lame, they would walk. It was a beautiful morning, with a diamond radiance of dew over everything. Her grandmother had curled Lily's hair more punctiliously than usual. The little face peeped like a rose out of two rows of golden spirals. Lily wore her new muslin dress with a pink sash, and her best hat of a fine white straw trimmed with a wreath of rosebuds; also the neatest black open-work stockings and pretty shoes. She even had white cotton gloves. When they set out, the old, heavily stepping woman, in her black gown and cape and bonnet, looked down at the little pink fluttering figure. Her face was full of the tenderest love and admiration, and yet there was something terrible about it. They crossed the new bridge – a primitive structure built of logs in a slovenly fashion. Old Woman Magoun pointed to a gap.

'Jest see that,' said she. 'That's the way men work.'

'Men ain't very nice, be they?' said Lily, in her sweet little voice.

'No, they ain't, take them all together,' replied her grandmother.

'That man that walked to the store with me was nicer than some, I guess,' Lily said, in a wishful fashion. Her grandmother reached down and took the child's hand in its small cotton glove. 'You hurt me, holding my hand so tight,' Lily said presently, in a deprecatory little voice.

The old woman loosened her grasp. 'Grandma didn't know how tight she was holding your hand,' said she. 'She wouldn't hurt you for nothin', except it was to save your life, or somethin' like that.' She spoke with an undertone of tremendous meaning which the girl was too childish to grasp. They walked along the country road. Just before they reached Greenham they passed a stone wall overgrown with blackberry-vines, and, an unusual thing in that vicinity, a lusty spread of deadly nightshade* full of berries.

'Those berries look good to eat, grandma,' Lily said.

At that instant the old woman's face became something terrible to see. 'You can't have any now,' she said, and hurried Lily along.

'They look real nice,' said Lily.

When they reached Greenham, Old Woman Magoun took her way straight to the most pretentious house there, the

residence of the lawyer, whose name was Mason. Old Woman
Magoun bade Lily wait in the yard for a few moments, and Lily
ventured to seat herself on a bench beneath an oak-tree; then
she watched with some wonder her grandmother enter the
lawyer's office door at the right of the house. Presently the
lawyer's wife came out and spoke to Lily under the tree. She
had in her hand a little tray containing a plate of cake, a glass
of milk, and an early apple. She spoke very kindly to Lily; she
even kissed her, and offered her the tray of refreshments, which
Lily accepted gratefully. She sat eating, with Mrs Mason watching her, when Old Woman Magoun came out of the lawyer's
office with a ghastly face.

'What are you eatin'?' she asked Lily, sharply. 'Is that a sour
apple?'

'I thought she might be hungry,' said the lawyer's wife, with
loving, melancholy eyes upon the girl.

Lily had almost finished the apple. 'It's real sour, but I like it;
it's real nice, grandma,' she said.

'You ain't been drinkin' milk with a sour apple?'

'It was real nice milk, grandma.'

'You ought never to have drunk milk and eat a sour apple,'
said her grandmother. 'Your stomach was all out of order this
mornin', an' sour apples and milk is always apt to hurt
anybody.'

'I don't know but they are,' Mrs Mason said, apologetically,
as she stood on the green lawn with her lavender muslin
sweeping around her. 'I am real sorry, Mrs Magoun. I ought to
have thought. Let me get some soda for her.'

'Soda never agrees with her,' replied the old woman, in a
harsh voice. 'Come,' she said to Lily, 'it's time we were goin'
home.'

After Lily and her grandmother had disappeared down the
road, Lawyer Mason came out of his office and joined his wife,
who had seated herself on the bench beneath the tree. She was
idle, and her face wore the expression of those who review joys
forever past. She had lost a little girl, her only child, years ago,
and her husband always knew when she was thinking about
her. Lawyer Mason looked older than his wife; he had a dry,
shrewd, slightly one-sided face.

'What do you think, Maria?' he said. 'That old woman came
to me with the most pressing entreaty to adopt that little girl.'

'She is a beautiful little girl,' said Mrs Mason, in a slightly husky voice.

'Yes, she is a pretty child,' assented the lawyer, looking pityingly at his wife; 'but it is out of the question, my dear. Adopting a child is a serious measure, and in this case a child who comes from Barry's Ford.'

'But the grandmother seems a very good woman,' said Mrs Mason.

'I rather think she is. I never heard a word against her. But the father! No, Maria, we cannot take a child with Barry blood in her veins. The stock has run out; it is vitiated physically and morally. It won't do, my dear.'

'Her grandmother had her dressed up as pretty as a little girl could be,' said Mrs Mason, and this time the tears welled into her faithful, wistful eyes.

'Well, we can't help that,' said the lawyer, as he went back to his office.

Old Woman Magoun and Lily returned, going slowly along the road to Barry's Ford. When they came to the stone wall where the blackberry-vines and the deadly nightshade grew, Lily said she was tired, and asked if she could not sit down for a few minutes. The strange look on her grandmother's face had deepened. Now and then Lily glanced at her and had a feeling as if she were looking at a stranger.

'Yes, you can set down if you want to,' said Old Woman Magoun, deeply and harshly.

Lily started and looked at her, as if to make sure that it was her grandmother who spoke. Then she sat down on a stone which was comparatively free of the vines.

'Ain't you goin' to set down, grandma?' Lily asked, timidly.

'No; I don't want to get into that mess,' replied her grandmother. 'I ain't tired. I'll stand here.'

Lily sat still; her delicate little face was flushed with heat. She extended her tiny feet in her best shoes and gazed at them. 'My shoes are all over dust,' said she.

'It will brush off,' said her grandmother, still in that strange voice.

Lily looked around. An elm-tree in the field behind her cast a spray of branches over her head; a little cool puff of wind came on her face. She gazed at the low mountains on the horizon, in the midst of which she lived, and she sighed, for no reason that she knew. She began idly picking at the blackberry-vines; there were no berries on them; then she put her little fingers on the berries of the deadly nightshade. 'These look like nice berries,' she said.

Old Woman Magoun, standing stiff and straight in the road, said nothing.

'They look good to eat,' said Lily.

Old Woman Magoun still said nothing, but she looked up into the ineffable blue of the sky, over which spread at intervals great white clouds shaped like wings.

Lily picked some of the deadly nightshade berries and ate them. 'Why, they are real sweet,' said she. 'They are nice.' She picked some more and ate them.

Presently her grandmother spoke. 'Come,' she said, 'it is time we were going. I guess you have set long enough.'

Lily was still eating the berries when she slipped down from the wall and followed her grandmother obediently up the road.

Before they reached home, Lily complained of being very thirsty. She stopped and made a little cup of a leaf and drank long at a mountain brook. 'I am dreadful dry, but it hurts me to swallow,' she said to her grandmother when she stopped drinking and joined the old woman waiting for her in the road. Her grandmother's face seemed strangely dim to her. She took hold of Lily's hand as they went on. 'My stomach burns,' said Lily, presently. 'I want some more water.'

'There is another brook a little farther on,' said Old Woman Magoun, in a dull voice.

When they reached that brook, Lily stopped and drank again, but she whimpered a little over her difficulty in swallowing. 'My stomach burns, too,' she said, walking on, 'and my throat is so dry, grandma.' Old Woman Magoun held Lily's hand more tightly. 'You hurt me holding my hand so tight, grandma,' said Lily, looking up at her grandmother, whose face she seemed to see through a mist, and the old woman loosened her grasp.

When at last they reached home, Lily was very ill. Old Woman Magoun put her on her own bed in the little bedroom out of the kitchen. Lily lay there and moaned, and Sally Jinks came in.

'Why, what ails her?' she asked. 'She looks feverish.'

Lily unexpectedly answered for herself. 'I ate some sour apples and drank some milk,' she moaned.

'Sour apples and milk are dreadful apt to hurt anybody,' said

Sally Jinks. She told several people on her way home that Old Woman Magoun was dreadful careless to let Lily eat such things.

Meanwhile Lily grew worse. She suffered cruelly from the burning in her stomach, the vertigo, and the deadly nausea. 'I am so sick, I am so sick, grandma,' she kept moaning. She could no longer see her grandmother as she bent over her, but she could hear her talk.

Old Woman Magoun talked as Lily had never heard her talk before, as nobody had ever heard her talk before. She spoke from the depths of her soul; her voice was as tender as the coo of a dove, and it was grand and exalted. 'You'll feel better very soon, little Lily,' said she.

'I am so sick, grandma.'

'You will feel better very soon, and then – '

'I am sick.'

'You shall go to a beautiful place.'

Lily moaned.

'You shall go to a beautiful place,' the old woman went on.

'Where?' asked Lily, groping feebly with her cold little hands. Then she moaned again.

'A beautiful place, where the flowers grow tall.'

'What color? Oh, grandma, I am so sick.'

'A blue color,' replied the old woman. Blue was Lily's favorite color. 'A beautiful blue color, and as tall as your knees, and the flowers always stay there, and they never fade.'

'Not if you pick them, grandma? Oh!'

'No, not if you pick them; they never fade, and they are so sweet you can smell them a mile off; and there are birds that sing, and all the roads have gold stones in them, and the stone walls are made of gold.'

'Like the ring grandpa gave you? I am so sick, grandma.'

'Yes, gold like that. And all the houses are built of silver and gold, and the people all have wings, so when they get tired walking they can fly, and – '

'I am so sick, grandma.'

'And all the dolls are alive,' said Old Woman Magoun. 'Dolls like yours can run, and talk, and love you back again.'

Lily had her poor old rag doll in bed with her, clasped close to her agonized little heart. She tried very hard with her eyes, whose pupils were so dilated that they looked black, to see her grandmother's face when she said that, but she could not. 'It is dark,' she moaned, feebly.

'There where you are going it is always light,' said the grandmother, 'and the commonest things shine like that breast-pin Mrs Lawyer Mason had on today.'

Lily moaned pitifully, and said something incoherent. Delirium was commencing. Presently she sat straight up in bed and raved; but even then her grandmother's wonderful compelling voice had an influence over her.

'You will come to a gate with all the colors of the rainbow,' said her grandmother; 'and it will open, and you will go right in and walk up the gold street, and cross the field where the blue flowers come up to your knees, until you find your mother, and she will take you home where you are going to live. She has a little white room all ready for you, white curtains at the windows, and a little white looking-glass, and when you look in it you will see – '

'What will I see? I am so sick, grandma.'

'You will see a face like yours, only it's an angel's: and there will be a little white bed, and you can lay down an' rest.'

'Won't I be sick, grandma?' asked Lily. Then she moaned and babbled wildly, although she seemed to understand through it all what her grandmother said.

'No, you will never be sick anymore. Talkin' about sickness won't mean anything to you.'

It continued. Lily talked on wildly, and her grandmother's great voice of soothing never ceased, until the child fell into a deep sleep, or what resembled sleep; but she lay stiffly in that sleep, and a candle flashed before her eyes made no impression on them.

Then it was that Nelson Barry came. Jim Willis waited outside the door. When Nelson entered he found Old Woman Magoun on her knees beside the bed, weeping with dry eyes and a might of agony which fairly shook Nelson Barry, the degenerate of a fine old race.

'Is she sick?' he asked, in a hushed voice.

Old Woman Magoun gave another terrible sob, which sounded like the gasp of one dying.

'Sally Jinks said that Lily was sick from eating milk and sour apples,' said Barry, in a tremulous voice. 'I remember that her mother was very sick once from eating them.'

Lily lay still, and her grandmother on her knees shook with her terrible sobs.

Suddenly Nelson Barry started. 'I guess I had better go to Greenham for a doctor if she's as bad as that,' he said. He went close to the bed and looked at the sick child. He gave a great start. Then he felt of her hands and reached down under the bedclothes for her little feet. 'Her hands and feet are like ice,' he cried out. 'Good God! why didn't you send for some one – for me – before? Why, she's dying; she's almost gone!'

Barry rushed out and spoke to Jim Willis, who turned pale and came in and stood by the bedside.

'She's almost gone,' he said, in a hushed whisper.

'There's no use going for the doctor, she'd be dead before he got here,' said Nelson, and he stood regarding the passing child with a strange, sad face – unutterably sad, because of his incapability of the truest sadness.

'Poor little thing, she's past suffering, anyhow,' said the other man, and his own face also was sad with a puzzled, mystified sadness.

Lily died that night. There was quite a commotion in Barry's Ford until after the funeral, it was all so sudden, and then everything went on as usual. Old Woman Magoun continued to live as she had done before. She supported herself by the produce of her tiny farm; she was very industrious, but people said that she was a trifle touched, since every time she went over the log bridge with her eggs or her garden vegetables to sell in Greenham, she carried with her, as one might have carried an infant, Lily's old rag doll.

Sister Liddy

1891

There were no trees near the almshouse; it stood in its bare, sandy lot, and there were no leaves or branches to cast shadows on its walls. It seemed like the folks whom it sheltered, out in the full glare of day, without any little kindly shade between itself and the dull, unfeeling stare of curiosity. The almshouse stood upon rising ground, so one could see it for a long distance. It was a new building, Mansard-roofed* and well painted. The village took pride in it: no town far or near had such a house for the poor. It was so fine and costly that the village did not feel able to give its insane paupers separate support in a regular asylum; so they lived in the almshouse with the sane paupers, and there was a padded cell in case they waxed too violent.

Around the almshouse lay the town fields. In summer they were green with corn and potatoes, now they showed ugly plough ridges sloping over the uneven ground, and yellow corn stubble. Beyond the field at the west of the almshouse was a little wood of elms and oaks and wild apple-trees. The yellow leaves had all fallen from the elms and the apple-trees, but most of the brown ones stayed on the oaks.

Polly Moss stood at the west window in the women's sitting-room and gazed over at the trees. 'It's cur'us how them oak leaves hang on arter the others have all fell off,' she remarked.

A tall old woman sitting beside the stove looked around suddenly. She had singular bright eyes, and a sardonic smile around her mouth. 'It's a way they allers have,' she returned, scornfully. 'Guess there ain't nothin' very cur'us about it. When the oak leaves fall off an' the others hang on, then you can be lookin' for the end of the world; that's goin' to be one of the signs.'

'Allers a-harpin' on the end of the world,' growled another old woman, in a deep bass voice. 'I've got jest about sick on't. Seems as if I should go crazy myself, hearin' on't the whole time.' She was sewing a seam in coarse cloth, and she sat on a stool on the other side of the stove. She was short and stout, and she sat with a heavy settle as if she were stuffed with lead.

The tall old woman took no further notice. She sat rigidly straight, and fixed her bright eyes upon the top of the door, and her sardonic smile deepened.

The stout old woman gave an ugly look at her; then she sewed with more impetus. Now and then she muttered something in her deep voice.

There were, besides herself, three old women in the room – Polly Moss, the tall one, and a pretty one in a white cap and black dress. There was also a young woman; she sat in a rocking-chair and leaned her head back. She was handsome, but she kept her mouth parted miserably, and there were ghastly white streaks around it and her nostrils. She never spoke. Her pretty black hair was rough, and her dress sagged at the neck. She had been living out at a large farm, and had overworked. She had no friends or relatives to take her in; so she had come to the almshouse to rest and try to recover. She had no refuge but the almshouse or the hospital, and she had a terrible horror of a hospital. Dreadful visions arose in her ignorant childish mind whenever she thought of one. She had a lover, but he had not been to see her since she came to the almshouse, six weeks before; she wept most of the time over that and her physical misery.

Polly Moss stood at the window until a little boy trudged into the room, bringing his small feet down with a clapping noise. He went up to Polly and twitched her dress. She looked around at him. 'Well, now, Tommy, what do ye want?'

'Come out-doors an' play hide an' coot wis me, Polly.'

Tommy was a stout little boy. He wore a calico tier that sagged to his heels in the back, and showed in front his little calico trousers. His round face was pleasant and innocent and charming.

Polly put her arms around the boy and hugged him. 'Tommy's a darlin',' she said; 'can't he give poor Polly a kiss?'

Tommy put up his lips. 'Come out-doors an' play hide an' coot wis me,' he said again, breathing the words out with the kiss.

'Now, Tommy, jest look out of the winder. Don't he see that it's rainin', hey?'

The child shook his head stubbornly, although he was looking straight at the window, which revealed plainly enough that long sheets of rain were driving over the fields. 'Come out-doors and play hide an' coot wis me, Polly.'

'Now, Tommy, jest listen to Polly. Don't he know he can't go out-doors when it's rainin' this way? He'd get all wet, an' Polly too. But I'll tell you what Polly an' Tommy can do. We'll jest go out in the hall an' we'll roll the ball. Tommy go run quick an' get his ball.'

Tommy raised a shout, and clapped out of the room; his sweet nature was easily diverted. Polly followed him. She had a twisting limp, and was so bent that she was not much taller than Tommy, her little pale triangular face seemed to look out from the middle of her flat chest.

'The wust-lookin' objeck,' growled the stout old woman when Polly was out of the room: 'looks more like an old cat that's had to airn its own livin' than a human bein'. It 'bout makes me sick to look at her.' Her deep tones travelled far; Polly, out in the corridor waiting for Tommy, heard every word.

'She is a dretful-lookin' cretur,' assented the pretty old woman. As she spoke she puckered her little red mouth daintily, and drew herself up with a genteel air.

The stout old woman surveyed her contemptuously. 'Well, good looks don't amount to much, nohow,' said she, 'if folks ain't got common-sense to balance 'em. I'd enough sight ruther know a leetle somethin' than have a dolly-face myself.'

'Seems to me she is about the dretfulest-lookin' cretur that I ever did see,' repeated the pretty old woman, quite unmoved. Aspersions on her intellect never aroused her in the least.

The stout old woman looked baffled. 'Jest turn your head a leetle that way, will you, Mis' Handy?' she said, presently.

The pretty old woman turned her head obediently. 'What is it?' she inquired, with a conscious simper.

'Jest turn your head a leetle more. Yes, it's funny I ain't never noticed it afore. Your nose is a leetle grain crooked – ain't it, Mis' Handy?'

Mrs Handy's face turned a deep pink – even her little ears and her delicate old neck were suffused; her blue eyes looked like an enraged bird's. 'Crooked! H'm! I shouldn't think that folks that's got a nose like some folks had better say much about other folks' noses. There can't nobody tell me nothin' about my nose; I know all about it. Folks that wouldn't wipe their feet on some folks, nor look twice at 'em, has praised it. My nose ain't crooked an' never was, an' if anybody says so it's 'cause they're so spity, 'cause they're so mortal homely themselves. Guess I know.' She drew breath, and paused for a return shot, but she got none. The stout old woman sewed and chuckled to herself, the tall one still fixed her eyes upon the top of the door, and the young woman leaned back with her lips parted, and her black eyes rolled.

The pretty old woman began again in defence of her nose; she talked fiercely, and kept feeling of it. Finally she arose and went out of the room with a flirt.

Then the stout old woman laughed. 'She's gone to look at her nose in the lookin'-glass, an' make sure it ain't crooked: if it ain't a good joke!' she exclaimed, delightedly.

But she got no response. The young woman never stirred and the tall old one only lowered her gaze from the door to the stove, which she regarded disapprovingly. 'I call it the devil's stove,' she remarked, after a while.

The stout old woman gave a grunt and sewed her seam; she was done with talking to such an audience. The shouts of children out in the corridor could be heard. 'Pesky young ones!' she muttered.

In the corridor Polly Moss played ball with the children. She never caught the ball, and she threw it with weak, aimless jerks; her back ached, but she was patient, and her face was full of simple childish smiles. There were two children besides Tommy – his sister and a little boy.

The corridor was long; doors in both sides led into the paupers' bedrooms. Suddenly one of the doors flew open, and a little figure shot out. She went down the corridor with a swift trot like a child. She had on nothing but a woollen petticoat and a calico waist; she held her head down, and her narrow shoulders worked as she ran; her mop of soft white hair flew out. The children looked around at her; she was a horrible caricature of themselves.

The stout old woman came pressing out of the sitting-room. She went directly to the room that the running figure had left, and peered in; then she looked around significantly. 'I knowed it,' she said; 'it's tore all to pieces agin. I'd jest been thinkin' to myself that Sally was dretful still, an' I'd bet she was pullin' her bed to pieces. There 'tis, an' made up jest as nice a few minutes ago! I'm goin' to see Mis' Arms.'

Mrs Arms was the matron. The old woman went off with an important air, and presently she returned with her. The matron was a large woman with a calm, benignant, and weary face.

Polly Moss continued to play ball, but several other old women had assembled, and they all talked volubly. They demonstrated that Sally had torn her bed to pieces, that it had been very nicely made, and that she should be punished.

The matron listened; she did not say much. Then she returned to the kitchen, where she was preparing dinner. Some of the paupers assisted her. An old man, with his baggy trousers hitched high, chopped something in a tray, an old woman peeled potatoes, and a young one washed pans at the sink. The young woman, as she washed, kept looking over her shoulder and rolling her dark eyes at the other people in the room. She was mindful of every motion behind her back.

Mrs Arms herself worked and directed the others. When dinner was ready the old man clanged a bell in the corridor, and everybody flocked to the dining-room except the young woman at the kitchen sink; she still stood there washing dishes. The dinner was coarse and abundant. The paupers, with the exception of the sick young woman, ate with gusto. The children were all hearty, and although the world had lost all its savor for the hearts and minds of the old ones, it was still somewhat salt to their palates. Now that their thoughts had ceased reaching and grasping, they could still put out their tongues, for that primitive instinct of life with which they had been born still survived and gave them pleasure. In this world it is the child only that is immortal.

The old people and the children ate after the same manner. There was a loud smacking of lips and gurgling noises. The rain drove against the windows of the dining-room, with its bare floor, its board tables and benches, and rows of feeding paupers. The smooth yellow heads of the children seemed to catch all the light in the room. Once in a while they raised imperious clamors. The overseer sat at one end of the table and served the beef. He was stout, and had a handsome, heavy face.

The meal was nearly finished when there was a crash of breaking crockery, a door slammed, and there was a wild shriek out in the corridor. The overseer and one of the old men who was quite able-bodied sprang and rushed out of the room. The matron followed, and the children tagged at her heels. The others continued feeding as if nothing had happened. 'That Agnes is wuss agin,' remarked the stout old woman. 'I've seed it a-comin' on fer a couple of days. They'd orter have put her in the cell yesterday; I told Mis' Arms so, but they're allers puttin' off, an' puttin' off.'

'They air a-takin' on her up to the cell now,' said the pretty old woman; and she brought around her knifeful of cabbage with a sidewise motion, and stretched her little red mouth to receive it.

Out in the corridor shriek followed shriek; there were loud voices and scuffling. The children were huddled in the doorway, peeping, but the old paupers continued to eat. The sick young woman laid down her knife and fork and wept.

Presently the shrieks and the scuffling grew faint in the distance; the children had followed on. Then, after a little, they all returned and the dinner was finished.

After dinner, when the women paupers had done their share of the clearing away, they were again assembled in their sitting-room. The windows were cloudy with fine mist; the rain continued to drive past them from over the yellow stubbly fields. There was a good fire in the stove, and the room was hot and close. The stout old woman sewed again on her coarse seam, the others were idle. There were now six old women present; one of them was the little creature whom they called Sally. She sat close to the stove, bent over and motionless. Her clothing hardly covered her. The sick young woman was absent; she was lying down on the lounge in the matron's room, and the children too were in there.

Polly Moss sat by the window. The old women began talking among themselves. The pretty old one had taken off her cap and had it in her lap, perking up the lace and straightening it. It was a flimsy rag, like a soiled cobweb. The stout old woman cast a contemptuous glance at it. She raised her nose and her upper lip scornfully. 'I don't see how you can wear that nasty thing nohow, Mis' Handy,' said she.

Mrs Handy flushed pink again. She bridled and began to speak, then she looked at the little soft soiled mass in her lap, and paused. She had not the force of character to proclaim black white while she was looking at it. Had the old cap been in the bureau drawer, or even on her head, she might have defended it to the death, but here before her eyes it silenced her.

But after her momentary subsidence she aroused herself; her blue eyes gleamed dimly at the stout old woman. 'It was a handsome cap when it was new, anyhow!' said she; 'better'n some folks ever had, I'll warrant. Folks that ain't got no caps at all can't afford to be flingin' at them that has, if they ain't quite so nice as they was. You'd orter have seen the cap I had when my daughter was married! All white wrought lace, an' bows of pink ribbon, an' long streamers, an' some artificial roses on't. I don't s'pose you ever see anythin' like it, Mis' Paine.'

The stout woman was Mrs Paine. 'Mebbe I ain't,' said she, sarcastically.

The tall old woman chimed in suddenly; her thin, nervous voice clanged after the others like a sharply struck bell. 'I ain't never had any caps to speak of,' she proclaimed; 'never thought much of 'em, anyhow; heatin' things; an' I never heard that folks in heaven wore caps. But I have had some good clothes. I've got a piece of silk in my bureau drawer. That silk would stand alone. An' I had a good thibet; there was rows an' rows of velvet ribbon on it. I always had good clothes; my husband, he wanted I should, an' he got 'em fer me. I airned some myself, too. I 'ain't got any now, an' I dunno as I care if I ain't, fer the signs are increasin'.'

'Allers a-harpin' on that,' muttered the stout old woman.

'I had a handsome blue silk when I was marri'd,' vouchsafed Mrs Handy.

'I've seen the piece of it,' returned the tall one; 'it ain't near so thick as mine is.'

The old woman who had not been present in the morning now spoke. She had been listening with a superior air. She was the only one in the company who had possessed considerable property, and had fallen from a widely differing estate. She was tall and dark and gaunt; she towered up next the pretty old woman like a scraggy old pine beside a faded lily. She was a single woman, and she had lost all her property through an injudicious male relative. 'Well,' she proclaimed, 'everybody knows I've had things if I ain't got 'em now. There I had a whole house, with Brussels carpets on all the rooms except the kitchen, an' stuffed furniture, an' beddin' packed away in chists, an' bureau drawers full of things. An' I ruther think I've had silk dresses an' bunnits an' caps.'

'I remember you had a real handsome blue bunnit once, but it warn't so becomin' as some you'd had, you was so dark-complected,' remarked the pretty old woman, in a soft, spiteful voice. 'I had a white one, drawn silk, an' white feathers on't, when I was married, and they all said it was real becomin'. I was allers real white myself. I had a white muslin dress with a flounce on it, once, too, an' a black silk spencer cape.'

'I had a fitch tippet an' muff that cost twenty-five dollars,' remarked the stout old woman, emphatically, '*an*' a cashmire shawl.'

'I had two cashmire shawls, an' *my* tippet cost fifty dollars,' retorted the dark old woman, with dignity.

'My fust baby had an elegant blue cashmire cloak, all worked with silk as deep as that,' said Mrs Handy. She now had the old cap on her head, and looked more assertive.

'Mine had a little wagon with a velvet cushion to ride in; an' I had a tea-set, real chiny, with a green sprig on't,' said the stout old woman.

'I had a Brittany teapot,' returned Mrs Handy.

'I had gilt vases as tall as that on my parlor mantelshelf,' said the dark old woman.

'I had a chiny figger, a girl with a basket of flowers on her arm, once,' rejoined the tall one; 'it used to set side of the clock. An' when I was fust married I used to live in a white house, with a flower-garden to one side. I can smell them pinks an' roses now, an' I s'pose I allers shall, jest as far as I go.'

'I had a pump in my kitchen sink, an' things real handy,' said the stout old one; 'an' I used to look as well as anybody, an' my husband too, when we went to meetin'. I remember one winter I had a new brown alpaca with velvet buttons, an' he had a new great-coat with a velvet collar.'

Suddenly the little cowering Sally raised herself and gave testimony to her own little crumb of past comfort. Her wits were few and scattering, and had been all her days, but the conversation of the other women seemed to set some vibrating into momentary concord. She laughed, and her bleared blue eyes twinkled. 'I had a pink caliker gownd once,' she quavered out. 'Mis' Thompson, she gin it me when I lived there.'

'Do hear the poor cretur,' said the pretty old woman, with an indulgent air.

Now everybody had spoken but Polly Moss. She sat by the misty window, and her little pale triangular face looked from her sunken chest at the others. This conversation was a usual one. Many and many an afternoon the almshouse old women sat together and bore witness to their past glories. Now they had nothing, but at one time or another they had had something over which to plume themselves and feel that precious pride of possession. Their present was to them a state of simple existence, they regarded their future with a vague resignation; they were none of them thinkers, and there was no case of rapturous piety among them. In their pasts alone they took real comfort, and they kept, as it were, feeling of them to see if they were not still warm with life.

The old women delighted in these inventories and comparing of notes. Polly Moss alone had never spoken. She alone had never had anything in which to take pride. She had been always deformed and poor and friendless. She had worked for scanty pay as long as she was able, and had then drifted and struck on the almshouse, where she had grown old. She had not even a right to the charity of this particular village: this was merely the place where her working powers had failed her; but no one could trace her back to her birthplace, or the town which was responsible for her support. Polly Moss herself did not know – she went humbly where she was told. All her life the world had seemed to her simply standing-ground; she had gotten little more out of it.

Every day, when the others talked, she listened admiringly, and searched her memory for some little past treasure of her own, but she could not remember any. The dim image of a certain delaine dress, with bright flowers scattered over it, which she had once owned, away back in her girlhood, sometimes floated before her eyes when they were talking, and she had a half-mind to mention that, but her heart would fail her. She feared that it was not worthy to be compared with the others' fine departed gowns; it paled before even Sally's pink calico. Polly's poor clothes, covering her pitiful crookedness, had never given her any firm stimulus to gratulation. So she was always silent, and the other old women had come to talk at her. Their conversation acquired a gusto from this listener who could not join in. When a new item of past property was given, there was always a side-glance in Polly's direction.

None of the old women expected to ever hear a word from Polly, but this afternoon, when they had all, down to Sally, testified, she spoke up:

'You'd orter have seen my sister Liddy,' said she; her voice was very small, it sounded like the piping of a feeble bird in a bush.

There was a dead silence. The other old women looked at each other. 'Didn't know you ever had a sister Liddy,' the stout old woman blurted out, finally, with an amazed air.

'My sister Liddy was jest as handsome as a pictur',' Polly returned.

The pretty old woman flushed jealously. 'Was she fair-complected?' she inquired.

'She was jest as fair as a lily – a good deal fairer than you ever was, Mis' Handy, an' she had long yaller curls a-hangin' clean down to her waist, an' her cheeks were jest as pink, an' she had the biggest blue eyes I ever see, an' the beautifulest leetle red mouth.'

'Lor'!' ejaculated the stout old woman, and the pretty old woman sniffed.

But Polly went on; she was not to be daunted; she had been silent all this time; and now her category poured forth, not piecemeal, but in a flood, upon her astonished hearers.

'Liddy, she could sing the best of anybody anywheres around,' she continued; 'nobody ever heerd sech singin'. It was so dretful loud an' sweet that you could hear it 'way down the road when the winders was shut. She used to sing in the meetin'-house, she did, an' all the folks used to sit up an' look at her when she begun. She used to wear a black silk dress to meetin', an' a white cashmire shawl, an' a bunnit with a pink wreath around the face, an' she had white kid gloves. Folks used to go to that meetin'-house jest to hear Liddy sing an' see her. They thought 'nough sight more of that than they did of the preachin'.

'Liddy had a feather fan, an' she used to sit an' fan her when she wa'n't singin', an' she allers had scent on her handkercher. An' when meetin' was done in the evenin' all the young fellars used to be crowdin' 'round, an' pushin' and bowin' an' scrapin', a-tryin' to get a chance to see her home. But Liddy she wouldn't look at none of them; she married a real rich fellar from Bostown. He was jest as straight as an arrer, an' he had black eyes an' hair, an' he wore a beautiful coat an' a satin vest, an' he spoke jest as perlite.

'When Liddy was married she had a whole chistful of clothes, real fine cotton cloth, all tucks an' laid-work, an' she had a pair of silk stockin's, an' some white shoes. An' her weddin' dress was white satin, with a great long trail to it, an' she had a lace veil, an' she wore great long ear-drops that shone like everythin'. *An'* she come out bride in a blue silk dress, an' a black lace mantilly, an' a white bunnit trimmed with lutestring ribbon.'

'Where did your sister Liddy live arter she was married?' inquired the pretty old woman, with a subdued air.

'She lived in Bostown, an' she had a great big house with a parlor an' settin'-room, an' a room to eat in besides the kitchen. An' she had real velvet carpets on all the floors down to the kitchen, an' great pictur's in gilt frames a-hangin' on all the walls. An' her furnitur' was all stuffed, an' kivered with red velvet, an' she had a pianner, an' great big marble images a-settin' on her mantel-shelf. An' she had a coach with lamps on the sides, an' blue satin cushings, to ride in, an' four horses to draw it, an' a man to drive. An' she allers had a hired girl in the kitchen. I never knowed Liddy to be without a hired girl.

'Liddy's husband, he thought everythin' of her; he never used to come home from his work without he brought her somethin', an' she used to run out to meet him. She was allers dretful lovin', an' had a good disposition. Liddy, she had the beautifu-lest baby you ever see, an' she had a cradle lined with blue silk to rock him in, an' he had a white silk cloak, an' a leetle lace cap – '

'I shouldn't think your beautiful sister Liddy an' her husband would let you come to the poor-house,' interrupted the dark old woman.

'Liddy's dead, or she wouldn't.'

'Are her husband an' the baby dead, too?'

'They're all dead,' responded Polly Moss. She looked out of the window again, her face was a burning red, and there were tears in her eyes.

There was silence among the other old women. They were at once overawed and incredulous. Polly left the room before long, then they began to discuss the matter. 'I dun know whether to believe it or not,' said the dark old woman.

'Well, I dun know, neither; I never knowed her to tell anythin' that wa'n't so,' responded the stout old one, doubtfully.

The old women could not make up their minds whether to believe or disbelieve. The pretty one was the most incredulous of any. She said openly that she did not believe it possible that such a 'homely cretur' as Polly Moss could have had such a handsome sister.

But, credulous or not, their interest and curiosity were lively. Every day Polly Moss was questioned and cross-examined concerning her sister Liddy. She rose to the occasion; she did not often contradict herself, and the glories of her sister were increased daily. Old Polly Moss, her little withered face gleaming with reckless enthusiasm, sang the praises of her sister Liddy as wildly and faithfully as any minnesinger his angel mistress, and the old women listened with ever-increasing bewilderment and awe.

It was two weeks before Polly Moss died with pneumonia that she first mentioned her sister Liddy, and there was not one afternoon until the day when she was taken ill that she did not relate the story, with new and startling additions, to the old women.

Polly was not ill long, she settled meekly down under the disease: her little distorted frame had no resistance in it. She died at three o'clock in the morning. The afternoon before, she seemed better; she was quite rational, and she told the matron that she wanted to see her comrades, the old women. 'I've got somethin' to tell 'em, Mis' Arms,' Polly whispered, and her eyes were piteous.

So the other old women came into the room. They stood around Polly's little iron bed and looked at her. 'I – want to – tell you – somethin',' she began. But there was a soft rush, and the sick young woman entered. She pressed straight to the matron; she disregarded the others. Her wan face seemed a very lamp of life – to throw a light over and above all present darkness, even of the grave. She moved nimbly; she was so full of joy that her sickly body seemed permeated by it, and almost a spiritual one. She did not appear in the least feeble. She caught the matron's arm. 'Charley has come, Mis' Arms!' she cried out. 'Charley has come! He's got a house ready. He's goin' to marry me, an' take me home, an' take care of me till I get well. I'm goin' right away!'

The old women all turned away from Polly and stared at the radiant girl. The matron sent her away, with a promise to see her in a few minutes. 'Polly's dyin',' she whispered, and the girl stole out with a hushed air, but the light in her face was not dimmed. What was death to her, when she had just stepped on a height of life where one can see beyond it?

'Tell them what you wanted to, now, Polly,' said the matron.

'I – want to tell you – somethin',' Polly repeated. 'I s'pose I've been dretful wicked, but I ain't never had nothin' in my whole life. I – s'pose the Lord orter have been enough, but it's dretful hard sometimes to keep holt of him, an' not look anywheres else, when you see other folks a-clawin' an' gettin' other things, an' actin' as if they was wuth havin'. I ain't never had nothin' as fur as them other things go; I don't want nothin' else now. I've – got past 'em. I see I don't want nothin' but the Lord. But I used to feel dretful bad an' wicked when I heerd you all talkin' 'bout things you'd had, an' I hadn't never had nothin', so – '

Polly Moss stopped talking, and coughed. The matron supported her. The old women nudged each other; their awed, sympathetic, yet sharply inquiring eyes never left her face. The children were peeping in at the open door; old Sally trotted past – she had just torn her bed to pieces. As soon as she got breath enough, Polly Moss finished what she had to say. 'I – s'pose I – was dretful wicked,' she whispered; 'but – I never had any sister Liddy.'

Miss Grief

1880

'A conceited fool' is a not uncommon expression. Now, I know
that I am not a fool, but I also know that I am conceited. But,
candidly, can it be helped if one happens to be young, well and
strong, passably good looking, with some money that one has
inherited and more that one has earned – in all, enough to make
life comfortable – and if upon this foundation rests also the
pleasant superstructure of a literary success? The success is
deserved, I think: certainly it was not lightly gained. Yet even
with this I fully appreciate its rarity. Thus, I find myself very
well entertained in life: I have all I wish in the way of society,
and a deep, though of course carefully concealed, satisfaction in
my own little fame; which fame I foster by a gentle system of
non-interference. I know that I am spoken of as 'that quiet
young fellow who writes those delightful little studies of society,
you know'; and I live up to that definition.

A year ago I was in Rome, and enjoying life particularly. I
had a large number of my acquaintances there, both American
and English, and no day passed without its invitation. Of course
I understood it: it is seldom that you find a literary man who is
good tempered, well dressed, sufficiently provided with money,
and amiably obedient to all the rules and requirements of
'society.' 'When found, make a note of it';* and the note was
generally an invitation.

One evening, upon returning to my lodgings, my man Simpson informed me that a person had called in the afternoon, and
upon learning that I was absent had left not a card, but her
name – 'Miss Grief.' The title lingered – Miss Grief! 'Grief has
not so far visited me here,' I said to myself, dismissing Simpson
and seeking my little balcony for a final smoke, 'and she shall
not now. I shall take care to be "not at home" to her if she

continues to call.' And then I fell to thinking of Isabel Abercrombie, in whose society I had spent that and many evenings: they were golden thoughts.

The next day there was an excursion; it was late when I reached my rooms, and again Simpson informed me that Miss Grief had called.

'Is she coming continuously?' I said, half to myself.

'Yes, sir: she mentioned that she should call again.'

'How does she look?'

'Well, sir, a lady, but not so prosperous as she was, I should say,' answered Simpson, discreetly.

'Young?'

'No, sir.'

'Alone?'

'A maid with her, sir.'

But once outside in my little high-up balcony with my cigar, I again forgot Miss Grief and whatever she might represent. Who would not forget in that moonlight, with Isabel Abercrombie's face to remember?

The stranger came a third time, and I was absent; then she let two days pass, and began again. It grew to be a regular dialogue between Simpson and myself when I came in at night: 'Grief today?'

'Yes, sir.'

'What time?'

'Four, sir.'

'Happy the man,' I thought, 'who can keep her confined to a particular hour!'

But I should not have treated my visitor so cavalierly if I had not felt sure that she was eccentric and unconventional – qualities extremely tiresome in a woman no longer young or attractive. If she were not eccentric, she would not have persisted in coming to my door day after day in this silent way, without stating her errand, leaving a note, or presenting her credentials in any shape. I made up my mind that she had something to sell – a bit of carving or some intaglio supposed to be antique. It was known that I had a fancy for oddities. I said to myself, 'She has read or heard of my "Old Gold" story, or else "The Buried God," and she thinks me an idealizing ignoramus upon whom she can impose. Her sepulchral name is at least not Italian; probably she is a sharp countrywoman of mine, turning, by means of the present aesthetic craze, an honest penny when she can.'

She had called seven times during a period of two weeks without seeing me, when one day I happened to be at home in the afternoon, owing to a pouring rain and a fit of doubt concerning Miss Abercrombie. For I had constructed a careful theory of that young lady's characteristics in my own mind, and she had lived up to it delightfully until the previous evening, when with one word she had blown it to atoms and taken flight, leaving me standing, as it were, on a desolate shore, with nothing but a handful of mistaken inductions wherewith to console myself. I do not know a more exasperating frame of mind, at least for a constructor of theories. I could not write, and so I took up a French novel (I model myself a little on Balzac).* I had been turning over its pages but a few moments when Simpson knocked, and, entering softly, said, with just a shadow of a smile on his well-trained face, 'Miss Grief.' I briefly consigned Miss Grief to all the Furies,* and then, as he still lingered – perhaps not knowing where they resided – I asked where the visitor was.

'Outside, sir – in the hall. I told her I would see if you were at home.'

'She must be unpleasantly wet if she had no carriage.'

'No carriage, sir: they always come on foot. I think she *is* a little damp, sir.'

'Well, let her in; but I don't want the maid. I may as well see her now, I suppose, and end the affair.'

'Yes, sir.'

I did not put down my book. My visitor should have a hearing, but not much more: she had sacrificed her womanly claims by her persistent attacks upon my door. Presently Simpson ushered her in. 'Miss Grief,' he said, and then went out, closing the curtain behind him.

A woman – yes, a lady – but shabby, unattractive, and more than middle-aged.

I rose, bowed slightly, and then dropped into my chair again, still keeping the book in my hand. 'Miss Grief?' I said interrogatively as I indicated a seat with my eyebrows.

'Not Grief,' she answered – 'Crief: my name is Crief.'

She sat down, and I saw that she held a small flat box.

'Not carving, then,' I thought – 'probably old lace, something that belonged to Tullia or Lucrezia Borgia.'* But, as she did not speak, I found myself obliged to begin: 'You have been here, I think, once or twice before?'

'Seven times; this is the eighth.'

A silence.

'I am often out; indeed, I may say that I am never in,' I remarked carelessly.

'Yes; you have many friends.'

' – Who will perhaps buy old lace,' I mentally added. But this time I too remained silent; why should I trouble myself to draw her out? She had sought me; let her advance her idea, whatever it was, now that entrance was gained.

But Miss Grief (I preferred to call her so) did not look as though she could advance anything: her black gown, damp with rain, seemed to retreat fearfully to her thin self, while her thin self retreated as far as possible from me, from the chair, from everything. Her eyes were cast down; an old-fashioned lace veil with a heavy border shaded her face. She looked at the floor, and I looked at her.

I grew a little impatient, but I made up my mind that I would continue silent and see how long a time she would consider necessary to give due effect to her little pantomime. Comedy? Or was it tragedy? I suppose full five minutes passed thus in our double silence; and that is a long time when two persons are sitting opposite each other alone in a small still room.

At last my visitor, without raising her eyes, said slowly, 'You are very happy, are you not, with youth, health, friends, riches, fame?'

It was a singular beginning. Her voice was clear, low, and very sweet as she thus enumerated my advantages one by one in a list. I was attracted by it, but repelled by her words, which seemed to me flattery both dull and bold.

'Thanks,' I said, 'for your kindness, but I fear it is undeserved. I seldom discuss myself even when with my friends.'

'I am your friend,' replied Miss Grief. Then, after a moment, she added slowly, 'I have read every word you have written.'

I curled the edges of my book indifferently; I am not a fop, I hope, but – others have said the same.

'What is more, I know much of it by heart,' continued my visitor. 'Wait: I will show you'; and then, without pause, she began to repeat something of mine word for word, just as I had written it. On she went, and I – listened. I intended interrupting her after a moment, but I did not, because she was reciting so well, and also because I felt a desire gaining upon me to see what she would make of a certain conversation which I knew was coming – a conversation between two of my characters which was, to say the least, sphinx-like, and somewhat incandescent as well. What won me a little, too, was the fact that the scene she was reciting (it was hardly more than that, though called a story) was secretly my favorite among all the sketches from my pen which a gracious public has received with favor. I never said so, but it was; and I had always felt a wondering annoyance that the aforesaid public, while kindly praising beyond their worth other attempts of mine, had never noticed the higher purpose of this little shaft, aimed not at the balconies and lighted windows of society, but straight up toward the distant stars. So she went on, and presently reached the conversation: my two people began to talk. She had raised her eyes now, and was looking at me soberly as she gave the words of the woman, quiet, gentle, cold, and the replies of the man, bitter, hot, and scathing. Her very voice changed, and took, though always sweetly, the different tones required, while no point of meaning, however small, no breath of delicate emphasis which I had meant, but which the dull types could not give, escaped an appreciative and full, almost overfull, recognition which startled me. For she had understood me – understood me almost better than I had understood myself. It seemed to me that while I had labored to interpret, partially, a psychological riddle, she, coming after, had comprehended its bearings better than I had, though confining herself strictly to my own words and emphasis. The scene ended (and it ended rather suddenly), she dropped her eyes, and moved her hand nervously to and fro over the box she held; her gloves were old and shabby, her hands small.

I was secretly much surprised by what I had heard, but my ill humor was deep-seated that day, and I still felt sure, besides, that the box contained something which I was expected to buy.

'You recite remarkably well,' I said carelessly, 'and I am much flattered also by your appreciation of my attempt. But it is not, I presume, to that alone that I owe the pleasure of this visit?'

'Yes,' she answered, still looking down, 'it is, for if you had not written that scene I should not have sought you. Your other

sketches are interiors – exquisitely painted and delicately finished, but of small scope. *This* is a sketch in a few bold, masterly
lines – work of entirely different spirit and purpose.'

I was nettled by her insight. 'You have bestowed so much of
your kind attention upon me that I feel your debtor,' I said,
conventionally. 'It may be that there is something I can do for
you – connected, possibly, with that little box?'

It was impertinent, but it was true; for she answered, 'Yes.'

I smiled, but her eyes were cast down and she did not see the
smile.

'What I have to show you is a manuscript,' she said after a
pause which I did not break; 'it is a drama. I thought that
perhaps you would read it.'

'An authoress! This is worse than old lace,' I said to myself in
dismay. – Then, aloud, 'My opinion would be worth nothing,
Miss Crief.'

'Not in a business way, I know. But it might be – an assistance
personally.' Her voice had sunk to a whisper; outside, the rain
was pouring steadily down. She was a very depressing object to
me as she sat there with her box.

'I hardly think I have the time at present – ' I began.

She had raised her eyes and was looking at me; then, when I
paused, she rose and came suddenly toward my chair. 'Yes, you
will read it,' she said with her hand on my arm – 'you will read
it. Look at this room; look at yourself; look at all you have.
Then look at me, and have pity.'

I had risen, for she held my arm, and her damp skirt was
brushing my knees.

Her large dark eyes looked intently into mine as she went on:
'I have no shame in asking. Why should I have? It is my last
endeavor; but a calm and well-considered one. If you refuse I
shall go away, knowing that Fate has willed it so. And I shall be
content.'

'She is mad,' I thought. But she did not look so, and she had
spoken quietly, even gently. 'Sit down,' I said, moving away
from her. I felt as if I had been magnetized; but it was only the
nearness of her eyes to mine, and their intensity. I drew forward
a chair, but she remained standing.

'I cannot,' she said in the same sweet, gentle tone, 'unless you
promise.'

'Very well, I promise; only sit down.'

As I took her arm to lead her to the chair, I perceived that she was trembling, but her face continued unmoved.

'You do not, of course, wish me to look at your manuscript now?' I said, temporizing; 'it would be much better to leave it. Give me your address, and I will return it to you with my written opinion; though, I repeat, the latter will be of no use to you. It is the opinion of an editor or publisher that you want.'

'It shall be as you please. And I will go in a moment,' said Miss Grief, pressing her palms together, as if trying to control the tremor that had seized her slight frame.

She looked so pallid that I thought of offering her a glass of wine; then I remembered that if I did it might be a bait to bring her here again, and this I was desirous to prevent. She rose while the thought was passing through my mind. Her pasteboard box lay on the chair she had first occupied; she took it, wrote an address on the cover, laid it down, and then, bowing with a little air of formality, drew her black shawl round her shoulders and turned toward the door.

I followed, after touching the bell. 'You will hear from me by letter,' I said.

Simpson opened the door, and I caught a glimpse of the maid, who was waiting in the anteroom. She was an old woman, shorter than her mistress, equally thin, and dressed like her in rusty black. As the door opened she turned toward it a pair of small, dim, blue eyes with a look of furtive suspense. Simpson dropped the curtain, shutting me into the inner room; he had no intention of allowing me to accompany my visitor further. But I had the curiosity to go to a bay window in an angle from whence I could command the street door, and presently I saw them issue forth in the rain and walk away side by side, the mistress, being the taller, holding the umbrella: probably there was not much difference in rank between persons so poor and forlorn as these.

It grew dark. I was invited out for the evening, and I knew that if I should go I should meet Miss Abercrombie. I said to myself that I would not go. I got out my paper for writing, I made my preparations for a quiet evening at home with myself; but it was of no use. It all ended slavishly in my going. At the last allowable moment I presented myself, and – as a punishment for my vacillation, I suppose – I never passed a more disagreeable evening. I drove homeward in a murky temper; it was foggy without, and very foggy within. What Isabel really was, now that she had broken through my elaborately built theories, I was not able to decide. There was, to tell the truth, a certain young Englishman – But that is apart from this story.

I reached home, went up to my rooms, and had a supper. It was to console myself; I am obliged to console myself scientifically once in a while. I was walking up and down afterward, smoking and feeling somewhat better, when my eye fell upon the pasteboard box. I took it up; on the cover was written an address which showed that my visitor must have walked a long distance in order to see me: 'A. Crief.' – 'A Grief,' I thought; 'and so she is. I positively believe she has brought all this trouble upon me: she has the evil eye.' I took out the manuscript and looked at it. It was in the form of a little volume, and clearly written; on the cover was the word 'Armor' in German text, and, underneath, a pen-and-ink sketch of a helmet, breastplate, and shield.

'Grief certainly needs armor,' I said to myself, sitting down by the table and turning over the pages. 'I may as well look over the thing now; I could not be in a worse mood.' And then I began to read.

Early the next morning Simpson took a note from me to the given address, returning with the following reply: 'No; I prefer to come to you; at four; A. Crief.' These words, with their three semicolons, were written in pencil upon a piece of coarse printing paper, but the handwriting was as clear and delicate as that of the manuscript in ink.

'What sort of a place was it, Simpson?'

'Very poor, sir, but I did not go all the way up. The elder person came down, sir, took the note, and requested me to wait where I was.'

'You had no chance, then, to make inquiries?' I said, knowing full well that he had emptied the entire neighborhood of any information it might possess concerning these two lodgers.

'Well, sir, you know how these foreigners will talk, whether one wants to hear or not. But it seems that these two persons have been there but a few weeks; they live alone, and are uncommonly silent and reserved. The people round there call them something that signifies "the Madames American, thin and dumb."'

At four the 'Madames American' arrived; it was raining again, and they came on foot under their old umbrella. The maid waited in the anteroom, and Miss Grief was ushered into my bachelor's parlor. I had thought that I should meet her with great deference; but she looked so forlorn that my deference changed to pity. It was the woman that impressed me then, more than the writer – the fragile, nerveless body more than the inspired mind. For it was inspired; I had sat up half the night over her drama, and had felt thrilled through and through more than once by its earnestness, passion, and power.

No one could have been more surprised than I was to find myself thus enthusiastic. I thought I had outgrown that sort of thing. And one would have supposed, too (I myself should have supposed so the day before), that the faults of the drama, which were many and prominent, would have chilled any liking I might have felt, I being a writer myself, and therefore critical; for writers are as apt to make much of the 'how,' rather than the 'what,' as painters, who, it is well known, prefer an exquisitely rendered representation of a commonplace theme to an imperfectly executed picture of even the most striking subject. But in this case, on the contrary, the scattered rays of splendor in Miss Grief's drama had made me forget the dark spots, which were numerous and disfiguring; or, rather, the splendor had made me anxious to have the spots removed. And this also was a philanthropic state very unusual with me. Regarding unsuccessful writers, my motto had been '*Væ victis!*'*

My visitor took a seat and folded her hands; I could see, in spite of her quiet manner, that she was in breathless suspense. It seemed so pitiful that she should be trembling there before me – a woman so much older than I was, a woman who possessed the divine spark of genius, which I was by no means sure (in spite of my success) had been granted to me – that I felt as if I ought to go down on my knees before her, and entreat her to take her proper place of supremacy at once. But there! one does not go down on one's knees, combustively, as it were, before a woman over fifty, plain in feature, thin, dejected, and ill dressed. I contented myself with taking her hands (in their miserable old gloves) in mine, while I said cordially, 'Miss Crief, your drama seems to me full of original power. It has roused my enthusiasm: I sat up half the night reading it.'

The hands I held shook, but something (perhaps a shame for having evaded the knees business) made me tighten my hold and bestow upon her also a reassuring smile. She looked at me for a moment, and then, suddenly and noiselessly, tears rose and rolled down her cheeks. I dropped her hands and retreated. I had not thought her tearful: on the contrary, her voice and face had seemed rigidly controlled. But now here she was bending herself over the side of the chair with her head resting on her arms, not sobbing aloud, but her whole frame shaken by the strength of her emotion. I rushed for a glass of wine; I pressed her to take it. I did not quite know what to do, but, putting myself in her place, I decided to praise the drama; and praise it I did. I do not know when I have used so many adjectives. She raised her head and began to wipe her eyes.

'Do take the wine,' I said, interrupting myself in my cataract of language.

'I dare not,' she answered; then added humbly, 'that is, unless you have a biscuit here or a bit of bread.'

I found some biscuit; she ate two, and then slowly drank the wine, while I resumed my verbal Niagara. Under its influence – and that of the wine too, perhaps – she began to show new life. It was not that she looked radiant – she could not – but simply that she looked warm. I now perceived what had been the principal discomfort of her appearance heretofore: it was that she had looked all the time as if suffering from cold.

At last I could think of nothing more to say, and stopped. I really admired the drama, but I thought I had exerted myself sufficiently as an anti-hysteric, and that adjectives enough, for the present at least, had been administered. She had put down her empty wineglass, and was resting her hands on the broad cushioned arms of her chair with, for a thin person, a sort of expanded content.

'You must pardon my tears,' she said, smiling; 'it was the revulsion of feeling. My life was at a low ebb: if your sentence had been against me, it would have been my end.'

'Your end?'

'Yes, the end of my life; I should have destroyed myself.'

'Then you would have been a weak as well as wicked woman,' I said in a tone of disgust. I do hate sensationalism.

'Oh no, you know nothing about it. I should have destroyed only this poor worn tenement of clay. But I can well understand how *you* would look upon it. Regarding the desirableness of life, the prince and the beggar may have different opinions. We will say no more of it, but talk of the drama instead.' As she spoke the word 'drama' a triumphant brightness came into her eyes.

I took the manuscript from a drawer and sat down beside her. 'I suppose you know that there are faults,' I said, expecting ready acquiescence.

'I was not aware that there were any,' was her gentle reply.

Here was a beginning! After all my interest in her – and, I may say under the circumstances, my kindness – she received me in this way! However, my belief in her genius was too sincere to be altered by her whimsies; so I persevered. 'Let us go over it together,' I said. 'Shall I read it to you, or will you read it to me?'

'I will not read it, but recite it.'

'That will never do; you will recite it so well that we shall see only the good points, and what we have to concern ourselves with now is the bad ones.'

'I will recite it,' she repeated.

'Now, Miss Crief,' I said bluntly, 'for what purpose did you come to me? Certainly not merely to recite: I am no stage manager. In plain English, was it not your idea that I might help you in obtaining a publisher?'

'Yes, yes,' she answered, looking at me apprehensively, all her old manner returning.

I followed up my advantage, opened the little paper volume and began. I first took the drama line by line, and spoke of the faults of expression and structure; then I turned back and touched upon two or three glaring impossibilities in the plot. 'Your absorbed interest in the motive of the whole no doubt made you forget these blemishes,' I said apologetically.

But, to my surprise, I found that she did not see the blemishes – that she appreciated nothing I had said, comprehended nothing. Such unaccountable obtuseness puzzled me. I began again, going over the whole with even greater minuteness and care. I worked hard: the perspiration stood in beads upon my forehead as I struggled with her – what shall I call it – obstinacy? But it was not exactly obstinacy. She simply could not see the faults of her own work, any more than a blind man can see the smoke that dims a patch of blue sky. When I had finished my task the second time, she still remained as gently impassive as before. I leaned back in my chair exhausted, and looked at her.

Even then she did not seem to comprehend (whether she agreed with it or not) what I must be thinking. 'It is such a heaven to me that you like it!' she murmured dreamily, breaking the silence. Then, with more animation, 'And *now* you will let me recite it?'

I was too weary to oppose her; she threw aside her shawl and bonnet, and standing in the center of the room, began.

And she carried me along with her: all the strong passages were doubly strong when spoken, and the faults, which seemed nothing to her, were made by her earnestness to seem nothing to me, at least for that moment. When it was ended, she stood looking at me with a triumphant smile.

'Yes,' I said, 'I like it, and you see that I do. But I like it because my taste is peculiar. To me originality and force are everything – perhaps because I have them not to any marked degree myself – but the world at large will not overlook as I do your absolutely barbarous shortcomings on account of them. Will you trust me to go over the drama and correct it at my pleasure?' This was a vast deal for me to offer; I was surprised at myself.

'No,' she answered softly, still smiling. 'There shall not be so much as a comma altered.' Then she sat down and fell into a reverie as though she were alone.

'Have you written anything else?' I said after a while, when I had become tired of the silence.

'Yes.'

'Can I see it?. Or is it *them*?'

'It is *them*. Yes, you can see all.'

'I will call upon you for the purpose.'

'No, you must not,' she said, coming back to the present nervously. 'I prefer to come to you.'

At this moment Simpson entered to light the room, and busied himself rather longer than was necessary over the task. When he finally went out, I saw that my visitor's manner had sunk into its former depression: the presence of the servant seemed to have chilled her.

'When did you say I might come?' I repeated, ignoring her refusal.

'I did not say it. It would be impossible.'

'Well, then, when will you come here?' There was, I fear, a trace of fatigue in my tone.

'At your good pleasure, sir,' she answered humbly.

My chivalry was touched by this: after all, she was a woman. 'Come tomorrow,' I said. 'By the way, come and dine with me then; why not?' I was curious to see what she would reply.

'Why not, indeed? Yes, I will come. I am forty-three: I might have been your mother.'

This was not quite true, as I am over thirty: but I look young, while she – Well, I had thought her over fifty. 'I can hardly call you "mother," but we might compromise upon "aunt,"' I said, laughing. 'Aunt what?'

'My name is Aaronna,' she gravely answered. 'My father was much disappointed that I was not a boy, and gave me as nearly as possible the name he had prepared – Aaron.'

'Then come and dine with me tomorrow, and bring with you the other manuscripts, Aaronna,' I said, amused at the quaint sound of the name. On the whole, I did not like 'aunt.'

'I will come,' she answered.

It was twilight and still raining, but she refused all offers of escort or carriage, departing with her maid, as she had come, under the brown umbrella. The next day we had the dinner. Simpson was astonished – and more than astonished, grieved – when I told him that he was to dine with the maid; but he could not complain in words, since my own guest, the mistress, was hardly more attractive. When our preparations were complete, I could not help laughing: the two prim little tables, one in the parlor and one in the anteroom, and Simpson disapprovingly going back and forth between them, were irresistible.

I greeted my guest hilariously when she arrived, and, fortunately, her manner was not quite so depressed as usual: I could never have accorded myself with a tearful mood. I had thought that perhaps she would make, for the occasion, some change in her attire; I have never known a woman who had not some scrap of finery, however small, in reserve for that unexpected occasion of which she is ever dreaming. But no: Miss Grief wore the same black gown, unadorned and unaltered. I was glad that there was no rain that day, so that the skirt did not at least look so damp and rheumatic.

She ate quietly, almost furtively, yet with a good appetite, and she did not refuse the wine. Then, when the meal was over and Simpson had removed the dishes, I asked for the new manuscripts. She gave me an old green copybook filled with short poems, and a prose sketch by itself; I lit a cigar and sat down at my desk to look them over.

'Perhaps you will try a cigarette?' I suggested, more for amusement than anything else, for there was not a shade of Bohemianism about her; her whole appearance was puritanical.

'I have not yet succeeded in learning to smoke.'

'You have tried?' I said, turning round.

'Yes: Serena and I tried, but we did not succeed.'

'Serena is your maid?'

'She lives with me.'

I was seized with inward laughter, and began hastily to look over her manuscripts with my back toward her, so that she might not see it. A vision had risen before me of those two forlorn women, alone in their room with locked doors, patiently trying to acquire the smoker's art.

But my attention was soon absorbed by the papers before me. Such a fantastic collection of words, lines, and epithets I had never before seen, or even in dreams imagined. In truth, they were like the work of dreams: they were *Kubla Khan*,* only more so. Here and there was radiance like the flash of a diamond, but each poem, almost each verse and line, was marred by some fault or lack which seemed wilful perversity, like the work of an evil sprite. It was like a case of jeweller's wares set before you, with each ring unfinished, each bracelet too large or too small for its purpose, each breastpin without its fastening, each necklace purposely broken. I turned the pages, marvelling. When about half an hour had passed, and I was leaning back for a moment to light another cigar, I glanced toward my visitor. She was behind me, in an easy chair before my small fire, and she was – fast asleep! In the relaxation of her unconsciousness I was struck anew by the poverty her appearance expressed; her feet were visible, and I saw the miserable worn old shoes which hitherto she had kept concealed.

After looking at her for a moment, I returned to my task and took up the prose story; in prose she must be more reasonable. She was less fantastic perhaps, but hardly more reasonable. The story was that of a profligate and commonplace man forced by two of his friends, in order not to break the heart of a dying girl who loves him, to live up to a high imaginary ideal of himself which her pure but mistaken mind has formed. He has a handsome face and sweet voice, and repeats what they tell them.

Her long, slow decline and happy death, and his own inward ennui and profound weariness of the role he has to play, made the vivid points of the story. So far, well enough, but here was the trouble: through the whole narrative moved another character, a physician of tender heart and exquisite mercy, who practiced murder as a fine art, and was regarded (by the author) as a second Messiah! This was monstrous. I read it through twice, and threw it down; then, fatigued, I turned round and leaned back, waiting for her to wake. I could see her profile against the dark hue of the easy chair.

Presently she seemed to feel my gaze, for she stirred, then opened her eyes. 'I have been asleep,' she said, rising hurriedly.

'No harm in that, Aaronna.'

But she was deeply embarrassed and troubled, much more so than the occasion required; so much so, indeed, that I turned the conversation back upon the manuscripts as a diversion. 'I cannot stand that doctor of yours,' I said, indicating the prose story; 'no one would. You must cut him out.'

Her self-possession returned as if by magic. 'Certainly not,' she answered haughtily.

'Oh, if you do not care – I had labored under the impression that you were anxious these things should find a purchaser.'

'I am, I am,' she said, her manner changing to deep humility with wonderful rapidity. With such alternations of feeling as this sweeping over her like great waves, no wonder she was old before her time.

'Then you must take out that doctor.'

'I am willing, but do not know how,' she answered, pressing her hands together helplessly. 'In my mind he belongs to the story so closely that he cannot be separated from it.'

Here Simpson entered, bringing a note for me: it was a line from Mrs Abercrombie inviting me for that evening – an unexpected gathering, and therefore likely to be all the more agreeable. My heart bounded in spite of me; I forgot Miss Grief and her manuscripts for the moment as completely as though they had never existed. But, bodily, being still in the same room with her, her speech brought me back to the present.

'You have had good news?' she said.

'Oh no, nothing especial – merely an invitation.'

'But good news also,' she repeated. 'And now, as for me, I must go.'

Not supposing that she would stay much later in any case, I had that morning ordered a carriage to come for her at about that hour. I told her this. She made no reply beyond putting on her bonnet and shawl.

'You will hear from me soon,' I said; 'I shall do all I can for you.'

She had reached the door, but before opening it she stopped, turned and extended her hand. 'You are good,' she said: 'I give you thanks. Do not think me ungrateful or envious. It is only that you are young, and I am so – so old.' Then she opened the door and passed through the anteroom without pause, her maid accompanying her and Simpson with gladness lighting the way. They were gone. I dressed hastily and went out – to continue my studies in psychology.

Time passed; I was busy, amused and perhaps a little excited (sometimes psychology is exciting). But, though much occupied with my own affairs, I did not altogether neglect my self-imposed task regarding Miss Grief. I began by sending her prose story to a friend, the editor of a monthly magazine, with a letter making a strong plea for its admittance. It should have a chance first on its own merits. Then I forwarded the drama to a publisher, also an acquaintance, a man with a taste for phantasms and a soul above mere common popularity, as his own coffers knew to their cost. This done, I waited with conscience clear.

Four weeks passed. During this waiting period I heard nothing from Miss Grief. At last one morning came a letter from my editor. 'The story has force, but I cannot stand that doctor,' he wrote. 'Let her cut him out, and I might print it.' Just what I myself had said. The package lay there on my table, travel worn and grimed; a returned manuscript is, I think, the most melancholy object on earth. I decided to wait, before writing to Aaronna, until the second letter was received. A week later it came. 'Armor' was declined. The publisher had been 'impressed' by the power displayed in certain passages, but the 'impossibilities of the plot' rendered it 'unavailable for publication' – in fact, would 'bury it in ridicule' if brought before the public, a public 'lamentably' fond of amusement, 'seeking it, undaunted, even in the cannon's mouth.' I doubt if he knew himself what he meant. But one thing, at any rate, was clear: 'Armor' was declined.

Now, I am, as I have remarked before, a little obstinate. I was determined that Miss Grief's work should be received. I would alter and improve it myself, without letting her know: the end justified the means. Surely the sieve of my own good taste, whose mesh had been pronounced so fine and delicate, would serve for two. I began; and utterly failed.

I set to work first upon 'Armor.' I amended, altered, left out, put in, pieced, condensed, lengthened; I did my best, and all to no avail. I could not succeed in completing anything that satisfied me, or that approached, in truth, Miss Grief's own work just as it stood. I suppose I went over that manuscript twenty times: I covered sheets of paper with my copies. But the obstinate drama refused to be corrected; as it was it must stand or fall.

Wearied and annoyed, I threw it aside and took up the prose story: that would be easier. But, to my surprise, I found that that apparently gentle 'doctor' would not out: he was so closely interwoven with every part of the tale that to take him out was like taking out one especial figure in a carpet: that is, impossible, unless you unravel the whole. At last I did unravel the whole, and then the story was no longer good, or Aaronna's: it was weak, and mine. All this took time, for of course I had much to do in connection with my own life and tasks. But, though slowly and at my leisure, I really did try my best as regarded Miss Grief, and without success. I was forced at last to make up my mind that either my own powers were not equal to the task, or else that her perversities were as essential a part of her work as her inspirations, and not to be separated from it. Once during this period I showed two of the short poems to Isabel, withholding of course the writer's name. 'They were written by a woman,' I explained.

'Her mind must have been disordered, poor thing!' Isabel said in her gentle way when she returned them – 'at least, judging by these. They are hopelessly mixed and vague.'

Now, they were not vague so much as vast. But I knew that I could not make Isabel comprehend it, and (so complex a creature is man) I do not know that I wanted her to comprehend it. These were the only ones in the whole collection that I would have shown her, and I was rather glad that she did not like even these. Not that poor Aaronna's poems were evil: they were simply unrestrained, large, vast, like the skies or the wind. Isabel was bounded on all sides, like a violet in a garden bed. And I liked her so.

One afternoon, about the time when I was beginning to see that I could not 'improve' Miss Grief, I came upon the maid. I was driving, and she had stopped on the crossing to let the carriage pass. I recognized her at a glance (by her general forlornness), and called to the driver to stop. 'How is Miss Crief?' I said. 'I have been intending to write to her for some time.'

'And your note, when it comes,' answered the old woman on the crosswalk fiercely, 'she shall not see.'

'What?'

'I say she shall not see it. Your patronizing face shows that you have no good news, and you shall not rack and stab her any more on *this* earth, please God, while I have authority.'

'Who has racked or stabbed her, Serena?'

'Serena, indeed! Rubbish! I'm no Serena: I'm her aunt. And as to who has racked and stabbed her, I say you, *you* – YOU literary men!' She had put her old head inside my carriage, and flung out these words at me in a shrill, menacing tone. 'But she shall die in peace in spite of you,' she continued. 'Vampires! you take her ideas and fatten on them, and leave her to starve. You know you do – *you* who have had her poor manuscripts these months and months!'

'Is she ill?' I asked in real concern, gathering that much at least from the incoherent tirade.

'She is dying,' answered the desolate old creature, her voice softening and her dim eyes filling with tears.

'Oh, I trust not. Perhaps something can be done. Can I help you in any way?'

'In all ways if you would,' she said, breaking down and beginning to sob weakly, with her head resting on the sill of the carriage window. 'Oh, what have we not been through together, we two! Piece by piece I have sold all.'

I am goodhearted enough, but I do not like to have old women weeping across my carriage door. I suggested, therefore, that she should come inside and let me take her home. Her shabby old skirt was soon beside me, and, following her directions, the driver turned toward one of the most wretched quarters of the city, the abode of poverty, crowded and unclean. Here, in a large bare chamber up many flights of stairs, I found Miss Grief.

As I entered I was startled: I thought she was dead. There seemed no life present until she opened her eyes, and even then they rested upon us vaguely, as though she did not know who we were. But as I approached a light came into them: she recognized me, and this sudden revivification, this return of the soul to the almost deserted body, was the most wonderful thing I ever saw. 'You have good news of the drama?' she whispered as I bent over her: 'tell me. I *know* you have good news.'

What was I to answer? Pray, what would you have answered, puritan?

'Yes, I have good news, Aaronna,' I said. 'The drama will appear.' (And who knows? Perhaps it will in some other world.)

She smiled, and her now brilliant eyes did not leave my face.

'He knows I'm your aunt: I told him,' said the old woman, coming to the bedside.

'Did you?' whispered Miss Grief, still gazing at me with a smile. 'Then please, dear Aunt Martha, give me something to eat.'

Aunt Martha hurried across the room, and I followed her. 'It's the first time she's asked for food in weeks,' she said in a husky tone.

She opened a cupboard door vaguely, but I could see nothing within. 'What have you for her?' I asked with some impatience, though in a low voice.

'Please God, nothing!' answered the poor old woman, hiding her reply and her tears behind the broad cupboard door. 'I was going out to get a little something when I met you.'

'Good Heavens! is it money you need? Here, take this and send; or go yourself in the carriage waiting below.'

She hurried out breathless, and I went back to the bedside, much disturbed by what I had seen and heard. But Miss Grief's eyes were full of life, and as I sat down beside her she whispered earnestly, 'Tell me.'

And I did tell her – a romance invented for the occasion. I venture to say that none of my published sketches could compare with it. As for the lie involved, it will stand among my few good deeds, I know, at the judgment bar.

And she was satisfied. 'I have never known what it was,' she whispered, 'to be fully happy until now.' She closed her eyes, and when the lids fell I again thought that she had passed away. But no, there was still pulsation in her small, thin wrist. As she perceived my touch she smiled. 'Yes, I am happy,' she said again, though without audible sound.

The old aunt returned; food was prepared, and she took some. I myself went out after wine that should be rich and pure. She rallied a little, but I did not leave her: her eyes dwelt upon me and compelled me to stay, or rather my conscience compelled me. It was a damp night, and I had a little fire made. The wine, fruit, flowers, and candles I had ordered made the bare place for the time being bright and fragrant. Aunt Martha dozed in her chair from sheer fatigue – she had watched many nights – but Miss Grief was awake, and I sat beside her.

'I make you my executor,' she murmured, 'as to the drama. But my other manuscripts place, when I am gone, under my head, and let them be buried with me. They are not many – those you have and these. See!'

I followed her gesture, and saw under her pillows the edges of two more copybooks like the one I had. 'Do not look at them – my poor dead children!' she said tenderly. 'Let them depart with me – unread, as I have been.'

Later she whispered, 'Did you wonder why I came to you? It was the contrast. You were young – strong – rich – praised – loved – successful: all that I was not. I wanted to look at you – and imagine how it would feel. You had success – but I had the greater power. Tell me, did I not have it?'

'Yes, Aaronna.'

'It is all in the past now. But I am satisfied.'

After another pause she said with a faint smile, 'Do you remember when I fell asleep in your parlor? It was the good and rich food. It was so long since I had had food like that!'

I took her hand and held it, conscience stricken, but now she hardly seemed to perceive my touch. 'And the smoking?' she whispered. 'Do you remember how you laughed? I saw it. But I had heard that smoking soothed – that one was no longer tired and hungry – with a cigar.'

In little whispers of this sort, separated by long rests and pauses, the night passed. Once she asked if her aunt was asleep, and when I answered in the affirmative she said, 'Help her to return home – to America: the drama will pay for it. I ought never to have brought her away.'

I promised, and she resumed her bright-eyed silence.

I think she did not speak again. Toward morning the change

came, and soon after sunrise, with her old aunt kneeling by her side, she passed away.

All was arranged as she had wished. Her manuscripts, covered with violets, formed her pillow. No one followed her to the grave save her aunt and myself; I thought she would prefer it so. Her name was not 'Crief,' after all, but 'Moncrief'; I saw it written out by Aunt Martha for the coffin plate, as follows: 'Aaronna Moncrief, aged forty-three years, two months, and eight days.'

I never knew more of her history than is written here. If there was more that I might have learned, it remained unlearned, for I did not ask.

And the drama? I keep it here in this locked case. I could have had it published at my own expense; but I think that now she knows its faults herself, perhaps, and would not like it.

I keep it; and, once in a while, I read it over – not as a *memento mori** exactly, but rather as a memento of my own good fortune, for which I should continually give thanks. The want of one grain made all her work void, and that one grain was given to me. She, with the greater power, failed – I, with the less, succeeded. But no praise is due to me for that. When I die 'Armor' is to be destroyed unread: not even Isabel is to see it. For women will misunderstand each other; and, dear and precious to me as my sweet wife is, I could not bear that she or anyone should cast so much as a thought of scorn upon the memory of the writer, upon my poor dead, 'unavailable,' unaccepted 'Miss Grief.'

At the Château of Corinne

1896

On the shores of Lake Leman there are many villas. For several centuries the vine-clad banks have been a favorite resting-place for visitors from many nations. English, French, Germans, Austrians, Poles, and Russians are found in the circle of strangers whose gardens fringe the lake northward from Geneva, eastward from Lausanne, and southward from Vevey, Clarens, and Montreux. Not long ago an American joined this circle. The American was a lady named Winthrop.

Mrs Winthrop's villa was not one of the larger residences. It was an old-fashioned square mansion, half Swiss, half French, ending in a high-peaked roof, which came slanting sharply down over several narrowed half-stories, indicated by little windows like dove-perches – four in the broadest part, two above, then one winking all alone under the peak. On the left side a round tower, inappropriate but picturesque, joined itself to the square outline of the main building; the round tower had also a peaked roof, which was surmounted by a contorted ornament of iron somewhat resembling a letter S. Altogether the villa was the sort of a house which Americans are accustomed to call 'quaint.' Its name was quaint also – Miolans la Tour, or, more briefly, Miolans. Cousin Walpole pronounced this 'Miawlins.'

Mrs Winthrop had taken possession of the villa in May, and it was now late in August; Lake Leman therefore had enjoyed her society for three long months. Through all this time, in the old lake's estimation, and notwithstanding the English, French, Germans, Austrians, Poles, and Russians, many of them titled, who were also upon its banks, the American lady remained an interesting presence. And not in the opinion of the old lake only, but in that also of other observers, less fluid and impersonal. Mrs Winthrop was much admired. Miolans had entertained numerous guests during the summer; today, however, it held only the *bona fide* members of the family – namely, Mrs

Winthrop, her cousin Sylvia, and Mr H. Walpole, Miss Sylvia's cousin. Mr H. Walpole was always called 'Cousin Walpole' by Sylvia, who took comfort in the name, her own (a grief to her) being neither more nor less than Pitcher. 'Sylvia Pitcher' was not impressive, but 'H. Walpole' could shine for two. If people supposed that H. stood for Horace, why, that was their own affair.*

Mrs Winthrop, followed by her great white dog, had strolled down towards the lake. After a while she came within sight of the gate; some one was entering. The porter's lodge was unoccupied save by two old busts that looked out from niches above the windows, much surprised that no one knew them. The newcomer surveyed the lodge and the busts; then opened the gate and came in. He was a stranger; a gentleman; an American. These three items Mrs Winthrop's eyes told her, one by one, as she drew nearer. He now caught sight of her – a lady coming down the water-path, followed by a shaggy dog. He went forward to meet her, raising his hat. 'I think this is Mrs Winthrop. May I introduce myself? I am John Ford.'

'Sylvia will be delighted,' said Mrs Winthrop, giving her hand in courteous welcome. 'We have been hoping that we should see you, Mr Ford, before the summer was over.'

They stood a few moments, and then went up the plane-tree avenue towards the house. Mrs Winthrop spoke the usual phrases of the opening of an acquaintance with grace and ease; her companion made the usual replies. He was quite as much at his ease as she was, but he did not especially cultivate grace. Sylvia, enjoying her conversation with Cousin Walpole, sat just within the hall door; she was taken quite by surprise. 'Oh, John, how you startled me! I thought you were in Norway. But how very glad I am to see you, my dear, dear boy!' She stood on tiptoe to kiss him, with a moisture in her soft, faded, but still pretty eyes.

Mrs Winthrop remained outside; there were garden chairs in the small porch, and she seated herself in one of them. She smiled a little when she heard Sylvia greet this mature specimen of manhood as a 'dear, dear boy.'

Cousin Walpole now came forward. 'You are welcome, sir,' he said, in his slender little voice. Then bethinking him of his French, he added, with dignity, 'Welcome to Miaw-lins – Miaw-lins-lay-Tower.'

Ford took a seat in the hall beside his aunt. She talked volubly: the surprise had excited her. But every now and then she looked at him with a far-off remembrance in her eyes: she was thinking of his mother, her sister, long dead. 'How much you look like her!' she said at last. 'The same profile – exact. And how beautiful Mary's profile was! Every one admired it.'

Ford, who had been gazing at the rug, looked up; he caught Mrs Winthrop's glance, and the gleam of merriment in it. 'Yes, my profile is like my mother's, and therefore good,' he answered, gravely. 'It is a pity that my full face contradicts it. However, I live in profile as much as possible; I present myself edgewise.'

'What *do* you mean, dear?' said Sylvia.

'I am like the new moon,' he answered; 'I show but a rim. All the rest I keep dark.'

Mrs Winthrop laughed; and again Ford caught her glance. What he had said of himself was true. He had a regular, clearly cut, delicately finished profile, but his full face contradicted it somewhat, showing more strength than beauty. His eyes were gray, without much expression, unless calmness can be called an expression; his hair and beard, both closely cut, were dark brown. As to his height, no one would have called him tall, yet neither would any one have described him as short. And the same phrasing might have been applied to his general appearance: no one would have called him handsome, yet neither would any one have classed him as ordinary. As to what is more important than looks, namely, manner, although his was quiet, and quite without pretension, a close observer could have discovered in it, and without much effort, that the opinions of John Ford (although never obtruded upon others) were in general sufficiently satisfactory to John Ford; and, furthermore, that the opinions of other people, whether accordant or discordant with his own, troubled him little.

After a while all went down to the outlook to see the afterglow on Mont Blanc. Mrs Winthrop led the way with Cousin Walpole, whose high, bell-crowned straw hat had a dignity which no modern head-covering could hope to rival.

Sylvia followed, with her nephew. 'You must come and stay with us, John,' she said. 'Katharine has so much company that you will find it entertaining, and even at times instructive. I am sure I have found it so; and I am, you know, your senior. We are alone today; but it is for the first time. Generally the house is full.'

'But I do not like a full house,' said Ford, smiling down upon the upturned face of the little 'senior' by his side.

'You will like this one. It is not a commonplace society – by no means commonplace. The hours, too, are easy; breakfast, for instance, from nine to eleven – as you please. As to the quality of the – of the bodily support, it is sufficient to say that Marches is housekeeper. You remember Marches?'

'Perfectly. Her tarts no one could forget.'

'Katharine is indebted to me for Marches,' continued Sylvia. 'I relinquished her to Katharine upon the occasion of her marriage, ten years ago; for she was totally inexperienced, you know – only seventeen.'

'Then she is now twenty-seven.'

'I should not have mentioned that,' said Miss Pitcher, instinctively. 'It was an inadvertence. Could you oblige me by forgetting it?'

'With the greatest ease. She is, then, sensitive about her age?'

'Not in the least. Why should she be? Certainly no one would ever dream of calling twenty-seven *old*!' (Miss Pitcher paused with dignity.) 'You think her beautiful, of course?' she added.

'She is a fine-looking woman.'

'Oh, John, that is what they always say of women who weigh two hundred! And Katharine is very slender.'

Ford laughed. 'I supposed the fact that Mrs Winthrop was handsome went without the saying.'

'It goes,' said Sylvia, impressively, 'but not without the saying; I assure you, by no means without the saying. It has been said this summer many times.'

'And she does not find it fatiguing?'

The little aunt looked at her nephew. 'You do not like her,' she said, with a fine air of penetration, touching his coat-sleeve lightly with one finger. 'I see that you do not like her.'

'My dear aunt! I do not know her in the least.'

'Well, how does she impress you, then, *not* knowing her?' said Miss Pitcher, folding her arms under her little pink shawl with an impartial air.

He glanced at the figure in front. 'How she impresses me?' he said. 'She impresses me as a very attractive, but very complete, woman of the world.'

A flood of remonstrance rose to Sylvia's lips; but she was obliged to repress it, because Mrs Winthrop had paused, and was waiting for them.

'Here is one of our fairest little vistas, Mr Ford,' she said as they came up, showing him an oval opening in the shrubbery, through which a gleam of blue lake, a village on the opposite shore, and the arrowy, snow-clad Silver Needle, rising behind high in the upper blue, were visible, like a picture in a leaf frame. The opening was so narrow that only two persons could look through it. Sylvia and Cousin Walpole walked on.

'But you have seen it all before,' said Mrs Winthrop. 'To you it is not something from fairy-land, hardly to be believed, as it is to me. Do you know, sometimes, when waking in the early dawn, before the prosaic little details of the day have risen in my mind, I ask myself, with a sort of doubt in the reality of it all, if this is Katharine Winthrop living on the shores of Lake Leman – herself really, and not her imagination only, her longing dream.' It was very well uttered, with a touch of enthusiasm which carried it along, and which was in itself a confidence.

'Yes – ah – quite so. Yet you hardly look like a person who would think that sort of thing under those circumstances,' said Ford, watching a bark, with the picturesque lateen-sails of Lake Leman, cross his green-framed picture from east to west.

Mrs Winthrop let the hand with which she had made her little gesture drop. She stood looking at him. But he did not add anything to his remark, or turn his glance from the lateen-sails.

'What sort of a person, then, do I look like?' she said.

He turned. She was smiling; he smiled also. 'I was alluding merely to the time you named. As it happened, my aunt had mentioned to me by chance your breakfast hours.'

'That was not all, I think.'

'You are very good to be interested.'

'I am not good; only curious. Pray tell me.'

'I have so little imagination, Mrs Winthrop, that I cannot invent the proper charming interpretation as I ought. As to bald truth, of course you cannot expect me to present you with that during a first visit of ceremony.'

'The first visit will, I hope, be a long one; you must come and stay with us. As to ceremony, if this is your idea of it – '

' – What must I be when unceremonious! I suppose you are thinking,' said Ford, laughing. 'On the whole, I had better make no attempts. The owl, in his own character, is esteemed an honest bird; but let him not try to be a nightingale.'

'Come as owl, nightingale, or what you please, so long as you come. When you do, I shall ask you again what you meant.'

'If you are going to hold it over me, perhaps I had better tell you now.'

'Much better.'

'I only meant, then, that Mrs Winthrop did not strike me as at all the sort of person who would allow anything prosaic to interfere with her poetical, heart-felt enthusiasms.'

She laughed gayly. 'You are delightful. You have such a heavy apparatus for fibbing that it becomes fairly stately. You do not believe I have any enthusiasms at all,' she added. Her eyes were dark blue, with long lashes; they were very fine eyes.

'I will believe whatever you please,' said John Ford.

'Very well. Believe what I tell you.'

'You include only what you tell in words?'

'Plainly, you are not troubled by timidity,' said the lady, laughing a second time.

'On the contrary, it is excess of timidity. It makes me desperate and crude.'

They had walked on, and now came up with the others. 'Does he amuse you?' said Sylvia, in a low tone, as Cousin Walpole in his turn walked onward with the new-comer. 'I heard you laughing.'

'Yes; but he is not at all what you said. He is so shy and ill at ease that it is almost painful.'

'Dear me!' said the aunt, with concern. 'The best thing, then, will be for him to come and stay with us. You have so much company that it will be good for him; his shyness will wear off.'

'I have invited him, but I doubt his coming,' said the lady of the manor.

The outlook was a little terrace built out over the water. Mrs Winthrop seated herself and took off her garden-hat (Mrs Winthrop had a very graceful head, and thick, soft, brown hair). 'Not so close, Gibbon,' she said, as the shaggy dog laid himself down beside her.

'You call your dog Gibbon?' said Ford.

'Yes; he came from Lausanne, where Gibbon* lived; and I think he looks just like him. But pray put on your hat, Mr Ford.

A man in the open air, deprived of his hat, is always a wretched object, and always takes cold.'

'I may be wretched, but I do not take cold,' replied Ford, letting his hat lie.

'John *does* look very strong,' said Sylvia, with pride.

'O fortunate youth – if he but knew his good-fortune!' said Cousin Walpole. 'From the Latin, sir; I do not quote the original tongue in the presence of ladies, which would seem pedantic. You do look strong indeed, and I congratulate you. I myself have never been an athlete; but I admire, and with impartiality, the muscles of the gladiator.'

'Sure, Cousin Walpole, there is nothing in common between John and a gladiator!'

'Your pardon, Cousin Sylvia. I was speaking generally. My conversation, sir,' said the bachelor, turning to Ford, 'is apt to be general.'

'No one likes personalities, I suppose,' replied Ford, watching the last hues of the sunset.

'On the contrary, I am devoted to them,' said Mrs Winthrop.

'Oh no, Katharine; you malign yourself,' said Sylvia. 'You must not believe all she says, John.'

'Mr Ford has just promised to do that very thing,' remarked Mrs Winthrop.

'Dear me!' said Sylvia. Her tone of dismay was so sincere that they all laughed. 'You know, dear, you have so much imagination,' she said, apologetically, to her cousin.

'Mr Ford has not,' replied the younger lady; 'so the exercise will do him no harm.'

The sky behind the splendid white mass of Mont Blanc was of a deep warm gold; the line of snowy peaks attending the monarch rose irregularly against this radiance from east to west, framed by the dark nearer masses of the Salève and Voirons.* The sun had disappeared, cresting with glory as he sank the soft purple summits of the Jura, and sending up a blaze of color in the narrow valley of the Rhone. Then, as all this waned slowly into grayness, softly, shyly, the lovely after-glow floated up the side of the monarch, tingeing all his fields of pure white ice and snow with rosy light as it moved onward, and resting on the far peak in the sky long after the lake and its shores had faded into night.

'This lake, sir,' said Cousin Walpole, 'is remarkable for the number of persons distinguished in literature who have at various times resided upon its banks. I may mention, cursorily, Voltaire, Sismondi, Gibbon, Rousseau, Sir Humphry Davy, D'Aubigné, Calvin, Grimm, Benjamin Constant, Schlegel, Châteaubriand, Byron, Shelley, the elder Dumas, and in addition that most eloquent authoress and noble woman Madame de Staël.'*

'The banks must certainly be acquainted with a large amount of fine language,' said Ford.

'And oh, how we have enjoyed Coppet, John! You remember Coppet?' said Miss Pitcher. 'We have had, I assure you, days and conversations there which I, for one, can never forget. Do you remember, Katharine, that moment by the fish-pond, when, carried away by the influences of the spot, Mr Percival exclaimed, and with such deep feeling, "*Etonnante femme!*"'*

'Meaning Mrs Winthrop?' said Ford.

'No, John, no; meaning Madame de Staël,' replied the little aunt.

Mr Ford did not take up his abode at Miolans, in spite of his aunt's wish and Mrs Winthrop's invitation. He preferred a little inn among the vineyards, half a mile distant. But he came often to the villa, generally rowing himself down the lake in a skiff. The skiff, indeed, spent most of its time moored at the water-steps of Miolans, for its owner accompanied the ladies in various excursions to Vevey, Clarens, Chillon,* and southward to Geneva.

'I thought you had so much company,' he said one afternoon to Sylvia, when they happened to be alone. 'I have been coming and going now for ten days, and have seen no one.'

'These ten days were reserved for the Storms,' replied Miss Pitcher. 'But old Mrs Storm fell ill at Baden-Baden, and what could they do?'

'Take care of her, I should say.'

'Gilbert Storm was poignantly disappointed. He is, I think, on the whole, the best among Katharine's *outside* admirers.'

'Then there are inside ones?'

'Several. You know Mr Winthrop was thirty-five years older than Katharine. It was hardly to be expected, therefore, that she should love him – I mean in the *true* way.'

'Whatever she might have done in the false.'

'You are too cynical, my dear boy. There was nothing false

about it; Katharine was simply a child. He was very fond of her, I assure you. And died most happily.'

'For all concerned.'

Sylvia shook her head. But Mrs Winthrop's step was now heard in the hall; she came in with several letters in her hand. 'Any news?' said Miss Pitcher.

'No,' replied the younger lady. 'Nothing ever happens any more.'

'As Ronsard sang,

> '"Le temps s'en va, le temps s'en va, ma dame!
> Las! le temps non; mais nous nous en allons,"'

said Ford, bringing forward her especial chair.

'That is true,' she answered, soberly, almost sombrely.

That evening the moonlight on the lake was surpassingly lovely; there was not a ripple to break the sheen of the water, and the clear outline of Mont Blanc rose like silver against the dark black-blue of the sky. They all strolled down to the shore; Mrs Winthrop went out with Ford in his skiff, 'for ten minutes.' Sylvia watched the little boat float up and down for twenty; then she returned to the house and read for forty more. When Sylvia was downstairs she read the third canto of 'Childe Harold';* in her own room she kept a private supply of the works of Miss Yonge. At ten Katharine entered. 'Has John gone?' said the aunt, putting in her mark and closing the Byronic volume.

'Yes; he came to the door, but would not come in.'

'I wish he would come and stay. He might as well; he is here every day.'

'That is the very point; he also goes every day,' replied Katharine.

She was leaning back in her chair, her eyes fixed upon the carpet. Sylvia was going to say something more, when suddenly a new idea came to her. It was a stirring idea; she did not often have such inspirations; she remained silent, investigating it. After a while, 'When do you expect the Carrols?' she said.

'Not until October.'

Miss Pitcher knew this perfectly, but she thought the question might lead to further information. It did. 'Miss Jay has written,' pursued Mrs Winthrop, her eyes still fixed absently on the carpet. 'But I answered, asking her to wait until October, when the Carrols would be here. It will be much pleasanter for them both.'

'She has put them off!' thought the little aunt. 'She does not want any one here just at present.' And she was so fluttered by the new possibilities rising round her like a cloud that she said goodnight, and went upstairs to think them over; she did not even read Miss Yonge.

The next day Ford did not come to Miolans until just before the dinner hour. Sylvia was disappointed by this tardiness, but cheered when Katharine came in; for Mrs Winthrop wore one of her most becoming dresses. 'She wishes to look her best,' thought the aunt. But at this moment, in the twilight, a carriage came rapidly up the driveway and stopped at the door. 'Why, it is Mr Percival!' said Sylvia, catching a glimpse of the occupant.

'Yes; he has come to spend a few days,' said Mrs Winthrop, going into the hall to greet her new guest.

Down fell the aunt's cloud-castle; but at the same moment a more personal feeling took its place in the modest little middle-aged breast; Miss Pitcher deeply admired Mr Percival.

'You know who it is, of course?' she whispered to her nephew when she had recovered her composure.

'You said Percival, didn't you?'

'Yes; but this is Lorimer Percival – Lorimer Percival, the poet.'

Katharine now came back. Sylvia sat waiting, and turning her bracelets round on her wrists. Sylvia's bracelets turned easily; when she took a book from the top shelf of the bookcase they went to her shoulders.

Before long Mr Percival entered. Dinner was announced. The conversation at the table was animated. From it Ford gathered that the new guest had spent several weeks at Miolans early in the season, and that he had also made since then one or two shorter visits. His manner was that of an intimate friend. The intimate friend talked well. Cousin Walpole's little candle illuminated the outlying corners. Sylvia supplied an atmosphere of general admiration. Mrs Winthrop supplied one of beauty. She looked remarkably well – brilliant; her guest – the one who was not a poet – noticed this. He had time to notice it, as well as several other things, for he said but little himself; the conversation was led by Mr Percival.

It was decided that they would all go to Coppet the next day

– 'dear Coppet,' as Sylvia called it. The expedition seemed to be partly sacred and partly sylvan; a pilgrimage-picnic. When Ford took leave, Mrs Winthrop and Mr Percival accompanied him as far as the water-steps. As his skiff glided out on the calm lake, he heard the gentleman's voice suggesting that they should stroll up and down awhile in the moonlight, and the lady's answer, 'Yes; for ten minutes.' He remembered that Mrs Winthrop's ten minutes was sometimes an hour.

The next day they went to Coppet; Mrs Winthrop and Mr Percival in the carriage, Sylvia and Cousin Walpole in the phaeton,* and Ford on horseback.

'Oh! isn't this almost *too* delightful!' said Miss Pitcher, when they reached the gates of the old Necker château. Cousin Walpole was engaged in tying his horse, and Mr Percival had politely stepped forward to assist her from the phaeton. It is but fair, however, to suppose that her exclamation referred as much to the intellectual influences of the home of Madame de Staël as to the attentions of the poet. 'I could live here, and I could die here,' she continued, with ardor. But as Mr Percival had now gone back to Mrs Winthrop, she was obliged to finish her sentence to her nephew, which was not quite the same thing. 'Couldn't *you*, John?' she said.

'It would be easy enough to die, I should say,' replied Ford, dismounting.

'We must all die,' remarked Cousin Walpole from the post where he was at work upon the horse. He tied that peaceful animal in such intricate and unexpected convolutions that it took Mrs Winthrop's coachman, later, fully twenty minutes to comprehend and unravel them.

The Necker homestead is a plain, old-fashioned château, built round three sides of a square, a court-yard within. From the end of the south side a long, irregular wing of lower outbuildings stretches towards the road, ending in a thickened, huddled knot along its margin, as though the country highway had refused to allow aristocratic encroachments, and had pushed them all back with determined hands. Across the three high, pale-yellow façades of the main building the faded shutters were tightly closed. There was not a sign of life, save in a little square house at the end of the knot, where, as far as possible from the historic mansion he guarded, lived the old custodian, who strongly resembled the portraits of Benjamin Franklin.

Benjamin Franklin knew Mrs Winthrop (and Mrs Winthrop's purse). He hastened through the knot in his shuffling woollen shoes, and unlocked the court-yard entrance.

'We must go all through the dear old house again, for John's sake,' said Sylvia.

'Do not sacrifice yourselves; I have seen it,' said her nephew.

'But not lately, dear John.'

'I am quite willing to serve as a pretext,' he answered, leading the way in.

They passed through the dark old hall below, where the white statue of Necker gleams in solitude, and went up the broad stairway, the old custodian preceding them, and throwing open the barred shutters of room after room. The warm sunshine flowed in and streamed across the floors, the dim tapestries, the spindle-legged, gilded furniture, and the Cupid-decked clocks. The old paintings on the walls seemed to waken slowly and survey them as they passed. Lorimer Percival seated himself in a yellow arm-chair, and looked about with the air of a man who was breathing a delicate aroma.

'This is the room where the "incomparable Juliette" danced her celebrated gavotte,' he remarked, 'probably to the music of that old harpsichord – or is it a spinet? – in the corner.'

'Pray tell us about it,' entreated Sylvia, who had seated herself gingerly on the edge of a small ottoman embroidered with pink shepherdesses on a blue meadow, and rose-colored lambs. Mrs Winthrop meanwhile had appropriated a spindle-legged sofa, and was leaning back against a tapestried Endymion.*

Percival smiled, but did not refuse Sylvia's request. He had not the objection which some men have to a monologue. It must be added, however, that for that sort of thing he selected his audience. Upon this occasion the outside element of John Ford, strolling about near the windows, was discordant, but not enough so to affect the admiring appreciation of the little group nearer his chair.

'Madame de Staël,' he began, with his eyes on the cornice, 'was a woman of many and generous enthusiasms. She had long wished to behold the grace of her lovely friend Madame Récamier,* in her celebrated gavotte, well known in the salons of Paris, but as yet unseen by the exile of Coppet. By great good-fortune there happened to be in the village, upon the occasion of a visit from Madame Récamier, a French dancing-master.

Madame de Staël sent for him, and the enchanted little man had the signal honor of going through the dance with the beautiful Juliette, in this room, in the presence of all the distinguished society of Coppet: no doubt it was the glory of his life. When the dance was ended, Corinne, carried away by admiration, embraced with transport – '

'The dancing-master?' said Cousin Walpole, much interested.

'No; her *ravissante amie.*'*

Cousin Walpole, conscious that he had made a mistake, betook himself to the portrait near by. 'Superb woman!' he murmured, contemplating it. 'Superb!'

The portrait represented the authoress of *Corinne* standing, her talented head crowned by a majestic aureole of yellow satin turban, whose voluminous folds accounted probably for the scanty amount of material left for the shoulders and arms.

'If I could have had the choice,' said Miss Pitcher, pensively gazing at this portrait, 'I would rather have been that noble creature than any one else on history's page.'

Later they went down to the old garden. It stretched back behind the house for some distance, shut in by a high stone wall. A long, straight alley, shaded by even rows of trees, went down one side like a mathematical line; on the other there was some of the stiff landscape-gardening of the last century. In the open space in the centre was a moss-grown fish-pond, and near the house a dignified little company of clipped trees. They strolled down the straight walk: this time Ford was with Mrs Winthrop, while Sylvia, Mr Percival, and Cousin Walpole were in front.

'I suppose she used to walk here,' observed Mrs Winthrop.

'In her turban,' suggested Ford.

'Perhaps she has sat upon that very bench – who knows? – and mused,' said Sylvia, imaginatively.

'Aloud, of course,' commented her nephew. But these irreverent remarks were in undertone; only Mrs Winthrop could hear them.

'No doubt they all walked here,' observed the poet; 'it was one of the customs of the time to take slow exercise daily in one of these dignified alleys. The whole society of Coppet was no doubt often here, Madame de Staël and her various guests, Schlegel, Constant, the Montmorency, Sismondi, Madame Récamier, and many others.'

'Would that I too could have been of that company!' said Cousin Walpole, with warmth.

'Which one of the two ladies would you have accompanied down this walk, if choice had been forced upon you?' said Mrs Winthrop.

'Which one? – Madame de Staël, of course,' replied the little bachelor, chivalrously.

'And you, Mr Percival?'

'With the one who had the intellect,' replied the poet.

'We must be even more lacking in beauty than we suppose, Sylvia, since they all chose the plain one,' said Katharine, laughing. 'But you have not spoken yet, Mr Ford: What would your choice have been?'

'Between the two, there would hardly have been one.'

'Isn't that a little enigmatical?'

'John means that he admires them equally,' explained the aunt.

'That is it,' said her nephew.

Lunch was spread upon the grass. Mrs Winthrop's coachman had made an impromptu carpet of carriage rugs and shawls. Percival threw himself down beside the ladies; Cousin Walpole, after trying various attitudes, took the one denominated 'cross-legged.' Ford surveyed their group for a moment, then went off and came back with a garden bench; upon this he seated himself comfortably, with his back against a tree.

'You are not sufficiently humble, Mr Ford,' said Katharine.

'It is not a question of humility, but of grace. I have not the gifts of Mr Percival.'

Percival said nothing. He was graceful; why disclaim it?

'But you are very strong, John,' said Sylvia, with an intention of consolation. 'And if not exactly graceful, I am sure you are very well shaped.'

Her hearers, including Ford himself, tried not to laugh, but failed. There was a burst of merriment.

'You think John does not need my encouragement?' said the little lady, looking at the laughers. 'You think I forget how old he is? It is quite true, no doubt. But I remember him *so* well, you know, in his little white frock, with his dear little dimpled shoulders! He always would have bread and sugar, whether it was good for him or not, and he was so pretty and plump!'

These reminiscences provoked another peal.

'You may laugh,' said Miss Pitcher, nodding her head sagely, 'but he did eat a great deal of sugar. Nothing else would content him but that bowl on the high shelf.'

'Do you still retain the same tastes, Mr Ford?' said Katharine. 'Do you still prefer what is out of reach – *on a high shelf?*'

'When one is grown,' said Ford, 'there is very little that is absolutely out of reach. It is, generally speaking, a question merely of determination, and – a long arm.'

The sun sank; his rays came slanting under their tree, gilding the grass in bars. The conversation had taken a turn towards the society of the eighteenth century. Percival said the most. But a poet may well talk in a memorial garden, hushed and sunny, on a cushioned carpet under the trees, with a long-stemmed wineglass near his hand, and fair ladies listening in rapt attention. Ford, leaning back against his tree, was smoking a cigarette; it is to be supposed that he was listening also.

'Here is something I read the other day, at least as nearly as I can recall it,' said the speaker. He was gazing at the tops of the trees on the other side of the pond. He had a habit of fixing his eyes upon something high above his hearers' heads when speaking. Men considered this an impertinence; but women had been known to allude to it as 'dreamy.'

'"Fair vanished ladies of the past,"' quoted the poet in his delightful voice, '"so charming even in your errors, do you merit the judgment which the more rigid customs of our modern age would pronounce upon you? Was that enthusiasm for virtue and for lofty sentiments with which your delicious old letters and memoirs, written in faded ink and flowing language, with so much wit and so much bad spelling, are adorned – was it all declamation merely, because, weighed in our severer balances, your lives were not always in accordance with it? Are there not other balances? And were you not, even in your errors, seeking at least an ideal that was fair? Striving to replace by a sensibility most devoted and tender a morality which, in the artificial society that surrounded you, had become well-nigh impossible? Let us not forget how many of you, when the dread hour came, faced with unfaltering courage the horrors of the Revolution, sustained by your example the hearts of strong men which had failed them, and atoned on the red guillotine for the errors and follies of your whole generation with your delicate lives."'

He paused. Then, in a lighter tone, added: 'Charming vanished dames, in your powder and brocade, I salute you! I, for one, enroll myself among your faithful and tender admirers.'

Mr Percival remained two weeks at Miolans. He was much with Mrs Winthrop. They seemed to have subjects of their own for conversation, for on several occasions when Ford came over in the morning they were said to be 'in the library,' and Miss Pitcher was obliged to confess that she did not feel at liberty to disturb them. She remarked, with a sigh, that it must be 'very intellectual,' and once she asked her nephew if he had not noticed the poet's 'brow.'

'Oh yes; he is one of those tall, slim, long-faced, talking fellows whom you women are very apt to admire,' said Ford.

Miss Pitcher felt as much wrath as her gentle nature allowed. But again her sentiments were divided, and she sacrificed her personal feelings. That evening she confided to Katharine, under a pledge of deepest secrecy, her belief that 'John' was 'jealous.'

Mrs Winthrop greeted this confidence with laughter. Not discouraged, the aunt the next day confided to her nephew her conviction that, as regarded the poet, Katharine had not yet 'at all made up her mind.'

'That is rather cruel to Percival, isn't it?' said Ford.

'Oh, he too has many, many *friends*,' said Sylvia, veering again.

'Fortunate fellow!'

At last Percival went. Ford was again the only visitor. And if he did not have long mornings in the library, he had portions not a few of afternoons in the garden. For if he came up the water-steps and found the mistress of the house sitting under the trees, with no other companion than a book, it was but natural that he should join her, and possibly make some effort to rival the printed page.

'You do not like driving?' she said, one day. They were in the parlor, and the carriage was coming round; she had invited him to accompany them, and he had declined.

'Not with a coachman, I confess.'

'There is always the phaeton,' she said, carelessly.

He glanced at her, but she was examining the border of her lace scarf. 'On the whole, I prefer riding,' he answered, as though it were a question of general preferences.

'And Katharine rides *so* well!' said Sylvia, looking up from her wax flowers. Sylvia made charming wax flowers, generally water-lilies, because they were 'so regular.'

'There are no good horses about here,' observed Ford. 'I have tried them all. I presume at home in America you keep a fine one?'

'Oh, in America! That is too far off. I do not remember what I did in America,' answered Mrs Winthrop.

A day or two later. 'You were mistaken about there being no good saddle-horses here,' she remarked. 'My coachman has found two; they are in the stable now.'

'If you are going to be kind enough to offer one of them to me,' he said, rather formally, after a moment's silence, 'I shall then have the pleasure of some rides with you, after all.'

'Yes,' answered Mrs Winthrop. 'As you say – after all!' She was smiling. He smiled too, but shook his head. Sylvia did not see this little by-play. Whatever it meant, however, it did not prevent Ford's riding with Mrs Winthrop several times, her groom following. Miss Pitcher watched these little excursions with much interest.

Meanwhile letters from Lorimer Percival came to Miolans almost daily. 'That is the Percival crest,' said Sylvia to her nephew, one of these epistles, which had just arrived, being on the hall table, seal upward, as they passed. 'So appropriate for a poet, I think – a flame.'

'Ah! I took it for steam,' said Ford.

Now the elder Percival had been a successful builder of locomotives. 'John,' said Miss Pitcher, solemnly, 'do you mean that for derision?'

'Derision, my dear aunt! There is nothing in the world so powerful as steam. If I only had more, I too might be a poet. Or if my father had had more, I too might have enjoyed a fortune.'

'Mr Percival enjoys no fortune,' said Sylvia, still solemnly.

'What has he done with it, then? Enjoyed it all out?'

'He tells me that it dissolved, like a mist, in his grasp.'

'Yes; they call it by various names,' said Ford.

Mrs Winthrop, dressed in her habit, now came down the stairway; she took the letter and put it in her pocket. That day the groom could not accompany them: the horse he rode was lame. 'We are sufficiently brave to do without him for one afternoon, are we not?' said the lady.

'I confess I am timid; but I will do my best,' answered Ford, assisting her to mount. Sylvia, standing in the doorway, thought this a most unfortunate reply.

They rode southward. 'Shall we stop for a few moments?' said Katharine, as they came towards Coppet.

'Yes; for ten,' he answered.

The old custodian let them in, and threw open the windows as before. The visitors went out on the little shelf-like balcony which opened from the drawing-room.

'You notice there is no view, or next to none,' said Ford, 'although we are on the shore of Lake Leman, and under the shadow of Mont Blanc. They did not care for views in the eighteenth century – that is, views of the earth; they were all for views of the 'soul.' Madame de Staël detested the country; to the last, Coppet remained to her a dreary exile. She was the woman who frankly said that she would not cross the room to look at the Bay of Naples, but would walk twenty miles to talk with an agreeable man.'

'They were as rare then, it seems, as they are now,' said Mrs Winthrop. 'But today we go more than twenty miles; we go to Europe.'

'She did the same – that is, what was the same in her day; she went to Germany. There she found two rather agreeable men – Goethe and Schiller.* Having found them, she proceeded to talk to them. They confessed to each other, long afterwards, the deep relief they felt when that gifted woman departed.'

'Ah, well, all she wanted, all she was seeking, was sympathy.'

'She should have waited until it came to her.'

'But if it never came?'

'It would – if she had not been so eager and voracious. The truth is, Corinne was an inordinate egotist. She expected all minds to defer to her superiority, while at the very moment she was engaged in extracting from them any poor little knowledge or ideas they might possess which could serve her own purposes. All her books were talked into existence; she talked them before she wrote them. It was her custom, at the dinner-table here at Coppet, to introduce the subject upon which she was engaged, and all her guests were expected, indeed forced, to discuss it with her in all its bearings, to listen to all she herself had to say, and never to depart from the given line by the slightest digression until she gave the signal. The next morning, closeted in her own room, she wrote out the results of all this, and it became a chapter.'

'She was a woman of genius, all the same,' said Mrs Winthrop, in a disagreeing tone.

'A woman of genius! And what is the very term but a stigma? No woman is so proclaimed by the great brazen tongue of the Public unless she has thrown away her birthright of womanly seclusion for the miserable mess of pottage called "fame."'

'The seclusion of a convent? or a prison?'

'Neither. Of a home.'

'You perhaps commend obedience, also?'

'In one way – yes.'

'I'm glad to know there are other ways.'

'I shall be very obedient to the woman I love in several of those other ways,' replied Ford, gathering some of the ripening grapes near the balcony rail.

Mrs Winthrop went back into the faded drawing-room. 'It is a pity there is no portrait here of Madame Récamier,' she remarked. 'That you might have admired.'

'The "incomparable Juliette" was at least not literary. But in another way she was as much before the public as though she had been what you call a woman of genius. It may be said, indeed, that she had genius – a genius for attracting admiration.'

'You are hard to please.'

'Not at all; I ask only the simple and retiring womanly graces. But anything retiring was hard to find in the eighteenth century.'

'You dislike literary women very much,' said Mrs Winthrop. She had crossed the room to examine an old mirror made of squares of glass, welded together by little leaden frames, which had once been gilded.

'Hardly. I pity them.'

'You did not know, then, that I was one?'

He had crossed the room also, and was now standing behind her; as she asked the question she looked at his image in the glass.

'I did not know it,' he answered, looking at hers.

'I am, anonymously.'

'Better anonymously than avowedly.'

'Will you read something I have written?'

'Thanks. I am not in the least a critic.'

'I know that; you are too prejudiced, too narrow, to be one. All the same, will you read?'

'If you insist.'

'I do insist. What is more, I have it with me. I have had it for several days, waiting for a good opportunity.' She drew from her pocket a small flat package, and gave it to him.

'Must it be now?'

'Here and now. Where could we find a more appropriate atmosphere?'

He seated himself and opened the parcel; within was a small square book in flexible covers, in decoration paper and type, a daintily rich little volume.

'Ah! I know this,' he said. 'I read it when it first came out.'

'So much the better. You can give me your opinion without the trouble of reading.'

'It received a good deal of praise, I remember,' he said, turning over the leaves.

She was silent.

'There was a charming little description somewhere – about going out on the Campagna* to gather the wild narcissus,' he went on, after a pause.

And then there was another silence.

'But – ' said Mrs Winthrop.

'But, as you kindly suggest, I am no judge of poetry. I can say nothing of value.'

'Say it, valuable or not. Do you know, Mr Ford, that you have scarcely spoken one really truthful word to me since we first met. Yet I feel sure that it does not come natural to you, and that it has cost you some trouble to – to – '

'To decorate, as I have, my plain speech. But if that is true, is it not a compliment?'

'And do I care for your compliments? I have compliments in abundance, and much finer ones than yours. What I want from you is the truth, your real opinion of that little volume in your hand. You are the only man I have met in years who seems to feel no desire to flatter me, to make me think well of myself. I see no reason why I should not think well of myself; but, all the same, I am curious. I can see that you judge me impartially, even severely.'

She paused. He did not look up or disclaim; he went on turning the pages of the little volume.

She had not seated herself; she was standing beside a table opposite him. 'I can see that you do not in the least like me,' she added, in a lower tone.

'My dear lady, you have so many to like you!' said Ford.

And then he did look up; their eyes met.

A flush came to her cheeks. He shut the little book and rose.

'Really, I am too insignificant a victim,' he said, bowing as he returned it.

'You mean that I – that I have tried – '

'Oh no; you do it naturally.'

For the moment her self-possession had failed her. But now she had it in hand again. 'If I *have* tried, naturally or artificially, I have made a failure – have I not?'

'It must be a novel experience for Mrs Winthrop.'

She turned away and looked at a portrait of Voltaire. After some moments, 'Let us come back to the real point between us,' she said, as he did not speak – 'that is, your opinion of my little book.'

'Is that the real point between us?'

'Of course it is. We will walk up and down Corrine's old rooms, and you shall tell me as we walk.'

'Why do you force me to say unpleasant things?'

'They are unpleasant, then? I knew it! Unpleasant for me.'

'For us both.'

'For you, I doubt it. For me, they cannot be more unpleasant than the things you have already said. Yet you see I forgive them.'

'Yes; but I have not forgiven you, Mrs Winthrop.'

'For what, pray?'

'For proposing to make me a victim.'

'Apparently you had small difficulty in escaping.'

'As you say – apparently. But perhaps I conceal my wounds.'

'You are trying to turn the subject, so that I will not insist about the little book.'

'I wish, indeed, that you would not insist.'

'But if I am the sort of woman you have indicated, I should think you would enjoy punishing me a little.'

'A little, perhaps. But the punishment would be too severe.'

They were walking slowly through the rooms; she turned her head and looked at him. 'I have listened to you, Mr Ford; I have let you say pretty much what you pleased to me, because it was amusing. But you cannot seriously believe that I really care for what you say, severe or otherwise?'

'Only as any right-minded woman must care.'

'Say on. Now I insist.'

'Goodbye to Miolans, then. You will never admit me within its gates again; that is, unless you have the unusual justice – unusual in a woman – to see that what I say is but the severity of a true friend.'

'A friend is not severe.'

'Yes, he is; in such a case as this, must be.'

'Go on. I will decide afterwards.'

They entered the third room. Ford reflected a moment; then began. 'The poem, which you now tell me is yours, had, as its distinguishing feature, a certain daring. Regarding its other points: its rhythm was crude and unmelodious; its coloring was exaggerated – reading it, one was cloyed with color; its logic – for there was an attempt at logic – was utterly weak.' He paused. Mrs Winthrop was looking straight before her at the wall across the end of the last room in the vista. Her critic did not lift his eyes, but transferred his gaze from one section of the dark old floor to the next as they walked onward.

'All this, however,' he resumed, 'could be forgiven. We do not expect great poems from women any more than we expect great pictures; we do not expect strong logic any more than we expect brawny muscle. A woman's poetry is subjective. But what cannot be forgiven – at least in my opinion – is that which I have called the distinguishing feature of the volume, a certain sort of daring. This is its essential, unpardonable sin. Not because it is in itself dangerous; it has not force enough for that; but because it comes, and can be recognized at once as coming, from the lips of a woman. For a woman should not dare in that way. Thinking to soar, she invariably descends. Her mental realm is not the same as that of man; lower, on the same level, or far above, it is at least different. And to see her leave it, and come in all her white purity, which must inevitably be soiled, to the garish arena where men are contending, where the dust is rising, and the air is tainted and heavy – this is indeed a painful sight. Every honest man feels like going to her, poor mistaken sibyl that she is, closing her lips with gentle hand, and leading her away to some far spot among the quiet fields, where she can learn her error, and begin her life anew. To the pity of it is added the certain truth that if the words she sang could be carried out to their logical end, if they were to be clothed in the hard realities of life and set up before her, they would strike first the poor creature who was chanting them, and crush her to the dust. Fortunately there is no danger of this; it is among the impossibilities. And sometimes the poor sibyls learn, and through the teachings of their own hearts, their great mistake.' As he ended, for the first time he lifted his eyes from the floor and looked at her.

Katharine Winthrop's face was flushed; the dark color extended over her forehead and dyed even her throat, and there was an expression as though only by a strong effort was a tremor of the lips controlled. This gave to her mouth a fixed look. She was so unlike herself, veiled in that deep, steady, painful blush, that, involuntarily and earnestly, Ford said, 'I beg you not to mind it so much.'

'I mind only that you should dare to say such things to me,' she answered, slowly, as though utterance was an effort.

'Remember that you forced me to speak.'

'I did not expect – this.'

'How could I know what you expected? But in one way I am glad you made me go on; it is well that you should have for once a man's true opinion.'

'All men do not think as you think.'

'Yes, they do; the honest ones.'

'Mr Percival does not.'

'Oh, Percival! He's effeminate.'

'So you judge him,' said Mrs Winthrop, to whose utterance anger had now restored the distinctness.

'We will not quarrel about Lorimer Percival,' said Ford; 'he is not worth it – at least, he is not worth it to me.' Then, as they entered the last room, 'Take it as I meant it, Katharine,' he said, the tone of his voice changing – 'take it as a true woman should. Show me the sweet side of your nature, the gentle, womanly side, and I will then be your suitor indeed, and a far more real and earnest one than though I had become the victim you intended me to be. You may not care for me; you may never care. But only let me see you accept for your own sake what I have said, in the right spirit, and I will at least ask you to care, as humbly and devotedly as man ever asked woman. For when she is her true self she is so far above us that we can only be humble.'

The flush still covered her forehead; her eyes looked at him, strangely and darkly blue in all this red.

'Curious, isn't it, how things come about?' she said. 'You have made me a declaration, after all.'

'A conditional one.'

'No, not conditional in reality, although you might have pleased yourself with the fancy. For I need not have been in earnest. I had only to pretend a little, to pretend to be the acquiescent creature you admire, and I could have turned you round my little finger. It is rather a pity I did not do it. It might have been entertaining.'

He had watched her as she spoke. 'I do not in the least believe you,' he said, gravely.

'It is not of much consequence whether you believe me or not. I think, on the whole, however, that I may as well take this occasion to tell you what you seem not to have suspected: I am engaged to Mr Percival.'

'Of course, then, you were angry when I spoke of him as I did. But I beg you will do me the justice to believe that I never for a moment dreamed that he was anything to Mrs Winthrop.'

'Your dreams must be unobservant.'

'I knew that he was with you, of course, and that you received his letters – there is one in your pocket now. But it made no impression upon me – that is, as far as you were concerned.'

'And why not? Even in the guise of an apology, Mr Ford, you succeed in insinuating your rudeness. What you have said, when translated, simply means that you never dreamed that Mrs Winthrop could be interested in Mr Percival. And why should she not be interested? But the truth is, there is such an infinite space between you that you cannot in the least comprehend him.' She turned towards the door which led to the stairway.

'That is very possible,' said Ford. 'But I have not now the honor to be a rival of Mr Percival's, even as an unfavored suitor; you did not comply with my condition.'

They went down the stairs, past the shining statue of Necker, and out into the sunshine. Benjamin Franklin brought forward the horses, and Ford assisted her to mount. 'You prefer that I should not go with you,' he said; 'but of course I must. We cannot always have things just as we wish them in this vexatious world, you know.'

The flush on her face was still deep; but she had recovered herself sufficiently to smile. 'We will select subjects that will act as safe conductors down to commonplace,' she said. They did. Only at the gate of Miolans was any allusion made to the preceding conversation.

He had said goodbye; the two riding-gloves had formally touched each other. 'It may be for a long time,' he remarked. 'I start towards Italy this evening; I shall go to Chambéry* and Turin.'

She passed him; her horse turned into the plane-tree avenue. 'Do not suppose that I could not have been, that I could not be – if I chose – all you described,' she said, looking back.

'I know you could. It was the possibilities in you which attracted me, and made me say what I did.'

'*That* for your possibilities!' she answered, making the gesture of throwing something lightly away.

He lifted his hat; she smiled, bowed slightly, and rode onward out of sight. He took his horse to the stables, went down to the water-steps, and unmoored his skiff. The next day Sylvia received a note from him; it contained his goodbye, but he himself was already on the way to Italy.

The following summer found Miss Pitcher again at Miolans. But although her little figure was still seen going down to the outlook at sunset, although she still made wax flowers and read (with a mark) 'Childe Harold,' it was evident that she was not as she had been. She was languid, mournful, and by August these adjectives were no longer sufficient to describe her condition, for she was now seriously ill. Her nephew, who was spending the summer in Scotland, was notified by a letter from Cousin Walpole. In answer he travelled southward to Lake Leman without an hour's delay; for Sylvia and himself were the only ones of their blood on the old side of the Atlantic, and if the gentle little aunt was to pass from earth in a strange land, he wished to be beside her.

But Sylvia did not pass. Her nephew read her case so skillfully, and with the others tended her so carefully, that in three weeks' time she was lying on a couch by the window, with 'Childe Harold' again by her side. But if she was now well enough for a little literature, she was also well enough for a little conversation.

'I suppose you were much surprised, John, to find Katharine still Mrs Winthrop?'

'No, not much.'

'But she told me that she had mentioned to you her engagement.'

'Yes, she mentioned it.'

'You speak as though she was one of the women who make and break engagements lightly. But she is not, I assure you; far from it.'

'She broke this one, it seems.'

'One breaking does not make a – breaker,' said Sylvia, thinking vaguely of 'swallows,' and nearly saying 'summer.' She paused, then shook her head sadly. 'I have never understood it,' she said, with a deep sigh. 'It lasted, I know, until the very end of June. I think I may say, without exaggeration, that I spent the entire month of July, day and night, picturing to myself his sufferings.'

'You took more time than he did. He was married before July was ended.'

'Simply despair.'

'Despair took on a cheerful guise. Some of the rest of us might not object to it in such a shape.'

But Miss Pitcher continued her dirge. 'So terrible for such a man! A mere child – only seventeen!'

'And he is – '

'Thirty-seven years, eight months, and nine days,' answered the lady, in the tone of an obituary. 'Twenty years younger than he is! Of course, she cannot in the least appreciate the true depth of his poetry.'

'He may not care for that, you know, if she appreciates him,' said Ford – Miss Pitcher thought, heartlessly.

During these three weeks of attendance upon his aunt he had, of course, seen Mrs Winthrop daily. Generally he met her in the sick-room, where she gave to the patient a tender and devoted care. If she was in the drawing-room when he came down, Cousin Walpole was there also; he had not once seen her alone. He was not staying at Miolans, although he spent most of his time there; his abode nominally was a farm-house near by. Sylvia improved daily, and early in September her nephew prepared for departure. He was going to Heidelberg. One beautiful morning he felt in the mood for a long farewell ride.

He sent word to Sylvia that he should not be at Miolans before evening, mounted, and rode off at a brisk pace. He was out all day under the blue sky, and enjoyed it. He had some wonderful new views of Mont Blanc, some exhilarating speed over tempting stretches of road, a lunch at a rustic inn among the vineyards, and the uninterrupted companionship of his own thoughts. Towards five o'clock, on his way home, he came by Coppet. Here the idle ease of the long day was broken by the small incident of his horse losing a shoe. He took him to the little blacksmith's shop in the village; then, while the work was in slow Swiss progress, he strolled back up the ascent towards the old château.

A shaggy white dog came to meet him; it was his friend Gibbon, and a moment later he recognized Mrs Winthrop's groom, holding his own and his mistress's horse. Mrs Winthrop was in the garden, so Benjamin Franklin said. He opened the high gate set in the stone wall and went down the long walk.

She was at the far end; her back was towards him, and she did not hear his step; she started when he spoke her name. But she recovered herself immediately, smiled, and began talking with much the same easy, graceful manner she had shown upon his first arrival at Miolans, when they met at the gate the year before. This meant that she had put him back as an acquaintance where he was then.

He did not seem unwilling to go. They strolled onward for ten minutes; then Mrs Winthrop said that she must start homeward; they turned towards the gate. They had been speaking of Sylvia's illness and recovery. 'I often think, when I look at my little aunt,' said Ford, 'how pretty she must have been in her youth. And, by-the-way, just before leaving Scotland I met a lady who reminded me of her, or rather of my idea of what she must have been. It was Mrs Lorimer Percival.'

'She is charming, I am told,' said the lady beside him.

'I don't know about the charming; I dislike the word. But she is very lovely and very lovable.'

'Did you see much of her?'

'I saw her several times; but only saw her. We did not speak.'

'You judge, then, by appearance merely.'

'In this case – yes. Her nature is written on her face.'

'All are at liberty to study it, then. Pray describe her.'

He was silent. Then, 'If I comply,' he said, 'will you bear in mind that I am quite well aware that that which makes this little lady's happiness is something that Mrs Winthrop, of her own accord, has cast aside as nothing worth?' As he rounded off this phrase he turned and looked at her.

But she did not meet his eyes. 'I will remember,' she answered.

He waited. But she said nothing more.

'Mrs Percival,' he resumed, 'is a beautiful young girl, with a face like a wild flower in the woods. She has an expression which is to me enchanting – an expression of sweet and simple goodness, and gentle, confiding trust. One is thankful to have even seen such a face.'

'You speak warmly. I am afraid you are jealous of poor Mr Percival.'

'He did not strike me as poor. If I was jealous, it was not the first time. He was always fortunate.'

'Perhaps there are other wild flowers in the woods; you must search more diligently.' She opened the gate, passed through, and signalled to her groom.

'That is what I am trying to do; but I do not succeed. It is terribly lonely work sometimes.'

'What a confession of weakness!'

He placed her in the saddle. 'It may be. At any rate, it is the truth. But women do not believe in truth for its own sake; it strikes them as crude.'

'You mean cruel,' said Katharine Winthrop. She rode off, the groom and Gibbon following. He went back to the blacksmith's shop. The next day he went to Heidelberg.

But he had not seen the last of Corinne's old château. On the 25th of October he was again riding up the plane-tree avenue of Miolans, this time under bare boughs.

'Oh, John! dear John!' said Miss Pitcher, hurrying into the drawing-room when she was told he was there. 'How glad I am to see you! But how did you know – I mean, how did you get here at this time of year?'

'By railway and on horseback,' he answered. 'I like autumn in the country. And I am very glad to see you looking so well, Aunt Sylvia.'

But if Sylvia was well in body, she was ill at ease in mind. She began sentences and did not finish them; she often held her little handkerchief to her lips as if repressing herself. Cousin Walpole had gone to Geneva, 'on business for Katharine.' No, Katharine was not with him; she was out riding somewhere. She was not well, and needed the exercise. Katharine, too, was fond of autumn in the country. But Sylvia found it rainy. After a while Ford took leave, promising to return in the evening. When he reached the country road he paused, looking up and down it for a moment; then he turned his horse southward. It was a dreary day for a ride; a long autumn rain had soaked the ground, clouds covered the sky, and a raw wind was blowing. He rode at a rapid pace, and when he came towards Coppet he again examined the wet track, then turned towards the château. He was not mistaken; Mrs Winthrop's horse was there. There was no groom this time; the horse was tied in the court-yard. Benjamin Franklin said that the lady was in the garden, and he said it muffled in a worsted cap and a long wadded coat that came to his heels. No doubt he permitted himself some wonder over the lady's taste.

The lady was at the end of the long walk as before. But today the long walk was a picture of desolation; all the bright leaves, faded and brown, were lying on the ground in heaps so sodden that the wind could not lift them, strongly as it blew. Across one end of this vista stretched the blank stone wall, its grayness streaked with wet spots; across the other rose the old château among the bare trees, cold, naked, and yellow, seeming to have already begun its long winter shiver. But men do not mind such things as women mind them. A dull sky and stretch of blank stone wall do not seem to them the end of the world – as they seemed at that moment to Katharine Winthrop. This time she heard his step; perhaps he intended that she should hear it. She turned.

Her face was pale; her eyes, with the dark shadows under them, looked larger than usual. She returned his greeting quietly; her trouble, whatever it was, did not apparently connect itself with him.

'You should not be walking here, Mrs Winthrop,' he said as he came up; 'it is too wet.'

'It is wet; but I am going now. You have been at Miolans?'

'Yes. I saw my aunt. She told me you were out riding somewhere. I thought perhaps you might be here.'

'Is that all she told you?'

'I think so. No; she did say that you were fond of autumn in the country. So am I. Wouldn't it be wise to stop at the old man's cottage, before remounting, and dry your shoes a little?'

'I never take cold.'

'Perhaps we could find a pair in the village that you could wear.'

'It is not necessary. I will ride rapidly; the exercise will be the best safeguard.'

'Do you know why I have come back?' he said, abandoning the subject of the shoes.

'I do not,' answered the lady. She looked very sad and weary.

'I have come back, Katharine, to tell you plainly and humbly that I love you. This time I make no conditions; I have none to make. Do with me as you please; I must bear it. But believe that I love you with all my heart. It has been against my will; I have not been willing to admit it to myself; but of late the certainty has forced itself upon me so overwhelmingly that I had no resource left save to come to you. I am full of faults; but – I love you. I have said many things that displeased you deeply; but – I love you. Do not deliberate. Send me away – if go I must – now. Keep me – if you will keep me – now. You can punish me afterwards.'

They had been walking onward, but now he stopped. She stopped also; but she said nothing; her eyes were downcast.

'It is a real love I offer you,' he said, in a low tone. Then, as still she did not speak, 'I will make you very happy, Katharine,' he added.

Her face had remained pale, but at this assertion of his a slight color rose, and a smile showed itself faintly. 'You are always so sure!' she murmured. And then she laughed, a little low, sweet, sudden laugh.

'Let him laugh who wins,' said Ford, triumphantly. The old streaked stone wall, if dreary, was at least high; no one saw him but one very wet and bedraggled little bird, who was in the tree above. This bird was so much cheered (it must have been that) that he immediately chirruped one note quite briskly, and coming out on a drier twig, began to arrange his soaked feathers.

'Now,' said Ford, 'we will have those shoes dried, whether you like it or not. No more imprudence allowed. How angry you were when I said we might find a pair in the village that you could wear! Of course I meant children's size.' He had drawn her hand through his arm, and was going towards the gate.

But she freed herself and stopped. 'It is all a mistake,' she said, hurriedly. 'It means nothing. I am not myself today. Do not think of it.'

'Certainly I shall not trouble myself to think of it much when – what is so much better – I have it.'

'No; it is nothing. Forget it. I shall not see you again. I am going back to America immediately – next week.'

He looked at her as she uttered these short sentences. Then he took her hands in his. 'I know about the loss of your fortune, Katharine; you need not tell me. No, Sylvia did not betray you. I heard it quite by chance from another source while I was still in Heidelberg. That is the reason I came.'

'The reason you came!' she repeated, moving from him, with the old proud light coming back into her eyes. 'You thought I would be overwhelmed – you thought that I would be so broken that I would be glad – you pitied me – you came to help me? And you were *sure* – ' She stopped; her voice was shaking.

'Yes, Katharine, I did pity you. Yes, I came to help you if you would let me. But I was not sure. I was sure of nothing but my own obstinate love, which burst out uncontrollably when I thought of you in trouble. I have never thought of you in that way before; you have always had everything. The thought has brought me straight to your side.'

But she was not softened. 'I withdraw all I have said,' she answered. 'You have taken advantage.'

'As it happens, you have said nothing. As to taking advantage, of course I took advantage: I was glad enough to see your pale face and sad eyes. But that is because you have always carried things with such a high hand. First and last, I have had a great deal of bad treatment.'

'That is not true.'

'Very well; then it is not. It shall be as you please. Do you want me to go down on my knees to you on this wet gravel?'

But she still turned from him.

'Katharine,' he said, in a graver tone, 'I am sorry on your account that your fortune is gone, or nearly gone; but on my own, how can I help being glad? It was a barrier between us, which, as I am, and as you are – but principally as you are – would have been, I fear, a hopeless one. I doubt if I should ever have surmounted it. Your loss brings you nearer to me – the woman I deeply love, love in spite of myself. Now if you are my wife – and a tenderly loved wife you will be – you will in a measure be dependent upon your husband, and that is very sweet to a self-willed man like myself. Perhaps in time I can even make it sweet to you.'

A red spot burned in each of her cheeks. 'It is very hard,' she said, almost in a whisper.

'Well, on the whole, life *is* hard,' answered John Ford. But the expression in his eyes was more tender than his words. At any rate, it seemed to satisfy her.

'Do you know what I am going to do?' he said, some minutes later. 'I am going to make Benjamin Franklin light a fire on one of those old literary hearths at the château. Your shoes shall be dried in the presence of Corinne herself (who must, however, have worn a much larger pair). And while they are drying I will offer a formal apology for any past want of respect, not only to Corinne, but to all the other portraits, especially to that blue-eyed Madame Necker in her very tight white satin gown. We will drink their healths in some of the native wine. If you insist, I will even make an effort to admire the yellow turban.'

He carried out his plan. Benjamin Franklin, tempted by the fee offered, and relying no doubt upon the gloomy weather as a barrier against discovery, made a bright fire upon one of the astonished hearths, and brought over a flask of native wine, a little loaf, and some fine grapes. Ford arranged these on a spindle-legged table, and brought forward an old tapestried arm-chair for Katharine. Then while she sat sipping her wine and drying her shoes before the crackling flame, he went gravely round the room, glass in hand, pausing before each portrait to bow ceremoniously and drink to its health and long life – probably in a pictorial sense. When he had finished the circuit, 'Here's to you all, charming vanished ladies of the past,' he said; 'may you each have every honor in the picturesque, powdered, unorthographic age to which you belong, and never by any possibility step over into ours!'

'That last touch has spoiled the whole,' said the lady in the tapestried chair.

But Ford declared that an expression in Madame Necker's blue eye approved his words.

He now came back to the hearth. 'This will never do,' he said. 'The shoes are not drying; you must take them off.' And with that he knelt down and began to unbutton them. But Katharine, agreeing to obey orders, finished the task herself. The old custodian, who had been standing in the doorway laughing at Ford's portrait pantomime, now saw an opportunity to make himself useful; he came forward, took one of the shoes, put it upon his hand, and, kneeling down, held it close to the flame. The shoes were little boots of dark cloth like the habit, slender, dainty, and made with thin soles; they were for riding, not walking. Ford brought forward a second arm-chair and sat down. 'The old room looks really cheerful,' he said. 'The portraits are beginning to thaw; presently we shall see them smile.'

Katharine too was smiling. She was also blushing a little. The blush and slight embarrassment made her look like a school-girl.

'Where shall we go for the winter?' said Ford. 'I can give you one more winter over here, and then I must go home and get to work again. And as we have so little foreign time left, I suggest that we lose none of it, and begin our married life at once. Don't be alarmed; he does not understand a word of English. Shall we say, then, next week?'

'No.'

'Are you waiting to know me better? Take me, and make me better.'

'What are your principal faults – I mean besides those I already know?' she said, shielding her face from the heat of the fire with her riding gauntlets.

'I have very few. I like my own way; but it is always a good way. My opinions are rather decided ones; but would you like an undecided man? I do not enjoy general society, but I am extremely fond of the particular. I think that is all.'

'And your obstinacy?'

'Only firmness.'

'You are narrow, prejudiced; you do not believe in progress of any kind. You would keep women down with an iron hand.'

'A velvet one.'

The custodian now took the other shoe.

'He will certainly stretch them with that broad palm of his,' said Ford. 'But perhaps it is as well; you have a habit of wearing shoes that are too small. What ridiculous little affairs those are! Will twelve pairs a year content you?'

A flush rose in her cheeks; she made no reply.

'It will be very hard for you to give up your independence, your control of things,' he said.

But she turned towards him with a very sweet expression in her eyes. 'You will do it all for me,' she answered.

He rose, walked about the room, coming back to lean over the gilded top of her chair and say, with emphasis, 'What in the world does that old wretch mean by staying here so persistently all this time?'

She laughed. Benjamin Franklin, looking up from his task, laughed too – probably on general principles of sociability and appreciation of his fee.

'To go back to your faults,' she said; 'please come and sit down, and acknowledge them. You have a very jealous nature.'

'You are mistaken. However, if you like jealousy, I can easily take it up.'

'It will not be necessary. It is already there.'

'You are thinking of some particular instance; of whom did you suppose I was jealous?'

But she would not say.

After a while he came back to it. 'You thought I was jealous of Lorimer Percival,' he said.

The custodian now announced that both shoes were dry; she put them on, buttoning them with an improvised button-hook made of a hair-pin. The old man stood straightening himself after his bent posture; he still smiled – probably on the same general principles. The afternoon was drawing towards its close; Ford asked him to bring round the horses. He went out; they could hear his slow, careful tread on each of the slippery stairs. Katharine had risen, she went to the mirror to adjust her riding-hat. Ford came up and stood behind her. 'Do you remember when I looked at you in the glass, in this same way, a year ago?' he said.

'How you talked to me that day about my poor little book! You made me feel terribly.'

'I am sorry. Forgive it.'

'But you do not forgive the book?'

'I will forget it, instead. You will write no more.'

'Always so sure! However, I will promise, if you acknowledge that you have a jealous disposition.'

She spoke gayly. He watched her in the glass a moment, then drew her away. 'Whether I have a jealous disposition or not I do not know,' he answered. 'But I was never jealous of Lorimer Percival; I held him in too light estimation. And I did not believe – no, not at any time – that you loved him; he was not a man whom you would love. Why you allowed yourself to become engaged to him I do not know; but I suspect it was because he flattered what you thought your literary talent. I do not believe you would ever have married him; you would have drawn back at the last moment. To be engaged to him was one thing, to marry him another. You kept your engagement along for months, when there was no reason at all for the delay. If you had married him I should have thought the less of you, but I should not have been jealous.' He paused. 'I might never have let you know it, Katharine,' he went on, 'but I prefer that there should be nothing but the truth between us. I know that it was Percival who broke the engagement at the last, and not you. I knew it when I was here in the summer. He himself told me when I met him in Scotland just after his marriage.'

She broke from him. 'How base are all men!' she said, in a voice unlike her own.

'In him it was simply egotism. He knew that I had known of his engagement to you, and he wished me to appreciate that in order to marry that sweet young girl, who was quite without fortune, he had been obliged to make, and had made, a great sacrifice.'

'Great indeed!' she commented, bitterly. 'You do well to commend him.'

'I do not commend him. I simply say that he was following out his nature. Being a poet, he is what is called sympathetic, you know; and he wanted my appreciation and sympathy – I will not say applause.'

She was standing with her back towards him. She now walked towards the door. But her courage failed, she sank into a chair and covered her face with her hands. 'It is too much,' she said. 'You wait until I have lost my fortune and am overwhelmed; you wait until I am rejected, cast aside; and then you come and win from me an avowal of my love, telling me afterwards – *afterwards*' – Her voice broke, she burst into tears.

'Telling you afterwards nothing but that I love you. Telling you afterwards that I have not had one really happy moment since our conversation in this old house a year ago. Telling you afterwards that my life has resolved itself into but one unceasing, tormenting wish – the wish, Katharine, that you would love me, I suppose I ought to say a little, but I mean a great deal. Look at me; is this humble enough for you?'

Her drew her hands away; she saw that he was kneeling at her feet; and, not only that, but she saw also something very like a mist in the gray eyes she had always thought too cold.

In the library of Mr John Ford, near New York, there hangs in the place of honor a water-color sketch of an old yellow château. Beneath it, ranged by themselves, are all the works of that eloquent authoress and noble woman, Madame de Staël.

'You admire her?' said a visitor recently, in some surprise. 'To me she always seemed a – a little antique, you know.'

'She is antiquity itself! But she once lent me her house, and I am grateful. By-the-way, Katharine, I never told you, although I found it out afterwards: Benjamin Franklin understood English, after all.'

SARAH ORNE JEWETT

A White Heron

1886

I

The woods were already filled with shadows one June evening, just before eight o'clock, though a bright sunset still glimmered faintly among the trunks of the trees. A little girl was driving home her cow, a plodding, dilatory, provoking creature in her behavior, but a valued companion for all that. They were going away from the western light, and striking deep into the dark woods, but their feet were familiar with the path, and it was no matter whether their eyes could see it or not.

There was hardly a night the summer through when the old cow could be found waiting at the pasture bars; on the contrary, it was her greatest pleasure to hide herself away among the high huckleberry bushes, and though she wore a loud bell she had made the discovery that if one stood perfectly still it would not ring. So Sylvia had to hunt for her until she found her, and call Co'! Co'! with never an answering Moo, until her childish patience was quite spent. If the creature had not given good milk and plenty of it, the case would have seemed very different to her owners. Besides, Sylvia had all the time there was, and very little use to make of it. Sometimes in pleasant weather it was a consolation to look upon the cow's pranks as an intelligent attempt to play hide and seek, and as the child had no playmates she lent herself to this amusement with a good deal of zest. Though this chase had been so long that the wary animal herself had given an unusual signal of her whereabouts, Sylvia had only laughed when she came upon Mistress Moolly at the swamp side, and urged her affectionately homeward with a twig of birch leaves. The old cow was not inclined to wander farther, she even turned in the right direction for once as they left the pasture, and stepped along the road at a good pace. She was quite ready to be milked now, and seldom stopped to browse.

Sylvia wondered what her grandmother would say because they were so late. It was a great while since she had left home at half past five o'clock, but everybody knew the difficulty of making this errand a short one. Mrs Tilley had chased the hornéd torment too many summer evenings herself to blame any one else for lingering, and was only thankful as she waited that she had Sylvia, nowadays, to give such valuable assistance. The good woman suspected that Sylvia loitered occasionally on her own account; there never was such a child for straying about out of doors since the world was made! Everybody said that it was a good change for a little maid who had tried to grow for eight years in a crowded manufacturing town, but, as for Sylvia herself, it seemed as if she never had been alive at all before she came to live at the farm. She thought often with wistful compassion of a wretched dry geranium that belonged to a town neighbor.

'"Afraid of folks,"' old Mrs Tilley said to herself, with a smile, after she had made the unlikely choice of Sylvia from her daughter's houseful of children, and was returning to the farm. '"Afraid of folks," they said! I guess she won't be troubled no great with 'em up to the old place!' When they reached the door of the lonely house and stopped to unlock it, and the cat came to purr loudly, and rub against them, a deserted pussy, indeed, but fat with young robins, Sylvia whispered that this was a beautiful place to live in, and she never should wish to go home.

The companions followed the shady woodroad, the cow taking slow steps, and the child very fast ones. The cow stopped long at the brook to drink, as if the pasture were not half a swamp, and Sylvia stood still and waited, letting her bare feet cool themselves in the shoal water, while the great twilight moths struck softly against her. She waded on through the brook as the cow moved away, and listened to the thrushes with a heart that beat fast with pleasure. There was a stirring in the great boughs overhead. They were full of little birds and beasts that seemed to be wide-awake, and going about their world, or else saying goodnight to each other in sleepy twitters. Sylvia herself felt sleepy as she walked along. However, it was not much farther to the house, and the air was soft and sweet. She was not often in the woods so late as this, and it made her feel as if she were a part of the gray shadows and the moving leaves. She was just thinking how long it seemed since she first came to the farm a year ago, and wondering if everything went on in the noisy town just the same as when she was there; the thought of the great red-faced boy who used to chase and frighten her made her hurry along the path to escape from the shadow of the trees.

Suddenly this little woods girl is horror stricken to hear a clear whistle not very far away. Not a bird's whistle, which would have a sort of friendliness, but a boy's whistle, determined, and somewhat aggressive. Sylvia left the cow to whatever sad fate might await her, and stepped discreetly aside into the bushes, but she was just too late. The enemy had discovered her, and called out in a very cheerful and persuasive tone, 'Halloa, little girl, how far is it to the road?' and trembling Sylvia answered almost inaudibly, 'A good ways.'

She did not dare to look boldly at the tall young man, who carried a gun over his shoulder, but she came out of her bush and again followed the cow, while he walked alongside.

'I have been hunting for some birds,' the stranger said kindly, 'and I have lost my way, and need a friend very much. Don't be afraid,' he added gallantly. 'Speak up and tell me what your name is, and whether you think I can spend the night at your house, and go out gunning early in the morning.'

Sylvia was more alarmed than before. Would not her grandmother consider her much to blame? But who could have foreseen such an accident as this? It did not appear to be her fault and she hung her head as if the stem of it were broken, but managed to answer 'Sylvy,' with much effort when her companion again asked her name.

Mrs Tilley was standing in the doorway when the trio came into view. The cow gave a loud moo by way of explanation.

'Yes, you'd better speak up for yourself, you old trial! Where'd she tuck herself away this time, Sylvy?' Sylvia kept an awed silence; she knew by instinct that her grandmother did not comprehend the gravity of the situation. She must be mistaking the stranger for one of the farmer lads of the region.

The young man stood his gun beside the door, and dropped a heavy game-bag beside it; then he bade Mrs Tilley goodevening, and repeated his wayfarer's story, and asked if he could have a night's lodging.

'Put me anywhere you like,' he said. 'I must be off early in the morning, before day; but I am very hungry, indeed. You can give me some milk at any rate, that's plain.'

'Dear sakes, yes,' responded the hostess, whose long slumbering hospitality seemed to be easily awakened. 'You might fare better if you went out on the main road a mile or so, but you're welcome to what we've got. I'll milk right off, and you make yourself at home. You can sleep on husks or feathers,' she proffered graciously. 'I raised them all myself. There's good pasturing for geese just below here towards the ma'sh. Now step round and set a plate for the gentleman, Sylvy!' And Sylvia promptly stepped. She was glad to have something to do, and she was hungry herself.

It was a surprise to find so clean and comfortable a little dwelling in this New England wilderness. The young man had known the horrors of its most primitive housekeeping, and the dreary squalor of that level of society which does not rebel at the companionship of hens. This was the best thrift of an old-fashioned farmstead, though on such a small scale that it seemed like a hermitage. He listened eagerly to the old woman's quaint talk, he watched Sylvia's pale face and shining gray eyes with ever growing enthusiasm, and insisted that this was the best supper he had eaten for a month; then, afterward, the new-made friends sat down in the doorway together while the moon came up.

Soon it would be berry time, and Sylvia was a great help at picking. The cow was a good milker, though a plaguy thing to keep track of, the hostess gossiped frankly, adding presently that she had buried four children, so that Sylvia's mother, and a son (who might be dead) in California were all the children she had left. 'Dan, my boy, was a great hand to go gunning,' she explained sadly. 'I never wanted for pa'tridges or gray squer'ls while he was to home. He's been a great wand'rer, I expect, and he's no hand to write letters. There, I don't blame him, I'd ha' seen the world myself if it had been so I could.

'Sylvia takes after him,' the grandmother continued affectionately, after a minute's pause. 'There ain't a foot o' ground she don't know her way over, and the wild creatur's counts her one o' themselves. Squer'ls she'll tame to come an' feed right out o' her hands, and all sorts o' birds. Last winter she got the jay birds to bangeing here, and I believe she'd 'a' scanted herself of her own meals to have plenty to throw out amongst 'em, if I hadn't kep' watch. Anything but crows, I tell her, I'm willin' to help support, – though Dan he went an' tamed one o' them that did seem to have reason same as folks. It was round here a good spell after he went away. Dan an' his father they didn't hitch, – but he never held up his head ag'in after Dan had dared him an' gone off.'

The guest did not notice this hint of family sorrows in his eager interest in something else.

'So Sylvy knows all about birds, does she?' he exclaimed, as he looked round at the little girl who sat, very demure but increasingly sleepy, in the moonlight. 'I am making a collection of birds myself. I have been at it ever since I was a boy.' (Mrs Tilley smiled.) 'There are two or three very rare ones I have been hunting for these five years. I mean to get them on my own ground if they can be found.'

'Do you cage 'em up?' asked Mrs Tilley doubtfully, in response to this enthusiastic announcement.

'Oh, no, they're stuffed and preserved, dozens and dozens of them,' said the ornithologist, 'and I have shot or snared every one myself. I caught a glimpse of a white heron three miles from here on Saturday, and I have followed it in this direction. They have never been found in this district at all. The little white heron, it is,' and he turned again to look at Sylvia with the hope of discovering that the rare bird was one of her acquaintances.

But Sylvia was watching a hop toad in the narrow footpath.

'You would know the heron if you saw it,' the stranger continued eagerly. 'A queer tall white bird with soft feathers and long thin legs. And it would have a nest perhaps in the top of a high tree, made of sticks, something like a hawk's nest.'

Sylvia's heart gave a wild beat; she knew that strange white bird, and had once stolen softly near where it stood in some bright green swamp grass, away over at the other side of the woods. There was an open place where the sunshine always seemed strangely yellow and hot, where tall, nodding rushes grew, and her grandmother had warned her that she might sink in the soft black mud underneath and never be heard of more. Not far beyond were the salt marshes and beyond those was the sea, the sea which Sylvia wondered and dreamed about, but never had looked upon, though its great voice could often be heard above the noise of the woods on stormy nights.

'I can't think of anything I should like so much as to find that heron's nest,' the handsome stranger was saying. 'I would give ten dollars to anybody who could show it to me,' he added desperately, 'and I mean to spend my whole vacation hunting for it if need be. Perhaps it was only migrating, or had been chased out of its own region by some bird of prey.'

Mrs Tilley gave amazed attention to all this, but Sylvia still watched the toad, not divining, as she might have done at some calmer time, that the creature wished to get to its hole under the doorstep, and was much hindered by the unusual spectators at that hour of the evening. No amount of thought, that night, could decide how many wished-for treasures the ten dollars, so lightly spoken of, would buy.

The next day the young sportsman hovered about the woods, and Sylvia kept him company, having lost her first fear of the friendly lad, who proved to be most kind and sympathetic. He told her many things about the birds and what they knew and where they lived and what they did with themselves. And he gave her a jackknife, which she thought as great a treasure as if she were a desert islander. All day long he did not once make her troubled or afraid except when he brought down some unsuspecting singing creature from its bough. Sylvia would have liked him vastly better without his gun; she could not understand why he killed the very birds he seemed to like so much. But as the day waned, Sylvia watched the young man with loving admiration. She had never seen anybody so charming and delightful; the woman's heart, asleep in the child, was vaguely thrilled by a dream of love. Some premonition of that great power stirred and swayed these young foresters who traversed the solemn woodlands with soft-footed silent care. They stopped to listen to a bird's song; they pressed forward again eagerly, parting the branches, – speaking to each other rarely and in whispers; the young man going first and Sylvia following, fascinated, a few steps behind, with her gray eyes dark with excitement.

She grieved because the longed-for white heron was elusive, but she did not lead the guest, she only followed, and there was no such thing as speaking first. The sound of her own unquestioned voice would have terrified her, – it was hard enough to answer yes or no when there was need of that. At last evening began to fall, and they drove the cow together, and Sylvia smiled with pleasure when they came to the place where she heard the whistle and was afraid only the night before.

2

Half a mile from home, at the farther edge of the woods, where the land was highest, a great pine tree stood, the last of its generation. Whether it was left for a boundary mark, or for what reason, no one could say; the woodchoppers who had felled its mates were dead and gone long ago, and a whole forest of sturdy trees, pines and oaks and maples, had grown again. But the stately head of this old pine towered above them all and made a landmark for sea and shore miles and miles away. Sylvia knew it well. She had always believed that whoever climbed to the top of it could see the ocean; and the little girl had often laid her hand on the great rough trunk and looked up wistfully at those dark boughs that the wind always stirred, no matter how hot and still the air might be below. Now she thought of the tree with a new excitement, for why, if one climbed it at break of day, could not one see all the world, and easily discover whence the white heron flew, and mark the place, and find the hidden nest?

What a spirit of adventure, what wild ambition! What fancied triumph and delight and glory for the later morning when she could make known the secret! It was almost too real and too great for the childish heart to bear.

All night the door of the little house stood open, and the whippoorwills came and sang upon the very step. The young sportsman and his old hostess were sound asleep, but Sylvia's great design kept her broad awake and watching. She forgot to think of sleep. The short summer night seemed as long as the winter darkness, and at last when the whippoorwills ceased, and she was afraid the morning would after all come too soon, she stole out of the house and followed the pasture path through the woods, hastening toward the open ground beyond, listening with a sense of comfort and companionship to the drowsy twitter of a half-awakened bird, whose perch she had jarred in passing. Alas, if the great wave of human interest which flooded for the first time this dull little life should sweep away the satisfactions of an existence heart to heart with nature and the dumb life of the forest!

There was the huge tree asleep yet in the paling moonlight, and small and hopeful Sylvia began with utmost bravery to mount to the top of it, with tingling, eager blood coursing the channels of her whole frame, with her bare feet and fingers, that pinched and held like bird's claws to the monstrous ladder reaching up, up, almost to the sky itself. First she must mount the white oak tree that grew alongside, where she was almost lost among the dark branches and the green leaves heavy and wet with dew; a bird fluttered off its nest, and a red squirrel ran to and fro and scolded pettishly at the harmless housebreaker. Sylvia felt her way easily. She had often climbed there, and knew that higher still one of the oak's upper branches chafed against the pine trunk, just where its lower boughs were set close together. There, when she made the dangerous pass from one tree to the other, the great enterprise would really begin.

She crept out along the swaying oak limb at last, and took the daring step across into the old pine tree. The way was harder than she thought; she must reach far and hold fast, the sharp dry twigs caught and held her and scratched her like angry talons, the pitch made her thin little fingers clumsy and stiff as she went round and round the tree's great stem, higher and higher upward. The sparrows and robins in the woods below were beginning to wake and twitter to the dawn, yet it seemed much lighter there aloft in the pine tree, and the child knew that she must hurry if her project were to be of any use.

The tree seemed to lengthen itself out as she went up, and to reach farther and farther upward. It was like a great mainmast to the voyaging earth; it must truly have been amazed that morning through all its ponderous frame as it felt this determined spark of human spirit creeping and climbing from higher branch to branch. Who knows how steadily the least twigs held themselves to advantage this light, weak creature on her way! The old pine must have loved his new dependent. More than all the hawks, and bats, and moths, and even the sweet-voiced thrushes, was the brave, beating heart of the solitary gray-eyed child. And the tree stood still and held away the winds that June morning while the dawn grew bright in the east.

Sylvia's face was like a pale star, if one had seen it from the ground, when the last thorny bough was past, and she stood trembling and tired but wholly triumphant, high in the treetop. Yes, there was the sea with the dawning sun making a golden dazzle over it, and toward that glorious east flew two hawks with slow-moving pinions. How low they looked in the air from that height when before one had only seen them far up, and dark against the blue sky. Their gray feathers were as soft as moths; they seemed only a little way from the tree, and Sylvia felt as if she too could go flying away among the clouds. Westward, the woodlands and farms reached miles and miles into the distance; here and there were church steeples, and white villages; truly it was a vast and awesome world.

The birds sang louder and louder. At last the sun came up bewilderingly bright. Sylvia could see the white sails of ships out at sea, and the clouds that were purple and rose-colored and yellow at first began to fade away. Where was the white heron's nest in the sea of green branches, and was this wonderful sight and pageant of the world the only reward for having climbed to such a giddy height? Now look down again, Sylvia, where the green marsh is set among the shining birches and dark hemlocks; there where you saw the white heron once you will see him again; look, look! a white spot of him like a single floating feather comes up from the dead hemlock and grows larger, and rises, and comes close at last, and goes by the landmark pine with steady sweep of wing and outstretched slender neck and crested head. And wait! wait! do not move a foot or a finger, little girl, do not send an arrow of light and consciousness from your two eager eyes, for the heron has perched on a pine bough not far beyond yours, and cries back to his mate on the nest, and plumes his feathers for the new day!

The child gives a long sigh a minute later when a company of shouting catbirds comes also to the tree, and vexed by their fluttering and lawlessness the solemn heron goes away. She knows his secret now, the wild, light, slender bird that floats and wavers, and goes back like an arrow presently to his home in the green world beneath. Then Sylvia, well satisfied, makes her perilous way down again, not daring to look far below the branch she stands on, ready to cry sometimes because her fingers ache and her lamed feet slip. Wondering over and over again what the stranger would say to her, and what he would think when she told him how to find his way straight to the heron's nest.

'Sylvy, Sylvy!' called the busy old grandmother again and again, but nobody answered, and the small husk bed was empty, and Sylvia had disappeared.

The guest waked from a dream, and remembering his day's

pleasure hurried to dress himself that it might sooner begin. He was sure from the way the shy little girl looked once or twice yesterday that she had at least seen the white heron, and now she must really be persuaded to tell. Here she comes now, paler than ever, and her worn old frock is torn and tattered, and smeared with pine pitch. The grandmother and the sportsman stand in the door together and question her, and the splendid moment has come to speak of the dead hemlock tree by the green marsh.

But Sylvia does not speak after all, though the old grandmother fretfully rebukes her, and the young man's kind appealing eyes are looking straight in her own. He can make them rich with money; he has promised it, and they are poor now. He is so well worth making happy, and he waits to hear the story she can tell.

No, she must keep silence! What is it that suddenly forbids her and makes her dumb? Has she been nine years growing, and now, when the great world for the first time puts out a hand to her, must she thrust it aside for a bird's sake? The murmur of the pine's green branches is in her ears, she remembers how the white heron came flying through the golden air and how they watched the sea and the morning together, and Sylvia cannot speak; she cannot tell the heron's secret and give its life away.

Dear loyalty, that suffered a sharp pang as the guest went away disappointed later in the day, that could have served and followed him and loved him as a dog loves! Many a night Sylvia heard the echo of his whistle haunting the pasture path as she came home with the loitering cow. She forgot even her sorrow at the sharp report of his gun and the piteous sight of thrushes and sparrows dropping silent to the ground, their songs hushed and their pretty feathers stained and wet with blood. Were the birds better friends than their hunter might have been, – who can tell? Whatever treasures were lost to her, woodlands and summer time, remember! Bring your gifts and graces and tell your secrets to this lonely country child!

The Town Poor

1890

Mrs William Trimble and Miss Rebecca Wright were driving along Hampden east road, one afternoon in early spring. Their progress was slow. Mrs Trimble's sorrel horse was old and stiff, and the wheels were clogged by clay mud. The frost was not yet out of the ground, although the snow was nearly gone, except in a few places on the north side of the woods, or where it had drifted all winter against a length of fence.

'There must be a good deal o' snow to the nor'ard of us yet,' said weather-wise Mrs Trimble. 'I feel it in the air; 't is more than the ground-damp. We ain't goin' to have real nice weather till the upcountry snow's all gone.'

'I heard say yesterday that there was good sleddin' yet, all up through Parsley,' responded Miss Wright. 'I shouldn't like to live in them northern places. My cousin Ellen's husband was a Parsley man, an' he was obliged, as you may have heard, to go up north to his father's second wife's funeral; got back day before yesterday. 'T was about twenty-one miles, an' they started on wheels; but when they'd gone nine or ten miles, they found 't was no sort o' use, an' left their wagon an' took a sleigh. The man that owned it charged 'em four an' six, too. I shouldn't have thought he would; they told him they was goin' to a funeral; an' they had their own buffaloes an' everything.'

'Well, I expect it's a good deal harder scratchin', up that way; they have to git money where they can; the farms is very poor as you go north,' suggested Mrs Trimble kindly. ''T ain't none too rich a country where we be, but I've always been grateful I wa'n't born up to Parsley.'

The old horse plodded along, and the sun, coming out from the heavy spring clouds, sent a sudden shine of light along the muddy road. Sister Wright drew her large veil forward over the high brim of her bonnet. She was not used to driving, or to being much in the open air; but Mrs Trimble was an active business woman, and looked after her own affairs herself, in all weathers. The late Mr Trimble had left her a good farm, but not much ready money, and it was often said that she was better off in the end than if he had lived. She regretted his loss deeply, however; it was impossible for her to speak of him, even to intimate friends, without emotion, and nobody had ever hinted that this emotion was insincere. She was most warm-hearted and generous, and in her limited way played the part of Lady Bountiful in the town of Hampden.

'Why, there's where the Bray girls lives, ain't it?' she exclaimed, as, beyond a thicket of witch-hazel and scrub-oak, they came in sight of a weather-beaten, solitary farmhouse. The barn was too far away for thrift or comfort, and they could see long lines of light between the shrunken boards as they came nearer. The fields looked both stony and sodden. Somehow, even Parsley itself could be hardly more forlorn.

'Yes'm,' said Miss Wright, 'that's where they live now, poor things. I know the place, though I ain't been up here for years. You don't suppose, Mis' Trimble – I ain't seen the girls out to meetin' all winter. I've re'lly been covetin'' –

'Why, yes, Rebecca, of course we could stop,' answered Mrs Trimble heartily. 'The exercises was over earlier 'n I expected, an' you're goin' to remain over night long o' me, you know. There won't be no tea till we git there, so we can't be late. I'm in the habit o' sendin' a basket to the Bray girls when any o' our folks is comin' this way, but I ain't been to see 'em since they moved up here. Why, it must be a good deal over a year ago. I know 't was in the late winter they had to make the move. 'T was cruel hard, I must say, an' if I hadn't been down with my pleurisy fever I'd have stirred round an' done somethin' about it. There was a good deal o' sickness at the time, an' – well, 't was kind o' rushed through, breakin' of 'em up, an' lots o' folks blamed the selec'*men*;* but when 't was done, 't was done, an' nobody took holt to undo it. Ann an' Mandy looked same 's ever when they come to meetin', 'long in the summer, – kind o' wishful, perhaps. They've always sent me word they was gittin' on pretty comfortable.'

'That would be their way,' said Rebecca Wright. 'They never was any hand to complain, though Mandy's less cheerful than Ann. If Mandy'd been spared such poor eyesight, an' Ann hadn't got her lame wrist that wa'n't set right, they'd kep' off the town fast enough. They both shed tears when they talked to me about havin' to break up, when I went to see 'em before I went over to brother Asa's. You see we was brought up neighbors, an' we went to school together, the Brays an' me. 'T was a special Providence brought us home this road, I've been so covetin' a chance to git to see 'em. My lameness hampers me.'

'I'm glad we come this way, myself,' said Mrs Trimble.

'I'd like to see just how they fare,' Miss Rebecca Wright continued. 'They give their consent to goin' on the town because they knew they'd got to be dependent, an' so they felt 't would come easier for all than for a few to help 'em. They acted real dignified an' right-minded, contrary to what most do in such cases, but they was dreadful anxious to see who would bid 'em off, town-meeting day; they did so hope 't would be somebody right in the village. I just sat down an' cried good when I found Abel Janes's folks had got hold of 'em. They always had the name of bein' slack an' poor-spirited, an' they did it just for what they got out o' the town. The selectmen this last year ain't what we have had. I hope they've been considerate about the Bray girls.'

'I should have be'n more considerate about fetchin' of you over,' apologized Mrs Trimble. 'I've got my horse, an' you're lame-footed; 't is too far for you to come. But time does slip away with busy folks, an' I forgit a good deal I ought to remember.'

'There's nobody more considerate than you be,' protested Miss Rebecca Wright.

Mrs Trimble made no answer, but took out her whip and gently touched the sorrel horse, who walked considerably faster, but did not think it worth while to trot. It was a long, round-about way to the house, farther down the road and up a lane.

'I never had any opinion of the Bray girls' father, leavin' 'em as he did,' said Mrs Trimble.

'He was much praised in his time, though there was always some said his early life hadn't been up to the mark,' explained her companion. 'He was a great favorite of our then preacher, the Reverend Daniel Longbrother. They did a good deal for the parish, but they did it their own way. Deacon Bray was one that did his part in the repairs without urging. You know 't was in his time the first repairs was made, when they got out the old soundin'-board an' them handsome square pews. It cost an awful sight o' money, too. They hadn't done payin' up that debt when they set to alter it again an' git the walls frescoed. My grandmother was one that always spoke her mind right out, an' she was dreadful opposed to breakin' up the square pews where she'd always set. They was countin' up what 't would cost in parish meetin', an' she riz right up an' said 't wouldn't cost nothin' to let 'em stay, an' there wa'n't a house carpenter left in the parish that could do such nice work, an' time would come when the great-grandchildren would give their eye-teeth to have the old meetin'-house look just as it did then. But haul the inside to pieces they would and did.'

'There come to be a real fight over it, didn't there?' agreed Mrs Trimble soothingly. 'Well, 't wa'n't good taste. I remember the old house well. I come here as a child to visit a cousin o' mother's, an' Mr Trimble's folks was neighbors, an' we was drawed to each other then, young 's we was. Mr Trimble spoke of it many's the time, – that first time he ever see me, in a leghorn hat* with a feather; 't was one that mother had, an' pressed over.'

'When I think of them old sermons that used to be preached in that old meetin'-house of all, I'm glad it's altered over, so's not to remind folks,' said Miss Rebecca Wright, after a suitable pause. 'Them old brimstone discourses, you know, Mis' Trimble. Preachers is far more reasonable, nowadays. Why, I set an' thought, last Sabbath, as I listened, that if old Mr Longbrother an' Deacon Bray could hear the difference they'd crack the ground over 'em like pole beans, an' come right up 'long side their headstones.'

Mrs Trimble laughed heartily, and shook the reins three or four times by way of emphasis. 'There's no gitting round you,' she said, much pleased. 'I should think Deacon Bray would want to rise, any way, if 't was so he could, an' knew how his poor girls was farin'. A man ought to provide for his folks he's got to leave behind him, specially if they're women. To be sure, they had their little home; but we've seen how, with all their industrious ways, they hadn't means to keep it. I s'pose he thought he'd got time enough to lay by, when he give so generous in collections; but he didn't lay by, an' there they be. He might have took lessons from the squirrels: even them little wild creatur's makes them their winter hoards, an' menfolks ought to know enough if squirrels does. "Be just before you are generous:"* that's what was always set for the B's in the copybooks, when I was to school, and it often runs through my mind.'

'"As for man, his days are as grass,"* – that was for A; the two go well together,' added Miss Rebecca Wright soberly. 'My good gracious, ain't this a starved-lookin' place? It makes me ache to think them nice Bray girls has to brook it here.'

The sorrel horse, though somewhat puzzled by an unexpected deviation from his homeward way, willingly came to a stand by the gnawed corner of the door-yard fence, which evidently served as hitching-place. Two or three ragged old hens were picking about the yard, and at last a face appeared at the kitchen window, tied up in a handkerchief, as if it were a case of toothache. By the time our friends reached the side door next this window, Mrs Janes came disconsolately to open it for them, shutting it again as soon as possible, though the air felt more chilly inside the house.

'Take seats,' said Mrs Janes briefly. 'You'll have to see me just as I be. I have been suffering these four days with the ague, and everything to do. Mr Janes is to court, on the jury. 'T was inconvenient to spare him. I should be pleased to have you lay off your things.'

Comfortable Mrs Trimble looked about the cheerless kitchen, and could not think of anything to say; so she smiled blandly and shook her head in answer to the invitation. 'We'll just set a few minutes with you, to pass the time o' day, an' then we must go in an' have a word with the Miss Brays, bein' old acquaintance. It ain't been so we could git to call on 'em before. I don't know 's you're acquainted with Miss R'becca Wright. She's been out of town a good deal.'

'I heard she was stopping over to Plainfields with her brother's folks,' replied Mrs Janes, rocking herself with irregular motion, as she sat close to the stove. 'Got back some time in the fall, I believe?'

'Yes'm,' said Miss Rebecca, with an undue sense of guilt and conviction. 'We've been to the installation over to the East Parish, an' thought we'd stop in; we took this road home to see if 't was any better. How is the Miss Brays gettin' on?'

'They're well's common,' answered Mrs Janes grudgingly. 'I was put out with Mr Janes for fetchin' of 'em here, with all I've got to do, an' I own I was kind o' surly to 'em 'long to the first of it. He gits the money from the town, an' it helps him out; but he bid 'em off for five dollars a month, an' we can't do much for 'em at no such price as that. I went an' dealt with the selec'men, an' made 'em promise to find their firewood an' some other things extra. They was glad to get rid o' the matter the fourth time I went, an' would ha' promised 'most anything. But Mr Janes don't keep me half the time in oven-wood, he's off so much, an' we was cramped o' room, any way. I have to store things up garrit a good deal, an' that keeps me trampin' right through their room. I do the best for 'em I can, Mis' Trimble, but 't ain't so easy for me as 't is for you, with all your means to do with.'

The poor woman looked pinched and miserable herself, though it was evident that she had no gift at house or home keeping. Mrs Trimble's heart was wrung with pain, as she thought of the unwelcome inmates of such a place; but she held her peace bravely, while Miss Rebecca again gave some brief information in regard to the installation.

'You go right up them back stairs,' the hostess directed at last. 'I'm glad some o' you church folks has seen fit to come an' visit 'em. There ain't been nobody here this long spell, an' they've aged a sight since they come. They always send down a taste out of your baskets, Mis' Trimble, an' I relish it, I tell you. I'll shut the door after you, if you don't object. I feel every draught o' cold air.'

'I've always heard she was a great hand to make a poor mouth. Wa'n't she from somewheres up Parsley way?' whispered Miss Rebecca, as they stumbled in the half-light.

'Poor meechin'* body, wherever she come from,' replied Mrs Trimble, as she knocked at the door.

There was silence for a moment after this unusual sound; then one of the Bray sisters opened the door. The eager guests stared into a small, low room, brown with age, and gray, too, as if former dust and cobwebs could not be made wholly to disappear. The two elderly women who stood there looked like captives. Their withered faces wore a look of apprehension, and the room itself was more bare and plain than was fitting to their evident refinement of character and self-respect. There was an uncovered small table in the middle of the floor, with some crackers on a plate; and, for some reason or other, this added a great deal to the general desolation.

But Miss Ann Bray, the elder sister, who carried her right arm in a sling, with piteously drooping fingers, gazed at the visitors with radiant joy. She had not seen them arrive.

The one window gave only the view at the back of the house, across the fields, and their coming was indeed a surprise. The next minute she was laughing and crying together. 'Oh, sister!' she said, 'if here ain't our dear Mis' Trimble! – an' my heart o' goodness, 't is 'Becca Wright, too! What dear good creatur's you be! I've felt all day as if something good was goin' to happen, an' was just sayin' to myself 't was most sundown now, but I wouldn't let on to Mandany I'd give up hope quite yet. You see, the scissors stuck in the floor this very mornin' an' it's always a reliable sign. There, I've got to kiss ye both again!'

'I don't know where we can all set,' lamented sister Mandana. 'There ain't but the one chair an' the bed; t' other chair's too rickety; an' we've been promised another these ten days; but first they've forgot it, an' next Mis' Janes can't spare it, – one excuse an' another. I am goin' to git a stump o' wood an' nail a board on to it, when I can git outdoor again,' said Mandana, in a plaintive voice. 'There, I ain't goin' to complain o' nothin', now you've come,' she added; and the guests sat down, Mrs Trimble, as was proper, in the one chair.

'We've sat on the bed many's the time with you, 'Becca, an' talked over our girl nonsense, ain't we? You know where 't was – in the little back bedroom we had when we was girls, an' used to peek out at our beaux through the strings o' mornin'-glories,' laughed Ann Bray delightedly, her thin face shining more and more with joy. 'I brought some o' them mornin'-glory seeds along when we come away, we'd raised 'em so many years; an' we got 'em started all right, but the hens found 'em out. I declare I chased them poor hens, foolish as 't was; but the mornin'-glories I'd counted on a sight to remind me o' home. You see, our debts was so large, after my long sickness an' all, that we didn't feel 't was right to keep back anything we could help from the auction.'

It was impossible for any one to speak for a moment or two; the sisters felt their own uprooted condition afresh, and their guests for the first time really comprehended the piteous contrast between that neat little village house, which now seemed a palace of comfort, and this cold, unpainted upper room in the remote Janes farmhouse. It was an unwelcome thought to Mrs Trimble that the well-to-do town of Hampden could provide no better for its poor than this, and her round face flushed with resentment and the shame of personal responsibility. 'The girls shall be well settled in the village before another winter, if I pay their board myself,' she made an inward resolution, and took another almost tearful look at the broken stove, the miserable bed, and the sisters' one hair-covered trunk, on which Mandana was sitting. But the poor place was filled with a golden spirit of hospitality.

Rebecca was again discoursing eloquently of the installation; it was so much easier to speak of general subjects, and the sisters had evidently been longing to hear some news. Since the late summer they had not been to church, and presently Mrs Trimble asked the reason.

'Now, don't you go to pouring out our woes, Mandy!' begged little old Ann, looking shy and almost girlish, and as if she insisted upon playing that life was still all before them and all pleasure. 'Don't you go to spoilin' their visit with our complaints! They know well's we do that changes must come, an' we'd been so wonted to our home things that this come hard at first; but then they felt for us, I know just as well's can be. 'T will soon be summer again, an' 't is real pleasant right out in the fields here, when there ain't too hot a spell. I've got to know a sight o' singin' birds since we come.'

'Give me the folks I've always known,' sighed the younger sister, who looked older than Miss Ann, and less even-tempered. 'You may have your birds, if you want 'em. I do re'lly long to go to meetin' an' see folks go by up the aisle. Now, I will speak of it, Ann, whatever you say. We need, each of us, a pair o' good stout shoes an' rubbers, – ours are all wore out; an' we've asked an' asked, an' they never think to bring 'em, an'' –

Poor old Mandana, on the trunk, covered her face with her arms and sobbed aloud. The elder sister stood over her, and patted her on the thin shoulder like a child, and tried to comfort her. It crossed Mrs Trimble's mind that it was not the first time one had wept and the other had comforted. The sad scene must have been repeated many times in that long, drear winter. She would see them forever after in her mind as fixed as a picture, and her own tears fell fast.

'You didn't see Mis' Janes's cunning little boy, the next one to the baby, did you?' asked Ann Bray, turning round quickly at last, and going cheerfully on with the conversation. 'Now, hush,

Mandy, dear; they'll think you're childish! He's a dear, friendly little creatur', an' likes to stay with us a good deal, though we feel 's if it was too cold for him, now we are waitin' to get us more wood.'

'When I think of the acres o' woodland in this town!' groaned Rebecca Wright. 'I believe I'm goin' to preach next Sunday, 'stead o' the minister, an' I'll make the sparks fly. I've always heard the saying, "What's everybody's business is nobody's business," an' I've come to believe it.'

'Now, don't you, 'Becca. You've happened on a kind of a poor time with us, but we've got more belongings than you see here, an' a good large cluset, where we can store those things there ain't room to have about. You an' Mis' Trimble have happened on a kind of poor day, you know. Soon's I git me some stout shoes an' rubbers, as Mandy says, I can fetch home plenty o' little dry boughs o' pine; you remember I was always a great hand to roam in the woods? If we could only have a front room, so 't we could look out on the road an' see passin', an' was shod for meetin', I don' know's we should complain. Now we're just goin' to give you what we've got, an' make out with a good welcome. We make more tea 'n we want in the mornin', an' then let the fire go down, since 't has been so mild. We've got a *good* cluset' (disappearing as she spoke), 'an' I know this to be good tea, 'cause it's some o' yourn, Mis' Trimble. An' here's our sprigged chiny cups that R'becca knows by sight, if Mis' Trimble don't. We kep' out four of 'em, an' put the even half dozen with the rest of the auction stuff. I've often wondered who'd got 'em, but I never asked, for fear 't would be somebody that would distress us. They was mother's, you know.'

The four cups were poured, and the little table pushed to the bed, where Rebecca Wright still sat, and Mandana, wiping her eyes, came and joined her. Mrs Trimble sat in her chair at the end, and Ann trotted about the room in pleased content for a while, and in and out of the closet, as if she still had much to do; then she came and stood opposite Mrs Trimble. She was very short and small, and there was no painful sense of her being obliged to stand. The four cups were not quite full of cold tea, but there was a clean old tablecloth folded double, and a plate with three pairs of crackers neatly piled, and a small – it must be owned, a very small – piece of hard white cheese. Then, for a treat, in a glass dish, there was a little preserved peach, the last – Miss Rebecca knew it instinctively – of the household stores brought from their old home. It was very sugary, this bit of peach; and as she helped her guests and sister Mandy, Miss Ann Bray said, half unconsciously, as she often had said with less reason in the old days, 'Our preserves ain't so good as usual this year; this is beginning to candy.' Both the guests protested, while Rebecca added that the taste of it carried her back, and made her feel young again. The Brays had always managed to keep one or two peach-trees alive in their corner of a garden. 'I've been keeping this preserve for a treat,' said her friend. 'I'm glad to have you eat some, 'Becca. Last summer I often wished you was home an' could come an' see us, 'stead o' being away off to Plainfields.'

The crackers did not taste too dry. Miss Ann took the last of the peach on her own cracker; there could not have been quite a small spoonful, after the others were helped, but she asked them first if they would not have some more. Then there was a silence, and in the silence a wave of tender feeling rose high in the hearts of the four elderly women. At this moment the setting sun flooded the poor plain room with light; the unpainted wood was all of a golden-brown, and Ann Bray, with her gray hair and aged face, stood at the head of the table in a kind of aureole. Mrs Trimble's face was all aquiver as she looked at her; she thought of the text about two or three being gathered together, and was half afraid.

'I believe we ought to 've asked Mis' Janes if she wouldn't come up,' said Ann. 'She's real good feelin', but she's had it very hard, an gits discouraged. I can't find that she's ever had anything real pleasant to look back to, as we have. There, next time we'll make a good heartenin' time for her too.'

The sorrel horse had taken a long nap by the gnawed fence-rail, and the cool air after sundown made him impatient to be gone. The two friends jolted homeward in the gathering darkness, through the stiffening mud, and neither Mrs Trimble nor Rebecca Wright said a word until they were out of sight as well as out of sound of the Janes house. Time must elapse before they could reach a more familiar part of the road and resume conversation on its natural level.

'I consider myself to blame,' insisted Mrs Trimble at last. 'I haven't no words of accusation for nobody else, an' I ain't one to take comfort in calling names to the board o' selec'*men*. I make no reproaches, an' I take it all on my own shoulders; but I'm goin' to stir about me, I tell you! I shall begin early tomorrow. They're goin' back to their own house, – it's been standin' empty all winter, – an' the town's goin' to give 'em the rent an' what firewood they need; it won't come to more than the board's payin' out now. An' you an' me'll take this same horse an' wagon, an' ride an' go afoot by turns, an' git means enough together to buy back their furniture an' whatever was sold at that plaguy auction; an' then we'll put it all back, an' tell 'em they've got to move to a new place, an' just carry 'em right back again where they come from. An' don't you never tell, R'becca, but here I be a widow woman, layin' up what I make from my farm for nobody knows who, an' I'm goin' to do for them Bray girls all I'm a mind to. I should be sca't to wake up in heaven, an' hear anybody there ask how the Bray girls was. Don't talk to me about the town o' Hampden, an' don't ever let me hear the name o' town poor! I'm ashamed to go home an' see what's set out for supper. I wish I'd brought 'em right along.'

'I was goin' to ask if we couldn't git the new doctor to go up an' do somethin' for poor Ann's arm,' said Miss Rebecca. 'They say he's very smart. If she could get so's to braid straw or hook rugs again, she'd soon be earnin' a little somethin'. An' may be he could do somethin' for Mandy's eyes. They did use to live so neat an' ladylike. Somehow I couldn't speak to tell 'em there that 't was I bought them six best cups an' saucers, time of the auction; they went very low, as everything else did, an' I thought I could save it some other way. They shall have 'em back an' welcome. You're real whole-hearted, Mis' Trimble. I expect Ann'll be sayin' that her father's child'n wa'n't goin' to be left desolate, an' that all the bread he cast on the water's comin' back through you.'

'I don't care what she says, dear creatur'!' exclaimed Mrs Trimble. 'I'm full o' regrets I took time for that installation, an' set there seepin' in a lot o' talk this whole day long, except for its kind of bringin' us to the Bray girls. I wish to my heart 't was tomorrow mornin' a'ready, an' I a-startin' for the selec'*men*.'

CHARLOTTE PERKINS GILMAN

The Yellow Wallpaper

1892

It is very seldom that mere ordinary people like John and myself secure ancestral halls for the summer.

A colonial mansion, a hereditary estate, I would say a haunted house, and reach the height of romantic felicity – but that would be asking too much of fate!

Still I will proudly declare that there is something queer about it.

Else, why should it be let so cheaply? And why have stood so long untenanted?

John laughs at me, of course, but one expects that in marriage.

John is practical in the extreme. He has no patience with faith, an intense horror of superstition, and he scoffs openly at any talk of things not to be felt and seen and put down in figures.

John is a physician, and *perhaps* – (I would not say it to a living soul, of course, but this is dead paper and a great relief to my mind) – *perhaps* that is one reason I do not get well faster.

You see he does not believe I am sick!

And what can one do?

If a physician of high standing, and one's own husband, assures friends and relatives that there is really nothing the matter with one but temporary nervous depression – a slight hysterical tendency – what is one to do?

My brother is also a physician, and also of high standing, and he says the same thing.

So I take phosphates or phosphites – whichever it is, and tonics, and journeys, and air, and exercise, and am absolutely forbidden to 'work' until I am well again.

Personally, I disagree with their ideas.

Personally, I believe that congenial work, with excitement and change, would do me good.

But what is one to do?

I did write for a while in spite of them; but it *does* exhaust me a good deal – having to be so sly about it, or else meet with heavy opposition.

I sometimes fancy that in my condition if I had less opposition and more society and stimulus – but John says the very worst thing I can do is to think about my condition, and I confess it always makes me feel bad.

So I will let it alone and talk about the house.

The most beautiful place! It is quite alone, standing well back from the road, quite three miles from the village. It makes me think of English places that you read about, for there are hedges and walls and gates that lock, and lots of separate little houses for the gardeners and people.

There is a *delicious* garden! I never saw such a garden – large and shady, full of box-bordered paths, and lined with long grape-covered arbors with seats under them.

There were greenhouses, too, but they are all broken now.

There was some legal trouble, I believe, something about the heirs and coheirs; anyhow, the place has been empty for years.

That spoils my ghostliness, I am afraid, but I don't care – there is something strange about the house – I can feel it.

I even said so to John one moonlight evening, but he said what I felt was a *draught*, and shut the window.

I get unreasonably angry with John sometimes. I'm sure I never used to be so sensitive. I think it is due to this nervous condition.

But John says if I feel so, I shall neglect proper self-control; so I take pains to control myself – before him, at least, and that makes me very tired.

I don't like our room a bit. I wanted one downstairs that opened on the piazza and had roses all over the window, and such pretty old-fashioned chintz hangings! but John would not hear of it.

He said there was only one window and not room for two beds, and no near room for him if he took another.

He is very careful and loving, and hardly lets me stir without special direction.

I have a schedule prescription for each hour in the day; he takes all care from me, and so I feel basely ungrateful not to value it more.

He said we came here solely on my account, that I was to have perfect rest and all the air I could get. 'Your exercise depends on your strength, my dear,' said he, 'and your food somewhat on your appetite; but air you can absorb all the time.' So we took the nursery at the top of the house.

It is a big, airy room, the whole floor nearly, with windows that look all ways, and air and sunshine galore. It was nursery first and then playroom and gymnasium, I should judge; for the windows are barred for little children, and there are rings and things in the walls.

The paint and paper look as if a boys' school had used it. It is stripped off – the paper – in great patches all around the head of my bed, about as far as I can reach, and in a great place on the other side of the room low down. I never saw a worse paper in my life.

One of those sprawling flamboyant patterns committing every artistic sin.

It is dull enough to confuse the eye in following, pronounced enough to constantly irritate and provoke study, and when you follow the lame uncertain curves for a little distance they suddenly commit suicide – plunge off at outrageous angles, destroy themselves in unheard of contradictions.

The color is repellent, almost revolting; a smouldering unclean yellow, strangely faded by the slow-turning sunlight.

It is a dull yet lurid orange in some places, a sickly sulphur tint in others.

No wonder the children hated it! I should hate it myself if I had to live in this room long.

There comes John, and I must put this away, – he hates to have me write a word.

We have been here two weeks, and I haven't felt like writing before, since that first day.

I am sitting by the window now, up in this atrocious nursery, and there is nothing to hinder my writing as much as I please, save lack of strength.

John is away all day, and even some nights when his cases are serious.

I am glad my case is not serious!

But these nervous troubles are dreadfully depressing.

John does not know how much I really suffer. He knows there is no *reason* to suffer, and that satisfies him.

Of course it is only nervousness. It does weigh on me so not to do my duty in any way!

I meant to be such a help to John, such a real rest and comfort, and here I am a comparative burden already!

Nobody would believe what an effort it is to do what little I am able, – to dress and entertain, and order things.

It is fortunate Mary is so good with the baby. Such a dear baby!

And yet I *cannot* be with him, it makes me so nervous.

I suppose John never was nervous in his life. He laughs at me so about this wallpaper!

At first he meant to repaper the room, but afterwards he said that I was letting it get the better of me, and that nothing was worse for a nervous patient than to give way to such fancies.

He said that after the wallpaper was changed it would be the heavy bedstead, and then the barred windows, and then that gate at the head of the stairs, and so on.

'You know the place is doing you good,' he said, 'and really, dear, I don't care to renovate the house just for a three months' rental.'

'Then do let us go downstairs,' I said, 'there are such pretty rooms there.'

Then he took me in his arms and called me a blessed little goose, and said he would go down to the cellar, if I wished, and have it whitewashed into the bargain.

But he is right enough about the beds and windows and things.

It is an airy and comfortable room as any one need wish, and, of course, I would not be so silly as to make him uncomfortable just for a whim.

I'm really getting quite fond of the big room, all but that horrid paper.

Out of one window I can see the garden, those mysterious deepshaded arbors, the riotous old-fashioned flowers, and bushes and gnarly trees.

Out of another I get a lovely view of the bay and a little private wharf belonging to the estate. There is a beautiful shaded lane that runs down there from the house. I always fancy I see people walking in these numerous paths and arbors, but John has cautioned me not to give way to fancy in the least. He says that with my imaginative power and habit of story-making, a nervous weakness like mine is sure to lead to all manner of excited fancies, and that I ought to use my will and good sense to check the tendency. So I try.

I think sometimes that if I were only well enough to write a little it would relieve the press of ideas and rest me.

But I find I get pretty tired when I try.

It is so discouraging not to have any advice and companionship about my work. When I get really well, John says we will ask Cousin Henry and Julia down for a long visit; but he says he would as soon put fireworks in my pillow-case as to let me have those stimulating people about now.

I wish I could get well faster.

But I must not think about that. This paper looks to me as if it *knew* what a vicious influence it had!

There is a recurrent spot where the pattern lolls like a broken neck and two bulbous eyes stare at you upside down.

I get positively angry with the impertinence of it and the everlastingness. Up and down and sideways they crawl, and those absurd, unblinking eyes are everywhere. There is one place where two breadths didn't match, and the eyes go all up and down the line, one a little higher than the other.

I never saw so much expression in an inanimate thing before, and we all know how much expression they have! I used to lie awake as a child and get more entertainment and terror out of blank walls and plain furniture than most children could find in a toy-store.

I remember what a kindly wink the knobs of our big, old bureau used to have, and there was one chair that always seemed like a strong friend.

I used to feel that if any of the other things looked too fierce I could always hop into that chair and be safe.

The furniture in this room is no worse than inharmonious, however, for we had to bring it all from downstairs. I suppose when this was used as a playroom they had to take the nursery things out, and no wonder! I never saw such ravages as the children have made here.

The wallpaper, as I said before, is torn off in spots, and it sticketh closer than a brother – they must have had perseverance as well as hatred.

Then the floor is scratched and gouged and splintered, the plaster itself is dug out here and there, and this great heavy bed which is all we found in the room, looks as if it had been through the wars.

But I don't mind it a bit – only the paper.

There comes John's sister. Such a dear girl as she is, and so careful of me! I must not let her find me writing.

She is a perfect and enthusiastic housekeeper, and hopes for no better profession. I verily believe she thinks it is the writing which made me sick!

But I can write when she is out, and see her a long way off from these windows.

There is one that commands the road, a lovely shaded winding road, and one that just looks off over the country. A lovely country, too, full of great elms and velvet meadows.

This wallpaper has a kind of sub-pattern in a different shade, a particularly irritating one, for you can only see it in certain lights, and not clearly then.

But in the places where it isn't faded and where the sun is just so – I can see a strange, provoking, formless sort of figure, that seems to skulk about behind that silly and conspicuous front design.

There's sister on the stairs!

Well, the Fourth of July is over! The people are all gone and I am tired out. John thought it might do me good to see a little company, so we just had Mother and Nellie and the children down for a week.

Of course I didn't do a thing. Jennie sees to everything now.

But it tired me all the same.

John says if I don't pick up faster he shall send me to Weir Mitchell in the fall.

But I don't want to go there at all. I had a friend who was in his hands once, and she says he is just like John and my brother, only more so!

Besides, it is such an undertaking to go so far.

I don't feel as if it was worth while to turn my hand over for anything, and I'm getting dreadfully fretful and querulous.

I cry at nothing, and cry most of the time.

Of course I don't when John is here, or anybody else, but when I am alone.

And I am alone a good deal just now. John is kept in town very often by serious cases, and Jennie is good and lets me alone when I want her to.

So I walk a little in the garden or down that lovely lane, sit on the porch under the roses, and lie down up here a good deal.

I'm getting really fond of the room in spite of the wallpaper. Perhaps *because* of the wallpaper.

It dwells in my mind so!

I lie here on this great immovable bed – it is nailed down, I believe – and follow that pattern about by the hour. It is as good as gymnastics, I assure you. I start, we'll say, at the bottom, down in the corner over there where it has not been touched, and I determine for the thousandth time that I *will* follow that pointless pattern to some sort of a conclusion.

I know a little of the principle of design, and I know this thing was not arranged on any laws of radiation, or alternation, or repetition, or symmetry, or anything else that I ever heard of.

It is repeated, of course, by the breadths, but not otherwise.

Looked at in one way each breadth stands alone, the bloated curves and flourishes – a kind of 'debased Romanesque'* with delirium tremens* – go waddling up and down in isolated columns of fatuity.

But, on the other hand, they connect diagonally, and the sprawling outlines run off in great slanting waves of optic horror, like a lot of wallowing seaweeds in full chase.

The whole thing goes horizontally, too, at least it seems so, and I exhaust myself in trying to distinguish the order of its going in that direction.

They have used a horizontal breadth for a frieze, and that adds wonderfully to the confusion.

There is one end of the room where it is almost intact, and there, when the crosslights fade and the low sun shines directly upon it, I can almost fancy radiation after all, – the interminable grotesques seem to form around a common centre and rush off in headlong plunges of equal distraction.

It makes me tired to follow it. I will take a nap I guess.

I don't know why I should write this.

I don't want to.

I don't feel able.

And I know John would think it absurd. But I *must* say what I feel and think in some way – it is such a relief!

But the effort is getting to be greater than the relief.

Half the time now I am awfully lazy, and lie down ever so much.

John says I mustn't lose my strength, and has me take cod liver oil and lots of tonics and things, to say nothing of ale and wine and rare meat.

Dear John! He loves me very dearly, and hates to have me sick. I tried to have a real earnest reasonable talk with him the other day, and tell him how I wish he would let me go and make a visit to Cousin Henry and Julia.

But he said I wasn't able to go, nor able to stand it after I got there; and I did not make out a very good case for myself, for I was crying before I had finished.

It is getting to be a great effort for me to think straight. Just this nervous weakness I suppose.

And dear John gathered me up in his arms, and just carried me upstairs and laid me on the bed, and sat by me and read to me till it tired my head.

He said I was his darling and his comfort and all he had, and that I must take care of myself for his sake, and keep well.

He says no one but myself can help me out of it, that I must use my will and self-control and not let any silly fancies run away with me.

There's one comfort, the baby is well and happy, and does not have to occupy this nursery with the horrid wallpaper.

If we had not used it, that blessed child would have! What a fortunate escape! Why, I wouldn't have a child of mine, an impressionable little thing, live in such a room for worlds.

I never thought of it before, but it is lucky that John kept me here after all, I can stand it so much easier than a baby, you see.

Of course I never mention it to them any more – I am too wise, – but I keep watch of it all the same.

There are things in that paper that nobody knows but me, or ever will.

Behind that outside pattern the dim shapes get clearer every day.

It is always the same shape, only very numerous.

And it is like a woman stooping down and creeping about behind that pattern. I don't like it a bit. I wonder – I begin to think – I wish John would take me away from here!

It is so hard to talk with John about my case, because he is so wise, and because he loves me so.

But I tried it last night.

It was moonlight. The moon shines in all around just as the sun does.

I hate to see it sometimes, it creeps so slowly, and always comes in by one window or another.

John was asleep and I hated to waken him, so I kept still and watched the moonlight on that undulating wallpaper till I felt creepy.

The faint figure behind seemed to shake the pattern, just as if she wanted to get out.

I got up softly and went to feel and see if the paper *did* move, and when I came back John was awake.

'What is it, little girl?' he said. 'Don't go walking about like that – you'll get cold.'

I thought it was a good time to talk, so I told him that I really was not gaining here, and that I wished he would take me away.

'Why darling!' said he, 'our lease will be up in three weeks, and I can't see how to leave before.

'The repairs are not done at home, and I cannot possibly leave town just now. Of course if you were in any danger, I could and would, but you really are better, dear, whether you can see it or not. I am a doctor, dear, and I know. You are gaining flesh and color, your appetite is better, I feel really much easier about you.'

'I don't weigh a bit more,' said I, 'nor as much; and my appetite may be better in the evening when you are here, but it is worse in the morning when you are away!'

'Bless her little heart!' said he with a big hug, 'she shall be as sick as she pleases! But now let's improve the shining hours by going to sleep, and talk about it in the morning!'

'And you won't go away?' I asked gloomily.

'Why, how can I, dear? It is only three weeks more and then we will take a nice little trip of a few days while Jennie is getting the house ready. Really dear you are better!'

'Better in body perhaps – ' I began, and stopped short, for he sat up straight and looked at me with such a stern, reproachful look that I could not say another word.

'My darling,' said he, 'I beg of you, for my sake and for our child's sake, as well as for your own, that you will never for one instant let that idea enter your mind! There is nothing so dangerous, so fascinating, to a temperament like yours. It is a false and foolish fancy. Can you not trust me as a physician when I tell you so?'

So of course I said no more on that score, and we went to sleep before long. He thought I was asleep first, but I wasn't, and lay there for hours trying to decide whether that front pattern and the back pattern really did move together or separately.

On a pattern like this, by daylight, there is a lack of sequence, a defiance of law, that is a constant irritant to a normal mind.

The color is hideous enough, and unreliable enough, and infuriating enough, but the pattern is torturing.

You think you have mastered it, but just as you get well underway in following, it turns a back-somersault and there you are. It slaps you in the face, knocks you down, and tramples upon you. It is like a bad dream.

The outside pattern is a florid arabesque, reminding one of a fungus. If you can imagine a toadstool in joints, an interminable string of toadstools, budding and sprouting in endless convolutions – why, that is something like it.

That is, sometimes!

There is one marked peculiarity about this paper, a thing nobody seems to notice but myself, and that is that it changes as the light changes.

When the sun shoots in through the east window – I always watch for that first long, straight ray – it changes so quickly that I never can quite believe it.

That is why I watch it always.

By moonlight – the moon shines in all night when there is a moon – I wouldn't know it was the same paper.

At night in any kind of light, in twilight, candle light, lamplight, and worst of all by moonlight, it becomes bars! The outside pattern I mean, and the woman behind it is as plain as can be.

I didn't realize for a long time what the thing was that showed behind, that dim sub-pattern, but now I am quite sure it is a woman.

By daylight she is subdued, quiet. I fancy it is the pattern that keeps her so still. It is so puzzling. It keeps me quiet by the hour.

I lie down ever so much now. John says it is good for me, and to sleep all I can.

Indeed he started the habit by making me lie down for an hour after each meal.

It is a very bad habit I am convinced, for you see I don't sleep.

And that cultivates deceit, for I don't tell them I'm awake – O no!

The fact is I am getting a little afraid of John.

He seems very queer sometimes, and even Jennie has an inexplicable look.

It strikes me occasionally, just as a scientific hypothesis, – that perhaps it is the paper!

I have watched John when he did not know I was looking, and come into the room suddenly on the most innocent excuses, and I've caught him several times *looking at the paper*! And Jennie too. I caught Jennie with her hand on it once.

She didn't know I was in the room, and when I asked her in a quiet, a very quiet voice, with the most restrained manner possible, what she was doing with the paper – she turned around as if she had been caught stealing, and looked quite angry – asked me why I should frighten her so!

Then she said that the paper stained everything it touched, that she had found yellow smooches on all my clothes and John's, and she wished we would be more careful!

Did not that sound innocent? But I know she was studying that pattern, and I am determined that nobody shall find it out but myself!

Life is very much more exciting now than it used to be. You see I have something more to expect, to look forward to, to watch. I really do eat better, and am more quiet than I was.

John is so pleased to see me improve! He laughed a little the other day, and said I seemed to be flourishing in spite of my wallpaper.

I turned it off with a laugh. I had no intention of telling him it was *because* of the wallpaper – he would make fun of me. He might even want to take me away.

I don't want to leave now until I have found it out. There is a week more, and I think that will be enough.

I'm feeling ever so much better! I don't sleep much at night, for it is so interesting to watch developments; but I sleep a good deal in the daytime.

In the daytime it is tiresome and perplexing.

There are always new shoots on the fungus, and new shades of yellow all over it. I cannot keep count of them, though I have tried conscientiously.

It is the strangest yellow, that wallpaper! It makes me think of all the yellow things I ever saw – not beautiful ones like buttercups, but old foul, bad yellow things.

But there is something else about that paper – the smell! I noticed it the moment we came into the room, but with so much air and sun it was not bad. Now we have had a week of fog and rain, and whether the windows are open or not, the smell is here.

It creeps all over the house.

I find it hovering in the dining-room, skulking in the parlor, hiding in the hall, lying in wait for me on the stairs.

It gets into my hair.

Even when I go to ride, if I turn my head suddenly and surprise it – there is that smell!

Such a peculiar odor, too! I have spent hours in trying to analyze it, to find what it smelled like.

It is not bad – at first, and very gentle, but quite the subtlest, most enduring odor I ever met.

In this damp weather it is awful, I wake up in the night and find it hanging over me.

It used to disturb me at first. I thought seriously of burning the house – to reach the smell.

But now I am used to it. The only thing I can think of that it is like is the *color* of the paper! A yellow smell.

There is a very funny mark on this wall, low down, near the mopboard. A streak that runs round the room. It goes behind every piece of furniture, except the bed, a long, straight, even *smooch*, as if it had been rubbed over and over.

I wonder how it was done and who did it, and what they did it for. Round and round and round – round and round and round – it makes me dizzy!

I really have discovered something at last.

Through watching so much at night, when it changes so, I have finally found out.

The front pattern *does* move – and no wonder! The woman behind shakes it!

Sometimes I think there are a great many women behind, and sometimes only one, and she crawls around fast, and her crawling shakes it all over.

Then in the very bright spots she keeps still, and in the very shady spots she just takes hold of the bars and shakes them hard.

And she is all the time trying to climb through. But nobody could climb through that pattern – it strangles so; I think that is why it has so many heads.

They get through, and then the pattern strangles them off and turns them upside down, and makes their eyes white!

If those heads were covered or taken off it would not be half so bad.

I think that woman gets out in the daytime!

And I'll tell you why – privately – I've seen her!

I can see her out of every one of my windows!

It is the same woman, I know, for she is always creeping, and most women do not creep by daylight.

I see her on that long road under the trees, creeping along, and when a carriage comes she hides under the blackberry vines.

I don't blame her a bit. It must be very humiliating to be caught creeping by daylight!

I always lock the door when I creep by daylight. I can't do it at night, for I know John would suspect something at once.

And John is so queer now, that I don't want to irritate him. I wish he would take another room! Besides, I don't want anybody to get that woman out at night but myself.

I often wonder if I could see her out of all the windows at once.

But, turn as fast as I can, I can only see out of one at one time.

And though I always see her, she *may* be able to creep faster than I can turn!

I have watched her sometimes away off in the open country, creeping as fast as a cloud shadow in a high wind.

If only that top pattern could be gotten off from the under one! I mean to try it, little by little.

I have found out another funny thing, but I shan't tell it this time! It does not do to trust people too much.

There are only two more days to get this paper off, and I believe John is beginning to notice. I don't like the look in his eyes.

And I heard him ask Jennie a lot of professional questions about me. She had a very good report to give.

She said I slept a good deal in the daytime.

John knows I don't sleep very well at night, for all I'm so quiet!

He asked me all sorts of questions, too, and pretended to be very loving and kind.

As if I couldn't see through him!

Still, I don't wonder he acts so, sleeping under this paper for three months.

It only interests me, but I feel sure John and Jennie are secretly affected by it.

Hurrah! This is the last day, but it is enough. John to stay in town over night, and won't be out until this evening.

Jennie wanted to sleep with me – the sly thing! but I told her I should undoubtedly rest better for a night all alone.

That was clever, for really I wasn't alone a bit! As soon as it was moonlight and that poor thing began to crawl and shake the pattern, I got up and ran to help her.

I pulled and she shook, I shook and she pulled, and before morning we had peeled off yards of that paper.

A strip about as high as my head and half around the room.

And then when the sun came and that awful pattern began to laugh at me, I declared I would finish it today!

We go away tomorrow, and they are moving all my furniture down again to leave things as they were before.

Jennie looked at the wall in amazement, but I told her merrily that I did it out of pure spite at the vicious thing.

She laughed and said she wouldn't mind doing it herself, but I must not get tired.

How she betrayed herself that time!

But I am here, and no person touches this paper but me, – not *alive*!

She tried to get me out of the room – it was too patent! But I said it was so quiet and empty and clean now that I believed I would lie down again and sleep all I could; and not to wake me even for dinner – I would call when I woke.

So now she is gone, and the servants are gone, and the things are gone, and there is nothing left but that great bedstead nailed down, with the canvas mattress we found on it.

We shall sleep downstairs tonight, and take the boat home tomorrow.

I quite enjoy the room, now it is bare again.

How those children did tear about here!

This bedstead is fairly gnawed!

But I must get to work.

I have locked the door and thrown the key down into the front path.

I don't want to go out, and I don't want to have anybody come in, till John comes.

I want to astonish him.

I've got a rope up here that even Jennie did not find. If that woman does get out, and tries to get away, I can tie her!

But I forgot I could not reach far without anything to stand on!

This bed will *not* move!

I tried to lift and push it until I was lame, and then I got so angry I bit off a little piece at one corner – but it hurt my teeth.

Then I peeled off all the paper I could reach standing on the floor. It sticks horribly and the pattern just enjoys it! All those strangled heads and bulbous eyes and waddling fungus growths just shriek with derision!

I am getting angry enough to do something desperate. To jump out of the window would be admirable exercise, but the bars are too strong even to try.

Besides I wouldn't do it. Of course not. I know well enough that a step like that is improper and might be misconstrued.

I don't like to *look* out of the windows even – there are so many of those creeping women, and they creep so fast.

I wonder if they all come out of that wallpaper as I did?

But I am securely fastened now by my well-hidden rope – you don't get *me* out in the road there!

I suppose I shall have to get back behind the pattern when it comes night, and that is hard!

It is so pleasant to be out in this great room and creep around as I please!

I don't want to go outside. I won't, even if Jennie asks me to.

For outside you have to creep on the ground, and everything is green instead of yellow.

But here I can creep smoothly on the floor, and my shoulder just fits in that long smooch around the wall, so I cannot lose my way.

Why there's John at the door!

It is no use, young man, you can't open it!

How he does call and pound!

Now he's crying for an axe.

It would be a shame to break down that beautiful door!

'John dear!' said I in the gentlest voice, 'the key is down by the front steps, under a plantain leaf!'

That silenced him for a few moments.

Then he said – very quietly indeed, 'Open the door, my darling!'

'I can't,' said I. 'The key is down by the front door under a plantain leaf!'

And then I said it again, several times, very gently and slowly, and said it so often that he had to go and see, and he got it of course, and came in. He stopped short by the door.

'What is the matter?' he cried. 'For God's sake, what are you doing!'

I kept on creeping just the same, but I looked at him over my shoulder.

'I've got out at last,' said I, 'in spite of you and Jane. And I've pulled off most of the paper, so you can't put me back!'

Now why should that man have fainted? But he did, and right across my path by the wall, so that I had to creep over him every time!

Turned

1911

In her soft-carpeted, thick-curtained, richly furnished chamber, Mrs Marroner lay sobbing on the wide, soft bed.

She sobbed bitterly, chokingly, despairingly; her shoulders heaved and shook convulsively; her hands were tight-clenched. She had forgotten her elaborate dress, the more elaborate bedcover; forgotten her dignity, her self-control, her pride. In her mind was an overwhelming, unbelievable horror, an immeasurable loss, a turbulent, struggling mass of emotion.

In her reserved, superior, Boston-bred life, she had never dreamed that it would be possible for her to feel so many things at once, and with such trampling intensity.

She tried to cool her feelings into thoughts; to stiffen them into words; to control herself – and could not. It brought vaguely to her mind an awful moment in the breakers at York Beach, one summer in girlhood when she had been swimming under water and could not find the top.

In her uncarpeted, thin-curtained, poorly furnished chamber on the top floor, Gerta Petersen lay sobbing on the narrow, hard bed.

She was of larger frame than her mistress, grandly built and strong; but all her proud young womanhood was prostrate now, convulsed with agony, dissolved in tears. She did not try to control herself. She wept for two.

If Mrs Marroner suffered more from the wreck and ruin of a longer love – perhaps a deeper one; if her tastes were finer, her ideals loftier; if she bore the pangs of bitter jealousy and outraged pride, Gerta had personal shame to meet, a hopeless future, and a looming present which filled her with unreasoning terror.

She had come like a meek young goddess into that perfectly

ordered house, strong, beautiful, full of goodwill and eager obedience, but ignorant and childish – a girl of eighteen.

Mr Marroner had frankly admired her, and so had his wife. They discussed her visible perfections and as visible limitations with that perfect confidence which they had so long enjoyed. Mrs Marroner was not a jealous woman. She had never been jealous in her life – till now.

Gerta had stayed and learned their ways. They had both been fond of her. Even the cook was fond of her. She was what is called 'willing,' was unusually teachable and plastic; and Mrs Marroner, with her early habits of giving instruction, tried to educate her somewhat.

'I never saw anyone so docile,' Mrs Marroner had often commented. 'It is perfection in a servant, but almost a defect in character. She is so helpless and confiding.'

She was precisely that: a tall, rosy-cheeked baby; rich womanhood without, helpless infancy within. Her braided wealth of dead-gold hair, her grave blue eyes, her mighty shoulders and long, firmly moulded limbs seemed those of a primal earth spirit; but she was only an ignorant child, with a child's weakness.

When Mr Marroner had to go abroad for his firm, unwillingly, hating to leave his wife, he had told her he felt quite safe to leave her in Gerta's hands – she would take care of her.

'Be good to your mistress, Gerta,' he told the girl that last morning at breakfast. 'I leave her to you to take care of. I shall be back in a month at latest.'

Then he turned, smiling, to his wife. 'And you must take care of Gerta, too,' he said. 'I expect you'll have her ready for college when I get back.'

This was seven months ago. Business had delayed him from week to week, from month to month. He wrote to his wife, long, loving, frequent letters, deeply regretting the delay, explaining how necessary, how profitable it was, congratulating her on the wide resources she had, her well-filled, well-balanced mind, her many interests.

'If I should be eliminated from your scheme of things, by any of those "acts of God" mentioned on the tickets, I do not feel that you would be an utter wreck,' he said. 'That is very comforting to me. Your life is so rich and wide that no one loss, even a great one, would wholly cripple you. But nothing of the sort is likely to happen, and I shall be home again in three weeks

– if this thing gets settled. And you will be looking so lovely, with that eager light in your eyes and the changing flush I know so well – and love so well! My dear wife! We shall have to have a new honeymoon – other moons come every month, why shouldn't the mellifluous kind?'

He often asked after 'little Gerta,' sometimes enclosed a picture postcard to her, joked his wife about her laborious efforts to educate 'the child,' was so loving and merry and wise –

All this was racing through Mrs Marroner's mind as she lay there with the broad, hemstitched border of fine linen sheeting crushed and twisted in one hand, and the other holding a sodden handkerchief.

She had tried to teach Gerta, and had grown to love the patient, sweet-natured child, in spite of her dullness. At work with her hands, she was clever, if not quick, and could keep small accounts from week to week. But to the woman who held a Ph.D., who had been on the faculty of a college, it was like baby-tending.

Perhaps having no babies of her own made her love the big child the more, though the years between them were but fifteen.

To the girl she seemed quite old, of course; and her young heart was full of grateful affection for the patient care which made her feel so much at home in this new land.

And then she had noticed a shadow on the girl's bright face. She looked nervous, anxious, worried. When the bell rang, she seemed startled, and would rush hurriedly to the door. Her peals of frank laughter no longer rose from the area gate as she stood talking with the always admiring tradesmen.

Mrs Marroner had labored long to teach her more reserve with men, and flattered herself that her words were at last effective. She suspected the girl of homesickness, which was denied. She suspected her of illness, which was denied also. At last she suspected her of something which could not be denied.

For a long time she refused to believe it, waiting. Then she had to believe it, but schooled herself to patience and understanding. 'The poor child,' she said. 'She is here without a mother – she is so foolish and yielding – I must not be too stern with her.' And she tried to win the girl's confidence with wise, kind words.

But Gerta had literally thrown herself at her feet and begged her with streaming tears not to turn her away. She would admit nothing, explain nothing, but frantically promised to work for Mrs Marroner as long as she lived – if only she would keep her.

Revolving the problem carefully in her mind, Mrs Marroner thought she would keep her, at least for the present. She tried to repress her sense of ingratitude in one she had so sincerely tried to help, and the cold, contemptuous anger she had always felt for such weakness.

'The thing to do now,' she said to herself, 'is to see her through this safely. The child's life should not be hurt any more than is unavoidable. I will ask Dr Bleet about it – what a comfort a woman doctor is! I'll stand by the poor, foolish thing till it's over, and then get her back to Sweden somehow with her baby. How they do come where they are not wanted – and don't come where they are wanted!' And Mrs Marroner, sitting alone in the quiet, spacious beauty of the house, almost envied Gerta.

Then came the deluge.

She had sent the girl out for needed air toward dark. The late mail came; she took it in herself. One letter for her – her husband's letter. She knew the postmark, the stamp, the kind of typewriting. She impulsively kissed it in the dim hall. No one would suspect Mrs Marroner of kissing her husband's letters – but she did, often.

She looked over the others. One was for Gerta, and not from Sweden. It looked precisely like her own. This struck her as a little odd, but Mr Marroner had several times sent messages and cards to the girl. She laid the letter on the hall table and took hers to her room.

'My poor child,' it began. What letter of hers had been sad enough to warrant that?

'I am deeply concerned at the news you send.' What news to so concern him had she written? 'You must bear it bravely, little girl. I shall be home soon, and will take care of you, of course. I hope there is not immediate anxiety – you do not say. Here is money, in case you need it. I expect to get home in a month at latest. If you have to go, be sure to leave your address at my office. Cheer up – be brave – I will take care of you.'

The letter was typewritten, which was not unusual. It was unsigned, which was unusual. It enclosed an American bill – fifty dollars. It did not seem in the least like any letter she had ever had from her husband, or any letter she could imagine him writing. But a strange, cold feeling was creeping over her, like a flood rising around a house.

She utterly refused to admit the ideas which began to bob and push about outside her mind, and to force themselves in. Yet under the pressure of these repudiated thoughts she went downstairs and brought up the other letter – the letter to Gerta. She laid them side by side on a smooth dark space on the table; marched to the piano and played, with stern precision, refusing to think, till the girl came back. When she came in, Mrs Marroner rose quietly and came to the table. 'Here is a letter for you,' she said.

The girl stepped forward eagerly, saw the two lying together there, hesitated, and looked at her mistress.

'Take yours, Gerta. Open it, please.'

The girl turned frightened eyes upon her.

'I want you to read it, here,' said Mrs Marroner.

'Oh, ma'am – No! Please don't make me!'

'Why not?'

There seemed to be no reason at hand, and Gerta flushed more deeply and opened her letter. It was long; it was evidently puzzling to her; it began 'My dear wife.' She read it slowly.

'Are you sure it is your letter?' asked Mrs Marroner. 'Is not this one yours? Is not that one – mine?'

She held out the other letter to her.

'It is a mistake,' Mrs Marroner went on, with a hard quietness. She had lost her social bearings somehow, lost her usual keen sense of the proper thing to do. This was not life; this was a nightmare.

'Do you not see? Your letter was put in my envelope and my letter was put in your envelope. Now we understand it.'

But poor Gerta had no antechamber to her mind, no trained forces to preserve order while agony entered. The thing swept over her, resistless, overwhelming. She cowered before the outraged wrath she expected; and from some hidden cavern that wrath arose and swept over her in pale flame.

'Go and pack your trunk,' said Mrs Marroner. 'You will leave my house tonight. Here is your money.'

She laid down the fifty-dollar bill. She put with it a month's wages. She had no shadow of pity for those anguished eyes, those tears which she heard drop on the floor.

'Go to your room and pack,' said Mrs Marroner. And Gerta, always obedient, went.

Then Mrs Marroner went to hers, and spent a time she never counted, lying on her face on the bed.

But the training of the twenty-eight years which had elapsed before her marriage; the life at college, both as student and teacher; the independent growth which she had made, formed a very different background for grief from that in Gerta's mind.

After a while Mrs Marroner arose. She administered to herself a hot bath, a cold shower, a vigorous rubbing. 'Now I can think,' she said.

First she regretted the sentence of instant banishment. She went upstairs to see if it had been carried out. Poor Gerta! The tempest of her agony had worked itself out at last as in a child, and left her sleeping, the pillow wet, the lips still grieving, a big sob shuddering itself off now and then.

Mrs Marroner stood and watched her, and as she watched she considered the helpless sweetness of the face; the defenseless, unformed character; the docility and habit of obedience which made her so attractive – and so easily a victim. Also she thought of the mighty force which had swept over her; of the great process now working itself out through her; of how pitiful and futile seemed any resistance she might have made.

She softly returned to her own room, made up a little fire, and sat by it, ignoring her feelings now, as she had before ignored her thoughts.

Here were two women and a man. One woman was a wife: loving, trusting, affectionate. One was a servant: loving, trusting, affectionate – a young girl, an exile, a dependent; grateful for any kindness; untrained, uneducated, childish. She ought, of course, to have resisted temptation; but Mrs Marroner was wise enough to know how difficult temptation is to recognize when it comes in the guise of friendship and from a source one does not suspect.

Gerta might have done better in resisting the grocer's clerk; had, indeed, with Mrs Marroner's advice, resisted several. But where respect was due, how could she criticize? Where obedience was due, how could she refuse – with ignorance to hold her blinded – until too late?

As the older, wiser woman forced herself to understand and extenuate the girl's misdeed and foresee her ruined future, a new feeling rose in her heart, strong, clear, and overmastering: a sense of measureless condemnation for the man who had done this thing. He knew. He understood. He could fully foresee and measure the consequences of his act. He appreciated to the full the innocence, the ignorance, the grateful affection, the habitual docility, of which he deliberately took advantage.

Mrs Marroner rose to icy peaks of intellectual apprehension, from which her hours of frantic pain seemed far indeed removed. He had done this thing under the same roof with her – his wife. He had not frankly loved the younger woman, broken with his wife, made a new marriage. That would have been heart-break pure and simple. This was something else.

That letter, that wretched, cold, carefully guarded, unsigned letter, that bill – far safer than a check – these did not speak of affection. Some men can love two women at one time. This was not love.

Mrs Marroner's sense of pity and outrage for herself, the wife, now spread suddenly into a perception of pity and outrage for the girl. All that splendid, clean young beauty, the hope of a happy life, with marriage and motherhood, honorable independence, even – these were nothing to that man. For his own pleasure he had chosen to rob her of her life's best joys.

He would 'take care of her,' said the letter. How? In what capacity?

And then, sweeping over both her feelings for herself, the wife, and Gerta, his victim, came a new flood, which literally lifted her to her feet. She rose and walked, her head held high. 'This is the sin of man against woman,' she said. 'The offense is against womanhood. Against motherhood. Against – the child.'

She stopped.

The child. His child. That, too, he sacrificed and injured – doomed to degradation.

Mrs Marroner came of stern New England stock. She was not a Calvinist, hardly even a Unitarian, but the iron of Calvinism was in her soul: of that grim faith which held that most people had to be damned 'for the glory of God.'

Generations of ancestors who both preached and practiced stood behind her; people whose lives had been sternly moulded to their highest moments of religious conviction. In sweeping bursts of feeling, they achieved 'conviction,' and afterward they lived and died according to that conviction.

When Mr Marroner reached home a few weeks later, following his letters too soon to expect an answer to either, he saw no wife upon the pier, though he had cabled, and found the house closed darkly. He let himself in with his latch-key, and stole softly upstairs, to surprise his wife.

No wife was there.

He rang the bell. No servant answered it.

He turned up light after light, searched the house from top to bottom; it was utterly empty. The kitchen wore a clean, bald, unsympathetic aspect. He left it and slowly mounted the stairs, completely dazed. The whole house was clean, in perfect order, wholly vacant.

One thing he felt perfectly sure of – she knew.

Yet was he sure? He must not assume too much. She might have been ill. She might have died. He started to his feet. No, they would have cabled him. He sat down again.

For any such change, if she had wanted him to know, she would have written. Perhaps she had, and he, returning so suddenly, had missed the letter. The thought was some comfort. It must be so. He turned to the telephone and again hesitated. If she had found out – if she had gone – utterly gone, without a word – should he announce it himself to friends and family?

He walked the floor; he searched everywhere for some letter, some word of explanation. Again and again he went to the telephone – and always stopped. He could not bear to ask: 'Do you know where my wife is?'

The harmonious, beautiful rooms reminded him in a dumb, helpless way of her – like the remote smile on the face of the dead. He put out the lights, could not bear the darkness, turned them all on again.

It was a long night –

In the morning he went early to the office. In the accumulated mail was no letter from her. No one seemed to know of anything unusual. A friend asked after his wife – 'Pretty glad to see you, I guess?' He answered evasively.

About eleven a man came to see him: John Hill, her lawyer. Her cousin, too. Mr Marroner had never liked him. He liked him less now, for Mr Hill merely handed him a letter, remarked, 'I was requested to deliver this to you personally,' and departed, looking like a person who is called on to kill something offensive.

'I have gone. I will care for Gerta. Goodbye. Marion.'

That was all. There was no date, no address, no postmark, nothing but that.

In his anxiety and distress, he had fairly forgotten Gerta and all that. Her name aroused in him a sense of rage. She had come between him and his wife. She had taken his wife from him. That was the way he felt.

At first he said nothing, did nothing, lived on alone in his house, taking meals where he chose. When people asked him about his wife, he said she was traveling – for her health. He would not have it in the newspapers. Then, as time passed, as no enlightenment came to him, he resolved not to bear it any longer, and employed detectives. They blamed him for not having put them on the track earlier, but set to work, urged to the utmost secrecy.

What to him had been so blank a wall of mystery seemed not to embarrass them in the least. They made careful inquiries as to her 'past,' found where she had studied, where taught, and on what lines; that she had some little money of her own, that her doctor was Josephine L. Bleet, M.D., and many other bits of information.

As a result of careful and prolonged work, they finally told him that she had resumed teaching under one of her old professors, lived quietly, and apparently kept boarders; giving him town, street, and number, as if it were a matter of no difficulty whatever.

He had returned in early spring. It was autumn before he found her.

A quiet college town in the hills, a broad, shady street, a pleasant house standing in its own lawn, with trees and flowers about it. He had the address in his hand, and the number showed clear on the white gate. He walked up the straight gravel path and rang the bell. An elderly servant opened the door.

'Does Mrs Marroner live here?'

'No, sir.'

'This is number twenty-eight?'

'Yes, sir.'

'Who does live here?'

'Miss Wheeling, sir.'

Ah! Her maiden name. They had told him, but he had forgotten.

He stepped inside. 'I would like to see her,' he said.

He was ushered into a still parlor, cool and sweet with the scent of flowers, the flowers she had always loved best. It almost brought tears to his eyes. All their years of happiness rose in his mind again – the exquisite beginnings; the days of eager longing before she was really his; the deep, still beauty of her love.

Surely she would forgive him – she must forgive him. He would humble himself; he would tell her of his honest remorse – his absolute determination to be a different man.

Through the wide doorway there came in to him two women. One like a tall Madonna, bearing a baby in her arms.

Marion, calm, steady, definitely impersonal, nothing but a clear pallor to hint of inner stress.

Gerta, holding the child as a bulwark, with a new intelligence in her face, and her blue, adoring eyes fixed on her friend – not upon him.

He looked from one to the other dumbly.

And the woman who had been his wife asked quietly:

'What have you to say to us?'

The Story of an Hour

1894

Knowing that Mrs Mallard was afflicted with a heart trouble, great care was taken to break to her as gently as possible the news of her husband's death.

It was her sister Josephine who told her, in broken sentences; veiled hints that revealed in half concealing. Her husband's friend Richards was there, too, near her. It was he who had been in the newspaper office when intelligence of the railroad disaster was received, with Brently Mallard's name leading the list of 'killed.' He had only taken the time to assure himself of its truth by a second telegram, and had hastened to forestall any less careful, less tender friend in bearing the sad message.

She did not hear the story as many women have heard the same, with a paralyzed inability to accept its significance. She wept at once, with sudden, wild abandonment, in her sister's arms. When the storm of grief had spent itself she went away to her room alone. She would have no one follow her.

There stood, facing the open window, a comfortable, roomy armchair. Into this she sank, pressed down by a physical exhaustion that haunted her body and seemed to reach into her soul.

She could see in the open square before her house the tops of trees that were all aquiver with the new spring life. The delicious breath of rain was in the air. In the street below a peddler was crying his wares. The notes of a distant song which some one was singing reached her faintly, and countless sparrows were twittering in the eaves.

There were patches of blue sky showing here and there through the clouds that had met and piled one above the other in the west facing her window.

She sat with her head thrown back upon the cushion of the

chair, quite motionless, except when a sob came up into her throat and shook her, as a child who has cried itself to sleep continues to sob in its dreams.

She was young, with a fair, calm face, whose lines bespoke repression and even a certain strength. But now there was a dull stare in her eyes, whose gaze was fixed away off yonder on one of those patches of blue sky. It was not a glance of reflection, but rather indicated a suspension of intelligent thought.

There was something coming to her and she was waiting for it, fearfully. What was it? She did not know; it was too subtle and elusive to name. But she felt it, creeping out of the sky, reaching toward her through the sounds, the scents, the color that filled the air.

Now her bosom rose and fell tumultuously. She was beginning to recognize this thing that was approaching to possess her, and she was striving to beat it back with her will – as powerless as her two white slender hands would have been.

When she abandoned herself a little whispered word escaped her slightly parted lips. She said it over and over under her breath: 'free, free, free!' The vacant stare and the look of terror that had followed it went from her eyes. They stayed keen and bright. Her pulses beat fast, and the coursing blood warmed and relaxed every inch of her body.

She did not stop to ask if it were or were not a monstrous joy that held her. A clear and exalted perception enabled her to dismiss the suggestion as trivial.

She knew that she would weep again when she saw the kind, tender hands folded in death; the face that had never looked save with love upon her, fixed and gray and dead. But she saw beyond that bitter moment a long procession of years to come that would belong to her absolutely. And she opened and spread her arms out to them in welcome.

There would be no one to live for her during those coming years; she would live for herself. There would be no powerful will bending hers in that blind persistence with which men and women believe they have a right to impose a private will upon a fellow-creature. A kind intention or a cruel intention made the act seem no less a crime as she looked upon it in that brief moment of illumination.

And yet she had loved him – sometimes. Often she had not. What did it matter! What could love, the unsolved mystery, count for in face of this possession of self-assertion which she suddenly recognized as the strongest impulse of her being!

'Free! Body and soul free!' she kept whispering.

Josephine was kneeling before the closed door with her lips to the keyhole, imploring for admission. 'Louise, open the door! I beg; open the door – you will make yourself ill. What are you doing, Louise? For heaven's sake open the door.'

'Go away. I am not making myself ill.' No; she was drinking in a very elixir of life through that open window.

Her fancy was running riot along those days ahead of her. Spring days, and summer days, and all sorts of days that would be her own. She breathed a quick prayer that life might be long. It was only yesterday she had thought with a shudder that life might be long.

She arose at length and opened the door to her sister's importunities. There was a feverish triumph in her eyes, and she carried herself unwittingly like a goddess of Victory. She clasped her sister's waist, and together they descended the stairs. Richards stood waiting for them at the bottom.

Someone was opening the front door with a latchkey. It was Brently Mallard who entered, a little travel-stained, composedly carrying his gripsack and umbrella. He had been far from the scene of accident, and did not even know there had been one. He stood amazed at Josephine's piercing cry; at Richards' quick motion to screen him from the view of his wife.

But Richards was too late.

When the doctors came they said she had died of heart disease – of joy that kills.

The Storm

A Sequel to 'At the 'Cadian Ball'

I

The leaves were so still that even Bibi thought it was going to rain. Bobinôt, who was accustomed to converse on terms of perfect equality with his little son, called the child's attention to certain sombre clouds that were rolling with sinister intention from the west, accompanied by a sullen, threatening roar. They were at Friedheimer's store and decided to remain there till the storm had passed. They sat within the door on two empty kegs. Bibi was four years old and looked very wise.

'Mama'll be 'fraid, yes,' he suggested with blinking eyes.

'She'll shut the house. Maybe she got Sylvie helpin' her this evenin',' Bobinôt responded reassuringly.

'No; she ent got Sylvie. Sylvie was helpin' her yistiday,' piped Bibi.

Bobinôt arose and going across to the counter purchased a can of shrimps, of which Calixta was very fond. Then he returned to his perch on the keg and sat stolidly holding the can of shrimps while the storm burst. It shook the wooden store and seemed to be ripping great furrows in the distant field. Bibi laid his little hand on his father's knee and was not afraid.

2

Calixta, at home, felt no uneasiness for their safety. She sat at a side window sewing furiously on a sewing machine. She was greatly occupied and did not notice the approaching storm. But she felt very warm and often stopped to mop her face on which the perspiration gathered in beads. She unfastened her white sacque at the throat. It began to grow dark, and suddenly realizing the situation she got up hurriedly and went about closing windows and doors.

Out on the small front gallery she had hung Bobinôt's Sunday clothes to air and she hastened out to gather them before the rain fell. As she stepped outside, Alcée Laballière rode in at the gate. She had not seen him very often since her marriage, and never alone. She stood there with Bobinôt's coat in her hands, and the big rain drops began to fall. Alcée rode his horse under the shelter of a side projection where the chickens had huddled and there were plows and a harrow piled up in the corner.

'May I come and wait on your gallery till the storm is over, Calixta?' he asked.

'Come 'long in, M'sieur Alcée.'

His voice and her own startled her as if from a trance, and she seized Bobinôt's vest. Alcée, mounting to the porch, grabbed the trousers and snatched Bibi's braided jacket that was about to be carried away by a sudden gust of wind. He expressed an intention to remain outside, but it was soon apparent that he might as well have been out in the open: the water beat in upon the boards in driving sheets, and he went inside, closing the door after him. It was even necessary to put something beneath the door to keep the water out.

'My! what a rain! It's good two years sence it rain' like that,' exclaimed Calixta as she rolled up a piece of bagging and Alcée helped her to thrust it beneath the crack.

She was a little fuller of figure than five years before when she married; but she had lost nothing of her vivacity. Her blue eyes still retained their melting quality; and her yellow hair, dishevelled by the wind and rain, kinked more stubbornly than ever about her ears and temples.

The rain beat upon the low, shingled roof with a force and clatter that threatened to break an entrance and deluge them there. They were in the dining room – the sitting room – the general utility room. Adjoining was her bed room, with Bibi's couch along side her own. The door stood open, and the room with its white, monumental bed, its closed shutters, looked dim and mysterious.

Alcée flung himself into a rocker and Calixta nervously began to gather up from the floor the lengths of a cotton sheet which she had been sewing.

'If this keeps up, *Dieu sait** if the levees goin' to stan' it!' she exclaimed.

'What have you got to do with the levees?'*

'I got enough to do! An' there's Bobinôt with Bibi out in that storm – if he only didn' left Friedheimer's!'

'Let us hope, Calixta, that Bobinôt's got sense enough to come in out of a cyclone.'

She went and stood at the window with a greatly disturbed look on her face. She wiped the frame that was clouded with moisture. It was stiflingly hot. Alcée got up and joined her at the window, looking over her shoulder. The rain was coming down in sheets obscuring the view of far-off cabins and enveloping the distant wood in a gray mist. The playing of the lightning was incessant. A bolt struck a tall chinaberry tree at the edge of the field. It filled all visible space with a blinding glare and the crash seemed to invade the very boards they stood upon.

Calixta put her hands to her eyes, and with a cry, staggered backward. Alcée's arm encircled her, and for an instant he drew her close and spasmodically to him.

'*Bonté!*'* she cried, releasing herself from his encircling arm and retreating from the window, 'the house'll go next! If I only knew w'ere Bibi was!' She would not compose herself; she would not be seated. Alcée clasped her shoulders and looked into her face. The contact of her warm, palpitating body when he had unthinkingly drawn her into his arms, had aroused all the old-time infatuation and desire for her flesh.

'Calixta,' he said, 'don't be frightened. Nothing can happen. The house is too low to be struck, with so many tall trees standing about. There! aren't you going to be quiet? say, aren't you?' He pushed her hair back from her face that was warm and steaming. Her lips were as red and moist as pomegranate seed. Her white neck and a glimpse of her full, firm bosom disturbed him powerfully. As she glanced up at him the fear in her liquid blue eyes had given place to a drowsy gleam that unconsciously betrayed a sensuous desire. He looked down into her eyes and there was nothing for him to do but to gather her lips in a kiss. It reminded him of Assumption.

'Do you remember – in Assumption, Calixta?' he asked in a low voice broken by passion. Oh! she remembered; for in Assumption he had kissed her and kissed and kissed her; until his senses would well nigh fail, and to save her he would resort to a desperate flight. If she was not an immaculate dove in those days, she was still inviolate; a passionate creature whose very defenselessness had made her defense, against which his honor forbade him to prevail. Now – well, now – her lips seemed in a manner free to be tasted, as well as her round, white throat and her whiter breasts.

They did not heed the crashing torrents, and the roar of the elements made her laugh as she lay in his arms. She was a revelation in that dim, mysterious chamber; as white as the couch she lay upon. Her firm, elastic flesh that was knowing for the first time its birthright, was like a creamy lily that the sun invites to contribute its breath and perfume to the undying life of the world.

The generous abundance of her passion, without guile or trickery, was like a white flame which penetrated and found response in depths of his own sensuous nature that had never yet been reached.

When he touched her breasts they gave themselves up in quivering ecstasy, inviting his lips. Her mouth was a fountain of delight. And when he possessed her, they seemed to swoon together at the very borderland of life's mystery.

He stayed cushioned upon her, breathless, dazed, enervated, with his heart beating like a hammer upon her. With one hand she clasped his head, her lips lightly touching his forehead. The other hand stroked with a soothing rhythm his muscular shoulders.

The growl of the thunder was distant and passing away. The rain beat softly upon the shingles, inviting them to drowsiness and sleep. But they dared not yield.

The rain was over; and the sun was turning the glistening green world into a palace of gems. Calixta, on the gallery, watched Alcée ride away. He turned and smiled at her with a beaming face; and she lifted her pretty chin in the air and laughed aloud.

3

Bobinôt and Bibi, trudging home, stopped without at the cistern to make themselves presentable.

'My! Bibi, w'at will yo' mama say! You ought to be ashame'. You oughtn' put on those good pants. Look at 'em! An' that mud on yo' collar! How you got that mud on yo' collar, Bibi? I never saw such a boy!' Bibi was the picture of pathetic resignation. Bobinôt was the embodiment of serious solicitude as he strove to remove from his own person and his son's the signs of their tramp over heavy roads and through wet fields. He scraped the mud off Bibi's bare legs and feet with a stick and carefully removed all traces from his heavy brogans. Then, prepared for the worst – the meeting with an over-scrupulous housewife, they entered cautiously at the back door.

Calixta was preparing supper. She had set the table and was dripping coffee at the hearth. She sprang up as they came in.

'Oh, Bobinôt! You back! My! but I was uneasy. W'ere you been during the rain? An' Bibi? he ain't wet? he ain't hurt?' She had clasped Bibi and was kissing him effusively. Bobinôt's explanations and apologies which he had been composing all along the way, died on his lips as Calixta felt him to see if he were dry, and seemed to express nothing but satisfaction at their safe return.

'I brought you some shrimps, Calixta,' offered Bobinôt, hauling the can from his ample side pocket and laying it on the table.

'Shrimps! Oh, Bobinôt! you too good fo' anything! and she gave him a smacking kiss on the cheek that resounded. *'J'vous réponds,** we'll have a feas' to night! umph-umph!'

Bobinôt and Bibi began to relax and enjoy themselves, and when the three seated themselves at table they laughed much and so loud that anyone might have heard them as far away as Laballière's.

4

Alcée Laballière wrote to his wife, Clarisse, that night. It was a loving letter, full of tender solicitude. He told her not to hurry back, but if she and the babies liked it at Biloxi, to stay a month longer. He was getting on nicely; and though he missed them, he was willing to bear the separation a while longer – realizing that their health and pleasure were the first things to be considered.

5

As for Clarisse, she was charmed upon receiving her husband's letter. She and the babies were doing well. The society was agreeable; many of her old friends and acquaintances were at the bay. And the first free breath since her marriage seemed to restore the pleasant liberty of her maiden days. Devoted as she was to her husband, their intimate conjugal life was something which she was more than willing to forgo for a while.

So the storm passed and every one was happy.

EDITH WHARTON

Souls Belated

1899

I

Their railway-carriage had been full when the train left Bologna;
but at the first station beyond Milan their only remaining
companion – a courtly person who ate garlic out of a carpet-bag
– had left his crumb-strewn seat with a bow.

Lydia's eye regretfully followed the shiny broadcloth of his
retreating back till it lost itself in the cloud of touts* and cab-
drivers hanging about the station; then she glanced across at
Gannett and caught the same regret in his look. They were both
sorry to be alone.

'Par-ten-za!'* shouted the guard. The train vibrated to a
sudden slamming of doors; a waiter ran along the platform with
a tray of fossilized sandwiches; a belated porter flung a bundle
of shawls and band-boxes into a third-class carriage; the guard
snapped out a brief *Partenza!* which indicated the purely orna-
mental nature of his first shout; and the train swung out of the
station.

The direction of the road had changed, and a shaft of sunlight
struck across the dusty red velvet seats into Lydia's corner.
Gannett did not notice it. He had returned to his *Revue de
Paris,** and she had to rise and lower the shade of the farther
window. Against the vast horizon of their leisure such incidents
stood out sharply.

Having lowered the shade, Lydia sat down, leaving the length
of the carriage between herself and Gannett. At length he missed
her and looked up.

'I moved out of the sun,' she hastily explained.

He looked at her curiously: the sun was beating on her
through the shade.

'Very well,' he said pleasantly; adding, 'You don't mind?' as he drew a cigarette-case from his pocket.

It was a refreshing touch, relieving the tension of her spirit with the suggestion that, after all, if he could *smoke* – ! The relief was only momentary. Her experience of smokers was limited (her husband had disapproved of the use of tobacco) but she knew from hearsay that men sometimes smoked to get away from things; that a cigar might be the masculine equivalent of darkened windows and a headache. Gannett, after a puff or two, returned to his review.

It was just as she had foreseen; he feared to speak as much as she did. It was one of the misfortunes of their situation that they were never busy enough to necessitate, or even to justify, the postponement of unpleasant discussions. If they avoided a question it was obviously, unconcealably because the question was disagreeable. They had unlimited leisure and an accumulation of mental energy to devote to any subject that presented itself; new topics were in fact at a premium. Lydia sometimes had premonitions of a famine-stricken period when there would be nothing left to talk about, and she had already caught herself doling out piecemeal what, in the first prodigality of their confidences, she would have flung to him in a breath. Their silence therefore might simply mean that they had nothing to say; but it was another disadvantage of their position that it allowed infinite opportunity for the classification of minute differences. Lydia had learned to distinguish between real and factitious silences; and under Gannett's she now detected a hum of speech to which her own thoughts made breathless answer.

How could it be otherwise, with that thing between them? She glanced up at the rack overhead. The *thing* was there, in her dressing-bag, symbolically suspended over her head and his. He was thinking of it now, just as she was; they had been thinking of it in unison ever since they had entered the train. While the carriage had held other travellers they had screened her from his thoughts; but now that he and she were alone she knew exactly what was passing through his mind; she could almost hear him asking himself what he should say to her. . . .

The thing had come that morning, brought up to her in an innocent-looking envelope with the rest of their letters, as they

were leaving the hotel at Bologna. As she tore it open, she and
Gannett were laughing over some ineptitude of the local guide-
book – they had been driven, of late, to make the most of such
incidental humors of travel. Even when she had unfolded the
document she took it for some unimportant business paper sent
abroad for her signature, and her eye travelled inattentively over
the curly *Whereases* of the preamble until a word arrested her:
– Divorce. There it stood, an impassable barrier, between her
husband's name and hers.

She had been prepared for it, of course, as healthy people are
said to be prepared for death, in the sense of knowing it must
come without in the least expecting that it will. She had known
from the first that Tillotson meant to divorce her – but what did
it matter? Nothing mattered, in those first days of supreme
deliverance, but the fact that she was free; and not so much (she
had begun to be aware) that freedom had released her from
Tillotson as that it had given her to Gannett. This discovery had
not been agreeable to her self-esteem. She had preferred to think
that Tillotson had himself embodied all her reasons for leaving
him; and those he represented had seemed cogent enough to
stand in no need of reinforcement. Yet she had not left him till
she met Gannett. It was her love for Gannett that had made life
with Tillotson so poor and incomplete a business. If she had
never, from the first, regarded her marriage as a full cancelling
of her claims upon life, she had at least, for a number of years,
accepted it as a provisional compensation, – she had made it
'do.' Existence in the commodious Tillotson mansion in Fifth
Avenue – with Mrs Tillotson senior commanding the approaches
from the second-story front windows – had been reduced to a
series of purely automatic acts. The moral atmosphere of the
Tillotson interior was as carefully screened and curtained as the
house itself: Mrs Tillotson senior dreaded ideas as much as a
draught in her back. Prudent people liked an even temperature;
and to do anything unexpected was as foolish as going out in
the rain. One of the chief advantages of being rich was that one
need not be exposed to unforeseen contingencies: by the use of
ordinary firmness and common sense one could make sure of
doing exactly the same thing every day at the same hour. These
doctrines, reverentially imbibed with his mother's milk, Tillotson (a model son who had never given his parents an hour's
anxiety) complacently expounded to his wife, testifying to his

sense of their importance by the regularity with which he wore
goloshes on damp days, his punctuality at meals, and his
elaborate precautions against burglars and contagious diseases.
Lydia, coming from a smaller town, and entering New York life
through the portals of the Tillotson mansion, had mechanically
accepted this point of view as inseparable from having a front
pew in church and a parterre box* at the opera. All the people
who came to the house revolved in the same small circle of
prejudices. It was the kind of society in which, after dinner, the
ladies compared the exorbitant charges of their children's teachers, and agreed that, even with the new duties on French clothes,
it was cheaper in the end to get everything from Worth;* while
the husbands, over their cigars, lamented municipal corruption,
and decided that the men to start a reform were those who had
no private interests at stake.

To Lydia this view of life had become a matter of course, just
as lumbering about in her mother-in-law's landau* had come to
seem the only possible means of locomotion, and listening every
Sunday to a fashionable Presbyterian divine the inevitable
atonement for having thought oneself bored on the other six
days of the week. Before she met Gannett her life had seemed
merely dull: his coming made it appear like one of those dismal
Cruikshank prints* in which the people are all ugly and all
engaged in occupations that are either vulgar or stupid.

It was natural that Tillotson should be the chief sufferer from
this readjustment of focus. Gannett's nearness had made her
husband ridiculous, and a part of the ridicule had been reflected
on herself. Her tolerance laid her open to a suspicion of
obtuseness from which she must, at all costs, clear herself in
Gannett's eyes.

She did not understand this until afterwards. At the time she
fancied that she had merely reached the limits of endurance. In
so large a charter of liberties as the mere act of leaving Tillotson
seemed to confer, the small question of divorce or no divorce
did not count. It was when she saw that she had left her husband
only to be with Gannett that she perceived the significance of
anything affecting their relations. Her husband, in casting her
off, had virtually flung her at Gannett: it was thus that the world
viewed it. The measure of alacrity with which Gannett would
receive her would be the subject of curious speculation over
afternoon-tea tables and in club corners. She knew what would

be said – she had heard it so often of others! The recollection bathed her in misery. The men would probably back Gannett to 'do the decent thing'; but the ladies' eye-brows would emphasize the worthlessness of such enforced fidelity; and after all, they would be right. She had put herself in a position where Gannett 'owed' her something; where, as a gentleman, he was bound to 'stand the damage.' The idea of accepting such compensation had never crossed her mind; the so-called rehabilitation of such a marriage had always seemed to her the only real disgrace. What she dreaded was the necessity of having to explain herself; of having to combat his arguments; of calculating, in spite of herself, the exact measure of insistence with which he pressed them. She knew not whether she most shrank from his insisting too much or too little. In such a case the nicest sense of proportion might be at fault; and how easy to fall into the error of taking her resistance for a test of his sincerity! Whichever way she turned, an ironical implication confronted her: she had the exasperated sense of having walked into the trap of some stupid practical joke.

Beneath all these preoccupations lurked the dread of what he was thinking. Sooner or later, of course, he would have to speak; but that, in the meantime, he should think, even for a moment, that there was any use in speaking, seemed to her simply unendurable. Her sensitiveness on this point was aggravated by another fear, as yet barely on the level of consciousness; the fear of unwillingly involving Gannett in the trammels of her dependence. To look upon him as the instrument of her liberation; to resist in herself the least tendency to a wifely taking possession of his future; had seemed to Lydia the one way of maintaining the dignity of their relation. Her view had not changed, but she was aware of a growing inability to keep her thoughts fixed on the essential point – the point of parting with Gannett. It was easy to face as long as she kept it sufficiently far off: but what was this act of mental postponement but a gradual encroachment on his future? What was needful was the courage to recognize the moment when, by some word or look, their voluntary fellowship should be transformed into a bondage the more wearing that it was based on none of those common obligations which make the most imperfect marriage in some sort a centre of gravity.

When the porter, at the next station, threw the door open,

Lydia drew back, making way for the hoped-for intruder; but
none came, and the train took up its leisurely progress through
the spring wheat-fields and budding copses. She now began to
hope that Gannett would speak before the next station. She
watched him furtively, half-disposed to return to the seat
opposite his, but there was an artificiality about his absorption
that restrained her. She had never before seen him read with so
conspicuous an air of warding off interruption. What could he
be thinking of? Why should he be afraid to speak? Or was it her
answer that she dreaded?

The train paused for the passing of an express, and he put
down his book and leaned out of the window. Presently he
turned to her with a smile.

'There's a jolly old villa out here,' he said.

His easy tone relieved her, and she smiled back at him as she
crossed over to his corner.

Beyond the embankment, through the opening in a mossy
wall, she caught sight of the villa, with its broken balustrades,
its stagnant fountains, and the stone satyr closing the perspective
of a dusky grass-walk.

'How should you like to live there?' he asked as the train
moved on.

'There?'

'In some such place, I mean. One might do worse, don't you
think so? There must be at least two centuries of solitude under
those yew-trees. Shouldn't you like it?'

'I – I don't know,' she faltered. She knew now that he meant
to speak.

He lit another cigarette. 'We shall have to live somewhere,
you know,' he said as he bent above the match.

Lydia tried to speak carelessly. '*Je n'en vois pas la nécessité!**
Why not live everywhere, as we have been doing?'

'But we can't travel forever, can we?'

'Oh, forever's a long word,' she objected, picking up the
review he had thrown aside.

'For the rest of our lives then,' he said, moving nearer.

She made a slight gesture which caused his hand to slip from
hers.

'Why should we make plans? I thought you agreed with me
that it's pleasanter to drift.'

He looked at her hesitatingly. 'It's been pleasant, certainly;

but I suppose I shall have to get at my work again some day. You know I haven't written a line since – all this time,' he hastily emended.

She flamed with sympathy and self-reproach. 'Oh, if you mean *that* – if you want to write – of course we must settle down. How stupid of me not to have thought of it sooner! Where shall we go? Where do you think you could work best? We oughtn't to lose any more time.'

He hesitated again. 'I had thought of a villa in these parts. It's quiet; we shouldn't be bothered. Should you like it?'

'Of course I should like it.' She paused and looked away. 'But I thought – I remember your telling me once that your best work had been done in a crowd – in big cities. Why should you shut yourself up in a desert?'

Gannett, for a moment, made no reply. At length he said, avoiding her eye as carefully as she avoided his: 'It might be different now; I can't tell, of course, till I try. A writer ought not to be dependent on his *milieu*; it's a mistake to humor oneself in that way; and I thought that just at first you might prefer to be – '

She faced him. 'To be what?'

'Well – quiet. I mean – '

'What do you mean by "at first"?' she interrupted.

He paused again. 'I mean after we are married.'

She thrust up her chin and turned toward the window. 'Thank you!' she tossed back at him.

'Lydia!' he exclaimed blankly; and she felt in every fibre of her averted person that he had made the inconceivable, the unpardonable mistake of anticipating her acquiescence.

The train rattled on and he groped for a third cigarette. Lydia remained silent.

'I haven't offended you?' he ventured at length, in the tone of a man who feels his way.

She shook her head with a sigh. 'I thought you understood,' she moaned. Their eyes met and she moved back to his side.

'Do you want to know how not to offend me? By taking it for granted, once for all, that you've said your say on this odious question and that I've said mine, and that we stand just where we did this morning before that – that hateful paper came to spoil everything between us!'

'To spoil everything between us? What on earth do you mean? Aren't you glad to be free?'

'I was free before.'

'Not to marry me,' he suggested.

'But I don't *want* to marry you!' she cried.

She saw that he turned pale. 'I'm obtuse, I suppose,' he said slowly. 'I confess I don't see what you're driving at. Are you tired of the whole business? Or was I simply a – an excuse for getting away? Perhaps you didn't care to travel alone? Was that it? And now you want to chuck me?' His voice had grown harsh. 'You owe me a straight answer, you know; don't be tender-hearted!'

Her eyes swam as she leaned to him. 'Don't you see it's because I care – because I care so much? Oh, Ralph! Can't you see how it would humiliate me? Try to feel it as a woman would! Don't you see the misery of being made your wife in this way? If I'd known you as a girl – that would have been a real marriage! But now – this vulgar fraud upon society – and upon a society we despised and laughed at – this sneaking back into a position that we've voluntarily forfeited: don't you see what a cheap compromise it is? We neither of us believe in the abstract "sacredness" of marriage; we both know that no ceremony is needed to consecrate our love for each other; what object can we have in marrying, except the secret fear of each that the other may escape, or the secret longing to work our way back gradually – oh, very gradually – into the esteem of the people whose conventional morality we have always ridiculed and hated? And the very fact that, after a decent interval, these same people would come and dine with us – the women who talk about the indissolubility of marriage, and who would let me die in a gutter today because I am "leading a life of sin" – doesn't that disgust you more than their turning their backs on us now? I can stand being cut by them, but I couldn't stand their coming to call and asking what I meant to do about visiting that unfortunate Mrs So-and-so!'

She paused, and Gannett maintained a perplexed silence.

'You judge things too theoretically,' he said at length, slowly. 'Life is made up of compromises.'

'The life we ran away from – yes! If we had been willing to accept them' – she flushed – 'we might have gone on meeting each other at Mrs Tillotson's dinners.'

He smiled slightly. 'I didn't know that we ran away to found a new system of ethics. I supposed it was because we loved each other.'

'Life is complex, of course; isn't it the very recognition of that fact that separates us from the people who see it *tout d'une pièce*?* If *they* are right – if marriage is sacred in itself and the individual must always be sacrificed to the family – then there can be no real marriage between us, since our – our being together is a protest against the sacrifice of the individual to the family.' She interrupted herself with a laugh. 'You'll say now that I'm giving you a lecture on sociology! Of course one acts as one can – as one must, perhaps – pulled by all sorts of invisible threads; but at least one needn't pretend, for social advantages, to subscribe to a creed that ignores the complexity of human motives – that classifies people by arbitrary signs, and puts it in everybody's reach to be on Mrs Tillotson's visiting-list. It may be necessary that the world should be ruled by conventions – but if we believed in them, why did we break through them? And if we don't believe in them, is it honest to take advantage of the protection they afford?'

Gannett hesitated. 'One may believe in them or not; but as long as they do rule the world it is only by taking advantage of their protection that one can find a *modus vivendi*.'*

'Do outlaws need a *modus vivendi*?'

He looked at her hopelessly. Nothing is more perplexing to man than the mental process of a woman who reasons her emotions.

She thought she had scored a point and followed it up passionately. 'You do understand, don't you? You see how the very thought of the thing humiliates me! We are together today because we choose to be – don't let us look any farther than that!' She caught his hands. '*Promise* me you'll never speak of it again; promise me you'll never *think* of it even,' she implored, with a tearful prodigality of italics.

Through what followed – his protests, his arguments, his final unconvinced submission to her wishes – she had a sense of his but half-discerning all that, for her, had made the moment so tumultuous. They had reached that memorable point in every heart-history when, for the first time, the man seems obtuse and the woman irrational. It was the abundance of his intentions that consoled her, on reflection, for what they lacked in quality.

After all, it would have been worse, incalculably worse, to have
detected any overreadiness to understand her.

2

When the train at night-fall brought them to their journey's end
at the edge of one of the lakes, Lydia was glad that they were
not, as usual, to pass from one solitude to another. Their
wanderings during the year had indeed been like the flight of
outlaws: through Sicily, Dalmatia, Transylvania and Southern
Italy they had persisted in their tacit avoidance of their kind.
Isolation, at first, had deepened the flavor of their happiness, as
night intensifies the scent of certain flowers; but in the new
phase on which they were entering, Lydia's chief wish was that
they should be less abnormally exposed to the action of each
other's thoughts.

She shrank, nevertheless, as the brightly-looming bulk of the
fashionable Anglo-American hotel on the water's brink began
to radiate toward their advancing boat its vivid suggestion of
social order, visitors' lists, Church services, and the bland
inquisition of the *table-d'hôte*.* The mere fact that in a moment
or two she must take her place on the hotel register as Mrs
Gannett seemed to weaken the springs of her resistance.

They had meant to stay for a night only, on their way to a
lofty village among the glaciers of Monte Rosa; but after the
first plunge into publicity, when they entered the dining-room,
Lydia felt the relief of being lost in a crowd, of ceasing for a
moment to be the centre of Gannett's scrutiny; and in his face
she caught the reflection of her feeling. After dinner, when she
went upstairs, he strolled into the smoking-room, and an hour
or two later, sitting in the darkness of her window, she heard
his voice below and saw him walking up and down the terrace
with a companion cigar at his side. When he came up he told
her he had been talking to the hotel chaplain – a very good sort
of fellow.

'Queer little microcosms, these hotels! Most of these people
live here all summer and then migrate to Italy or the Riviera.
The English are the only people who can lead that kind of life
with dignity – those soft-voiced old ladies in Shetland shawls
somehow carry the British Empire under their caps. *Civis*

Romanus sum.* It's a curious study – there might be some good things to work up here.'

He stood before her with the vivid preoccupied stare of the novelist on the trail of a 'subject.' With a relief that was half painful she noticed that, for the first time since they had been together, he was hardly aware of her presence.

'Do you think you could write here?'

'Here? I don't know.' His stare dropped. 'After being out of things so long one's first impressions are bound to be tremendously vivid, you know. I see a dozen threads already that one might follow – '

He broke off with a touch of embarrassment.

'Then follow them. We'll stay,' she said with sudden decision.

'Stay here?' He glanced at her in surprise, and then, walking to the window, looked out upon the dusky slumber of the garden.

'Why not?' she said at length, in a tone of veiled irritation.

'The place is full of old cats in caps who gossip with the chaplain. Shall you like – I mean, it would be different if – '

She flamed up.

'Do you suppose I care? It's none of their business.'

'Of course not; but you won't get them to think so.'

'They may think what they please.'

He looked at her doubtfully.

'It's for you to decide.'

'We'll stay,' she repeated.

Gannett, before they met, had made himself known as a successful writer of short stories and of a novel which had achieved the distinction of being widely discussed. The reviewers called him 'promising,' and Lydia now accused herself of having too long interfered with the fulfilment of his promise. There was a special irony in the fact, since his passionate assurances that only the stimulus of her companionship could bring out his latent faculty had almost given the dignity of a 'vocation' to her course: there had been moments when she had felt unable to assume, before posterity, the responsibility of thwarting his career. And, after all, he had not written a line since they had been together: his first desire to write had come from renewed contact with the world! Was it all a mistake then? Must the most intelligent choice work more disastrously than the blundering combinations of chance? Or was there a still more humiliating answer to her perplexities? His sudden impulse of activity so exactly coincided with her own wish to withdraw, for a time, from the range of his observation, that she wondered if he too were not seeking sanctuary from intolerable problems.

'You must begin tomorrow!' she cried, hiding a tremor under the laugh with which she added, 'I wonder if there's any ink in the inkstand?'

Whatever else they had at the Hotel Bellosguardo,* they had, as Miss Pinsent said, 'a certain tone.' It was to Lady Susan Condit that they owed this inestimable benefit; an advantage ranking in Miss Pinsent's opinion above even the lawn tennis courts and the resident chaplain. It was the fact of Lady Susan's annual visit that made the hotel what it was. Miss Pinsent was certainly the last to underrate such a privilege: – 'It's so important, my dear, forming as we do a little family, that there should be some one to give *the tone*; and no one could do it better than Lady Susan – an earl's daughter and a person of such determination. Dear Mrs Ainger now – who really *ought*, you know, when Lady Susan's away – absolutely refuses to assert herself.' Miss Pinsent sniffed derisively. 'A bishop's niece! – my dear, I saw her once actually give in to some South Americans – and before us all. She gave up her seat at table to oblige them – such a lack of dignity! Lady Susan spoke to her very plainly about it afterwards.'

Miss Pinsent glanced across the lake and adjusted her auburn front.

'But of course I don't deny that the stand Lady Susan takes is not always easy to live up to – for the rest of us, I mean. Monsieur Grossart, our good proprietor, finds it trying at times, I know – he has said as much, privately, to Mrs Ainger and me. After all, the poor man is not to blame for wanting to fill his hotel, is he? And Lady Susan is so difficult – so very difficult – about new people. One might almost say that she disapproves of them beforehand, on principle. And yet she's had warnings – she very nearly made a dreadful mistake once with the Duchess of Levens, who dyed her hair and – well, swore and smoked. One would have thought that might have been a lesson to Lady Susan.' Miss Pinsent resumed her knitting with a sigh. 'There are exceptions, of course. She took at once to you and Mr Gannett – it was quite remarkable, really. Oh, I don't mean that either – of course not! It was perfectly natural – we *all* thought you so charming and interesting from the first day – we knew at once that Mr Gannett was intellectual, by the magazines you took in; but you know what I mean. Lady Susan is so very – well, I won't say prejudiced, as Mrs Ainger does – but so prepared *not* to like new people, that her taking to you in that way was a surprise to us all, I confess.'

Miss Pinsent sent a significant glance down the long laurus-tinus alley* from the other end of which two people – a lady and gentleman – were strolling toward them through the smiling neglect of the garden.

'In this case, of course, it's very different; that I'm willing to admit. Their looks are against them; but, as Mrs Ainger says, one can't exactly tell them so.'

'She's very handsome,' Lydia ventured, with her eyes on the lady, who showed, under the dome of a vivid sunshade, the hour-glass figure and superlative coloring of a Christmas chromo.

'That's the worst of it. She's too handsome.'

'Well, after all, she can't help that.'

'Other people manage to,' said Miss Pinsent skeptically.

'But isn't it rather unfair of Lady Susan – considering that nothing is known about them?'

'But, my dear, that's the very thing that's against them. It's infinitely worse than any actual knowledge.'

Lydia mentally agreed that, in the case of Mrs Linton, it possibly might be.

'I wonder why they came here?' she mused.

'That's against them too. It's always a bad sign when loud people come to a quiet place. And they've brought van-loads of boxes – her maid told Mrs Ainger's that they meant to stop indefinitely.'

'And Lady Susan actually turned her back on her in the *salon*?'

'My dear, she said it was for our sakes: that makes it so unanswerable! But poor Grossart *is* in a way! The Lintons have taken his most expensive *suite*, you know – the yellow damask drawing-room above the portico – and they have champagne with every meal!'

They were silent as Mr and Mrs Linton sauntered by; the lady with tempestuous brows and challenging chin; the gentleman, a

blond stripling, trailing after her, head downward, like a reluctant child dragged by his nurse.

'What does your husband think of them, my dear?' Miss
Pinsent whispered as they passed out of earshot.

Lydia stooped to pick a violet in the border.

'He hasn't told me.'

'Of your speaking to them, I mean. Would he approve of
that? I know how very particular nice Americans are. I think
your action might make a difference; it would certainly carry
weight with Lady Susan.'

'Dear Miss Pinsent, you flatter me!'

Lydia rose and gathered up her book and sunshade.

'Well, if you're asked for an opinion – if Lady Susan asks you
for one – I think you ought to be prepared,' Miss Pinsent
admonished her as she moved away.

3

Lady Susan held her own. She ignored the Lintons, and her little
family, as Miss Pinsent phrased it, followed suit. Even Mrs
Ainger agreed that it was obligatory. If Lady Susan owed it to
the others not to speak to the Lintons, the others clearly owed it
to Lady Susan to back her up. It was generally found expedient,
at the Hotel Bellosguardo, to adopt this form of reasoning.

Whatever effect this combined action may have had upon the
Lintons, it did not at least have that of driving them away.
Monsieur Grossart, after a few days of suspense, had the
satisfaction of seeing them settle down in his yellow damask
*premier** with what looked like a permanent installation of
palm-trees and silk sofa-cushions, and a gratifying continuance
in the consumption of champagne. Mrs Linton trailed her
Doucet* draperies up and down the garden with the same
challenging air, while her husband, smoking innumerable cigarettes, dragged himself dejectedly in her wake; but neither of
them, after the first encounter with Lady Susan, made any
attempt to extend their acquaintance. They simply ignored their
ignorers. As Miss Pinsent resentfully observed, they behaved
exactly as though the hotel were empty.

It was therefore a matter of surprise, as well as of displeasure,
to Lydia, to find, on glancing up one day from her seat in the

garden, that the shadow which had fallen across her book was that of the enigmatic Mrs Linton.

'I want to speak to you,' that lady said, in a rich hard voice that seemed the audible expression of her gown and her complexion.

Lydia started. She certainly did not want to speak to Mrs Linton.

'Shall I sit down here?' the latter continued, fixing her intensely-shaded eyes on Lydia's face, 'or are you afraid of being seen with me?'

'Afraid?' Lydia colored. 'Sit down, please. What is it that you wish to say?'

Mrs Linton, with a smile, drew up a garden-chair and crossed one open-work ankle above the other.

'I want you to tell me what my husband said to your husband last night.'

Lydia turned pale.

'My husband – to yours?' she faltered, staring at the other.

'Didn't you know they were closeted together for hours in the smoking-room after you went upstairs? My man didn't get to bed until nearly two o'clock and when he did I couldn't get a word out of him. When he wants to be aggravating I'll back him against anybody living!' Her teeth and eyes flashed persuasively upon Lydia. 'But you'll tell me what they were talking about, won't you? I know I can trust you – you look so awfully kind. And it's for his own good. He's such a precious donkey and I'm so afraid he's got into some beastly scrape or other. If he'd only trust his own old woman! But they're always writing to him and setting him against me. And I've got nobody to turn to.' She laid her hand on Lydia's with a rattle of bracelets. 'You'll help me, won't you?'

Lydia drew back from the smiling fierceness of her brows.

'I'm sorry – but I don't think I understand. My husband has said nothing to me of – of yours.'

The great black crescents above Mrs Linton's eyes met angrily.

'I say – is that true?' she demanded.

Lydia rose from her seat.

'Oh, look here, I didn't mean that, you know – you mustn't take one up so! Can't you see how rattled I am?'

Lydia saw that, in fact, her beautiful mouth was quivering beneath softened eyes.

'I'm beside myself!' the splendid creature wailed, dropping into her seat.

'I'm so sorry,' Lydia repeated, forcing herself to speak kindly; 'but how can I help you?'

Mrs Linton raised her head sharply.

'By finding out – there's a darling!'

'Finding what out?'

'What Trevenna told him.'

'Trevenna – ?' Lydia echoed in bewilderment.

Mrs Linton clapped her hand to her mouth.

'Oh, Lord – there, it's out! What a fool I am! But I supposed of course you knew; I supposed everybody knew.' She dried her eyes and bridled. 'Didn't you know that he's Lord Trevenna? I'm Mrs Cope.'

Lydia recognized the names. They had figured in a flamboyant elopement which had thrilled fashionable London some six months earlier.

'Now you see how it is – you understand, don't you?' Mrs Cope continued on a note of appeal. 'I knew you would – that's the reason I came to you. I suppose *he* felt the same thing about your husband; he's not spoken to another soul in the place.' Her face grew anxious again. 'He's awfully sensitive, generally – he feels our position, he says – as if it wasn't *my* place to feel that! But when he does get talking there's no knowing what he'll say. I know he's been brooding over something lately, and I *must* find out what it is – it's to his interest that I should. I always tell him that I think only of his interest; if he'd only trust me! But he's been so odd lately – I can't think what he's plotting. You will help me, dear?'

Lydia, who had remained standing, looked away uncomfortably.

'If you mean by finding out what Lord Trevenna has told my husband, I'm afraid it's impossible.'

'Why impossible?'

'Because I infer that it was told in confidence.'

Mrs Cope stared incredulously.

'Well, what of that? Your husband looks such a dear – any one can see he's awfully gone on you. What's to prevent your getting it out of him?'

Lydia flushed.

'I'm not a spy!' she exclaimed.

'A spy – a spy? How dare you?' Mrs Cope flamed out. 'Oh, I don't mean that either! Don't be angry with me – I'm so miserable.' She essayed a softer note. 'Do you call that spying – for one woman to help out another? I do need help so dreadfully! I'm at my wits' end with Trevenna, I am indeed. He's such a boy – a mere baby, you know; he's only two-and-twenty.' She dropped her orbed lids. 'He's younger than me – only fancy! a few months younger. I tell him he ought to listen to me as if I was his mother; oughtn't he now? But he won't, he won't! All his people are at him, you see – oh, I know *their* little game! Trying to get him away from me before I can get my divorce – that's what they're up to. At first he wouldn't listen to them; he used to toss their letters over to me to read; but now he reads them himself, and answers 'em too, I fancy; he's always shut up in his room, writing. If I only knew what his plan is I could stop him fast enough – he's such a simpleton. But he's dreadfully deep too – at times I can't make him out. But I know he's told your husband everything – I knew that last night the minute I laid eyes on him. And I *must* find out – you must help me – I've got no one else to turn to!'

She caught Lydia's fingers in a stormy pressure.

'Say you'll help me – you and your husband.'

Lydia tried to free herself.

'What you ask is impossible; you must see that it is. No one could interfere in – in the way you ask.'

Mrs Cope's clutch tightened.

'You won't, then? You won't?'

'Certainly not. Let me go, please.'

Mrs Cope released her with a laugh.

'Oh, go by all means – pray don't let me detain you! Shall you go and tell Lady Susan Condit that there's a pair of us – or shall I save you the trouble of enlightening her?'

Lydia stood still in the middle of the path, seeing her antagonist through a mist of terror. Mrs Cope was still laughing.

'Oh, I'm not spiteful by nature, my dear; but you're a little more than flesh and blood can stand! It's impossible, is it? Let you go, indeed! You're too good to be mixed up in my affairs, are you? Why, you little fool, the first day I laid eyes on you I saw that you and I were both in the same box – that's the reason I spoke to you.'

She stepped nearer, her smile dilating on Lydia like a lamp through a fog.

'You can take your choice, you know; I always play fair. If you'll tell I'll promise not to. Now then, which is it to be?'

Lydia, involuntarily, had begun to move away from the pelting storm of words; but at this she turned and sat down again.

'You may go,' she said simply. 'I shall stay here.'

4

She stayed there for a long time, in the hypnotized contemplation, not of Mrs Cope's present, but of her own past. Gannett, early that morning, had gone off on a long walk – he had fallen into the habit of taking these mountain-tramps with various fellow-lodgers; but even had he been within reach she could not have gone to him just then. She had to deal with herself first. She was surprised to find how, in the last months, she had lost the habit of introspection. Since their coming to the Hotel Bellosguardo she and Gannett had tacitly avoided themselves and each other.

She was aroused by the whistle of the three o'clock steamboat as it neared the landing just beyond the hotel gates. Three o'clock! Then Gannett would soon be back – he had told her to expect him before four. She rose hurriedly, her face averted from the inquisitorial façade of the hotel. She could not see him just yet; she could not go indoors. She slipped through one of the overgrown garden-alleys and climbed a steep path to the hills.

It was dark when she opened their sitting-room door. Gannett was sitting on the window-ledge smoking a cigarette. Cigarettes were now his chief resource: he had not written a line during the two months they had spent at the Hotel Bellosguardo. In that respect, it had turned out not to be the right *milieu* after all.

He started up at Lydia's entrance.

'Where have you been? I was getting anxious.'

She sat down in a chair near the door.

'Up the mountain,' she said wearily.

'Alone?'

'Yes.'

Gannett threw away his cigarette: the sound of her voice made him want to see her face.

'Shall we have a little light?' he suggested.

She made no answer and he lifted the globe from the lamp and put a match to the wick. Then he looked at her.

'Anything wrong? You look done up.'

She sat glancing vaguely about the little sitting-room, dimly lit by the pallid-globed lamp, which left in twilight the outlines of the furniture, of his writing-table heaped with books and papers, of the tea-roses and jasmine drooping on the mantel-piece. How like home it had all grown – how like home!

'Lydia, what is wrong?' he repeated.

She moved away from him, feeling for her hat-pins and turning to lay her hat and sunshade on the table.

Suddenly she said: 'That woman has been talking to me."

Gannett stared.

'That woman? What woman?'

'Mrs Linton – Mrs Cope.'

He gave a start of annoyance, still, as she perceived, not grasping the full import of her words.

'The deuce! She told you – ?'

'She told me everything.'

Gannett looked at her anxiously.

'What impudence! I'm so sorry that you should have been exposed to this, dear.'

'Exposed!' Lydia laughed.

Gannett's brow clouded and they looked away from each other.

'Do you know *why* she told me? She had the best of reasons. The first time she laid eyes on me she saw that we were both in the same box.'

'Lydia!'

'So it was natural, of course, that she should turn to me in a difficulty.'

'What difficulty?'

'It seems she has reason to think that Lord Trevenna's people are trying to get him away from her before she gets her divorce – '

'Well?'

'And she fancied he had been consulting with you last night as to – as to the best way of escaping from her.'

Gannett stood up with an angry forehead.

'Well – what concern of yours was all this dirty business? Why should she go to you?'

'Don't you see? It's so simple. I was to wheedle his secret out of you.'

'To oblige that woman?'

'Yes; or, if I was unwilling to oblige her, then to protect myself.'

'To protect yourself? Against whom?'

'Against her telling every one in the hotel that she and I are in the same box.'

'She threatened that?'

'She left me the choice of telling it myself or of doing it for me.'

'The beast!'

There was a long silence. Lydia had seated herself on the sofa, beyond the radius of the lamp, and he leaned against the window. His next question surprised her.

'When did this happen? At what time, I mean?'

She looked at him vaguely.

'I don't know – after luncheon, I think. Yes, I remember; it must have been at about three o'clock.'

He stepped into the middle of the room and as he approached the light she saw that his brow had cleared.

'Why do you ask?' she said.

'Because when I came in, at about half-past three, the mail was just being distributed, and Mrs Cope was waiting as usual to pounce on her letters; you know she was always watching for the postman. She was standing so close to me that I couldn't help seeing a big official-looking envelope that was handed to her. She tore it open, gave one look at the inside, and rushed off upstairs like a whirlwind, with the director shouting after her that she had left all her other letters behind. I don't believe she ever thought of you again after that paper was put into her hand.'

'Why?'

'Because she was too busy. I was sitting in the window, watching for you, when the five o'clock boat left, and who should go on board, bag and baggage, valet and maid, dressing-bags and poodle, but Mrs Cope and Trevenna. Just an hour and a half to pack up in! And you should have seen her when they started. She was radiant – shaking hands with everybody – waving her handkerchief from the deck – distributing bows and smiles like an empress. If ever a woman got what she wanted just in the nick of time that woman did. She'll be Lady Trevenna within a week, I'll wager.'

'You think she has her divorce?'

'I'm sure of it. And she must have got it just after her talk with you.'

Lydia was silent.

At length she said, with a kind of reluctance, 'She was horribly angry when she left me. It wouldn't have taken long to tell Lady Susan Condit.'

'Lady Susan Condit has not been told.'

'How do you know?'

'Because when I went downstairs half an hour ago I met Lady Susan on the way – '

He stopped, half smiling.

'Well?'

'And she stopped to ask if I thought you would act as patroness to a charity concert she is getting up.'

In spite of themselves they both broke into a laugh. Lydia's ended in sobs and she sank down with her face hidden. Gannett bent over her, seeking her hands.

'That vile woman – I ought to have warned you to keep away from her; I can't forgive myself! But he spoke to me in confidence; and I never dreamed – well, it's all over now.'

Lydia lifted her head.

'Not for me. It's only just beginning.'

'What do you mean?'

She put him gently aside and moved in her turn to the window. Then she went on, with her face turned toward the shimmering blackness of the lake, 'You see of course that it might happen again at any moment.'

'What?'

'This – this risk of being found out. And we could hardly count again on such a lucky combination of chances, could we?'

He sat down with a groan.

Still keeping her face toward the darkness, she said, 'I want you to go and tell Lady Susan – and the others.'

Gannett, who had moved towards her, paused a few feet off.

'Why do you wish me to do this?' he said at length, with less surprise in his voice than she had been prepared for.

'Because I've behaved basely, abominably, since we came here: letting these people believe we were married – lying with every breath I drew – '

'Yes, I've felt that too,' Gannett exclaimed with sudden energy.

The words shook her like a tempest: all her thoughts seemed to fall about her in ruins.

'You – you've felt so?'

'Of course I have.' He spoke with low-voiced vehemence. 'Do you suppose I like playing the sneak any better than you do? It's damnable.'

He had dropped on the arm of a chair, and they stared at each other like blind people who suddenly see.

'But you have liked it here,' she faltered.

'Oh, I've liked it – I've liked it.' He moved impatiently. 'Haven't you?'

'Yes,' she burst out; 'that's the worst of it – that's what I can't bear. I fancied it was for your sake that I insisted on staying – because you thought you could write here; and perhaps just at first that really was the reason. But afterwards I wanted to stay myself – I loved it.' She broke into a laugh. 'Oh, do you see the full derision of it? These people – the very prototypes of the bores you took me away from, with the same fenced-in view of life, the same keep-off-the-grass morality, the same little cautious virtues and the same little frightened vices – well, I've clung to them, I've delighted in them, I've done my best to please them. I've toadied Lady Susan, I've gossiped with Miss Pinsent, I've pretended to be shocked with Mrs Ainger. Respectability! It was the one thing in life that I was sure I didn't care about, and it's grown so precious to me that I've stolen it because I couldn't get it in any other way.'

She moved across the room and returned to his side with another laugh.

'I who used to fancy myself unconventional! I must have been born with a card-case in my hand. You should have seen me with that poor woman in the garden. She came to me for help, poor creature, because she fancied that, having 'sinned,' as they call it, I might feel some pity for others who had been tempted in the same way. Not I! She didn't know me. Lady Susan would have been kinder, because Lady Susan wouldn't have been afraid. I hated the woman – my one thought was not to be seen with her – I could have killed her for guessing my secret. The one thing that mattered to me at that moment was my standing with Lady Susan!'

Gannett did not speak.

'And you – you've felt it too!' she broke out accusingly. 'You've enjoyed being with these people as much as I have; you've let the chaplain talk to you by the hour about "The Reign of Law" and Professor Drummond.* When they asked you to hand the plate in church I was watching you – *you wanted to accept*.'

She stepped close, laying her hand on his arm.

'Do you know, I begin to see what marriage is for. It's to keep people away from each other. Sometimes I think that two people who love each other can be saved from madness only by the things that come between them – children, duties, visits, bores, relations – the things that protect married people from each other. We've been too close together – that has been our sin. We've seen the nakedness of each other's souls.'

She sank again on the sofa, hiding her face in her hands.

Gannett stood above her perplexedly: he felt as though she were being swept away by some implacable current while he stood helpless on its bank.

At length he said, 'Lydia, don't think me a brute – but don't you see yourself that it won't do?'

'Yes, I see it won't do,' she said without raising her head.

His face cleared.

'Then we'll go tomorrow.'

'Go – where?'

'To Paris; to be married.'

For a long time she made no answer; then she asked slowly, 'Would they have us here if we were married?'

'Have us here?'

'I mean Lady Susan – and the others.'

'Have us here? Of course they would.'

'Not if they knew – at least, not unless they could pretend not to know.'

He made an impatient gesture.

'We shouldn't come back here, of course; and other people needn't know – no one need know.'

She sighed. 'Then it's only another form of deception and a meaner one. Don't you see that?'

'I see that we're not accountable to any Lady Susans on earth!'

'Then why are you ashamed of what we are doing here?'

'Because I'm sick of pretending that you're my wife when you're not – when you won't be.'

She looked at him sadly.

'If I were your wife you'd have to go on pretending. You'd have to pretend that I'd never been – anything else. And our friends would have to pretend that they believed what you pretended.'

Gannett pulled off the sofa-tassel and flung it away.

'You're impossible,' he groaned.

'It's not I – it's our being together that's impossible. I only want you to see that marriage won't help it.'

'What will help it then?'

She raised her head.

'My leaving you.'

'Your leaving me?' He sat motionless, staring at the tassel which lay at the other end of the room. At length some impulse of retaliation for the pain she was inflicting made him say deliberately:

'And where would you go if you left me?'

'Oh!' she cried.

He was at her side in an instant.

'Lydia – Lydia – you know I didn't mean it; I couldn't mean it! But you've driven me out of my senses; I don't know what I'm saying. Can't you get out of this labyrinth of self-torture? It's destroying us both.'

'That's why I must leave you.'

'How easily you say it!' He drew her hands down and made her face him. 'You're very scrupulous about yourself – and others. But have you thought of me? You have no right to leave me unless you've ceased to care – '

'It's because I care – '

'Then I have a right to be heard. If you love me you can't leave me.'

Her eyes defied him.

'Why not?'

He dropped her hands and rose from her side.

'Can you?' he said sadly.

The hour was late and the lamp flickered and sank. She stood up with a shiver and turned toward the door of her room.

5

At daylight a sound in Lydia's room woke Gannett from a troubled sleep. He sat up and listened. She was moving about softly, as though fearful of disturbing him. He heard her push back one of the creaking shutters; then there was a moment's silence, which seemed to indicate that she was waiting to see if the noise had roused him.

Presently she began to move again. She had spent a sleepless night, probably, and was dressing to go down to the garden for a breath of air. Gannett rose also; but some undefinable instinct made his movements as cautious as hers. He stole to his window and looked out through the slats of the shutter.

It had rained in the night and the dawn was gray and lifeless. The cloud-muffled hills across the lake were reflected in its surface as in a tarnished mirror. In the garden, the birds were beginning to shake the drops from the motionless laurustinus-boughs.

An immense pity for Lydia filled Gannett's soul. Her seeming intellectual independence had blinded him for a time to the feminine cast of her mind. He had never thought of her as a woman who wept and clung: there was a lucidity in her intuitions that made them appear to be the result of reasoning. Now he saw the cruelty he had committed in detaching her from the normal conditions of life; he felt, too, the insight with which she had hit upon the real cause of their suffering. Their life was 'impossible,' as she had said – and its worst penalty was that it had made any other life impossible for them. Even had his love lessened, he was bound to her now by a hundred ties of pity and self-reproach; and she, poor child! must turn back to him as Latude returned to his cell* . . .

A new sound startled him: it was the stealthy closing of Lydia's door. He crept to his own and heard her footsteps passing down the corridor. Then he went back to the window and looked out.

A minute or two later he saw her go down the steps of the porch and enter the garden. From his post of observation her face was invisible, but something about her appearance struck him. She wore a long travelling cloak and under its folds he detected the outline of a bag or bundle. He drew a deep breath and stood watching her.

She walked quickly down the laurustinus alley toward the gate; there she paused a moment, glancing about the little shady square. The stone benches under the trees were empty, and she seemed to gather resolution from the solitude about her, for she crossed the square to the steamboat landing, and he saw her pause before the ticket-office at the head of the wharf. Now she was buying her ticket. Gannett turned his head a moment to look at the clock: the boat was due in five minutes. He had time to jump into his clothes and overtake her –

He made no attempt to move; an obscure reluctance restrained him. If any thought emerged from the tumult of his sensations, it was that he must let her go if she wished it. He had spoken last night of his rights: what were they? At the last issue, he and she were two separate beings, not made one by the miracle of common forbearances, duties, abnegations, but bound together in a *noyade** of passion that left them resisting yet clinging as they went down.

After buying her ticket, Lydia had stood for a moment looking out across the lake; then he saw her seat herself on one of the benches near the landing. He and she, at that moment, were both listening for the same sound: the whistle of the boat as it rounded the nearest promontory. Gannett turned again to glance at the clock: the boat was due now.

Where would she go? What would her life be when she had left him? She had no near relations and few friends. There was money enough ... but she asked so much of life, in ways so complex and immaterial. He thought of her as walking barefooted through a stony waste. No one would understand her – no one would pity her – and he, who did both, was powerless to come to her aid ...

He saw that she had risen from the bench and walked toward the edge of the lake. She stood looking in the direction from which the steamboat was to come; then she turned to the ticket-office, doubtless to ask the cause of the delay. After that she went back to the bench and sat down with bent head. What was she thinking of?

The whistle sounded; she started up, and Gannett involuntar-

ily made a movement toward the door. But he turned back and
continued to watch her. She stood motionless, her eyes on the
trail of smoke that preceded the appearance of the boat. Then
the little craft rounded the point, a dead-white object on the
leaden water: a minute later it was puffing and backing at the
wharf.

The few passengers who were waiting – two or three peasants
and a snuffy priest – were clustered near the ticket-office. Lydia
stood apart under the trees.

The boat lay alongside now; the gang-plank was run out and
the peasants went on board with their baskets of vegetables,
followed by the priest. Still Lydia did not move. A bell began to
ring querulously; there was a shriek of steam, and some one
must have called to her that she would be late, for she started
forward, as though in answer to a summons. She moved
waveringly, and at the edge of the wharf she paused. Gannett
saw a sailor beckon to her; the bell rang again and she stepped
upon the gang-plank.

Half-way down the short incline to the deck she stopped
again; then she turned and ran back to the land. The gang-plank
was drawn in, the bell ceased to ring, and the boat backed out
into the lake. Lydia, with slow steps, was walking toward the
garden . . .

As she approached the hotel she looked up furtively and
Gannett drew back into the room. He sat down beside a table;
a Bradshaw* lay at his elbow, and mechanically, without
knowing what he did, he began looking out the trains to
Paris . . .

WILLA CATHER

Paul's Case

A Study in Temperament

1905

It was Paul's afternoon to appear before the faculty of the
Pittsburgh High School to account for his various misdemean-
ors. He had been suspended a week ago, and his father had
called at the Principal's office and confessed his perplexity about
his son. Paul entered the faculty room suave and smiling. His
clothes were a trifle outgrown, and the tan velvet on the collar
of his open overcoat was frayed and worn; but for all that there
was something of the dandy about him, and he wore an opal
pin in his neatly knotted black four-in-hand,* and a red carnation in his buttonhole. This latter adornment the faculty somehow felt was not properly significant of the contrite spirit
befitting a boy under the ban of suspension.

Paul was tall for his age and very thin, with high, cramped
shoulders and a narrow chest. His eyes were remarkable for a
certain hysterical brilliancy, and he continually used them in a
conscious, theatrical sort of way, peculiarly offensive in a boy.
The pupils were abnormally large, as though he were addicted
to belladonna,* but there was a glassy glitter about them which
that drug does not produce.

When questioned by the Principal as to why he was there Paul
stated, politely enough, that he wanted to come back to school.
This was a lie, but Paul was quite accustomed to lying; found it,
indeed, indispensable for overcoming friction. His teachers were
asked to state their respective charges against him, which they
did with such a rancor and aggrievedness as evinced that this
was not a usual case. Disorder and impertinence were among
the offences named, yet each of his instructors felt that it was

scarcely possible to put into words the real cause of the trouble, which lay in a sort of hysterically defiant manner of the boy's; in the contempt which they all knew he felt for them, and which he seemingly made not the least effort to conceal. Once, when he had been making a synopsis of a paragraph at the blackboard, his English teacher had stepped to his side and attempted to guide his hand. Paul had started back with a shudder and thrust his hands violently behind him. The astonished woman could scarcely have been more hurt and embarrassed had he struck at her. The insult was so involuntary and definitely personal as to be unforgettable. In one way and another he had made all his teachers, men and women alike, conscious of the same feeling of physical aversion. In one class he habitually sat with his hand shading his eyes; in another he always looked out of the window during the recitation; in another he made a running commentary on the lecture, with humorous intention.

His teachers felt this afternoon that his whole attitude was symbolized by his shrug and his flippantly red carnation flower, and they fell upon him without mercy, his English teacher leading the pack. He stood through it smiling, his pale lips parted over his white teeth. (His lips were continually twitching, and he had a habit of raising his eyebrows that was contemptuous and irritating to the last degree.) Older boys than Paul had broken down and shed tears under that baptism of fire, but his set smile did not once desert him, and his only sign of discomfort was the nervous trembling of the fingers that toyed with the buttons of his overcoat, and an occasional jerking of the other hand that held his hat. Paul was always smiling, always glancing about him, seeming to feel that people might be watching him and trying to detect something. This conscious expression, since it was as far as possible from boyish mirthfulness, was usually attributed to insolence or 'smartness.'

As the inquisition proceeded one of his instructors repeated an impertinent remark of the boy's, and the Principal asked him whether he thought that a courteous speech to have made a woman. Paul shrugged his shoulders slightly and his eyebrows twitched.

'I don't know,' he replied. 'I didn't mean to be polite or impolite, either. I guess it's a sort of way I have of saying things regardless.'

The Principal, who was a sympathetic man, asked him

whether he didn't think that a way it would be well to get rid
of. Paul grinned and said he guessed so. When he was told that
he could go he bowed gracefully and went out. His bow was but
a repetition of the scandalous red carnation.

His teachers were in despair, and his drawing master voiced
the feeling of them all when he declared there was something
about the boy which none of them understood. He added: 'I
don't really believe that smile of his comes altogether from
insolence; there's something sort of haunted about it. The boy is
not strong, for one thing. I happen to know that he was born in
Colorado, only a few months before his mother died out there
of a long illness. There is something wrong about the fellow.'

The drawing master had come to realize that, in looking at
Paul, one saw only his white teeth and the forced animation of
his eyes. One warm afternoon the boy had gone to sleep at his
drawing board, and his master had noted with amazement what
a white, blue-veined face it was; drawn and wrinkled like an old
man's about the eyes, the lips twitching even in his sleep, and
stiff with a nervous tension that drew them back from his teeth.

His teachers left the building dissatisfied and unhappy; humil-
iated to have felt so vindictive toward a mere boy, to have
uttered this feeling in cutting terms, and to have set each other
on, as it were, in the gruesome game of intemperate reproach.
Some of them remembered having seen a miserable street cat set
at bay by a ring of tormentors.

As for Paul, he ran down the hill whistling the 'Soldiers'
Chorus' from *Faust*,* looking wildly behind him now and then
to see whether some of his teachers were not there to writhe
under his lightheartedness. As it was now late in the afternoon
and Paul was on duty that evening as usher at Carnegie Hall, he
decided that he would not go home to supper. When he reached
the concert hall the doors were not yet open and, as it was chilly
outside, he decided to go up into the picture gallery – always
deserted at this hour – where there were some of Raffelli's* gay
studies of Paris streets and an airy blue Venetian scene or two
that always exhilarated him. He was delighted to find no one in
the gallery but the old guard, who sat in one corner, a newspaper
on his knee, a black patch over one eye and the other closed.
Paul possessed himself of the place and walked confidently up
and down, whistling under his breath. After a while he sat down
before a blue Rico* and lost himself. When he bethought him to

look at his watch, it was after seven o'clock, and he rose with a
start and ran downstairs, making a face at Augustus,* peering
out from the cast room, and an evil gesture at the *Venus de
Milo** as he passed her on the stairway.

When Paul reached the ushers' dressing room half a dozen
boys were there already, and he began excitedly to tumble into
his uniform. It was one of the few that at all approached fitting,
and Paul thought it very becoming – though he knew that the
tight, straight coat accentuated his narrow chest, about which
he was exceedingly sensitive. He was always considerably
excited while he dressed, twanging all over to the tuning of the
strings and the preliminary flourishes of the horns in the music
room; but tonight he seemed quite beside himself, and he teased
and plagued the boys until, telling him that he was crazy, they
put him down on the floor and sat on him.

Somewhat calmed by his suppression, Paul dashed out to the
front of the house to seat the early comers. He was a model
usher; gracious and smiling he ran up and down the aisles;
nothing was too much trouble for him; he carried messages and
brought programs as though it were his greatest pleasure in life,
and all the people in his section thought him a charming boy,
feeling that he remembered and admired them. As the house
filled, he grew more and more vivacious and animated, and the
color came to his cheeks and lips. It was very much as though
this were a great reception and Paul were the host. Just as the
musicians came out to take their places, his English teacher
arrived with checks for the seats which a prominent manufac-
turer had taken for the season. She betrayed some embarrassment when she handed Paul the tickets, and a hauteur which
subsequently made her feel very foolish. Paul was startled for a
moment, and had the feeling of wanting to put her out; what
business had she here among all these fine people and gay
colors? He looked her over and decided that she was not
appropriately dressed and must be a fool to sit downstairs in
such togs. The tickets had probably been sent her out of
kindness, he reflected as he put down a seat for her, and she had
about as much right to sit there as he had.

When the symphony began Paul sank into one of the rear
seats with a long sigh of relief, and lost himself, as he had done
before the Rico. It was not that symphonies, as such, meant
anything in particular to Paul, but the first sigh of the instru-

ments seemed to free some hilarious and potent spirit within him; something that struggled there like the genie in the bottle found by the Arab fisherman.* He felt a sudden zest of life; the lights danced before his eyes and the concert hall blazed into unimaginable splendor. When the soprano soloist came on Paul forgot even the nastiness of his teacher's being there and gave himself up to the peculiar stimulus such personages always had for him. The soloist chanced to be a German woman, by no means in her first youth, and the mother of many children; but she wore an elaborate gown and a tiara, and above all she had that indefinable air of achievement, that world-shine upon her, which, in Paul's eyes, made her a veritable queen of Romance.

After a concert was over Paul was always irritable and wretched until he got to sleep, and tonight he was even more than usually restless. He had the feeling of not being able to let down, of its being impossible to give up this delicious excitement which was the only thing that could be called living at all. During the last number he withdrew and, after hastily changing his clothes in the dressing room, slipped out to the side door where the soprano's carriage stood. Here he began pacing rapidly up and down the walk, waiting to see her come out.

Over yonder, the Schenley, in its vacant stretch, loomed big and square through the fine rain, the windows of its twelve stories glowing like those of a lighted cardboard house under a Christmas tree. All the actors and singers of the better class stayed there when they were in the city, and a number of the big manufacturers of the place lived there in the winter. Paul had often hung about the hotel, watching the people go in and out, longing to enter and leave schoolmasters and dull care behind him forever.

At last the singer came out, accompanied by the conductor, who helped her into her carriage and closed the door with a cordial *auf wiedersehen* which set Paul to wondering whether she were not an old sweetheart of his. Paul followed the carriage over to the hotel, walking so rapidly as not to be far from the entrance when the singer alighted, and disappeared behind the swinging glass doors that were opened by a Negro in a tall hat and a long coat. In the moment that the door was ajar it seemed to Paul that he, too, entered. He seemed to feel himself go after her up the steps, into the warm, lighted building, into an exotic, tropical world of shiny, glistening surfaces and basking ease. He reflected upon the mysterious dishes that were brought into the dining room, the green bottles in buckets of ice, as he had seen them in the supper party pictures of the *Sunday World* supplement. A quick gust of wind brought the rain down with sudden vehemence, and Paul was startled to find that he was still outside in the slush of the gravel driveway; that his boots were letting in the water and his scanty overcoat was clinging wet about him; that the lights in front of the concert hall were out and that the rain was driving in sheets between him and the orange glow of the windows above him. There it was, what he wanted – tangibly before him, like the fairy world of a Christmas pantomime – but mocking spirits stood guard at the doors, and, as the rain beat in his face, Paul wondered whether he were destined always to shiver in the black night outside, looking up at it.

He turned and walked reluctantly toward the car tracks. The end had to come sometime; his father in his nightclothes at the top of the stairs, explanations that did not explain, hastily improvised fictions that were forever tripping him up, his upstairs room and its horrible yellow wallpaper, the creaking bureau with the greasy plush collarbox, and over his painted wooden bed the pictures of George Washington and John Calvin, and the framed motto, 'Feed my Lambs,' which had been worked in red worsted by his mother.

Half an hour later Paul alighted from his car and went slowly down one of the side streets off the main thoroughfare. It was a highly respectable street, where all the houses were exactly alike, and where businessmen of moderate means begot and reared large families of children, all of whom went to Sabbath school and learned the shorter catechism, and were interested in arithmetic; all of whom were as exactly alike as their homes, and of a piece with the monotony in which they lived. Paul never went up Cordelia Street without a shudder of loathing. His home was next to the house of the Cumberland minister. He approached it tonight with the nerveless sense of defeat, the hopeless feeling of sinking back forever into ugliness and commonness that he had always had when he came home. The moment he turned into Cordelia Street he felt the waters close above his head. After each of these orgies of living he experienced all the physical depression which follows a debauch; the loathing of respectable beds, of common food, of a house penetrated by kitchen odors; a shuddering repulsion for the flavorless, colorless mass of everyday existence; a morbid desire for cool things and soft lights and fresh flowers.

The nearer he approached the house, the more absolutely unequal Paul felt to the sight of it all: his ugly sleeping chamber; the cold bathroom with the grimy zinc tub, the cracked mirror, the dripping spiggots; his father, at the top of the stairs, his hairy legs sticking out from his nightshirt, his feet thrust into carpet slippers. He was so much later than usual that there would certainly be inquiries and reproaches. Paul stopped short before the door. He felt that he could not be accosted by his father tonight; that he could not toss again on that miserable bed. He would not go in. He would tell his father that he had no carfare and it was raining so hard he had gone home with one of the boys and stayed all night.

Meanwhile, he was wet and cold. He went around to the back of the house and tried one of the basement windows, found it open, raised it cautiously, and scrambled down the cellar wall to the floor. There he stood, holding his breath, terrified by the noise he had made, but the floor above him was silent, and there was no creak on the stairs. He found a soapbox, and carried it over to the soft ring of light that streamed from the furnace door, and sat down. He was horribly afraid of rats, so he did not try to sleep, but sat looking distrustfully at the dark, still terrified lest he might have awakened his father. In such reactions, after one of the experiences which made days and nights out of the dreary blanks of the calendar, when his senses were deadened, Paul's head was always singularly clear. Suppose his father had heard him getting in at the window and had come down and shot him for a burglar? Then, again, suppose his father had come down, pistol in hand, and he had cried out in time to save himself, and his father had been horrified to think how nearly he had killed him? Then, again, suppose a day should come when his father would remember that night, and wish there had been no warning cry to stay his hand? With this last supposition Paul entertained himself until daybreak.

The following Sunday was fine; the sodden November chill was broken by the last flash of autumnal summer. In the morning Paul had to go to church and Sabbath school, as always. On seasonable Sunday afternoons the burghers of

Cordelia Street always sat out on their front stoops and talked
to their neighbors on the next stoop, or called to those across
the street in neighborly fashion. The men usually sat on gay
cushions placed upon the steps that led down to the sidewalk,
while the women, in their Sunday 'waists,' sat in rockers on the
cramped porches, pretending to be greatly at their ease. The
children played in the streets; there were so many of them that
the place resembled the recreation grounds of a kindergarten.
The men on the steps – all in their shirt sleeves, their vests
unbuttoned – sat with their legs well apart, their stomachs
comfortably protruding, and talked of the prices of things, or
told anecdotes of the sagacity of their various chiefs and
overlords. They occasionally looked over the multitude of
squabbling children, listened affectionately to their high-pitched,
nasal voices, smiling to see their own proclivities reproduced in
their offspring, and interspersed their legends of the iron kings
with remarks about their sons' progress at school, their grades
in arithmetic, and the amounts they had saved in their toy
banks.

On this last Sunday of November Paul sat all the afternoon
on the lowest step of his stoop, staring into the street, while his
sisters, in their rockers, were talking to the minister's daughters
next door about how many shirtwaists they had made in the last
week, and how many waffles someone had eaten at the last
church supper. When the weather was warm, and his father was
in a particularly jovial frame of mind, the girls made lemonade,
which was always brought out in a red-glass pitcher, orna-
mented with forget-me-nots in blue enamel. This the girls
thought very fine, and the neighbors always joked about the
suspicious color of the pitcher.

Today Paul's father sat on the top step, talking to a young
man who shifted a restless baby from knee to knee. He happened
to be the young man who was daily held up to Paul as a model,
and after whom it was his father's dearest hope that he would
pattern. This young man was of a ruddy complexion, with a
compressed, red mouth, and faded, nearsighted eyes, over which
he wore thick spectacles, with gold bows that curved about his
ears. He was clerk to one of the magnates of a great steel
corporation, and was looked upon in Cordelia Street as a young
man with a future. There was a story that, some five years ago –
he was now barely twenty-six – he had been a trifle dissipated,

but in order to curb his appetites and save the loss of time and strength that a sowing of wild oats might have entailed, he had taken his chief's advice, oft reiterated to his employees, and at twenty-one had married the first woman whom he could persuade to share his fortunes. She happened to be an angular schoolmistress, much older than he, who also wore thick glasses, and who had now borne him four children, all nearsighted, like herself.

The young man was relating how his chief, now cruising in the Mediterranean, kept in touch with all the details of the business, arranging his office hours on his yacht just as though he were at home, and 'knocking off work enough to keep two stenographers busy.' His father told, in turn, the plan his corporation was considering, of putting in an electric railway plant in Cairo. Paul snapped his teeth; he had an awful apprehension that they might spoil it all before he got there. Yet he rather liked to hear these legends of the iron kings that were told and retold on Sundays and holidays; these stories of palaces in Venice, yachts on the Mediterranean, and high play at Monte Carlo appealed to his fancy, and he was interested in the triumphs of these cash boys who had become famous, though he had no mind for the cash-boy stage.

After supper was over and he had helped to dry the dishes, Paul nervously asked his father whether he could go to George's to get some help in his geometry, and still more nervously asked for carfare. This latter request he had to repeat, as his father, on principle, did not like to hear requests for money, whether much or little. He asked Paul whether he could not go to some boy who lived nearer, and told him that he ought not to leave his schoolwork until Sunday; but he gave him the dime. He was not a poor man, but he had a worthy ambition to come up in the world. His only reason for allowing Paul to usher was that he thought a boy ought to be earning a little.

Paul bounded upstairs, scrubbed the greasy odor of the dishwater from his hands with the ill-smelling soap he hated, and then shook over his fingers a few drops of violet water from the bottle he kept hidden in his drawer. He left the house with his geometry conspicuously under his arm, and the moment he got out of Cordelia Street and boarded a downtown car, he shook off the lethargy of two deadening days and began to live again.

The leading juvenile of the permanent stock company which

played at one of the downtown theaters was an acquaintance of Paul's, and the boy had been invited to drop in at the Sunday-night rehearsals whenever he could. For more than a year Paul had spent every available moment loitering about Charley Edwards's dressing room. He had won a place among Edwards's following not only because the young actor, who could not afford to employ a dresser, often found him useful, but because he recognized in Paul something akin to what churchmen term 'vocation.'

It was at the theater and at Carnegie Hall that Paul really lived; the rest was but a sleep and a forgetting. This was Paul's fairy tale, and it had for him all the allurement of a secret love. The moment he inhaled the gassy, painty, dusty odor behind the scenes, he breathed like a prisoner set free, and felt within him the possibility of doing or saying splendid, brilliant, poetic things. The moment the cracked orchestra beat out the overture from *Martha*,* or jerked at the serenade from *Rigoletto*,* all stupid and ugly things slid from him, and his senses were deliciously, yet delicately fired.

Perhaps it was because, in Paul's world, the natural nearly always wore the guise of ugliness, that a certain element of artificiality seemed to him necessary in beauty. Perhaps it was because his experience of life elsewhere was so full of Sabbath-school picnics, petty economies, wholesome advice as to how to succeed in life, and the inescapable odors of cooking, that he found this existence so alluring, these smartly clad men and women so attractive, that he was so moved by these starry apple orchards that bloomed perennially under the limelight.

It would be difficult to put it strongly enough how convinc-ingly the stage entrance of that theater was for Paul the actual portal of Romance. Certainly none of the company ever sus-pected it, least of all Charley Edwards. It was very like the old stories that used to float about London of fabulously rich Jews, who had subterranean halls there, with palms, and fountains, and soft lamps and richly appareled women who never saw the disenchanting light of London day. So, in the midst of that smoke-palled city, enamored of figures and grimy toil, Paul had his secret temple, his wishing carpet, his bit of blue-and-white Mediterranean shore bathed in perpetual sunshine.

Several of Paul's teachers had a theory that his imagination had been perverted by garish fiction, but the truth was that he scarcely ever read at all. The books at home were not such as would either tempt or corrupt a youthful mind, and as for reading the novels that some of his friends urged upon him – well, he got what he wanted much more quickly from music; any sort of music, from an orchestra to a barrel organ. He needed only the spark, the indescribable thrill that made his imagination master of his senses, and he could make plots and pictures enough of his own. It was equally true that he was not stagestruck – not, at any rate, in the usual acceptation of that expression. He had no desire to become an actor, any more than he had to become a musician. He felt no necessity to do any of these things; what he wanted was to see, to be in the atmosphere, float on the wave of it, to be carried out, blue league after blue league, away from everything.

After a night behind the scenes Paul found the schoolroom more than ever repulsive; the bare floors and naked walls; the prosy men who never wore frock coats, or violets in their buttonholes; the women with their dull gowns, shrill voices, and pitiful seriousness about prepositions that govern the dative. He could not bear to have the other pupils think, for a moment, that he took these people seriously; he must convey to them that he considered it all trivial, and was there only by way of a jest, anyway. He had autographed pictures of all the members of the stock company which he showed his classmates, telling them the most incredible stories of his familiarity with these people, of his acquaintance with the soloists who came to Carnegie Hall, his suppers with them and the flowers he sent them. When these stories lost their effect, and his audience grew listless, he became desperate and would bid all the boys goodby, announcing that he was going to travel for a while; going to Naples, to Venice, to Egypt. Then, next Monday, he would slip back, conscious and nervously smiling; his sister was ill, and he should have to defer his voyage until spring.

Matters went steadily worse with Paul at school. In the itch to let his instructors know how heartily he despised them and their homilies, and how thoroughly he was appreciated else-where, he mentioned once or twice that he had no time to fool with theorems; adding – with a twitch of the eyebrows and a touch of that nervous bravado which so perplexed them – that he was helping the people down at the stock company; they were old friends of his.

The upshot of the matter was that the Principal went to Paul's
father, and Paul was taken out of school and put to work. The
manager at Carnegie Hall was told to get another usher in his
stead; the doorkeeper at the theater was warned not to admit
him to the house; and Charley Edwards remorsefully promised
the boy's father not to see him again.

The members of the stock company were vastly amused when
some of Paul's stories reached them – especially the women.
They were hard-working women, most of them supporting
indigent husbands or brothers, and they laughed rather bitterly
at having stirred the boy to such fervid and florid inventions.
They agreed with the faculty and with his father that Paul's was
a bad case.

The eastbound train was plowing through a January snowstorm;
the dull dawn was beginning to show gray when the engine
whistled a mile out of Newark. Paul started up from the seat
where he had lain curled in uneasy slumber, rubbed the breath-
misted window glass with his hand, and peered out. The snow
was whirling in curling eddies above the white bottom lands,
and the drifts lay already deep in the fields and along the fences,
while here and there the long dead grass and dried weed stalks
protruded black above it. Lights shone from the scattered
houses, and a gang of laborers who stood beside the track waved
their lanterns.

Paul had slept very little, and he felt grimy and uncomfortable.
He had made the all-night journey in a day coach, partly because
he was ashamed, dressed as he was, to go into a Pullman, and
partly because he was afraid of being seen there by some
Pittsburgh businessman, who might have noticed him in Denny
& Carson's office. When the whistle awoke him, he clutched
quickly at his breast pocket, glancing about him with an
uncertain smile. But the little, clay-bespattered Italians were still
sleeping, the slatternly women across the aisle were in open-
mouthed oblivion, and even the crumby, crying babies were for
the nonce stilled. Paul settled back to struggle with his
impatience as best he could.

When he arrived at the Jersey City station he hurried through
his breakfast, manifestly ill at ease and keeping a sharp eye
about him. After he reached the Twenty-third Street station, he
consulted a cabman and had himself driven to a men's-furnish-

ings establishment that was just opening for the day. He spent
upward of two hours there, buying with endless reconsidering
and great care. His new street suit he put on in the fitting room;
the frock coat and dress clothes he had bundled into the cab
with his linen. Then he drove to a hatter's and a shoe house. His
next errand was at Tiffany's, where he selected his silver and a
new scarf pin. He would not wait to have his silver marked, he
said. Lastly, he stopped at a trunk shop on Broadway and had
his purchases packed into various traveling bags.

It was a little after one o'clock when he drove up to the
Waldorf, and after settling with the cabman, went into the
office. He registered from Washington; said his mother and
father had been abroad, and that he had come down to await
the arrival of their steamer. He told his story plausibly and had
no trouble, since he volunteered to pay for them in advance, in
engaging his rooms; a sleeping room, sitting room, and bath.

Not once, but a hundred times, Paul had planned this entry
into New York. He had gone over every detail of it with Charley
Edwards, and in his scrapbook at home there were pages of
description about New York hotels, cut from the Sunday papers.
When he was shown to his sitting room on the eighth floor he
saw at a glance that everything was as it should be; there was
but one detail in his mental picture that the place did not realize,
so he rang for the bellboy and sent him down for flowers. He
moved about nervously until the boy returned, putting away his
new linen and fingering it delightedly as he did so. When the
flowers came he put them hastily into water, and then tumbled
into a hot bath. Presently he came out of his white bathroom,
resplendent in his new silk underwear, and playing with the
tassels of his red robe. The snow was whirling so fiercely outside
his windows that he could scarcely see across the street, but
within the air was deliciously soft and fragrant. He put the
violets and jonquils on the taboret beside the couch, and threw
himself down, with a long sigh, covering himself with a Roman
blanket. He was thoroughly tired; he had been in such haste, he
had stood up to such a strain, covered so much ground in the
last twenty-four hours, that he wanted to think how it had all
come about. Lulled by the sound of the wind, the warm air, and
the cool fragrance of the flowers, he sank into deep, drowsy
retrospection.

It had been wonderfully simple; when they had shut him out

of the theater and concert hall, when they had taken away his bone, the whole thing was virtually determined. The rest was a mere matter of opportunity. The only thing that at all surprised him was his own courage – for he realized well enough that he had always been tormented by fear, a sort of apprehensive dread that, of late years, as the meshes of the lies he had told closed about him, had been pulling the muscles of his body tighter and tighter. Until now he could not remember the time when he had not been dreading something. Even when he was a little boy it was always there – behind him, or before, or on either side. There had always been the shadowed corner, the dark place into which he dared not look, but from which something seemed always to be watching him – and Paul had done things that were not pretty to watch, he knew.

But now he had a curious sense of relief, as though he had at last thrown down the gauntlet to the thing in the corner.

Yet it was but a day since he had been sulking in the traces; but yesterday afternoon that he had been sent to the bank with Denny & Carson's deposit, as usual – but this time he was instructed to leave the book to be balanced. There was above two thousand dollars in checks, and nearly a thousand in the bank notes which he had taken from the book and quietly transferred to his pocket. At the bank he had made out a new deposit slip. His nerves had been steady enough to permit of his returning to the office, where he had finished his work and asked for a full day's holiday tomorrow, Saturday, giving a perfectly reasonable pretext. The bankbook, he knew, would not be returned before Monday or Tuesday, and his father would be out of town for the next week. From the time he slipped the bank notes into his pocket until he boarded the night train for New York, he had not known a moment's hesitation. It was not the first time Paul had steered through treacherous waters.

How astonishingly easy it had all been; here he was, the thing done; and this time there would be no awakening, no figure at the top of the stairs. He watched the snowflakes whirling by his window until he fell asleep.

When he awoke, it was three o'clock in the afternoon. He bounded up with a start; half of one of his precious days gone already! He spent more than an hour in dressing, watching every stage of his toilet carefully in the mirror. Everything was quite perfect; he was exactly the kind of boy he had always wanted to be.

When he went downstairs Paul took a carriage and drove up Fifth Avenue toward the Park. The snow had somewhat abated; carriages and tradesmen's wagons were hurrying soundlessly to and fro in the winter twilight; boys in woolen mufflers were shoveling off the doorsteps; the avenue stages made fine spots of color against the white street. Here and there on the corners were stands, with whole flower gardens blooming under glass cases, against the sides of which the snowflakes stuck and melted; violets, roses, carnations, lilies of the valley – somehow vastly more lovely and alluring that they blossomed thus unnaturally in the snow. The Park itself was a wonderful stage winterpiece.

When he returned, the pause of the twilight had ceased and the tune of the streets had changed. The snow was falling faster, lights streamed from the hotels that reared their dozen stories fearlessly up into the storm, defying the raging Atlantic winds. A long, black stream of carriages poured down the avenue, intersected here and there by other streams, tending horizontally. There were a score of cabs about the entrance of his hotel, and his driver had to wait. Boys in livery were running in and out of the awning stretched across the sidewalk, up and down the red velvet carpet laid from the door to the street. Above, about, within it all was the rumble and roar, the hurry and toss of thousands of human beings as hot for pleasure as himself, and on every side of him towered the glaring affirmation of the omnipotence of wealth.

The boy set his teeth and drew his shoulders together in a spasm of realization; the plot of all dramas, the text of all romances, the nerve-stuff of all sensations was whirling about him like the snowflakes. He burnt like a faggot in a tempest.

When Paul went down to dinner the music of the orchestra came floating up the elevator shaft to greet him. His head whirled as he stepped into the thronged corridor, and he sank back into one of the chairs against the wall to get his breath. The lights, the chatter, the perfumes, the bewildering medley of color – he had, for a moment, the feeling of not being able to stand it. But only for a moment; these were his own people, he told himself. He went slowly about the corridors, through the writing rooms, smoking rooms, reception rooms, as though he were exploring the chambers of an enchanted palace, built and peopled for him alone.

When he reached the dining room he sat down at a table near a window. The flowers, the white linen, the many-colored wineglasses, the gay toilettes of the women, the low popping of corks, the undulating repetitions of the *Blue Danube* from the orchestra, all flooded Paul's dream with bewildering radiance. When the roseate tinge of his champagne was added – that cold, precious, bubbling stuff that creamed and foamed in his glass – Paul wondered that there were honest men in the world at all. This was what all the world was fighting for, he reflected; this was what all the struggle was about. He doubted the reality of his past. Had he ever known a place called Cordelia Street, a place where fagged-looking businessmen got on the early car; mere rivets in a machine they seemed to Paul, – sickening men, with combings of children's hair always hanging to their coats, and the smell of cooking in their clothes. Cordelia Street – Ah, that belonged to another time and country; had he not always been thus, had he not sat here night after night, from as far back as he could remember, looking pensively over just such shimmering textures and slowly twirling the stem of a glass like this one between his thumb and middle finger? He rather thought he had.

He was not in the least abashed or lonely. He had no especial desire to meet or to know any of these people; all he demanded was the right to look on and conjecture, to watch the pageant. The mere stage properties were all he contended for. Nor was he lonely later in the evening, in his lodge at the Metropolitan. He was now entirely rid of his nervous misgivings, of his forced aggressiveness, of the imperative desire to show himself different from his surroundings. He felt now that his surroundings explained him. Nobody questioned the purple; he had only to wear it passively. He had only to glance down at his attire to reassure himself that here it would be impossible for anyone to humiliate him.

He found it hard to leave his beautiful sitting room to go to bed that night, and sat long watching the raging storm from his turret window. When he went to sleep it was with the lights turned on in his bedroom; partly because of his old timidity, and partly so that, if he should wake in the night, there would be no wretched moment of doubt, no horrible suspicion of yellow wallpaper, or of Washington and Calvin above his bed.

Sunday morning the city was practically snowbound. Paul breakfasted late, and in the afternoon he fell in with a wild San Francisco boy, a freshman at Yale, who said he had run down for a 'little flyer' over Sunday. The young man offered to show Paul the night side of the town, and the two boys went out together after dinner, not returning to the hotel until seven o'clock the next morning. They had started out in the confiding warmth of a champagne friendship, but their parting in the elevator was singularly cool. The freshman pulled himself together to make his train, and Paul went to bed. He awoke at two o'clock in the afternoon, very thirsty and dizzy, and rang for ice-water, coffee, and the Pittsburgh papers.

On the part of the hotel management, Paul excited no suspicion. There was this to be said for him, that he wore his spoils with dignity and in no way made himself conspicuous. Even under the glow of his wine he was never boisterous, though he found the stuff like a magician's wand for wonder-building. His chief greediness lay in his ears and eyes, and his excesses were not offensive ones. His dearest pleasures were the gray winter twilights in his sitting room; his quiet enjoyment of his flowers, his clothes, his wide divan, his cigarette, and his sense of power. He could not remember a time when he had felt so at peace with himself. The mere release from the necessity of petty lying, lying every day and every day, restored his self-respect. He had never lied for pleasure, even at school; but to be noticed and admired, to assert his difference from other Cordelia Street boys; and he felt a good deal more manly, more honest, even, now that he had no need for boastful pretensions, now that he could, as his actor friends used to say, 'dress the part.' It was characteristic that remorse did not occur to him. His golden days went by without a shadow, and he made each as perfect as he could.

On the eighth day after his arrival in New York he found the whole affair exploited in the Pittsburgh papers, exploited with a wealth of detail which indicated that local news of a sensational nature was at a low ebb. The firm of Denny & Carson announced that the boy's father had refunded the full amount of the theft and that they had no intention of prosecuting. The Cumberland minister had been interviewed, and expressed his hope of yet reclaiming the motherless lad, and his Sabbath-school teacher declared that she would spare no effort to that end. The rumor had reached Pittsburgh that the boy had been seen in a New York hotel, and his father had gone East to find him and bring him home.

Paul had just come in to dress for dinner; he sank into a chair, weak to the knees, and clasped his head in his hands. It was to be worse than jail, even; the tepid waters of Cordelia Street were to close over him finally and forever. The gray monotony stretched before him in hopeless, unrelieved years; Sabbath school, Young People's Meeting, the yellow-papered room, the damp dish-towels; it all rushed back upon him with a sickening vividness. He had the old feeling that the orchestra had suddenly stopped, the sinking sensation that the play was over. The sweat broke out on his face, and he sprang to his feet, looked about him with his white, conscious smile, and winked at himself in the mirror. With something of the old childish belief in miracles with which he had so often gone to class, all his lessons unlearned, Paul dressed and dashed whistling down the corridor to the elevator.

He had no sooner entered the dining room and caught the measure of the music than his remembrance was lightened by his old elastic power of claiming the moment, mounting with it, and finding it all-sufficient. The glare and glitter about him, the mere scenic accessories had again, and for the last time, their old potency. He would show himself that he was game, he would finish the thing splendidly. He doubted, more than ever, the existence of Cordelia Street, and for the first time he drank his wine recklessly. Was he not, after all, one of those fortunate beings born to the purple, was he not still himself and in his own place? He drummed a nervous accompaniment to the Pagliacci music* and looked about him, telling himself over and over that it had paid.

He reflected drowsily, to the swell of the music and the chill sweetness of his wine, that he might have done it more wisely. He might have caught an outbound steamer and been well out of their clutches before now. But the other side of the world had seemed too far away and too uncertain then; he could not have waited for it; his need had been too sharp. If he had to choose over again, he would do the same thing tomorrow. He looked affectionately about the dining room, now gilded with a soft mist. Ah, it had paid indeed!

Paul was awakened next morning by a painful throbbing in his head and feet. He had thrown himself across the bed without undressing, and had slept with his shoes on. His limbs and hands were lead heavy, and his tongue and throat were parched and burnt. There came upon him one of those fateful attacks of clearheadedness that never occurred except when he was physically exhausted and his nerves hung loose. He lay still, closed his eyes, and let the tide of things wash over him.

His father was in New York; 'stopping at some joint or other,' he told himself. The memory of successive summers on the front stoop fell upon him like a weight of black water. He had not a hundred dollars left; and he knew now, more than ever, that money was everything, the wall that stood between all he loathed and all he wanted. The thing was winding itself up; he had thought of that on his first glorious day in New York, and had even provided a way to snap the thread. It lay on his dressing table now; he had got it out last night when he came blindly up from dinner, but the shiny metal hurt his eyes, and he disliked the looks of it.

He rose and moved about with a painful effort, succumbing now and again to attacks of nausea. It was the old depression exaggerated; all the world had become Cordelia Street. Yet somehow he was not afraid of anything, was absolutely calm; perhaps because he had looked into the dark corner at last and knew. It was bad enough, what he saw there, but somehow not so bad as his long fear of it had been. He saw everything clearly now. He had a feeling that he had made the best of it, that he had lived the sort of life he was meant to live, and for half an hour he sat staring at the revolver. But he told himself that was not the way, so he went downstairs and took a cab to the ferry.

When Paul arrived in Newark he got off the train and took another cab, directing the driver to follow the Pennsylvania tracks out of the town. The snow lay heavy on the roadways and had drifted deep in the open fields. Only here and there the dead grass or dried weed stalks projected, singularly black, above it. Once well into the country, Paul dismissed the carriage and walked, floundering along the tracks, his mind a medley of irrelevant things. He seemed to hold in his brain an actual picture of everything he had seen that morning. He remembered every feature of both his drivers, of the toothless old woman from whom he had bought the red flowers in his coat, the agent from whom he had got his ticket, and all of his fellow passengers on the ferry. His mind, unable to cope with vital matters near at hand, worked feverishly and deftly at sorting and grouping these images. They made for him a part of the ugliness of the world, of the ache in his head, and the bitter burning on his tongue. He stooped and put a handful of snow into his mouth as he walked, but that, too, seemed hot. When he reached a little hillside, where the tracks ran through a cut some twenty feet below him, he stopped and sat down.

The carnations in his coat were drooping with the cold, he noticed, their red glory all over. It occurred to him that all the flowers he had seen in the glass cases that first night must have gone the same way, long before this. It was only one splendid breath they had, in spite of their brave mockery at the winter outside the glass; and it was a losing game in the end, it seemed, this revolt against the homilies by which the world is run. Paul took one of the blossoms carefully from his coat and scooped a little hole in the snow, where he covered it up. Then he dozed awhile, from his weak condition, seemingly insensible to the cold.

The sound of an approaching train awoke him, and he started to his feet, remembering only his resolution, and afraid lest he should be too late. He stood watching the approaching locomotive, his teeth chattering, his lips drawn away from them in a frightened smile; once or twice he glanced nervously sidewise, as though he were being watched. When the right moment came, he jumped. As he fell, the folly of his haste occurred to him with merciless clearness, the vastness of what he had left undone. There flashed through his brain, clearer than ever before, the blue of Adriatic water, the yellow of Algerian sands.

He felt something strike his chest, and that his body was being thrown swiftly through the air, on and on, immeasurably far and fast, while his limbs were gently relaxed. Then, because the picture-making mechanism was crushed, the disturbing visions flashed into black, and Paul dropped back into the immense design of things.

A Jury of Her Peers

1916

When Martha Hale opened the storm-door and got a cut of the north wind, she ran back for her big woolen scarf. As she hurriedly wound that round her head her eye made a scandalized sweep of her kitchen. It was no ordinary thing that called her away – it was probably farther from ordinary than anything that had ever happened in Dickson County. But what her eye took in was that her kitchen was in no shape for leaving: her bread all ready for mixing, half the flour sifted and half unsifted.

She hated to see things half done; but she had been at that when the team from town stopped to get Mr Hale, and then the sheriff came running in to say his wife wished Mrs Hale would come too – adding, with a grin, that he guessed she was getting scarey and wanted another woman along. So she had dropped everything right where it was.

'Martha!' now came her husband's impatient voice. 'Don't keep folks waiting out here in the cold.'

She again opened the storm-door, and this time joined the three men and the one woman waiting for her in the big, two-seated buggy.

After she had the robes tucked around her she took another look at the woman who sat beside her on the back seat. She had met Mrs Peters the year before at the county fair, and the thing she remembered about her was that she didn't seem like a sheriff's wife. She was small and thin and didn't have a strong voice. Mrs Gorman, sheriff's wife before Gorman went out and Peters came in, had a voice that somehow seemed to be backing up the law with every word. But if Mrs Peters didn't look like a sheriff's wife, Peters made it up in looking like a sheriff. He was to a dot the kind of man who could get himself elected sheriff –

a heavy man with a big voice, who was particularly genial with
the law-abiding, as if to make it plain that he knew the difference
between criminals and non-criminals. And right there it came
into Mrs Hale's mind, with a stab, that this man who was so
pleasant and lively with all of them was going to the Wrights'
now as a sheriff.

'The country's not very pleasant this time of year,' Mrs Peters
at last ventured, as if she felt they ought to be talking as well as
the men.

Mrs Hale scarcely finished her reply, for they had gone up a
little hill and could see the Wright place now, and seeing it did
not make her feel like talking. It looked very lonesome this cold
March morning. It had always been a lonesome-looking place.
It was down in a hollow, and the poplar trees around it were
lonesome-looking trees. The men were looking at it and talking
about what had happened. The county attorney was bending to
one side of the buggy, and kept looking steadily at the place as
they drew up to it.

'I'm glad you came with me,' Mrs Peters said nervously, as
the two women were about to follow the men in through the
kitchen door.

Even after she had her foot on the door-step, her hand on the
knob, Martha Hale had a moment of feeling she could not cross
that threshold. And the reason it seemed she couldn't cross it
now was simply because she hadn't crossed it before. Time and
time again it had been in her mind. 'I ought to go over and see
Minnie Foster' – she still thought of her as Minnie Foster,
though for twenty years she had been Mrs Wright. And then
there was always something to do and Minnie Foster would go
from her mind. But *now* she could come.

The men went over to the stove. The women stood close together
by the door. Young Henderson, the county attorney, turned
around and said, 'Come up to the fire, ladies.'

Mrs Peters took a step forward, then stopped. 'I'm not – cold,'
she said.

And so the two women stood by the door, at first not even so
much as looking around the kitchen.

The men talked for a minute about what a good thing it was
the sheriff had sent his deputy out that morning to make a fire
for them, and then Sheriff Peters stepped back from the stove,

unbuttoned his outer coat, and leaned his hands on the kitchen table in a way that seemed to mark the beginning of official business. 'Now, Mr Hale,' he said in a sort of semi-official voice, 'before we move things about, you tell Mr Henderson just what it was you saw when you came here yesterday morning.'

The county attorney was looking around the kitchen.

'By the way,' he said, 'has anything been moved?' He turned to the sheriff. 'Are things just as you left them yesterday?'

Peters looked from cupboard to sink; from that to a small worn rocker a little to one side of the kitchen table.

'It's just the same.'

'Somebody should have been left here yesterday,' said the county attorney.

'Oh – yesterday,' returned the sheriff, with a little gesture as of yesterday having been more than he could bear to think of. 'When I had to send Frank to Morris Center for that man who went crazy – let me tell you, I had my hands full *yesterday*. I knew you could get back from Omaha by to-day, George, and as long as I went over everything here myself – '

'Well, Mr Hale,' said the county attorney, in a way of letting what was past and gone go, 'tell just what happened when you came here yesterday morning.'

Mrs Hale, still leaning against the door, had that sinking feeling of the mother whose child is about to speak a piece. Lewis often wandered along and got things mixed up in a story. She hoped he would tell this straight and plain, and not say unnecessary things that would just make things harder for Minnie Foster. He didn't begin at once, and she noticed that he looked queer – as if standing in that kitchen and having to tell what he had seen there yesterday morning made him almost sick.

'Yes, Mr Hale?' the county attorney reminded.

'Harry and I had started to town with a load of potatoes,' Mrs Hale's husband began.

Harry was Mrs Hale's oldest boy. He wasn't with them now, for the very good reason that those potatoes never got to town yesterday and he was taking them this morning, so he hadn't been home when the sheriff stopped to say he wanted Mr Hale to come over to the Wright place and tell the county attorney his story there, where he could point it all out. With all Mrs Hale's other emotions came the fear now that maybe Harry wasn't dressed warm enough – they hadn't any of them realized how that north wind did bite.

'We come along this road,' Hale was going on, with a motion of his hand to the road over which they had just come, 'and as we got in sight of the house I says to Harry, "I'm goin' to see if I can't get John Wright to take a telephone." You see,' he explained to Henderson, 'unless I can get somebody to go in with me they won't come out this branch road except for a price *I* can't pay. I'd spoke to Wright about it once before; but he put me off, saying folks talked too much anyway, and all he asked was peace and quiet – guess you know about how much he talked himself. But I thought maybe if I went to the house and talked about it before his wife, and said all the women-folks liked the telephones, and that in this lonesome stretch of road it would be a good thing – well, I said to Harry that that was what I was going to say – though I said at the same time that I didn't know as what his wife wanted made much difference to John –'

Now, there he was! – saying things he didn't need to say. Mrs Hale tried to catch her husband's eye, but fortunately the county attorney interrupted with:

'Let's talk about that a little later, Mr Hale. I do want to talk about that, but I'm anxious now to get along to just what happened when you got here.'

When he began this time, it was very deliberately and carefully:

'I didn't see or hear anything. I knocked at the door. And still it was all quiet inside. I knew they must be up – it was past eight o'clock. So I knocked again, louder, and I thought I heard somebody say, "Come in." I wasn't sure – I'm not sure yet. But I opened the door – this door,' jerking a hand toward the door by which the two women stood, 'and there, in that rocker' – pointing to it – 'sat Mrs Wright.'

Everyone in the kitchen looked at the rocker. It came into Mrs Hale's mind that that rocker didn't look in the least like Minnie Foster – the Minnie Foster of twenty years before. It was a dingy red, with wooden rungs up the back, and the middle rung was gone, and the chair sagged to one side.

'How did she – look?' the county attorney was inquiring.

'Well,' said Hale, 'she looked – queer.'

'How do you mean – queer?'

As he asked it he took out a notebook and pencil. Mrs Hale did not like the sight of that pencil. She kept her eye fixed on her husband, as if to keep him from saying unnecessary things that would go into that notebook and make trouble.

Hale did speak guardedly, as if the pencil had affected him too.

'Well, as if she didn't know what she was going to do next. And kind of – done up.'

'How did she seem to feel about your coming?'

'Why, I don't think she minded – one way or other. She didn't pay much attention. I said, "Ho' do, Mrs Wright? It's cold, ain't it?" And she said, "Is it?" – and went on pleatin' at her apron.

'Well, I was surprised. She didn't ask me to come up to the stove, or to sit down, but just set there, not even lookin' at me. And so I said: "I want to see John."

'And then she – laughed. I guess you would call it a laugh.

'I thought of Harry and the team outside, so I said, a little sharp, "Can I see John?" "No," says she – kind of dull like. "Ain't he home?" says I. Then she looked at me. "Yes," says she, "he's home." "Then why can't I see him?" I asked her, out of patience with her now. "'Cause he's dead," says she, just as quiet and dull – and fell to pleatin' her apron. "Dead?" says I, like you do when you can't take in what you've heard.

'She just nodded her head, not getting a bit excited, but rockin' back and forth.

'"Why – where is he?" says I, not knowing *what* to say.

'She just pointed upstairs – like this' – pointing to the room above.

'I got up, with the idea of going up there myself. By this time I – didn't know what to do. I walked from there to here; then I says: "Why, what did he die of?"

'"He died of a rope round his neck," says she; and just went on pleatin' at her apron.'

Hale stopped speaking, and stood staring at the rocker, as if he were still seeing the woman who had sat there the morning before. Nobody spoke; it was as if every one were seeing the woman who had sat there the morning before.

'And what did you do then?' the county attorney at last broke the silence.

'I went out and called Harry. I thought I might – need help. I got Harry in, and we went upstairs.' His voice fell almost to a whisper. 'There he was – lying over the – '

'I think I'd rather have you go into that upstairs,' the county attorney interrupted, 'where you can point it all out. Just go on now with the rest of the story.'

'Well, my first thought was to get that rope off. It looked – '

He stopped, his face twitching.

'But Harry, he went up to him, and he said, "No, he's dead all right, and we'd better not touch anything." So we went downstairs.

'She was still sitting that same way. "Has anybody been notified?" I asked. "No," says she, unconcerned.

'"Who did this, Mrs Wright?" said Harry. He said it businesslike, and she stopped pleatin' at her apron. "I don't know," she says. "You don't *know*?" says Harry. "Weren't you sleepin' in the bed with him?" "Yes," says she, "but I was on the inside." "Somebody slipped a rope round his neck and strangled him, and you didn't wake up?" says Harry. "I didn't wake up," she said after him.

'We may have looked as if we didn't see how that could be, for after a minute she said, "I sleep sound."

'Harry was going to ask her more questions, but I said maybe that weren't our business; maybe we ought to let her tell her story first to the coroner or the sheriff. So Harry went fast as he could over to High Road – the Rivers' place, where there's a telephone.'

'And what did she do when she knew you had gone for the coroner?' The attorney got his pencil in his hand all ready for writing.

'She moved from that chair to this one over here' – Hale pointed to a small chair in the corner – 'and just sat there with her hands held together and looking down. I got a feeling that I ought to make some conversation, so I said I had come in to see if John wanted to put in a telephone; and at that she started to laugh, and then she stopped and looked at me – scared.'

At sound of a moving pencil the man who was telling the story looked up.

'I dunno – maybe it wasn't scared,' he hastened; 'I wouldn't like to say it was. Soon Harry got back, and then Dr Lloyd came, and you, Mr Peters, and so I guess that's all I know that you don't.'

*

He said that last with relief, and moved a little, as if relaxing. Everyone moved a little. The county attorney walked toward the stair door.

'I guess we'll go upstairs first – then out to the barn and around there.'

He paused and looked around the kitchen.

'You're convinced there was nothing important here?' he asked the sheriff. 'Nothing that would – point to any motive?'

The sheriff too looked all around, as if to re-convince himself.

'Nothing here but kitchen things,' he said, with a little laugh for the insignificance of kitchen things.

The county attorney was looking at the cupboard – a peculiar, ungainly structure, half closet and half cupboard, the upper part of it being built in the wall, and the lower part just the old-fashioned kitchen cupboard. As if its queerness attracted him, he got a chair and opened the upper part and looked in. After a moment he drew his hand away sticky.

'Here's a nice mess,' he said resentfully.

The two women had drawn nearer, and now the sheriff's wife spoke.

'Oh – her fruit,' she said, looking to Mrs Hale for sympathetic understanding. She turned back to the county attorney and explained: 'She worried about that when it turned so cold last night. She said the fire would go out and her jars might burst.'

Mrs Peters' husband broke into a laugh.

'Well, can you beat the woman! Held for murder, and worrying about her preserves!'

The young attorney set his lips.

'I guess before we're through with her she may have some-thing more serious than preserves to worry about.'

'Oh, well,' said Mrs Hale's husband, with good-natured superiority, 'women are used to worrying over trifles.'

The two women moved a little closer together. Neither of them spoke. The county attorney seemed suddenly to remember his manners – and think of his future.

'And yet,' said he, with the gallantry of a young politician, 'for all their worries, what would we do without the ladies?'

The women did not speak, did not unbend. He went to the sink and began washing his hands. He turned to wipe them on the roller towel – whirled it for a cleaner place.

'Dirty towels! Not much of a housekeeper, would you say, ladies?'

He kicked his foot against some dirty pans under the sink.

'There's a great deal of work to be done on a farm,' said Mrs Hale stiffly.

'To be sure. And yet' – with a little bow to her – 'I know there are some Dickson County farm houses that do not have such roller towels.' He gave it a pull to expose its full length again.

'Those towels get dirty awful quick. Men's hands aren't always as clean as they might be.'

'Ah, loyal to your sex, I see,' he laughed. He stopped and gave her a keen look. 'But you and Mrs Wright were neighbors. I suppose you were friends, too.'

Martha Hale shook her head.

'I've seen little enough of her of late years. I've not been in this house – it's more than a year.'

'And why was that? You didn't like her?'

'I liked her well enough,' she replied with spirit. 'Farmers' wives have their hands full, Mr Henderson. And then – ' She looked around the kitchen.

'Yes?' he encouraged.

'It never seemed a very cheerful place,' said she, more to herself than to him.

'No,' he agreed; 'I don't think any one would call it cheerful. I shouldn't say she had the home-making instinct.'

'Well, I don't know as Wright had, either,' she muttered.

'You mean they didn't get on very well?' he was quick to ask.

'No; I don't mean anything,' she answered, with decision. As she turned a little away from him, she added: 'But I don't think a place would be any the cheerfuler for John Wright's bein' in it.'

'I'd like to talk to you about that a little later, Mrs Hale,' he said. 'I'm anxious to get the lay of things upstairs now.'

He moved toward the stair door, followed by the two men.

'I suppose anything Mrs Peters does'll be all right?' the sheriff inquired. 'She was to take in some clothes for her, you know – and a few little things. We left in such a hurry yesterday.'

The county attorney looked at the two women whom they were leaving alone there among the kitchen things.

'Yes – Mrs Peters,' he said, his glance resting on the woman who was not Mrs Peters, the big farmer woman who stood behind the sheriff's wife. 'Of course Mrs Peters is one of us,' he said, in a manner of entrusting responsibility. 'And keep your eye out, Mrs Peters, for anything that might be of use. No telling; you women might come upon a clue to the motive – and that's the thing we need.'

Mr Hale rubbed his face after the fashion of a show man getting ready for a pleasantry.

'But would the women know a clue if they did come upon it?' he said; and, having delivered himself of this, he followed the others through the stair door.

The women stood motionless and silent, listening to the foot-steps, first upon the stairs, then in the room above them.

Then, as if releasing herself from something strange, Mrs Hale began to arrange the dirty pans under the sink, which the county attorney's disdainful push of the foot had deranged.

'I'd hate to have men comin' into my kitchen,' she said testily – 'snoopin' round and criticizin'.'

'Of course it's no more than their duty,' said the sheriff's wife, in her manner of timid acquiescence.

'Duty's all right,' replied Mrs Hale bluffly; 'but I guess that deputy sheriff that come out to make the fire might have got a little of this on.' She gave the roller towel a pull. 'Wish I'd thought of that sooner! Seems mean to talk about her for not having things slicked up, when she had to come away in such a hurry.'

She looked around the kitchen. Certainly it was not 'slicked up.' Her eye was held by a bucket of sugar on a low shelf. The cover was off the wooden bucket, and beside it was a paper bag – half full.

Mrs Hale moved toward it.

'She was putting this in there,' she said to herself – slowly.

She thought of the flour in her kitchen at home – half sifted, half not sifted. She had been interrupted, and had left things half done. What had interrupted Minnie Foster? Why had that work been left half done? She made a move as if to finish it, – unfinished things always bothered her, – and then she glanced around and saw that Mrs Peters was watching her – and she didn't want Mrs Peters to get that feeling she had got of work begun and then – for some reason – not finished.

'It's a shame about her fruit,' she said, and walked toward the cupboard that the county attorney had opened, and got on the chair, murmuring: 'I wonder if it's all gone.'

It was a sorry enough looking sight, but 'Here's one that's all right,' she said at last. She held it toward the light. 'This is cherries, too.' She looked again. 'I declare I believe that's the only one.'

With a sigh, she got down from the chair, went to the sink, and wiped off the bottle.

'She'll feel awful bad, after all her hard work in the hot weather. I remember the afternoon I put up my cherries last summer.'

She set the bottle on the table, and, with another sigh, started to sit down in the rocker. But she did not sit down. Something kept her from sitting down in that chair. She straightened – stepped back, and, half turned away, stood looking at it, seeing the woman who had sat there 'pleatin' at her apron.'

The thin voice of the sheriff's wife broke in upon her: 'I must be getting those things from the front room closet.' She opened the door into the other room, started in, stepped back. 'You coming with me, Mrs Hale?' she asked nervously. 'You – you could help me get them.'

They were soon back – the stark coldness of that shut-up room was not a thing to linger in.

'My!' said Mrs Peters, dropping the things on the table and hurrying to the stove.

Mrs Hale stood examining the clothes the woman who was being detained in town had said she wanted.

'Wright was close!' she exclaimed, holding up a shabby black skirt that bore the marks of much making over. 'I think maybe that's why she kept so much to herself. I s'pose she felt she couldn't do her part; and then, you don't enjoy things when you feel shabby. She used to wear pretty clothes and be lively – when she was Minnie Foster, one of the town girls, singing in the choir. But that – oh, that was twenty years ago.'

With a carefulness in which there was something tender, she folded the shabby clothes and piled them at one corner of the table. She looked up at Mrs Peters, and there was something in the other woman's look that irritated her.

'She don't care,' she said to herself. 'Much difference it makes to her whether Minnie Foster had pretty clothes when she was a girl.'

Then she looked again, and she wasn't so sure; in fact, she hadn't at any time been perfectly sure about Mrs Peters. She had that shrinking manner, and yet her eyes looked as if they could see a long way into things.

'This all you was to take in?' asked Mrs Hale.

'No,' said the sheriff's wife; 'she said she wanted an apron. Funny thing to want,' she ventured in her nervous little way, 'for there's not much to get you dirty in jail, goodness knows. But I suppose just to make her feel more natural. If you're used to wearing an apron – . She said they were in the bottom drawer of this cupboard. Yes – here they are. And then her little shawl that always hung on the stair door.'

She took the small gray shawl from behind the door leading upstairs, and stood a minute looking at it.

Suddenly Mrs Hale took a quick step toward the other woman.

'Mrs Peters!'

'Yes, Mrs Hale?'

'Do you think she – did it?'

A frightened look blurred the other thing in Mrs Peters' eyes.

'Oh, I don't know,' she said, in a voice that seemed to shrink away from the subject.

'Well, I don't think she did,' affirmed Mrs Hale stoutly. 'Asking for an apron, and her little shawl. Worryin' about her fruit.'

'Mr Peters says – .' Footsteps were heard in the room above; she stopped, looked up, then went on in a lowered voice: 'Mr Peters says – it looks bad for her. Mr Henderson is awful sarcastic in a speech, and he's going to make fun of her saying she didn't – wake up.'

For a moment Mrs Hale had no answer. Then, 'Well, I guess John Wright didn't wake up – when they was slippin' that rope under his neck,' she muttered.

'No, it's *strange*,' breathed Mrs Peters. 'They think it was such a – funny way to kill a man.'

She began to laugh; at sound of the laugh, abruptly stopped.

'That's just what Mr Hale said,' said Mrs Hale, in a resolutely natural voice. 'There was a gun in the house. He says that's what he can't understand.'

'Mr Henderson said, coming out, that what was needed for the case was a motive. Something to show anger – or sudden feeling.'

'Well, I don't see any signs of anger around here,' said Mrs Hale. 'I don't – '

She stopped. It was as if her mind tripped on something. Her eye was caught by a dish-towel in the middle of the kitchen table. Slowly she moved toward the table. One half of it was wiped clean, the other half messy. Her eyes made a slow, almost unwilling turn to the bucket of sugar and the half empty bag beside it. Things begun – and not finished.

After a moment she stepped back, and said, in that manner of releasing herself:

'Wonder how they're finding things upstairs? I hope she had it a little more red up there. You know,' – she paused, and feeling gathered, – 'it seems kind of *sneaking*: locking her up in town and coming out here to get her own house to turn against her!'

'But, Mrs Hale,' said the sheriff's wife, 'the law is the law.'

'I s'pose 'tis,' answered Mrs Hale shortly.

She turned to the stove, saying something about that fire not being much to brag of. She worked with it a minute, and when she straightened up she said aggressively:

'The law is the law – and a bad stove is a bad stove. How'd you like to cook on this?' – pointing with the poker to the broken lining. She opened the oven door and started to express her opinion of the oven; but she was swept into her own thoughts, thinking of what it would mean, year after year, to have that stove to wrestle with. The thought of Minnie Foster trying to bake in that oven – and the thought of her never going over to see Minnie Foster – .

She was startled by hearing Mrs Peters, say: 'A person gets discouraged – and loses heart.'

The sheriff's wife had looked from the stove to the sink – to the pail of water which had been carried in from outside. The two women stood there silent, above them the footsteps of the men who were looking for evidence against the woman who had worked in that kitchen. That look of seeing into things, of seeing through a thing to something else, was in the eyes of the sheriff's wife now. When Mrs Hale next spoke to her, it was gently:

'Better loosen up your things, Mrs Peters. We'll not feel them when we go out.'

Mrs Peters went to the back of the room to hang up the fur

tippet she was wearing. A moment later she exclaimed, 'Why, she was piecing a quilt,' and held up a large sewing basket piled high with quilt pieces.

Mrs Hale spread some of the blocks out on the table. 'It's log-cabin pattern,' she said, putting several of them together. 'Pretty, isn't it?'

They were so engaged with the quilt that they did not hear the footsteps on the stairs. Just as the stair door opened Mrs Hale was saying:

'Do you suppose she was going to quilt it or just knot it?'

The sheriff threw up his hands.

'They wonder whether she was going to quilt it or just knot it!'

There was a laugh for the ways of women, a warming of hands over the stove, and then the county attorney said briskly:

'Well, let's go right out to the barn and get that cleared up.'

'I don't see as there's anything so strange,' Mrs Hale said resentfully, after the outside door had closed on the three men – 'our taking up our time with little things while we're waiting for them to get the evidence. I don't see as it's anything to laugh about.'

'Of course they've got awful important things on their minds,' said the sheriff's wife apologetically.

They returned to an inspection of the block for the quilt. Mrs Hale was looking at the fine, even sewing, and preoccupied with thoughts of the woman who had done that sewing, when she heard the sheriff's wife say, in a queer tone:

'Why, look at this one.'

She turned to take the block held out to her.

'The sewing,' said Mrs Peters, in a troubled way. 'All the rest of them have been so nice and even – but – this one. Why, it looks as if she didn't know what she was about!'

Their eyes met – something flashed to life, passed between them; then, as if with an effort, they seemed to pull away from each other. A moment Mrs Hale sat there, her hands folded over that sewing which was so unlike all the rest of the sewing. Then she had pulled a knot and drawn the threads.

'Oh, what are you doing, Mrs Hale?' asked the sheriff's wife, startled.

'Just pulling out a stitch or two that's not sewed very good,' said Mrs Hale mildly.

'I don't think we ought to touch things,' Mrs Peters said, a little helplessly.

'I'll just finish up this end,' answered Mrs Hale, still in that mild, matter-of-fact fashion.

She threaded a needle and started to replace bad sewing with good. For a little while she sewed in silence. Then, in that thin, timid voice, she heard:

'Mrs Hale!'

'Yes, Mrs Peters?'

'What do you suppose she was so – nervous about?'

'Oh, *I* don't know,' said Mrs Hale, as if dismissing a thing not important enough to spend much time on. 'I don't know as she was – nervous. I sew awful queer sometimes when I'm just tired.'

She cut a thread, and out of the corner of her eye looked up at Mrs Peters. The small, lean face of the sheriff's wife seemed to have tightened up. Her eyes had that look of peering into something. But next moment she moved, and said in her thin, indecisive way:

'Well, I must get those clothes wrapped. They may be through sooner than we think. I wonder where I could find a piece of paper – and string.'

'In that cupboard, maybe,' suggested Mrs Hale, after a glance around.

One piece of the crazy sewing remained unripped. Mrs Peters' back turned, Martha Hale now scrutinized that piece, compared it with the dainty, accurate sewing of the other blocks. The difference was startling. Holding this block made her feel queer, as if the distracted thoughts of the woman who had perhaps turned to it to try and quiet herself were communicating themselves to her.

Mrs Peters' voice roused her.

'Here's a bird-cage,' she said. 'Did she have a bird, Mrs Hale?'

'Why, I don't know whether she did or not.' She turned to look at the cage Mrs Peters was holding up. 'I've not been here in so long.' She sighed. 'There was a man round last year selling canaries cheap – but I don't know as she took one. Maybe she did. She used to sing real pretty herself.'

Mrs Peters looked around the kitchen.

'Seems kind of funny to think of a bird here.' She half laughed

– an attempt to put up a barrier. 'But she must have had one –
or why would she have a cage? I wonder what happened to it.'

'I suppose maybe the cat got it,' suggested Mrs Hale, resuming
her sewing.

'No; she didn't have a cat. She's got that feeling some people
have about cats – being afraid of them. When they brought her
to our house yesterday, my cat got in the room, and she was
real upset and asked me to take it out.'

'My sister Bessie was like that,' laughed Mrs Hale.

The sheriff's wife did not reply. The silence made Mrs Hale
turn round. Mrs Peters was examining the bird-cage.

'Look at this door,' she said slowly. 'It's broke. One hinge has
been pulled apart.'

Mrs Hale came nearer.

'Looks as if someone must have been – rough with it.'

Again their eyes met – startled, questioning, apprehensive. For
a moment neither spoke nor stirred. Then Mrs Hale, turning
away, said brusquely:

'If they're going to find any evidence, I wish they'd be about
it. I don't like this place.'

'But I'm awful glad you came with me, Mrs Hale.' Mrs Peters
put the bird-cage on the table and sat down. 'It would be
lonesome for me – sitting here alone.'

'Yes, it would, wouldn't it?' agreed Mrs Hale, a certain
determined naturalness in her voice. She had picked up the
sewing, but now it dropped in her lap, and she murmured in a
different voice: 'But I tell you what I *do* wish, Mrs Peters. I
wish I had come over sometimes when she was here. I wish – I
had.'

'But of course you were awful busy, Mrs Hale. Your house –
and your children.'

'I could've come,' retorted Mrs Hale shortly. 'I stayed away
because it weren't cheerful – and that's why I ought to have
come. I' – she looked around – 'I've never liked this place.
Maybe because it's down in a hollow and you don't see the
road. I don't know what it is, but it's a lonesome place, and
always was. I wish I had come over to see Minnie Foster
sometimes. I can see now – ' She did not put it into words.

'Well, you mustn't reproach yourself,' counseled Mrs Peters.
'Somehow, we just don't see how it is with other folks till –
something comes up.'

'Not having children makes less work,' mused Mrs Hale, after a silence, 'but it makes a quiet house – and Wright out to work all day – and no company when he did come in. Did you know John Wright, Mrs Peters?'

'Not to know him. I've seen him in town. They say he was a good man.'

'Yes – good,' conceded John Wright's neighbor grimly. 'He didn't drink, and kept his word as well as most, I guess, and paid his debts. But he was a hard man, Mrs Peters. Just to pass the time of day with him – .' She stopped, shivered a little. 'Like a raw wind that gets to the bone.' Her eye fell upon the cage on the table before her, and she added, almost bitterly: 'I should think she would've wanted a bird!'

Suddenly she leaned forward, looking intently at the cage. 'But what do you s'pose went wrong with it?'

'I don't know,' returned Mrs Peters; 'unless it got sick and died.'

But after she said it she reached over and swung the broken door. Both women watched it as if somehow held by it.

'You didn't know – her?' Mrs Hale asked, a gentler note in her voice.

'Not till they brought her yesterday,' said the sheriff's wife.

'She – come to think of it, she was kind of like a bird herself. Real sweet and pretty, but kind of timid and – fluttery. How – she – did – change.'

That held her for a long time. Finally, as if struck with a happy thought and relieved to get back to everyday things, she exclaimed:

'Tell you what, Mrs Peters, why don't you take the quilt in with you? It might take up her mind.'

'Why, I think that's a real nice idea, Mrs Hale,' agreed the sheriff's wife, as if she too were glad to come into the atmosphere of a simple kindness. 'There couldn't possibly be any objection to that, could there? Now, just what will I take? I wonder if her patches are in here – and her things.'

They turned to the sewing basket.

'Here's some red,' said Mrs Hale, bringing out a roll of cloth. Underneath that was a box. 'Here, maybe her scissors are in here – and her things.' She held it up. 'What a pretty box! I'll warrant that was something she had a long time ago – when she was a girl.'

She held it in her hand a moment; then, with a little sigh, opened it.

Instantly her hand went to her nose.

'Why – !'

Mrs Peters drew nearer – then turned away.

'There's something wrapped up in this piece of silk,' faltered Mrs Hale.

'This isn't her scissors,' said Mrs Peters, in a shrinking voice.

Her hand not steady, Mrs Hale raised the piece of silk. 'Oh, Mrs Peters!' she cried. 'It's – '

Mrs Peters bent closer.

'It's the bird,' she whispered.

'But, Mrs Peters!' cried Mrs Hale. '*Look* at it! Its *neck* – look at its neck! It's all – other side to.'

She held the box away from her.

The sheriff's wife again bent closer.

'Somebody wrung its neck,' said she, in a voice that was slow and deep.

And then again the eyes of the two women met – this time clung together in a look of dawning comprehension, of growing horror. Mrs Peters looked from the dead bird to the broken door of the cage. Again their eyes met. And just then there was a sound at the outside door.

Mrs Hale slipped the box under the quilt pieces in the basket, and sank into the chair before it. Mrs Peters stood holding to the table. The county attorney and the sheriff came in from outside.

'Well, ladies,' said the county attorney, as one turning from serious things to little pleasantries, 'have you decided whether she was going to quilt it or knot it?'

'We think,' began the sheriff's wife in a flurried voice, 'that she was going to – knot it.'

He was too preoccupied to notice the change that came in her voice on that last.

'Well, that's very interesting, I'm sure,' he said tolerantly. He caught sight of the bird-cage. 'Has the bird flown?'

'We think the cat got it,' said Mrs Hale in a voice curiously even.

He was walking up and down, as if thinking something out.

'Is there a cat?' he asked absently.

Mrs Hale shot a look up at the sheriff's wife.

'Well, not *now*,' said Mrs Peters. 'They're superstitious, you know; they leave.'

She sank into her chair.

The county attorney did not heed her. 'No sign at all of any-one having come in from the outside,' he said to Peters, in the manner of continuing an interrupted conversation. 'Their own rope. Now let's go upstairs again and go over it, piece by piece. It would have to have been someone who knew just the – '

The stair door closed behind them and their voices were lost.

The two women sat motionless, not looking at each other, but as if peering into something and at the same time holding back. When they spoke now it was as if they were afraid of what they were saying, but as if they could not help saying it.

'She liked the bird,' said Martha Hale, low and slowly. 'She was going to bury it in that pretty box.'

'When I was a girl,' said Mrs Peters, under her breath, 'my kitten – there was a boy took a hatchet, and before my eyes – before I could get there – ' She covered her face an instant. 'If they hadn't held me back I would have' – she caught herself, looked upstairs where footsteps were heard, and finished weakly – 'hurt him.'

Then they sat without speaking or moving.

'I wonder how it would seem,' Mrs Hale at last began, as if feeling her way over strange ground – 'never to have had any children around?' Her eyes made a slow sweep of the kitchen, as if seeing what that kitchen had meant through all the years. 'No, Wright wouldn't like the bird,' she said after that – 'a thing that sang. She used to sing. He killed that too.' Her voice tightened.

Mrs Peters moved uneasily.

'Of course we don't know who killed the bird.'

'I knew John Wright,' was Mrs Hale's answer.

'It was an awful thing was done in this house that night, Mrs Hale,' said the sheriff's wife. 'Killing a man while he slept – slipping a thing round his neck that choked the life out of him.'

Mrs Hale's hand went out to the bird-cage.

'His neck. Choked the life out of him.'

'We don't *know* who killed him,' whispered Mrs Peters wildly. 'We don't *know*.'

Mrs Hale had not moved. 'If there had been years and years of – nothing, then a bird to sing to you, it would be awful – still – after the bird was still.'

It was as if something within her not herself had spoken, and it found in Mrs Peters something she did not know as herself.

'I know what stillness is,' she said, in a queer, monotonous voice. 'When we homesteaded in Dakota, and my first baby died – after he was two years old – and me with no other then – '

Mrs Hale stirred.

'How soon do you suppose they'll be through looking for the evidence?'

'I know what stillness is,' repeated Mrs Peters, in just that same way. Then she too pulled back. 'The law has got to punish crime, Mrs Hale,' she said in her tight little way.

'I wish you'd seen Minnie Foster,' was the answer, 'when she wore a white dress with blue ribbons, and stood up there in the choir and sang.'

The picture of that girl, the fact that she had lived neighbor to that girl for twenty years, and had let her die for lack of life, was suddenly more than she could bear.

'Oh, I *wish* I'd come over here once in a while!' she cried. 'That was a crime! That was a crime! Who's going to punish that?'

'We mustn't take on,' said Mrs Peters, with a frightened look toward the stairs.

'I might 'a' *known* she needed help! I tell you, it's *queer*, Mrs Peters. We live close together, and we live far apart. We all go through the same things – it's all just a different kind of the same thing! If it weren't – why do you and I *understand*? Why do we *know* – what we know this minute?'

She dashed her hand across her eyes. Then, seeing the jar of fruit on the table, she reached for it and choked out:

'If I was you I wouldn't *tell* her her fruit was gone! Tell her it *ain't*. Tell her it's all right – all of it. Here – take this in to prove it to her! She – she may never know whether it was broke or not.'

She turned away.

Mrs Peters reached out for the bottle of fruit as if she were glad to take it – as if touching a familiar thing, having something to do, could keep her from something else. She got up, looked about for something to wrap the fruit in, took a petticoat from the pile of clothes she had brought from the front room, and nervously started winding that round the bottle.

'My!' she began, in a high, false voice, 'it's a good thing the men couldn't hear us! Getting all stirred up over a little thing like a – dead canary.' She hurried over that. 'As if that could have anything to do with – with – My, wouldn't they *laugh*?'

Footsteps were heard on the stairs.

'Maybe they would,' muttered Mrs Hale – 'maybe they wouldn't.'

'No, Peters,' said the county attorney incisively; 'it's all perfectly clear, except the reason for doing it. But you know juries when it comes to women. If there was some definite thing – something to show. Something to make a story about. A thing that would connect up with this clumsy way of doing it.'

In a covert way Mrs Hale looked at Mrs Peters. Mrs Peters was looking at her. Quickly they looked away from each other. The outer door opened and Mr Hale came in.

'I've got the team round now,' he said. 'Pretty cold out there.'

'I'm going to stay here awhile by myself,' the county attorney suddenly announced. 'You can send Frank out for me, can't you?' he asked the sheriff. 'I want to go over everything. I'm not satisfied we can't do better.'

Again, for one brief moment, the two women's eyes found one another.

The sheriff came up to the table.

'Did you want to see what Mrs Peters was going to take in?'

The county attorney picked up the apron. He laughed.

'Oh, I guess they're not very dangerous things the ladies have picked out.'

Mrs Hale's hand was on the sewing basket in which the box was concealed. She felt that she ought to take her hand off the basket. She did not seem able to. He picked up one of the quilt blocks which she had piled on to cover the box. Her eyes felt like fire. She had a feeling that if he took up the basket she would snatch it from him.

But he did not take it up. With another little laugh, he turned away, saying:

'No; Mrs Peters doesn't need supervising. For that matter, a sheriff's wife is married to the law. Ever think of it that way, Mrs Peters?'

Mrs Peters was standing beside the table. Mrs Hale shot a look up at her; but she could not see her face. Mrs Peters had turned away. When she spoke, her voice was muffled.

'Not – just that way,' she said.

'Married to the law!' chuckled Mrs Peters' husband. He moved toward the door into the front room, and said to the county attorney:

'I just want you to come in here a minute, George. We ought to take a look at these windows.'

'Oh – windows,' said the county attorney scoffingly.

'We'll be right out, Mr Hale,' said the sheriff to the farmer, who was still waiting by the door.

Hale went to look after the horses. The sheriff followed the county attorney into the other room. Again – for one final moment – the two women were alone in that kitchen.

Martha Hale sprang up, her hands tight together, looking at that other woman, with whom it rested. At first she could not see her eyes, for the sheriff's wife had not turned back since she turned away at that suggestion of being married to the law. But now Mrs Hale made her turn back. Her eyes made her turn back. Slowly, unwillingly, Mrs Peters turned her head until her eyes met the eyes of the other woman. There was a moment when they held each other in a steady, burning look in which there was no evasion nor flinching. Then Martha Hale's eyes pointed the way to the basket in which was hidden the thing that would make certain the conviction of the other woman – that woman who was not there and yet who had been there with them all through that hour.

For a moment Mrs Peters did not move. And then she did it. With a rush forward, she threw back the quilt pieces, got the box, tried to put it in her handbag. It was too big. Desperately she opened it, started to take the bird out. But there she broke – she could not touch the bird. She stood there helpless, foolish.

There was the sound of a knob turning in the inner door. Martha Hale snatched the box from the sheriff's wife, and got it in the pocket of her big coat just as the sheriff and the county attorney came back into the kitchen.

'Well, Henry,' said the county attorney facetiously, 'at least we found out that she was not going to quilt it. She was going to – what is it you call it, ladies?'

Mrs Hale's hand was against the pocket of her coat.

'We call it – knot it, Mr Henderson.'

NOTES

Catharine Sedgwick

'*Cacoethes Scribendi*'

p. 3 *Glory and gain the industrious tribe provoke*: Alexander Pope, 'The Dunciad: To Dr Jonathan Swift' (Book the Second, 33).

p. 3 '. . . But 'tis a spirit': Shakespeare, *The Tempest* I. ii. 413–15.

p. 5 **Georgics and Pastorals:** Georgics are poems dealing with agricultural and rural affairs (after Virgil's *Georgics*); Pastorals tell of the life of shepherds and rural life.

p. 5 **a Crichton:** James Crichton (1560–82), called 'the Admirable Crichton', a Scottish scholar and adventurer who was celebrated for his extraordinary accomplishments and attainments in the languages, sciences and arts.

p. 7 *North American Review*: monthly magazine printed in New York from 1799–1800 featuring essays and stories.

p. 8 **Atalanta:** the fleet-footed daughter of Schoeneus who promised to marry any man who could outrun her. Hippomenes won her hand by throwing three golden apples (given to him by Aphrodite) in front of her, causing her to delay and pick them up. However, Hippomenes' failure to thank Aphrodite led to the pair being changed into lions.

p. 10 '**Full many a gem of purest ray serene,**' etc.: Thomas Gray, 'Elegy Written in a Country Churchyard' (53).

p. 10 *cacoethes scribendi*: an uncontrollable urge to write.

p. 10 **La Roche:** Maria Sophie La Roche (1731–1807), German sentimental novelist.

p. 10 **Meg Merrilies:** weird and masculine Gypsy woman in Sir Walter Scott's *Guy Mannering* (1815).

p. 10 **Ichabod Crane:** awkward country schoolmaster in 'The Legend of Sleepy Hollow', by Washington Irving (1820).

p. 11 **Otway:** Thomas Otway (1652–85), tragic poet of the English Classical school.

p. 11 **Tasso:** Bernardo Tasso (1544–95), Italian poet famous for *Jerusalem Delivered* (1581).

p. 11 **Mr D'Israeli:** Isaac D'Israeli (1766–1848), English miscellaneous writer, father of Benjamin Disraeli.

p. 12 **blue stocking:** women having or pretending to have literary tastes (after eighteenth-century literary clubs whose members occasionally wore blue stockings).

Harriet Prescott Spofford

'Circumstance'

p. 37 **demesnes:** possession of land as one's own, or an estate occupied, controlled and worked for the exclusive use of one owner.

p. 38 **the Indian Devil:** a jaguar.

p. 43 **Lady Margaret:** the heroine of 'Lay of the Last Minstrel' (1805) by Sir Walter Scott.

p. 49 **the world was all before them, where to choose:** alludes to the departure of Adam and Eve from Eden at the end of Milton's *Paradise Lost*.

Rebecca Harding Davis

'Life in the Iron Mills'

p. 51 **Is this ... redress:** modeled after Alfred Lord Tennyson's *In Memoriam* (1850), 56. 25–7.

p. 51 **rain-butts:** casks to collect rainwater.

p. 51 *la belle rivière!*: the beautiful river!

p. 52 **puddler:** person who refines molten crude ore by stirring.

p. 53 **Egoist, or Pantheist, or Arminian:** one who is self-interested; one who believes God is in all things; one who believes in free will.

p. 53 **picker:** person who separates cotton fibers.

p. 53 **feeder:** person who shovels ore to the processor.

p. 54 **on the spools:** working on winding cotton.

p. 55 **Milesian:** Irish.

p. 55 **flitch:** salt bacon.

p. 59 *Korl:* slag.

p. 61 **Farinata:** one of the heretics in Canto 10 of the *Inferno*.

p. 62 **sinking-fund:** fund used to pay off debt.

p. 62 **Kant, Novalis, Humboldt:** Immanuel Kant (1724–1804), German philosopher; Friedrich Leopold von Hardenberg (1772–1801), naturalist, statesman, explorer; Friedherr von Willhelm Humboldt (1767–1835), German language scholar, philosopher, diplomat.

p. 65 *Ce n'est pas mon affaire:* that's no business of mine.

p. 66 **'What shall we do to be saved?':** Acts 16:30.

p. 67 *'De profundis clamavi':* Out of the depths I cry (Psalm 130).

p. 67 **'I am innocent of the blood of this man':** Matthew 27:24.

p. 67 **'Inasmuch as ye did it unto one of the least of these, ye did it unto me':** Matthew 25:40.

p. 67 *n'est ce pas?:* isn't that true?

p. 68 **Saint-Simonian:** Louis de Rouvroy Saint-Simon (1760–1825), first French socialist.

p. 69 **Magdalens:** prostitutes (Matthew 15:39).

p. 69 **Baconian theories, Goethe schemes:** Francis Bacon (1521–1626), English philosopher and scientist; Goethe – see note to 'At the Château of Corinne' (p. 309).

p. 69 **their Jean Paul, their Cromwell:** Jean Paul Richter (1763–1825), German novelist; Oliver Cromwell (1599–1658), leader of the parliamentary forces during the English Civil War and ruler of England from 1649 until his death.

p. 79 **chaffering:** bargaining.

p. 82 **'How long, O Lord? how long?'** Thomas Babington Macaulay (1800–59), *Marriage of Tirzah and Ahirad*.

p. 83 **'Father, forgive them, for they know not what they do!':** Jesus's words on the Cross, Luke 23:24.

p. 84 frick: fresh.

p. 85 Esau: the son of Isaac and Rebecca, who was cheated out of his birthright by his brother Jacob (Genesis 25:25).

p. 85 Aphrodite: Greek goddess of love.

'Marcia'

p. 90 Gérôme: Jean Léon Gérôme (1824–1904), French painter, sculptor and teacher.

p. 90 Boughton: George Henry Boughton (1834–1905), American genre and landscape artist.

Louisa May Alcott

'My Contraband'

p. 95 Contraband: a negro slave who during the Civil War either escaped to or was brought within Union lines.

p. 98 Michael Angelo's bronze prisoner: bronze statue of Julius (1507), which was destroyed in 1771.

p. 99 the bat in Æsop's fable: in the war between the animals and the birds, the bat gave himself up to the animals as the likely victors. However, the arrival of the eagle allowed the birds to win, and the bat was sentenced to have his feathers removed and to fly at night away from the light.

p. 100 'F.F.Vs': the First Families of Virginia (the social elite).

p. 110 the attack on Fort Wagner: part of the July 1862 siege of Charleston, South Carolina, eventually won by the Union side, led by the 54th Massachusetts, the first all-black Union army regiment.

p. 113 Jeff, Beauregard, an' Lee: Pierre Gustave Toutant Beauregard (1818–93), American Confederate general; Robert E. Lee (1731–82), American revolutionary general.

'Behind a Mask: or, A Woman's Power'

p. 119 Rachel: wife of Jacob, Genesis 24–35.

p. 121 Juno: in Roman mythology the Queen of heaven and sister and wife of Jupiter. She is the protectress of marriage and the guardian of women.

p. 127 **Hector:** in Greek myth the son of Priam and Hecuba and brother of Paris. Hector was the greatest Trojan warrior, killing Patroclus before being slain by Achilles.

p. 138 **barcarole:** a boat song (especially as sung by Venetian gondoliers).

p. 159 *Peerage*: *Burke's Peerage*, a heraldic dictionary of the peerage and Baronetage of the UK, first compiled by John Burke in 1826.

p. 161 **Roundhead damsel:** Roundheads were members of the Parliamentary party during the English Civil War.

p. 162 **'The Marriage à la Mode':** series of six paintings by William Hogarth in 1745 depicting the disastrous consequences of aristocratic marriage without love.

p. 164 **Queen Bess:** Queen Elizabeth I (1533–1601).

p. 164 **Essex:** Lord Essex (1566–1601), a favorite of Elizabeth I who was beheaded for treason.

p. 164 **bonny Prince Charlie:** The Young Pretender (1720–88), last serious Stuart claimant to the British throne and leader of the unsuccessful Jacobite rebellion of 1745–6.

p. 181 **Hercules:** in Greek legend a mighty hero possessing extraordinary strength and courage, who accomplished twelve tasks to win immortality.

p. 207 **Lady Tartuffe:** character in Molière comedy *Tartuffe* (1667).

p. 207 **Vashti:** proud queen of Ahasuerus mentioned in the Book of Esther.

Mary E. Wilkins Freeman

'A Poetess'

p. 231 **an old delaine:** a lightweight wool, or wool and cotton dress.

'Old Woman Magoun'

p. 240 **hands of tobacco:** small bunches of tobacco leaves.

p. 240 **passel:** group.

p. 242 **dredge:** to scrape up from the bottom.

p. 251 **deadly nightshade:** poisonous weeds.

'Sister Liddy'

p. 258 Mansard-roofed: a roof having two slopes on all sides with the lower slope steeper than the upper one.

Constance Fenimore Woolson

'Miss Grief'

p. 271 'When found, make a note of it': Dickens, *Dombey and Son* ch. 15.

p. 273 Balzac: Honoré de Balzac (1799–1850), French novelist most famous for his *Comédie Humaine*.

p. 273 the Furies: goddesses of vengeance who in Greek myth lived in the underworld.

p. 274 Tullia or Lucrezia Borgia: members of a Spanish-Italian family of great prominence in Europe from the late-fourteenth to the early-sixteenth century, noted amongst other things for excessive cruelty and ambition.

p. 279 'Væ victis!': woe to the vanquished.

p. 284 *Kubla Khan*: 1797 poem by Samuel Taylor Coleridge.

p. 291 *memento mori*: a reminder of death.

'At the Château of Corinne'

p. 293 If people supposed that H. stood for Horace: Horace Walpole (1717–97), English author notable for *The Castle of Otranto*.

p. 297 Gibbon: Edward Gibbon (1737–94), historian famous for his *History of the Decline and Fall of the Roman Empire*.

p. 298 Voirons: town in southeast France situated on the Morge river, north of Grenoble.

p. 299 Voltaire ... Madame de Staël: Voltaire–assumed name of François Marie Aouet (1694–1778), French writer and historian; Jean Charles Léonard Simond de Sismondi (1773–1842), Swiss historian and economist; Jean Jacques Rousseau (1712–78), French writer and philosopher famous for his *Confessions* (1772) amongst many other writings; Sir Humphrey Davy (1778–1829), English scientist; Charles François D'Aubigney (1817–78), French landscape painter; John Calvin

(1509–64), Protestant reformer and theologian; Friedrich Melchior von Grimm (1723–1807), German diplomatic and literary figure; Benjamin Constant de Magalhaês (1838–91), Brazilian republican; August Wilhelm von Schlegel (1767–1845), German poet and critic; François René Châteaubriand (1768–1848), French author and statesman; George Gordon Noel Byron (1788–1824), English poet; Percy Bysshe Shelley (1792–1822), English poet who married Mary Godwin; Alexandre Dumas (1802–70), French novelist and dramatist; Madame de Staël (1766–1817), French writer best known for *De l'Allemagne*.

p. 299 *Etonnante femme!*: wonderful woman.

p. 299 **Vevey, Clarens, Chillon**: Vevey and Clarens are Swiss towns on Lake Geneva; Chillon is a castle on Lake Geneva made famous in literature and song by, amongst others, Byron.

p. 300 **'Childe Harold'**: 1812 poem by Byron.

p. 302 **phaeton**: four-wheeled horse-drawn vehicle.

p. 303 **Endymion**: beautiful youth who spent much of his time in perpetual sleep.

p. 303 **Madame Récamier**: (1777–1849), French leader of society during Napoleonic era.

p. 304 *ravissante amie*: a beautiful or ravishing lady.

p. 309 **Goethe and Schiller**: Johann Wolfgang von Goethe (1749–1832), German poet, dramatist, novelist, philosopher, statesman and scientist, most famous for his epic poem *Faust*; Johann Christoph Friedrich von Schiller (1759–1805), German poet, dramatist and historian.

p. 311 **the Campagna**: level, open country.

p. 316 **Chambéry**: city in southeast France.

Sarah Orne Jewett

'The Town Poor'

p. 340 **selec'*men***: board of officers chosen to transact and administer general and public business in New England towns.

p. 342 **leghorn hat**: hat made from fine plaited straw that is usually cut green and bleached.

p. 342 **'Be just before you are generous'**: Richard Sheridan, *The School for Scandal* IV. i (1777).

p. 343 **'As for man, his days are as grass'**: Psalm 103, 15–16.

p. 344 **meechin'**: furtive or cringing manner.

Charlotte Perkins Gilman

'The Yellow Wallpaper'

p. 357 **Romanesque:** style of architecture characterized by profuse ornament.

p. 357 **delirium tremens:** a violent delirium with tremors induced by excessive and prolonged use of alcohol.

Kate Chopin

'The Storm'

p. 381 *Dieu sait*: God knows.

p. 381 **the levees:** embankments designed to prevent flooding.

p. 382 *Bonté!*: Goodness!

p. 384 *J'vous réponds*: I will respond.

Edith Wharton

'Souls Belated'

p. 387 **cloud of touts:** group of men soliciting custom.

p. 387 *'Par-ten-za!'*: all aboard!

p. 387 *Revue de Paris*: literary review (1829–89).

p. 390 **parterre box:** a box behind the orchestra on the ground floor.

p. 390 **Worth:** Charles Frederick Worth (1825–95), Parisian dressmaker and fashion-setter.

p. 390 **landau:** carriage.

p. 390 **Cruikshank prints:** George Cruikshank (1792–1878), political satirist and caricaturist.

p. 392 *Je n'en vois pas la nécessité!*: it does not matter to me.

p. 395 *tout d'une pièce*: all of a piece.

p. 395 *modus vivendi*: way of being in the world.

p. 396 *table-d'hôte*: ordinary people.

p. 396–7 *Civis Romanus sum*: I am a citizen of Rome.

p. 398 **Hotel Bellosguardo:** hotel with a good view, or where the viewing is good.

p. 399 **laurustinus alley:** alley covered with evergreen shrub.

p. 400 *premier*: best rooms in the hotel.

p. 400 **Doucet:** French dress designer.

p. 409 **'The Reign of Law' and Professor Drummond:** James Lawson Drummond (1783–1853) famously pronounced that 'The Reign of Law in nature is universal.'

p. 411 **as Latude returned to his cell:** Henri Masers de Latude (1725–1805), French prisoner who was the model for Dumas's *The Man in the Iron Mask*.

p. 412 *noyade*: drowning.

p. 413 **Bradshaw:** Bradshaw's Railway Guide.

Willa Cather

'Paul's Case'

p. 415 **four-in-hand:** necktie tied in a slipknot with long ends overlapping in front.

p. 415 **belladonna:** medicinal extract from eponymous European poisonous plant.

p. 417 **'Soldiers' Chorus' from *Faust*:** 1859 opera composed by Charles Gounod.

p. 417 **Raffelli:** Jean François Rafelli (1850–1923), French painter.

p. 417 **Rico:** Martin Rico (1835–1908), Spanish landscape painter.

p. 418 **Augustus:** Gaius Octavius (63BC–14AD), first Roman emperor.

p. 418 *Venus de Milo*: Greek statue of a majestic woman with her arms broken off.

p. 419 **the genie in the bottle found by the Arab fisherman**: 'The History of the Fisherman and the genie' in *The Arabian Nights' Entertainment*.

p. 424 *Martha*: opera by Friedrich von Flotow (1847).

p. 424 *Rigoletto*: opera by Giuseppe Verdi (1851).

p. 432 **Pagliacci music**: opera by Ruggiero Leoncavallo (1892).

Nathaniel Hawthorne, letter to his publisher, William Ticknor, 19 January 1855, *The Centenary Edition of the works of Nathaniel Hawthorne*, vol. XVII (Ohio State University Press, 1987).

> America is now wholly given over to a d——d mob of scribbling women, and I should have no chance of success while the public taste is occupied with their trash – and should be ashamed of myself if I did succeed.

Catharine Sedgwick

Edgar Allan Poe, 'Catharine M. Sedgwick', *Godey's Lady's Book*, vol. XXXIII, no. 9 (September 1846), pp. 130–32.

> Miss Sedgwick is not only one of our most celebrated and most meritorious writers, but attained reputation at a period when American reputation in letters was regarded as a phenomenon; and thus, like Irving, Cooper, Paulding, Bryant, Halleck, and one or two others, she is indebted, certainly, for some portion of the esteem in which she was held and is held, to [. . .] patriotic pride and gratitude [. . .] for which we must make reasonable allowance in estimating the absolute merit of our literary pioneers. [. . .]
> She has neither the vigor of Mrs Stephens nor the vivacious grace of Miss Chubbuck, nor the pure style of Mrs Embury, nor the classic imagination of Mrs Child, nor the naturalness of Mrs Annan, nor the thoughtful and suggestive originality of Miss Fuller; but in many of the qualities mentioned she excels, and in no one of them is she particularly deficient. She is an author of marked talent, but by no means of such decided genius as would entitle her to that precedence among our female writers which, under the circumstances to which I have alluded, *seems* to be yielded her by the voice of the public.

Judith Fetterly, *Provisions* (Bloomington: Indiana University Press, 1989), pp. 43–4.

> Sedgwick was remarkable in her day for the degree of positive, and even enthusiastic, critical acclaim accorded her works. During her lifetime, critics consistently linked her name with those of Cooper, Washington Irving, and William Cullen Bryant and identified her as one of the founders of American literature. The sources of her popularity and reputation are perhaps fairly easy to define. To Sydney Smith's notorious question of 1820, 'in the four quarters of the globe, who reads an American book,' Sedgwick provided an answer. Her novels were noteworthy for their use of American materials – settings, characters, manners, history – and frequently for their realism in the handling of these materials. In addition, they reflected a commitment to the current mythology of American democracy – that is, to the belief that the only operative basis for class distinction in America was that of manners. Moreover, in marked contrast to Cooper's male-centered world, infiltrated by the occasional 'female,' Sedgwick's fictional world centered on women and contained a variety of female characters, often both interesting and realistic but always larger and more complex than the current literary stereotypes [. . .] Sedgwick's fictional prose is notable for its ease, grace, clarity, and directness. In sum, Sedgwick gave her country a writer to be proud of, a writer who could answer Smith's question, and to whom Americans could point as an example of what American genius could do with American materials.

Elizabeth Stuart Phelps

Judith Fetterly, *Provisions* (Bloomington: Indiana University Press, 1989), pp. 203–8.

> The career of Elizabeth Stuart Phelps offers a fit emblem of the degree to which the talent and the life of the mid-nineteenth-century American woman of genius was sacrificed by and to a culture that had no place for the woman artist. 'The Angel Over The Right Shoulder' articulates and documents this sacrifice [. . .] Phelps, of a disposition inherently gloomy and imaginatively dominated throughout childhood by the fear of her mother's death, forced herself as a woman and a Christian to write of and from 'the sunny side.' That 'power of blackness' which Herman

Melville recognized in Nathaniel Hawthorne as the sign of genius was, in fact, a masculine prerogative. [. . .]

Not surprisingly, the ending of 'The Angel Over The Right Shoulder' is weak and unconvincing. The invocation of domestic iconography – 'wish you a happy new year, mamma' – carries even less conviction after our exposure to its cost. And the proposition that Mrs James can choose both self and family is belied by the structure of her dream, which dramatizes the incompatibility of these alternatives and sharply distinguishes between their respective moral value. And, finally, though the dream may provide temporary relief, for continued effectiveness it requires a set of impossible conditions, not the least of which is a constant backward glance to make sure that the angels are still there and still writing.

The 'real' end of the story occurs somewhat earlier. It indicates the degree to which the dream has, in fact, evaded rather than confronted the reality of the dreamer's life and registers the alienation from self inherent in its 'solution': 'Eager to warn the traveller of what she had seen, she touched her. The traveller turned, and she recognized or seemed to recognize *herself*. Startled and alarmed, she awoke in tears.' Privileged during her dream to be among, indeed, behind, the angel authors, Mrs James' tears signal her despair at resigning herself to the role of character. It is her best, perhaps her only solution, but it will take a lot of dreaming to keep her on the sunny side of this particular grave.

Frances Harper

Phebe A. Hanford, *Daughters of America; or, Women of the Century* (B. B. Russell, 1882), p. 326.

Frances E. W. Harper is one of the most eloquent women lecturers in the country. As one listens to her clear, plaintive, melodious voice, and follows the flow of her musical speech in her logical presentation of truth, he cannot but be charmed with her oratory and rhetoric, and forgets that she is of the race once enslaved in our land. She is one of the colored women of whom white women may be proud, and to whom the abolitionists can point and declare that a race which could show such women ought never to have been held in bondage. She lectures on temperance, equal rights, and religious themes, and has shown herself able in the use of the pen.

Frances Smith Foster, 'Frances E. W. Harper', *African American Writers*, ed., Valerie Smith (New York: Scribner's and Sons, 1991), pp. 163–7.

Harper maintained the dominant themes in her early lectures and writings for the rest of her career: Christian living, civil rights, and racial pride. [. . .]

The themes, situations, and images that appear in 'The Two Offers' are consistent with those in Harper's poetry and lectures. In poems such as 'Saved by Faith,' 'The Contrast,' and 'The Drunkard's Child' (all in her 1854 volume), Harper emphasizes the importance of personal faith and self-discipline, warning against the tragic results of neglecting those virtues. In 'Advice to the Girls' (also in the 1854 volume), she specifically cautions against choosing a husband by his appearance [. . .]

Harper argued that the future of the nation depended upon the ability of its citizens to unite behind a common goal. 'Between the white people and the colored there is a community of interests,' she asserted, 'and the sooner they find it out, the better it will be for both parties, but that community of interests does not consist in increasing the privileges of one class and curtailing the rights of the other, but in getting every citizen interested in the welfare, progress, and durability of the state.' Her other theme, and the one that increasingly dominated her published writings, was that the Emancipation had opened a new era, a time for blacks, particularly black women, to 'consecrate their lives to the work of upbuilding the race.'

Joanne Braxton, 'Frances E. W. Harper', *Modern American Women Writers*, ed., Elaine Showalter (New York: Scribner's and Sons, 1991), p. 203.

'Critics have accepted Harper's historical significance' [Maryemma] Graham asserts, 'but have had difficulty with the aggressive link she made between poetry and politics.' Because Harper's politics were both racial and sexual, Graham suggests that critics have also had difficulty in identifying the tradition in which Harper should be placed, 'genteel,' 'black liberation,' or 'prefeminist.' The answer, perhaps, is all three. Like other black 'prefeminists' of Harper's era, such as Anne Julia Cooper, Gertrude

Mossell, and Ida B. Wells, Harper took race, not gender, as her point of departure and, in the words of Paula Giddings, 'redefined the meaning of what was called "true womanhood."' Harper's tools were the lecture, the political essay, the narrative poem, and the sentimental novel, all of which she used to achieve the same purpose, the uplift of the men and women of her race and of women of all races. She pursued this goal tirelessly, seeking new challenges in her full maturity, at an age when she might have rested comfortably on her earlier accomplishments. Even today, Harper's life and work stand as a model of social and artistic commitment that women both black and white might strive to emulate.

Harriet Prescott Spofford

Judith Fetterly, *Provisions* (Bloomington: Indiana University Press, 1989), pp. 264–7.

'I read Miss Prescott's "Circumstance," but it followed me in the Dark – so I avoided her.' So wrote Emily Dickinson to Thomas Wentworth Higginson on 25 April 1862. To her sister-in-law, Sue Gilbert Dickinson, she wrote, 'Sue, it is the only thing I have ever read in my life that I didn't think I could have imagined myself,' and despite her comment to Higginson, she begged Sue to 'send me everything she writes.' [. . .]

Nathaniel Hawthorne wanted women's literature to exhibit women's bodies, naked, without the restraint of decency; 'Circumstance' expresses the violence behind that desire. Made to sing to please the beast, for whom the pleasure has a distinctly sexual connotation, this woman experiences a sense of shame and loathing at such enforced and public exposure. [. . .]

When we examine the nature of the woman's response to this sudden attack in the night from one whom she is powerless to resist and can only hope to placate, the sexual context is intensified. A 'quivering disgust' far worse than physical pain or fear of death defines this woman's nightmare. Her revulsion derives from her idea of the beast: a 'living lump of appetites,' 'the strength of our lower natures let loose,' possessed of the hideous 'vitality' of 'foaming chaps' and 'slaver.' In the context of mid-nineteenth-century America; this language constitutes a familiar code for referring to unrestrained male sexuality, that lower nature often let loose on the bodies of women. The women's experience can be read, then, as an experience of 'rape,' a nightmare as likely to occur in the home as in the woods. [. . .]

Anna Dalke, ' "Circumstance" and the Creative Woman: Harriet Prescott Spofford', *Arizona Quarterly* 41:1 (Spring 1985), pp. 71–85.

Spofford suggests in ['Circumstance'] that the 'realist school,' which James commends in his review, is inadequate to encompass the exigencies of female circumstance. The story thus functions not only as a defense but as an early sample of a tradition of American writing by women, a tradition which is concerned with exploring extreme states of consciousness. That tradition includes names as long known as that of Emily Dickinson, and as newly rediscovered as that of Charlotte Perkins Gilman. [. . .]

James faults Spofford, finally, not only because her tales are 'marvelously void of human nature and false to actual society' but because she creates, in place of a duplication of the world as he saw it, something entirely new and other [. . .] She imagines another world altogether, and presents it in a new language as well. Her 'inordinate fondness for the picturesque' obstructs what should be her prime function: 'an author's paramount charge is the cure of souls, to the subjection, and if need be to the exclusion of the picturesque.'

Spofford begs to differ. In 'Circumstance' she concerns herself quite literally with the salvation of her protagonist's soul, a salvation which is accomplished precisely by the means James condemns. Spofford moves in her story beyond the mere 'perception of the actual' to imagine the extreme and urgent requirements of a woman's situation. The story posits a very different view of female fluency from that described by James: it is not 'pernicious,' but salutary, preservative, even redemptive.

Walking on the edge of the woods, at the edge of evening, this young woman slips over the margin and encounters her own worst self in the forest. She fights in the dark woods not something other, but her own lower self. [. . .]

This realist [Spofford] confronts, then, the extreme margins of realism: the naturalistic rendering of the self as no more than animal, as an entirely physical being which eats, which stinks, which drools and slobbers, and which, when it is finished, will assimilate itself – and whatever imagination she may have of a self better than that which he represents – into himself. [. . .]

In his review, James praises Balzac for his minute description and condemns Spofford for her lack of the same. But Spofford, unlike Poe and Hawthorne, is interested in fidelity of another sort. She is attempting to be true, not to external features, but to an inward reality of extreme experience. In her story she refuses the limits and structure of realism for a very different sort of literary endeavour, one which attempts to record not mere changes in fashion but the revision of a soul. She records not what is but what could and should be.

Rebecca Harding Davis

Anonymous, ' "Waiting for the Verdict" ', *The Nation*, no. 125 (21 November 1867), pp. 410–11.

Mrs Davis has written a number of short stories, chiefly of country life in Virginia and Pennsylvania, all distinguished by a certain severe and uncultured strength, but all disfigured by an injudicious straining after realistic effects which leave nature and reality at a certain distance behind and beside them. The author has made herself the poet of poor people – laborers, farmers, mechanics, and factory hands. She has attempted to reproduce in dramatic form their manners and habits and woes and wants. The intention has always been good, but the execution has, to our mind, always been monstrous. The unfortunate people whom she transfers into her stories are as good material for the story-teller's art as any other class of beings, but not a bit better. [...] They are worth reading about only as long as they are studied with a keen eye versed in the romance of human life, and described in the same rational English which we exact from writers on other subjects. Mrs Davis' manner is in direct oppugnancy to this truth. She drenches the whole field beforehand with a flood of lachrymose sentimentalism and riots in the murky vapors which rise in consequence of the act. [...] In her desire to impart such reality to her characters as shall make them appeal successfully to our feelings, she emphasizes their movements and gestures to that degree that all vocal sounds, all human accents, are lost to the ear, and nothing is left but a crowd of ghastly, frowning, grinning automatons. The reader, exhausted by the constant strain upon his moral sensibilities, cries aloud for the good, graceful 'fashionable novel.

Sharon M. Harris, *Rebecca Harding Davis and American Realism* (Philadelphia: University of Pennsylvania Press, 1991), pp. 27–34.

Davis scholarship has centered on 'life' as a landmark in American literary history. [. . .] Yet these scholars have not known quite what to make of this ['Life in the Iron Mills'] early example of American realism and naturalism. All agree that it is grimly realistic, that it is a pioneering work. But many question the passages that seem to offer religion as a panacea for Hugh Wolfe and the 'lower' class, passages that use the language of romanticism and seem to deny the determinism of Hugh's fate. [. . .]

Davis's purpose in the narrative frame is to lure readers into this new form of fiction without alienating them before they descend with the narrator into the lower realms. [. . .] In 1861, Davis also insisted that readers acknowledge this oppressed class within their midst, and her narrator asserts this in a tone of indictment and challenge. [. . .]

To delineate Deb's world as intermediary is not to deny her victimization. The debilitation of this life is physically symbolized in Deborah herself, who is 'deformed, almost a hunchback.' There is no beauty in Deborah's life and none in her face, which is 'ghastly' because of her blue lips and watery eyes. This 'Zolaesque' description, preceding the French naturalist's work by half a dozen years, shatters the tradition of the blue-eyed, fair-haired heroines typical of the mid-nineteenth-century American romanticism of Cooper, Hawthorne, and Melville, among others. Instead, Deborah becomes one of American fiction's earliest realistic grotesques, a precursor to those depicted in Sherwood Anderson's *Winesburg, Ohio.* In Anderson's portrayals, a person's physical disabilities often represent a gentle human spirit caught in the webs of a particular obsession. For Deb, the obsession is Hugh, and she becomes the first in a series of 'thwarted woman's forms' that Davis depicts in her fiction and nonfiction. The significance of Deb's 'hunger' swells to overwhelming proportions in 'Life.' Like all the workers, Deb is physically hungry, but she is also sexually and emotionally deprived because of her deformity. Further, both Hugh and Deb are hungry 'to know,' to have that secret forever released from the silence of the upper classes which will allow the oppressed to rise socially and economically. Most importantly, both victims are spiritually hungry – Hugh for a means to express his creative voice and Deb for an unnamed fulfillment which she believes only Hugh can effectuate.

Louisa May Alcott

Henry James, review of *Moods*, *North American Review* 101 (July 1865), pp. 276–81.

What shall we call this quality [Alcott's 'decided cleverness']? Imagination does not seem to us too grand a word. For, in the absence of knowledge, our authoress has derived her figures, as the German derived his camel, from the depths of her moral consciousness. If they are on this account the less real, they are also on this account the more unmistakably instinct with a certain beauty and grace. If Miss Alcott's experience of human nature has been small, as we should suppose, her admiration for it is nevertheless great. [...] She has the rare merit [...] of seldom being puerile. For inanimate nature, too, she has a genuine love, together with a very pretty way of describing it. With these qualities there is no reason why Miss Alcott should not write a very good novel, provided she will be satisfied to describe only that which she has seen. When such a novel comes, as no doubt it eventually will, we will be among the first to welcome it. With the exception of two or three celebrated names, we know not, indeed, to whom, in this country, unless to Miss Alcott, we are to look for a novel above the average.

Abigail A. Hamblen, 'Louisa May Alcott and the Racial Question', *University Review* 37 (Kansas City: Missouri University Press, 1971), pp. 307–13.

'My Contraband' is perhaps the most marked example of [Alcott's] passionate adherence to one side of the conflict. Here she is explicit in pointing out the faults of both brothers: Marse Ned is selfish, authoritarian, dissolute; Bob is bitter, vengeful, murderous. The former she dismisses simply as a being of unmitigated evil; the latter, however, shows what nobility he might have been capable of had he not been blighted by slavery, crushed by the iron hand of his owner. In other words, this octoroon is the product of the 'peculiar institution.'

The reflective reader is willing to admit the truth of her

assertion. But he might wonder about Marse Ned, and *his* character. If Bob is the result of his slavery, is not his young master equally the result? If his formative years had made Bob what he is, have not Ned's done the same for him?

But Miss Alcott gives him no quarter. She is not interested in excusing the misdeeds of white men – only applauding the good deeds of blacks. For her, Fort Wagner marks an important epoch: 'The future must show how well that fight was fought; for though Fort Wagner once defied us, public prejudice is down; and through the cannon-smoke of that black night the manhood of the colored race shines before many eyes that would not see, rings in many ears that would not hear, wins many hearts that would not hitherto believe.'

Her first glimpse of Bob shows her that he has 'an eye full of the passionate melancholy which in such men always seems to utter a mute protest against the broken law that doomed them at their birth.' At first reading, one imagines that she is referring to miscegenation – 'the broken law.' But recalling 'M.L.' with its picture of black man and white woman happily made parents, we realize that the 'broken law' must mean slavery. Such a name for it shows the northern attitude only; if in Northern eyes the South broke some 'law' in upholding slavery, it must be recalled that many Southerners felt that divine approval hallowed the institution. Again, in the true spirit of the dedicated protagonist, Miss Alcott passes over any theory that might oppose hers. [. . .]

And so, no matter what one's persuasion, one cannot help respecting a writer who both sincerely and relentlessly took up the cudgels in a battle which she confidently expected to end in victory for the 'right.' She could not foresee that a hundred years later it would still be raging.

Ruth K. MacDonald, *Louisa May Alcott* (Boston: Twayne Publishers, 1983), pp. 95–9.

Louisa May Alcott stands as one of the great American practitioners of the girls' novel and the family story. Her novels for children show her originality, especially when compared to other novels for children in her time. Alcott's child heroes and heroines are always flawed; though the faults of Rose Campbell and Polly Milton may simply be added on to their otherwise excellent characters, Jo March's temper and Dan Kean's violence are integral parts of their characters which are improved upon only by protracted struggle. It is their willingness to struggle with their faults, and the persistence of these faults in spite of all efforts to correct them that make Alcott's most successful stories survive. [. . .]

Alcott may be best known for her juvenile novels, but her works for adults are remarkably good, again for the same reasons that her children's novels succeed: skill in building character and then an equal skill in letting the character act out his or her own fate, however unpopular or unusual the course of action might be. [. . .] In her adult novels Alcott was more adventurous in investigating the difficulties that the sentimental novels for children ignored. The social issues which may be lightly touched on in the juveniles are explored in greater depth in the adult works. [. . .]

The plight of a woman confined by social status, sexual prejudice, defect in character, or poverty in spite of her obvious worth was a popular theme; Alcott's protagonists overcome their limitations by hard work and faith in God. Becoming a wife, mother, and good Christian at the end of the novel shows not so much a character capitulating to literary stereotype but more the power of that character to overcome seemingly impossible barriers to such earthly happiness and success.

Martha Saxon, 'The Secret Imaginings of Louisa Alcott', *Critical Essays on Louisa May Alcott*, ed., Madeline B. Stern (Boston: G. K. Hall & Co., 1984), pp. 256–61.

'Behind a Mask' [. . .] reveals much about the author. Jean Muir is probably the most complex and human of the A. M. Barnard heroines – a thirty-year-old actress with a disreputable past who seduces her way through an entire family before marrying an elderly lord. Jean is two people, one who performs her governess and companion duties perfectly while turning the heads of all the household males by her apparent frankness, youth, and charm. The other, the real Jean, is dangerous, vengeful, unscrupulous, and bent on getting her own way. She is, above all, hidden, keeping every true feeling inside and displaying only those which will forward her cause. [. . .]

One of the beauties of this story, in terms of both writing and psychology, is that the reader understands and forgives Jean. Alcott has made her 'bad' heroine attractive to us. Technically, she does it by keeping the 'good' Jean on stage most of the time, while we only experience the 'bad' Jean in letters and secondhand reports. She also makes Jean's judgments of people accurate [...]

Jean's industry, right or wrong, triumphs over aristocratic lethargy. [...] Like any good Alcott heroine, she teaches all of [the Coventry family] little moral lessons in the process of getting what she wants. The fact that she has a scandalous past is morally balanced out by the Coventrys' tendency to self-indulgence and arrogance.

Mary E. Wilkins Freeman

Anonymous, 'New England in the Short Story', *The Atlantic Monthly*, vol. LCVII, no. CCCIV (June 1891), pp. 845–50.

Of the genuine originality of these stories it is hard to speak too strongly. There is, indeed, a common character to the whole series, an undertone of hardship, of loss, of repressed life, of sacrifice, of the idolatry of duty, but we suspect this is due more to the prevailing spirit of New England life than to any determining force of Miss Wilkins' genius. For the most part, she brings to light some pathetic passage in a strongly marked individuality, and the variety of her characterizations is noticeable. Now and then she touches a very deep human nature, and opens to view a secret of the human heart which makes us cry out that here is a poet, a seer. [...] Always there is a freedom from commonplace, and a power to hold the interest to the close which is owing, not to a trivial ingenuity, but to the spell which her personages cast over the reader's mind as soon as they come within his ken. He wonders what they will do; and if he is surprised at any conclusion, the surprise is due, not to any trick in the author, but to the unexpected issue of an original conception, which reflection always shows to be logical and reasonable.

The humor which is a marked feature of Miss Wilkins' stories is of a pungent sort. Every story has it, and it is a savior which prevents some, that otherwise would be rather painful, from oppressing the reader unduly.

Kate Gardner, 'The Subversion of Genre in the Short Stories of Mary Wilkins Freeman', *New England Quarterly* 65:3 (September 1992), pp. 447–68.

Decay, desiccation, decline, degeneration, and death – these have been the key words of traditional Freeman criticism. This emphasis has obscured the vitality of both the stories and their characters and has instead cast Freeman as a pessimistic anthropologist who, lacking even the strength of her bleak vision, simply tacked happy endings onto the reports of her findings.

The past decade, with the burgeoning of feminist approaches, has seen the publication of many sympathetic, complex, and demanding studies of Freeman and her female contemporaries. All of these studies recognize the power – often the subversive power and too often the frustrated power – of Freeman's women, and they recognize too that in dismissing these women as 'marginal,' earlier critics were merely repeating, even compounding, the very crimes of insensitivity that the stories expose and condemn. In making the poor, the old, the peculiar, the unmarried, and the female central to her stories, Freeman after all challenges the designation 'marginal.'

The title of [. . .] 'A Poetess' identifies the heroine by her occupation. When she loses that, she loses her identity as well; she ceases to exist; she dies. The separate spheres of men and women – where women die of broken hearts and men put their hearts into their work – have been set spinning and collide. Freeman's women have usurped the male province of work and of dedication to it while retaining territorial rights to feminine sensibility. Freeman transforms that sensibility, traditionally associated with weakness and frailty, into a strength.

Marjorie Pryse, 'An Uncloistered "New England Nun"', *Studies in Short Fiction* 20 (Summer 1983), pp. 289–95.

When Louisa Ellis reconsiders marriage to Joe Dagget, she aligns herself against the values he represents. Her resulting unconventionality makes it understandably difficult for historians, themselves the intellectual and emotional products of a society which has long enshrined these values, to view her either perceptively or sympathetically. For Louisa Ellis rejects the concept of manifest destiny and her own mission within it; she establishes her own home as the limits of her world, embracing rather than fleeing domesticity, discovering in the process that she can retain her autonomy; and she expands her vision by preserving her virginity, an action which can only appear if not 'foolish' at least threatening to her biographers and critics, most of whom have been men.

In analyzing 'A New England Nun' without bias against solitary women, the reader discovers that within the world Louisa inhabits, she becomes heroic, active, wise, ambitious, and even transcendent, hardly the woman Freeman's critics and biographers have depicted. In choosing solitude, Louisa creates an alternative pattern of living for a woman who possesses, like her, 'the enthusiasm of an artist.' [. . .] 'A New England Nun' dramatizes change in Louisa Ellis. A situation she has long accepted now becomes one she rejects. The story focuses on what she stands to lose, and on what she gains by her rejection. [. . .]

In appearing to accept her long wait, she has actually made a turn away from the 'old winds of romance' which had 'never more than murmured' for her anyway. Now, when she sews wedding clothes, she listens with 'half-wistful attention' to the stillness which she must soon leave behind. For she has no doubt that she will lose, not gain, in marrying Joe Dagget. She knows, first, that she must lose her own house. [. . .] She will also lose the freedom to express herself in her own art. [. . .]

In rejecting marriage to Joe Dagget, Louisa feels 'fairly steeped in peace.' She gains a transcendent selfhood, an identity which earns her membership in a 'sisterhood of sensibility.' [. . .]

Freeman's choice of concluding image – that Louisa is both nun-like in her solitude yet 'uncloistered' by her decision not to marry Joe Dagget – documents the author's perception that in marriage Louisa would have sacrificed more than she would have gained.

Norma Johnsen, 'Pieces: Artist and Audience in Three Mary Wilkins Freeman Stories', *Colby Quarterly* 29:1 (March 1993), pp. 43–56.

'Sister Liddy' is about a storyteller in the process of telling a story [. . .] Wilkins dramatizes the artist who writes not out of an inner sense of a story she wants to share with a responsive listener, but out of a need to fabricate a self that will earn the approval of a hostile, uncaring audience. This artist, Polly Moss, dies from a falseness to herself personified in a dummy 'sister' she creates and clothes to mediate with her audience. In describing this creation, Mary Wilkins writes of a painful and destructive state which she knew something about. [. . .]

Sister Liddy is the ultimate sentimental heroine, a veritable catalog of female fantasy. [. . .] Polly creates this paragon for an audience of women, but [. . .] her audience of paupers is hostile, calling her 'the wust-lookin' objeck,' delighting in her deformity because it enables them to look down on her. Thus, when Polly speaks of Sister Liddy, she gets back at the women in her audience: She says to a vain woman, 'She was jest as fair as a lily – a good deal fairer than you ever was, Mis' Handy . . .' Polly confronts her audience like a lion tamer with a whip, expanding and adding accessories to her story of Sister Liddy until the strain of the fabrication leads to her death.

Mary Wilkins describes Polly as an artist, based on a male model: 'Old Polly Moss, her little withered face gleaming with reckless enthusiasm, sang the praises of her sister Liddy as wildly and faithfully as any minnesinger his angel mistress.' As an artist, Polly successfully asserts herself. Tired of being the passive listener to their boasting, she tells her story to compete with the other women, but the gender of her model suggests its ultimate falseness. Nevertheless, this desperate effort earns the respect of her audience, as we know by the way they listen 'with ever-increasing bewilderment and awe.' She tells her tale to impress an audience, to project an image of herself, sharing in the reflected glory of such a sister. But what she cobbles together is a false persona, a dressed-up monster, a Frankenstein who eventually destroys her. Instead of 'making [her characters] true' and recounting events as truthfully as she can, instead of sharing her scripture, Polly manufactures grandiose details of impossible splendours, not to bring her past into the future, not to create, not to share, but to impress.

Ann Douglas Wood, 'The Literature of Impoverishment: The Women Local Colorists in America, 1865–1914', *Women's Studies* I (1972), pp. 3–45.

In 'Sister Liddy,' one of the most powerful short stories written in America, Freeman bitterly exhibits the aged female occupants of a small town almshouse as a spectrum of obsolete and frustrated womanhood. The almshouse itself, standing in a 'bare, sandy lot' with 'no trees,' naked in its shabbiness, is an emblem of the barrenness of its occupants. Two of these inhabitants stand out with the vividness and precision of a nightmare. Old Polly Moss is utterly friendless, and 'so bent that [. . .] her little pale triangular face seemed to look out from the middle of her flat chest.' She can do little but daydream and play ball with the almshouse children: 'She never caught the ball, and she threw it back with weak, aimless jerks; her back ached, but she was patient, and her face was full of simple, childish smiles.' The insane as well as the poor are here, particularly one small and ancient madwoman who passes quickly in and out of the story but cannot be forgotten: 'Suddenly one of the doors flew open, and a little figure shot out. She went down the corridor with a swift trot like a child. She had on nothing but a woollen petticoat and a calico waist; she held her head down, and her narrow shoulders worked as she ran; her mop of soft white hair flew out.' She is womanhood so deprived, so denied as to become demonic. Witchlike, she has found in the very extreme of her impoverishment her revenge.

Susan Allen Toth, 'Defiant Light: A Positive View of Mary Wilkins Freeman', *New England Quarterly* 46 (March 1973), pp. 82–93.

Although [judgments of Mary Wilkins Freeman as a pessimistic recorder of New England's decline] have sound basis, their cultural and historical focus on gloom, misery, decay, and extinction has obscured the real dramatic conflict at the heart of Freeman's best stories. It is a conflict whose positive aspects need to be recognized. Many of her characters suffer, but they also fight their way to significant victories. Living in drab poverty, they still struggle with courageous spirit towards self-expression and independence. This vital struggle is far from being dated as a past or purely local condition that existed in New England in the decades following the Civil War.

Freeman has a surprisingly modern and complex sense of the constant, mutual adjustment necessary between individual and community, between need for independence and social insistence on conformity, between private fulfillment and social duties. Her men and women must assert themselves in ingenious ways to maintain their integrity in the face of community pressures, and Freeman records their varying successes with a wry but sympathetic spirit. [. . .]

Individual and community clash intensely in Freeman's world because organized society is inherently hostile to the needs and demands of its constituents. [. . .] Unlike the idealized communities of Deephaven or Dunnet Landing in Sarah Orne Jewett's fiction, unlike Alice Brown's placid Tiverton, or even Harriet Beecher Stowe's earlier pictures of bustling Oldtown, Freeman's isolated villages are far from harmonious social groups.

Constance Fenimore Woolson

William Dean Howells, review of *Castle Nowhere: Lake Country Sketches* and *Rodman the Keeper: Southern Sketches*, *Harper's New Monthly Magazine* 74 (February 1887), p. 482.

The reader of Miss C. F. Woolson's short stories, lately reprinted in two volumes, must have felt the mastery which she shows in them. [. . .] Something more and something better than the literary instinct helped our author to the perception of things which gives both of these books their uncommon claim to remembrance; she has made them necessary to any one who would understand the whole meaning of Americanism, or would know some of its most recondite phases by virtue of qualities which are felt in all her work [. . .] These qualities, which are above artistry, to our thinking, need not make one indifferent to that; one would lose a great deal that is beautiful and valuable if they did. Miss Woolson deals with nature and with human nature in a fresh way, or at least a way of her own, which is at once simple in its kindliness and conscious of the limitations of all human judgment, where it ceases to be a question of sufferer, sinner, lover, and hater, with their relation to the frame of things, and to that material aspect of the universe, which now seems so deaf and blind to humanity, and now so full of poignant sympathy.

Joan Myers Weimer, 'Woman Artists as Exiles in the Fiction of Constance Fenimore Woolson', *Legacy* 3:2 (Fall 1986), pp. 3–15.

When Woolson presents women artists realistically, rather than fantastically, she envisions them as she does most of her women characters – as exiles. And she furthers her exploration alienation by presenting their proper subject matter as other exiles.

Some of Woolson's female characters begin as voluntary exiles, leaving their homes in order to become painters or preachers, only to find themselves involuntarily exiled from love and self-respect. Some are exiles from their own painful feelings of inadequacy; some from self-knowledge; some from relationships whose loss leads to such devastation that solitude is preferable. The women artists, whether mediocre or brilliant, are ultimately exiled from their own art. [. . .]

Woolson apparently mistrusted her own success. When she

imagined a woman writer of real genius, she called her 'Miss Grief' and made her work incomprehensible to the reading public. Her other women artists attract the love of masterful men who insist they give up their art. Their decisions to marry these men are presented [in 'Dorothy'] as a 'great downfall.' [. . .]

Woolson imagined another male mentor persuading a woman to give up her artistic ambitions, not because her writing is bad – Woolson never reveals its quality – but because he believes that genius in a woman is a disfigurement or a delusion.

But a real cultural ambivalence about these female geniuses emerges in the warning in a popular magazine that while women with minds 'equal to any human undertaking' exist, 'happily these giants are rare.' Such women have unsexed themselves. By going beyond male-defined limitations they have become monsters, not women at all. [. . .]

Since ['Miss Grief'] depicts a woman genius whose tragic failure is the fault of society and not herself, perhaps the publishers [who left the story out of two Woolson anthologies issued after her death] felt that like Miss Grief's own work, Woolson's account would not be acceptable to the public. [. . .]

But it would be a mistake to see her death as a mark of professional despair. Although her stories show that both genius and mediocrity, love and lovelessness, disable women artists, she herself managed not to be disabled but to remain productive and successful by making art out of those dilemmas. And it would be equally wrong to dismiss her analysis of the excruciating dilemmas of women artists as merely a symptom of her own depressions. Several of her women contemporaries depicted those struggles as equally harrowing.

Cheryl B. Torsney, *Constance Fenimore Woolson: The Grief of Artistry* (Athens: The University of Georgia Press, 1989), pp. 75, 81, 86, 90.

'Miss Grief' becomes a paradigmatic story of nineteenth-century woman's artistry, a narrative that, given late twentieth-century hindsight, offers an ironic comment on the canonization of literary texts by implying that many powerful works by women were, in effect, suppressed by those male readers, editors, and publishers in positions of power. [. . .]

[W]e can read 'Miss Grief' as a script of classic class conflict. The lower classes have the potential for power, but the upper class can rob them of it because political convention is on its side. Since in this story the upper class is male and the underclass female, the dimension of gender becomes primary. The underclass female has the potential for revolutionary power; the conservative male upper class recognizes this and manages to maintain its firm grip on institutions and conventions by rendering the underclass helpless. [. . .]

Other elements in the story suggest a role reversal and overturning of the contemporary domestic romance, a nineteenth-century form that featured a heroine's rather than a hero's script. [. . .] 'Miss Grief,' however, violates all of these conventions. The heroine is not pretty; she has large dark eyes and is forty-three years old though the narrator thinks her over fifty; she is 'plain in feature, thin, dejected, and ill dressed.' Nor does the narrative end happily ever after: her manuscripts – her children – are buried alive. Miss Grief violates all of the narrator's expectations about the conventions of women and women writers. [. . .]

These 'authoresses' could, of course, scribble, but they could not control [. . .] For Woolson, a fluent speaker of French, the story of Aaronna Moncrief is *her* grief, for it will remain, for some time, 'unlearned,' because the male establishment neglects to ask the proper questions about her history. The subversive subtext of 'Miss Grief' insists on the woman artist's potential for power. In Woolson's day, however, that promise was not to be realized. For writers like Aaronna Moncrief and Constance Fenimore Woolson, artistry would bring grief, rather than triumph [. . .]

'At the Château of Corinne,' for all of its connections with the history of women's writing, seems to be a reflection on the business of women's artistry and on the history of women as readers and writers, rather than a happy romance. It is a narrative account of the fall of women's writing into the abyss after the demise of the Cult of True Womanhood and before the advent of the new Woman; it is also, more broadly, the tragic story of how all women in all ages, the women of genius serving as representative for all of her sisters, are appropriated, their subversive voices silenced, by the patriarchy.

Sarah Orne Jewett

Edward M. Chapman, 'The New England of Sarah Orne Jewett', *The Yale Review* (Fall 1913), pp. 157–72.

[From] description at a distance, mental, moral, or physical, Miss Jewett was beautifully free. She was of New England ancestry, birth, and training. Her home was in a New England village and she always kept it there. The 'atmosphere' of her books was the atmosphere that she breathed. Her 'types' were not so much the result of study and abstraction from observed subjects as the transcription of direct appeals which the life of her neighbors made to her own heart. Born thus through contact of life with life, they not only embody various human qualities, but they really possess souls. The reader can rarely speak of them as 'quaint' or 'bleak' or anything else that merely accords with literary convention. They are too personal to submit themselves to easy definition; so human, indeed, as generally to be humane.

Like Jane Austen, Sarah Orne Jewett was at her best when [. . .] painting her 'two square inches of ivory.' She exercised, too, an artist's privilege in choosing subjects that seemed to her worth painting. There is no realistic setting forth of rustic squalor, though degeneracy exists in New England hamlets as in most rural communities.

Josephine Donovan, *New England Local Color Literature* (New York: Continuum Press, 1988), pp. 99–118.

Jewett adds to the gallery of strong and authentic female characters developed by the local colorists. [. . .]

Yet Jewett's world was not an escapist Utopia. She did not leave the stubborn and painful realities behind. It is indeed the tension between the 'fallen,' alienated world of real experience and the transcending vision of a supportive, fulfilling community that gives power to her greatest work. The sense of elegy which so many have remarked in Jewett's work is a lamentation for the tentative nature of human accomplishment – and especially for the artificially limited possibilities of emotional and intellectual development afforded women – but at the same time there is a celebration of the transfiguring moments in which the human community – again sustained primarily by women – coheres.

In order to understand Jewett's accomplishment it is necessary to review her theory of literature, a theory whose originality has not been sufficiently appreciated. For it was this theory that enabled her to reach beyond her predecessors and to create an imaginative realm that passes beyond the historical limitations to women's condition and prevails as an intuition of being. [. . .]

Jewett wrote, [. . .] 'It is [. . .] those unwritable things that the story holds in its heart, if it has any, that makes the true soul of it, and these must be understood, and yet how many a story goes lame for lack of understanding' (*Letters*, Fields, ed., 112). This then is the meaning of the term 'imaginative realism'; it is writing that stirs one's imagination, that makes one dream. [. . .]

The tension between city and country runs through Jewett's work. [. . .] The second central theme [. . .] is that of individualism versus community.

Sarah Orne Jewett created a symbolic universe which expressed the longing of late-nineteenth-century women that the matriarchal world of the mothers be sustained. By her use of 'imaginative realism' she carried the themes of the earlier local colorists to a powerful and complex conclusion. Hers is perhaps the last fully female-identified vision in women's literature. For later women writers such as Wharton, Cather, and Gertrude Stein, the world of men was too much with them for this kind of imaginative construction. Jewett's vision, therefore, remains a powerful response to the transitions that were happening in women's lives at the turn of the century. Mary E. Wilkins Freeman formulated another, more extreme.

Marilyn S. Mobley, 'Rituals of Flight and Return: Ironic Journeys of Sarah Orne Jewett's Female Characters', *Colby Library Quarterly* 22 (March 1986), pp. 36–42.

In light of Sarah Orne Jewett's expressed affection for the rural villages of Maine, it might seem inconsistent that she so often uses flight imagery to describe the real and imaginary journeys of her female characters. Though seemingly contradictory, this characteristic imagery belies an ambivalence toward her native region, and demonstrates an unflinching admiration for its self-reliant women. Challenging the notion that range is masculine and that confinement is feminine, Jewett portrays women who continually contemplate and/or embark on journeys outside the confines of their rural domestic communities. While a different form of flight predominates in each text, certain patterns emerge in her numerous references to birds, holidays, and excursions that signify Jewett's attempt to acquaint her readers with the range of experience available to her New England women. The most significant of these patterns – the flight from one's environment to the outside world and the inevitable return home – has the mythic characteristics of ritual and reveals Jewett's complex response to this region, to its women and to her own role as a regional writer. Although inevitable, this return is not a resignation to limitations or failure, but a heroic expression of the desire to remain connected to one's cultural roots; thus, like flight, it is an act of self-affirmation. [. . .]

The nature of [Sylvia's] triumph – successfully making the solitary passage from ignorance to knowledge of the world – rehearses the traditional metaphor for the initiatory experience in American literature. If we understand initiation as the first existential ordeal, crisis, or encounter with experience in the life of a youth, or more simply as a 'viable mode of confronting adult realities,' then we might say Sylvia undergoes an initiation. Yet the traditional pattern of the initiatory journey – that of separation or departure, trial, communication of communal secrets, and return to the community – is not what we have in this story. Although Sylvia returns to her home, her departure has been both real and imaginative, both complete and abortive. In realistic terms, she moves upward but not outward. Only figuratively and psychically does her journey broaden her horizons. [. . .]

By using the rituals of flight and return in carefully devised circular narrative structures, she exposes the ironies that characterized the lives of many rural women in her time. On her own literary journey, Jewett discovered that she need not be limited by the local color medium; instead she could transform it through her essentially affirmative vision. Indeed, she journeyed beyond the comprehensive landscape we associate with myth. The achievement of her fiction is that she does not deny the contradictions that emerge, but seeks instead to hold them in balance before us.

Elizabeth Ammons, 'The Shape of Violence in Jewett's "A White Heron"', *Colby Library Quarterly* 22:1 (March 1986), pp. 6–16.

'A White Heron' represents an anti-bildungsroman. It is a rite-of-passage story in which the heroine refuses to make the passage. Choosing the world of her grandmother over the world of the alluring young man, Sylvia chooses not to pass over into the world of adult female sexuality as it is defined by the culture. The nine-year-old child, a girl about to enter puberty, refuses to enter into the transaction that everyone – the hunter, her grandmother – expects her to make.

'A White Heron' says that heterosexuality requires the female to offer up body itself as prey. All Sylvia has to do is offer up the body of the bird – a free, beautiful creature like herself – to the hunter and she will receive money, social approval, and the affection of a man. Clearly the heron in this story symbolizes the heroine, and the exchange Sylvia is expected to make at the age of nine, with her heart set throbbing by the handsome young man, is the transition from childhood to the threshold of womanhood, the wrench from little girl identification with the mother (in this case the maternal earth itself) to big girl identification with a man. Sylvia is expected to offer her freedom, her true nature, indeed life itself to a predator, who will pierce, stuff, and then own and admire the beautiful corpse. (Ornithology as a metaphor for male heterosexual predation is one of the brilliant strokes of 'A White Heron.' The combination of violence, voyeurism, and commercialism contained in the gun-wielding science, the goal of which is to create living death, is chilling.) Tempted – and Jewett *does* make the hunter with his money and charm and social privilege tempting – Sylvia says no.

In 'A White Heron' Jewett creates a threshold story about choosing not to step across. Sylvia won't give the bird over to the hunter, won't give herself over to him, won't enter the body-for-money bargain the culture expects of her. She chooses the world of her grandmother, a place defined as free, healthy, and 'natural' in this story, over the world of heterosexual favor and violence represented by the hunter.

Jewett's choice of a fairy tale to tell this story is perfect since one major purpose of this classic, white, western fairy tale is to teach heterosexuality.

Charlotte Perkins Gilman

William Dean Howells, ed., *The Great Modern American Stories: An Anthology* (New York: Boni & Liveright, 1920), p. vii.

Horace Scudder (then of *The Atlantic*) said in refusing ['The Yellow Wallpaper'] that it was so terribly good that it ought never to be printed. But terrible and too wholly dire as it was, I could not rest until I had corrupted the editor of *The New England* magazine into publishing it. Now that I have got it into my collection here, I shiver over it as much as I did when I first read it

in manuscript, though I agree with the editor of *The Atlantic* of
the time that it was too terribly good to be printed.

Jeffrey Berman, *The Talking Cure: Literary Representations of
Psychoanalysis* (New York: New York University Press, 1985),
pp. 35–59.

Despite the pre-Freudian world of 'The Yellow Wallpaper,' and
Charlotte Perkins Gilman's subsequent condemnation of psychoanalysis, the story is startlingly modern in its vision of mental
illness. Anticipating Freudian discoveries, the story suggests that
psychological illness worsens when it is not acknowledged as real
and that the rest cure is antithetical both to the talking cure and
to the therapeutic value of artistic creation. Moreover, 'The
Yellow Wallpaper' portrays mental illness as originating from
childhood experiences. Unlike Breuer's 'Fräulein Anna O.,' 'The
Yellow Wallpaper' shows the social and political as well as the
psychological implications of madness. Gilman rejects not psycho-
therapy, which Freud was introducing, but pseudotherapy, which
has always been with us. Gilman's narrator is one of the first in a
long line of benumbed and bedeviled patients in American literature who search desperately for understanding but who, following
the accepted medical advice of the time, lose their mind.

Denise D. Knight, ed., *'The Yellow Wallpaper' and Selected
Stories of Charlotte Perkins Gilman* (Newark: University of
Delaware Press, 1994), pp. 22–9.

Although Gilman hoped that her stories would be entertaining,
her primary goal in writing fiction was not to entertain the
reader. [. . .] But if Gilman wasn't a consistently eloquent writer,
she was at least a prolific one who used her fiction as an
opportunity to show her readers the possibilities of a world
reformed: in short, her stories recreate the world according to her
vision of the ideal.

Like her contemporaries, Gilman wanted her literature to
produce an effect upon the reader. But unlike many of her
contemporaries, she was less concerned with capturing realistic
dialect than in demonstrating the possibilities for effecting social
change. Rather, she attempts to proselytize the reader by infusing
her stories with socialist and feminine ideology. [. . .]

A significant part of Gilman's strategy, then, in writing short fiction was to demonstrate viable alternatives to long-ingrained and oppressive social habits. [. . .]

One of Gilman's complaints about existing literature was that the story of the 'conscientious woman' – the strong and self-reliant female who would leave an abusive husband and risk poverty, loneliness, and disgrace rather than endure a destructive marriage – had not been adequately told. [. . .]

The depiction of an ideal world is one that is repeated frequently in Gilman's fiction. If we consider her entire body of fiction, in fact, and consider the political and philosophical influences informing her writing, we can conclude that Gilman was *primarily*, but not exclusively, a writer of idealism – a loosely defined branch of literature based on a system of philosophy that seeks to show the author's conception of the ideal.

Kate Chopin

Anonymous, Review of *A Night in Acadie*, *The Nation*, vol. LXVI, no. 1719 (9 June 1898), p. 447.

Kate Chopin tells a story like a poet, and reproduces the spirit of a landscape like a painter. Her stories are to the bayous of Louisiana what Mary Wilkins's are to New England, with a difference, to be sure, as the Cape jessamine is different from the cinnamon rose, but like in seizing the heart of her people and showing the traits that come from their surroundings; like, too, in giving without a wasted word the history of main crises in their lives. That Cape jessamine is sometimes thought too heavy is perhaps inevitable in the heated South. But enough there is of artistic in the best sense to hold the reader from cover to cover, transported for the time to a region of fierce passions, mediaeval chivalry, combined with rags and bad grammar, a soft, sliding Creole accent, and the tragedies and comedies that loom with special meaning in a sparsely settled country.

Mary E. Papke, *Verging on the Abyss: The Social Fiction of Kate Chopin and Edith Wharton* (New York: Greenwood Press, 1990), pp. 29–30.

One insurpassable obstacle in Chopin studies [. . .] is the fact that Chopin does not, in her critical essays, ever overtly state her central subject or theme. Most critics, nevertheless, readily agree that her major theme is the defiance of women against social convention and hegemonic ideology. Emily Toth, in her dissertation, links Chopin with the domestic and plantation traditions but, more importantly, delineates the all-pervasiveness of the woman question in the social criticism and fiction of the day. Further, since the ideology of true womanhood was central in Chopin's life, it is not surprising that this might be the major impression or truth she would express. What is astonishing is that she had the temerity to do so, to present implicit critiques of social conventions and ideology within her fiction. Her subversive artistry can best be understood as an extension of her private philosophy and pessimistic world view. She did not believe in either ethical absolutes or the total absence of ethics. Neither did she see her world as necessarily progressive or retrogressive. For Chopin, each individual – particularly each woman – possessed infinite potential for self-fulfillment and expression but also, at the same time, the greater possibility for self-compromise and self-destruction. And these two faces of the same coin were not purely determined by nature but also of nurture: 'Human impulses do not change and cannot so long as men and women continue to stand in the relation to one another which they have occupied since our knowledge of their existence began.' Her finest fiction, like Edith Wharton's, posits the possibility of changing those relations. She does so by presenting to the reader women who defy those longstanding socio-sexual relations even though because of that defiance they fall at last into abysses of solitude and self-alienation.

Peggy Skaggs, *Kate Chopin* (Boston: Twayne Publishers, 1985), pp. 112–13.

Chopin focuses with increasing clarity on the special problems that women face in reconciling their often conflicting needs for place and love on the one hand and individual sovereignty on the other. This focal point begins to emerge in her first story, 'Wiser than a God,' and becomes sharp in such later stories as 'Lilacs' and 'The Story of an Hour.' 'Regret' develops the theme that the fully realized feminine existence cannot be based altogether on personal freedom but must also include maternal love. And 'A Respectable Woman' makes clear that sexual desire is an important part of the complete woman. But 'Athenaise,' 'The Story of an Hour,' and many other stories both early and late insist that to live fully a woman must recognize herself to be a discrete and autonomous individual. In 'The Storm,' Chopin's last important story, which remained unpublished until 1969, the author portrays a woman who simply satisfies her three basic needs without reflecting upon the conflicts among them; but the primary tension of the story derives from the awareness that Calixta's method of fulfilling those needs will almost certainly lead to explosive consequences.

Finally, in *The Awakening*, the novel that both climaxed and foreclosed her brief but brilliant literary career, Kate Chopin puts all her favorite fictional pieces together. [. . .]

Chopin lived and wrote approximately three quarters of a century before her time. So long as she confined her work to innocuous local-color stories, her contemporaries accepted her work and indeed praised it. But when she dared to expose the conflicts raging inside of wives and mothers, her contemporaries insulted her personally and, even worse, banned her novel.

Today, however, Chopin's reputation stands high. [. . .] Critics are claiming that her work exemplifies whatever school or approach they favor at the moment, whether it be romanticism, realism, naturalism, existentialism, or feminism.

Actually, however, Chopin stands alone, a solitary figure among all those 'ism's.' [. . .] Her work defies classification as she portrays the dilemma of the modern woman, freed at last from her centuries of drudgery but groping uncertainly for a new place in society where she can be accepted as a unique individual and fulfill her needs for both love and autonomy.

Per Seyersted, *Kate Chopin: A Critical Biography* (New York: Octagon Books, 1980), pp. 196–9.

She took her writing seriously. While she had the commercial instinct and wanted her work to succeed even financially, literary integrity was her paramount concern. She was one of the utterly few who wrote to suit their own taste, and she made practically no concessions to the public and did not aspire to reaching beyond the group who would be in sympathy with her. Partly because she did not write in self-justification as Mmes. de Staël and Sand had done, she could do away with both their militancy in the portrayals of female emancipation and their protestations that their works were moral. Her courage is even more remarkable when we consider that she did not have her predecessors' influential friends and that she lived in a country where intellectual genius – even in a man – did not count for much.

The great achievement of Kate Chopin was that she broke new ground in American literature. She was the first woman writer in her country to accept passion as a legitimate subject for serious, outspoken fiction. Revolting against tradition and authority; with a daring which we can hardly fathom today; with an uncompromising honesty and no trace of sensationalism, she undertook to give the unsparing truth about woman's submerged life. She was something of a pioneer in the amoral treatment of sexuality, of divorce, and of woman's urge for an existential authenticity. She is in many respects a modern writer, particularly in her awareness of the complexities of truth and the complications of freedom. With no desire to reform, but only to understand; with the clear conscience of the rebel, yet unembittered by society's massive lack of understanding, she arrived at her culminating achievements, *The Awakening* and 'The Storm.' [. . .]

Kate Chopin is a rare, transitional figure in modern literature. In her illustrations of the female condition she forms a link between George Sand and Simone de Beauvoir. In her descriptions of the power of sexuality she reflects the ideas of such a work as *Hippolytus* and foreshadows the forceful 20th-century treatments of Eros. [. . .]

Mrs Chopin had a daring and a vision all her own, a unique pessimistic realism applied to woman's unchanging condition.

Edith Wharton

Carl Van Doren, 'An Elder America', *The Nation*, vol. 111 (3 November 1920), pp. 510–11.

We can no more do without some notion or other of an age more golden than our own than we can do without bread. There must be, we assure ourselves, a more delectable day yet to come, or there must have been one once. The evidence of prophecy, however, is stronger than that of history, which somehow fails to find the perfect age. Mrs Wharton has never ranged herself with the prophets, contented, apparently, with being the most intellectual of our novelists and surveying with level, satirical eyes the very visible world. [. . .]

Mrs Wharton's structure and methods show no influence of the impressionism now broadening the channel of fiction [. . .] she knows her world. In lonely contrast to the many who write about what they know without understanding it or interpreting it, she brings a superbly critical disposition to arrange her knowledge in significant forms. These characters who move with such precision and veracity through the ritual of a frozen caste are here as real as their actual lives would ever have let them be. They are stiff with ceremonial garments and heavy with the weight of imagined responsibilities. Mrs Wharton's triumph is that she had described these rites and surfaces and burdens as familiarly as if she loved them and as lucidly as if she hated them.

Mary E. Papke, *Verging on the Abyss: The Social Fiction of Kate Chopin and Edith Wharton* (New York: Greenwood Press, 1990), p. 104.

[Wharton] reconstructs that metamorphosis of her supposedly genteel world into a modern, seemingly barbaric society in that she both censures 'genteel' society for its own rapacious material-ism, for its willingness to sacrifice its own ethics and traditions for hard cash, as well as rebuking the new materialist society for its own perverse form of amorality. In all her fiction, the social use and prescribed roles of women act as a thermometer by which to measure the heat of the social battle and the changes in social consciousness. Wharton, of course, does not rest with symbolic use of women; instead she also delimits the reality of women during this period, a time of social transformation and ideological mutation.

Katherine Joslin, *Edith Wharton* (New York: St Martin's Press, 1991), pp. 29–30.

Identity for Wharton is inextricably bound to culture, to one's material and social environment. [. . .]

The bond between the individual and the social group, 'the web of customs, manners, culture', lies at the heart of Edith Wharton's fiction. Her novels and short stories depict individuals enmeshed in what she metaphorically called the social 'web' or 'net', an elaborate weave of manners, mores, rituals, expectations, gestures as well as physical environment, houses, streets, rooms, decor, costume that define the parameters of human experience, even human nature. As she knew from her own experience, as a woman in Old New York, society is a 'hieroglyphic world', a coded world of signs that individuals must learn in order to make the personal adjustments, however difficult, between individual desire and social necessity. Human nature, for her, was clothed in the social fabric: she saw no possibility for life denuded of that garment, no essential 'human nature' outside the elaborately woven social context. The story she had to tell in her fiction delineated the dialectic features of the social bond: the bonds or restrictions society places on the individual and the resulting bond or covenant between the two.

John Lowe, 'Edith Wharton', *Modern American Women Writers*, ed., Elaine Showalter (New York: Scribner's and Sons, 1991), pp. 555–6.

Clearly, Wharton is emerging as one of the most important American writers; we now see that throughout her career she was fascinated, as most great writers have been, by the tension that exists in America between the needs of democracy and of individualism, and the dramatic situations that develop when seismic encounters between these two realms create catastrophe. Simultaneously, although it is often forgotten [. . .] she excelled in the comedy of manners and social satire, and all of her best books draw much of their strength from this resource, especially her powerful sense of irony and her ability to create believable comic dialogue.

It would be wrong, however, to pigeonhole Wharton as a novelist of manners, as is often done. Her vast oeuvre ranges fearlessly across the spectrum of American culture, sometimes in areas she knew little about, but always with a penetrating eye, a devastating wit, and an abundance of compassion. Her feminine protagonists offer unusually compelling and widely varying illustrations of the difficulty of finding fulfillment as a woman in America, a country whose rapid changes frequently brought only new modes of oppression for its women. [. . .]

Wharton was almost as effective, however, with her male protagonists (especially Newland Archer and Ethan Frome), and her best novels go beyond gender issues, the comedy of manners, and other categories; they are, *au fond*, quests of identity, in the classical American tradition. Her characters struggle with society and each other, but ultimately arrive at a knowledge of who they are – and frequently, who they might have been – through a final conflict with their souls. As such, they eloquently chart the course of what Wharton called 'the eternal struggle between man's contending impulses.'

Willa Cather

H. L. Mencken, review of *Youth and the Bright Medusa*, *The Smart Set*, vol. LXIII, no. 4 (December 1920), pp. 9–10.

[*Youth and the Bright Medusa*] is made up of eight stories, and all of them deal with artists. It is Miss Cather's peculiar virtue that she represents the artist in terms of his own thinking – that she does not look *at* him through a peep-hole in the studio door, but looks *with* him at the life that he is so important and yet so isolated and lonely a part of. One finds in every line of her writing a sure-footed and civilized culture; it gives her an odd air of foreignness, particularly when she discusses music, which is often. [. . .] They are stories that lift themselves completely above the level of current American fiction, even of good fiction. They are the work of a woman who, after a long apprenticeship, has got herself into the front rank of American novelists, and is still young enough to have her best writing ahead of her. I call *My Ántonia* to your attention once more. It is the finest thing of its sort ever done in America.

Deborah Carlin, 'Willa Cather', *Modern American Women Writers*, ed., Elaine Showalter (New York: Scribner's and Sons, 1991), pp. 49–50.

Willa Cather remains an anomaly in American literature. Her novels have been embraced by the general public, both in her time and in ours. . . . [Yet] despite such widespread and sustained popular acceptance of her work, Cather has fared less well in critical studies and in the American literary canon. While her fiction is perceived to be significant in some vague way, she has never been accorded the status of a 'major' twentieth-century writer along the lines of William Faulkner or F. Scott Fitzgerald. In part this is because she is difficult to place. Neither a realist or a modernist, Cather wrote novels that confound easy categorization and, by extension, canonization. [. . .] Cather's literary reputation, as Sharon O'Brien has documented, suffered in the 1930s and 1940s, when critics defined her work solely in terms of nostalgia, elegy, escape, and a rejection of the modern world.

As a consequence, half of Cather's oeuvre remains unread. Her critical reputation is defined by region, in the best, and, paradoxically, most limiting sense of the word. [. . .] It is both curious and ironic that a writer who is so difficult to place in the canon is finally relegated to a specific regional place which then becomes the prevailing 'meaning' of her work.

It might instead be more accurate to understand Cather not by specific geographical place but by those strategies which the child, girl, woman, and writer adopted in order to create places of possibility, of self-expression, and of self-definition within the spheres of family, work, and nation. And for Cather, much like her critical reputation, these are places of ambiguity, of ambivalence, and even of anomaly.

Deborah Carlin, *Cather, Canon, and the Politics of Reading* (Amherst: University of Massachusetts Press, 1992), pp. 6–8.

Such passionate devotion [on behalf of a minority of readers to Cather's novels] constitutes simply one of the reading communities in which the person and prose of Willa Cather are appropriated, claimed, and somehow signified. Such reading communities organize themselves unconsciously around what Barbara Herrnstein Smith has termed 'contingencies of value,' an evaluative frame of reference in which an object, a text, or an author 'is likely to perform certain particular (though taken-for-granted) functions for some particular (though only implicitly defined) set of subjects under some particular (unspecified but assumed) set or range of conditions.' Though some significations of value characterize virtually all critical treatments of 'major' writers, Cather, because she 'belongs to no school,' is especially subject to the revision, reification, and renunciation of widely disparate readerly contingents. Whether viewed as an American icon, a woman writer, a lesbian, a cosmopolitan Midwesterner, a conservative Republican, a scathing journalist, an antimodernist, or an embittered elegiast, Cather remains an anomaly in American literature and her fiction is particularly hard to place. Despite her popular appeal, Cather lingers in the margins of the American literary canon. [. . .]

Cather has made it into some versions of an American literary canon. But what soon becomes apparent about canonical inclusions of Cather is that they are limited to the first half of her oeuvre, those early pioneer novels – *O Pioneers!* (1913), *The*

Song of the Lark (1915), and *My Ántonia* (1918) – that cele-
brate American manifest destiny and the settling of the West.
Spanning both popular and critical assessments, Cather's canonical value resides in the historical myth of national destiny that a
vast array of readers recognize in these early novels. [. . .] Why,
for instance, are the majority of Cather's later fictions rigorously
unread? [. . .]

Looking at Willa Cather as the consummate artist whose works
are best understood as being fundamentally about art itself is the
most prevalent approach in Cather studies, and with good
reason. [. . .] Investigations of Cather's artistry locate recurring
biographical and thematic issues that center around what Cather
firmly believed was the exceptional and necessary role of the
artist in society: to preserve that which is true and good by a
careful attention to human nature and a command of one's artistic
medium.

Sally Harvey, *Redefining the American Dream: The Novels of*
Willa Cather (Toronto: Associated University Press, 1995),
pp. 19–20.

In [Sinclair] Lewis's [Nobel acceptance] speech, he highlighted a
particular problem for the American artist, a problem to which
Cather's increasing focus on community may be an unconscious
or perhaps at times a carefully crafted, response. The writer in
America, Lewis noted, 'has no institution, no group, to which
he can turn for inspiration.' We see this, of course, in the
exodus of writers from the United States after World War I,
but Cather did not expatriate. Cather in her novels, however,
does seem intent – whether consciously so or not – on finding
and defining her artistic 'group,' not particularly within America
but within a tradition of artists, past, present, and future, representative of the broader Western traditions that she learned to
revere early in her life, but not excluding earlier native American
traditions, to which Cather became strongly attracted when she
visited the Southwest. We see in her later novels an increasing concern with defining, and then aligning herself to, such an
artistic community, as many of her characters become actively
involved in securing a place for themselves within the larger
community that Archibald MacLeish described as 'riders on the
earth together, brothers on that bright loveliness in the eternal
cold.'

Susan Glaspell

Bartholow V. Crawford, 'Susan Glaspell', *The Palimpsest*, vol. XI, no. 12 (December 1930), pp. 517–21.

The work of Susan Glaspell reveals considerable variety in form, setting, and style; but there is also a degree of continuity and coherence in ideals and point of view. In her early volume of stories, *Lifted Masks*, in her novel, *Brook Evans*, and in her play, *The Inheritors*, she exhibits a sensitiveness to human injustice, an insight into human nature, and a realization of the unceasing struggle between idealism and the animal which is not cynical but sympathetic. [. . .]

Suffice it to say that in Susan Glaspell Iowa claims an author of wide experience, varied capabilities, and undoubted genius. The middle Western scene was for her not something to be lived down or forgotten, but one of her richest resources; and in every reference to the region of her birth, there is affectionate under-standing and sympathy.

Mary E. Papke, *Susan Glaspell: A Research and Production Sourcebook* (Westport, Connecticut: Greenwood Press, 1993), pp. 10–13.

It is ironic that feminist criticism itself has also played a part in [Glaspell's] continued marginalization, no doubt counter to its intentions, in its perhaps too great attention on *Trifles* as her masterwork, that work or 'A Jury of Her Peers' offered as her passport into the canon. It is no mystery why *Trifles* and its companion short story were the works most receptive to recla-mation in the 1970s. Those works boldly reflect feminist political concerns of that time and in the terms through which those concerns were stated – how the patriarchy suppresses matriarchy, how it effects the trivialization of women's work, experience, and desires. Anthologized in 1973 by Mary Anne Ferguson in her *Images of Women in Literature* and by Lee Edwards and Arlyn Diamond in their *American Voices, American Women*, the play and the story provide an almost too easily made accounting of gender antagonisms. [. . .]

Critics need to reread Glaspell's opus in terms of her 'American-ness.' I would argue that her vision of what it means to be an American was as important to her as what it means to be a woman in America. Finally, critics need to incorporate and to invent new perspectives on reading and staging theatre, ones which address directly issues of collaboration, experimentation, political contextualization, and the use of the theatre as a staging ground for ideological debates, for if, as the early Pulitzer Prize stipulations argue, 'the original American play[s] which shall best represent the educational value and power of the stage' are those we should value most, Glaspell's plays, one already so honored, certainly all merit renewed critical attention.

Veronica Makowsky, *Susan Glaspell's Century of American Women: A Critical Interpretation of Her Work* (New York: Oxford University Press, 1993), pp. 4–10.

Glaspell was an idealist, a believer in truth and beauty. [. . .] In contrast to the cosmopolitan modernists, she was a profoundly American writer in the transcendental tradition of Emerson and Whitman. Like them, she sought self-knowledge or truth in the often 'obscure reveries of the inward gaze.' In contrast with the despondent, elitist modernists, she shared Whitman's democratic optimism about the potential for human progress and so cel-ebrated the so-called 'common people,' though she acknowledged their faults and the obstacles with which entrenched society confronted them. [. . .]

Glaspell and her ilk may be damned by Hawthorne and his successors for what they did write about women and their lives, but she is also damned, in fame and sales, for what she did not do, namely, fit the paradigm of today's 'women novel,' the supermarket romance novel, whether Harlequin or another brand, in which the heroine's ultimate goal is getting the hero to take care of her. In contrast, Glaspell's heroines take responsibility for themselves and are able to nurture others, including men, only after they have achieved self-reliance. [. . .]

Her novels are generally conventional omniscient narrations with clearly comprehensible characterization, time schemes, and diction, and, of course, well-made, interesting plots. They are not fragmented, convoluted, allusive, or obscure; in short, they are generally quite easy and pleasant to read and readily convey Glaspell's beliefs. Inopportunely for her place in literary history, difficulty, not clarity, was valued by those exponents of modern-ism, the New Critics, who reigned in the academy well into the 1960s. [. . .]

Glaspell differs from most of her nineteenth-century predecessors in the tentativeness of her happy endings. [. . .] Her heroines' success is their ability to hope for a better world, not the achievement of that world, despite a few seemingly improved men. [. . .]

Glaspell differs from much of this nineteenth-century fiction in her emphasis on mature woman as mother, not on young girl as daughter. Indeed, Glaspell's treatment of maternity is particularly relevant to current debates within feminism. [. . .] Glaspell's maternal metaphor is at once conservative and revolutionary. The women want to save what is best in the town, its future, progress in the form of children, but Glaspell represents their unconventional lives and relinquishment of society's comforts as indications of the direction in which the future should go, toward the innovative, the original, the 'outside.'

Victoria Aarons, 'A Community of Women: Surviving Marriage in the Wilderness', *Portraits of Marriage in Literature*, ed., Anne C. Hargrove and Maurine Magliocco (Macomb, Illinois: Western Illinois University Press, 1984) pp. 44–66.

[In] 'A Jury of Her Peers' . . . [a]n immediate bond is established between the two women, a kind of intimacy that is not built from long-term acquaintance. Instead, it is a bond created of necessity in the face of life on the prairies where farmhouses are at a great distance from one another, and human contact rare. [. . .]

The two women recognize much more than the blatant fact that Minnie Wright killed her husband. They realize, without articulating it aloud, that she had no choice but to kill him. [. . .]

The stillness, the isolation, and the social exclusion that Minnie Wright must have endured, bound to a marriage ill-suited to her, yet an institution that permitted no escape, drove her to such an extreme act of violence. Both Mrs Hale and Mrs Peters respond to this knowledge with a shared experience, a common bond. The reader finds the two women positioning themselves in silent collusion against their husbands, on the side of the exiled Mrs Wright, their sense of justice having been fulfilled. [. . .]

As the women recognize the kind of existence Minnie Wright must have endured they feel an enormous amount of guilt. They identify with her in a way the men cannot. They see what their husbands fail to see, and so are shamed by their neglect of the lonely, stoic woman. They, too, are to blame. [. . .]

[T]he men in 'A Jury of Her Peers' are deprived of an awakening sensitivity. They remain short-sighted and never come to understand the hidden force behind Minnie Wright's oppressed position. Throughout the story the men view their wives as weak, keepers of a domestic arena which is insignificant. [. . .]

But the women's shared vision of domestic affairs – of cooking, sewing, and cleaning – as a source of power and accomplishment, alienates them from their husbands. [. . .] The women's attention to domestic affairs is a way of constructing order, of finding the only place possible given the societal restrictions placed on women. It is here they can excel, make sense of experience and give their lives meaning. This is why the first clue for the women in 'A Jury of Her Peers' is Minnie Wright's disorganized kitchen. They sense immediately that something is amiss. Their husbands, however, cannot see this because they don't recognize the value of domestic concerns. Moreover, they view themselves and their place in society as superior to that of their wives.

SUGGESTIONS FOR FURTHER READING

Catharine Sedgwick

Readers wishing to know more about Catharine Sedgwick's life and work should turn to *Three Wise Virgins*, by Gladys Brooks (New York: Dutton, 1957); *Catharine Maria Sedgwick*, by Edward H. Foster (New York: Twayne Publishers, 1974); and two short articles by Mary Kelley, 'A Woman Alone: Catharine Maria Sedgwick's Spinsterhood in Nineteenth-Century America', in *New England Quarterly* 51 (1978): 209–25, and 'Catharine Maria Sedgwick' *Legacy* 6 (1989): 45–50.

The following works offer interesting material on Sedgwick's prose including 'Cacoethes Scribendi':

Nina Baym, *Woman's Fiction* (Ithaca: Cornell University Press, 1978).

Michael D. Bell, 'History and Romance Convention in Catharine Sedgwick's *Hope Leslie*', *American Quarterly* 22 (1970): 213–21.

Judith Fetterly, *Provisions* (Bloomington: Indiana University Press, 1989).

Thomas H. Fick, 'Catharine Sedgwick's "Cacoethes Scribendi": Romance in Real Life', *Studies in Short Fiction* 27:4 (Fall 1990): 567–76.

Mary Kelley, *Private Women: Public Stage* (New York: Oxford University Press, 1984).

Elizabeth Stuart Phelps

Readers who wish to know more about Elizabeth Stuart Phelps's life and work should consult Austin Phelps's 'Memorial' in *The Last Leaf from Sunny Side* (Boston: Phillips, Samson, 1853); Phelps's own *Chapters from a Life* (Boston: Houghton, Mifflin, 1896); Carol Farley Kessler's *Elizabeth Stuart Phelps* (Boston: Twayne Publishers, 1982); and 'A Literary Legacy: Elizabeth Stuart Phelps, Mother and Daughter' in *Frontiers* 3 (1980): 28–33.

The following works specifically address 'The Angel Over The Right Shoulder':

Margo Culley, 'Vain Dreams: The Dream Convention and Women's Fiction', *Frontiers* 1 (1976): 94–102.

Judith Fetterly, *Provisions* (Bloomington: Indiana University Press, 1989).

Carol Holly, 'Shaming the Self in "The Angel Over The Right Shoulder"', *American Literature* 60:1 (March 1988): 42–60.

Linda Huf, *A Portrait of the Artist as a Young Woman: The Writer as Heroine in American Literature* (New York: Ungar, 1983).

Frances Harper

Readers who wish to know more about Frances Harper should begin by turning to *A Brighter Coming Day: A Frances Ellen Watkins Harper Reader*, edited by Frances Smith Foster (New York: Feminist Press, 1990); Joanne Braxton's 'Frances E. W. Harper', in *Modern American Women Writers*, edited by Elaine Showalter (New York: Scribner's and Sons, 1991); Frances Smith Foster's 'Frances E. W. Harper', in *African American Writers*, edited by Valerie Smith (New York: Scribner's and Sons, 1991); and *Discarded Legacy: Politics and Poetics in the Life of Frances E. W. Harper* by Melba-Joyce Boyd (Detroit: Wayne State University Press, 1994).

The following articles are relevant both to Harper's work in general and to 'The Two Offers' in particular:

Paul Lauter, 'Is Frances Ellen Watkins Harper Good Enough To Teach?', *Legacy* 5:1 (Spring 1988): 27–32.

Maggie Sale, 'Critiques from within: Antebellum Projects of Resistance', *American Literature* 64:4 (December 1992): 695–718.

William J. Scheick, 'Strategic Ellipses in Harper's "The Two Offers"', *Southern Literary Journal* 23:2 (Spring 1991): 14–18.

Harriet Prescott Spofford

Readers who wish to know more about Harriet Prescott Spofford should begin by reading *Our Famous Women* by Rose Terry Cooke (Hartford: Worthington, 1884); Elizabeth K. Halbeisen's *Harriet Prescott Spofford: A Romantic Survival* (Philadelphia: University of Pennsylvania Press, 1935); and *American*

Fiction by Arthur Hobson Quinn (New York: Appleton Century, 1936).

The following articles are relevant to 'Circumstance':

Anna Dalke, '"Circumstance" and the Creative Woman: Harriet Prescott Spofford', *Arizona Quarterly* 41:1 (Spring 1985): 71–85.

Judith Fetterly, *Provisions* (Bloomington: Indiana University Press, 1989).

Maryanne Garbowsky, 'A Maternal Muse for Emily Dickinson', *Dickinson Studies* 41 (1987): 12–17.

Thelma J. Shinn, 'Harriet Prescott Spofford: A Reconsideration', *Turn-of-the-Century Women* 1:1 (Summer 1984): 36–45.

Rebecca Harding Davis

Readers who wish to know more about Rebecca Harding Davis should read *American Fiction*, by Arthur Hobson Quinn (New York: Appleton Century, 1936); *The Rebecca Harding Davis Years: A Biography of a Mother and Son*, by Gerald Langford (New York: Holt, Rinehart and Winston, 1961); *Rebecca Harding Davis and American Realism* (Philadelphia: University of Pennsylvania Press, 1991); 'Rebecca Harding Davis', *Legacy* 7 no. 2 (Fall, 1990) 39–45, by Sharon M. Harris; and Jane Atteridge Rose's *Rebecca Harding Davis* (New York: Twayne Publishers, 1993).

The following works represent interesting criticism of 'Life in the Iron Mills' and 'Marcia', as well as of the author's work in general:

Walter Heresford, 'Literary Contexts of "Life in the Iron Mills"', *American Literature* 49 (1977): 70–85.

Tillie Olsen, 'A Biographical Interpretation', *Life in the Iron Mills and Other Stories* (Old Westbury, New York: Feminist Press, 1985).

Jean Pfaelzer, '"Marcia" by Rebecca Harding Davis', *Legacy* 4:1 (Spring 1987): 3–10.

——'Rebecca Harding Davis: Domesticity, Social Order, and the Industrial Novel', *International Journal of Women's Studies* 4 (1981): 234–44.

William Shurr, '"Life in the Iron Mills": A Nineteenth-Century Conversion Narrative', *American Transcendental Quarterly* 5:4 (December 1991): 245–57.

Louisa May Alcott

Readers who wish to know more about Louisa May Alcott's life and work should read *Louisa May: A Modern Biography of Louisa May Alcott*, by Martha Saxton (Boston: Houghton Mifflin, 1977); *Communities of Women*, by Nina Auerbach (Cambridge: Harvard University Press, 1978); Madelon Beldell's *The Alcotts: Biography of a Family* (New York: C. N. Potter, 1980); and *Louisa May Alcott*, by Ruth K. MacDonald (Boston: Twayne Publishers, 1983). For specific information on the author and her most famous novel, *Little Women*, see *A Hunger for Home: Louisa May Alcott and Little Women* by Sarah Elbert (Philadelphia: Temple University Press, 1984) and, more recently, *Sister's Choice: Tradition and Change in American Women's Writing*, by Elaine Showalter (New York: Oxford University Press, 1991).

The following contain interesting critiques of Alcott's work generally and articles relevant to 'My Contraband' and 'Behind a Mask' specifically:

Mary Capello, '"Looking about Me with All My Eyes": Censored Viewing, Carnival, and Louisa May Alcott's Hospital Sketches', *Arizona Quarterly* 50:3 (Autumn 1994): 59–88.

Mary Elliot, 'Outperforming Femininity: Public Conduct and Private Enterprise in Louisa May Alcott's "Behind a Mask"', *American Transcendental Quarterly* 8:4 (December 1994): 299–310.

Abigail A. Hamblen, 'Louisa May Alcott and the Racial Question', *University Review* 37 (1971): 307–13.

Jane E. Schultz, 'Embattled Care: Narrative Authority in Louisa May Alcott's Hospital Sketches', *Legacy* 9:2 (Fall 1992): 104–18.

Madeline B. Stern, ed., *Critical Essays on Louisa May Alcott* (Boston: G. K. Hall & Co., 1984).

Mary E. Wilkins Freeman

Readers who wish to know more about Mary E. Wilkins Freeman's life and literature should refer to *Mary E. Wilkins Freeman*, by Edward Foster (Amherst, Massachusetts: Green Knight, 1956); Ann Hamblen's *The New England Art of Mary Wilkins Freeman* (New York: Hendricks House, 1956); and *Mary Wilkins Freeman*, by Perry D. Westbrook (Boston: Twayne

Publishers, 1988). More recent studies include *New England Local Color Literature*, by Josephine Donovan (New York: Ungar, 1983) and the essay 'Mary Wilkins Freeman' by Marjorie Pryse in *Modern American Women Writers*, edited by Elaine Showalter (New York: Scribner's and Sons, 1991).

The following all contain interesting material on the four short stories excerpted in the anthology:

Kate Gardner, 'The Subversion of Genre in the Short Stories of Mary Wilkins Freeman', *New England Quarterly* 65:3 (September 1992): 447–68.

David H. Hirsch, 'Subdued Meaning in "A New England Nun"', *Studies in Short Fiction* 2 (1965): 124–36.

Norma Johnsen, 'Pieces: Artist and Audience in Three Mary Wilkins Freeman Stories', *Colby Quarterly* 29:1 (March 1993): 43–56.

Shirley Marchalonis, ed., *Critical Essays on Mary Wilkins Freeman* (Boston: G. K. Hall, 1991).

Marjorie Pryse, 'An Uncloistered "New England Nun"', *Studies in Short Fiction* 12 (Summer 1983): 61–4.

Ann Romines, 'A Place for "A Poetess"', *Markham Review* 12 (Summer 1983): 61–4.

Susan Allen Toth, 'Defiant Light: A Positive View of Mary Wilkins Freeman', *New England Quarterly* 46 (March 1973): 82–93.

Ann Douglas Wood, 'The Literature of Impoverishment: The Women Local Colorists in America, 1865–1914', *Women's Studies* I (1972): 3–45.

Constance Fenimore Woolson

Readers interested in discovering more about the life and work of Constance Fenimore Woolson should begin with John Dwight Kern's *Constance Fenimore Woolson* (Philadelphia: 1934); *Constance Fenimore Woolson* by Rayburn S. Moore (New York: Twayne, 1963); and Cheryl B. Torsney's *Constance Fenimore Woolson: The Grief of Artistry* (Athens: The University of Georgia Press, 1989). Also of interest is Henry James's article 'Miss Constance Fenimore Woolson', reprinted in *American Essays of Henry James*, edited by Leon Edel (New York: Vintage Books, 1956).

The following all contain interesting readings of Woolson's two short stories included in this anthology:

Cheryl B. Torsney, ed., *Critical Essays on Constance Fenimore Woolson* (New York: G. K. Hall & Co., 1992).
——Introduction to 'Miss Grief', *Legacy* 4:1 (Spring 1987): 11–25.
Joan Myers Weimer, 'Woman Artists as Exiles in the Fiction of Constance Fenimore Woolson', *Legacy* 3:2 (Fall 1986): 3–15.

Readers interested in the literary and personal relationship between Woolson and Henry James should read:

Mary P. Edwards Kitterman, 'Henry James and the Artist-Heroine in the Tales of Constance Fenimore Woolson', *Nineteenth-Century Women Writers of the English-Speaking World* (Westport, Connecticut: Greenwood Press, 1986): 45–59.
Cheryl B. Torsney, 'The Traditions of Gender: Constance Fenimore Woolson and Henry James', *Patrons and Protégées: Gender, Friendship, and Writing in Nineteenth-Century America*, ed. Shirley Marchalonis (New Brunswick: Rutgers University Press, 1994): 161–83.

Sarah Orne Jewett

Readers who wish to know more about Sarah Orne Jewett and her art should read Josephine Donovan's *Sarah Orne Jewett* (New York: Ungar Publishing Co., 1980); *Sarah Orne Jewett: A New England Persephone*, by Sarah W. Sherman (Hanover: University Press of New England, 1989); Elizabeth Silverthorne's *Sarah Orne Jewett: A Writer's Life* (Woodstock, New York: Overlook Press, 1993); and *Sarah Orne Jewett: Her World and Her Work* by Paula Blanchard (Reading, Massachusetts: Addison-Wesley, 1994).
    The following works contain interesting readings of 'A White Heron':

Elizabeth Ammons, 'The Shape of Violence in Jewett's "A White Heron"', *Colby Library Quarterly* 22:1 (March 1986): 6–16.
Richard Cary, ed., *An Appreciation of Sarah Orne Jewett* (Waterville, Maine: Colby College Press, 1973).
Josephine Donovan, *New England Local Color Literature* (New York: Continuum Press, 1988).
Marilyn S. Mobley, *Folk Roots and Mythic Wings in Sarah Orne Jewett and Toni Morrison: Cultural Function of Narrative?* (Baton Rouge: Louisiana State University Press, 1991).

—— 'Rituals of Flight and Return: Ironic Journeys of Sarah Orne Jewett's Female Characters', *Colby Library Quarterly* 22 (March 1986): 36–42.

Gwen L. Nagel, ed., *Critical Essays on Sarah Orne Jewett* (Boston: G. K. Hall & Co., 1984).

Louis A. Renza, *'A White Heron' and the Question of Minor Literature* (Madison: University of Wisconsin Press, 1984).

Margaret Roman, *Sarah Orne Jewett: Reconstructing Gender* (Tuscaloosa: University of Alabama Press, 1992).

Charlotte Perkins Gilman

Readers who wish to know more about Charlotte Perkins Gilman may be interested in Mary A. Mill's *Charlotte Perkins Gilman: The Making of a Radical Feminist, 1860–1896* (Philadelphia: Temple University Press, 1980); *Charlotte Perkins Gilman*, by Gary Scharnhorst (Boston: Twayne Publishers, 1985); and Ann J. Lane's *To Herland and Beyond: the Life and Work of Charlotte Perkins Gilman* (New York: Pantheon Books, 1990). Other recent works of note include *That Kind of Woman*, edited by Bronte Adams and Trudi Tate (New York: Caroll & Graff, 1992); *Critical Essays on Charlotte Perkins Gilman*, edited by Joanne B. Karpinski (New York: G. K. Hall & Co., 1992); and Carol Farley Kessler's *Charlotte Perkins Gilman: Her Progress Toward Utopia with Selected Writings* (New York: Syracuse University Press, 1995).

The following works specifically deal with 'The Yellow Wallpaper':

Catherine Golden, 'The Writing of "The Yellow Wallpaper": A Double Palimpsest', *Studies in American Fiction* 17:2 (Autumn 1989): 193–201.

Beverly A. Hume, 'Gilman's "Interminable Grotesque": The Narrator of "The Yellow Wallpaper"', *Studies in Short Fiction* 28:4 (Fall 1991): 477–84.

Greg Johnson, 'Gilman's Gothic Allegory: Rage and Redemption in "The Yellow Wallpaper"', *Studies in Short Fiction* 26:4 (Fall 1989): 521–30.

Denise D. Knight, ed., *'The Yellow Wallpaper' and Selected Stories of Charlotte Perkins Gilman* (Newark: University of Delaware Press, 1994).

Kate Chopin

Readers who wish to know more about Kate Chopin's life and work should begin with any of the four most recent biographies: Per Seyersted's *Kate Chopin: A Critical Biography* (New York: Octagon Books, 1980); Peggy Skaggs's *Kate Chopin* (Boston: Twayne Publishers, 1985); *Kate Chopin*, by Barbara C. Ewell (New York: Ungar Publishing Co., 1986); or Emily Toth's *Kate Chopin* (New York: Morrow, 1990). Other interesting works include Elaine Showalter's *Sister's Choice: Tradition and Change in American Women's Writing* (New York: Oxford University Press, 1991), and *Kate Chopin Reconsidered: Beyond the Bayou* by Linda S. Boren and Sara de Saussure Davis (Baton Rouge: Louisiana State University Press, 1992).

For material concerning Chopin's short stories, and specifically 'The Story of an Hour' and 'The Storm', see:

Christopher Baker, 'Chopin's "The Storm"', *Explicator* 52:4 (Summer 1994): 225–6.

Anna Shannon Elfenbein, *Women on the Color Line: Evolving Stereotypes and the Writings of George Washington Cable, Grace King, Kate Chopin* (Charlottesville: University Press of Virginia, 1994).

Angelyn Mitchell, 'Feminine Double Consciousness in Kate Chopin's "The Story of an Hour"', *CEA Magazine* 5:1 (Fall 1992): 59–64.

Mary E. Papke, *Verging on the Abyss: The Social Fiction of Kate Chopin and Edith Wharton* (New York: Greenwood Press, 1990).

Helen Taylor, *Gender, Race, and Region in the Writings of Grace King, Ruth McEnery Stuart, and Kate Chopin* (Baton Rouge: Louisiana State University Press, 1989).

Harbour Winn, 'Echoes of Literary Sisterhood: Louisa May Alcott and Kate Chopin', *Studies in American Fiction* 20:2 (Autumn 1992): 205–8.

Edith Wharton

Readers who wish to know more about Edith Wharton's work should begin with R. W. B. Lewis's *Edith Wharton: A Biography* (New York: Harper & Row, 1975); *Edith Wharton* (Boston: Twayne Publishers, 1991 revised edn.), by Margaret McDowell; Cynthia Griffin Wolff's *A Feast Of Words: The Triumph of Edith Wharton* (New York: Oxford University Press, 1977); and

John Lowe's essay 'Edith Wharton' in *Modern American Women Writers*, edited by Elaine Showalter (New York: Scribner's and Sons, 1991).

The following offer highly interesting readings of Wharton's work, some of which deal with 'Souls Belated':

Elizabeth Ammons, *Edith Wharton's Argument with America* (Athens: The University of Georgia Press, 1980).

Penelope Vita Finzi, *Edith Wharton and the Art of Fiction* (New York: St Martin's Press, 1990).

Judith Fryer, *Felicitous Space: The Imaginative Structures of Edith Wharton and Willa Cather* (Chapel Hill: University of North Caroline Press, 1986).

Janet Goodwyn, *Edith Wharton: Traveller in the Land of Letters* (New York: St Martin's Press, 1990).

David Holbrook, *Edith Wharton and the Unsatisfactory Man* (New York: St Martin's Press, 1991).

Katherine Joslin, *Edith Wharton* (New York: St Martin's Press, 1991).

Mary E. Papke, *Verging on the Abyss: The Social Fiction of Kate Chopin and Edith Wharton* (New York: Greenwood Press, 1990).

Willa Cather

Readers who wish to know more about Willa Cather should perhaps begin with the three recent biographies: *Willa Cather: The Emerging Voice* (New York: Oxford University Press, 1987), by Sharon O'Brien; James Woodress's *Willa Cather: A Literary Life* (Lincoln: University of Nebraska Press, 1987); and *Willa Cather: Double Lives*, by Hermione Lee (New York: Pantheon, 1989). Other useful starting points include Deborah Carlin's essay 'Willa Cather' in *Modern American Women Writers*, edited by Elaine Showalter (New York: Scribner's and Sons, 1991), and Carlin's recent *Cather, Canon, and the Politics of Reading* (Amherst: University of Massachusetts Press, 1992).

The following works offer highly interesting readings of both Cather's work in general and 'Paul's Case' in particular:

Judith Fryer, *Felicitous Space: The Imaginative Structures of Edith Wharton and Willa Cather* (Chapel Hill: University of North Carolina Press, 1986).

Sally Harvey, *Redefining the American Dream: The Novels of Willa Cather* (Toronto: Associated University Press, 1995).

Jo Ann Middleton, *Willa Cather's Modernism: A Study of Style and Technique* (Rutherford, New Jersey: Fairleigh Dickinson University Press, 1990).

Susan J. Rosowski, *The Voyage Perilous: Willa Cather's Romanticism* (Lincoln: University of Nebraska Press, 1986).

Michael N. Salda, 'What Really Happens in Cather's "Paul's Case"?', *Studies in Short Fiction* 29:1 (Winter 1992): 113–19.

Eve Kosofsky Sedgwick, 'Across Gender, Across Sexuality: Willa Cather and Others', *South Atlantic Quarterly* 88:1 (Winter 1989): 53–72.

Loretta Wasserman, 'Is Cather's Paul a Case?', *Modern Fiction Studies* 36:1 (Spring 1990): 103–19.

Susan Glaspell

Readers who wish to know more about Susan Glaspell should consult Arthur E. Waterman's *Susan Glaspell* (New York: Twayne, 1966); Mary E. Papke's *Susan Glaspell: A Research and Production Sourcebook* (Westport, Connecticut: Greenwood Press, 1993); Veronica Makowsky's *Susan Glaspell's Century of American Women: A Critical Interpretation of Her Work* (New York: Oxford University Press, 1993); and *Susan Glaspell: Essays on Her Theater and Fiction* (Ann Arbor: University of Michigan Press, 1995), edited by Linda Ben-Zvied.

For readings concentrating on 'A Jury of Her Peers' readers are directed to:

Victoria Aarons, 'A Community of Women: Surviving Marriage in the Wilderness', *Portraits of Marriage in Literature*, ed., Anne C. Hargrove and Maurine Magliocco (Macomb, Illinois: Western Illinois University Press, 1984).

Karen Alkalay-Gut, '"Jury of Her Peers": The Importance of Trifles', *Studies in Short Fiction* 21:1 (Winter 1984): 1–9.

Elaine Hedges, 'Small Things Reconsidered: Susan Glaspell's "A Jury of Her Peers"', *Women's Studies* 12:1 (1986): 89–110.

Leonard Mustazza, 'Generic Translation and Thematic Shift in Susan Glaspell's "Trifles" and "A Jury of Her Peers"', *Studies in Short Fiction* 26:4 (Fall 1989): 489–96.

ACKNOWLEDGEMENTS

The editor and publishers wish to thank the following for permission to use copyright material:

Arizona Quarterly for material from Anna Dalke, ' "Circumstance" and the Creative Woman: Harriet Prescott Spofford', *Arizona Quarterly*, 41:1 (Spring 1985), pp. 71–85;

Colby Library Quarterly for material from Norma Johnsen, 'Pieces: Artist and Audience in Three Mary Wilkins Freeman Stories', *Colby Quarterly*, 29:1 (March 1993), pp. 43–56; Elizabeth Ammons, 'The Shape of Violence in Jewett's "A White Heron"', *Colby Library Quarterly*, 22:1 (March 1986), pp. 6–16; and Marilyn S. Mobley, 'Rituals of Flight and Return: Ironic Journeys of Sarah Orne Jewett's Female Characters', *Colby Library Quarterly*, 22 (March 1986), pp. 36–42;

The Continuum Publishing Company for material from Josephine Donovan, *New England Color Literature*, Continuum Press (1988);

Indiana University Press for material from Judith Fetterly, *Provisions* (1989);

Oxford University Press, Inc for material from Veronica Makowsky, *Susan Glaspell's Century of American Women: A Critical Interpretation of Her Work*, pp. 4–9. Copyright © 1993 by Oxford University Press, Inc;

Studies in Short Fiction for material from Marjorie Pryse, 'An Uncloistered "New England Nun"', *Studies in Short Fiction*, 20 (1983), pp. 289–95. Copyright © 1983 by Newberry College;

The University of Georgia Press for material from Cheryl B. Torsney, *Constance Fenimore Woolson: The Grief of Artistry* (1989), pp. 75, 81, 86, 90;

The University of Massachusetts Press for material from Deborah Carlin, *Cather, Canon, and the Politics of Reading* (1992), pp. 6–8. Copyright © 1992 by The University of Massachusetts Press;

The University of Pennsylvania Press for material from Sharon M. Harris, *Rebecca Harding Davis and American Realism* (1991), pp. 27–34.

Every effort has been made to trace all the copyright holders but if any have been inadvertently overlooked the publishers will be pleased to make the necessary arrangement at the first opportunity.